11/
01

THREE RIVERS
PUBLIC LIBRARY DISTRICT

Channahon, IL 60410

815-467-6200

DEMCO

ARMITAGE'S MANUAL OF ANNUALS, BIENNIALS, AND HALF-HARDY PERENNIALS

ARMITAGE'S MANUAL OF ANNUALS, BIENNIALS, AND HALF-HARDY PERENNIALS

Allan M. Armitage

Illustrations by Asha Kays and Chris Johnson

TIMBER PRESS
Portland, Oregon

All photographs are by Allan M. Armitage

Printed in Singapore

Published in 2001 by
Timber Press, Inc.
The Haseltine Building
133 S.W. Second Avenue, Suite 450
Portland, Oregon 97204, U.S.A.

ISBN 0-88192-505-5

Library of Congress Cataloging-in-Publication Data

Armitage, A.M. (Allan M.)
      Armitage's manual of annuals, biennials, and half-hardy perennials /
  Allan M. Armitage; illustrations by Asha Kays and Chris Johnson.
        p.   cm.
      Includes bibliographical references (p.   ).
      ISBN 0-88192-505-5
      1. Annuals (Plants) 2. Biennials (Plants) 3. Perennials. I. Title.

  SB422.A66 2001
  635.9'31—dc21

                                                              00-066789

To the most patient and most supportive person I know—my wife, Susan. Life is a wonderful journey, made richer by her presence and by the knowledge that when we are together, there need be no destination.

CONTENTS

Color photographs follow page 256

ACKNOWLEDGMENTS

Many thanks to Asha Kays and Chris Johnson, whose drawings educate, entertain, and make my descriptions far more sensible; to Suzy Bales, Stephanie Anderson, and Meg Green, for their comments, additions, and corrections to the text; and to my editor, Franni Bertolino Farrell—it is obvious to me that the more I write, the more important her assistance becomes.

PREFACE

What is an annual?

An annual may be defined botanically as a plant that completes its entire life cycle within the space of a year: it grows, flowers, produces seed, and then dies, regardless of temperature or other environmental conditions. Gardeners, however, do not use that definition in defining annuals and perennials. From a gardening standpoint, an annual is usually defined as a plant that dies because it is unable to survive extremes of cold or heat, that is, the winter is too cold or the summer is too hot—and that is what I mean when I use the word "annual" in this book. When a typical garden annual, such as a geranium or a petunia, is grown in a greenhouse, it will flower and produce seed many times over, surviving for years.

The difficulty of the gardener's definition of annuals is obvious: winters and summers vary depending on latitude and altitude. Is an annual in Duluth still an annual in Miami, even though it survives winters perfectly well in Florida? Or conversely, will a perennial in Fargo be a perennial in New Orleans, even though it dies because of summer heat? For better or worse, I have made an arbitrary decision as to what most people accept as a garden annual. Using the USDA hardiness zone map as a guide, I consider all plants that are "usually" killed by winters in zones 1 to 7 (global warming and recent mild winters notwithstanding) annuals. That includes all Canada (except its west coast) and at least three-quarters of the land mass of the United States. According to the USDA zone map, winter temperatures in zone 7 (the southernmost zone in my definition) range from 0 to 10°F, although most "annuals" die when sustained temperatures of 20°F are experienced. Many of the plants I have included in this book may be considered perennials in Portland, Vancouver, Atlanta, or Tallahassee; in the Appendix, I offer a list of half-hardy perennials that fall into this gray area.

Other plants, commonly used as winter annuals in southern zones, are later pulled out because they cannot tolerate warm summers. These same plants may be fine summer annuals in cool summers. Such a group would include pansies, violas, English daisies, pot marigold, snapdragons, and hybrid pinks (the Appendix includes a list of these winter annuals as well). Gardeners in the southernmost areas of the country, in such gardening oases as Houston, San Diego, or Key West, may find this book more useful as a guide to perennials rather than as a guide to annuals.

No matter what we call these wonderful plants, let's enjoy the beauty they provide.

On gardening

If gardeners had to settle on one banner to describe their experiences, it would probably be "Wait until next year!" or perhaps "You should have been here last week." We are a tough lot, putting up with droughts, floods, heat waves, frosts, voracious pests, and diseases. We get frustrated, we throw up our hands, we burn those glossy catalogs, we even swear off this stuff. But come the first hint of spring, we are like Pavlov's dogs, salivating over catalogs retrieved from the recycling bin. And off we go again, to box store and garden center. It is a way of life, and as a leopard cannot change its spots, a gardener cannot *not* love plants. Once the garden bug has bitten, we will be there, year after year.

On serious gardeners

"Serious gardeners"—the very combination is an oxymoron. Gardening is something to be enjoyed, not a competitive sport. A great deal of sweat, toil, money, and frustration go into making a garden, but when all is said and done, the pleasure should be worth the pain. Let the weeds grow occasionally. So what if the asters sprawl a little? Who would deny a few bugs a little dinner every now and then? (I too draw the line at deer, voles, and moles, and heaven help those accursed Japanese beetles, as I lie in wait with a brick in each hand.) Whatever your garden is, one thing it will never be is finished, so enjoy the pieces you already have. Have fun, smell the flowers, stretch out on the grass, and feed the birds. If you wish, take learning seriously, but take nothing else about gardening seriously.

On plant material

I enjoy all kinds of plants, from the noble beech to the golden marigold, and I believe a garden is most interesting when a diversity of plant materials makes up its "bones." I don't like rose gardens, but I love roses incorporated *in* the garden, and I can say the same for iris gardens, herb gardens, daylily gardens, and dwarf conifer gardens. All these "gardens" are nothing more than collections. While I enjoy collecting (haven't we all gone through the salvia stage of life?), I don't think collections are gardens.

On plant pronunciation

Despite the good number of snobs in this area, most of our intimidation is self-inflicted. We look at these long words and immediately become tongue-tied, especially if the other person in the room is an "expert." It doesn't matter whether you pronounce *Tagetes* "ta jee′ teez" or "ta je′ teez," or *majus* "ma′ yoos" or "may′ jus"—it simply is not important. The key to plant pronunciation is to get the syllables in the right order and fire away. If you were obtaining your Ph.D. in taxonomy at a British university, pronunciation might figure in; until then, enjoy rolling these long names off your tongue.

On annuals

The myth that all annuals are bedding plants has been smashed by gardeners asking, "What else is there?" The flower breeding industry spent millions of dollars successfully improving the habits, color, and availability of impatiens, geraniums, and petunias for the landscaper and gardener—and as a result, other annuals receded from the American landscape. Many floral researchers, present company included, worked on the important bedding plants exclusively. No one championed the other guys, those plants excluded from the "bedding club." Hundreds of wonderful, lonely annuals, from *Angelonia* to *Xeranthemum*, were all but ignored.

Slowly but surely, however, the voices of gardeners, who were spending their money at mail-order firms and specialty nurseries, were heard. Breeders, researchers, and plant collectors heard the murmurs and saw the dollar bills. Because of the gardener, not the industry, dozens of more "unusual" annuals are now available in the local garden shop. Doubtless a real effort must be made before the eye peels off red geraniums to search out some *Strobilanthes*, but the tide has turned.

On the renaissance in American gardening

What led me to write this book in the first place was not so much the great renaissance in the use of annuals as it was—and is—the renaissance in gardening. American gardeners have shown that they are not monochromatic, nor monoplantmatic, nor mono-anything. If a plant is colorful and if it performs well, we want it. The key phrase in that last sentence is this: "if it performs well." From breeders to box stores, the industry realizes that the consumer will continue to buy its product only if the product performs. Hardly a new concept in commerce—but one which is not always as easy to attain as it is to say. Annual or perennial, it matters little as long as the plant provides pleasure.

On plant snobbery

Don't plant snobs just rot your socks? A plant snob, by definition, is an intimidator, condescending and oh-so-opinionated—about the wrong combinations in a beginner's garden, the wrong plants, or the wrong place at which the plants were purchased. I come across these intimidators when perennials are the subject ("Oh, *that* daylily—never!" or "Isn't the color of that astilbe simply ghastly!"), but the condescension is much more likely to surface when annuals are discussed. "Annual" seems to be a bad word, seldom uttered in the polite company of snobs (another oxymoron). Such people turn into raving lunatics when they hear the words "marigold" and "petunia," and "impatiens" doesn't fare much better: all three cause a reaction only slightly less severe than "poison oak." The key is simply to nod your head in complete agreement—then do what you want.

On plant labeling

Speaking of rotten socks, the dreadful job of labeling being done out there keeps me overstocked, with matching pairs. Trees, shrubs, and even many perennials come with large labels featuring colorful photos, reasonably good planting directions, and plant preferences: the industry thus turns out not only an excellent plant but an educated consumer. And when that plant succeeds, the gardener goes back next year and buys a dozen more. In most cases, labels in bedding plants are a joke; they are difficult to see and harder to read, with photographs so small they could be almost anything.

In my opinion, generic labels like "white impatiens" or "yellow marigold" should be banished from the gardening world forever. Such a dumbing-down of the product is an insult to the gardener, and worst of all, if the "red geranium" succeeds, how in the world will that gardener ever find that plant again? Next year's red geraniums are likely to be a totally new cultivar—last year's "blue car" was a Dodge and now it's a Pinto. Absolutely arrogant and nonsensical. Granted, the labels for non-bedding annuals are usually far more creative than they are for the bedding plants: the growers of these products want to obtain some of that bedding market. The good news is that progressive growers and retailers are using better signage and labeling—a good reason to visit your local retail center. Plant capitalism at its best.

Sources of seeds and plants

Obviously the best place to start is your local area, where retail outlets, box stores, and specialty nurseries may carry, or be able to find, the plant you seek. The greenhouse business is taking the demand for new annuals very seriously, and simply because your favorite plant was not offered last year does not mean it is not out there now. Scour your local outlets, and if disappointment sets in, ever onward!

Mail-order sources too provide outstanding choice and reliability. I am surrounded by catalogs that list dozens of annuals, from the most common to the most obscure. No matter how much material I have gathered, however, I am smart enough to know I have overlooked even more. The only source I will mention, therefore, is Barbara Barton's *Gardening by Mail*, now in its fifth edition, available in bookstores and online. You will find your own favorite sources eventually, and once you do, be loyal to them and they will be the same to you.

The Internet has rapidly become a most useful option—click "gardening" and away you go, to Never Never Land and back. An incredible amount of resources is available online; the depth of information and the number of outlets selling products are overwhelming. It's only a matter of how much time you wish to spend in front of the screen.

On box stores and garden centers

Research clearly shows that people who show up at the garden center have already been to a box store, or will soon be going. I do the same. The box store has cheaper plants simply because it has put the squeeze on the grower, whose profitability shrinks even more. The low prices at the box store artificially keep prices lower everywhere. Remember, though, that some box stores only sell hoses, they don't use them. If you wish to buy good plants at the local box or other mass market outlet, meet the plant truck.

Any garden center worth a darn should have better-trained people, a better selection of plants, and better service. If they don't, go back to the box. New plants, such as many of those described in this book, are more often found in good garden centers, particularly those which grow their own material; these grower-retailers are able to experiment on their own and so provide new material before others. But in future, box stores will have more diversity and creativity. The managers who run their plant departments are not stupid; they know that new products sell and that the same people who couldn't find anything but red petunias at the garden center will soon be visiting them. Keep the good garden centers in business but continue to check in on the box stores.

On the non-gardening spouse

People who attend my lectures always ask my wife about her gardening skills, realizing that behind every good man is a better woman. Susan, who really doesn't have quite the same obsession for this stuff as I do, used to explain about picking up branches, raking leaves, or other essential but rather mundane tasks—which did not seem to elicit much excitement from the questioners. One day she read an article and realized she was simply using the wrong jargon. Now when she is asked the same question, she replies with confidence, "I am the groundskeeper." And everybody is impressed. So if you have a non-practicing spouse, tell them they can come along as the groundskeeper. They will always be welcomed.

On Laura and Ray

Laura is my oldest daughter—intelligent, beautiful, one of my treasures. She recently married Ray; as individuals they are terrific and together they are the greatest. Having recently purchased a small house with an overgrown yard, they have become gardeners. Laura and Ray readily admit they don't really know what they are doing, but they have made a garden out of their yard. Plant names are not yet important to them; they simply want plants that work. But even as they discover the bread-and-butter plants, I see them looking around at other material and asking, "What is that?" and "Can we grow it?" I am in seventh heaven, standing back as the garden bug bites this neat couple, and I'll enjoy watching to see if the bite is serious. I have learned a lot more about plants and gardening as I look at the garden through their eyes; I am a better plantsman because of them.

Nuts and bolts of simple propagation

Almost every plant in this book can be propagated by seed or by cuttings. These methods are simple and fun to do, don't require much equipment, and provide great satisfaction. As rewarding as propagating your own plants can be, however, you will undoubtedly run into a few problems along the way.

Propagation by seed

Gathering seeds from the garden is a good idea if you want to be sure the plants in your garden continue every year. (It's the only idea if commercial seed is not available.)

Examine fruit to determine if seed is ripe. In most cases, seed darkens in color as it matures. Another indication of ripeness is the shriveling or changing color of the fruit itself.

Collect seed in a small bag. Many fruit capsules release all the seed at one time, often overnight, and in many cases, seed may be shot from the capsule for long distances. Wrap fruit in a piece of cheesecloth or other gauzy material to catch the seeds when they are released. Some work is required to wrap the fruit, but—sore thumbs nothwithstanding—this is an effective seed-harvesting method.

In most cases, annual seed may be sown at the time it is released from the fruit. If seed is sown immediately, sowing time will vary according to the maturity time of the plant. Seed can also be stored until the next spring in a cool, dry location. The rule of thumb for seed storage is temperature (F) + humidity (%) < 100. In general, annual seed need not be stored in the refrigerator.

Buying annual seed is more of an option than most people realize, but one must work to find the unusual material. Seed packages abound in every garden center and box store in late winter; in general, the seed is relatively inexpensive and the quality is reasonable, if not excellent. For bedding plants like impatiens and geraniums, the highest quality seed usually goes to the commercial industry, but if only 50% germination is obtained at home rather than the 90% germination demanded by greenhouse operators, does it really matter? How many seedlings do you want to plant, anyway?

The greatest choice of species and cultivars is found in the seed listings of mail-order catalogs or on the Internet. The downside of being offered such a wide range of seed is that the more unusual seeds may have been stored for a long time. By the time they are purchased, they may have lost significant vigor. They are also quite expensive: prices of $0.50 to $1.50 a seed are not uncommon. But no sense complaining—these venues are at least giving you an opportunity to obtain the plant. Once plants are thriving in the garden, their seed can be collected or cuttings rooted for longevity. Also, by buying rather than gathering seed, you can sow it when you want.

Sowing time is important, particularly if sowing is done in the home. A rule of thumb is to sow seed later rather than earlier. Many a gardener sows seeds too early only to be confronted with tall, skinny, chlorotic seedlings in February—

and then wonders how to keep them until spring planting season. In general, sowing six to eight weeks before planting out works well for those who don't have greenhouses. As to actually sowing the seeds, if you have a greenhouse, life is certainly easier. But since most of us do not, we must take over significant areas of the basement, garage, or kitchen. Reacquaint your spouse with your marriage vows before you start.

Any container with drainage holes will suit. Fill it with a soilless mix, which is sold at most retail stores. Most mixes consist of peat, perlite or peat, and vermiculite or pine bark—and sometimes, to all appearances, whatever could be scraped off the floor. Do not get cheap on this item: cheap soilless mixes are terrible, soon taking on the properties of concrete and equally useless. Buy professional mixes whenever possible. Do not use garden soil; it does not work in small containers.

Since seeds germinate at different rates and must be transplanted at different times, sow only one kind of seed per container. If you are using seed flats, do your best to separate seeds so you don't sow twenty seeds in one spot. With large seeds, this is fairly easy. With tiny seeds, get a small container (I use an old film canister), put a few pinches of dry sand in it, and add the small seeds. Put a small hole in the cap of the container, mix the sand and seed up, then slowly pour the mixture in rows on top of the prepared soilless mix. This provides visibility and some separation for the seeds.

Depth of planting is based on the diameter of the seed. The rule of thumb for depth is to plant the seed three times its diameter, but who measures? If the seeds are tiny, place them on top of the medium. They will find cracks and crevices of their own. In general, small seeds require light to germinate and burying them results in reduced germination. I sprinkle some coarse vermiculite (sold at most outlets) in a thin layer over the top of the seeds, so they don't dry out. If the seeds are large, make a little trough with a stick, sow them in the furrow, then fill it.

Moisture and heat are the keys to germination. Moist (not wet) conditions need be maintained. To maintain a solid marriage as well, wet the medium somewhere outdoors first and let it drain there. Then sow the seeds. Make a small greenhouse by covering the entire container with a clear plastic bag or wrap. This maintains humidity and moisture and allows you to see what is popping through the soil.

Germination is greatly enhanced if the soil in the containers can reach 70–77°F: put the containers in a warm room, put lights over the containers to provide heat, or situate the containers over heating cables or some other source of heat. If temperatures are cold (60°F, say), germination will be much slower and less uniform. Uniformity is nice because then seedlings in that container can all be transplanted at the same time. If germination is not uniform, which will be normal for unusual taxa, take off the plastic when the early germinators appear ready to be watered on their own; early germinators become tall and skinny if they are kept under the plastic too long. Water the open seed flat carefully. If you prefer to use a hose, use a mist nozzle.

Suddenly the seedlings have tripled in size, and this is the tricky part: transplanting. The easiest way to accomplish transplanting is to purchase small pots (such as 4″ wide containers) or peat pots; if many plants are desired, purchase standard plant flats (which measure about 11 × 22″) with inserts of eighteen to seventy-two cells. See what is available and get it. Transplant the seedling to the final container only when at least one true leaf has fully expanded. Do this carefully, so as not to break the seedling's root or the stem. It is preferable, but not necessary, to put one seedling per container. To separate every seedling from another as they come out of the seed tray is tiresome and boring—and results in significant damage to the lone survivor. Plant a clump, if that is all that you have; take scissors later and simply cut off the runts. In nature, seeds fall in the same spot and no one separates them. The strong survive, especially when you wield those scissors.

Keep the transplant moist, but do not overwater. Use the finger test to check moisture level: if when you put your finger in the soil, it comes out black, do not water. If it comes out dry, time to water. The rate of growth—and thereby the rate at which water is taken up by the transplants—is determined by light. And in the house, light is the limiting factor.

Provide as much light—in windows, in sun rooms, by your spouse's reading lamp, your son's desk (he doesn't study anyway), or in the hamster cage below the warming light—as possible. Shelves of fluorescent lights are most common. The lank, limp, stretched seedlings that occur when light is poor seldom make robust plants when transplanted to the garden. Placing the transplants in cool rooms (<60°F) reduces the stretch; high light plus cool temperatures is the best combination, but one that is difficult to find in most homes. It is best to time sowing so that the transplants can go outside during the day to "harden off" before placing in the garden; do bring them in at night if temperatures go below 40°F. A cold frame also works wonders (see "Propagation by cuttings"). When they are big enough to handle, transplants may be placed in the garden once the threat of frost has passed.

Propagation by cuttings

By taking cuttings, a simple means of propagation, you are sure to reproduce the same plant from year to year. But cuttings must be overwintered—not the easiest thing to do with frost-sensitive annuals. And with the length of time the plants must be kept indoors, light is even more important a consideration than it is in seed propagation. Required materials are similar to those suggested for seed propagation.

Take a terminal cutting, that is, the end portion of a stem, preferably without flowers (remove them, if present) and 1–2″ long. If the leaves are large, cut them in half. If the stem is woody or somewhat so, dip the ends in a rooting hormone (obtainable at any plant outlet) and knock off the excess powder or liquid before planting. Put the cut end in a soilless mix, and place a clear plastic bag or wrap over it to maintain moisture.

Maintain a cultural environment similar to that recommended for seed propagation. Rooting will take place in seven to twenty days. Light is essential if the good quality of the developing plant is to be maintained once transplanted. A heated cold frame will do wonders for the propagator in the family; it is nothing more than an inexpensive outdoor shelter, with a glass or other clear cover through which light can enter and a heat source (a heater on a thermostat in the North, perhaps nothing more than an incandescent light in the South) to keep temperatures above 40°F during the winter. In any case, if cuttings are taken in the fall, and plants will not return to the garden until the spring, light must be provided and temperatures should not fall beneath 40°F for any length of time. If a cold frame is not possible, keep the plants as cool as possible (>40°F) in an area with as much incoming light as possible. They may be planted to the garden once the threat of frost has passed.

How to use this book

Generic entries give an informal pronunciation guide, a common name (where applicable), and the plant family. Species entries provide another pronouncer (this time for the specific epithet); common name(s); average height/spread; flowering time and/or season of interest; flower color or foliage; and origin.

A-to-Z GENERA

Abelmoschus (a bel mos′ kus)   Malvaceae

The generic name comes from the Arabic, *abu-i-misk* ("the father of musk"), an allusion to the smell of *Abelmoschus moschatus* (musk mallow) seeds. Consisting of approximately fifteen species, the genus is best known for okra (*A. esculentus*), loved only by those who were force-fed it as infants in their pablum. All species are characterized by the red, pink, and yellow hibiscus-like flowers, often up to 4″ across. The flowers have five colorful petals and a calyx (attached sepals), which usually has five spatula-shaped lobes or teeth; above the calyx is the epicalyx, a structure that resembles bracts and surrounds the base of the petals. The reason for including this incredibly boring description is that the calyx and epicalyx help separate the genus from the similar and more familiar *Hibiscus*.

Some ornamental forms of okra may occasionally be found, but the most common choices available to the gardener are musk mallow and manihot.

Quick guide to *Abelmoschus* species

	Height	Flower color	Flower width
A. esculentus	2–5′	yellow with reddish center	2–3″
A. manihot	4–7′	pale yellow with purple center	4–9″
A. moschatus	1–4′	yellow with crimson center	2–3″

-manihot (man′ ee hot)   yellow mallow, okra   4–7′/3′
   summer   pale yellow   east Asia

This species, occasionally seen as an architectural feature in the garden, manages to maintain a modicum of class despite its large size. The best part of this relative of the hibiscus is the lovely pale yellow color of the five-petaled, 5″ wide flowers, each with a purple throat; they begin to open in mid summer and continue flowering most of the season, each persisting for about a day. The flower color reminds me of a soft moonlit night, that is, until I lean back against the leaves. The hairy, almost spiny leaves pop my moonlit bubble and replace it with less romantic thoughts. The large leaves, which may be 8–12″ across, are palmately divided (like fingers) into five to nine long narrow segments of variable widths and dentation. The leaves are edible and still cultivated in some east Asian countries. The 3″ long fruit (capsule) is nearly ellipsoid, hairy, and obviously five-sided.

Plants should be placed in full sun and provided with consistent irrigation. Although a dozen can be planted at a time, a single well-grown specimen of *Abelmoschus manihot* is sufficient. Propagate by seed.

| *-moschatus* (mos ka′ tus) | musk mallow, ornamental okra | 2–3′/2′ |
| all season | yellow, red, pink | India |

The common name of musk mallow is a reference to the distinct musky odor of the long narrow fruit. Curious as to what "musky" really was, I looked the word up in the dictionary; here I learned that musk is an odorous substance, secreted by an Asian deer, used in perfumery. Not only does that Asian deer secrete such musk, so do the muskrat and musk ox. Picturing these smelly, shaggy mammals does not perk my nostrils like lavender or thyme. Maybe that is why I can't get the hang of okra.

Neither common name does a great deal to enamor *Abelmoschus moschatus* to gardeners and landscapers, but names notwithstanding, the plants are quite ornamental, particularly some of the cultivars that have been bred. The species itself bears axillary 2–3″ wide light yellow flowers with purple blotching within. The flowers are up to 3″ across, consisting of five petals and the characteristic columnar pistil, to which the many stamens are attached. Each flower persists but one day, relinquishing its place in the sun to the next in line. The leaves consist of widely spread, thin, toothed lobes, but they occasionally look more maple-like; they are sparsely hairy on both sides, and while the foliage can itch, it is not prickly. The thin fruit (capsule) is among the shortest of the genus, only 2–3″ long, and yes, it does smell. Capsules and flowers appear together throughout the season, as some flowers finish while others are opening. The species can grow to 5′ tall; cultivars are significantly shorter.

Plants require full sun for best performance; shade results in taller stems and fewer flowers. Propagate by seed. If seed is collected, it must be scarified for uniform germination. Scarification can be accomplished by putting seeds in a sandpaper-lined can and shaking the can for five to ten minutes. Purchased seed is usually already scarified.

CULTIVARS

'Pacific Light Pink' bears 2–3″ wide pink flowers on 12–18″ tall bushy plants. Its dwarf habit makes it much easier to include in the landscape.

'Pacific Orange Scarlet' is actually scarlet, closer to red than orange. Otherwise similar to 'Pacific Light Pink'.

Alternative species

Abelmoschus esculentus (es kew len′ tus; okra), a relative of *A. moschatus*, is farmed for the fruit, mainly in the South, but several interesting ornamental cultivars have been made available. The flowers are smaller than other species but have handsome yellow petals with a purple center. A dwarf cultivar with purple leaves and purple fruit has captured the imaginations of many gardeners at the trial grounds at the University of Georgia (UGA). The fruit is edible, and its purple fruit can mess up your soup just as well as okra bought at the grocer's. Cheaper too.

Quick key to *Abelmoschus* species

A. Fruit 3" or less
    B. Plant 2–3′ tall, fruit slightly five-sided . . . .*A. moschatus*
    BB. Plant 4–7′ tall, fruit obviously five-sided . . . .*A. manihot*
AA. Fruit >4" long . . . .*A. esculentus*

Additional reading

Anonymous. 1996. Some like it hot. *Southern Living* 31(6):91.
Armitage, Allan M. 1997. Ornamental okra. *Greenhouse Grower* 15(10):105–106.
Lee, Rand B. 1998. A feast of mallows. *American Cottage Gardener* 5(3):5–7.

Abutilon (ab yew′ tih lon)   flowering maple   Malvaceae

Using the majestic maple's name as the common name for this genus is stretching common sense a bit, although one could argue that the leaves of *Abutilon* look more like maple leaves than, say, oak leaves. Many species are native to South America but are spread throughout warm areas in both hemispheres. The alternate leaves are in general palmately lobed and attached to the stems with long petioles. The solitary flowers are pendulous in the leaf axils, consisting of five sepals and petals, in yellow, orange, rose, and occasionally white. Where they are native, or in countries where plants are perennial, species such as *A. vitifolium* and the hybrid *A.* ×*suntense* are shrubs and may grow 20′ tall. Approximately 150 species of *Abutilon* have been described, but the dwarf forms used in containers and gardens are hybridized and go under the name of *A.* ×*hybridum*. Companies interested in the landscape and garden trade have been intensely breeding more colors and better forms. In general, the better forms are in flower all summer (all year if brought inside in the winter).

Quick guide to *Abutilon* species

	Habit	Flower color
A. ×hybridum	upright	varied
A. megapotamicum	trailing	yellow petals, red sepals
A. pictum	upright, trailing	yellow, orange

-×*hybridum* (hi′ brih dum)   Chinese lantern, parlor maple   1–3′/2′
   summer   yellow, orange, rose, white   hybrid

This species was a favorite plant in the Victorian era, when parlors were an important room of the household. The many cultivars of that day nearly went the way of the parlor, but they are making a comeback in the garden and the patio container, leaving silk and plastic to occupy the foyer. A good trade, I would say. The hybrids are a variable complex of species including *Abutilon striatum*, *A. darwinii*, and others. In general, plants may be up to 5′ in height, although modern hybrids are seldom more than 2′ tall. The leaves may be unlobed but are often three- or occasionally five-lobed. The margins are serrate to dentate, and the leaves may be smooth or softly hairy underneath. The drooping bell-shaped flowers are held in axillary peduncles (flower stems), and the colored blooms are often obviously veined. In many hybrids, the sepals are darker than the petals, an additional ornamental aspect.

I have trialed several of the hybrids for outdoor use. If purchased as standards (plants trained on a single stem), plants may be excellent performers. As traditional plants, however, they are not sufficiently strong and require a good deal of soil preparation and care before they can be added to the garden. Their place seems to be in large containers and window boxes, where the flowers can be viewed more easily and the soil, moisture, and fertility are more reliably controlled. Flowers persist many days in water and do well even out of water, and therefore may be picked for nosegays.

Full sun in the North, full sun for most cultivars in the South. Forms with variegated foliage benefit from some afternoon shade in the South. Maintain moist soils; do not allow to dry out. Fertilize at least three times during the season with a complete fertilizer. Pinch once to stimulate bushiness.

Propagate by semi-hardwood, two- or three-node terminal cuttings. Remove all flowers from the axils and place in bottom heat (72–75°F) in a well-drained medium. Smooth-leaved forms may be put under mist; hairy-leaved forms should be rooted in a sweat tent (structure covered with plastic but no mist).

CULTIVARS

'Apricot Belle' has salmon flowers with darker venation and pubescent leaves. Appears similar to 'Apricot Glow' and 'Apricot'.

'Bartley Schwartz' is an excellent selection for growing as a standard or basket. The pendulous yellow-orange flowers are borne in abundance throughout the season.

Bella Hybrids were developed by the late Claude Hope, the great plantsman, at Linda Vista, Costa Rica. They are wonderfully compact (perfect for containers and window boxes) and have been bred in many colors. I use them in the container plantings at the University of Georgia trial grounds, and they are excellent. Not to be confused with the older Belle series.

'Benary's Giant' is a seed-propagated mix of 1½′ tall plants.

'Clementine' produces crimson-red flowers for hanging baskets and containers. Hybridized by Logee's Greenhouses, Ltd., Danielson, Connecticut. A form with marbled white leaves, 'Clementine Variegated', is also sold.

'Crimson Belle' has royal red flowers.

'Dwarf Red' has red-orange flowers with dark green leaves. Excellent branching habit.

'Hardy Orange' is an old-fashioned rangy orange-flowered form.

'Huntington Pink' has light pink bell-shaped flowers with deeper pink veins.

'Kentish Belle', more often seen in the United Kingdom than here, has large bright orange flowers on 2–3' tall plants.

'Marion Stewart', introduced by Plants Delight Nursery, bears 1½" wide orange bell-shaped flowers with red veins. Plants can grow up to 5' in height.

'Mobile Pink' bears soft pink flowers with dark pink venation on compact plants. Floriferous.

'Moonchimes' has been described as having intense yellow flowers. Those I have seen have soft yellow blooms on dwarf (2' tall) plants.

'Pink Belle' bears bright pink flowers with darker veins. Probably the same as 'Satin Pink Belle'.

'Pink Blush', introduced by Dennis Schrader and Bill Smith of Land Craft Nursery, Long Island, New York, has a mounding habit with soft pink flowers and a light yellow center.

'Savitzii', a popular plant during the foliage boom, bears leaves that are heavily marbled with creamy white. Every now and then orange flowers are produced. More showy than 'Souvenir de Bonn' but may not produce as many flowers.

'Snow Belle' has clean white flowers with contrasting yellow stamens. Similar to (may be the same as) 'Snowfall'. This is a more compact form of the difficult-to-find but beloved old 'Boule de Neige' ('Snowball').

'Snowfall', a compact plant, produces small pure white flowers. Terrific for containers.

'Souvenir de Bonn' has salmon to orange flowers that contrast with the white marbling on the large leaves. Sometimes the edging is less defined, and the leaves appear mottled.

'Summer Sherbet' is a seed-propagated hybrid mix with 3–4" wide flowers in lemon, rose, pink, apricot, and red. Useful for containers and baskets.

'Tangerine' produces large golden orange flowers with bright pink veins. Quite a combination! Also sold as 'Tangerine Belle'.

'Variegatum' has soft green leaves mottled creamy white. The salmon to soft orange flowers have crimson veins.

'Yellow Belle' has flowers of bright yellow.

-megapotamicum (meg a po tam' ee kum)

	trailing abutilon, Chinese lantern	1'/4–5'
summer	yellow	Brazil

Everyone who grows this trailing form of the flowering maple counts it a favorite. Suitable as a standard specimen, basket, or window box plant, it can grow up or fall over other plants, complementing most everything as it goes. The small, 2–3" long pointed leaves are shallowly three-lobed and almost horizontal, so much so that the plant appears to grow almost in a single plane. The

2–3″ long, narrow flowers consist of lemon-yellow petals surrounded at the base by bright red sepals. The column of pistil and attached stamens conspicuously protrudes from the petals, making a stunning combination.

CULTIVARS

'Variegatum' has similar flowers and yellow-mottled leaves. Extremely popular.

'Victor's Folley' produces flowers with wine-colored sepals and deeply veined, soft peach petals.

'Wisley Red' bears rich red flowers.

Alternative species

Abutilon indicum is related to *A. megapotamicum*. It has soft 4″ long leaves that are usually shallowly three-lobed; they are white on the undersides and hairy on both sides. The yellow chalice flowers are borne in the leaf axils. Plants are big, growing 4–8′ tall.

Abutilon pictum (pik′ tum; syn. *A. striatum*) is similar to *A. ×hybridum*; it can grow up to 10′ tall, but the forms selected for gardeners and landscapers are less than 3′ tall. They are often trained as standard specimens but can also be used in containers and baskets. The species generally has yellow to orange flowers; selections can vary. 'Aureo-maculatum' is an excellent form, whose velvety green leaves, hairy on the underside, are splattered with yellow; the leaves are five-lobed and toothed; the flowers are coral red with darker veins but are not produced as freely as in the hybrids. 'Gold Dust' has light green leaves with heavy golden mottling; the orange flowers are produced abundantly. 'Thomsonii' is an upright grower with salmon-orange flowers and maple-like leaves (five to seven lobes), mottled in soft yellow. 'Victory', my favorite selection of *A. pictum*, has yellow blooms with red centers hanging from almost every leaf node.

Quick key to *Abutilon* species

A. Plant trailing, yellow petals with red calyx, pistil
   obviously protruding . . . . *A. megapotamicum*
AA. Plant upright or mounding, many colors, pistil not obviously protruding
   B. Leaves usually three-lobed, middle lobe broadest at base,
      flowers orange or yellow . . . . *A. pictum*
   BB. Leaves either unlobed or more or less three-lobed,
      flowers many colors . . . . *A. ×hybridum*

Additional reading

Emsweller, S. E., P. Brierley, D. V. Lumsden, and F. L. Mulford. 1937. Improvements in flowers by breeding. USDA Yearbook: 890–998.

Abutilon megapotamicum 'Variegatum'   ASHA KAYS

Acalypha (a kal′ ee fa)   Euphorbiaceae

More than 430 species of woody plants occur in this genus, all native to tropical areas of the world, where they are also used as hedging or large shrubs in the landscape. In the woody species, mainly *Acalypha wilkesiana* (copperleaf), the multicolored foliage provides the ornamental value; the small red flowers are essentially inconspicuous. The main species found in North American gardens is *A. hispida* (chenille plant), in which the bright red flowers are borne in long, pendent, tassel-like spikes.

Quick guide to *Acalypha* species

	Grown for	Use
A. godseffiana	colorful foliage	container, garden
A. hispida	flowers	container, basket
A. wilkesiana	colorful foliage	container, garden

-*hispida* (his′ pid a)   chenille plant   15–18″/3′
   summer   red   New Guinea, Malaya

I remember when I first saw this plant in flower: I was a young boy and couldn't help but think of the long braids on the snooty red-haired girl who sat in front of me in fourth grade. Except that the plant wasn't snooty. Plants are nearly always grown as baskets and containers but may also be trained as an upright standard. The flowers are longer than the leaves and distinctive enough to cause most visitors to do a double take.

The pointed alternate leaves are 3–4″ long and half as wide, wider in the middle and slightly hairy above. The plants are dioecious, that is, they carry male and female flowers on separate plants. The flowers lack petals; the bright red effect is from the long branched styles of the female flowers. The many small flowers are held in drooping tassel-like spikes, some 20″ long and 1″ wide. Each inflorescence is formed in the upper leaf axils.

These tropical plants are best grown in the light shade of pines or other open shade with good air circulation. Provide with consistent water, particularly when they are grown in baskets, or they will decline rapidly.

Propagate by two- or three-node cuttings. Plants root with bottom heat (72–75°F) in ten to fourteen days.

CULTIVARS

'Alba' bears long tassels of creamy white flowers tinged pink. Not as easy to find and not as showstopping.

var. *pendula* (syn. *Acalypha repens*; trailing redtails, strawberry firetails) is prostrate (6–10″ tall) and has smaller leaves and short fuzzy red tails that elongate to 2″ at most.

'Summer Love' is a selection with short pink tails. It may be a selection of var. *pendula*.

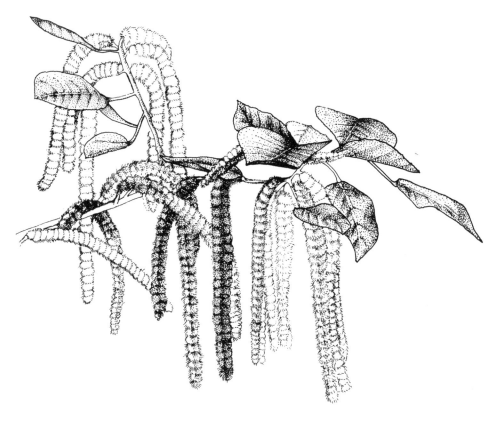

Acalypha hispida   CHRIS JOHNSON

-*wilkesiana* (wilks ee an' a)   copperleaf   3–6'/3'
  summer   red   New Guinea, Malaya

While living in Perth, Western Australia, I walked by 10' tall shrubs and long
semiformal hedges of this colorful species. In the tropics, where it grows 8–15'
tall, copperleaf is a common landscape and privacy plant, in demand for its multicolored foliage. The species bears 4–6" long elliptical, serrated leaves that are
copper-green, often blotched with red or crimson. The small red flowers are
borne on slender 8" long spikes—not nearly as showy as those of chenille plant,
perhaps because they have to compete with the showy leaves. These monoecious
plants (they carry male and female flowers on the same plant) bear the name of
American scientist and explorer Admiral Charles Wilkes (1801–1877).

   Plants are gaining popularity as a container item whose brightly painted
leaves can complement surrounding flowers, and they are in demand by landscapers as accent plants. They grow rapidly in warm summers, attaining 3–4' in
height; in cool summers, foliage may be more vibrant, but plants are smaller.

They are easily produced in warm greenhouses and should be purchased as mature plants. Plant in full sun, after all threat of frost has passed.

Propagate by two- or three-node cuttings. Plants root with bottom heat (72–75°F) in ten to fourteen days.

CULTIVARS

Because they are based on foliage patterns, all cultivars are likely to be mixed up in the trade.

'Ceylon' has somewhat twisted coppery leaves with pink to whitish margins. Quite popular.

'Haleakala' has twisted bronze leaves with fringed margins. Interesting, to say the least.

'Hoffman's' bears narrow twisted leaves with ivory lobes. Also sold as 'Hoffmaniana'.

'Kana Coast' has large bright yellow leaves flecked and spotted with green. Often some reversion occurs, and the green takes up an entire half of the leaf.

'Kilauea' is a dwarf form with small narrow leaves blotched with red and copper-pink. The edges of the foliage are creamy white. Also sold as 'Miniature Firedragon'.

'Macrophylla' (heart copperleaf) has wide russet leaves splashed with bronze-red and copper.

'Marginata', the most popular form and probably the one most people know as the true copperleaf, produces leaves with crimson or other colored margins.

'Musaica' has orange and red markings on the green leaves.

'Obovata' (heart copperleaf) produces bronzy green leaves with bright pink to orange margins.

'Petticoat' has large, highly ruffled, copper-colored leaves, with earth-tone margins.

Alternative species

Acalypha godseffiana is not easily distinguished from *A. wilkesiana*. It is a dwarf form with a bushy, mounding habit and short, narrow, green to yellow spikes. The branches droop down, and the glossy green leaves are usually creamy white with pale yellow margins. 'Heterophylla' is a particularly ugly form with narrow, ragged, yellow-edged leaves on drooping branches. Stunning to some—it's all in the eye of the beholder. Grows about 12″ tall.

Quick key to *Acalypha* species

- A. Leaves green, spikes 1″ wide, flower spikes much longer than leaves . . . . *A. hispida*
- AA. Leaves splashed in colors, spikes much shorter than the leaves
    - B. Green leaves margined in cream, flowers greenish yellow . . . . *A. godseffiana*
    - BB. Colors more conspicuous, flowers some shade of red . . *A. wilkesiana*

Adlumia (ad loom' ee a)   climbing fumitory   Fumariaceae

The sole representative of this monotypic genus is the climbing biennial vine *Adlumia fungosa* (climbing fumitory), native to the northeastern United States (thus its other common names, mountain fringe and Allegheny vine). Every gardener who enjoys plant names must have this plant. The generic name is so beautiful, it is actually fun to tell people that you have it in your garden. If parents can name their little girls Chantilly, then I soon expect some sweet, little Adlumias out there as well.

The delicate light green foliage is thrice pinnate and fern-like. Plants use the petioles of new leaves to clamber and scramble over shrubs and bushes; they may also be trained up arbors. The pale pink and whitish flowers, similar in appearance to those of bleeding heart (*Dicentra*), are formed in hanging clus-

Adlumia fungosa   ASHA KAYS

ters at the axils. After flowering, seeds are expelled and germinate in the summer and fall of the same year. These biennials are low and bushy the first year, but with one winter under their belt, they climb as fast as helium balloons released from the football stadium, growing 10–12′ tall in a few weeks. Definitely a plant that should be put in the ground and left alone. Plants are hardy to zone 3 and may be grown as far south as zone 7.

Provide some afternoon shade for best performance. This may never be a mainstream garden plant, but it is fun and easy to grow.

Propagate by seed; plants self-sow where they are happy.

Agastache (a ga sta′ kee)   giant hyssop   Lamiaceae

Most hyssops are considered short-lived perennials and do well into zone 6; but several annuals are also available, all characterized by opposite aromatic foliage, with at least some hint of anise.

-*foeniculum* (fo nik′ yew lum)   anise hyssop   2–4′/2′
   summer   purple, white   North America

Usually only one or two main stems emerge, each bearing opposite ovate leaves, 2–3″ long and 1–2″ wide; the margins are serrate, and the upper surface is smooth and green while the lower surface is hairy. Break off a leaf and smell the fragrance of anise, which, depending on the selection, you may find pleasant or perhaps a little too strong. The fragrance provides the common name, but plants are poor substitutes for *Hyssopus officinalis*, the herb hyssop. The whorled flowers are densely held in a compact upright pubescent spike, 2–4″ long; each whorl is subtended by small pointed bracts. The overall flower color is lavender to purple, but creamy white selections are also common.

Plants make a fine grouping in the garden, providing many months of flowers and fragrant foliage. They may also be used as cut flowers, persisting well for about a week; harvest when inflorescence is about two-thirds open. Deadheading keeps plants looking fresh after they have flowered. Mildew can be a problem in certain areas. Plants are cold hardy to about 23°F.

Full sun, propagate by seed.

CULTIVARS

'Alabaster' is a common creamy white form, about 3′ tall.

'Honey Bee Blue' has lavender-blue flowers and stands 2–2½′ tall. An excellent plant with persistent flowering and a good habit.

'Honey Bee White' is similar but with creamy white flowers. An improvement on 'Alabaster'.

'Licorice Blue' and 'Licorice White' bear lavender-blue and creamy white flowers, respectively, on 3–4′ tall plants. Good as cut flowers.

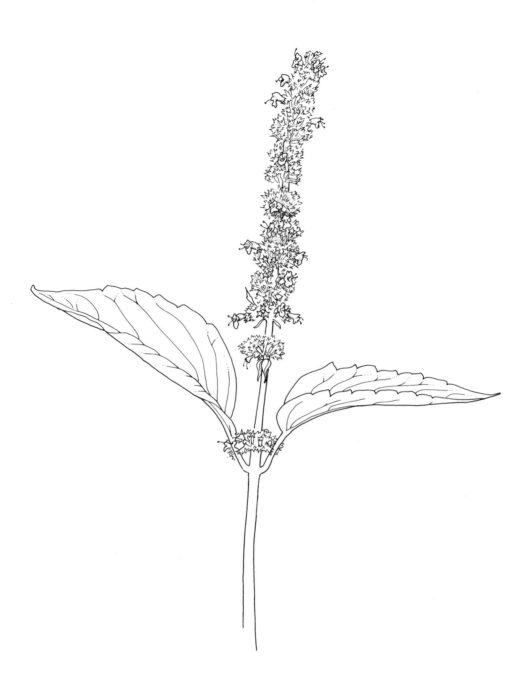

Agastache foeniculum 'Honey Bee White'   ASHA KAYS

Alternative species

Agastache mexicana (Mexican hyssop) is similar but has a creeping rootstock and many stems. The rose flowers are usually interrupted on 12″ long spikes. Not as cold hardy.

Ageratum (a jer ay′ tum)   Asteraceae

The genus consists of about forty species, all native to Central and South America. *Ageratum conyzoides*, a common weed in the tropics, and *A. corymbosum*, a 4–6′ tall shrubby plant with blue, lavender, or white flat-topped flowers, are seldom seen in cultivation. Only the bedding floss flower, *A. houstonianum*, is common in American landscapes. This species has been subject to intense breeding by the bedding plant industry since the 1970s.

-houstonianum (yew sto nee a′ num)		floss flower	1–3′/1–2′
all season	lavender		West Indies, Mexico

I have a love-hate relationship with many bedding plants, mainly concerning the lack of creativity in their use. Seeing little blue meatballs lining walk after walk in the American front yard became a little boring—that's the price of success, I guess. Nothing to do with the fine Texas city, *Ageratum houstonianum* is rather named for William Houston, an American physician who collected the species in the Antilles and Mexico. The opposite leaves are usually heart-shaped at the base and rounded at the apex, with crenate (wavy) margins. Flower stems are borne in the upper axils and terminal apex and are made up of heads of five to fifteen densely clustered tubular flowers. Each flower is five-lobed, usually spreading, giving the flower head a tassel-like appearance (the species is also known as tassel flower).

Plants are generally sold in small containers in the spring, ready for transplanting; place 9–12″ apart in full sun and well-drained soils. In the North, plants usually persist all season; in the South, the dense flowers may trap too much moisture, and the combination of heat and humidity often results in poor performance by mid summer. In the Deep South, however, they may be put out in the fall and flower all winter. Consistent moisture is helpful; a plant's vigor and flowering period is much reduced when soil dries out.

The ornamental plant industry has been breeding ageratum for some time; in 1940 Waller-Franklin Seed Co. introduced 'Midget Blue', which was honored with a prestigious All-America Selection award that year—the only ageratum ever to receive that award in AAS history. Most bedding plants, including ageratum, are F_1 hybrids, which provide more uniformity to the grower, a characteristic not as important to the gardener. Collecting the seed of F_1 hybrids is an exercise in futility as seeds will not breed true. Package seed is available for sale to the gardener and may be sown at 70–75°F in moist conditions. Terminal cuttings may also be taken in the fall and maintained inside over the winter, but

Ageratum houstonianum   CHRIS JOHNSON

with so many cultivars available at the garden center, it is far more efficient and less expensive to buy some in the spring. All available cultivars are propagated by seed, and the majority are F_1 hybrids.

CULTIVARS

'Adriatic' is 4–6″ tall, bearing mid blue flowers.

'Bavaria' bears white and blue bicolored flowers on 10–12″ tall plants.

'Blue Blazer', an early flowerer, provides uniformity of production and performance. Plants are about 6″ tall and produce mid-blue flowers.

'Blue Bouquet' is an intermediate form with 16–20″ tall stems and lavender flowers. Taller than bedding forms but shorter than 'Blue Horizon'.

'Blue Horizon' is an excellent tall (2–3′) lavender form suitable for the garden and cut flowers. It is a triploid, which means it is vigorous and essentially sterile.

'Blue Lagoon' grows 8–10″ tall and is covered with light blue flowers.

'Blue Mink' is an open-pollinated tetraploid form with powder-blue flowers. Larger leaves and flowers but not as uniform as other hybrids.

'Capri' is an unusual bicolor selection with light blue flowers and white centers. Plants are 12–15″ tall, with normal mounding habit.

Champion series consists of 'Blue Champion', 'Light Blue Champion', and 'White Champion', each about 6" tall.

Danube series consists of 'Blue Danube' (also sold as 'Blue Puffs') and 'White Danube', which plants, mounding 9–12", are covered with lavender and off-white flowers, respectively. A most popular series.

Fields series consists of mounded many-branched plants. 'Fields Blue' and 'Fields White' are offered.

'Garden Leader True Blue' is about 7" tall with dark blue flowers.

Hawaii series is similar and consists of 'Blue Hawaii', 'Royal Hawaii' (deep lavender), and 'White Hawaii'.

'Neptune Blue' bears lavender-blue flowers on 6–8" tall plants.

'Pacific Plus' has some of the richest colors of the group. They are blue-red but sufficiently different from other blues and whites in the species. Also sold as 'Pacific Rose'.

Pearls series consists of 'Azure Pearl', with light blue flowers, and 'Silver Pearl' with silvery white blooms.

'Pinky' and 'Pinky Improved' are 6–8" tall and bear dusky pink flowers.

'Red Sea' produces 2' tall plants with dark red flower buds, opening to purple-red flowers.

'Southern Cross' is 12" tall with blue and white bicolor flowers. Unique.

'Summer Snow' is a white-flowered form consisting of 6–8" tall plants.

'Summit' bears flowers of deep blue.

Tycoon series bears many flowers on 7–9" tall plants. Available in blue and purple.

'White Ball' provides white flowers on 10" bedding plants.

Additional reading

Latimer, J. G., and R. D. Oetting. 1998. Greenhouse conditioning affects landscape performance of bedding plants. *J. Env. Hort.* 16(3):138–142.

Agrostemma (ag ro stem' a)   corn-cockle   Caryophyllaceae

Corn-cockle was so named because of its tendency to occur as a weed in grain crops in England and the Continent, and the entire genus of approximately four species was treated as a field weed, especially when its seeds were discovered to contain the poison saponin. It was dangerous to consume flour that had been been contaminated with seeds of *Agrostemma*; no wonder the genus was not held in high esteem by gardeners. With the advent of herbicides and better seed-cleaning techniques, however, corn-cockle is much less a field weed, and its ornamental characteristics can be enjoyed more fully. The genus is occasionally confused with *Lychnis*, but the five styles (female part of the flower) of *Agrostemma* are opposite the petals, whereas in *Lychnis*, the styles are between the petals. Most people simply read the label. The only species available to gardeners is *A. githago*, popular as a garden plant and highly regarded as a cut flower.

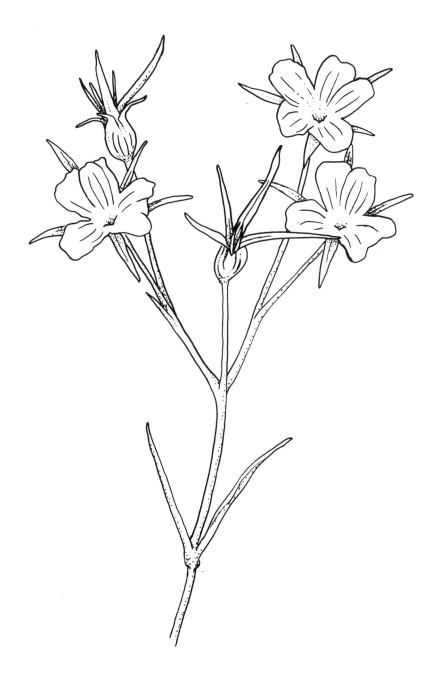

Agrostemma githago 'Milas'   ASHA KAYS

-githago (gih tha' go)	corn-cockle	3–4'/1'
summer	magenta	Europe

Calling plants tall and skinny, with few branches, is not exactly flattering, but that is what they are. The opposite linear to lanceolate leaves are covered with short grayish white hairs. The five-petaled flowers are large (2" wide) and usually magenta (although some softer colors have been selected); they are solitary, on long hairy flower stems. In the garden, plants should be placed close to each other; some don't branch well and they will need their fellows for company. Harvest them for cut flowers as the flowers begin to open. Flowers persist about five days in water, longer in floral preservative.

Full sun, propagate by seed *in situ* or in a warm greenhouse.

CULTIVARS

'Milas' has plum-pink flowers.

'Milas Cerise' and 'Milas Rosea' bear flowers of deep red and lilac-pink, respectively. They are otherwise similar to the species.

'Ocean Pearl' produces white flowers with black speckled markings on 3' tall plants.

Additional reading

Armitage, Allan M. 1993. *Specialty Cut Flowers*. Timber Press, Portland, Ore.

Alcea (al see' a) hollyhock Malvaceae

Approximately sixty species of annual, biennial, and short-lived perennial species constitute this genus, some of them exceptionally popular. Hollyhocks have been gracing gardens for centuries and are presently enjoying a renaissance in the United States. All species are found in sunny, well-drained habitats and provide exceptional color for short periods of time. Flowers are usually large and appear singly or in racemes, and the stems are hairy. All are best grown as biennials (to zone 3) and require little more than sun and good air circulation. *Alcea rosea* is the best-known member.

-rosea (ro zay' a)	hollyhock	4–8'/2'
spring, early summer	many colors	Turkey, Asia

My mother knew very little about gardening, other than that the lawnmower was a good way to keep her sons out of trouble. But how she loved her hollyhocks. They grew with their backs up the stucco wall of our garage, held up with ugly white strings, which extended from rusty nails on either side. Like tape measures across a boxer's chest, these strings were often more visible than the plants themselves. But every year, a few seedlings would come up, and every year we would put some seeds in the ground. They provided a riot of color along an

Alcea rosea   ASHA KAYS

otherwise drab path but by mid summer, the leaves were eaten up by rust. By that time, other activities, like burning down the woods behind our house, occupied us, and the hollyhocks were forgotten until they reappeared once again.

My mother would be pleased to see the current renaissance in hollyhocks. The old red single flowers are still around, but so are many other colors and forms, including double flowers 5″ across. Plants are generally 3–6′ tall, but 8′ monsters are not rare. They are unbranched, rather pole-like even, and the stems are hairy to the point of being bristly. The leaves have three, five, or seven lobes, and the flowers occur in terminal racemes, made up of three to ten flowers. The six to nine bracts beneath the flowers are joined together and turn brown as the flowers mature. Modern cultivars are also less susceptible to my mother's nemesis, hollyhock rust, which is caused by the fungus *Puccinia malvacearum*. If my mother had known that the spores that caused those orange-brown pustules on the undersides of the leaves and stems overwintered on the blistered leaves by the garage, she would have removed them. Actually, she would have told her sons to do it, and we would probably have taken the trusty Lawn Boy to them. Fungal sprays are now available; it is equally effective and more satisfying to simply remove any affected leaves and try a different cultivar next year.

Hollyhocks are mostly biennials and can be transplanted in the fall or sown in site about two months before frost. Mulch if necessary during the winter, but plants are winter hardy to zone 3. In cool climates, they will bloom early to mid summer. In warmer areas (zones 8 to 10), they will flower in spring if planted in fall. They may also be sown directly in the prepared soil immediately after the last frost date or in containers about two weeks before that time, but cold is still needed for best flowering. If sowing in containers, place the container at 72–75°F and cover the moist soil with plastic until the seedlings emerge. Do not germinate the seeds too early or plants will be weak and stretched before the transplant date. First-year plants overwinter well, particularly if good snow cover occurs.

CULTIVARS

Single flowers

'Barnyard Pink-Red' is offered by an enterprising nursery that claims seeds were collected from an old barnyard in Vermont. They are single, tall, and old-fashioned. I bet they collected them from my mother's plants.

'Indian Spring' is available in white, yellow, rose, and pink. Plants are 7–8′ tall.

'Nigra' has some of the deepest purple flowers of any cultivar. Plants attain a height of about 6′. Also sold as 'Black Beauty'.

'Simplex' is a mixture of colors on 4–5′ tall stems.

Double and semi-double flowers

Chaters Double Hybrids occur in a range of colors. Each double flower resembles a ruffled peony. Plants with single colors include 'Chaters Pink', 'Chaters Scarlet', 'Chaters Purple', 'Chaters White', and 'Chaters Yellow'.

'Majorette' has semi-double lacy flowers on 3′ tall stems.

'Nigrita' has dark, almost purple-red double flowers.

'Pinafore' is more branched and compact than other cultivars and bears semi-double flowers in numerous colors. Plants are 3–4' tall.

'Powder Puffs' grow 6–8' tall and produce 4" wide fully double flowers in white, yellow, rose, and red.

'Summer Carnival' is a mixture of colors with double blooms on 2½–3' tall plants.

Alternative species

Alcea rugosa (Russian hollyhock), with its classical nature and resistance to hollyhock rust, is increasingly popular. The large single flowers are pale yellow, and the leaves are deeply five-lobed. The 5–6' tall stems are hairy all over.

Related genera

Althaea, also known as hollyhock, is often confused with *Alcea*, for obvious reasons. Most of the ornamental hollyhocks belong to *Alcea*. The flowers of *Althaea* are smaller (seldom exceeding 1½" wide) and usually rose or rose-pink, occasionally white. While not as flashy as *Alcea*, they are useful for naturalistic plantings. Approximately twelve species are known, the 3–5' tall *Althaea officinalis*, which has small rose, pink, or white flowers, is best known. The roots of this species were the original source of marshmallows.

Additional reading

Ganter, Mary N. 1996. Hollyhocks, the straight skinny. *Flower and Garden* 40(4): 24–26.

Lee, Rand B. 1998. A feast of mallows. *American Cottage Gardener* 5(3):5–7.

Allamanda (a la man' da)   Apocynaceae

These wonderful tropical South American vines for indoor and outdoor enjoyment rapidly cover pergolas, pillars, and fences once temperatures warm up. Approximately twelve species are known, all with whorled leaves, entire margins, and showy flowers. People who encounter *Allamanda* often confuse it with *Mandevilla*: both are summer-flowering and usually found covering some mailbox or other. In general, leaves of *Mandevilla* are more shiny, not as vigorous, and usually bear flowers in shades of red or purple. The common flower colors of *Allamanda* are yellow or gold, although one species produces burgundy flowers. For those who must be absolutely sure, check the stamens. They are united with the stigma in *Mandevilla*, separate from the stigma in *Allamanda*. Tedious but effective.

-cathartica (ka thar' tih ka)   golden trumpet   vine
   summer   golden yellow   South America

These vigorous plants reach heights of 50' in their native habitats, but in most parts of this country, the untropical climate renders these vines a little less vigorous. Leaves occur in whorls of three to four, each leaf growing about 5" long and 1" wide, with a pointed tip and somewhat wavy margin. The leaves are smooth except on the veins beneath. The foliage is reasonably handsome, but it is the flowers that keep gardeners coming back. They occur in summer in few-flowered inflorescences at the ends of branches. The sepals occur in five unequal lobes, and the petals are golden yellow with white markings in the throat. The mouths of the flowers are up to 5" in diameter, which then taper to a long cylindrical tube.

Fertilize regularly, place in consistently moist soils in full sun. Tie around a strong structure and enjoy the flowers all summer. Take cuttings, or dig plants up in the fall if they must be overwintered. To overwinter, cut back the dug-up plant, place in a container in bright light, and allow the plant to remain on the dry side. Temperatures should remain above 45°F. Plants should be pruned to two or three fat, vigorous shoots prior to replanting. Unless a greenhouse or sun room is available, it makes more sense to purchase plants again in the spring.

CULTIVARS

'Flore Plena' is characterized by the double golden yellow flowers. More interesting than handsome—why mess up the beautiful single flowers normally offered?

'Grandiflora' (var. *grandiflora*) has thin wiry stems and 4" wide lemon-yellow flowers.

'Hendersonii' (var. *hendersonii*) has thick leathery leaves and abundant 4–5" wide flowers. The entire plant is smooth.

'Williamsii' (var. *williamsii*) has 2–3" wide yellow flowers with a reddish brown throat. The stems and the leaves are pubescent.

Alternative species

Allamanda violacea (syn. *A. blanchetii*; purple allamanda) is less vigorous than *A. cathartica* and is considered a weak climber. The 3–4" wide leaves are whorled in fours and are obviously pointed. The flowers are also 3–4" wide and rosy purple, darker in the throat. 'Chocolate Cherry' offers flowers in the burgundy and wine range, with a brownish throat.

Alocasia (al o kay' see a)   elephant ear   Araceae

The desire for big and tropical has brought the diverse plants of this genus to America. The seventy species show a terrific amount of variability, but they are all characterized by long sheathed petioles, arising from a tuber or rhizome, that carry the large leaves. Leaves may be blotched or mottled, or the veins and midrib may be brightly colored, but subtle they are not. The leaves are usually peltate, at least when plants are young, but the peltate characteristic is less obvious as the plants mature. The flowers are typical aroid flowers, with a narrow spadix surrounded by a white- to cream-colored spathe. If the plant ever flowers, look at the spadix: you will notice the female flowers on the bottom of the cylinder, a row or two of odd-looking flowers called staminodes, then the male flowers above those. In most spadixes, there is also an essentially sterile area at the top. Interesting for the morbidly curious, and fascinating for the botanically hungry. But make no mistake about it: plants are garden-grown for the leaves, not the flowers.

When these plants first sprang upon the landscape market, gardeners and the occasional grower wanted to know how to tell *Alocasia* from the closely related *Colocasia*. The name *Alocasia* is simply a variant of *Colocasia*—and if they borrowed each other's name, they are closely related indeed. Unfortunately, there is no easy way to tell them apart. Two subtle differences do occur in the flower: the position of the ovules in *Alocasia* are basal but are borne on the side of the ovary in *Colocasia*; and the sterile section one can see at the top of the spadix in *Alocasia* is absent in *Colocasia*. Now such characteristics might help a taxonomist, but in my garden, these suckers never flower, so what am I supposed to look at? I look at the mature leaves. They are always peltate in *Colocasia* but less so in *Alocasia*. Not much to go on, but as I said, there is no easy way. After a while, one simply memorizes one's favorites and, like a pro, bids neighbors, "Come see my magnificent alocasia."

Quick guide to *Alocasia* species

	Height	Leaf color	Leaf margin
A. cuprea	3'	glossy green	entire
A. macrorrhiza	10'	green	undulate
A. micholitziana	3'	dark green	undulate

-cuprea (kew pree′ a)   copper alocasia   2–4′/3′
   summer   purple to green spathe   Borneo, Malaya

The foliage of copper alocasia is among the most beautiful in the genus, resembling burnished metal. Two-foot-long petioles hold the oval, pointed leaf blades. The thick leaves are about 18″ long and 12″ wide, dark metallic green on the upper surface, and deep purple beneath, and puckered along the prominent veins. The upper lobes are almost united, forming a notched leaf base, accentuating the peltate nature. But it is the broad heavily shaded (almost black) midrib and arched silvery veins that make the plant so appealing.

Partial shade.

-*macrorrhiza* (ma kro ri′ za)   elephant ear   8–12′/4′
summer   green to light yellow spathe   India, Malaya

Among the larger species in the genus, *Alocasia macrorrhiza* has for centuries
been cultivated in the tropics for its large edible rhizome (*macrorrhiza* means
"large root") and shoots. In the ornamental garden, plants can grow up to 15′
tall in areas of high heat and humidity; in most areas of the country, 6–8′ is
usual. Unlike most alocasias, this species can make a significant stem, up to 6′
in height. The leaf blades are 5–6′ long and 3–4′ wide, in the shape of an arrowhead (sagittate), with the short lobes pointing up. They are peltate only when
plants are young. The margins of these huge bright green leaves are somewhat
wavy, and the conspicuous midrib is broad and depressed. The nine to twelve
pairs of veins may be green or white, and blotches of color often occur between
the veins in named cultivars.

Elephant ears must be placed in full sun; anything less results in long
stretched petioles that are insufficiently strong to support the large leaves.
Hardy in zone 9.

Propagate by division, but use strong equipment—a kitchen knife won't do it.

CULTIVARS

'Black Stem' offers purple petioles.

'Variegata', the most common cultivar, bears leaves with areas of dark green,
gray-green, and ivory. Each leaf is a little different; some may be almost totally
white. The petioles are longitudinally striped with green and white.

'Violacea' has violet-tinged leaves.

-*micholitziana* (mich o litz ee a′ na)   wavy alocasia   2–4′/2′
summer   greenish spathe   Philippines

A far more refined plant than *Alocasia macrorrhiza*, this species bears narrow
sagittate leaves with obvious wavy margins. The soft-textured leaves are rich
green above and dull green below, showing off clean white to cream veins. The
petioles are marbled with brown or purple. Plants are more useful for smaller
gardens, growing only to about 3′, although more vigor is seen in warmer summers. Primitive and sophisticated at the same time. Plants were named for W.
Micholitz, who collected in Southeast Asia for the British nursery owned by
Henry Sander (1847–1920).

Full sun, consistently moist soils.

CULTIVARS

'Maxkowskii', a more common form, has broader and darker leaves than the
species (some say they are almost black). The velvety leaves are less wavy and
heart-shaped, with non-marbled petioles. Their beauty lies in the wonderful
stylized pure white veins which contrast beautifully with the rest of the leaf
blade. Also sold as 'African Mask', 'Green Velvet', and 'Green Goddess'.

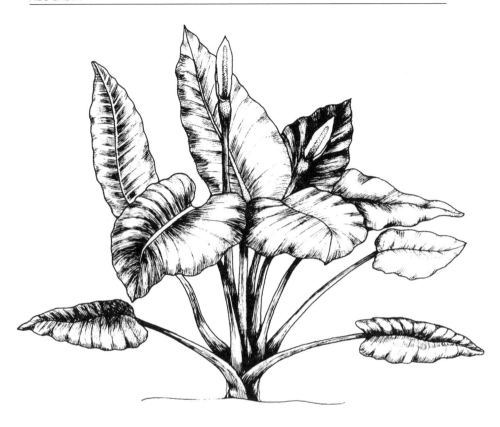

Alocasia macrorrhiza   CHRIS JOHNSON

Alternative species

Alocasia odora is similar to *A. macrorrhiza* and often confused in the trade. It may be distinguished by its consistently peltate leaves, which are held stiffly upright. Plants may even be a little larger than *A. macrorrhiza*. No cultivars are known.

Alocasia plumbea (black taro) is also similar to *A. macrorrhiza*, but its vegetative parts are colored or tinged purple. 'Metallica' has leaves with a purple sheen, 'Nigra' bears dark green, almost black, leaves, and 'Rubra' produces leaves tinged with red. Plants grow 2–3′ tall.

Alocasia zebrina (zebra taro), related to *A. cuprea*, has triangular green leaves above and beneath, and grows to 3′ in height. It is easy to identify because of the pale green and purple stripes on the petioles. 'Glaucous' has blue-green foliage. Extraordinary.

Quick key to *Alocasia* species

A. Leaf blades 2–4' long . . . . *A. macrorrhiza*
AA. Leaf blades <2' long
    B. Basal lobes of leaves united for nearly entire length,
       leaf blades deep purple beneath . . . . *A. cuprea*
    BB. Basal lobes shortly united, leaf blades pale green
       beneath . . . . *A. micholitziana*

Alocasia hybrids

Many selections of *Alocasia* have been offered to the gardening public, from the Midwest to Florida and the Deep South. The upsurge in interest in foliage plants has made some selections darlings of the landscape industry throughout the country and crazy-gardener must-haves.

×*amazonica* is a hybrid between *Alocasia lowii*, a Malaysian species with metallic bluish green leaves, and *A. sanderiana*, a species with triangular cream-veined leaves, deeply notched. Also sold as *A. amazonica* or 'Amazonica', it has an upright habit and long leaves with a wavy margin; the velvety leaves are 2' long and 1' wide, dark green above with silvery veins, purple beneath. 'Polly' bears deep green lacquered leaves with white veins.

'Aquino' has long arrowhead-shaped silvery green leaves with sunken veins.

'Black Velvet' is a compact grower with dark velvet green leaves and contrasting silver veins.

'Frydek' has rich dark green soft-textured foliage, painted with creamy white veins. The leaves have obvious lobes at the base and points at the tips. About 3' tall and equally wide. This may be a cultivar of *Alocasia micholitziana*.

'Hilo Beauty' is 2–3' tall with black stems and thin, 8–12" long green leaves mottled with lime-yellow and silvery gray blotches. A water lover.

Additional reading

Bown, Deni. 2000. *Aroids*, 2nd ed. Timber Press, Portland, Ore.
Riffle, Robert Lee. 1998. *The Tropical Look*. Timber Press, Portland, Ore.

Alonsoa (a lon zo' a)   mask flower   Scrophulariaceae

The genus consists of about twelve species, most of which are 1–2' tall and herbaceous, although the shrubby orange-flowered *Alonsoa linearis* can be 3' tall. The flowers, held in terminal racemes, consist of an irregular five-lobed corolla (petals) and five sepals. Twisting of the individual flower stems (pedicel) results in the largest lobe being uppermost on each flower. The leaves are usually opposite or in threes. Exceptionally vivid in massed displays, they catch one's eye even in tubs and pots. There has been very little interest in this genus in American landscapes—an oversight on the part of plant breeders and niche nurseries, I think. Perhaps as plants become more common in retail and garden centers, more gardeners and landscapers may give them a try.

-warscewiczii (war sha vich' ee i)   mask flower   1–2'/18"
   all   season scarlet, salmon   Peru

I first saw mask flower used as a garden and pot plant in Denmark in the 1980s. Plants stood about 1' tall and held numerous salmon flowers in inflorescences above the leaves. They were quite beautiful. I obtained a little seed and did some experimenting in the greenhouse, but our temperatures proved to be too warm, or I proved to be too incompetent, to reproduce the beauty of the plants I saw. But my incompetence should not discourage others from experimenting in the garden. Plants bear opposite, oval to heart-shaped, pointed leaves with doubly serrated margins. If grown well, dozens of flower stems will occur in late spring and continue off and on most of the season under cool summers. Plant in full sun to partial shade in deep containers and reasonably moist soils. They can be used throughout the summer in the North but are better as spring and early summer plants in the South (they died again by mid July in UGA trials). Mask flower is a nice change but not nearly as weather-tolerant as common bedding plants.

CULTIVARS

'Alba' is a white-flowered form.

Alternative species

Alonsoa meridionalis is a highly branched 1–2' tall plant. I don't see too many mask flowers in my travels, but I came across this scarlet to dull orange form in containers in an English garden several years ago, and I was smitten again. Plants are available in this country, and in particular the handsome pink-flowered 'Shell Pink' should be tried. I also have enjoyed 'Salmon Beauty', whose yellow stamens contrast well with the salmon flowers. Full sun in the North, partial shade in the South.

Quick key to *Alonsoa* species

A. Individual flowers up to 1" wide, flowers longer than
   pedicels, filament crooked . . . . *A. warscewiczii*
AA. Individual flowers smaller, pedicels longer than flowers,
    filament not obviously crooked . . . . *A. meridionalis*

Alpinia (al pin' ee a)   ginger lily   Zingiberaceae

Many genera of gingers have become popular as landscape features, providing a tropical look in the midst of other annuals or perennials. The ginger family provides such variation of flower and foliage and has a great future in gardening and design. In recent years, ginger lilies have been rediscovered by landscapers and gardeners outside Florida and Texas, and although most are not hardy north of zone 8, they grow just fine as annuals in temperate climates, and roots can withstand temperatures in the teens, if not sustained. Alpinias are tall plants from the forest verges of China, India, Southeast Asia, and tropical Australia. They are grown for their showy flowers, which resemble seashells, but since plants require two years to flower, gardeners north of zone 9 must appreciate them for their foliage. Of the 200 species, only three or four have broken away from tropical areas and can be considered garden plants in this country.

Quick guide to *Alpinia* species

	Height	Flower color
A. japonica	2–3'	red and white
A. galanga	6–7'	yellow
A. purpurata	7–10'	red
A. zerumbet	2–4'	whitish

-purpurata (per per a' ta)	red ginger	7–10'/3'
late summer	red	SE Pacific

The flowering forms of red ginger require long summers, sufficient heat, and two-year-old plants before flowering will occur. In zones 8 to 10, they are often used as cut flowers that persist for weeks in water. They grow excessively tall in hot climates (>12') but are better behaved in temperate gardens. The terminal inflorescences are up to 2' long; the showy part is the bright red bracts, which surround the small white flowers. In northern gardens, flowering probably won't occur, however, and plants should be enjoyed for the tropical look of the foliage, rather than the flowers. The glossy green leaves, which can be up to 3' long and 6" wide, are borne at right angles to the reed-like stems and have a distinctly lighter-colored midrib.

Place in full sun, provide lots of water. Propagate by division or from young plantlets formed in the inflorescence. Most plants in the trade are raised through tissue culture.

CULTIVARS

'Dwarf Pink' is a more dwarf form, growing only 3–4' tall and bearing light pink inflorescences.

'Fire and Ice' has pink and white inflorescences.

'Fireball' bears red and white flowers.

'Hot Pink' grows to full height with bright pink inflorescences.

'Jungle Queen' bears pale pink, almost white inflorescences.

'Pink Ginger' is 6–7' tall with pink inflorescences.

'Tahitian Ginger' has short, fat inflorescences of a darker red.

-zerumbet (ze rum' bet)	shell ginger	4–6'/3'
late summer	white	east Asia

The 2' long lanceolate leaves have hairy margins and are sessile. The flowers are pendulous from the leaf axils and consist of pink bract-like structures around white flowers. The flowers are noticeably fragrant but will probably not be appreciated except in a greenhouse or conservatory, north of zone 8. In the tropics, plants can reach a height of 12', with 1' long inflorescences. In temperate climates, 4–6' is more common. I include this species only for its variegated leaf form, which is an exceptional plant for the landscape.

CULTIVARS

'Variegata' has wonderful dark green leaves with bright yellow bands or stripes. The best of all alpinias for temperate gardens, it grows about 3' tall. Excellent for the tropical look that is pleasing to the eye even without the whitish flowers.

Alternative species

Alpinia galanga (ga lan' ga; Thai spice ginger) is well known in Asia, particularly Thailand, where its rhizomes (sold as galangel, Laos root, and Siamese ginger) are used in cooking. The 5–7' tall plant, a relative of *A. purpurata*, produces small pale yellow flowers with maroon stripes on 12" long inflorescences. Reasonably cold hardy, it flowers after frosts. Hardy to zone 8, perhaps to zone 7.

Alpinia japonica is related to *A. zerumbet*. Best known for the cultivar 'Kinisiana' (peppermint stick), plants bear long wavy leaves that are markedly hairy on the undersides. The flowers are held in spikes and consist of red and white peppermint flowers. They grow to about 2' tall in shade.

Additional reading

Chapman, Timothy. 1995. *Ornamental Gingers*. 6920 Bayou Paul Rd., St. Gabriel, LA 70776.
San Felasco Nurseries: www.sanfelasco.com
Stokes Tropicals: www.stokestropicals.com
Wight Nurseries of North Carolina: www.wightnurseries.com

Alternanthera (al ter nan' the ra)   calico plant   Amaranthaceae

The approximately 200 species of this rather nondescript genus occur in an amazing diversity of habitat in tropical and subtropical America. Included in this number are "normal" garden plants as well as the invasive aquatic species, *Alternanthera philoxeroides* (alligator weed). With that many species, it is a cinch that one or two of them will be useful as landscape subjects. Alternantheras were popular in Victorian times, when formal gardens demanded plants which could be shaped and clipped to within 6" of the ground. The most common

species is the low-growing *A. ficoidea* (fih koy' dee a), which is grown for its variously colored leaves. Other species found in the trade are *A. bettzichiana*, which
is similar to *A. ficoidea*, and *A. dentata*, a highly useful species with sprawling and
upright forms. The generic name was suggested by the alternately arranged
anthers inside the small flowers.

Quick guide to *Alternanthera* species

	Habit	Height	Use
A. bettzichiana	edging, shaping	9–24"	formal design, container
A. dentata	sprawling to upright	1–3'	garden, container
A. ficoidea	edging, shaping	6–9"	formal design, container

-dentata (den ta′ ta)	upright calico plant	1–3′/2′
all season	foliage	West Indies

Historically plants in the genus have been thought of as edging, shaping plants,
but *Alternanthera dentata* has strong upright to pendulous stems and is quite
useful as a garden plant or in large containers, complementing other annuals or
perennials. The stems bear linear to lanceolate leaves, 3–4″ long and 2″ wide,
either rounded or coming to a point at the base. In the species, the leaves are
dark green, pale green beneath, and slightly dentate; in selections, however,
leaves are often entire, particularly those of the purple-leaved forms. The white
to greenish flowers occur in short spikes in the leaf axils.

Full sun, well-drained soils. Propagate by two- or three-node cuttings.

CULTIVARS

'Gail's Choice' was discovered by Gail Kahle of Plano, Texas. Plants are dwarf
(<15″ tall) and spread at least double the height. They bear 2–3″ long leaves all
season, regardless of heat. An outstanding plant, similar to 'Wave Hill' but less
leggy and with leaves of a more lustrous deep purple.

'Rubiginosa' (indoor clover) may often be found as a houseplant. With its
sprawling habit and reddish purple leaves, it makes a terrific filler in the container, and cut stems are useful for bouquet color. Quite similar to 'Gail's
Choice' but not as red nor as dwarf. Also sold as 'Ruby' and 'Versicolor'.

'Wave Hill', an exceptional foliage plant, is named for the excellent garden of
the same name in the Bronx, New York. The large purple leaves are borne on
strong 2–3′ long stems. Taller than and not as shiny in leaf as 'Gail's Choice'
but still highly useful for containers and mixing in the landscape. Introduced by
Saul's Nursery of Atlanta, Georgia.

-ficoidea (fih koy′ dee a)	joseph's coat	6–9″/1′
all season	foliage	Mexico, South America

There is a small but passionate audience for *Alternanthera ficoidea* (joseph's coat),
particularly where floral designs are part of the landscape palette. Municipalities

using floral designs in parks or town halls need small formal colorful plants for success. In some provinces of Canada and the northern states, perpetual care in cemeteries includes floral designs on grave sites. My first job was in a Jewish cemetery in Montreal; in the decrepit tiny greenhouse there, I propagated joseph's coat for formal plantings on grave sites. Digging the grave was difficult, but it was a joy to see the pleasure in the faces of the loved ones when they saw the colorful manicured plots. I believed their pain was lessened for a short time.

The best form for clipped edging plants is *Alternanthera ficoidea* var. *amoena* (a mee' na; syn. *A. amoena*; parrot plant); these were mainstays in Victorian times and are still used in floral clocks and other plant design masterpieces. Cultivars of this variety are usually offered in a mix, although separate colors may be available; foliar colors occur in orange, rose, carmine, and pink.

The ½–1″ opposite linear to obovate leaves of the species taper at the base and are usually green, variously blotched with an assortment of colors. The white to creamy flowers are solitary or in few globe-like flower clusters, held in the axils. They are seldom noticed, so hidden are they by the foliage. Plant in full sun.

Propagate by two-node cuttings. Use a mild concentration of rooting hormone, and place in moist media at 73–77°F, preferably under mist or a sweat tent. Rooting occurs in twelve to twenty days, depending on season and presence or absence of bottom heat.

CULTIVARS

'Christmas Tree' is a tiny-leaved mounding selection of *Alternanthera ficoidea* var. *amoena* with gray-green leaves. One of the smallest, most compact forms offered.

'Filigree' is small and slow-growing, with narrow red-bronze leaves.

'Frizzy', a well-named plant, has very narrow, almost thread-like light green leaves. The uppermost ones turn yellow as the season progresses. Plants grow 4–8″ tall.

'Green Machine' is a low (2–3″) form with wide puckered green leaves. Off-white bracts occur in the leaves most of the season.

'Krinkle' is about 6″ tall, with crinkled rust-colored leaves marked with green and yellow.

'Rosea Nana' (pygmy parrot plant), another var. *amoena* cultivar, has small spatula-shaped rose-colored leaves on reasonably bushy plants.

'Snowball' is a many-branched plant with delicate green leaves splashed with white. Quite handsome.

'Tricolor' has relatively large leaves of purple, variegated in pink. This is occasionally listed, incorrectly, as *Alternanthera purpurea* 'Tricolor'. Quite handsome.

'White Carpet' has small puckered leaves with creamy white margins.

Alternative species

Alternanthera bettzichiana (bet sich ee an' a; red calico plant) is more upright than of *A. ficoidea*. Its venation pattern differs subtly, and the petiole is longer relative to the leaf blade; however, they are sufficiently similar botanically that some authorities lump this species in with *A. ficoidea*.

'Aurea Nana' is only about 4" tall and consists of grassy foliage, splashed with cream, yellow, and dark green. May be a hybrid with *Alternanthera ficoidea*. Also sold as 'Aurea Supernana'.

'Big Red' bears larger leaves in red to bronze hues. Similar to 'Brilliantissima'.

'Brilliantissima' bears coppery red leaves with pink centers and purple veins.

'True Yellow' (golden calico plant) produces wide chartreuse-yellow foliage— a good yellow form. This and other related forms have really caught on with landscapers who are into the chartreuse stage of their lives. I have often seen 'True Yellow' combined with 'Margarita' sweet potato and 'Amazon' coleus, the three together making a single Dantesque inferno.

Quick key to *Alternanthera* species

A. Plant <12" tall, leaves generally blotched in many colors
  B. Petiole less than half as long as leaf blade . . . . *A. ficoidea*
  BB. Petiole at least half as long or longer than leaf blade . . . .
  . . . . *A. bettzichiana*
AA. Plant >12" tall, usually 2–3', stems sprawling or upright . . . . . *A. dentata*

Additional reading

Shi, W. X., and X. C. Wang. 1990. *The Purifying Efficiency and Mechanism of Aquatic Plants in Ponds*. Pergamon Press, New York.

Amaranthus (a ma ran' thus)   amaranth   Amaranthaceae

This genus of sixty widely distributed species is probably best known for the omnipresent red root pigweed, *Amaranthus retroflexus*, and some of the tumble-weeds, such as *A. albus*, that spread eastward with the railroads. Some of the most exotic-looking greenhouse and garden plants can be found under this genus. To many, "exotic" is a euphemism for "weird" and "ugly," and these plants have seldom been accused of being pretty. Some of the gaudiest culti-vated forms, particularly varieties of *A. tricolor*, are favorites of municipal plant-ings and landscape islands, and their flowers and foliage are seldom passed with-out comment. The pendulous forms, such as *A. caudatus*, are generally seen in conservatories or botanical gardens but are also useful for hanging baskets.

The young leaves of many species enjoy a culinary reputation, especially those of red root pigweed, while the young foliage of *Amaranthus caudatus*, *A. tricolor*, and *A. cruentus* are widely cultivated in tropical zones as leaf vegetables.

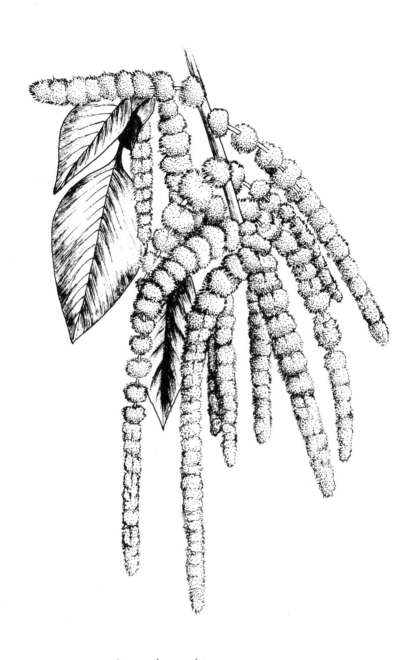

Amaranthus caudatus   CHRIS JOHNSON

Quick guide to *Amaranthus* species

	Flowers	Flower color	Height
A. caudatus	drooping	red	up to 4' in baskets
A. cruentus	drooping to erect	red	3–6'
A. hypochondriacus	erect	red	3–6'
A. tricolor	erect	colors from upper leaves	1–2'

-caudatus (kaw′ da tus)	love-lies-bleeding, tassel flower	3–5'/1–2'
summer	red	Peru, Africa, India

As an eight-year-old boy, I remember seeing screaming red pigtails hanging down from a large container, and I thought they looked kind of violent. Then I read the common name and knew I was not too far off the mark. I said to myself, "Who would name a plant love-lies-bleeding?" It was a very bad day for either the explorer or a country western singer.

Plants grow 2–6' tall with oval, pointed leaves, 3–5" wide, and drooping spikes of blood-red flowers that resemble knotted strands of rope. The spikes are terminal or in the leaf axils and may extend 1' or so in length. Most of the time, they are planted in baskets to show off the drooping flower strands, and in that case, the plants themselves become pendulous, rather than growing upright. The hanging tassels are useful as cut flowers, adding colorful flowers and foliage to many a tired bouquet. The flowers also dry well, so the tassels may be enjoyed for months on end.

Full sun to partial shade. If you use baskets, which tend to dry out, place the basket in morning sun and afternoon shade. Rich soils are not necessary, but fertilizing at half strength at least twice during the season insures the plants will remain leafy and not yellow out. Plants are better in the North than in the South, where the heat and humidity combine to shorten their ornamental effectiveness. Keep the container moist.

Propagate by two-node cuttings or by seed. Germinate at approximately 72°F under mist or in a sweat tent. Seeds germinate in two to three weeks. Barely cover seeds, as they germinate better when exposed to light.

CULTIVARS

'Green Thumb' has vivid green flowers. Similar to 'Viridis' but a brighter green.

'Love-Lies-Bleeding' is a name given to all plants with long (up to 2') drooping blood-red tassels and dark green leaves.

'Summer Love' is a dwarf form, growing only about 15" tall, with 4–8" long pink tassels.

'Viridis' has the same flower form as 'Summer Love', but the flowers are chartreuse-green. Not as colorful but equally effective.

-hypochondriacus (hi po kon dree a' kus) prince's feather 3-6'/3'
summer red Mexico, India, China

These spectacular, colorful plants show off both foliage and flowers during the summer, and under cool summer conditions, remain colorful until frost. *Amaranthus hypochondriacus* (syn. *A. erythostachys*) is known as prince's feather, and individual selections are also sold under that name, despite the range of variability in flower and foliage at both levels. These are upright, architectural garden plants, with dark green foliage that is sometimes deeply flushed purple. The deep crimson axillary flower spikes stand upright above the foliage, like popping fireworks. You cover your ears when you see them. As garish as these plants are, they are more graceful than love-lies-bleeding.

Place in full sun. Pinch in early spring to encourage branching prior to flowering; fertilize occasionally with half-strength fertilizer in mid summer. Propagate by seed or terminal cuttings.

CULTIVARS

'Prince's Feather' is a 3-5' tall generic blood-red selection.
'Pygmy Torch' is 2-3' tall, with deep maroon flowers and purple foliage.

-tricolor (tri' kul er) joseph's coat, tampala, Chinese spinach 1-3'/1'
all season foliage Indonesia

If you look up the word "gaudy" in an illustrated dictionary, selections of this plant will likely be pictured as examples. That is the neat thing about gardening: there is room for all tastes. Plants are erect, with alternate oval leaves 8-10" long and about 3" wide. The 1" long flower spikes are found in most of the leaf axils but are insignificant compared to the uppermost foliage. In the species, the upper leaves are deeper green or purple, but selections have so expanded the color range that well-grown plants are visible to onlookers speeding by at 55 mph, hanging out the window. Plant in full sun in the North; a little afternoon shade does not hurt in the South. Plants are like fireworks, bursting forth in a dazzling display of color but rapidly fading when afternoon rains appear. Summer rain and humidity result in short seasons; heat without humidity is seldom a problem, however, and the fireworks are tremendous while the show goes on!

Most purchased plants are propagated from seed, and occasionally seed of good selections is offered for sale. Sow at 75°F; germination will take eight to ten days. May also be propagated from terminal cuttings.

CULTIVARS

'Aurora' is 4-5' tall and has spectacular creamy yellow uppermost leaves. A 55-mph plant, easily seen from a distance.
'Early Splendor' bears bright crimson uppermost leaves and bronze bottom foliage.
'Flaming Fountain' has thin willow-like leaves of carmine, crimson, and bronze.

'Illumination' almost looks like a poinsettia, with large orange to scarlet upper leaves with golden centers. The lower leaves are green to bronze.

'Intense Purple' is just that, with leaves veined deep purple to red and intense red-purple tassels.

'Molten Fire' has a scarlet growing center over green to bronze leaves.

'Splendens' is among the most colorful, if not the showiest, cultivars; the leaves are deep red, those uppermost a brilliant light red. An even more exotic blend is 'Splendens Tricolor', whose uppermost leaves combine red and gold in a gaudy but not uninteresting combination; also sold as 'Splendens Perfecta'.

Alternative species

Amaranthus cruentus (purple amaranth, red amaranth) is similar enough to also be called prince's feather, but in the name of clarity, that name should be associated only with *A. hypochondriacus*. The leaves are smooth above, coarsely hairy beneath, and the sharp apex usually terminates in a soft "spine." The flowers are greenish red and droop from the leaf axils. Taxonomy on the genus is terribly mixed up, and this plant has been called *A. paniculatus*, *A. hybridus*, and a few others. Full sun.

'Bronze Standard' has bronze flower spikes and deep green foliage.

'Foxtail' carries long deep red spike-like racemes of flowers over bronze foliage. Plants grow 2–3' tall.

'Hot Biscuits' is a favorite of mine, among the neatest plants I have seen. The plants grow 5–6' tall, and the 2' plumes of earthy cinnamon-feathered flowers are exceptional.

'Komo' is completely burgundy-colored, growing 5–6' tall. Outstanding!

'Oeschberg' grows to 6' in height, with dark scarlet flower spikes.

'Red Cathedral' is 4–5' tall with bronze-red leaves and large flowers of shocking burgundy.

Quick key to *Amaranthus* species

A. Flower clusters small, color coming from uppermost leaves   . . . *A. tricolor*
AA. Flowers in large spikes or panicles, erect or pendulous
    B. Plant 3–6' tall, flowers in panicles
        C. Flowers erect in broad panicles . . . . *A. hypochondriacus*
        CC. Flowers erect to drooping, not as broad . . . . *A. cruentus*
    BB. Flowers in long narrow drooping spikes . . . . *A. caudatus*

Ammi (a′ mee)   Apiaceae

I attended a wedding recently and did what all dads with twenty-year-old daughters do: took notes. The wedding was lovely, the bride was crying and the groom was clueless—all was normal. Later in the reception hall, I met some of my students, and we immediately had a quiz on the flowers in the arrangements. That is what gardeners do at weddings. The yellow sunflowers, the deep green fennel, and the mums were beautifully set off by some airy white flowers that looked like the roadside flower, queen anne's lace (*Daucus carota*). Surprise, surprise, most of my students knew we were looking at false queen anne's lace, *Ammi majus*. The arrival of the happy bride and groom, and the smell of cooked meatballs, pulled us from our plant reveries of roadside look-alikes.

Every now and then plants appear under the name of bishop's flower, but that name is better reserved for the common perennial *Aegopodium podagraria*. The genus has been studied extensively, particularly in pharmaceutical circles. Numerous flavonols, alkaloids (some poisonous to livestock), and cumarins have been isolated from leaves and fruit of *Ammi majus*. The fruit of *A. visnaga* contains visnadine, which affects peripheral and coronary vasodilator activity and has been used in the treatment of angina pectoris.

Ammi majus is usually grown by cut flower growers, appearing at the florist's after harvest, but it can just as easily attain its 2–3' of height in the garden. The leaves are pinnately compound, and the flowers are white and umbrella-like, similar to those of queen anne's lace but larger (4–6" wide). The foliage is more open and delicate, and the leaves are smaller and less coarse. It is as adaptable to Alabama as to Arizona. When cutting the stems, use gloves and long sleeves. The sap of the cut stems may result in contact dermatitis in sensitive individuals. Plant in full sun.

Propagate by seed (chill seed at 40–45°F for one to two weeks prior to sowing). Probably less than 50% of the seeds will germinate, but seedlings will appear in one to two weeks. They may be sown in the garden in the fall and will emerge in early spring.

CULTIVARS

'Queen of Africa' is 3–4' tall but otherwise differs little from the species.
'Snowflake' has 2–3" wide flowers and grows 3' tall.
'White Dill' bears flowers that are slightly whiter than *A. majus*.

Alternative species

Ammi visnaga (green mist) is a much bigger, coarser, and, in my opinion, more beautiful form than false queen anne's lace. The chartreuse flowers open slowly and are outstanding in the garden. Flowers are useful as cuts as well. Difficult to locate but well worth the search.

Additional reading

Armitage, Allan M. 1993. *Specialty Cut Flowers*. Timber Press, Portland, Ore.

Ammobium (a mo' bee um)   winged everlasting   Asteraceae

Another of the many genera of everlasting flowers. The only species in commerce is *Ammobium alatum*, easily distinguished from other everlastings (see at *Helipterum*) by its winged stems. Plants are native to eastern Australia, and do well only in warm areas with cool nights and a minimum of afternoon rains. Although they can be as handsome in the garden as they are in the arrangement, they are mainly grown so that their flowers may be cut and dried. When cut and hung to dry, every part of the flower dries perfectly, and they persist forever in the vase. Cut the stems before the flowers are fully expanded.

The leaves, which look a little like a dandelion's, are basal or alternate; they are about 6″ long and 2″ wide, with apices as sharp as a javelin's point. In early to mid summer, weird winged flower stems arise like David Copperfield from the haze. The white flowers are about 1½″ across and characterized by dry, chaffy silvery bracts. If the stems are cut, additional wings will take flight—no need to fear a shortage of flowers for the garden or the vase.

Full sun, propagate by seed. Seed can be germinated in the spring at 72–75°F under mist or high humidity conditions. It can also be sown directly outdoors in the spring. Although commonly grown as annuals, plants can be treated as biennials by sowing seeds outdoors in late summer and early fall. Plants fare better in the North than in the South, where high heat and humidity, combined with afternoon rains, result in significant disease problems.

CULTIVARS

'Bikini' bears white flowers ¾″ wide with yellow centers. Plants are only about 15″ tall and quite useful for the smaller garden.

Anagallis (a na ga′ lis)   pimpernel   Primulaceae

Now here is a plant we could all use, particularly on Mondays. The generic name comes from the Greek, *anagelao* ("to laugh"); plants were thought to possess the ability to dispel sadness. When I see a good basket of pimpernel in the garden, I am ecstatic. Works for me.

Only two or three of the approximately twenty known species of *Anagallis* are ever seen in American gardens, and even they are not common.

-monellii (mon el′ ee i)	blue pimpernel	1–2′/2′
summer	blue	Mediterranean

The free-branching plants are especially useful for containers and baskets, with long angled stems flowing up, out, and over. The ovate to elliptical leaves are opposite, occasionally whorled, and entire, about 1″ long and not as wide. The small dark blue flowers (ca. ½″ wide) are borne in the upper axils of the plants and consist of five rounded petals and five small sepals. Flowers are generally tinged with a little red. The plants used in American gardens are sometimes seen in rock gardens or other well-drained areas but also in containers and baskets.

Plant in full sun in the North, afternoon shade in the South. Provide consistent moisture, but not wet soils, for best performance. Propagate named cultivars by terminal cuttings, species by seed (bottom heat and humidity are useful).

'African Sunset' is vigorous and bears flowers of brilliant blue.

'Blue Light' grows vigorously and flowers well. Similar to 'Skylover'.

'Skylover', the most common cultivar, is used almost exclusively in containers. The plants are self-branching and make large plants over time. The 1″ wide flowers are blue with violet-pink centers. Plants have done well in trials around the country and can be recommended for long flowering times and handsome flowers.

Alternative species

Anagallis arvensis (common pimpernel; scarlet pimpernel) is trailing, with branches growing out and long. A European field weed, it is seldom thought of as an ornamental plant for the garden. The flowers, which tend to close at the approach of bad weather, were known as poor man's weatherglass. The small flowers are usually scarlet, sometimes white, but in var. *caerulea*, the flowers are sky blue and similar to *A. monellii*. Plants are best used for baskets.

Anchusa (an koo′ sa) alkanet Boraginaceae

Few of the approximately thirty known species of this genus are suitable for the garden. All these are biennials or short-lived (two or three years) perennials and provide flowers in the blue range, a color effect that is often difficult to find in the spring and summer garden. Members of *Anchusa* are characterized by alternate leaves, hairy stems, and a scorpioid cyme (flowers arranged together in the shape of a scorpion's tail). The best known is the perennial *A. azurea* (Italian alkanet), but at least one annual form is also available.

| *-capensis* (ka pen′ sis) | annual alkanet | 1–3′/1′ |
| spring, summer | lavender, blue | South Africa |

I brought back some seeds of this biennial from England a few years ago and put them by the entrance of the UGA Horticulture Gardens. A few leaves and some flowers in blue and pink hues came up that first year, but since other flowers covered them up, I hardly remembered they were there. The second year's leaves, however, appeared in very early spring and soon gave way to long stems with beautiful gentian-blue to pink flowers.

Plants grow to 2′ tall with 4–6″ long alternate, hairy, linear to lanceolate leaves. The flowers are numerous and occur in compound inflorescences in spring and early summer. After flowering, small fruit is formed, which releases many seeds. Seedlings will appear in fall or early spring, and flowering will occur the same year. Plants persist longer in cool than in warm climes.

I am sowing more seeds, since those original plants were mistaken for weeds by one of my students and received a lethal dose of herbicide. We washed, scrubbed, and provided life support as soon as we discovered the error, but plants succumbed nevertheless. Lesson learned, life goes on.

Full sun, propagate by seed.

CULTIVARS

'Blue Angel' has dark blue to ultramarine flowers on 9–12" tall plants.
'Blue Bird' is about 18" tall and bears dark blue flowers. A 1935 All-America Selection.
'Dawn' is a mixture of pink, white, and blue flowers on 18–24" tall plants.
'Pink Bird' is about 18" tall and has pink flowers.

Angelica (an jel' ih ka)   Apiaceae

These biennials are better known for their angelic medicinal properties (from which the generic name comes) than as ornamental garden plants. The fifty or so species are found in the northern United States and Canada, Japan, and Europe. In general, they are tall, stout, and at home in semi-shaded moist areas. The leaves are ternate (in threes) to pinnate, and the petioles are usually sheathed around the stem. The available garden forms are impressive but often short-lived.

Quick guide to *Angelica* species

	Height	Flower color
A. *archangelica*	5–6'	creamy white
A. *gigas*	3–5'	purple

-archangelica (ar kan jel' ih ka)	wild parsnip	5–6'/4'
early summer	creamy white	Europe, Asia

Say the name *Angelica archangelica* a few times and it begins to take on poetic qualities of its own. The specific name came from the archangel Raphael. The plant has been cultivated for generations in Asia and Europe for its confectionery properties and as a vegetable. The stems and petioles may be candied or crystallized, and the young shoots can be prepared as you would asparagus, or cooked with rhubarb to reduce the tartness. But don't let your taste (or lack thereof) for rhubarb limit the use of this plant! As a cultivated plant, it lends a stateliness of its own to the garden. The large flat, creamy white to greenish compound umbels are handsome enough, but the resulting seed heads can be absolutely majestic. These large plants can take over an area and will reseed if allowed to do so. Plants are monocarpic, meaning they die after seeding. Some gardeners have found that removing the flowers before they go to seed increases the chance of perennialization. Seedlings require two years to flower. They can be grown as biennials as far north as zone 5.

Angelica archangelica   ASHA KAYS

-*gigas* (jee′ gas)   purple parsnip   3–5′/4′
   late summer,   fall purple   Japan, Korea, China

This large coarse plant, introduced to this country from Korea by Barry Yinger, is no longer a rarity in American nurseries. An exciting biennial plant for the late summer and fall garden, it never fails to draw attention when in flower. The light green leaves are attached to the thick stems with inflated purple sheaths. The flowers are deep purple, in umbels 3–4″ across. The drying seed heads are as magical as those of *Angelica archangelica*. The plant is tolerant of shade, but the dark flowers get lost if the shade is too heavy. Plants love moisture and will be stunted in dry summers. They will self-sow in favorable conditions and may be considered "perennial" biennials. Seed-grown plants generally require two years before flowering. In the shaded Armitage garden, plants were magnificent in June and July, although the seed heads never developed as well as I would have liked. The quality of the seed heads increases with sunny areas, cool night temperatures, and low humidity. First-year plants overwinter in zone 5, occasionally zone 4, but this species is often treated as an annual.

Quick key to *Angelica* species

  A. Petioles tinged purple, flowers deep purple . . . . *A. gigas*
  AA. Petioles not tinged purple, flowers creamy white to
      greenish white . . . . *A. archangelica*

Angelonia (an jel o′ nee a)   summer snapdragon   Scrophulariaceae

Plants are native to tropical and subtropical areas, where they are often cultivated as perennials or subshrubs. They are found wild in damp areas of the savannah and other open places, and although they naturalize in damp areas, they are quite drought-tolerant. The genus has become popular throughout the United States for its upright form, lovely long flower stems, and season-long flowering. Of the thirty species, only *Angelonia angustifolia* has received significant breeding or attention in the commercial world. The leaves are simple, opposite, and usually entire. The flowers are lipped and remind some people of small snapdragons; this look, combined with their heat tolerance, has provided a common name for the entire genus.

-*angustifolia* (an gus tih fo′ lee a)   summer snapdragon   2–4′/2′
   all season   blue, purple   Central America

I first saw this plant in 1994, in landscape containers designed by Kathy Pufahl. This fine grower had picked up some seed and produced a few plants at her Long Island nursery, Beds and Borders; the color she had planted was a handsome bicolor, and it looked great. I noted its snapdragon-like appearance and how well it handled the summertime heat, and I bet I showed that plant in

Angelonia angustifolia 'Angel Mist Pink'   ASHA KAYS

dozens of lectures and seminars around the country. Mostly I received vacant stares—until the spring of 1997, when Kathy's vision sprang on the retail scene in certain locations like a cheetah on the hunt. As we speak, availability is increasing. This is a no-brainer. Find it, grow it.

I have no problem with summer snapdragon as a common name, but *Angelonia angustifolia* rolls so sweetly off the tongue, we don't really need one. I'm sure someone will insult our intelligence and make up a four- or five-letter common name (watch out for "angel flower"), in the belief that anything with more than six letters can't be pronounced by the gardening public.

The alternate leaves work their way up the stems, and the inflorescences (flower stems) are made up of about a dozen individual lipped flowers, 1″ wide. Their heat tolerance is welcome throughout the country, and their drought tolerance too is appreciated. They reach 3′ in height, depending on cultivar and amount of heat; they can sprawl but require no staking. Plants are useful in the garden bed as well as in containers. They are not particularly adaptable to baskets.

Full sun, well-drained soils for best performance; plants are otherwise reasonably trouble free. Cutting back of spent flowers is not necessary, and plants will continue to flower under sunny warm conditions. Place on 9–12″ centers in the landscape; plants fill in two to three weeks after planting, depending on temperatures. They work in garden situations but do even better in large patio containers. Their biggest problem is that they may be too vigorous and may require a serious cutback during the summer. They associate well with gray-leaved plants, such as dusty miller, lamb's ears, or silver plectranthus. The blue forms look outstanding with yellow marigolds or lantanas, the whites with almost anything. My good friend and fine author Suzanne Bales brings them into her home. "They have a soft scent," she says, "and are wonderful as a cut flower, where they can be viewed up close."

Plants can be propagated by terminal cuttings, but virus has been a major problem with the genus, particularly in the bicolor forms. Buying greenhouse-grown material in the spring from reputable sources is the best bet. No seed is available.

CULTIVARS

'Alba' is a white-flowered form, highly diverse but not as vigorous as the blue forms.

Angel Mist series, a Ball Seed Co. introduction, offers upright vigorous plants in blue, purple, pink, bicolor, and white. The best news about this series is that plants are virus indexed and clean, which greatly reduces the possibility of spreading virus around the garden.

'Blue Pacific' has been around the longest, with its long spikes of blue and white flowers. Similar to 'Hilo Princess'.

'Light Blue' bears the prettiest flowers in a light blue. Plants are bushy and more compact.

'Mandiana Blue' is a vigorous well-branched lavender-blue form.

'Pandiana' has light pink flowers on 3′ tall stems. Excellent for cut flowers.

Princess series is made up of three cultivars, all of which are 2–3′ tall and bloom all summer. 'Hilo Princess' bears blue to purple flowers; 'Pink Princess' provides pink flowers and is among the tallest of the genus; 'Tiger Princess' is a lanky lavender-blue and white bicolor.

'Purple' has also graced our shores for some time. Purple flowers are held on vigorous, well-branched plants.

Additional reading

Armitage, Allan M. 1997. Angelonia. *Greenhouse Grower* 15(12):79–80.

Anisodontea (a nis o don′ tee a)   African mallow   Malvaceae

What does one do with nineteen species of African mallow, mostly from the Cape Province of South Africa? The answer is, not much. Gardeners have blissfully ignored the genus, characterized by its three-lobed leaves and mallow-like flowers. No species are common in gardens in North America, but *Anisodontea* ×*hypomandarum* (hybrid African mallow) is finding its way here and there. It is a vigorous shrub but not sufficiently cold hardy; plants die to the ground (may return zone 7 and higher), and gardeners have to start all over again. This is not a bad thing, as these plants can easily rise to 5′ in height and 3–4′ wide. The three-lobed leaves are 1–2″ long and toothed. The pink to rose flowers have darker veins and are produced in the upper axils. They are only about 1″ wide and are generally borne singly (sometimes in groups of two or three).

Plants look particularly good when grown as standards, that is, training the plant to a single stem and then pinching at 3–4′ to make a bush at the top. Perhaps that sounds like too much trouble, but shaping the plant, at the very least, will keep it in bounds. A pinch or two will do the trick. Natural root stress will help contain the plant if it is grown in a container. Not useful for baskets.

Full sun, propagate by cuttings or division.

Alternative species

Anisodontea capensis (ka pen′ sis) is woody at the base and grows to about 3′ in height. Flowers are produced in a raceme and consist of pale to deep magenta petals with darker veins and a basal spot. Individual flowers are less than 1″ wide. Full sun.

Anoda (a no′ da)   Malvaceae

This little-known genus consists of about ten species of annuals and perennials native to Central and South America. Of the ten species, *Anoda cristata* is becoming better known to American growers and gardeners. Before one gets too excited about this plant, it should be known that it is a problematic weed, par-

Anisodontea ✕*hypomandarum*   ASHA KAYS

ticularly troublesome in agricultural fields, where it reduces yields and costs hundreds of thousands of dollars in lost produce. Seed remains viable for many months, so the plant may be with you for a while. It is pretty, nevertheless, and the several excellent rediscovered selections have improved our perception of this annoying weed.

Plants grow 2–3′ tall and consist of variable triangular leaves, which are usually entire but may be coarsely toothed, and may or may not be lobed. The cup-shaped flowers are held in the axils of the upper leaves and are usually solitary or in pairs. They are 1–2″ wide and occur in lavender, white, or lavender-blue. If breeders can reduce the size of these plants, it is likely we will encounter them more frequently in garden centers.

Full sun, propagate by seed.

CULTIVARS

'Opal Cup' bears lavender-pink flowers with darker veins on 2–3′ tall plants.

'Snow Cup' has white to alabaster white flowers. Also sold as 'Silver Cup' and 'Snowdrop'.

Alternative species

Anoda wrightii is a 2–3′ tall plant, bearing rough stems and cordate leaves. The yellow flowers are only ½–1″ wide but bloom over a long period of time. 'Butter Cup' has butter-yellow flowers.

Antirrhinum (an tih ri′ num)   Scrophulariaceae

Although the common snapdragon, *Antirrhinum majus*, is by far the most common member of the genus, about forty species reside under the *Antirrhinum* banner. In general, the leaves are linear to lanceolate and usually alternate, although they may occasionally be opposite near the bottom of the stems.

The flowers are usually held in terminal racemes and are characterized by upper and lower lips, which look like a snapping dragon.

| *-majus* (may′ jus) | snapdragon | 1–4′/1′ |
| cool seasons | many colors | Mediterranean |

The snapdragon was a mainstay in great grandmother's garden and will be in your grandson's as well. Growing up in Montreal, my mother dutifully bought snapdragons at the corner market in the spring, and they flowered all summer. Then they got rust all over the leaves. I assumed that everyone put in snaps in the summer, and rust was just a leaf color. When I moved to balmy Michigan, I found the snaps were not doing as well in the heat of the summer there but still looked okay and still got rust. When we lived in north Georgia, people were planting them in the fall, to be enjoyed in the spring and early summer; in the summer, they were pulled out of the garden, as a humanitarian gesture. They didn't get much rust in the South because they weren't there at all.

Snaps are said to be perennial in the North and, with good snow cover, may very well be. In Montreal, the rust took most of them out, and anyway, who wants to overwinter snapdragons when you can start fresh the next spring? But their cold tolerance has made them favorites in southern landscapes, where they complement pansies as fall-planted annuals. They don't flower until early May when "perennialized," but they are handsome in leaf during the winter. In Long Island, plants overwinter only in mild winters, but when they do, flowering is more robust.

Plants have long narrow smooth leaves and lipped flowers held in a terminal raceme, but the size of flower, leaf, and plant varies significantly.

Serious breeding efforts have been expended on snapdragons, and most garden plants are F_1 hybrids, which provide vigor and uniformity of growth. Cultivars are 1–4' in height. Many of the taller forms have been bred for cut flower production, and large greenhouse ranges in North America, South America, and Europe produce hundreds of thousands of stems for floral work every week of the year. In the garden, a few large cultivars may also be found, which are useful as cut flowers for visitors or vases.

Full sun, well-drained soils. Plant in the fall in zone 7 and south, in the spring in zone 7 and north. Rust is a fungal disease caused by *Puccinia antirrhi*, and its severity differs with cultivar and location. It occurs more frequently under cool moist conditions. Breeding for rust-resistant cultivars has helped a great deal, and providing sufficient spacing in the garden (at least 1' apart) adds the circulation that reduces rust's incidence. Propagation by cuttings is not recommended because the fungi too will be propagated. Fungicides are also available.

Propagate by seed, using bottom heat and high humidity. It makes far more sense, however, to purchase plants at the garden center each fall or spring.

CULTIVARS

Most common bedding plants have been bred to within an inch of their lives, and in some cases, like geraniums and petunias, hundreds of named cultivars are available to the greenhouse grower. But remember: breeding is focused on improving seed quality and performance in the greenhouse; other objectives include compact height and reducing time on the greenhouse bench. These are all worthy objectives to the commercial grower, and bedding plants are far better than they were in 1990. Few of these breeding goals, however, significantly affect garden performance, and outdoor descriptions of many selections are similar. And, sadly, due to poor labeling in the retail outlets, it is difficult to find the cultivar of your choice anyway. It is ironic that breeding companies spend an average of seven years to get the next "great" named variety to the market, where it is sold merely as a generic color—a "red geranium."

My descriptions of common snapdragon cultivars are by necessity brief, and I may omit some well-known grower favorites.

Tall forms (>30")

'Madame Butterfly' is a mixture of upright flower colors. The flowers are not as "lipped" as they are in common forms, bearing a closer resemblance to a butterfly than a snapping dragon.

Panorama Mix, an F$_2$ hybrid often seen in seed packages, occurs in a mix of colors. Plants grow about 3' tall.

Rocket series is the most common tall form, growing 3–5' tall. Seed packages are available in seven colors (seldom available in the garden center) and a mix. This is the most popular cut flower form of snapdragon when grown outdoors.

Intermediate forms (18–30")

'Black Prince' is among the finer cultivars I have tested. The leaves are almost black, and the flowers are crimson-red. Outstanding.

'Brazilian Carnival' is a mixture of bicolors, similar to the Princess series. Plants grow 2½–3' tall.

Crown series is quite beautiful, in about six colors and a mix. I think this could become a winner, although flowering is still a little late. About 20" tall. 'Crown Pink Appleblossom' is excellent.

Freesong series is about 18" tall, with early flowering central spikes and good branching habit. Six colors and a mix have been developed.

LaBella series is about 2' tall, with butterfly-like flowers that more closely resemble a large butterfly than the normal snapping dragon. A favorite of mine, an outstanding performer in the University of Georgia trials. Available in ten colors and a mix.

Liberty series grows 2½–3' tall, and the flower stems require no support. Among the best of all snapdragons in winter trials at the University of Georgia.

Montego series is 14–18" tall in six colors.

Princess series consists of intermediate to tall plants in unique bicolors. Each flower has two colors; one of my favorites is 'Princess White with Purple Eye'.

Sonnet series, among the best for garden and landscape, grows about 3' tall. Upright but not floppy, plants make good, if not the tallest, cut flowers as well. Available in nine colors and a mix. Plants are big enough for landscape plantings and also effective in large containers.

Short forms (6–18")

Bells series consists of open-flowered butterfly-type F$_1$ hybrids (see 'Madame Butterfly' in the list of tall forms) that grow 10–12" tall in the garden. Sold in seven colors and a mix.

Chandelier series followed the Lampion series. 'Deep Pink', 'Lilac Blush', 'Lemon Blush', 'Pearl White', 'Primrose Vein', 'Rose Pink', and 'Yellow' are among the selections, all carried over soft gray-green foliage. Excellent for baskets and containers.

Chimes series consists of F$_1$ hybrids with normal snapdragon flowers growing 9–12" tall. Bred in eight colors and a mix.

Floral Carpet series is about 1' tall, available in six colors and a mix. 'Rose Carpet' was an All-America Selection in 1965. Useful as container items.

Floral Showers series, another fine dwarf form, has been bred in thirteen colors and two mixes. 'Floral Showers Bicolor' and 'Floral Showers Wine Bicolor' received Fleuroselect awards, the European equivalent of All-America Selections, in 1998. Useful as container items.

Antirrhinum majus 'Ribbon Yellow'   ASHA KAYS

Jamaican Mix consists of open butterfly flowers in pastel colors such as apricot, peach, and pink.

Kim series is a short group with bright colors. Scarlet and orange are outstanding color forms.

Lampion is an outstanding series, the first trailing snapdragon with either *Antirrhinum hispanicum* or *A. molle*, or both, in the parentage. Gray leaves and numerous flower colors have been introduced. Best suited for baskets and containers.

Magic Carpet is an open-pollinated series that grows 6–8″ tall.

Montego series is early to flower, about 8″ tall and available in fourteen colors plus a mix.

'Powys Pride' is, to my knowledge, the only green-and-white variegated-leaved snapdragon. Plants are 12–18″ tall and produce scarlet-red flowers. Seed-propagated.

Ribbon series, which grows close to 18″ tall, could be classified as either short or intermediate. Available in crimson, lavender, light pink, purple, rose, yellow, and white. Quite a good series.

Tahiti series is less than 8″ tall and is grown in twelve colors, two bicolors, and a mix.

Alternative species

Antirrhinum hispanicum (his pa′ nih kum) and *A. molle* (mol′ ee) have terrific potential for gardeners who like snapdragons but are looking for something a little different. Both are spreaders rather than upright growers and are most useful for baskets and containers. They are characterized by hairy, often gray foliage, which makes for a highly ornamental plant even when they are not in flower. Flowers are smaller than common snapdragon and occur in white, pink, and yellow, often with two colors on each flower. Pink is probably the most common color, at least in *A. molle*. Breeding of these species continues, and named series may become popular. Full sun, excellent drainage.

Arctotis (ark to′ tis)   African daisy   Asteraceae

Native to South Africa, these up-and-coming daisies in the American garden scene are useful for warm climates but do not require a great deal of heat to perform well. About fifty species are known; all have basal rosettes, usually pinnately divided, and handsome daisy-like flowers, usually borne singly.

I don't mean to be a spoilsport, but how does one tell all these daisies apart? With calendulas and asters, or sunflowers and coreopsis, there are enough visual clues to make a reasonable guess. But many South African daisies, like *Arctotis*, *Arctotheca*, *Gazania*, and *Ursinia*, are so similar to the naked eye that the guess lacks reason. Some of these genera have been lumped together or split apart so many times that even the academics are confused. It is difficult to find

Arctotis for sale in garden outlets, but if you do, it will likely be as cultivars of *Arctotis* ×*hybrida*.

All common South African daisies belong to the Arctotis tribe in the family Asteraceae, meaning they are well and truly related, so we are in deep trouble if we really want to figure them out. For a start, *Arctotis* is generally single-flowered, often black-centered, with few contrasting marks on the ray flowers; *Gazania* is low-growing, often with a black ring immediately around the central disk; *Ursinia* is less hairy than others; and *Arctotheca* looks more like a dandelion than a garden plant. But all this is surely not enough to please serious plant splitters, so with the help of L. H. Bailey, here are some of the characteristics which separate these four genera. With a hand lens or a small microscope, look closely at the leaves, particularly the undersides, the flower head (receptacle), and the bracts at the base of the receptacle.

Quick key to South African daisy genera

    A. Foliage tomentose (long hairs)
        B. Outer involucre bracts united to form cup or tube . . . . *Gazania*
        BB. Outer involucre bracts free or united only at base
            C. Stemless, disk flowers yellow, deeply five-lobed . . . . . *Arctotheca*
            CC. Stems occasionally present, disk flowers usually
                black, five-lobed . . . . *Arctotis*
    AA. Foliage glabrous or pubescent (short hairs) . . . . *Ursinia*

The flowers may be cut but seldom persist more than a couple of days in the vase. Plant in full sun; provide good drainage or place in large containers for best performance. Seed may be propagated on species and hybrids, under 72°F and humid conditions. As breeders discover the potential of this genus for the American market place, improvements in performance will occur rapidly.

| -×***hybrida*** (hi′ brih da) | African daisy | 1–3′/2′ |
| summer, fall | many colors | hybrid |

These hybrids (syn. ×*Venidioarctotis*) between *Arctotis venusta* and *A. fastuosa* (syn. *Venidium fastuosum*) are excellent plants for sunny areas and produce a profusion of brilliantly colored flowers on long flower stems. Once flowering occurs, plants remain in bloom throughout the summer and fall. Most daisies consist of 2–2½″ wide flowers with many ray flowers and usually a colorful center. The alternate silvery gray woolly leaves are also handsome and provide a lovely backdrop to the colorful flowers. As with many South African species, the flowers tend to close in the early afternoon and remain partially closed on dull days. Newer cultivars are less prone to this annoying habit. Plants do well in moderate summers in the North and should perform well where high humidity is not a concern. In the South, summer performance is mixed due to the combination of high night temperatures, humidity, and common afternoon rains. Flowering is generally better in late summer and fall; blooming can continue even through the first frost.

Plant in full sun; provide good drainage or place in large containers for best performance. Seed-propagate under 72°F and humid conditions.

CULTIVARS

'China Rose' has handsome gray-green foliage and rose to pink flowers on 9–12″ long stems.

'Circus-Circus', a selection of *Arctotis venusta* (blue-eyed African daisy), is a mixture of flower colors including bronze, pink, lavender, orange, pink, yellow, and white, all surrounding blue-red disk flowers.

Glistening Mix consists of a mixed bag of colors, about 16″ tall.

Harlequin Hybrids have brilliant orange to pale pink flowers, most with dark centers, held on 6–12″ long peduncles (flower stems). The foliage ranges from dull green to silvery gray and can be handsome even when not in flower. Some cultivar names, which describe the flower color, include 'Apricot', 'Dark Red', 'Flame' (salmon-orange), 'Mahogany' (burnt orange), 'Pink', 'Rosita' (dull pink), 'Tangerine', and 'Wine' (burgundy). All are excellent. My favorites are 'Flame' and 'Wine'.

'Nicolas Hind' bears cherry-rose flowers with narrow petals surrounding a green center.

'Salmon Queen' provides salmon to peach flowers.

Sinuata Mix is 12–14″ tall in several bright colors.

'Zulu Prince' is a beautiful flower of silvery white with a large contrasting dark black central ring. The deeply lobed leaves are silvery white.

Related genera

Arctotheca (ark to thee′ ka) is a South African daisy I found growing everywhere in Perth, Western Australia. *Arctotheca calendula* is a weed there, similar to our dandelion only much prettier, with its pale yellow flowers. Plants go dormant in the summer under conditions of heat and drought. I doubt it will become a popular plant, but who knows?

Argemone (ar je′ mo nee)   prickly poppy   Papaveraceae

These coarse annuals are not exactly serene in nature (the common name provides a hint as to their disposition). On most of the twenty-eight species of prickly poppy, the leaves are lobed to divided and can be as prickly as a porcupine at the tips or on the undersides. How did such plants ever make their entrance into the gardening scene? Like many others, they were believed to have some medicinal value. The Latin *argema* means "cataract," and these plants were thought, incorrectly, to alleviate that eye problem. Since nobody is cultivating these plants for what they don't do, why would anyone want to grow the awful sounding things? It is simple: if you can stand the size and the pain, the yellow to white 4–5″ wide flowers are unlike any others. They are showy, if not exactly user-friendly. All plants ooze copious amounts of yellow sap when broken.

Quick guide to *Argemone* species

	Height	Flower color	Spiny
A. grandiflora	3–5'	white	no
A. mexicana	1–3'	yellow	yes
A. platyceras	2–4'	white	yes

-*grandiflora* (gran dih flor´ a)   large-flowered prickly poppy   3–5'/3'
   summer   white   Mexico

The many-branched plants do not need pinching. The margins of lower 3–5"
long leaves are deeply lobed, the upper more wavy. The lower veins are prickly,
the margins are softly spiny, and the stems are weakly spined. All in all, the plant
is more friendly than most other species, and with the white-veined foliage, one
can enjoy the plant even when no flowers are present. If you pull off a leaf, the
yellow sap will quickly become obvious. The white cup-shaped flowers are about
4" across, with a satiny luster. They usually occur in groups of three to six; each
blossom consists of three to six sepals, two whorls of three petals, and more
than 150 stamens. Flowering continues as long as the flowers are deadheaded.
The capsules, which form after the flowers, are about 1" long and slightly spiny.
I really like this plant, from a distance, and it surely provokes comment.

    Seed can be purchased and either sown in place or in a peat-based container
that can be transplanted with the seedling. Self-sown seedlings may also occur,
which is great if they fall in the right place; if they fall in the middle of the path,
not so good.

    Full sun, well-drained soils. If the plant is in too much shade, the stems will
be too weak to support it and an awful mess ensues. Do not fertilize unless
grown in sandy soils; too much fertility results in weak-stemmed plants.

CULTIVARS

    var. *lutea* is a yellow-flowered, rather uncommon form.

-*mexicana* (meks ih ka´ na)   Mexican prickly poppy, devil's fig   2–3'/3'
   summer   yellow   Mexico

The smaller stature of the Mexican poppy makes it a little easier to use, but it is
also more sprawling in habit than *Argemone grandiflora*. The spiny stems (look at
those common names again) branch from near the base of the plant, and the
lobed leaves are beautifully blue-green, the blue hue being particularly striking
over the veins. The margins are spiny, and the apex of the leaf is sharp, so keep
the gloves on. The flowers, of course, are the reason gardeners invite this sadis-
tic thing home, and they are rewarded with pale to bright yellow (occasionally
orange) 2–3" wide flowers in the summer. The flowers consist of six petals, three
to six sepals, and thirty to fifty stamens.

    Full sun, propagate by seed *in situ*. Fertilize sparingly.

Argemone mexicana   CHRIS JOHNSON

CULTIVARS

'Alba' bears white flowers over bluish silver foliage.

'Sanguinea' has orangish red flowers.

'Yellow Lustre' is the beauty of the group, with lemon-yellow flowers on 18–24" tall plants. The blue-green foliage is veined in silver.

Alternative species

Argemone platyceras (play tee seer' as; crested poppy) may occasionally be confused with *A. grandiflora* because they both have white flowers. It is much more spiny, however, and quite variable. The flowers are generally 2–3" across, and the stems may be up to 4' tall, although 2–3' is more common. The 1–2" long capsules are covered in rigid spines.

Argemone polyanthemos (pa lee an' the mos) is native to the western United States and also has large (up to 4" in diameter) white or pale mauve flowers. If for no other reason, its wonderful common name, cowboy's fried egg, merits its inclusion in the garden. The divided leaves are blue-green (glaucous) and more succulent than *A. platyceras*. The good news is that the leaves and in fact the entire plant is less spiny than either Mexican prickly poppy or crested poppy. Plants stand 3–4' tall.

Quick key to *Argemone* species

A. Flowers white or usually so
    B. Plant softly spiny, fruit with few spines
        C. Leaves glaucous, uppermost leaves tightly
           clasping stem . . . . *A. polyanthemos*
        CC. Leaves not glaucous, uppermost leaves not
            tightly clasping stem . . . . *A. grandiflora*
    BB. Plant densely spiny, fruit covered in spines . . . . *A. platyceras*
AA. Flowers usually yellow . . . . *A. mexicana*

Additional reading

Springer, Lauren. 1997. Parade of poppies. *Horticulture* 94(6):41–45.

Argyranthemum (ar je ran' tha mum)   marguerite daisy   Asteraceae

A genus of about twenty-three species, the marguerites were very popular as a greenhouse cut flower crop and as a pot plant in the 1940s and 1950s. Slowly replaced, beginning in the 1960s, by roses, florist mums, and carnations imported from overseas, they had all but disappeared from the radar screen of American horticulture by the 1990s. And they were further abused when the comfortable name *Chrysanthemum* was replaced with *Argyranthemum*. Marguerites are still available as cut flowers, mainly field grown from California, but their popularity has recently soared as a landscape annual, hybridized from about three species.

Quick guide to *Argyranthemum* species

	Leaf color	Flower color
A. foeniculaceum	blue-green	white
A. frutescens	green	white
A. maderense	green	pale yellow

-foeniculaceum (fo nik yew lay' see um)   lace-leaf marguerite   2–3'/3'
   summer   white   Canary Islands

The lacy blue-green foliage of this species means plants are as pretty when not in flower as they are when covered with white flowers. The leaves are deeply divided, usually alternate, and if the plant is grown in the garden or in a large container, the upright fern-like appearance of its foliage provides a see-through effect. The single flowers almost always consist of white ray flowers with yellow centers. I love seeing these plants in patio containers, and they always bring to mind the fine plantings at Sissinghurst Garden in England and my neighbor's house in Perth, Western Australia. They are best grown in areas of moderate climate, where humidities are not stifling.

Full sun, propagate by cuttings.

CULTIVARS

'Blue Haze' is a fine blue-green foliage form with single white flowers.

'Jamaica Primrose' and 'Jamaica Snowstorm' bear pale yellow and white flowers, respectively, on 2' tall plants.

-frutescens (froo te' senz)   marguerite daisy   1–3'/2'
   summer   white, yellow   Canary Islands

This species, the real old-fashioned marguerite grown as a cut flower, boasts single white or yellow flowers. The dark green leathery leaves are pinnately divided, and plants can reach more than 3' in height. The flowers of some of the garden forms are occasionally doubled and have enjoyed some popularity. Plants always do better in cool weather, forgetting to flower in the heat of the summer.

Full sun, propagate by terminal cuttings.

CULTIVARS

'Dana' is about 20" tall with clean white shasta daisy-type flowers.

'Edelweiss' produces large white double flowers.

'Mary Cheek' produces semi-double to double pink flowers.

'Pink Champagne' bears semi-double pincushion flowers of pale pink over ferny foliage.

'Quinta White' has double white flowers.

'Vancouver' produces double pink flowers on 2' tall stems.

'Vera' is about 2' tall, with 1" white daisies with yellow centers. The foliage is blue-green and lacy. Looks fabulous trained as a standard.

Alternative species

Argyranthemum maderense is related to *A. frutescens*. Plants are usually about 2' tall; the pale yellow ray flowers surround a darker disk, and the green leaves are lobed, not divided as in *A. foeniculaceum*.

Quick key to *Argyranthemum* species

A. Flowers white or nearly always so
  B. Leaves deeply divided, often blue-green . . . . *A. foeniculaceum*
  BB. Leaves less deeply divided, more lobed, leaves green . . . *A. frutescens*
AA. Flowers pale yellow or nearly always so . . . . *A. maderense*

Argyranthemum hybrids

The dominant form of the genus offered to consumers is not the cultivars of the aforementioned species, but the hybrids, originating from breeding stations around the world, including Europe and Australia. When hybrids from the Cobbity Research Station of the University of Sydney, Australia, were put on the market, breeders used the name Cobbity daisy, and it has stuck. Some exceptional forms are offered, from single daisy to semi-double pom-pom flowers, from dark green to silver leaves, all on well-branched plants. Plants are best grown in large containers, where they can be combined with more floriferous plants. The hybrids flower far more profusely in cool weather; they are fabulous in coastal California and pretty darn good in Colorado and Minnesota, but only a few can be recommended further south: hot summers result in shrubby foliage and few flowers. Aggressive breeding, combined with trialing in warm areas, particularly at the University of Georgia, is reducing this problem, but a good choice of heat-tolerant hybrids is still a few years away.

'Butterfly', the best of all cultivars, has single butter-yellow flowers. The 1–2' tall plants continue to flower throughout the summer and are the standard by which other hybrids are judged.

'Comet Pink' has wonderful blue-green foliage and nicely formed single pink flowers, which can smother the plant when in bloom.

'Comet White' produces tall single white flowers with a prominent yellow center over handsome blue-green foliage. The silvery foliage of both the Comets looks good even in the absence of flowers.

'Harvest Snow', about 14″ tall, bears single white flowers with a yellow center.

'Lemon Delight' bears single lemon-yellow flowers over silvery foliage. About 8″ tall.

'Midas Gold' is a favorite of mine and a proven performer in the UGA Horticulture Gardens, not an easy feat. Light off-yellow flowers, 8–12″ tall. Almost as good as 'Butterfly'.

'Petite Pink' is only 12–15″ tall with pale pink daisies.

'Stars Pink' is a handsome plant with soft pink flowers, 2–3″ wide. When not in flower, which is most of the time, plants have the best-looking foliage we have trialed. Gray-green, very dense, and outstanding in containers.

'Sugar Baby' has single white flowers with yellow centers. Plants are compact and flower well in the spring, but flowering is significantly curtailed in hot weather.

'Summer Angel' provides semi-double white flowers with yellow centers. The leaves are silvery green.

Argyranthemum 'Midas Gold'   ASHA KAYS

'Summer Eyes' is an interesting flower. White ray flowers surround the large burgundy center, which is flecked with gold. The leaves are compact and green. Plants performed well in the UGA Horticulture Gardens.

'Summer Melody', bred by Mal Morgan in eastern Australia, bears double pink-lavender flowers on compact (1' tall) plants. An excellent habit for containers.

'Summer Pink' provides single pink flowers with prominent yellow centers.

'Surprise Party' provides semi-double lavender-pink ray flowers around a burgundy and white center.

Artanema (ar ta nee' ma)   Scrophulariaceae

When I first planted a representative of this genus, I had no idea what it was. Since that is pretty common these days, I decided it should be treated like all the others I never heard of. So I tossed it in the ground, watered and fertilized, and then left it alone in the back forty. Plants did well using this Armitage technique, producing dozens of tubular dark blue flowers with a yellow throat on 12″ tall plants. The species I had received was *Artanema fimbriata*, which is native to coastal regions of Australia from northeastern Queensland to northeastern New South Wales, where it is usually found on swamp margins. Although it won't make for a drift of color, *A. fimbriata* does have potential in American gardens as a container and basket plant. The flowers are five-lobed, the upper two smaller than the lower three. They look a bit like a yawning snapdragon and somewhat resemble those of wishbone flower (*Torenia*).

Full sun to partial shade, propagate by seed or cuttings. Plants flower well, appear to tolerate full sun and plenty of heat, and are definitely worth a try. Expect more cultivars from Australia soon.

CULTIVARS

'Opal Blue' has lovely mid blue flowers.

Artemisia (ar tih mee' zee a)   wormwood, sagebrush   Asteraceae

From the medicinal gardens of the Middle Ages to our present fine perennials, this large genus of 200 species is well known as a symbol of the West (sagebrush), an ingredient of a liquor (absinthe), a dispeller of worms (wormwood), and a wonderful culinary herb (tarragon). The annual *Artemisia annua* (sweet annie, sweet wormwood) is no slouch either when it comes to medicinal properties and has been studied extensively as a source of artemisinin, which is used in the treatment of malaria. New tissue culture techniques have increased the percentage of extractable artemisinin from 0.08% to nearly 0.2% (on a dry weight basis).

Artemisia annua, although not well known, is an impressive 4–6' tall plant that grows vigorously and fits well into larger gardens. It is erect, with 1–2½" long leaves, divided into one or two deeply cut segments. As a general rule, the aroma of artemisia foliage is not particularly welcome indoors; but the fragrance of this species is much more pleasant, even sweet-smelling, as Annie would say, and the fragrance lingers even after drying. The species is popular in the potpourri and wreath-making trade and can be cut throughout the season and hung to dry. Its tiny yellow flowers, which are produced in loose spreading panicles in the summer, are quite forgettable.

Full sun, well-drained soils. Propagate by seed or cuttings.

Asarina (a sa ree' na)   twining snapdragon   Scrophulariaceae

Of the sixteen species in the genus, the ones we occasionally see are the vining, twining forms.

-scandens (skan' denz)   climbing snapdragon   vine
     summer   blue, pink   Mexico

This most popular twining species gets woody at the base and can grow up to 9', but 6' is more common in temperate gardens. The alternate heart- to arrow-shaped leaves have entire margins and are widely spread apart. It climbs by its twisting stems, which are best trained around narrow bamboo poles or a rough

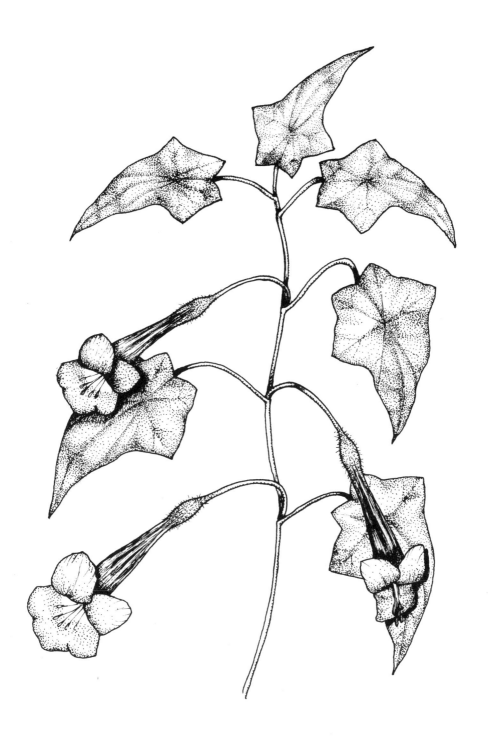

Asarina barclaiana   CHRIS JOHNSON

trellis. The 1″ long trumpet-like axillary flowers consist of five smooth sepals and a funnel-like lipped corolla (fused petals); they range in color from pale violet to lavender to pink, but generally darken to a deeper purple.

I really like these vines, but their vigor varies considerably, depending on where you garden. In the South, I find they don't grow as rapidly as perennial vines like *Clematis* or other annual vines like *Cobaea* or *Thunbergia*. But Suzanne Bales, whose home on Long Island is a sanctuary for vines of all kinds, finds *Asarina* a most vigorous participant, so dense as to look like "a living body stocking." Plants grow quickly once established, wherever the garden. Flowering occurs best in late summer and fall.

Full sun to partial shade.

CULTIVARS

Jewel Mix provides a mix of indigo, blue, pink, and white flowers.
'Joan Loraine' bears deep purple flowers with a white throat.
'Mystic Pink' has soft pink flowers.
Satin Mix has flowers in blue, pink, and white on different plants. 'Satin Pink' bears bright pink 1½″ bells on 10′ tall plants.

Alternative species

Asarina antirrhinifolia (an tih ri nih fo′ lee a; violet twining snapdragon) bears showy trumpet-shaped bluish flowers. More of a trailer than a climber.

Asarina barclaiana (bar clay a′ na) is similar to *A. scandens* and differs only by having hairy sepals and darker flowers.

Asarina erubescens (er oo bes′ enz; creeping gloxinia) has large pink flowers swollen on one side. The entire plant is softly hairy, unlike the smooth plants just described.

Asarina procumbens (pro kum′ benz; creeping snapdragon), a white-flowered trailer, is quite beautiful spilling over rocks or out of containers in areas of cool summers. It can spread aggressively by underground runners and may become invasive. Generally treated as an annual, but in well-drained gardens, plants can return in zone 7 (6 with protection).

Asarina purpusii (per poos′ ee i; purple twining snapdragon) also trails when left to its own devices. It cascades from baskets and pots. 'Victoria Falls' has cherry-purple trumpet-shaped flowers. Not a great climber.

Asclepias (as klee′ pee as)   milkweed   Asclepiadaceae

Next time someone stumps you with a trivia question, fire back by asking who the son of Apollo was. The son of Apollo and Coronis was Asklepios, the god of medicine and healing in Greek mythology. Who says gardeners don't know their history? Most gardeners know the perennial forms of milkweed such as butterfly weed (*Asclepias tuberosa*) and swamp milkweed (*A. incarnata*). The annual forms, however, are equally beautiful and flower for a much longer time. All members of the genus have a milky sap, which some people find allergenic. An interesting feature to help identify the genus, but don't taste it.

-*curassavica* (ker a sa′ vee ka)   blood flower   3–4′/2′
   summer   red with yellow   South America

This outstanding eye-catching annual grows about 3′ tall and produces flowers all summer: they are cinnabar red, with yellow, so the common name is most appropriate. The shiny 6″ long lanceolate leaves are opposite and often have a white midrib, so the plant is handsome even when it is not in flower. The flowers are made up of five sepals and five lobes on the fused petals, often reflexed when they open. The "hooded" appearance of each flower makes for most interesting and beautiful inflorescences (cymes). The flowers are formed in the axils and terminally in mid summer and will continue to open throughout the summer. Hummingbirds, bees, and moths love the nectar-rich blossoms. After flowering, long narrow seed pods (follicles) form, which open along their edges to

Asclepias curassavica   ASHA KAYS

reveal seeds crowned by a tuft of white silky hairs (accounting for another common name, silkweed).

Plants are weedy in the tropics and can be a problem in southern gardens as well. The main problem in the garden is aphids, which congregate every year for their season-long meeting on the stems of every species in the genus. I use a spray of water to dislodge them and hope the ladybugs are hungry.

Full sun, well-drained soils. Propagate by seed.

CULTIVARS

'Red Butterfly' has vibrant red and orange bicolored flowers. About 3' tall.

'Silky Gold' is an excellent name for this selection, with flowers of golden orange. Plants grow about 3' tall and have fruit similar to the species. Quite beautiful.

Alternative species

Asclepias physocarpa (swan plant) is better known for its fruit than its flowers. Plants are shrubby, up to 6' tall, with narrow-lanceolate leaves and creamy to green-white clusters of flowers. The inflated fruit is softly spiny and looks like the graceful neck of a swan, thus the common name. Full sun.

Asperula (as per' yew la) woodruff Rubiaceae

The genus consists of about a hundred species of dwarf annual and perennial plants with square stems and opposite to whorled leaves. Most have terminal or axillary cymes of white or blue flowers. The best-known woodruff is no longer in *Asperula*: *A. odorata*, sweet woodruff, was moved to the genus *Galium* (*G. odoratum*). A little-used plant for American gardeners is blue woodruff, *A. orientalis*, a native of Europe and the Far East. Plants grow 9–12" tall and are covered with lavender-blue flowers for months at a time. The lance-shaped hairy leaves are whorled, and the tubular flowers are delicately fragrant. Excellent in the ground or in containers. A potential gem in the rough.

Full sun to partial shade, propagate by seed.

CULTIVARS

'Blue Surprise', offered from seed, grows about 12" tall and is totally covered with lavender-blue flowers. Struggles in hot, humid climates.

Asteriscus (a ster is' kus) Asteraceae

The genus name comes from the Greek for "star," a reference to the flowers. This relative of the aster is much less known and is characterized by the orange-yellow daisy flowers. The only species occasionally offered is *Asteriscus maritimus*, native to Portugal, Greece, and the Canary Islands. Plants are well suited to warm, dry pockets in well-drained soils and are probably best in rock gardens or sandy soils. The tuft-forming plants grow about 1′ tall and produce many branches, the crown of which produces a shaggy daisy flower consisting of many narrow rays surrounding a darker yellow center.

I like this plant but have had little success with it in my garden. In areas where the climate is non-Mediterranean, it is better suited to container culture, which allows for the addition of soils more suitable than the awful clay I must contend with. Afternoon rains and high humidity don't do a whole lot for it either. Others have been far more successful.

Full sun, porous soils. Propagate by seed or cuttings.

CULTIVARS

'Gold Coin', a more robust and compact form, is otherwise similar to the species. Also sold as 'Compact Gold Coin'.

Asystasia (as is tay′ zee a)   Acanthaceae

It is always a lesson in humility when I come across an exceptional plant in a genus I have never heard of, especially one that contains seventy species. This time the plant in question—the one that made me realize once again how truly little I know—was *Asystasia gangetica* (Ganges primrose), sent me by Alan Shapiro, an excellent Florida nurseryman. I placed a plant in the UGA trial garden and off it went, making a vigorous ground cover in about three weeks. The simple 2″ long, ovate opposite leaves are thin and borne on long stems. The 1″ long bell-shaped lavender-pink flowers have open-flared lobes and are held on one-sided axillary racemes. Flowers are borne profusely in spring, less so in the heat of a hot summer, and more so again in fall. Although native to the tropics of the eastern hemisphere, the species exhibits inhibited flowering during hot summers. Plants do thrive in the summer, however, and many stems are produced, making plants suitable for the landscape or for baskets and containers, where they may spill over the sides. The term "sprawly" comes to mind, but I think this species will be an excellent seller as soon as landscapers and gardeners discover it. A yellow-flowered form is also available.

Full sun, normal soils. Propagate by cuttings.

Atriplex (a′ trih pleks)   saltbush, orach   Chenopodiaceae

Yet again, a genus better known for its uses outside the ornamental garden has found favor with gardeners and designers for some of its more handsome members. Many species are native to western North America; *Atriplex canescens*, for example, likes windy, dry, saline settings. Desert holly (*A. hymenelyta*) is native to deserts and alkaline soils of the West, while white thistle (*A. lentiformis*) may be found in southwestern United States. All are tough and handsome in their own right, but only one, *A. hortensis* (orach), has made the transition to the ornamental garden. Orach is better known for the culinary uses of its succulent leaves and as an alternative to spinach than as a garden plant. White-leaved varieties are said to have the tenderest leaves with the sweetest flavor.

The garden plant used most often is the upright, 2–3' tall *Atriplex hortensis* var. *rubra* (red orach), for the foil it provides its green-leaved neighbors. The triangular purple-red leaves are alternate to opposite, about 4" long and usually entire or just slightly dentate. The minute pinkish flowers that occur in terminal racemes in summer are best removed; they will reseed if not. Other variants may sometimes be found, a copper-leaved form and a lighter almost pink-leaved form, but neither are as effective as var. *rubra*. All can be weedy.

Full sun to partial shade, propagate by seed.

B

Ballota (ba law' ta) horehound Lamiaceae

Ballota is a loose translation of the Greek word for the black horehound, *B. nigra*, which was then known as "ballote"—hence, the generic name. The common name requires a bit more head-scratching. The "hore" part refers to the leaves, which have slightly whitish hairs (as in "hoarfrost"), but I have not unearthed the "hound" part. Any help will be appreciated. Deep thinkers are always welcome in horticulture.

The genus, which contains about thirty-five species, is closely related to *Stachys* and *Marrubium*, with opposite leaves, four-sided stems, and small two-lipped flowers held in whorls. Species are mainly Mediterranean in origin and therefore tend to perform well in dry, temperate climes.

Quick guide to *Ballota* species

	Height	Leaf color	Use
B. acetabulosa	2'	gray-green	container
B. nigra	3'	green	garden
B. pseudodictamnus	1–2'	gray-green	container

-nigra (ni' gra) black horehound 2–4'/2'
summer white, lilac Greece, North Africa

Few people actually grow this small shrubby species, but a couple of its selections have improved the offerings. The plant resembles *Lamium* (dead nettle), with 1–1½" long ovate leaves. About twelve whorled white, lilac, or pale pink flowers occur over the 2–4' tall plants. Plants are quite variable, with stems ranging from tall to short, and although they are native to faraway lands, they have become naturalized in the Northeast.

Full sun, dry, well-drained soils. Propagate by seed or cuttings.

CULTIVARS

'Variegata' is the best form, consisting of 1–1½' tall plants with white streaks and spots on the green leaves. The flowers are purple. Also sold as 'Archer's Variety'.

'Zanzibar' is about 3' tall, with spotted leaves.

-pseudodictamnus (soo do dik tam' nus)   false dittany   12–15"/24"
     summer   foliage   Greece, Crete

This terrific little architectural plant, grown mainly for its small slightly wavy, gray-woolly leaves, is best suited for containers or protected areas in which drainage can be improved. The woolly stems resemble pipe cleaners and can grow up to 2' long, but 12–18" is normal. The small leaves are less than ½" wide but are produced in abundance, forming a handsome mound as the plant matures. If plants get a little leggy, simply give them a haircut. New foliage will emerge readily. About six to twelve small whorled flowers, whitish with purple markings, are produced in summer. They look like coleus flowers; most people simply ignore them or remove them. Plants are always said to be tender, but their cold hardiness is surprising: they often come back as far north as zone 6. They have been perennial favorites at New York's Wave Hill Garden for years.

Full sun, dry, well-drained soils. Propagate by seed or cuttings.

Alternative species

Ballota acetabulosa (a se tab yew lo' sa) is similar to *B. pseudodictamnus*, and the two are probably mixed up in the trade. *Ballota acetabulosa* differs by having larger leaves, usually heart-shaped, with obviously scalloped margins. Plants are also taller, growing to 2' tall. Otherwise the flowers and foliar color are similar.

Quick key to *Ballota* species

A. Plant 1–2' tall, tomentose, leaves gray-woolly .... *B. pseudodictamnus*
AA. Plant >1–2' tall, not tomentose, leaves green .... *B. nigra*

Ballota hybrids

'All Hallow's Green' is a low grower with fine-textured lime-green to gray-green leaves. Found by Valerie Finnis, a grand dame of England, and named for Halloween. Different and worth a try. Tolerates a little shade.

Barleria (bar leer' ee a)   Acanthaceae

The generic name honors the life and work of French monk and botanist Jacques Barrelier (1606–1673). The genus consists of more than 200 species, with opposite leaves, upright habit, and late summer flowers, ranging from violet to yellow to purple. The main form in American landscapes is *Barleria cristata* (Philippine violet), which has terrific merit for the late summer and fall garden.

-cristata (kris ta' ta)	Philippine violet	3–4'/3'
fall	blue-violet	India, Burma

I have grown this species for years, and since I learned what to expect, I have come to look forward to it every time. The opposite, oblong to elliptical leaves are about 4" long and 1" wide, a handsome dull green. Plants grow slowly in the spring, but as temperatures warm up, they expand rapidly. People are disappointed when they look for early flowering and all they see is a green shrub throughout spring and summer; however, a little patience helps. Plants begin to bud up in late summer and fall, and the 2" long tubular flowers appear as terminal and axillary spikes. The flowers, which consist of four unequal sepals and a corolla tube with five rounded lobes, continue until frost. This is an excellent shrubby annual which freshens up the fall garden, and appears to be disease and insect free.

Full sun, propagate by cuttings.

CULTIVARS

'Alba' is a white-flowered form.

'Variegata' produces the same blue flowers, but the leaves are variegated with splotches of yellow and green.

Alternative species

Barleria obtusa (ob tus' a) is shorter than *B. cristata*, about 2' tall, with elliptical leaves, 2½–3" long. Flowers are purple. 'Amethyst Lights' has interesting green, white, and pink foliage and small lavender-blue flowers; it tends to be much more pendulous.

Barleria repens (re' penz) is 2–3' tall, with a mounding habit of glossy green leaves. The coral-red trumpet flowers occur in late summer.

Basella (ba sel' a)   Malabar nightshade   Basellaceae

The five species of rampant, twining vines can provide some interesting ornamental value. The species offered in the American trade is *Basella alba* (Malabar spinach), with glossy dark green foliage. The alternate leaves may be harvested and treated as a sweet culinary spinach. The oblong rounded 4–6" leaves, which resemble spinach, are produced rapidly on the twining stems as temperatures warm up. Flowers are white, rose, or red but are seldom seen in the landscape because they do not flower in long daylengths.

Start seed in place when temperatures warm up, after all threat of frost has passed. They may be trained on strong supports, pergolas, or arches, or grown as a full-bodied hanging basket. Plants will grow rapidly attaining 20–25′ in a single season. Light bamboo poles from the market won't cut it.

Full sun, propagate by seed. Provide lots of water; these are heavy drinkers.

CULTIVARS

'Rubra', the best form, is characterized by brilliant red to fuchsia-colored stems and petioles. A lot of fun to try.

Begonia (be go′ nee a)   Begoniaceae

Begonia was named after Michel Begon (1638–1710), a patron of botany and the governor of French Canada, later the province of Quebec. It is a huge genus of more than 900 species of mostly herbaceous plants, used mainly as houseplants or pot plants. It is a little surprising that with such a large number of species, more would not have frost tolerance. Only *Begonia grandis* has sufficiently consistent toughness to be considered a perennial in large portions of the country. *Begonia octopetala*, a tuberous form, occasionally overwinters in milder areas. Many species are native to South America (Brazil and Peru are centers of origin); however, Central America, Mexico, Sumatra, South Africa, southern Asia, KwaZulu-Natal, and the Himalayas all claim their fair share.

Begonia nitida was thought to be the first begonia introduced to England (1777). Few other plants have been improved or varied so rapidly, yielding the great numbers of interesting forms that make begonias so strongly appealing to collectors and fanciers. Unfortunately, the great private collections of the past have not been maintained, and many species are no longer in culture. Of the great mass of species, it is interesting to note that few are seen outside the confines of botanical gardens, greenhouses, or the houseplant trade; taxonomists have tried to make some sense them all, and the best way to learn more about the beauty and diversity is to join a begonia society or a working group at a local botanical garden. My good friend Janet Welsh, of Pennsylvania, is a begonia aficionado and is forever scolding me about my miserable treatment of this great genus. Please, for my sake, if you'd like more information, contact the American Begonia Society (see "Additional reading"). That way, Janet won't beat up on me quite so much.

From the gardener's perspective, the genus is most easily divided into fibrous-rooted forms (*Begonia semperflorens-cultorum*, wax begonia), tuberous forms (*B. tuberhybrida-cultorum*, tuberous begonia), rhizomatous forms (*B. rex-cultorum*, rex begonia), and cane-stemmed forms (*B.* ×*argenteoguttata*, angel-wing begonia). These divisions are convenient but by no means all-inclusive. The first three classifications are common in landscapes, and members of the fourth are placed in containers for summer diversity and color.

The leaves of most species discussed here are ear-shaped, some the size of a mouse's ear, others like an elephant's. All begonias are monoecious (male and female flowers are borne on the same plant). The male flowers generally consist of four petals, two of which are smaller than the others, and the females usually have five. Flowers have been doubled in many ornamental introductions, particularly in the tuberous begonias. The winged fruit (capsule) contains many minute dust-like seeds.

Quick guide to *Begonia* species

	Grown for	Height	Use
cane-stemmed (angel wings)	foliage, flowers	1–4'	container
fibrous-rooted (wax begonias)	flowers	6–12"	garden
rhizomatous (rex begonias)	foliage	1–3'	container
tuberous (tuberous begonias)	flowers	1–3'	container, basket

Angel-wing begonia (*B.* ×*argenteoguttata* and others)   angel wings   1–4'/2'
    all season   foliage   garden

The diversity of leaf pattern and color in this group of begonias, beloved of all houseplant fans, is remarkable. Angel wings are extraordinary in their ease of propagation, growth, and flowering and have been included in warm low-light

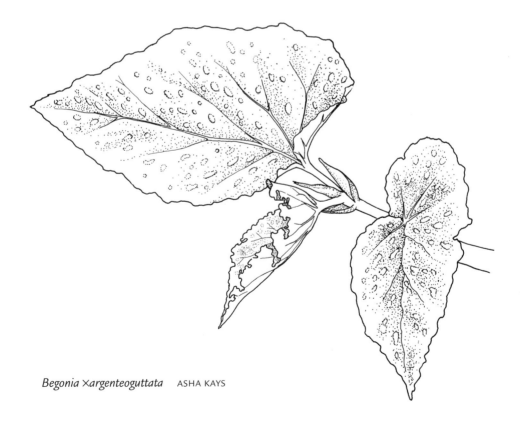

Begonia ×*argenteoguttata*   ASHA KAYS

households for many years. They are horticulturally classified as cane-stemmed begonias because of their long, bamboo-like stems, from which arise the oblique (one side is longer than the other) elephant-ear leaves. The leaves are often dark green, spotted with silver on the upperside and dark red beneath, but mind-boggling variability in foliage design can be found. The pendulous flowers are often pink, and the male flowers (in the middle of the inflorescence) open first. The females later give way to three-winged fruit, which persist for many weeks.

In the garden, angel wings can attain some serious height, 3–4' not being uncommon. They may be pruned back if the canes are too long or if the plant becomes top heavy. More dwarf forms, with heights of 1–2', are now available, and these fit a little more comfortably into most gardens. Plants may be placed in large containers or in protected areas of the garden, always in shaded areas. Some cultivars may tolerate some direct sun, but afternoon shade is a must.

CULTIVARS

Some of the many cultivars grown by the houseplant trade have simply been recycled for gardeners. Here is a brief sampling; plants grow 1½–2½' unless otherwise noted.

'Anna Christine' bears deep bronze ruffled leaves with coral flowers.

'Anna Feile' has dark green jagged leaves with a purple back and many clusters of salmon-pink flowers.

'Bubbles' has large pointed dark green leaves with white polka dots and reddish pink flowers.

'Coral Chime' is an 8–12" tall form with coral flowers and white-spotted leaves.

'Corliss Engle' produces dark green leaves with white spots and clusters of salmon-pink flowers. A terrific plant named for a terrific lady.

'Cracklin' Rose' produces 6" leaves that twist somewhat, revealing their deep red backs. Among the darkest green-leaved forms available. Pink flowers.

'Dragon Wing' is a seed-propagated introduction that grows only about 18" tall and has red flowers all season. This is a great plant. The leaves are a lustrous green, and plant performance has been excellent around the country. Highly recommended.

'Ebony' bears green leaves with chocolate-brown reverse and bright pink flowers.

'Elaine' is a compact form with frilled narrow leaves and large pink pendulous flowers. Excellent for hanging baskets.

'Ester Albertine' has large feathery apple-green leaves splashed with white. Flowers are pale pink.

'Florence Rita' produces soft green pointed leaves and pink flowers.

'Honeysuckle' bears clusters of salmon-pink flowers amid long angel-wing foliage. Wonderful honeysuckle fragrance.

'Kismet', a dwarf angel wing whose silver leaves have darker silver veins and red-purple lower sides, has the look of a rex begonia. Absolutely outstanding.

'Lois Burks' is a heavily branched low grower with foliage streaked silver and showy soft pink flowers. Useful for baskets and containers.

'Looking Glass' bears silver-green olive-veined leaves that are cranberry-red beneath. Quite a combination.

'Lucerne' ('Lucerna') has dark green leaves with silver markings on the top, dark red beneath, and dark pink flowers. Outstanding.

'Pink Cane' has pink flowers on canes that are more vertical than upright. Vigorous, 3–4′ tall.

'Sophia' produces sharply pointed green leaves with silver and pink splotches. Pink flowers. Also sold as 'Sophie Irene'.

'Torch' is only about 12″ tall and bears thick green leaves, with red undersides, and red flowers.

'Withlacoochee' is a cascading form with elongated soft olive-green leaves, red undersides, and a crazy name. White flowers.

'Zorro' is a small plant with soft pink flowers and silver dots on the green leaves.

Fibrous-rooted begonias (*B. semperflorens-cultorum*)

	wax begonias	6–12″/12″
all season	many colors	garden

Wax begonias, the most common form in the genus, are omnipresent in American landscapes, so much so that one is tempted to believe there are no other plants for the landscaper to use. I have seen seas of red flowers around the bases of entire buildings as well as grotesque animal shapes (peacock seems to be a favorite), clothed in begonias of all colors. While one may be a little tired of seeing wax begonias, it is impossible to condemn the plant's success. From the commercial landscaper's point of view, the low maintenance requirements of wax begonias make them preferable to petunias or marigolds. Home gardeners too have embraced wax begonias, for the issue of low maintenance is almost as high a concern for them.

Plants are similar to other begonias; they are monoecious and have ear-shaped leaves. They are successful because of their tough waxy leaves, often dark green or bronze, and their continuous production of red, white, or pink flowers from spring until frost. The waxy coating on the foliage reduces water loss from the leaves, resulting in excellent drought tolerance. Plants are a complex of hybrids first derived from *Begonia cucullata* var. *hookeri* and *B. schmidtiana* but now including *B. fuchsioides*, *B. gracilis*, and *B. minor*. The roots are fibrous, stems are numerous, more or less smooth, and leaves are shiny, with ciliate margins. The foliage often has red margins.

Begonias were always assumed to be plants for shade, and tolerate shade they do. They are commonly placed in full sun, however, even in the South, and their environmental tolerance is broad. In the sun, flower colors are brighter, and plants are shorter and more compact. In the shade, plants are more open, taller, and not as floriferous. That is the strength of these hybrids: they grow well with little care, almost anywhere.

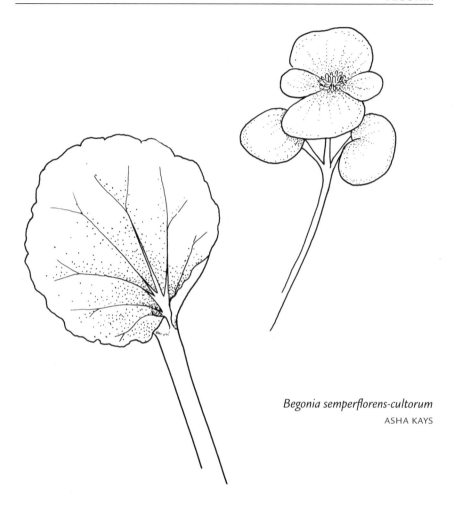

Begonia semperflorens-cultorum
ASHA KAYS

CULTIVARS

My descriptions of common begonia cultivars are by necessity brief, and I may omit some well-known grower favorites. Plants grow 6–12" tall unless otherwise noted.

Ambassador series consists of green-leaved members in seven individual flower colors.

Atlanta series consists of many colors and has performed well in the University of Georgia trials.

Belle Vista series has green foliage and individuals bear rose-pink ('Linda'), deep scarlet ('Scarlanda'), light scarlet ('Scarletta'), and white flowers ('Viva').

Bingo series has bronze foliage with flowers of red, pink, salmon, or white.

Cocktail series is by far the most common and well-known group of begonias. They are all bronze-leaved and short in stature. Light pink ('Brandy'), rose

('Gin'), white edged with red ('Rum'), red ('Vodka'), white ('Whisky'), and a mixture of flower colors are available. Good plants, better marketing.

Devil series consist of bronze-leaved forms with light pink, pink and white, red, rose, or white flowers.

Encore series is another popular group, taller and more vigorous than many others. Individual green- or bronze-leaved forms with pink, red, and white flowers are available; the pink and white bicolor is available with bronze leaves only.

Eureka series is available in bronze- and green-leaved forms, each in five flower colors.

'Gloire de Sceaux' is an old-fashioned form with dark pink flowers over bronzed leaves.

Harmony series consists of bronze-leaved begonias in pink, scarlet, white, and a mix.

Inferno series forms mounds of flowers in bright colors.

Olympia series, a well-established group, has mostly green foliage with light pink, pink, red, rose, salmon, red and white ('Starlet'), and white flowers. Also sold as Super Olympia series, a reference to greenhouse-performance improvements.

Organdy series is a mixture of flower colors and green and bronze leaves.

Party series, among the most vigorous groups, grows 12–15″ tall and is available in five colors. A 55-mph series.

Prelude series has green leaves available in six separate colors and a mix.

'Richmondensis' (syn. *Begonia richmondensis*) is an interspecific cross between *B. semperflorens-cultorum* and *B. fuchsioides*. Plants have glossy wing-like leaves on arching cascading stems and are excellent for hanging baskets. Flowers are generally pink. *Begonia richmondensis* var. *purpurea* has reddish coppery leaves with pink flowers tinged with white; var. *alba* produces white flowers.

Royale series is also a mixture, similar to Organdy.

Senator series consists of five individual colors and a mix with bronze foliage.

Starra series is a fine group of begonias, with smaller flowers that nevertheless cover the plants totally in the summer.

Victory series includes bronze- and green-leaved forms in pink, scarlet, white, and rose flowers.

Tuberous begonias (*B. tuberhybrida-cultorum*)   tuberous begonia   1–2′/2′
all season   many colors   garden

I remember on my first trip to Butchart Gardens on Vancouver Island being blown away by the size, diversity, and sheer beauty of tuberous begonias. Perhaps because of my wintery roots in Montreal, tuberous begonias and I became connected. On March 1, we ritually planted tubers in baskets, signifying the beginning of the end of winter, at least mentally. Having them slowly emerge helped get us through the three more blizzards we invariably had in late March and April. While they didn't compare with those at Butchart, they pushed away more than a few snowbanks. Now that I live in Georgia and am able to raise all sorts of things that I couldn't in Montreal, I can't grow tuberous begonias worth a darn. It is about the only thing I miss about March in Quebec.

Begonia tuberhybrida-cultorum   ASHA KAYS

The many species of tuberous begonias include the perennial *Begonia grandis* and the beautiful orange-flowered *B. sutherlandii* from KwaZulu-Natal. Intense hybridization by Veitch and Sons of England in the early 1900s of Central American species such as *B. bolivensis*, *B. clarkei*, *B. davisii*, *B. pearcei*, and *B. veitchii* yielded the earliest of the dozens of large-flowered plants we call tuberous begonias. This rich mélange is classified under the catch-all *B. tuberhybrida-cultorum*. The tubers are large, often concave above. The stems of tuberous begonias are occasionally upright and often pendulous, and the ear-shaped leaves are often pointed at the apex. The leaves are usually green but may also be streaked or spotted. The flowers occur in threes, with the two female flowers flanking the male. For the showiest display, the two females are removed to allow the male to strut its stuff. The males may reach 6″ across and are usually double, the females, smaller and single.

If you are raising plants from dry tubers, place the concave side up in a suitable container and water well. Plants are generally grown in containers and baskets and are not as appropriate for the garden. The upright forms need staking; use thick stakes, as these plants can get quite heavy. Pendulous forms are always best for baskets.

Plants may also be grown from seed. The compact bedding forms, often referred to as Non-Stops, are grown from seed and can be used with reasonable success in the garden or landscape. If you'd like to try to keep the tubers for the next year, allow them to dry down at the end of the season. This will occur naturally under shorter days and cooler temperatures. Store clean tubers at about 40°F in dry peat or sawdust until you are ready to pot them up again in the spring or during a blizzard in March. Many cultivars are now available at garden centers, and storage of the tuber may not be worth the time or effort.

CULTIVARS

Dozens of colors and forms can be bought as dry tubers or young plants. They are classified into thirteen groups, based on shape, color, or form of flower and stems. Join a begonia group to learn more; see Janet Welsh of the American Begonia Society (www.begonias.org).

Charisma series is a seed-propagated group whose dominant parent is *Begonia elatior*. Plants do poorly in the ground but well in containers or baskets. They have many semi and fully double flowers, in scarlet, pink, and salmon-orange.

Fortune Mix and Galaxy Mix are seed-propagated forms with numerous colors.

Illumination series is a pendulous group of tuberous begonias, suited for baskets. The semi-double flowers occur in apricot, light pink, orange, and rose.

Non-Stop series consists of compact plants with double camellia-like flowers in ten colors and a mix.

Ornament series bears single and semi-double flowers with bronze leaves.

Rhizomatous begonias (*B. rex-cultorum*)	rex begonia	1–3′/3′
summer	foliage	garden

Grown strictly for the stunning foliage, this group of plants has been part of the houseplant and conservatory scene for many years. All members of this group are said to have originated from a single imported plant of *Begonia rex* to England in 1856, and subsequent hybridization with related Asian species has resulted in the many forms currently available. It is unlikely that true *B. rex* is in cultivation. The plants are mainly rhizomatous, with colored obliquely ovate pointed leaves. Sometimes the base of the leaf appears to be spiraled. The morphology of the leaves can be described in boring detail, but who needs it? When we come across a well-grown hybrid, we see only the incredible combinations of silver, gray, bronze, purple, red, brown, and green, to name just a few of the colors that create such rich patterns. The small white or pink flowers are seldom conspicuous but are similar in form to other species.

Plants cannot tolerate temperatures lower than 55°F for any length of time, but they may be used in shaded containers during the summer. Place in shade;

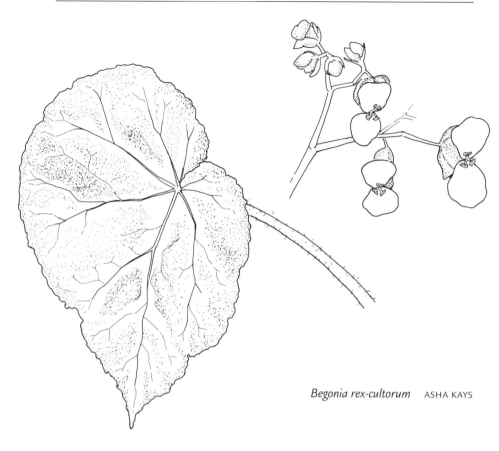

Begonia rex-cultorum   ASHA KAYS

plants quickly lose their metallic luster if placed in too much sun. Fertilize sparingly but at regular intervals.

Propagate by leaf cuttings. Detach a healthy mature leaf, and make incisions in the leaf across the main veins. Lay the leaf on a fine propagating medium, so that the medium is in close contact with the cut portions. Place at 75–80°F. Plantlets will form at the severed veins, after which they can be detached and potted. Alternatively, leaves may be cut into 1 × 1 cm pieces, each small piece including a portion of the principal vein. Insert the leaf piece vertically, vein down, into the medium. Plants can also be propagated from petiole cuttings (like an African violet) or from seed.

CULTIVARS

Hundreds have been developed, but most come and go, and it is the rare nursery that handles a diverse range of cultivars. Your best sources are specialist nurseries and conservatories at botanical gardens (volunteer to help shape the plants, and you might come away with a leaf for propagating). Plants are often divided into those with small (<3″ long), medium (6″), and large (>6″) leaves. These meager descriptions do not do these plants justice. All have been historically grown indoors, but outdoor container culture in protected sites should be considered.

'Comtesse Louise Erdody' dates back to the 1800s. The spiraled leaves with dark green venation are silver and pink and covered with coarse pink hairs.

'Fireworks' produces large maroon leaves, marked white blending to purple between the veins. Plants are more upright than others.

'Lalomie' bears large silvery leaves with deep green veins and pink margins.

'Merlin' has small leaves with spiraled bases in many colors.

'Peace' produces silver leaves with a handsome rose blush.

'Persian Swirl' bears large plum-colored leaves with a white lacy pattern throughout.

'Purple Petticoats' has medium spiraled leaves, silver with lilac along the margins and veins.

'Raspberry Swirl' has large raspberry-red leaves with silver and pink.

'Uncle Remus' is a dwarf form with multicolored leaves in silver, green, and red. Only 6–10″ tall.

'Venetian Red' bears large deep red leaves with contrasting dull black veins.

'Vista' is a medium-leaved form, with black to brown foliage dappled with deep coral.

'Wood Nymph' bears small rounded leaves of a rich brown speckled with silver.

Alternative species

Begonia dregei (syn. *B. parvifolia*; grape-leaf begonia, maple-leaf begonia) is a tuberous species best known for its large, lobed shiny green leaves on a 3–4′ tall plant. Leaf color varies; some plants may have white to gray spots and purple veins, and red undersides on the leaves. Flowers are few and white. Shade to partial shade.

Begonia fuchsioides (fuchsia begonia) is an undiscovered gem with small red fuchsia-like flowers. They have performed well in containers in our trials in Georgia. A pink form is also available.

Begonia masoniana (iron-cross begonia) is a rhizomatous species, with wrinkled leaves, 10–14″ long, covered with stiff red projections. The green leaves have large finger-like chocolate-brown markings, with arms (the German iron cross) radiating along the main veins. Plants can be used outdoors in areas protected from rain and wind. Many small green-white flowers are produced, but it is the foliage that people remember.

Begonia sutherlandii is a graceful tuberous species that should be better known. Plants are 1–2′ tall, with lobed lanceolate green leaves, 4–6″ long, with red veins and margins. The many single copper to salmon-orange flowers bloom all summer. Useful for partial shade in container or garden. A keeper!

Quick key to *Begonia* species

A. Roots tuberous . . . . *B. tuberhybrida-cultorum*
AA. Roots fibrous or rhizomatous
    B. Roots fibrous
        C. Leaves >2" long, showy, flowers with long
           peduncles, usually pendulous . . . . *B. ×argenteoguttata*
        CC. Leaves <2" long, not showy, flowers with
           short peduncles, not pendulous . . . . . . *B. semperflorens-cultorum*
    BB. Plant with prominent or creeping stems, rhizomes . . . *B. rex-cultorum*

Additional reading

American Begonia Society: www.begonias.org
Bender, Steve. 1989. Flowers through thick and thin. *Southern Living* 24(5):106–108.
Floyd, John. 1999. An angel but a dragon too. *Southern Living* 34(5):18GA.
Gilbert, Richard. 1994. Bewitched by begonias. *The Garden* 119(9):428–431.
Jimerson, Douglas A. 1989. Simply sensational summer bulbs. *Better Homes and Gardens* 67(4):95–100.
Lancaster, Roy. 1994. *Begonia sutherlandii. The Garden* 119(10):478–479.
Martin, Tovah. 1996. Rex begonias. *Horticulture* 74(1):42–43.

Bellis (bel′ is)   English daisy   Asteraceae

The prim and proper English daisy is a turf weed in the British Isles, only a few inches tall and with a small white flower. The genus consists of seven species, but only *Bellis perennis* is cultivated. The bright green oblanceolate to spathe-shaped leaves are basal, and rosettes grow unobtrusively throughout the summer in cool summers, and through the winter in areas of mild winters. The small (<1" wide) flowers bloom in cool seasons, spring to summer in the North, early spring in the South. Plants are quite cold hardy, surviving temperatures to about 8°F; they are often listed as perennials but should be treated as annuals in the North and biennials in the South.

Plants are seldom more than 1' tall and are used as edging, or as companions in container plantings. In the South, they are planted in the fall, along with pansies, to provide flowers in April. In early summer they often decline badly and are removed. Plants are useful in the rock garden, as good drainage is a definite advantage to their performance. In the North, early spring planting results in flowers through mid to late summer, depending on heat.

Full sun. Propagate by seed or, in the case of sterile forms, by division.

CULTIVARS

Carpet series is a terrific group, with 1" wide flowers on 6–9" tall plants. Among the most profuse flowerers for fall planting in the UGA trial grounds. 'White Carpet' is especially good.

Bellis perennis   CHRIS JOHNSON

Goliath series bears 3″ wide fully double flowers in a red, salmon, pink, and white.

Habanera series is one of the best for large flowers and good performance. Blooms are 1½–2″ wide and can be found in red, rose, white, and a lovely white with red tips.

'Kito' bears deep cherry-red flowers.

Medici series provides excellent well-branched compact plants, about 9″ tall. Six to ten semi-double flowers in red and white, with yellow centers, per plant.

Monstrosa series is made up of big suckers, with chrysanthemum-like 2″ wide flowers on 8″ tall plants. Plants have been selected with red, rose, or white flowers. Often found in seed packets.

Pomponette series is a dwarf form with small pom-pom flowers in red, rose, and white as well as a mix of colors.

Radar Mix is a mixture of about four colors on 12″ tall plants.

'Robella' bears 2″ wide flowers of salmon-pink. Among the largest-flowered forms.

Tasso series is similar to the Pomponettes but with larger flowers. Rose, deep rose, red, and white flowers occur.

Bidens (bi´ denz) beggar's tick, pitchforks Asteraceae

The common names refer to the hooked fruit of the plant, whose two barbs stick to anything that touches them. The generic name comes from the Latin, *bis* ("twice") and *dens* ("tooth"), again referring to the loathsome fruit and their habit of biting you. Many are native to this country; the Southwest is the hotbed of *Bidens*. *Bidens laevis* (bur-marigold) is a common tall-growing species often seen in Texas gardens.

In reading about the genus, one would think there was nothing ornamental about it, that it should be dismissed as an obnoxious weed. As well it should! And was—until some reasonable breeding work was done with *B. ferulifolia* (fer oo lih fo´ lee a; fennel-leaf tick). This species, native to southern Arizona, is grown for the fennel-like foliage, which means the 3˝ long, opposite leaves are pinnately compound or divided. The golden yellow cosmos-like flowers are 1– 1½˝ wide and are held on four-sided flower stems arising from the upper axils. Plants are generally floppy—a positive attribute when they are placed in hanging baskets.

I have seen selections of bidens hanging down from baskets in England, the West Coast, and the Northeast, and the yellow flowers, often combined with other annuals, are outstanding. The keys to good, persistent flowering are cool summers and well-maintained moisture level in the baskets. Plants are too leggy in heat and humidity, and many cultivars cannot be recommended for locations that experience hot summers.

CULTIVARS

'Golden Goddess' is the best-known cultivar, bearing 2˝ wide sunny yellow flowers on long flower stems. Bigger leaves, longer flower stems, and bigger flowers than 'Goldmarie'.

'Goldmarie' has dozens of small (1–1½˝ wide) bright yellow flowers on vigorous cascading plants. Excellent for window boxes and baskets.

'Peter's Gold Carpet' has very much impressed me with its vigorous "controlled" growth in the UGA trials. Plants grow rapidly, but the internode length is shorter than it is on 'Golden Goddess' and 'Goldmarie', which makes it an excellent choice for hot, humid summers.

'Smiley' is similar in flower to the others listed here but is more trailing than 'Peter's Gold Carpet'. Plants struggled early in our trials but recovered nicely in late summer and fall.

Alternative species

Bidens cernua is closely related to *B. laevis*; however, it can be shaped much more easily. I saw mounded specimens of this plant in the Zurich Botanical Garden, and I couldn't believe how colorful and beautiful they were. Plant breeders, get going on this one!

Bidens ferulifolia
'Peter's Gold Carpet'
ASHA KAYS

Brachycome (brak ee ko' mee)   Swan River daisy   Asteraceae

Most of the seventy species of this daisy-flowered genus (*Brachyscome* to a few authorities, but I prefer the shorter version) are native to southern and western Australia. The common name refers to the Swan River, which runs through Perth, Western Australia, and empties into the Indian Ocean at Freemantle. Several species are occasionally found in nurseries and garden shops, but the majority of plants offered are hybrids, which perform significantly better than they did in the early 1990s.

-iberidifolia (i ber id ih fo' lee a)   Swan River daisy   1–2'/2'
    summer   mauve, violet   Western Australia

A graceful little annual with many 3–4" long pinnately divided leaves, each narrow segment with entire margins. The 1" wide flowers of mauve, violet, rose, or white are held above the foliage on 3–4" long flower stems. The plant is slightly pubescent.

All in all, the species is cute but nothing to write home about. No doubt when plants were grown well, the profusion of sweetly fragrant flowers made them excellent for borders or for small cut flowers. Too often, however, when plants of the species were placed in American gardens, they rotted due to poor drainage or struggled because temperatures were too hot or too cool.

The newer hybrids are much more vigorous and, if placed in well-drained containers, can be excellent garden performers. They are better suited to window boxes, containers, or well-drained rock garden environments than they are to "normal" garden situations. All "brachys" benefit from a shearing in mid summer if they become a little too lanky. They will return in a week or two, and the shearer will be rewarded with additional flower production.

Full sun, excellent drainage. Propagate by seed or vegetative cuttings. Most of the newer hybrids are vegetatively propagated, which has contributed to garden vigor.

Alternative species

Brachycome multifida also grows 1–2' tall but has larger leaves and flowers. Flowers are generally purple, although white and pink occasionally occur.

Brachycome hybrids

Hybrids (between *Brachycome multifida*, *B. iberidifolia*, and other species) have been developed, mostly in Australia and Europe.

'Amethyst', about 12" tall, has large pink-mauve daisy flowers. *Brachycome multifida* is the dominant parent.

'Blue Mist' has narrow daisy-like flowers.

Bravo series is a seed-propagated group of short plants in some excellent colors. 'Bravo Deep Blue with Black Eye' is quite lovely. 'Bravo Violet with Black Center' describes another. Not as vigorous as vegetative forms. Cultivars of *Brachycome iberidifolia*.

'Bright Eyes', only 3–6" tall, has finely divided leaves and a profusion of blue-mauve flowers with yellow centers.

'City Lights' is a seed-propagated form with lavender-blue flowers and yellow centers. About 6–9" tall.

'Fernleaf White' is a spreading 6–10" tall form with narrow fern-like foliage and 1" wide creamy white flowers.

'Jumbo Mauve' is a beautiful plant, with large chrysanthemum-like flowers. Grows about 18" tall and 2' across. Excellent in our trials.

'Jumbo Misty Lilac' and 'Jumbo Misty Pink' are large-flowered forms with flowers blushed pink and lilac-white, respectively.

'Lemon Drop' was first seen in Australia, and I am not sure if it arrived here under another name. It is similar to 'Sunburst' in color.

'Mauve Delight' appears to have *Brachycome multifida* as the dominant parent. Dozens of small mauve flowers cover this 12" tall plant. The best in UGA trials.

'Mini Yellow' has small leaves and small flowers in a good clear yellow hue. Only about 8" tall and a bit more lanky than 'Mauve Delight'.

Brachycome 'City Lights'   ASHA KAYS

'Moonlight' has small white flowers, with narrow divided foliage. Spreads wonderfully well, grows 6–10″ tall. Outstanding in the UGA trial gardens. Also sold as 'Billabong Moonlight'.

'Purple Splendor', an older seed-propagated form, has handsome deep purple flowers with purple eye. Probably a cultivar of *Brachycome iberidifolia*. Also found as a mix (Splendor Mix) with blue, white, and sky blue.

'Strawberry Mousse' is less than 12″ tall with mauve-pink flowers.

'Sunburst' is a vigorous form growing 12–18″ tall with bright yellow to cream-colored daisy flowers. Also sold as 'Billabong Sunburst'.

'Toucan Tango' has deep lavender daisies on 6–8″ tall plants. Formerly sold as 'Ultra'.

'White Splendor' bears white flowers with a dark eye.

Additional reading

Armitage, Allan M. 1998. Swan River daisy. *Greenhouse Grower* 16(6):49–50.

Brassica (bras′ ih ka)   Brassicaceae

This economically important genus includes lettuce, mustard, chard, oilseed, brussels sprouts, kohlrabi, cauliflower, broccoli, cabbage, and kale. It is quite amazing how many ornamental forms of vegetables have appeared in landscapes since the 1990s. Perhaps it is a time of more open minds and an "anything goes" attitude, but from ornamental okra to variegated corn, ornamental forms of vegetables have caught on with gardeners and landscapers. Probably the most common form of embellished food is the ornamental kale.

The leaves of the kales and cabbages are held in loose rosettes, whose margins may be entire, wavy, or scalloped. Kale and cabbage are horticultural terms based on morphological differences in the species *Brassica oleracea*. Kale, whose leaves remain open and don't form a head, belongs to the Acephala (no head) Group. Cabbage, whose leaves generally fold over on themselves, belongs to the Capitata Group. The colors of the leaves can be extraordinarily decorative, in combinations of white, purple, mauve, and pink. The flowers bolt (flower stems arise rapidly from the center of the plant) when temperatures warm up. The presence of the flowers generally denotes the end of the useful life of the plant; removing them prolongs the ornamental life somewhat.

Ornamental kales have become quite popular in areas where late fall color is appreciated and are usually planted with the pansies in the fall. There is no sense transplanting too early in the fall, as warm temperatures result in poor quality and poor leaf color. Color gets better as temperatures fall into the fifties and below. Plants can persist through a few light frosts, surviving occasional dips to 15–20°F, if autumn temperatures have been falling slowly, hardening plants off. If, however, the fall is warm, a night temperature of 28°F can turn the plants into cabbage soup. The delay of bolting is a positive characteristic in the breeding of additional varieties. Plants are terrific subjects for the fall landscape and any late fall or winter color is a bonus. Some people argue that the flowers are another bonus, providing additional interest in an otherwise uninteresting time of year. I am not one of them. The onset of bolting detracts from the plant's appearance, and flowers should be removed.

As a group, kale and cabbage are biennials, and plants require cool temperatures to flower. In the South, they often go through the winter and are pulled out in early April; in the North, they may be buried by snow before they bolt. Cool temperatures are necessary for best growth, and so, like the leafy vegetables in our salad bowl, these plants do best when produced in times of cool temperatures. They are sold in the fall, occasionally in early spring.

CULTIVARS

Kale cultivars

'Lacinato' has thick crinkled blue-green leaves. About 2' tall.

Northern Lights series has frilled edges in white, red, and rose.

'Redbor' is an exquisite red leafy kale, much more vigorous and lively than other forms. Stands about 3' tall. An eye-catcher.

'Red Russian' is 2–3' tall with a deep purple hue in winter.

The following are the results of University of Georgia kale trials, fall-planted. All are seed-propagated and greenhouse-grown in the fall or winter for fall or spring sale. They range from compact forms like the Kamone series to large ruffled-leaved forms like the Feather series. Leaf colors are red, white, rose, and pink. Overall rating is based on a scale of 1 to 5, with 5 being excellent.

	Spread	Overall rating	Bolting date
'Feather Red'	13"	3.9	Apr. 10
'Feather White'	15"	3.9	Mar. 14
'Kamone Red'	9"	3.4	Mar. 14
'Kamone White'	8"	3.1	Mar. 7
Nagoya Mix	10"	3.3	Mar. 14
'Nagoya Red'	10"	3.2	Mar. 7
'Nagoya White'	9"	3.0	Mar. 2
Osaka Mix	11"	3.6	Feb. 19
'Osaka Pink'	9"	3.7	Feb. 2
'Osaka Red'	10"	3.6	Feb. 18
'Osaka White'	10"	3.1	Feb. 19
'Pigeon Red'	8"	3.3	Mar. 14
'Pigeon White'	10"	3.4	Mar. 2
'Prima Donna'	9"	3.2	Feb. 25
'Sparrow Red'	8"	2.8	Mar. 7
'Sparrow White'	8"	2.7	Mar. 14
Tokyo Mix	12"	3.3	Apr. 2
'Tokyo Pink'	9"	3.0	Apr. 4
'Tokyo Red'	12"	3.3	Mar. 14
'Tokyo White'	7"	3.1	Apr. 10

Other veggie cultivars

Several highly ornamental forms of mustard, chard (subspecies of *Beta vulgaris*), chicory (*Cichorium intybus*), and even ornamental beets (*B. vulgaris*) have become available. Their value as food crops is surpassed only by their value as ornamental companions to other cool-loving plants. Most are used in areas where pansies and violas are planted in the fall and make outstanding displays in beds or in containers, as companions for winter crops or as features on their own.

'Argentata' is an heirloom chard with wide silvery white midribs and deep green leaves.

'Bright Lights' is an outstanding selection of chard (probably *Beta vulgaris* var. *flavescens*), with bright colored petioles of yellow, gold, pink, and crimson. The leaves are dark green to bronze. Fantastic in the garden as an edible ornamental. An All-America Selection in 1998, and one which even I can get excited about.

'Macgregor's Favorite' is a strap-leaved Swiss chard with brilliant metallic purple leaves. Good for early spring show in containers and with pansies.

'Red Giant' is an exceptional mustard, with large leaves of violet red. Plants maintain a good low wide garden form well into spring.

'Rossana', a chicory, bears deep dark wine-colored leaves with white midribs.

'Ruby Red' is another fabulous form of chard, with bright red petioles that shimmer in the spring. Highly ornamental.

'Spadona', another chicory, produces handsome green foliage.

Additional reading

Dunbar, Rebecca. 1998. Bizarre brassicas. *The Garden* 123(3):191–193.

Breynia (bray′ nee a)   Euphorbiaceae

I first encountered *Breynia* in a conservatory in Canada and was intrigued with
the color of the foliage but wondered what it had to do with brains. Did people
eat it to get smarter? Or were the flowers like brainy celosias? Turns out the
genus was named for seventeenth-century German botanist J. P. Breyn. Many
years later, I encountered *B. nivosa* (syn. *B. distacha*; snow bush) grown as a wonderful 4′ tall hedge in Perth, Western Australia, and realized this shrub was
indeed useful in areas of frost-free winters and, for the rest of us, as a conservatory or porch plant. When grown singly, for the stems and painted leaves, it is
more interesting than ornamental. The flexible branches are coral pink to bright
red and occur in a zigzag pattern. The ovate leaves are alternate and entire and
only about 1″ long. Along with the stems, the leaves provide the color for this
plant; they are richly mottled and variegated white, with green veins. The small
flowers are tinged green on long pedicels but not particularly notable.

Breynia nivosa is quite wonderful when placed in containers and under-
planted with other annuals or perennials. They are more colorful when young
but always of interest.

Full sun, propagate by cuttings.

CULTIVARS

'Atropurpurea' has dark purple leaves. Plants are a little too dark for my taste
and not as handsome as the species.

'Dwarf White' is smaller in every way, with green-and-white leaves on 18″ tall
plants.

'Rosea-Picta' has leaves with pink and red mottling.

Browallia (bro wal′ ee a)   bush violet   Solanaceae

Not everyone thought that Linnaeus's system for binomial nomenclature was
the best way to name plants, and significant opposition arose in Europe after
publication of *Species Plantarum* in 1753. One of his supporters was J. Browall, of
Abo, Sweden, a bishop who was rewarded by having his name on this fine genus.
Sadly, the relationship between these two men was not a tranquil one. The good
times were reflected in Linnaeus's naming one species *elata*, exalting their early
intimacy; one *demissa*, for the rupture of their relationship; and another, finally,
alienata, for their permanent estrangement. So goes the story. Modern treatment of the genus has reduced it to a few species, including *Browallia speciosa*
and *B. americana*, into which those storied species have been folded.

Quick guide to *Browallia* species

	Habit	Height
B. americana	upright	1½–2′
B. speciosa	cascading, upright	2–3′
B. viscosa	upright	1–2′

-*americana* (a mer ih ka′ na)   browallia   1½–2′/2′
    summer   blue, violet   South America

Browallia americana, once common, is now offered only by specialty nurseries. The upright plants, well-branched and free-flowering, can reach 2′ tall. They are somewhat hairy and slightly sticky on the stems. The leaves are about 2″ long and wide, usually ovate. The 2″ wide star-shaped flowers are single or sometimes in twos or threes. The blue to violet petals are notched, resulting in two lobes per petal.

    Partial shade, well-drained soils. Propagate by seed or cuttings.

CULTIVARS

    'Caerulea' has pale blue flowers.
    'Grandiflora' and 'Major' have larger flowers.
    'Nana' is a dwarf form, growing less than 1′ tall.

-*speciosa* (spee see o′ sa)   bush violet   1–3′/3′
    summer   blue, deep purple   Colombia

Browallia speciosa is often seen as a garden plant but has never achieved mainstream status. Perhaps because it is more subtle than gaudy and does not enjoy the reputation of tougher showier plants such as petunias or begonias. The alternate 2–3″ long leaves are ovate and entire, and the flowers are borne in the upper leaf axils. Flowers have four stamens and a cylindrical corolla tube. They are usually violet or deep purple with a white eye. The species is woody at the base and can grow to 3′ tall, but extensive breeding has resulted in cascading forms suitable for baskets and dwarf forms for edging. Gardeners will find more baskets being offered for sale than they will potted plants.

    Morning sun, afternoon partial shade, well-drained soils. Propagate by seed or cuttings.

CULTIVARS

    'Blue Bells' is a cascading form most suitable for baskets or containers. 'Heavenly Bells' (pale blue), 'Jingle Bells' (mixed colors), 'Marine Bells' (deep indigo blue), and 'Silver Bells' (white) are also available.

    'Blue Troll' is an upright form with a compact self-branching habit. 'White Troll' is its white companion.

    'Daniella' bears flowers of deep blue, close to violet.

    'Major', a longtime favorite, has large sapphire-colored flowers with white eyes. Also sold as 'Sapphire Flower'.

'Starlight Blue', an upright form with a 6–9″ stature, is often used as an edging plant. A pinch on the plants helps make them more bushy. 'Starlight Sky Blue' (light blue) and 'Starlight White' are also available.

'Vanja' has large deep blue flowers with white eye.

'Violetta' has flowers of dark violet.

Alternative species

Browallia viscosa, a relative of *B. americana*, is so named because of the sticky (viscous) calyx on the young growth. Plants are 1–2′ tall with 1″ ovate leaves and many violet-blue flowers with a white eye. The lobes of the flowers are deeply notched. Good for garden or container. Partial shade. 'Alba' is a white-flowered form; 'Sapphire' is a violet selection.

Quick key to *Browallia* species

A. Corolla segments long, not notched, tube about 1″ long . . . . . *B. speciosa*
AA. Corolla segments short, notched, tube <1″ long
    B. Calyx slightly hairy . . . . *B. americana*
    BB. Calyx sticky . . . . *B. viscosa*

Brugmansia (brug man′ zee a)   angel's trumpet   Solanaceae

On my first trip to Costa Rica, I wandered around the grounds of a nursery with plant breeder Grace Price, and everywhere my friend and I commented on the fabulous species of *Solanum*, *Salvia*, *Arachis*, and the wonderful brugmansias. Most of what we saw were plantings of *Brugmansia arborea* and *B. aurea*. Approximately five species of tropical shrubs and trees are known; normally they reach up to 8′ tall, although in their native South and Central America, plants may grow 30′ in height. Plants, generally offered in containers that limit their growth, are seen more and more in large landscapes or in gardens where a relatively large plant can be used to advantage. They seldom flower until about 3′ tall and benefit from ample water and fertility. Plants are obviously tropical, but who cares? Plant out after threat of frost, and enjoy a little Andean habitat in the garden.

The alternate leaves, 6–8″ long, are entire or slightly dentate or pubescent. The flowers, 6–12″ long, are usually borne singly and are always pendulous. The buds of the funnel-shaped flowers are pleated, and the five flower lobes are often slightly reflexed. Five equal stamens attached to the petals and a fruit in the form of a capsule characterize the genus.

I was always a little confused about the difference between this genus and the better known *Datura*, so I didn't feel so bad when I learned that all members of *Brugmansia* used to be part of that genus. The differences between the two are somewhat subtle, as the following table shows.

	Flowers	Flower color	Fruit
Brugmansia	pendulous	white, yellow, peach	smooth, not dehiscent
Datura	upright	usually white, with purple	prickly, dehiscent

Another difference is the leaf odor: according to Suzy Bales, leaves of *Datura* smell like rotting garbage, those of *Brugmansia* do not. And the flowers of *Datura* open only for a night whereas those of *Brugmansia* are more persistent.

-×*candida* (kan′ dih da)	angel's trumpet	4–5′/5′
summer	yellow to white	hybrid

This hybrid between *Brugmansia aurea*, a white- to yellow-flowered species, and *B. versicolor*, a white-flowered species, is popular in American gardens. It is a small tree with finely hairy branches bearing 8–10″ long leaves. The corolla (attached petals) is recurved, up to 12″ long and twice the length of the calyx (attached sepals). The flowers are exceedingly fragrant and often open yellow then mature to white, rarely pink. Plants may be pruned in the spring for additional growth or to provide cuttings for propagation.

Minimum temperature for plants is about 40°F, so be patient prior to planting and remove the plants before the first frost. If plants are removed from the garden in the fall and placed in containers in a frost-free area, they will defoliate but should start to grow again in the spring, when water is provided and temperatures warm up.

Full sun, propagate by cuttings. Provide bottom heat for rooting.

CULTIVARS

'Double Blackcurrant Swirl' has double lilac-mauve flowers with frilled margins. Quite different.

'Double Golden Queen' provides large double frilled canary-yellow flowers.

'Double White Lady' is just that.

'Ecuador' produces an abundance of double white flowers.

'Ecuador Pink' has long deep pink flowers with upturned fluted edges.

-*sanguinea* (san gwin′ ee a)	red angel's trumpet	6–8′/4′
summer	orange-red	South America

This is a large shrubby species of angel's trumpet, with alternate, undulated leaves that are softly hairy when young. The pendulous orange-red flowers are 10″ long, with a yellow-green base and five lobes, each recurved a little. This species is more unusual than the white forms and more difficult to find, but the flowers are quite distinct. Probably not as floriferous as some of the others but worth a try nevertheless.

Full sun, propagate by seed or cuttings.

CULTIVARS

'Eagle Tree' has pendulous reddish orange flowers, 8–10" long.

-suaveolens (sway vee o' lenz)	angel's trumpet	8–10'/5'
summer	white	Brazil

A fairly common offering with half pendulous (not quite hanging down) 12" long white flowers, this species is wonderfully fragrant, more so in the evening than during the day. The calyx is smooth, not pubescent, and the lobes of the flowers are about 1" long. The points of the corolla are slightly recurved. The 8" long ovate leaves are hairless and pointed at the apex. These architectural gems are a marvelous addition to the garden.

Full sun, propagate by seed or cuttings.

CULTIVARS

'Pink' is like the species but with 12" long pink flowers that release a similar wonderful fragrance.

'Variegata' has white-margined leaves and pure white flowers.

Alternative species

Brugmansia ×insignis (in sig' nis) is quite similar to and often confused with *B. suaveolens*. This hybrid (*B. suaveolens* × *B. versicolor*) differs by having a slightly hairy, rather than a smooth, calyx. The lobes of the flowers are about 3" long, and flowers are white to pink. If you are not interested in checking out hairy sepals and other subtle differences, worry not; these plants can be used in the landscape just like other angel's trumpets. Full sun, propagate by cuttings. Cultivars include 'Orange', with large orange-yellow flowers, and 'Pink' ('Frosty Pink'), with salmon-pink blossoms.

Brugmansia versicolor, another relative of *B. suaveolens*, has large flowers which start out as creamy white and change to a pink-apricot color. Quite distinctive. 'Alba' tends to hold its white color longer but will still "blush out."

Quick key to *Brugmansia* species

    A. Corolla mainly white, although may open yellow or gold
        B. Calyx hairy
            C. Flowers open yellow, often turn to white . . . . *B. ×candida*
            CC. Flowers remain white . . . . *B. ×insignis*
        BB. Calyx smooth . . . . *B. suaveolens*
    AA. Corolla red . . . . *B. sanguinea*

Brugmansia hybrids

'Charles Grimaldi' has large, wide-open, salmon-pink flowers. Wonderful fragrance, abundant flowering. A terrific selection.

Brugmansia suaveolens
CHRIS JOHNSON

'Cypress Gardens' bears an abundance of hanging white trumpets. Flowers early on 3–4' tall plants. Excellent for containers.

'Dr. Seuss' is blessed with bell-shaped yellow-orange flowers. A great plant named for a great storyteller.

'Jamaican Yellow' bears wonderful creamy yellow flowers that are more elongated than others.

'Peaches and Cream' combines variegated foliage and creamy peach flowers, pendulous and fragrant. Introduced by Logee's Greenhouses, Ltd., Danielson, Connecticut.

'Sunray', developed by Kyle Courtney of Norwalk, Iowa, has wonderfully fragrant deep yellow flowers, which tend to be more outward-facing than pendulous.

Additional reading

Ellis, David. 1995. Devil in angel's petals. *American Horticulturist* 74(5):7.
Kellum, Jo. 1997. Grow heaven on earth. *Southern Living* 32(7):71.
Shear, William A. 1999. Angel's trumpet. *Flower and Garden* 43(2):28–30.

C

Caladium (ka lay' dee um) Araceae

Caladiums are colorful leafy summer plants that people love to hate. The flowers are essentially nonexistent, the leaves are gaudy, and it has to be about 90°F outside before you can enjoy them. That the previous statement is a wee bit extreme is obvious from the success of this plant in many gardens. The foliage arises from a spherical or cylindrical tuber, which goes dormant annually. The leaves vary in size and shape but are usually blotched, mottled, painted, or spotted with various colors. They can be accused of many things, but subtlety is not one of them. About seven species of this tuberous genus are known, but the one that has received all the breeders' attention is *Caladium bicolor*, which focus has resulted in dozens of selections for the shady garden.

-bicolor (bi' kul er)

		2-3'/2'
summer	foliage	South America

This specific name encompasses the hybrids sometimes known as *Caladium ×hortulanum*. The tuber is depressed and ranges 2–6″ in diameter. The leaves are usually shaped like an arrowhead (sagittate), and the petiole is often attached in the middle of the leaf (peltate); the margins are usually wavy. Variously colored, the leaves possess a rainbow of hues reminiscent of a three-year-old's finger painting. Populating the plant to such an extent that the whitish green flowers are seldom noticed, the leaves have inspired a great deal of hybridization: the peltate forms are usually called fancy-leaf forms, those with lanceolate leaves are referred to as strap-leaf forms.

Tubers can be purchased in the spring but should not be planted outdoors until night temperatures are at least 65°F, otherwise they will probably be dug up by curious squirrels and rodents before the first leaf emerges. They may be started indoors by placing the pot in the warmest area of the home. They respond well to heat but sit and look at you if temperatures are below 65°F. Starting them indoors is rewarding; once foliage starts to emerge, keep the plants moist but not wet and maintain warm temperatures. Wherever you plant them, be sure to place the tops of the tubers at least 3″ below the surface, as covering the tuber encourages new roots. Once three to five leaves have emerged and temperatures remain summer-like, they may be placed in a shady area of the garden. Full sun should be avoided, as the foliage will burn up around the margins. Organic matter is highly recommended, particularly the use of well-rotted compost or cow manure.

As fall moves toward winter, the leaves begin to fade. Water should be reduced and the tubers lifted once dormancy occurs, and certainly before the onset of frost. Lift, clean, and sort the lifted tubers. Separate the small tubers from the larger ones; the large ones will emerge faster in the spring, and the smaller ones can be placed outdoors in an area where they can be expanded. Store the lifted tubers at 55-70°F in slightly moist peat moss or sphagnum. Once temperatures warm up again, begin watering and provide heat to start again.

When I was young and foolish and living in Montreal, I ordered some tubers, placed them outside in late May, and waited for them to look like the catalogs. It was obvious those photos were not taken in Montreal. They are warm-lovers, that is simply the way it is. Great plants for summer color. Some of the white-leaved forms truly brighten up the shade, and the darker leaved forms too can be spectacular.

CULTIVARS

White fancy-leaf forms
'Aaron' has white leaves with an irregular green edge.

'Fantasy' bears creamy white leaves with red veins.

'June Bride' has large white leaves with green margins.

'Mrs. Arno Nehrling' bears white leaves with dark green venation and margins. The main veins are shaded red.

'White Christmas' produces leaves with large white blotches and green veins.

'White Queen' has white leaves with deep red primary veins and green margins.

Pink fancy-leaf forms
'Calypso' bears leaves with pink mottling and red venation.

'Carolyn Whorton' produces bright pink leaves with red veins and dark green marbling toward the margins.

'Elise' bears light pink leaves with green margins.

'Florida Sweetheart' produces heart-shaped pink leaves with light green edges on dwarf plants.

'Fannie Munson' has pale pink leaves, deeper pink veins, and a thin green margin.

'Kathleen' bears centers of salmon-pink and green borders.

'Pink Beauty' has pink marbling in the center of the green leaves and along the red veins.

'Pink Symphony' sends up light pink leaves with white blotches and green venation.

'Rosebud' produces leaves with pink venation and pink centers fading to white, then light green.

Red fancy-leaf forms

'Blaze' is a dwarf form with shiny dark red leaves and green margins.
'Florida Cardinal Red' produces dark red leaves and green margins.
'Frieda Hempel' bears bright red leaves with dark green margins.
'Irene Dahl' has medium red leaves and dull green margins.
'Postman Joiner' produces pale red leaves with darker veins and green margins.
'Red Flash' is dull green with brilliant red centers and white blotching.

Strap-leaf forms

'Candidum' is a popular form with white leaves and green veins and margins. 'Candidum Junior' is a smaller form.
'Clarice' bears pink leaves with darker pink venation, green margins, and white blotches.
'Gingerland' has grayish green leaves with white veins, dark green margins, and maroon spotting.
'Miss Muffet' is a dwarf green form with white veins, red centers, and red blotches.
'Red Frill' produces dark red leaves and green margins on short plants.
'White Wing' has wide dark green margins around the white leaves.

Additional reading

Jimerson, Douglas A. 1989. Simply sensational summer bulbs. *Better Homes and Gardens* 67(4):95-100.
Miller, Carol Bishop. 1997. Tuber talk. *Horticulture* 94(4):48.

Calandrinia (kal an drin' ee a)   Portulacaceae

The genus consists of about 150 species of annuals and perennials, native to South America, North America, and Australia. The foliage is alternate, entire, and fleshy, and the brilliantly colored flowers consist of five to seven petals and two persistent sepals. This is not a common annual in most of the country; in fact, plants are known only in California and parts of the Southwest, although widely used throughout tropical and other warm areas.

-umbellata (um be la' ta)	rock purslane	4-6"/12"
summer	red, crimson	Peru

This species is reasonably winter hardy to zone 7, but it is better treated as an annual. Plants grow in tufted compact masses of leaves along with red-tinged stems. The basal narrow leaves are gray-green and slightly hairy. The 1" wide saucer-shaped flowers are an intense glowing crimson-magenta and carried over long periods of the summer. They are held in a short umbel-like inflorescence (actually a many-flowered corymb). Flowers close in the evening and open the next morning.

Plants are best used in sunny rock gardens or well-drained areas in sandy or poor soil. They work well on slopes, even when quite dry. They do better in warm dry climates, like the Southwest, and rot freely in summers where significant rain and humidity occur. Plants flower the first year from seed; reseeding maintains plants in the garden. Propagate by seed or cuttings.

Alternative species

Calandrinia ciliata var. *manziesii* (redmaids) is native to the Southwest and grows to 2' in height (although 12–15" is more common). The crimson to rosy red flowers are held in leafy racemes. The leaves are about 4" long. A white form is occasionally found.

Calandrinia polyandra is native to Western Australia. I came across plantings of this species in King's Park, the magnificent botanical garden in Perth, where the pink to mauve flowers, 1" wide, could be seen a hundred yards away.

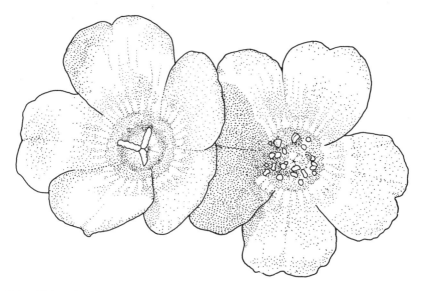

Calandrinia polyandra   ASHA KAYS

Calceolaria (kal see o lar' ee a)   pocketbook flower   Scrophulariaceae

The pocketbook flower, so named because it supposedly resembles a purse, has spent much of its ornamental history as a pot plant—presented as a gift that then slowly dies from neglect. The gift plant is part of the *Calceolaria* Herbeohybrida Group, complex hybrids of at least three species. They can surely be beautiful, with inflated flowers of many colors, but they have seldom been used in the garden. A few other species have been tried as window box or container specimens, or used in combination plantings in cool climes. The word "cool" is the functional word here, as all species of *Calceolaria* do poorly in hot summers. Representatives of the Herbeohybrida Group may be plunked down in the garden every now and then, but the species making the most headway in garden recognition is the yellow-flowered *C. biflora*.

-biflora (bi flor′ a)	pocketbook flower	1–2′/1′
summer	yellow	Chile, Argentina

The 1–2″ wide yellow flowers are held on many scapes, in pairs or three flowers per scape. The leaves are hairy above and on the lower veins, and lanceolate to ovate in shape. They are all basal, and when the flowers appear they stand well away from the foliage. This species is exceptional combined with other plants, the bright yellow enhancing other colors. It combines beautifully with verbena and red geraniums and, flowing down from containers, with petunias and heliotrope; it is especially terrific in states, provinces, or countries where summers are cool, like the west coast of Canada and the United States, New Zealand, and the British Isles. That is not to say that plants cannot be used in Atlanta, or St. Louis, but as they appear right now, they will melt out by mid to late June. Breeders should be incorporating other species, like the more heat-tolerant *Calceolaria mexicana*, to provide additional heat tolerance.

Full sun to partial shade, propagate by seed. Keep cool.

CULTIVARS

'Goldcrest' bears deep yellow flowers. Floriferous and quite popular.

'Triomphe de Versailles' may be no different, but such a glamorous name deserves inclusion. The low-trailing plants bear clusters of bright yellow flowers.

Calendula (kal end′ yew la)   marigold   Asteraceae

The Romans noticed how some species of marigolds seemed to flower continuously, remaining in bloom through the passing of many *calendae* (the first days of each month, on which interest on borrowed monies was due). Hence, the marigold was known, in Latin, as the flower of the calends, and the juice of the flowers was used by Romans as a cure for warts. In Mexico, where it arose like the Flanders poppy in areas disturbed by war, it was known as the flower of death. *Calendula* was grown as an herbal plant long before it became an ornamental; its yellow color suggested to suggestible seventeenth-century scientists that it be used as a treatment for jaundice as well as for measles and smallpox. Although some of the traditional medicinal strategies seem a little crazy now, many such uses for calendula are still widely accepted: a lotion made from calendula flowers is recommended as a salve for cuts, bruises, and diaper rash (anybody with a red-bottomed baby can appreciate that last news), and the petals are still used as a garnish for salads, soups, and drinks, although they can be harmful if ingested in too great a quantity. And you thought this was just a simple bedding plant!

-officinalis (o fih shih na' lis)   pot marigold   9–18"/12"
   spring, summer   yellow, gold   unknown

Although twenty species in the genus are known, the most widely grown are the many cultivars derived from *Calendula officinalis*. The alternate simple oblong leaves are more or less hairy, and the solitary flowers up to 3" wide. Breeding has resulted in dense double-flowered forms in cream to deep orange. I categorize pot marigolds as cool-loving annuals that should be planted early in the spring or late winter. Plants can tolerate frost of 22°F if properly hardened off before planting. This means that if plants are exposed for a week or so to temperatures of 40°F prior to frost, they are highly tolerant of light freezes; if not hardened off, the same temperatures will kill the plant. The cool-loving label makes plants suitable for full-season flowering in the areas where summer temperatures are moderate. In most of the country, however, calendula is best suited for early spring planting, to be enjoyed in the cool spring and then replaced by

Calendula officinalis   CHRIS JOHNSON

warm-loving plants in late spring and summer. In the Deep South, plants are put out in the fall, with pansies, and flower in March and April.

Flowers are produced abundantly, particularly if old flowers are removed before seed forms. Some of the taller forms have historically been used as cut flowers and still are brought indoors from the garden. They are also produced as winter- and spring-flowering pot plants, to be enjoyed indoors like pot mums and then put outdoors. *Calendula* was quite common as a pot plant years ago, as shown by the common name, but has been displaced by chrysanthemums, poinsettias, African violets, and Easter lilies. The heyday of recognition for *Calendula* was probably in the 1930s, when three cultivars were All-America Selections: 'Sunshine' (1934), 'Orange Shaggy' (1935), and 'Orange Fantasy' (1938). Although these particular cultivars are no longer available, their genes are seen in the many modern cultivars.

Full sun, propagate by seed. Seed can be sown *in situ*, but many of the better cultivars are only found as flowering or budded plants in the garden center.

CULTIVARS

'Bon Bon Orange' and 'Bon Bon Yellow' were the first dwarf forms with double flowers. An apricot and light yellow have since become available.

'Calypso Orange with Black Center', a compact form, has 2″ wide flowers with a handsome black center. 'Calypso Yellow with Black Center' is similar but with yellow flowers.

'Fiesta Gitana' is a mixture of colors ranging from creamy yellow through lemon and gold to deep orange. Reselected recently by Kieft Seed, a Dutch company, it is an impressive dwarf offering.

'Greenheart Orange' has serrated orange petals around a lime-green center.

'Indian Prince' has vivid orange flowers with a red underside. Prince Mix includes yellow, orange, and gold flowers.

Kablouna Mix has large crested flower heads in which the darker centers are wider than the ray flowers.

'Lemon Gem' has beautiful soft yellow flowers on a compact 12–15″ frame.

'Mandarin' is available in orange and yellow.

Pacific Beauty Mix is a blend of orange, yellow-apricot, and cream flowers on 2′ tall plants. 'Pacific Apricot' is one of the best.

'Pink Surprise' provides orange flowers with pink shades throughout.

'Touch of Red' produces plants in which each flower petal (including such colors as buff, orange, and yellow) is tipped in red. Distinctive and lovely.

Additional reading

Broadhurst, C. Leigh. 1998. Marigold: the little flower that could. *Better Nutrition* 60(11):26–28.

Dickson, Charles. 1999. Curing the common contusion. *Mother Earth News* 174: 24.

Duke, James A. 1998. Healing herbs from the garden. *Organic Gardening* 45(1): 50–53.

Taylor, Joy, and Doug Jimerson. 1989. Edible flowers, savory choices to buy or grow. *Better Homes and Gardens* 67(4):142.

Calibrachoa (kal ih bra' ko a)   trailing petunia   Solanaceae

To find the name *Calibrachoa* in any serious horticultural reference is almost impossible. In no book on annuals, in no encyclopedic book, including *Hortus*, *RHS Dictionary of Gardening*, and *Manual of Cultivated Plants*, could I even find it listed. Is the name just a figment of our horticultural imagination? *Calibrachoa* was separated from *Petunia* in 1825, but I thought that some reference would have at least a passing mention of it. Many taxonomists believe that all species of *Calibrachoa* and *Petunia* should be lumped together under one genus, but in 1985, species of *Calibrachoa* were found to have $2n = 18$ chromosomes, whereas *Petunia* had $2n = 14$. Other discernible differences were that species of *Calibrachoa* were small shrubs and had incised calyx lobes, whereas representatives of *Petunia* were large herbs with deeply incised calyx lobes. In 1990, the genus *Calibrachoa* was again separated from *Petunia* and called *Petunia* sensu ("in the sense of") Wijsman, the Dutch taxonomist who accomplished the split. Scientific literature holds it likely the genus *Calibrachoa* consists of about twenty-five species, but horticultural and gardening references do not recognize it as a separate genus. (Maybe it is because *Petunia* sensu Wijsman has no poetry about it.) Exist it does, nevertheless and legitimately, and this reference is recognizing *Calibrachoa*.

Garden introductions of *Calibrachoa* ×*hybrida* have been accepted greedily by the gardening public. Plants provide small petunia-like flowers on prostrate low-growing plants. Introduced via Japanese breeders, the 3–6″ tall plants have excellent weather tolerance—they just keep on flowering. The stems vary 6–20″ in length and cover square yards in a matter of four to six weeks. The leaves are about 1″ wide and 1½″ long, with entire margins. Each flower is only about 1″ wide, but they occur profusely at the nodes once days lengthen. They flower more under long-day conditions, so early spring flowering may be a little less than expected. But flower they will.

Plants can be used at the front of the garden, in a rock garden, or in containers and baskets. Full sun is necessary for good flowering; shady conditions reduce flowering significantly. Plants have proven to be consistently winter hardy in our trials in Athens (zone 7), so in southern gardens they may be planted in the fall as well.

Plants may easily be propagated by cuttings or division—just don't sell any of the propagules (all plants bought at the garden center are patented and propagation is frowned upon, but so is removing the label from a new pillow). Little or no seed is produced.

CULTIVARS

Colorburst series, from The Flower Fields group of plants, produces flowers that are a little larger than other series. Colors include cherry, red, rose, and violet.

Calibrachoa   ASHA KAYS

Lirica Showers, the lowest-growing series, offers flowers in blue, blush white
(an excellent soft white with blush throat), lemon-yellow, pink, rose (with a yellow throat), and white. Excellent performance.

Million Bells is a little taller than Lirica Showers and includes cherry pink,
trailing blue, trailing orchid pink, trailing pink, and trailing white. 'Terra Cotta'
is the most beautiful flower color, on vigorous plants.

'Yellow' is a gorgeous light yellow color, sure to be a winner. Also sold as
'Lemon-lime'.

Additional reading

University of Georgia Trial Reports: www.uga.edu/ugatrial

Watanabe, H., T. Ando, E. Nishono, H. Kokubun, T. Tsukamoto, G. Hashimoto,
and E. Marchesi. 1999. Three groups of species in *Petunia* sensu Jessieu (Solanaceae) inferred from the intact seed morphology. *Amer. J. Bot.* 86(2):302–
310.

Wijsman, H. J. W. 1990. On the inter-relationships of certain species of *Petunia*.
Part 6: new names for the species of *Calibrachoa* formerly included in *Petunia*
(Solanaceae). *Acta Botanica Neerlandica* 39:101–102.

Wijsman, H. J. W., and J. H. de Jong. 1985. On the inter-relationships of certain species of *Petunia*. Part 4: hybridization between *P. linearis* and *P. calycina* and nomenclatorial consequences in the *Petunia* group. *Acta Botanica Neerlandica* 34:337–349.

Callistephus (kal ih stef' us)   China aster   Asteraceae

This monotypic genus is far better known by cut flower growers than by gardeners. The China asters (*Callistephus chinensis*) are grown in cut flower farms and sold to florists throughout America. Gardeners are rewarded with 2–3' tall ornamental plants as well as an inexpensive source of cut flowers for entertainment.

Callistephus chinensis   ASHA KAYS

The branched stems bear alternate, triangular leaves with coarse teeth on the margins. The flowers are usually double and occur in late summer and fall, as the days become shorter. Flowers develop most rapidly when a period of long days (LD) is followed by short days (SD). That is, plants are "primed" or induced to flower under LD and then develop more rapidly under SD. This is particularly true for older cultivars, but so much breeding has occurred that newer cultivars flower even in mid summer. The more they are cut, the more they will flower.

Plants are easily grown from seed and flower the first year from seed. Unfortunately, a couple of serious diseases have kept China asters out of the gardening mainstream. Aster yellows results in distorted flowers (flowers partly or entirely greenish and yellow), spindly stems, and the yellowing of all or part of the plant. It is generally spread by leafhoppers, which carry the virus. Infected plants must be discarded. Plants afflicted with aster wilt (caused by the aster wilt fungus, *Fusarium conglutinans callistephi*) suddenly wilt, usually near maturity. The stem completely rots at the soil line, and often a streak of blackened tissue extends up one side. The advent of wilt-resistant cultivars has greatly reduced the severity of this problem.

Full sun, well-drained soils. Propagate by seed. Maintain excellent cleanliness around plants (no aphids, no overwintering weeds).

CULTIVARS

American Beauty Mix produces 3″ wide double flowers on 2–3′ tall stems in many colors.

Ball Florist Mix is an old favorite consisting of 3″ wide white, pink, blue, rose, and purple flowers.

Bouquet series (Bouquet Powderpuffs) has 2–2½″ wide fully double flowers with no yellow centers. Bred for wilt resistance. Plants grow 2–2½′ tall. Other Bouquet types are available in separate colors, such as azure, crimson, peach blossom, purple, rose-pink, scarlet, and white.

Chrestia Mix has 2″ large heads with tiny disk flowers and long spoon-shaped ray flowers. In blue, rose, pink, and yellow.

'Crego' bears a many-colored mixture of feathery 3″ wide flowers on 2′ tall plants.

Dwarf Queen Mix is only 12″ tall, with fully double flowers. The bedding plant of China asters.

Emperor series bears 2½″ wide flowers on 2–3′ high stems. 'Emperor Carmine' and 'Emperor Red' have carmine and deep red flowers, respectively.

Fireworks Mix consists of quilled ray flowers on 2′ tall plants, in white, rose, blue, pink and scarlet.

Florette Strain is available in separate colors, including deep pink, pale pink, crimson, blue, and a pastel champagne color. The 2–3″ wide flowers consist of fully double quill forms and are produced on 3′ tall stems.

Galaxy series is 4–8″ tall with large double 2–3″ wide flowers in many colors.

Matador series is similar to Matsumoto, but its flowers are slightly smaller. Separate colors and a mix are available. 'Matador Salmon-Pink' is particularly outstanding.

Matsumoto, a leading series of asters for cut flower production, produces sprays of 2–2½″ wide flowers with distinctive yellow centers. Mixes and separate colors are available. Plants have good wilt resistance.

Milady series is a dwarf form growing only 12″ tall with fully double blooms in numerous colors, including blue, red-rose, rose, scarlet, and white.

'Perfection' is a mixture of 3–4″ wide fully double flowers with incurved petals on 2½–3′ tall plants. Also sold as 'Giant Perfection'.

'Pixie Princess', only 8″ tall, is a good choice for the front of the garden. Fully double, pastel blooms occur in late summer and fall.

Pompom is a bicolor series with small rounded flowers. 'Pompom Blue and White' and 'Pompom Red and White' are two good selections.

Pot 'n' Patio Mix bears double 2½" wide flowers on 6–9" tall plants. In lavender, pink, and scarlet.

Princess and Super Princess series are 3–3½' tall with quilled petals. The "Super" designation refers to the larger flowers and stronger stems of these many selections. Separate colors found under the Super Princess logo include 'Alice' (light blue), 'Hilda' (light yellow), 'Scarlatto' (copper-scarlet), and 'Victoria' (scarlet).

Prinette series has long thin curved outer petals and small tubular center flowers. Flowers are available in pink and red.

Rainbow Mix may be ordered in single or double-flowered forms. Flowers generally have a prominent yellow eye and are borne on 2–3' tall stems.

Roundabout Mix consists of 6–8" tall plants with large flowers in many colors.

Seastar Mix has large flowers consisting of curled narrow (sometimes called "tiger paw") petals. Plants grow about 2' tall.

Serene series bears pompom spray flowers on 2' tall stems. Plants flower about fourteen weeks after sowing. Light blue, red, and rose colors are available.

'Sparkler' has double incurved flowers on 2–3' tall stems. Flowers are mainly available as a mixture.

Totem Pole Mix are large plants with many stems topped by fully double 3–4" wide flowers. Mixture of blue, cherry, rose-pink, and white.

Additional reading

Armitage, Allan M. 1993. *Specialty Cut Flowers*. Timber Press, Portland, Ore.

Campanula (kam pan' yew la)   bellflower   Campanulaceae

Campanula is a wonderfully large genus with plants for all people in nearly all parts of the country. Most popular bellflowers are perennials, but a number of fine annuals and biennials are sold. Campanulas can be identified by their alternate leaves, bell-shaped flowers, and pleated (like the pleats in your pants) flower buds.

Quick guide to *Campanula* species

	Height	Use
C. isophylla	6–9"	basket, container
C. medium	2–4'	garden, container
C. pyramidalis	3–5'	garden, cut flower

-isophylla (ih sa' fil a)   Italian bellflower, falling stars   6–9"/12"
          summer   lavender   Italy

This species is probably the least known of available bellflowers to gardeners, lost in a sea of the many perennials being sold. Look for it in the garden center as a hanging basket—about the only way it is produced. The procumbent plants consist of woody rootstocks with 6″ soft stems and 2″ long leaves. The 1–2″ wide lavender-blue flowers are borne profusely and often in loose clusters.

Place baskets in full morning sun, partial shade in afternoon. Maintain consistent moisture.

CULTIVARS

'Alba' bears white rather than lavender flowers.

'Balchiniana' has creamy stripes along the green leaves and lavender flowers. Also sold as 'Variegata'.

'Caerulea' produces clear blue flowers.

'Kristal Blue' and 'Kristal White' are popular with greenhouse growers, therefore the blue and white flowers, respectively, are often seen in retail centers.

'Mayi' has larger flowers and gray-pubescent leaves.

'Stella' is a highly popular selection bearing 1″ wide star-shaped flowers. Not significantly different from the Kristals.

| *-medium* (may′ dee um) | Canterbury bells | 2–4′/2′ |
| spring, summer | blue | southern Europe |

When plants carry single flowers up the 3′ tall stem, they are known as Canterbury bells; when they produce double flowers of white, rose, or purple, they are known as cup and saucer plants. Canterbury bells and cup and saucer plants were among grandmother's favorites, but plants are less available than in her day. The species is biennial, rather nondescript the first year but eye-catching the next. Plants produce a stout taproot and erect stems and then branch from the main stems. The flowers, mainly held in terminal racemes, sometimes in the leaf axils, are among the most dramatic and beautiful in the genus. Plant one-year-old plants in the fall; flowers will occur next spring or early summer.

Full sun, well-drained soils. Propagate by seed.

CULTIVARS

'Alba' has white flowers.

'Caerulea' bears clear blue flowers.

'Calycanthema' is the cup and saucer plant, with double-flowered forms in numerous colors. The base of the flowers is extended, forming the "saucer."

Champion series consists of 1–1½″ wide single flowers on 2–2½′ long flower stems. Available in pink and blue; other colors will soon be bred. Without doubt the best selections for cut flowers from the garden, they have been quickly embraced by cut flower growers and appear in florist shops in late summer and fall.

'Dwarf Musical Bells' was developed for the 6–12″ tall plants in a mix of single colors.

'Flore Pleno' is a hose-in-hose double form, without the saucer.

Campanula medium   ASHA KAYS

-pyramidalis (peer a mih da′ lis)   chimney bellflower   3–5′/3′
     summer   blue, white   southern Europe

This plant should be treated as a biennial, as it deteriorates badly after the second year. The 2″ long heart-shaped basal leaves have 6–8″ long petioles and dentate margins. Racemose panicles, 12–15″ long, of bell-shaped blue flowers arise from the axil of each stem leaf. More flowers open at the base of the flower stem than at the top, resulting in the pyramidal shape of the inflorescence.

As with most other upright *Campanula* species, pull out after flowering. Chimney bellflower does not tolerate heat and humidity and struggles as far north as zone 6. Whatever the locale, stems are brittle, and the plant should be supported. A good species for large patio containers.

Full sun, propagate by seed.

CULTIVARS

'Alba' is similar to the type but with clear white flowers.
'Aureo-variegata' has yellow variegated foliage.
'Compacta' is a dwarf form, 2–3′ tall. It is easier to manage in the garden and requires less room than the type but lacks the characteristic pyramidal shape.

Quick key to *Campanula* species

 A. Plant <18″ tall . . . . *C. isophylla*
AA. Plant >18″ tall
       B. Flowers in elongated raceme, corolla >1½″ long . . . . *C. medium*
       BB. Flowers in branched panicle, corolla <1½″ long . . . . . *C. pyramidalis*

Canna (kan′ a)   canna lily   Cannaceae

The old red-flowered, green-leaved canna lily, grown for mass plantings, was a tired symbol of horticulture's lack of interest in vegetative annuals. Not that anything is particularly wrong with red cannas, other than being boring, but far more exciting cultivars have now been developed. Many species are known— *Canna glauca* (blue canna), *C. indica* (indian shot), and *C. iridiflora* (Peruvian canna) are even occasionally offered—and hybridization has occurred with them all. In most cases the canna you purchase is likely a hybrid in which an aforementioned species is the obvious dominant parent. Each species (or its hybrids) has obvious advantages (*Canna glauca* and its hybrids can be grown in ponds, for instance), and for the connoisseur, they make an elegant departure from the stronger hybrids normally available. The bluish green foliage of *C. glauca*; the narrow stature and small red flowers of *C. indica* and its outstanding purple-leaved form, 'Purpurea'; or the fabulous pendent flowers of *C. iridiflora* are well worth looking for. Although "subtle canna" would strike most people as an oxymoron, these plants are indeed subtle but wonderful. The following chart may help distinguish the species, which are difficult to tell apart.

Quick guide to *Canna* species

	Leaf color	Flowers	Flower color
C. glauca	bluish	upright	yellow
C. indica	green	upright	red
C. iridiflora	green	pendulous	rosy red

-×*generalis* (jen er al′ is)	hybrid canna lily	3–8′/3′
summer	many colors	garden

The garden hybrids listed as *Canna* ×*generalis* are easily available and provide flowers and foliage of wonderful diversity. The resurgence of cannas can be attributed to believers who never lost faith that cannas deserved a place in American gardens; Jim Waddick, Herb Kelly, Johnnie Johnson, Jan Potgeither, Jack and Jo Roberson, and Bob Hayes introduced stunning hybrids, which forward-looking nurseries have picked up and promoted. They are cold hardy in zones 7

Canna ×*generalis*   CHRIS JOHNSON

to 10 but can be dug and stored further north. Fertilize heavily in the spring and once again in late summer with half as much. Plants are excellent for wet areas, even shallow ponds. In the UGA Horticulture Gardens, we put cannas in poorly drained areas where other plants languish.

Plant in the spring, after danger of frost, in full sun. In the South, plants arise in late March or early April. In most areas, tubers should be lifted after frost has knocked down the foliage. Dig up the roots, allowing soil to remain. Root division should be accomplished while the weather is still warm and dry enough to allow the cut ends to "cure" or heal before storing for the winter. If insufficient time is available for curing, then wait until spring to divide.

Quick key to *Canna* species

A. Flowers pendulous or nearly so . . . . *C. iridiflora*
AA. Flowers not pendulous
    B. Leaves blue-green to glaucous, flowers usually yellow . . . . . *C. glauca*
    BB. Leaves many colors, not blue-green, flowers many
        colors . . . . *C.* ×*generalis*

Canna hybrids

'Aida' has dark green foliage and soft pink flowers on 2½–3' tall plants.

'Ambassador' bears wonderful creamy white flowers on 5' tall plants.

'Australia' has satiny purple foliage with large deep red flowers on 4–5' tall plants. Quite remarkable.

'Bengal Tiger' is a most popular canna hybrid, with good reason. The clean yellow-and-green variegated foliage is outstanding, and the orange flowers too are handsome. Also sold as 'Pretoria'.

'Black Knight' is about 2½' tall with deep red flowers and burgundy leaves.

'Cap Camarata' has intense red flowers over green leaves.

'Chanteclerc' has bronze purple leaves and scarlet flowers.

'City of Portland' is 3–4' tall, with coral-pink flowers on green foliage.

'Cleopatra', a most interesting canna hybrid, bears green foliage with bronze stripes and yellow flowers with red speckles. You either love it or hate it.

'Conestoga' grows up to 5' tall, with large green leaves and yellow flowers.

'Confetti' has creamy flowers spotted with pink.

'Dollar' produces unique orange flowers, covered with red spots, and dull green foliage.

'Durban' is most unusual, producing leaves with deep red and orange stripes radiating from dark green central midribs. The leaves mature to a hodgepodge of red, olive, violet, and rose. Flowers are orange-red, plants are 4–5' tall.

'Ehemanni' is an 8–10' tall plant with pendulous cherry-red flowers. A hybrid of *Canna iridiflora*. A most interesting and valuable selection but not for the small garden.

'Emblem' has deep scarlet blooms and bronze foliage.

'Fireside' bears fiery red flowers over green leaves.

'Futurity Pink' is 2½–3' tall with pure pink flowers on deep burgundy foliage. 'Futurity Red' is taller and has scarlet-red flowers on burgundy foliage. 'Futurity Yellow' has yellow flowers with green leaves.

'Grande' is big and tall, well over 6' in height, and has small orange flowers, wide green leaves with red margins, and bronze stems.

'Intrigue' produces deep purple lance-shaped foliage and orange flowers on 6–9' tall plants.

'Kansas City' bears large handsome leaves, with alternating green and white sections, which I suppose could be called variegated. Bright yellow flowers hover over the 4–6' tall plants. An absolute knockout.

'King Humbert' has bright orange-red flowers and bronze-red leaves on 5–6' tall plants. 'Yellow King Humbert' is shorter with butter-yellow flowers and green foliage.

'La Garoule' produces light peach flowers over green foliage.

'Liberty series, developed by Jack and Jo Roberson of American Daylilies, includes 'Liberty Scarlet' (red flowers, bronze leaves), 'Liberty Pink', 'Liberty Coral Pink' (coral flowers, bronze foliage), 'Liberty Sun' (yellow flowers), and the fascinating 'Liberty Bugle Boy' (bicolor flowers).

'Louis Cayeau' bears scarlet flowers over green leaves.

'Matador' is a short plant with green foliage and many salmon flowers.

'Omega' produces large tropical green leaves with small flowers that start yellow and turn orange to pink as they mature. Plants are 8–10' tall.

'Panache', a hybrid of *Canna glauca*, grows to 6' in height with lovely narrow blue-green leaves and somewhat pendulous light pink flowers.

'Pink Beauty' is about 2' tall, with pink flowers edged in gold over glossy, green leaves.

'Pink Sunburst', a favorite of mine, grows 2' tall with foliage striped pink, bronze, and green and large pink flowers. Outstanding.

'Red Stripe' is another weird canna, with small orange-red flowers and large foliage that moves between green and red. A hybrid of *Canna indica*. Plants are 5–8' tall.

'Red Velvet' is 4–6' tall with large deep velvet-red flowers and bright green leaves. The leaves have purple margins and venation.

'Richard Wallace' is about 4' tall, with light green leaves and yellow flowers.

'Stadt Feltbach' bears peach-colored flowers and green leaves.

'Stuttgart' is an unusual selection with variegated green-and-white leaves and pink flowers. Plants are not suitable for full sun, and partial shade is needed, particularly in the afternoon. Leaves become necrotic at the edges when plants are in too much sun.

'Talisman' provides salmon-pink flowers over green foliage.

'The President' is a tried-and-true cultivar with green leaves and red flowers on 3–3½' tall plants.

'Tropical Red' is a seed-propagated form, the first really good dwarf to hit the garden scene. Plants are 12–18" tall with red flowers and green leaves. 'Tropical Rose', an All-America Selection in 1992, is similar with rosy pink flowers. Both are excellent for small areas.

'Tropicana' ('Phaison') is an excellent plant for deep bronze and pink leaves. Plants are vigorous, among the most outstanding in the UGA Horticulture Gardens. Gaudy orange flowers on 5–7' tall plants.

'Wyoming', one of the best-known selections, produces orange flowers over bronze-red foliage on 3' tall plants.

Additional reading

Jimerson, Douglas A. 1989. Simply sensational summer bulbs. *Better Homes and Gardens* 67(4):95–100.

Capsicum (kap' sih kum)   pepper   Solanaceae

The nine species of this well-known genus provide green pepper, red pepper, chili pepper, tabasco pepper, paprika, and cayenne pepper. But all belong to *Capsicum annuum*, a species from which so many forms have been developed that, as with *Brassica oleracea* (and its potpourri of cabbage, kale, and broccoli), five horticultural groups based on shape of the fruit have been identified. All are grown for the fruit, in green, red, yellow, and purple, and in many shapes and sizes. The crispy fruit of sweet peppers (Grossum Group) has a sweet flavor and is rich in vitamins A and C. The pungency and heat of hot peppers, which may occur in all groups, is concentrated in the seeds and inner surfaces of the fruit. Gardeners who enjoy combining the edible with the ornamental may enjoy planting some of the wonderful cultivars of cayenne and chili peppers. These plants belong to the Longum Group, and many cultivars have been transformed into highly ornamental, and spicy, plants.

I recall planting about twenty different cultivars of ornamental peppers in a trial at the University of Georgia. They became quite ornamental over time, developing fruit in various colors and shapes, all simply exuding heat. A few of my students tasted the fruit, and through sweaty brow and burning tongue, discovered that ornamental still meant heat. We invited our garden visitors to partake as well; most declined, but some from Cajun country, some from Mexico, and a few from the Middle East showed us what wimps we really were. Taste at your own peril. Some people are so highly sensitive that they had a reaction simply by handling the fruit and then rubbing their faces or eyes. Be careful.

Ornamental peppers are grown from seed, which can be collected from the fruit if it is allowed to ripen; however, seed is available in packages in the spring, and plants are sold through most garden centers. Full sun, lots of water.

CULTIVARS

'Aurora' is only about 4" tall, with purple fruit changing to bright red.

'Bellingrath Gardens Purple' is a tall plant (2½') with small satiny leaves of purple-green splashed with shades of purple, green, and white. The fruit evolves from purplish to fiery red.

'Black Prince', among the most popular forms, has purple foliage and handsome purple fruit.

'Bonfire' has conical fruit that begins pale green and changes to bright red.

Explosive series includes such plants as 'Blast' (fabulous, with purple leaves and fruit), 'Ember', and 'Ignite'. All hot.

'Fiesta' has thin, curved fruit that starts cream-colored, changes to orange, and finishes bright red.

'Fireworks' is a compact form, around 1' tall, with creamy white slightly inflated fruit that ripens to red.

'Fish' is an awful name for a variegated pepper with hot red fruit.

'Gion Red' produces large conical red fruit.

'Holiday Cheer' bears small round fruit that elongates as it turns from cream to red. An All-America Selection in 1979.

'Holiday Flame' has elongated red fruit and a compact habit.

'Holiday Time' produces round red fruit. An All-America Selection in 1980.

'Hot Bed' is a compact plant with elongated red fruit.

'Korona' is a beautiful low-growing form with inflated conical orange fruit.

'Masquerade' is 10–15″ tall and bears yellow fruit maturing to red.

'Medusa', a dwarf form with long narrow fruit, is (according to the fabulous Meg Green, who runs the UGA Horticulture Gardens) "very cool."

'Piccolo' has leaves variegated in green and white, with globose black-purple fruit.

'Prairie Fire' has upright conical fruit that matures from yellow to orange to red. Plants are 6–9″ tall.

'Pretty in Purple', a wonderful form, has dark purple foliage, with occasional green variegation, and orange to red fruit at maturity. A terrific plant in the UGA trials.

'Pylon Red' bears slender fruit that is quite similar to 'Fiesta'.

'Rainbow' produces an array of fruit colors, from white to purple and red. Compact.

'Red Missile' grows in a compact habit with large conical red fruit.

'Royal Black' has dark purple foliage and red to purple bullet-like fruit. About 3' tall.

'Teno' has some of the brightest red fruit we trialed. Compact.

'Thai Variegated' has conical peppers, lovely foliage splashed in white and pink, and a compact habit.

'Treasures Red' has deep green foliage and erect fruit that starts white and turns red. Absolutely stunning in our trial beds. One of the best.

'Triton' looks a little weird, with huge orange inflated fruit on a small 6–9″ tall plant. A little too unbalanced for my taste.

'Variegated Purple' has purple leaves and fruit variegated white and purple, turning red. Also sold as 'Variegated'.

Additional reading

Starbuck, Jamison. 1998. Hawthorn, garlic and cayenne: three herbs for health. *Better Nutrition* 60(2):50–58.

University of Georgia Trial Reports: www.uga.edu/ugatrial

Cardiospermum (kar dee o sper' mum)   love-in-a-puff   Sapindaceae

Fourteen species of tendril-climbing vines with alternate biternate leaves make up this genus, but the only species seen in American gardens is *Cardiospermum halicacabum* (hal ee ka ka' bum; heart pea, balloon vine)—the epitome of fun. The only reason to grow this vine is to enjoy its weird and wonderful fruit: it is not colorful, the flowers are insignificant, and the foliage does not shout out to be noticed, but I, for one, just love to put it by the hollies and let it climb. The sprawling plants grow 7–10' in a single season, and small white flowers are produced during the summer. Its notoriety stems from the inflated green papery fruit, inside which are three magical black seeds with a heart-shaped white spot on each. Now you know what puffy love looks like—a great treat for kids and visitors. If you'd like to gather seeds for next year's plants, wait until the puffs are brown and crisp; the seeds within will otherwise be insufficiently mature for good germination. Plants are native to India, Africa, and South America but have escaped in the southern United States.

Cardiospermum grandiflorum (heartseed) is occasionally found in seed catalogs. It is more vigorous than *C. halicacabum* (it grows through tree canopies in the tropics, to which it is native) and has larger creamy white fragrant flowers. Fruit is larger and almost triangular.

Full sun, propagate by seed.

Carpanthea (kar pan' thee a)   yellow blanket flower   Aizoaceae

This little-known genus in a little-known family is represented by *Carpanthea pomeridiana* (pom er id ee a' na), native to South Africa. Plants, sold under the cultivar name 'Golden Carpet', offer an abundance of yellow daisy-like flowers on 6" tall plants. The many-petaled flowers have a feathery appearance, the twelve to twenty stamens providing most of their 2" wide bulk. Flowers open wide only in bright sunlight. The alternate leaves are lanceolate and somewhat succulent.

This species, which was once part of the genus *Mesembryanthemum*, does best in cool nights and dry soils. It is a good plant for a rockery, as an edging, or at the base of a well-drained area. Plants flower mainly in the spring and are at their best in the cool temperatures of spring and fall. They may be cold hardy to about zone 7 but are mostly grown as annuals.

Full sun, propagate by seed ten to twelve weeks before transplanting.

Carthamus (kar' tha mus)   Asteraceae

The most common of the fourteen species is *Carthamus tinctorius* (safflower), from the flower petals of which a yellow dye was obtained. The generic name comes from the Arabic, *qurtom*, and the Hebrew, *qarthami* ("to paint"), which accounts for this species' other common name, false saffron. The 3' tall plants are now common cut flowers for summer and fall cutting.

Carthamus tinctorius   ASHA KAYS

The lower leaves are ovate, usually simple with entire or slightly spiny-toothed margins; the upper stem leaves are sessile, lance-shaped to ovate with entire or somewhat spiny-toothed margins as well. The flowers are 1–1½″ wide and look like a messy, wet dog—a wet orange dog at that. I have no idea why people like these flowers so much, but it does make sense that most cut stems are dried before use, thereby providing them with an excuse for looking so bad. I have seen nice fields of safflower; I have seldom seen a garden with safflower as an important member. But far be it for me to understand the mind-set of all gardeners or cut flower lovers. All of us who love flowers realize there is no accounting for taste. Grow it and have fun.

Full sun, well-drained soils. All cultivars are grown from seed. It is best to start seeds early in containers and transplant to the garden rather than direct-sow.

CULTIVARS

'Goldtuft' bears fuzzy balls of golden orange on 2–3′ stems. A popular cultivar for cutting.

'Grenade' is a mixture of cream, yellow, and orange flowers with spineless stems (a definite advantage).

'Lasting Orange', 'Lasting Tangerine', and 'Lasting White' are spineless and grow about 3′ tall.

'Orange and Cream' has flowers in those colors, 2–3′ tall.

'Tall Splendid Orange' bears yellow-orange flowers on 3–3½′ tall stems.

Caryopteris (kar ee op′ te ris)   bluebeard   Verbenaceae

Bluebeard is best known for the perennial form, *Caryopteris* ×*clandonensis*, a hybrid of *C. mongolica* and *C. incana*. This perennial and its cultivars are really the only ones known by most gardeners, but people are missing out if they haven't tried the less cold hardy *C. incana*. Here is a terrific but almost unknown plant that stands 3–5′ tall, with opposite coarsely serrated leaves and dozens of lavender to purple flowers. The ovate leaves are pubescent, 3–4″ long and held to the stiff stems by a short petiole. Although individual flowers are small, many are held in axillary cymes, generally one cyme at each node, accounting for the whorled look of the flowers as they ascend the stem. New stems arise from the upper axils, particularly if the terminal is cut, and flowers form in the nodes of the new breaks.

We studied the potential of *Caryopteris incana* for cut flowers and found it to be a better cut flower than *C.* ×*clandonensis*. Unfortunately, it is difficult to find seeds, and almost impossible to find plants, of this excellent annual. It is a marvelous plant, providing dozens of long-lasting flowers in and out of the garden, and sure to please.

Full sun, propagate by seed. Collect seed if possible to guarantee a supply for next year's plants.

'Summer Mist' is a seed-propagated form with whorls of lavender-blue flowers on 2–2½' plants. Some plants will have pink or whitish flowers.

Additional reading

Armitage, Allan M. 1993. *Specialty Cut Flowers*. Timber Press, Portland, Ore.

Catharanthus (ka tha ran' thus)   periwinkle   Apocynaceae

In the bedding plant world, an incredible eddy of activity has swirled about *Catharanthus roseus* (Madagascar periwinkle, vinca), producing new forms and cultivars. The pink pinwheel flowers have evolved into large phlox-like flowers in many colors. At the same time, a parallel and equally aggressive program to conserve and protect native tracts of this species has occurred, for it contains alkaloids that retard the development of leukemia. If anybody still questions the importance of conservation, tell them about Madagascar periwinkle.

As a garden plant, *Catharanthus roseus* provides season-long flowering over leathery dark green opposite leaves on 6–12" tall plants. Flowers are five-petaled, with a long throat extending from the small sepals. The stamens are carried just below the mouth of the throat and are not visible to the eye unless the petals are

Catharanthus roseus   ASHA KAYS

ripped apart. Current large-flowered, free-flowering hybrids hardly resemble the native Madagascar plants; in particular, the petals of modern hybrids often overlap and look more like a phlox flower than the open spread-out flowers common to the original plants and early garden cultivars.

Although many positive strides have been achieved in its breeding, *Catharanthus roseus* remains difficult to produce and to grow in the garden. From a production standpoint, it must be treated as warm-loving plant in the greenhouse; growers raise temperatures—and are therefore forced to spend more money on fuel. If grown beside other cool-loving crops, such as geraniums and marigolds, vinca does poorly and inferior plants result. Symptoms of overly cold production temperatures are stunted plants, small flowers, and yellow leaves, particularly the bottom ones. Stay away from these at the retail shop; even though the price may be right, it is unlikely plants will recover once placed in the garden. The other problem is that vinca loves dry climates and sandy soils. Growing it in well-drained soils is a necessity. Do not use an automatic sprinkler system that waters turf in the middle of the night; if vinca receives the same amount of water that the lawn gets (assuming the lawn is green), it will likely rot and die. This is of course more of a problem for landscapers, who maintain large turf areas, than it is for gardeners; most self-respecting gardeners find their lawn area diminishing over time. Warm temperatures, good drainage, and full sun are needed for best performance of these fine plants.

CULTIVARS

'Apricot Delight', one of my favorites, has flowers with soft apricot petals and a red eye.

'Blue Pearl' is an independent color, with large light blue flowers with white eye. Excellent hybrid.

Carpet series was among the first and best spreading forms. Plants are harder to find but some beautiful colors and habits were available. If you can find them, give them a try.

'Cascade Appleblossom' is a spreading form of vinca, with light pink flowers and white eyes.

Cooler series is an outstanding group of plants with wide flowers and excellent performance. 'Grape Cooler' and 'Peppermint Cooler' (white with a red eye), two of the earliest offerings, have now been joined by blush (bluish pink), coconut (pure white), icy pink (light pink with rose eye), pink, raspberry red, rose, and strawberry.

Heatwave series consists of deep rose, grape, orchid, peppermint, pink, white, and a mixture of colors. Plants are 10–12″ tall with 2″ wide flowers.

'Lemon Meringue' is a little different, with white flowers and solid yellow foliage. The leaves will either be loved or confused with the common yellowing of leaves caused by stressful conditions.

Little series is a dwarf and compact group, only about 4″ tall. They are better as ground covers than as clumpers. Colors include 'Linda' (rose), 'Blanche' (white), 'Bright Eye' (pure white with rosy red eye), 'Delicata' (white with rose-red eye), and 'Pinkie' (rosy pink with deeper eye).

Mediterranean is a low-growing, almost ground-hugging series. Several colors, including deep rose with a light eye, are available.

Pacifica series is among the finest and should be asked for by name. 'Pacifica Red' is the best red-flowered vinca on the market and definitely on my top ten list of favorite bedding plants. Other colors include blush, deep orchid, lilac, polka dot (white with red eyes), punch (rosy pink with darker eyes), and white.

'Parasol' bears 2″ white flowers with rose-red eyes. With plants 18–20″ tall, it is among the largest selections of vinca available.

'Santa Fe Deep Salmon' provides salmon-pink flowers on 10″ tall plants.

Tropicana, a breakthrough vinca, was the building block of current large-flowered series. It consists of plants with large phlox-like flowers in blush, pink, and white.

Victory, an upright series, includes such colors as grape, apricot, white, carmine-rose, purple with white eye, and cranberry.

Additional reading

University of Georgia Trial Reports: www.uga.edu/ugatrial

Celosia (sel o′ see a)   cockscomb   Amaranthaceae

About sixty species of *Celosia* from the tropics of Asia, Africa, and America are known, but only one, *Celosia argentea*, is used as an annual in American gardens. The leaves are alternate, mostly narrow and entire. Individual flowers occur in terminal and axillary spikes, the heads of some forms being convoluted, resembling a cock's comb, while others occur as feathery spikes. Taxonomists are as confused as horticulturists and gardeners as to how to group the various forms of celosia. Most refer the ornamental celosias to *C. argentea* var. *cristata*. Within this variety are four groups gardeners may recognize. The most common is the Cristata Group, the common cockscomb, whose distorted flower heads make one stare in fascination or in stunned silence. I find that my students remember them more easily when I refer to them as colored brains. They are monstrous, the epitome of how artificial and plastic-looking some bedding plants have become, but before gardeners scoff, they should remember that such flower forms occur naturally—and flower breeders have merely provided additional choices. The second most common form is the Plumosa Group, typified by feathery plumose spike flowers; its more civilized look is available in various heights and flower colors. The Spicata Group (wheat celosia) is generally about 3′ tall, with feathery earth-tone flowers in long slender terminal and axillary spikes; these plants make excellent fresh and dried cut flowers. The Childsii Group, an uncommon form in horticultural circles, is characterized by globose heads of flowers; it is somewhat similar to the Cristata Group.

Since 1935, eleven *Celosia* cultivars have been All-America Selections, the latest being 'Prestige Scarlet' in 1997.

Grow in full sun, fertilize well early in the spring. Too much rain and humidity causes flowers to rot; well-drained soils are a must, and occasional fungicide applications are useful in warm, humid climates.

CULTIVARS

Childsii Group

Sparkler series is part of a small group of plants with globose flowers. Plants grow 3′ tall and consist of carmine, cream, orange, red, wine, and yellow colors. 'Wine Sparkler' is outstanding. Recommended for cut flowers.

Cristata Group

'Amigo Mahogany Red' has deep purple leaves with red veins topped with a velvet red cockscomb. Plants are only about 8″ tall. Other colors will soon be available.

Bombay series is a convoluted form available in ten colors. Big, strong, and vigorous—among the most popular cut flowers in the world.

Chief series was introduced as a large plant for the garden and, when the 3–4′ tall plants are closely spaced, is a great success as a cut flower. Strong stems carry wonderful brightly colored flowers of carmine, fire, gold, persimmon, red, rose, and a bicolor. Only 'Bicolor Chief' (red and yellow) is nauseous, the others are terrific.

'Fireglow' is about 2′ tall with cardinal-red flowers. An All-America Selection in 1964.

Jewel Box Mix consists of 4–5″ tall plants smothered with big colored brains. An awful thing.

'Prestige Scarlet' is about 1′ tall with 3″ wide deep red flowers and bronze-green leaves. An All-America Selection in 1997.

'Red Velvet' has crimson heads 10″ across on 2–3′ tall plants.

'Treasure Chest' consists of 8–10″ tall plants with cockscombs 8–10″ across. Available as a mixture of red, scarlet, gold, pink, and salmon.

Plumosa Group

'Apricot Brandy' has apricot-orange feathers on 18–24″ tall plants. A 1991 All-America Selection. Quite striking.

Castle series has 8″ plumes on dwarf 12″ plants. Available in orange, pink, scarlet, and yellow.

Century series has more meat to it than other series, consisting of free-branching 24″ tall plants in fire (deep red), red (bronze leaves), rose, and yellow. Flower plumes are about 12″ long.

Fairy Fountains Mix was one of the first popular dwarf (10–12″ tall) plume forms used for bedding. It occurs as a mix of colors only.

'Forest Fire' is among the tallest of the plume types. The 2½′ tall plants have scarlet feathers and bronze foliage. Quite brilliant.

Geisha series is a dwarf form, growing only 6–8″ tall. As ugly as Jewel Box but at least without the brains.

Kimono series is also tiny (6–8″ tall). Little 2″ long feathers of cherry red, cream, orange, red (with bronze foliage), rose, salmon-pink, scarlet, and yellow

Celosia 'Prestige Scarlet'   ASHA KAYS

may be found in the series. Plants look better at the retail store than they do in the garden.

'New Look' is an outstanding cultivar, bearing deep scarlet plumes over bronze foliage. Well-branched plants are a landscaper's dream. A Georgia Garden Gold Winner from the UGA Horticulture Gardens in 1998.

'Pampas Plume' grows 2½–3' tall in a mixture of colors.

'Red Glow' has rosy red flowers on 10" tall plants.

'Wine Sparkler' bears red plumes, red stems, and wine-red foliage on 2–3' tall plants.

Spicata Group

'Amazon' produces narrow ruby-red plumes, resembling those of the grass *Pennisetum*. Bronze foliage sets off this wonderful form even more. Plants grow 3–4' tall.

'Enterprise Dark Pink' has many flowers open at once, making a most impressive show.

'Flamingo Feather', 2–3' tall, was the first introduction of an upright series of plants. The flowers are light pink fading to a wheat-straw white. Outstanding for cut flowers, fresh or dry.

'Flamingo Purple' is 3–4' tall and has purple leaves and rosy purple plumes. Although flowering does not occur until mid to late summer, and plants can reseed all over the place, it is still a terrific plant, beautiful in all respects—even when not in flower.

'Pink Candle' has rose-pink flowers on 2–3' tall plants.

'Startrek Lilac' and 'Startrek Rose-Pink' are two exciting forms in which the central flower plume is surrounded by equal plumes, resulting in a star-shaped inflorescence. Very interesting, useful for cut flowers.

'Venezuela' is a dwarf form with rose-wine flowers. Outstanding.

Additional reading

Kellum, Jo. 1998. Celosia worth a second look. *Southern Living* 33(6):82.

Kleine, Adele. 1992. Color in the garden: the return to red. *Flower and Garden* 36 (1):56–58.

Raworth, Jenny, and Susan Berry. 1995. A shelf full of color. *Horticulture* 73(10): 56–57.

University of Georgia Trial Reports: www.uga.edu/ugatrial

Centaurea (sen tor′ ee a)   cornflower, bachelor's buttons   Asteraceae

Centaureas seem to grow everywhere. This tendency to grow wherever empty space presents itself has resulted in such wonderful old-fashioned names as bluet, hurtsickle, ragged sailor, and French pink; common names generally reflect local lore, and this plant is dripping in it. Its usefulness as buttonhole flower, particularly for courting young gentlemen, provided the name of bachelor's buttons. The genus was said to have healed Chiron, who was a centaur (the half-man, half-horse beasts of Greek mythology)—hence the generic name. Chiron went on to teach many Greek heroes, including Achilles. Not bad for that simple little roadside flower.

Better known for such perennial species as *Centaurea montana* (mountain bluet), *C. hypoleuca* (knapweed), and *C. macrocephala* (basket flower), the genus does offer several annual forms that have nevertheless been perennial favorites in gardens and landscapes. The most common is the lovely cornflower, *C. cyanus*, one of the best blues ever put on earth, but other annuals have also found their way into gardeners' hearts. American basket flower (*C. americana*) and sweet sultan (*C. moschata*) are commonly found in florist shops, as they are grown for cut flowers in many parts of the country. For best results in the garden, they should be sown in great drifts, in succession. That is, as the first planting gets a little ragged, sow again. All species benefit from multiple sowings and will flower until frost.

A characteristic of all species of *Centaurea* is the involucre at the base of the flowers. The involucre is made up of small bracts, which overlap like shingles. Some species are characterized by bracts that are fringed or slightly hairy, while others are entire. A boring way to spend your day, perhaps, but looking at the bract margins is an easy way to identify different species.

Quick guide to *Centaurea* species

	Height	Flower color
C. americana	3–4'	pink
C. cyanus	1–2'	blue, lavender
C. moschata	2–3'	varied

-americana (a mer ih ka' na)	American basket flower	3–4'/2'
spring, summer	pink	SE United States

Grown mostly as a cut flower, this species is difficult to find in American gardens. That is a shame, because its tall stout stems carry some remarkable flowers. We grew hundreds of plants in our cut flower trials in Georgia, and stems lengths of 2–3' with long-lasting flowers were the rule of the day. The sessile 3 × 1½" leaves are lanceolate and usually entire, or with widely spaced teeth on the margins. The flowers are generally solitary and 3–4" in diameter. The large involucre at the base of the flower is about 2" across. The flowers are pink to purple and, if cut, persist four to five days in the vase.

In the garden, direct sow or place transplants near the back, in full sun.

CULTIVARS

'Aloha' has 3" wide lilac-rose flowers on 3' tall stems.

'Jolly Joker' bears 3" wide lavender-pink flowers on 4' tall stems.

-cyanus (si an' us)	cornflower, bachelor's buttons	1–2'/2'
spring, summer	lavender	SE Europe

This slender annual produces many branches with linear lanceolate leaves, which are mostly entire. Many small ray flowers, providing the look of a fully double flower, occur in spring and continue until early summer. If you look at the base of the flower, you will see the many tightly held bracts. The 1½–2" wide flowers are generally lavender-blue, but other colors have been selected. (When plants escape, however, they are almost invariably blue.) Stick your nose in a bouquet of cornflowers, and you may be rewarded with a pleasant ephemeral fragrance. Flowers may be picked and enjoyed fresh or air-dried. If flowers are pre-dried for about half an hour in the oven at 175°F, the color is better retained.

This is a great plant for fillers or for the vase. Grow in full sun, provide decent drainage, and get out of the way. With luck, plants will reseed and can be enjoyed for many years. They are always propagated by seed.

CULTIVARS

'Black Gem', an old-fashioned seed selection, is gaining a foothold in American gardens once again. Silvery leaves and dark maroon flowers on 2' tall plants.

'Blue Bottle' is only about 12" tall with deep blue flowers.

'Blue Diadem' provides 2½" wide flowers with blue petals and dark blue to black centers.

Dwarf Midget is a mixture containing pink, mauve, red, blue, and white 1″ wide flowers on 12″ tall plants. Plants may also be obtained in separate colors ('Blue Midget', for example).

'Emperor William' is 2–3′ tall with single dark blue flowers and gray-green foliage.

Florence series is a group of plants which grow about 18″ tall. Colors include blue, lavender, pink, red, violet, and white.

'Frosty' is available in a mix of colors, each with white-edged petals. About 20″ tall. Also sold as 'Frosted Queen'.

'Garnet' has rich burgundy flowers on 2′ tall plants.

'Jubilee Gem', a 1937 All-America Selection, bears many double bright blue flowers on 2′ tall plants.

'Pinkie' has light pink flowers.

Polka Dot Mix is about 2′ tall with a mixture of double flowers.

'Red Boy' bears rosy red flowers on 2½′ tall plants.

'Snowman' has creamy white flowers on 2½–3′ tall plants.

| *-moschata* (mos ka′ ta) | sweet sultan | 2–3′/2′ |
| spring, summer | many colors | SW Asia |

Some taxonomists have changed the name of this plant to *Amberboa moschata*; until it is accepted by all, however, let's leave well enough alone. Commonly grown in Europe as a cottage flower and as a cut flower, this species is known for its long slender stems and sweet honey-like fragrance. The sultan of Constantinople wore it for its beauty and fragrance, hence the common name. The basal leaves are generally undivided and toothed; the stem leaves are lobed or divided. The rounded double flowers occur in numerous colors, but pink, carmine, and white are most common. The honey-sweet fragrance is strongest in cool weather, especially in early morning and early evening. Bringing the flowers indoors occasionally overwhelms wimpy noses. Open a window.

They are undemanding in the garden; placed in full sun and reasonably drained soil, plants are easy to grow. Seed may be sowed direct, or well-developed seedlings can be planted out after frost.

CULTIVARS

'Antique Lace' grows about 2′ tall with flowers in pastel shades of pink, lilac, and lavender.

'Dairy Maid' is but one name given to the 1–2′ tall yellow-flowered form that used to be called subsp. *suaveolens*. That name has been discontinued, but the flowers are terrific nonetheless. Some say they smell like chocolate, but my nose must be chocolate-challenged.

'Imperialis' is a common mix with flowers from white to yellow-pinks to carmine and purple on 3–4′ tall stems.

'Lucida' produces dark red flowers on 2′ tall stems.

'The Bride' bears clean white flowers.

Alternative species

Centaurea cineraria (syn. *C. gymnocarpa*), a relative of *C. moschata*, is one of the many plants with the common name of dusty miller. The common bedding-plant dusty miller is usually classified as *Senecio cineraria*, but other silver-leaved species also find their way into the sales area as dusty miller, including this one. *Centaurea cineraria* has felty white, softly hairy foliage, each 6–8″ long leaf pinnately dissected and arching away from the central stem. The small purple flowers are insignificant and usually hidden by the foliage. I like this plant even more than *Senecio cineraria*, and it is becoming more available. Sometimes grown under the name 'Gloucester White'. Full sun, propagate by seed or cuttings.

Centaurea rothrockii (roth rok′ ee i) is related to *C. americana*. It has pink-purple ray flowers surrounding a yellow disk. Some people think it the most exotic species of all the cornflowers. Stout stems are 3–4′ tall but seldom need staking. Particularly useful as a cut flower.

Quick key to *Centaurea* species

A.   Bracts of involucre entire . . . . *C. moschata*
AA. Bracts of involucre fringed or hairy
  B.   Plant 3–4′ tall, flowers 3–4″ wide . . . . *C. americana*
  BB. Plant 2–3′ tall, flowers 1½–2″ wide . . . . *C. cyanus*

Additional reading

Bushnell, Dick. 1999. The queen of cornflowers. *Sunset Magazine* 202(3):80.
Lee, Rand B. 1996. Centaureas. *American Cottage Gardener* 3(1):19–21.
——. 1998. Scintillating centaureas. *American Gardener* 77(4):36–40.

Centradenia (sen tra deen′ ee a)   Melastomataceae

Belonging to the same family as *Tibouchina* and *Heterocentron*, this genus is even less well-known a garden plant than those genera are. The approximately six classified species would generally be found as understory plants in conservatories or in botanical gardens, if noticed at all. These handsome tropical plants from Mexico and South America, with their opposite showy leaves and pink to fuchsia flowers, have only recently been trialed to any extent as a landscape plant. All have eight stamens and four petals, and all but *Centradenia floribunda* have unequal stamens.

Quick guide to *Centradenia* species

	Height	Flower color
C. grandifolia	2′	light rose
C. inaequilateralis	1′	pink
C. ovata	1′	rose to fuchsia

-ovata (o vay′ ta)   9–12″/12″
   spring   rose to fuchsia   Central America

Although garden information on this species is scanty, it will probably be available to gardeners soon. The plants I have looked at have nearly smooth, opposite, ovate leaves, each about 1½″ long. The stems are somewhat procumbent (trailing loosely), and the leaves and stems are flushed dull to rosy red throughout. The ¼″ long petioles and the pointed sepals are also fuchsia-red. The sparsely produced flowers remind me of those of *Heterocentron* (Spanish shawl) in number and appearance. They are handsome from a distance but absolutely fascinating up close. Four of the eight stamens are straight, and four appear to have a sickle attached to them. Easy to see if you are so inclined. The fuchsia-colored flowers, which are made up of four obovate petals, are about 1½″ wide and held in clusters, although often only one flower is open at a time. Quite unlike most other plants on the market.

    Many centradenias tend to flower in winter or early spring. In our trials in Georgia, plants of this species flowered in the greenhouse in early spring, but the

Centradenia ovata   ASHA KAYS

foliage had to sustain our interest in the summer, because nary another flower was seen until late fall. They are sprawlers, however, and because of this will be useful for baskets and containers. Good red fall color too. Worth a try, but don't expect a lot of flowers.

Full sun. Propagate by terminal cuttings.

Alternative species

Centradenia grandifolia, the most cultivated species, is a shrubby plant. The light rose flowers bloom for a longer period of time, into the summer. The branches are winged, and the 3–6″ leaves are curved, ending in a long acuminate apex.

Centradenia inaequilateralis (in ay kwih lat er al′ is) is also handsome, with leaves that are ovate to lanceolate, hairy and oblique (base of unequal dimensions). They are lighter red on the undersides. If the genus becomes popular, hybrids involving this species will be selected.

Quick key to *Centradenia* species

  A. Leaves >2″ long, with long narrow acuminate apex . . . . *C. grandifolia*
AA. Leaves <2″ long, apex not obviously acuminate
      B. Leaf bases obviously oblique, leaves ovate-
          lanceolate . . . . *C. inaequilateralis*
    BB. Leaf bases not oblique, leaves broad ovate . . . . *C. ovata*

Centratherum (sen tra′ ther um)   Brazilian button flower   Asteraceae

This little-known genus bears bluish lavender flowers that look a little like thistles. I have grown *Centratherum punctatum* (syn. *C. intermedium*) for many years and always enjoy the carefree flowering on open, sprawling plants. The alternate ovate to linear leaves are serrated and are often spotted with tiny purple pinpoints (punctate). Plants grow 15–18″ tall and provide fillers for more formal plantings. They are tender but often self-sow readily, appearing here and there where comfortable, and thus become a long-term visitor to the garden.

Full sun, propagate by seed. No cultivars have been named.

Ceratotheca (ser a to theek′ a)   Pedaliaceae

Only five species are found in the genus, the name of which comes from the Greek, *kera* ("horn") and *theke* ("case"), a reference to the horns on the fruit. In general, leaves are opposite; the upper ones may be alternate, more or less three-lobed. The species usually seen in American gardens is *Ceratotheca triloba*, native to South Africa and aptly named African foxglove by one its biggest fans, Ann Armstrong of Charlotte, North Carolina.

The 3' tall plants bear light lavender flowers in the upper leaf axils, each 2½" wide flower consisting of a five-lobed corolla, four stamens, and a shortened nonfunctional stamen called a staminode. The flowers, often tinged pink or white, are turned to one side of the upper stem and are held by short flower stems. They are as tough as nails in abusive conditions, particularly in heat and drought. Seeds often overwinter. In mild climates, plants may be placed in the garden along with winter-planted pansies and snapdragons and treated as a biennial. Ann mentions that they are beautiful combined with *Lantana trifolia*, *Verbena bonariensis*, and *Alternanthera* 'Rubiginosa'.

Plants are easily grown from seed and may be transplanted to the sunny garden when the threat of frost has passed. Place in a sunny area in well-drained soils. Fertilize well in the spring as temperatures warm up.

Cerinthe (ser in' thee)   honeywort   Boraginaceae

The first time I saw this weird plant was in a private garden in Dublin, Ireland. We all gathered around these 12" tall purple things, oohing and aahing. Then disaster struck. All eyes turned to me, and the questions—"What is it, Allan?" "Can I grow it, Allan?" "Where do I get it, Allan?"—were like tracer bullets on a dark night. Of course, Allan had absolutely no idea. But like all good teachers, I quietly asked my all-knowing hostess, Helen Dillon, who whispered, "*Cerinthe major*." Without hesitation, I repeated the name to the onlookers, who once again realized I knew nothing but politely thanked me anyway. Thank goodness for knowledgeable hostesses.

These are really fascinating plants, with 2–4" long smooth blue-green leaves and arching stems that terminate in wild-looking yellow flowers. The fascinating blooms consist of a purple tube, surrounded by purple bracts, equal in size to or larger than the sepals. The lobes of the flowers are strongly recurved. It is difficult to describe the flowers; suffice it to say that most people want to try them, once seen—they are that unusual. Plants are grown commercially as cut flower fillers and may be similarly enjoyed when cut from the garden. *Cerinthe major*, the more common species, is similar to *C. retorta*, which differs by having pale yellow, nonreflexed flowers and larger leaves. Unfortunately, hot summers are not to their liking; they perform well until mid summer and then fade away. Gardeners in the North and West can expect success.

Afternoon shade and well-drained but moisture-retentive soils are recommended. A little lime around the plants is also useful.

CULTIVARS

'Purpurascens', a selection of *Cerinthe major*, has purple foliage and purple flowers. Also sold as 'Kiwi Blue'.

Yellow Gem Strain offers yellow flowers hanging from purple bracts. Fascinating.

Additional reading

Lovejoy, Ann. 1999. Blue notes. *Horticulture* 96(2):42–45.

## *Chrysanthemum* (kris an' tha mum)								Asteraceae

The generic name comes from the Greek, *chrysos* ("gold") and *anthos* ("flower"), probably referring to the yellow *Chrysanthemum coronarium*. Chrysanthemums have been cultivated in China for more than 2500 years, but lovers of perennials and pot plants have watched this large genus being pared off by taxonomists and placed in genera all over the map. The florist mum was switched to *Dendranthema*; even Luther Burbank's shasta daisy was traded to *Leucanthemum*. The good news concerning that taxonomic assault, however, is that the annual species remain intact and can still be called mums. (Turns out that some changes are being struck down anyway, so Luther may eventually rest in peace again.) In the garden, the annuals may be interspersed among taller plants or planted in drifts of their own. Free-flowering and quite wonderful, they perform better in cool, dry summers and struggle in hot, humid ones. With so many other mums out there, they have been unjustly ignored in American gardens. It is time to reverse this decline, dust a few off, and reacquaint ourselves with these brilliant plants.

Quick guide to *Chrysanthemum* species

	Ray flower color	Height
C. carinatum	white with yellow base	2–3'
C. coronarium	light yellow	2–4'
C. segetum	golden yellow	1–2'

-carinatum (kar ih nay' tum)				tricolor daisy				2–3'/2'
  summer						white with yellow				North Africa

This erect bushy species from Morocco has long stiff stems and deeply cut alternate leaves. The somewhat succulent leaves are pinnatisect (pinnately divided), and the lobes are linear. The 2–2½" wide flowers consist of white rays and a yellow ring at the base, forming a circle above the central disk. They are generally purple in the center, which neat profusion of color accounts for its common name and also explains why the plant is still occasionally listed as *Chrysanthemum tricolor*.

Plants flower summer to early fall and persist for at least eight weeks. It is likely that they will require support, either by staking or as provided by neighboring plants. Gardeners who sow canned wildflower mixes for roadsides or pastures may find this species listed as part of the contents. Plants are also quite successful as cut flowers.

Propagate by seed, which if sowed indoors at 62–65°F will emerge in about ten days. Seed may also be directly sown in the garden when threat of frost has passed, or in the fall in areas of mild winters. Remove seedlings to retain an 8–12″ spacing in the garden. They tolerate light frosts but not prolonged exposure to winters woes. Full sun.

CULTIVARS

'Dunnetti' is a mixture of colorful single and double flowers banded with red, purple, or yellow. Plants are 2–3′ tall.

'German Flag' provides dozens of scarlet flowers with a yellow band at the base of the petals and a dark center. Quite striking.

Merry Mix is similar to 'Dunnetti', with a range of flower colors on 2–3′ tall plants.

'Monarch Court Jesters' is an old-fashioned mixture of large flowers with attractive zonation on 2′ tall plants.

'Northern Star' produces white flowers with yellow bands. Excellent choice.

'Polar Skies' has handsome cream-colored flowers.

-coronarium (kor a nar′ ee um)	crown daisy	2–4′/2′
summer	yellow	Portugal

Although not particularly well known today, this species was used to fashion garlands (the Latin *coronarius* roughly translates to "used in garlands") to ward off devils in the Mediterranean areas to which it is native. A short leafy form of crown daisy, *Chrysanthemum coronarium* var. *spatiosum*, is grown as a green vegetable, like spinach; its young leaves are widely used in Chinese, Vietnamese, and Japanese cooking. The ornamental forms can grow up to 4′, but in gardens, heights of about 2′ are more common. They are coarse, with alternate, divided leaves that tend to remain a lighter green than those of other annual mums, even when fertilized vigorously. The base of the leaves is slightly clasped around the stem, a characteristic which helps to separate this species from *C. carinatum*. The 1½–2″ wide flowers are typically light yellow, the disk being darker than the rays; deeper yellow forms have been selected, however. The species itself bears single flowers, but the double forms, which were more popular for cut flowers, have predominated. To me, the singles are more classy and tolerate inclement weather better. Plants may require staking in rich soils. Flowers appear in mid summer and continue if deadheading is practiced.

Plant in full sun in the North. A little afternoon shade helps in southern climates. Propagate as with *Chrysanthemum carinatum*.

CULTIVARS

'Flore Plenum' has double light yellow to white flowers on 2½′ tall plants.

'Golden Gem', only about 1′ tall, is a popular form for bedding or pot plant use. The flowers are golden yellow.

'Primrose Gem' produces dome-shaped 2′ tall plants with primrose-yellow flowers. The center is a darker yellow. Quite handsome.

-segetum (se jet' um)   corn marigold   1–2'/2'
    summer   yellow   Mediterranean

This species is native to the eastern Mediterranean and western Africa but became established throughout Europe. Prior to the widespread use of herbicides, it was common in pastures and fields, particularly where soils were disturbed for planting, thus its common name.

The leaves are oblong to oblong-obovate; the upper leaves are entire, the middle and lower leaves, deeply cut. Flowers are about 2½" wide and are usually held in terminal sprays. They are always yellow but may vary from light to golden and are almost always single.

Corn marigold is a common ingredient in wildflower mixes, along with corn-cockle (*Agrostemma githago*), cornflower (*Centaurea cyanus*), and common poppy (*Papaver rhoeas*).

Full sun. Propagate as with *Chrysanthemum carinatum*.

CULTIVARS

'Eastern Star' bears primrose-yellow flowers with a brown disk.
'Evening Star' produces bright golden yellow flowers.
'Prado' is a terrific 3' tall plant with 2" wide golden yellow flowers with a dark red center.

Quick key to *Chrysanthemum* species

A. Ray flowers ringed with yellow or red . . . . *C. carinatum*
AA. Ray flowers not ringed, generally yellow or white
    B. Leaves linear lobed and deeply incised, plants usually
        >2' tall . . . . *C. coronarium*
    BB. Leaves not reduced to linear lobes, plants usually
        <2' tall . . . . *C. segetum*

Chrysocephalum (kri so seph' a lum)   Nullarbor buttons   Asteraceae

I first stumbled across this little gem in New South Wales, Australia, where it was growing in landscapes and being sold in pots. As I approached the nursery, I saw what looked like bright yellow balls on 12–18" tall plants, and sure enough, these were the flowers—dozens of them on each plant. Formerly sold as *Helichrysum ramosissimum* and *H. apiculatum*, it became known as golden buttons or Nullarbor buttons, for the Nullarbor Plain in southwestern Australia, from which it is native. Confused as usual, I checked with Rodger and Gwen Elliot, the smartest plants people I know in Australia, and they determined that it was not a *Helichrysum* at all, but should be labeled *Chrysocephalum apiculatum* (a pik yew lay' tum).

My scant knowledge of Australian names aside, I knew this species had a future in America. Imagining how the country would pat me on the back for my

Chrysocephalum apiculatum 'Golden Buttons'   ASHA KAYS

great find, I sent some plants home. Six months later the same plant was introduced to America by the Paul Ecke Ranch of Encinitas, California. Once again, a nickel short and a dollar late. However the plant got here, I am pleased to see it in our country. Sure enough, it has done as well as I hoped it would, flowering so profusely and brightly that it's easily included on my 55-mph plant list. I have grown it for years and always will, it is such a great worker. Heat and humidity are non-issues.

The foliage is alternate and green, although it does have some silver in it. The flowers are little rounded balls, only ½" wide but clustered in groups of three or more and continuously in flower. Their small scale demands they be placed in front, but they seem to take care of themselves otherwise. Not as colorful as petunias or impatiens, I suppose, but how many plants do you have that come from the Nullarbor Plain in Australia? Definitely one of my favorites.

Full sun, well-drained soils. Propagate from cuttings.

CULTIVARS

'Baby Gold', 'Golden Buttons', and 'Nullarbor Golden Buttons' are essentially the same as the species but with prettier names.

Cirsium (ser' see um)　　　　　plume thistle　　　　　Asteraceae

"Who in their right mind plants thistles?" one of my brighter students asked me when we were transplanting seedlings in the research plots at the University of Georgia. Canada thistle, bull thistle, pasture thistle, and spiny thistle are only a few of the plants that sane people and animals avoid like the plague—or approach only with a very long scythe and leather gloves. So I suppose that my student's question was valid, but I could not come up with a rapid comeback and simply mumbled that this one might be a good cut flower. He went back to planting, secure in the belief that he was in the company of an idiot.

We were planting Japanese thistle, *Cirsium japonicum*, which is in fact far less spiny than most thistles. Data were eventually collected, and a few florists tried Japanese thistle, which turned out to be a long-lasting cut flower that, when prepared properly, persists well in bouquets. Plants are perennial but are usually considered biennials or annuals.

I prefer to use these handsome and colorful flowers in the garden. (I may be crazy but I am not stupid: I certainly didn't relish harvesting the stuff.) The terminal flowers are produced in the summer and continue for at least eight weeks. Plants grow 2–3' tall, and the alternate, dentate to pinnate leaves have short spines on the undersides. They compete well with other plants in the bed, and they don't have the aggressive tendencies of other thistles. A good choice for something a little different in the way of color and conversation. They are really quite wonderful when, allowed to reseed, they appear here and there throughout the garden.

Full sun, propagate by seed. Place seedlings in the fall or early spring. Frost is not a problem once roots are established. Cold is not necessary for flower production, but plants produce better in cool summers than in hot, humid ones.

'Pink Beauty' bears pink flower heads on 2–2½' tall plants.
'Red Beauty' has carmine-red flowers.

Cladanthus (kla dan' thus)   Asteraceae

This genus of four annual species is seldom seen in North American gardens. I
have, however, grown and seen *Cladanthus arabicus*, which I think may be a
worthwhile plant for the sunny border or open area. Native to southern Spain
and northwestern Africa, plants used to be known as *Anthemis arabica* and are
still grown under that name. They were removed because of slight differences in
floral morphology.

Plants are covered with fine minute hairs and are quite pungent (break off a
small piece of leaf and sniff), with alternate leaves divided into two or three linear to subdivided lobes. The upper leaves are whorled, and the whorled effect
beneath the yellow flowers results in a compact "full-bodied" plant. The golden
yellow cup-shaped flowers are 1½–2″ wide and often have a reddish band at the
base of the ray petals. The disk is a dark orange. Flowers occur from early summer through frost. This species needs to be tried in more locations.

Full sun, propagate by seed.

CULTIVARS

'Criss Cross' is about 12″ tall with handsome golden flowers and deeply
divided dark green foliage.

Clarkia (klar' kee a)   godetia   Onagraceae

Clarkia and *Godetia* are used interchangeably, and one genus is often sold as the
other. Most taxonomists have rolled everything into *Clarkia*; however, some
authorities have split one from the other. According to the splitters, the petals
of *Clarkia* are distinctly clawed (bottom half of the petal much more narrow
than upper half) while those of *Godetia* are scarcely clawed. For garden purposes,
consider *Clarkia* the correct genus and godetia the common name. I like the
generic name—we need a good plant to commemorate Capt. William Clark, the
great explorer of our West.

The genus bears showy flowers arranged in racemes or spikes. All thirty-three
species, native to the West Coast, mainly California and Oregon, are most often
used as cut flowers from the field or in greenhouses, particularly in the West.
Nearly all the garden forms are derived from *Clarkia amoena*.

-*amoena* (a mee' na)   satin flower   16–30″/15″
   summer   many colors   western North America

The stems of this species, usually unbranched or slightly branched, are slightly
pubescent above and smooth beneath. The ½–2½″ long leaves vary from linear

to lanceolate in shape and are held on short petioles. The pointed erect flower buds are also handsome, giving rise to the 1–2″ wide flowers borne in the leaf axils. Flowers consist of four smooth petals, which gave rise to the common name; four united sepals, which turn to one side at the base of the flower as it opens; eight stamens; and a four-lobed pistil. The satiny petals are often lobed or clawed. Flowers are usually crimson to light pink, with a large central blotch at the base of the petals.

Satin flower is among the most beautiful plants I know when grown in a suitable environment: cool nights, warm days, and low humidity. So much for the East and the South. All resent hot, humid summers; in such areas, they do well if transplanted early in the spring and then removed as they decline in mid summer. They also do well if transplanted in late summer for fall flowering. Fertilize sparingly, as high nitrogen favors foliage at the expense of flowers.

The flowers may be cut to bring indoors. Cut them as soon as the buds swell. Individual flowers may last only five or six days, but flower buds continue to open without fading. The more flowers present on the stem, therefore, the longer the vase life. A vase life of two weeks is not uncommon when a floral preservative is used.

Plant in full sun, provide excellent drainage. Propagate by seed; direct sow in early spring if ground is well prepared.

CULTIVARS

Single flowers

'Aurora' has salmon-orange flowers.

'Furora' bears crimson-scarlet flowers on 2½′ tall stems.

'Gloria' produces clear pink flowers.

Grace series is an F_1 hybrid, and although seed is more expensive than open-pollinated forms, uniformity and color selection are excellent. The upright habit, 2–3′ height, and the availability of both individual cultivars (with light pink, rose-pink, salmon, red, and lavender flowers) and a formula mix make the series particularly attractive.

'Memoria' bears clean white flowers on 2′ tall stems.

Satin series consists of 12″ plants with 2″ flowers in six colors. Seed-propagated.

subsp. *whitneyi* is a lower-growing form, with large flowers. The petals are lavender, somewhat lighter below, with a bright red spot in the center.

Double flowers

Azaleaflora Mix is available as a mix or in several single colors, including 'Maidenblush' (bright rose), 'Ruddigore' (crimson-red), 'White Bouquet' (white), 'Brilliant' (carmine), 'Sweetheart' (pink), and 'Orange Glory' (orange). Plants generally flower on 1–2′ tall stems.

'Grandiflora' is taller (2½′) than Azaleaflora but only available as a mixture of colors.

Cleome (klee o' mee)   spider flower   Capparidaceae

The 150 species of the genus can be found throughout the tropics, in nearly all kinds of soil and microclimates. With all that diversity, it is strange that *Cleome hassleriana*, native to South America, has for so long been the only species around. The alternate leaves are palmate and divided into five to seven leaflets, each oblong-lanceolate in shape. At the base of each leaf petiole is a thorn or spine, which causes significant pain if carelessly handled. The presence of the spine accounted for the original specific name, *C. spinosa*. The wonderfully scented flowers have four petals and sepals and are borne at the end of the stems on long flower stems (pedicels). The pedicels and the stamens, which project beyond the petals of the many flowers, result in a spider web of bloom, while the dangling seed pods, at least to some, look like the legs of a spider. Let us not get too carried away with this spider thing, however: it is simply a neat-looking flower. Its delicate grace and the remarkable way its parts are put together should increase our awe of life's diversity.

Plants usually stand 3–5′ tall; I have seen them provide backdrops for hedges or anchor a planting simply by their dominance when in flower. In the garden, plants can vigorously reseed and become quite a nuisance. In warm climates, they tend to decline by late summer, but in most places and times, free-form cleome isn't such a bad sight. Plant in full sun as transplants or sow *in situ* after the soil has warmed up. Great old-fashioned plants.

CULTIVARS

'Helen Campbell' is about 4′ tall with clean white flowers.

Queen series provides the most common selections today. 'Cherry Queen' is a cherry rose; pink ('Pink Queen' was a 1942 All-America Selection), violet, and white are also offered. Plants grow at least 4′ tall.

'Sparkler Bush' is about 3′ tall with handsome rosy pink flowers.

Alternative species

Cleome marshallii (syn. *Polanisia dodecandra*), a dwarf species, grows only 1–2′ tall. Neither the flowers nor the plant itself is as impressive as *C. hassleriana*, but there is always something to be said for short plants. 'White Spider' is a rather washed-out white.

Cleome rosea var. *bicolor* is a gem of a little cleome and just possibly the next great plant for American gardeners. Leaves in threes, no spines, and gorgeous small rose to purple flowers present all summer. Compact plants begin flowering around 12″ tall but keep growing and getting fatter throughout the season, never exceeding about 3′ in height. I obtained seed from my gardening friends Ann Armstrong and Linde Wilson of Charlotte, North Carolina, and Larry Mellichamp identified it. It never went out of flower in our trials. Seed is available; named cultivars will be offered in the next few years. I recommend it highly.

Cleome serrulata (Rocky Mountain bee plant), an annual native to western North America, has leaves in threes and flowers that range from purple to pink

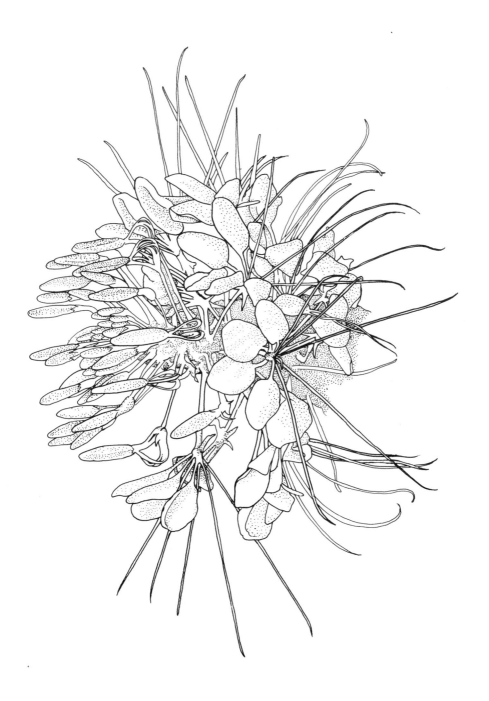

Cleome hassleriana   ASHA KAYS

to white. The long narrow seed pods are held on long stalks and arguably add additional ornamental value. (I would argue against that: they tend to go to seed too quickly.) The flowers are not particularly nose-friendly, as the other common name of skunkweed attests. 'Solo' has white flowers and is thornless. Plants are about 1½' tall.

Additional reading

Loewer, Peter. 1998. Cleomes. *Early American Homes* (spring):68–69.
Maurer, Mary. 1995. Cleomes: garden royalty. *Flower and Garden* 39(3):24.

Clerodendrum (kle ro den' drum)   Verbenaceae

Many medicinal properties were associated with the 400 or so species of this genus, and so from the Greek, *kleros* ("chance") and *dendron* ("tree"), arose the generic name. The genus consists of trees, shrubs, and vines, all woody in their native tropical habitat. In most North American gardens, wood is formed during the summer, but few species have sufficient cold hardiness to survive the winter. The hardiest are probably the shrubby glory bower, *Clerodendrum bungei* (to about 15°F), and the harlequin glory bower, *C. trichotomum* (to about 5°F). These large woody shrubs flower in late summer and fall, and if winters allow for them in the garden, they are spectacular. They benefit from being cut to the ground in the spring. When flowering is heavy, removal of the fruit results in fewer seedlings the next year, a problem where these plants, especially *C. trichotomum*, are successful.

Most tropical forms are best for the greenhouse and conservatory, but how many of us have conservatories? The best known of the greenhouse plants is *Clerodendrum thomsoniae*, whose pure white sepals and crimson petals resulted in the macabre common name of bleeding heart vine. To add further insult to injury, a variegated leaf form is also sold, and its combination of bleeding flowers and cream-and-green leaves is, unfortunately, unforgettable. Plants flower in the winter and are usually sold as a basket plant for a sunny window. Unfortunately, they prefer temperatures no lower than 55°F, below which they start dropping leaves and go into an unwanted dormancy.

A few species are occasionally seen in botanical gardens or public showplaces for summer color outdoors, but availability and lack of information have limited their entry into gardens. Two species in particular, other than the shrubby forms just mentioned, deserve more widespread use in summer gardens.

Quick guide to *Clerodendrum* species

	Habit	Flower color	Flowering time
C. speciosissimum	shrub	scarlet	summer, fall
C. splendens	twining	red, scarlet	fall, winter
C. ugandense	shrub	blue	summer

-speciosissimum (spee see o sis′ ih mum)   showy clerodendrum   6–8′/3′
   late summer, fall   scarlet   Java

In their native habitat, plants grow upright and reach 10–12′ without difficulty, and they'll do the same in a greenhouse. In American gardens, however, 3–4′ in the ground and 2–3′ in a container is more realistic. The first time I saw this species was at Cheekwood Gardens in Nashville; it was fall, and it was flowering its head off. The specific name means "most showy," and most showy the flowers are. The orange-red flowers are borne in dense panicles and, if temperatures are above 65°F, will continue to flower until frost. Handsome dark blue fruit will be formed as well. The four-sided stems bear 8–10″ long opposite heart-shaped leaves, which are densely pubescent. Their dark green color provides an excellent contrast to the showy blooms. The grayish exudate that often occurs on the undersides of leaves makes for a less-than-desirable shabbiness, but not much can be done about it, unfortunately.

If plants can be purchased in flower, they will likely continue to flower throughout the season and may be brought in to bright light to continue through the winter. Container plants can be moved indoors in the spring if temperatures decline and brought indoors for the winter. Whether in the ground or in containers, plants need full sun to achieve their best blooming effect.

Propagate by seed or by cuttings before stems become too woody.

-ugandense (yew gan den′ see)   blue butterfly bush   2–4′/2′
   summer, fall   light blue   tropical Africa

When I grew this species in the early 1990s in the UGA Horticulture Gardens, I was taken with the beautiful light blue butterfly-like blossoms and the reasonable growth habit of the plant, which resembles a small shrub. It did not appear it would get out of hand, like some shrubby members are prone to do. I also hoped that it had some cold tolerance and could survive a zone 7 winter (it did not).

The flowers consist of distinct, beautifully contrasting lobes of light blue and violet-blue, which catch the eye of all who pass by; even the anthers and the filaments are violet-blue. The blooms were all I could have hoped for, formed in summer on 3–4″ long panicles and continuing for much of the summer. Plants, however, were too lanky, and the foliage was a little disappointing: whatever I did, it remained a light, almost anemic green color. The opposite narrow, obovate leaves are dentate and only slightly pubescent. Plants do best in containers, where growth can be optimized; in the ground, they are not particularly vigorous. I still enjoy the flowers but have been disappointed in the plant as a whole.

Plant in full sun, propagate by tip cuttings.

Alternative species

Clerodendrum splendens is as beautiful as *C. speciosissimum*, bearing bright red to scarlet flowers. It is more viney in habit, growing twining stems that climb about 9′ in height. Plants tend to flower only in the fall and winter and are more useful indoors than out. In the South, they stand a chance of flowering before frost. High humidity reduces burning around the edges of their leaves. Finally—something good to be said for humidity.

Quick key to *Clerodendrum* species

A. Twining habit, red to scarlet flowers . . . . *C. splendens*
AA. Not twining, scarlet or blue flowers
    B. Scarlet flowers, pubescent foliage . . . . *C. speciosissimum*
    BB. Blue flowers, foliage mostly glabrous . . . . *C. ugandense*

Additional reading

Martin, Tovah. 1995. Bowers of glory. *Horticulture* 73(1):30–32.

Clitoria (klih tor' ee a)   Fabaceae

Clitoria is a marvelous, relatively unknown genus of climbers, most native to the tropics in Asia but naturalized throughout the tropics and subtropics. At least two species are native to the eastern United States, *C. mariana* (4' tall with light blue flowers) and *C. fragrans* (a short-growing plant with pale purple flowers), but neither are used in the garden. Of the seventy species recorded in the genus, only *C. ternatea* (butterfly pea) is seen and that only occasionally, in botanical gardens and conservatories; it is rare in gardens. But that's no excuse for not giving this beautiful vine a try. We grew it in Athens, and everybody stopped to stare.

The plants climb by smooth twining stems, attached to which are 1″ long petioles holding the alternate 4–5″ long leaves. The leaves consist of five (occasionally seven) elliptical to rounded leaflets, each slightly downy on the underside. The vine is not grown for the foliage, however, but for its rich blue flowers, which are produced in the axils of the leaves. This most beautiful blue gives way to a white-yellow eye at the center. Flowers are generally produced singly or in pairs and share the keeled structure seen in other members of the pea family.

Learning plant names is a great excuse for learning about things in general— the great people commemorated in generic or specific names, outmoded medical practices, folklore, even geography. In this plant's case I expected the specific epithet referred to leaves in threes (ternate), but when I studied *Clitoria ternatea*, I found no ternate leaves on it. Out came the plant books, where I learned that the species is found on Ternate, one of the hundreds of islands and atolls that make up the Molucca Islands, part of the vast island country of Indonesia. The Moluccas, Ternate included, were part of the major trade routes established by Europeans, mainly Dutch, who imported spices for Europe; collectively they became known as the Spice Islands. I love this stuff.

Plants often overwinter in southern Florida and parts of the Southwest, but they are annuals in the rest of the country. Place in full sun, propagate by seed in spring.

CULTIVARS

'Blue Sails' bears semi-double dark blue flowers.

Cobaea (ko bee′ a)   missionary bells   Polemoniaceae

The genus was named for B. Cobo (1572–1659), a Jesuit priest and naturalist who visited monasteries in Peru and Mexico. Although approximately twenty species are known, the most common by far is *Cobaea scandens* (cup and saucer vine), native to mountain habitats in Mexico. The vines consist of large alternate pinnate leaves, usually four to six segments per leaf, each measuring 3–4″ long. The leaves have large leaf-like bracts at the base and a hook-shaped tendril at the end, which grabs any structure within grasp. Like kids climbing ropes in a gym class, the plants quickly shinny up any pole, post, or trellis. The 2–3″ long flowers can be quite beautiful; each five-lobed corolla is greenish on emergence then becomes blushed with violet-purple at maturity. The large sepals are like saucers cupping the base of the corolla, producing the "cup and saucer" look of the blossoms. Flowers occur in late summer and fall; they are held on slender pedicels from the leaf axils and stand well out from the foliage.

Warning: this is not a plant for the squeamish gardener. Plants are heavy growers, approaching dutchman's pipe vine (*Aristolochia macrophylla*) for vigor.

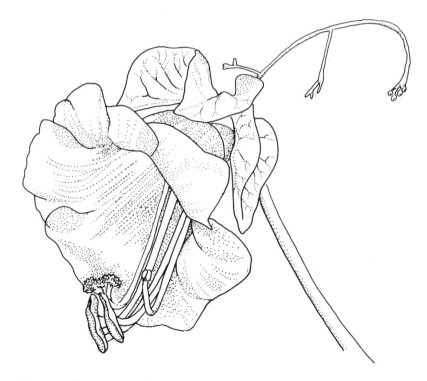

Cobaea scandens ASHA KAYS

They can enclose a small balcony in a single day and grow 15–30′ in a single season. Household string will not suffice for a climbing structure.

Plants grow more vigorously in areas of cool nights and warm days; hot, humid weather tends to slow growth. Cooler nights also yield more flowers; hot climates result in a wonderful leafy screen but less abundant flowering.

Grow in full sun, water copiously, and fertilize sparingly, especially once vigorous growth begins: high nitrogen means heavy leaf production at the expense of flower production. Propagate by seed *in situ* about 1″ deep when threat of frost has passed and the ground has warmed up. Soaking the seed overnight may aid uniformity and germination percentage. Early outdoor seeding does nothing but give local critters more chance to dig up the seeds. Seeds may be sown indoors at 70–75°F then transplanted after one or two true leaves have appeared.

CULTIVARS

'Alba', a white-flowered form, can be grown from seed.

'Variegata' has variegated foliage. It is much more difficult to find than *Cobaea scandens* and not as vigorous. Plants must be propagated by cuttings.

Additional reading

Halpin, Anne. 1997. Annual vines. *Horticulture* 94(4):60–64.

Coleus (ko′ lee us)   Lamiaceae

I remember the good old days, when *Coleus* (syn. *Solenostemon*)—grown from seed—was just another shade-loving bedding plant. Lessons in plant selection were minimal in our early years, but we were taught that the big three annuals for the shade were begonia, impatiens, and coleus—and that coleus was the shade-lover of choice. Our teachers were half wrong. Current hybrid offerings of coleus perform well in shade but are even better in full sun. This is true from Miami to Montreal, particularly of the vegetatively propagated cultivars. The old seed-propagated forms, such as the Sabers, Wizards, and Rainbows, are still fine plants, likely to be found in bedding plant flats at the local box store; they tolerate shade better than sun but also work in sun.

For years, seed companies found it more profitable to work with flowering bedding plants, such as geraniums, marigolds, and impatiens; the seed-propagated coleus remained stagnant. Interest was rekindled in the early 1990s, when older vegetative material resurfaced. Most rediscoveries were in the Southeast and the Southwest, where the old favorite 'Alabama Sunset' was routinely planted in botanical gardens and landscapes. In Florida, seed-propagated plants had never left the sunny landscape, but they needed stronger, more colorful forms as well. It did not take long for the new material to be embraced in the Midwest and Northeast. By the mid 1990s, breeders, landscapers, and gardeners had led coleus from its shady closet and into the mainstream of American gardens.

So what to choose? The incredible surge in the popularity of this old-fashioned plant means that it warrants significant shelf space at the retail nursery, and one mail-order nursery catalog lists 126 cultivars of hybrid coleus and then tries to describe the colors as well! Disdain has turned to must-have, side-yard plants have become collector items, boredom is cutting edge. I must admit that I too entered this cultivar craze; when I released eight cultivars in 1993, I had no idea that the genie was being released by others at the same time.

Most new cultivars are vegetatively propagated rather than seed-grown. Many of the vegetative cultivars perform better in full sun than in shade, with better coloration and stronger stems (shade tolerance still exists, but not the necessity for shade); many offer less summer flowering and more vigor than the seed-propagated forms. In fact, seed breeders are presently using vegetative material as part of the germ plasm to provide additional color, vigor, and weather tolerance to their plants.

Most selections and hybrids are grouped under the banner of *Coleus blumei*, but a few other species, such as the trailing *C. pumilus* and its cultivars, have entered the marketplace as well. Seems everyone wants a piece of coleus: taxonomists have also been tinkering with it, and they decided that the coleus genus does not really exist—it was just a figment of crazed gardeners' imaginations. We should now call all those 126 cultivars *Solenostemon scutellarioides*. In your dreams.

CULTIVARS

If you prefer shopping by mail, your choice of cultivars immediately expands; in the retail outlets, only a few cultivars are offered, and a handful of series and independents are more common than others. But I must issue a public service announcement, whatever your shopping preference: beware of vegetatively propagated coleus names—they are incredibly mixed up. Consider the dilemma of describing multicolored foliage in a mail-order catalog: the result is often an exercise in fiction, well meaning though it may be. You may think you know the "proper" name and so try ordering more plants, from another source this time, but what you get may be quite different from what you received before. Buying in person is sometimes no better: the name on the plant at the garden center may be the same as the one you bought there last year, but the plant is obviously different. Coleus is notoriously fickle; it changes colors under different light intensities, or just for spite. If half the fun in life is guessing just what's a-comin' next, then coleus provides a lot of amusement. Try to keep your healthy sense of garden curiosity—what you end up with may be quite good, if unexpected.

Within the broader categories of vegetative and seed-propagated, a cultivar may be further described as one of three types. Landscape types are upright and generally less than 24″ tall. Novelties offer interesting leaf shape or color; it's subjective, but these are usually eyepoppers. Ground covers, which are more likely to flower in the summer than other types, include both mounding forms and long-stemmed forms, suitable for baskets and containers. Here are a few of my favorites; forgive the omission of some of yours.

Vegetative

Ducksfoot series, a mounding ground cover, provides plants with flattened foliage, somewhat resembling a duck's foot, in many colors.

	Height	Flowering
'Indian Frills'	13"	none
'Inky Fingers'	18"	none
'Purple'	18"	none

Other cultivars, mostly in darker colors, are emerging in the Ducksfoot series. For sure, more will follow even these in the ground cover line.

Solar series, a landscape type, was introduced in 1994 by George Griffith of Hatchett Creek Farms, Gainesville, Florida. Its members were so different from other cultivars, they became popular immediately.

	Height	Flowering
Eclipse	32"	medium
Flare	38"	medium
Furnace	34"	light
Morning Mist	25"	light
Red	33"	light
Shade	29"	heavy
Spectrum	28"	none
Storm	30"	light
Stormy Weather	40"	light
Sunrise	40"	light

In general, availability in garden centers is good. I love 'Solar Morning Mist' and 'Solar Sunrise', but my favorite is 'Solar Flare'. They are all terrific.

Sunlover series arose in 1993 from plants that had been researched at USDA facilities in the South. We evaluated many, many different forms at the UGA Horticulture Gardens and greenhouses and named and released eight cultivars. They all perform well in full sun and grow rapidly. All are landscape types, with the exception of 'Thumbellina', a mounding ground cover.

	Height	Flowering
'Collin's Gold'	28"	light
'Cranberry Salad'	36"	medium
'Freckles'	38"	medium
'Gay's Delight'	36"	light
'Olympic Torch'	36"	medium
'Red Ruffles'	31"	light
'Rustic Orange'	34"	light
'Thumbellina'	19"	medium

The most popular Sunlovers have been 'Red Ruffles', 'Gay's Delight' (a 55-mph plant), 'Rustic Orange', and 'Thumbellina'. 'Red Ruffles', which appears nationally under the banner Athens Select, should be widely available.

Trailing coleus (*Coleus pumilus* forms) are uncommon but, as mounding ground covers, are great fun in baskets and containers. Stems can trail 3'; a few pinches will produce well-branched plants. Full sun. 'Compact Red' has been around for years and produces small red-purple leaves, closely arranged to each other; 'Dark Heart' bears a purple heart in the center of the green leaves—quite vigorous; 'Tell Tale Heart' is a compact plant whose small green leaves have a heart-shaped burgundy center; 'Trailing Red' has small burgundy leaves with tiny green edges; 'Trailing Rose' has dark burgundy leaves with rose-pink centers.

Finally, but tiny samplings of my favorite "independent" vegetative forms of coleus, with their whimsical, magical, and outrageous names.

	Type	Height	Flowering
'Alabama Sunset'	landscape	36"	light
'Amazon'	landscape	26"	light
'Aurora'	landscape	24–36"	light
'Big Red'	landscape	36"	medium
'Blusher'	landscape	12–24"	light
'Cardinal'	landscape	24–36"	light
'Defiance'	landscape	12–24"	light
'Flirting Skirts'	novelty	36"	medium
'Florida Sunrise'	landscape	24–36"	light
'Glennis'	landscape	18–30"	light
'Inky Fingers'	landscape	12–24"	light
'Kingwood'	novelty	24–30"	light
'Kiwi Fern'	novelty	18–24"	medium
'Leopard'	landscape	28"	heavy
'Max Levering'	landscape	18–24"	light
'Othello'	landscape	12–24"	light
'Pat Martin'	landscape	40"	medium
'Pineapple'	landscape	31"	none
'Red Ulrich'	landscape	48"	medium
'Religious Radish'	landscape	36"	light
'St. Valentines'	landscape	36"	heavy
'Sunset'	landscape	24"	light
'Swiss Sunshine'	ground cover	10"	medium
'Tilt A Whirl'	novelty	36–48"	medium

I think 'Alabama Sunset' is still unbeatable, and even in the shade, where its leaves turn almost red in color, it is terrific. 'Aurora' has wonderful parchment-colored leaves. 'Pat Martin' adds an element of class to this gaudy group of independents, each clamoring to be number one. There are dozens of others, each with their own fan club, but neither time nor space allows for them all.

Seed-propagated

No major mixup of names occurs in the seed material: all are the result of breeding programs, not backyard selection. All are shorter, better suited for partial shade, and flower more heavily than most vegetative forms. They tend to be a mix of colors and, in the garden center, are more often sold in bedding flat containers than in single pots. All those listed here are landscape types.

	Height	Flowering
'Black Dragon'	15–18"	medium
Brilliant Mix	18–24"	medium
Carefree Mix	12"	medium
'Color Pride'	24"	light
Fairway Mix	10–12"	medium
Sabre Mix	10–12"	medium
'Volcano'	12–15"	medium
Wizard Mix	8–12"	heavy

Additional reading

Armitage, Allan M. *Herbaceous Plants Photo Library*: www.plantamerica.com
———. 1999. The best coleus under the sun. *Organic Gardening* 46(4):36–39.
Bubel, Nancy. 1989. Coleus from seed. *Horticulture* 67(1):34–35.
Glasshouse Works: www.rareplants.com or www.glasshouseworks.com
Hartlage, Richard W. 1997. Coleus. *Horticulture* 94(3):60–61.
Thomason, Julia H. 1994. Richly colored coleus. *Southern Living* 29(5):108.

Colocasia (kol o kay′ see a)   taro, dasheen   Araceae

Colocasias are an important staple carbohydrate in wet, hot areas of the world, where they are grown in low-lying areas along the banks of streams and rivers. The young leaves as well as the root stalks are eaten boiled, baked, or roasted. In temperate areas, they are grown as annuals for their outstanding leaves. They are more water-loving than their quite-similar relative *Alocasia* (which see) and can be grown in boggy areas with great success.

Although the smaller-leaved *Colocasia affinis* can sometimes be found, the only species of *Colocasia* easily available to the American gardener is *C. esculenta* (cocoyam, taro, dasheen). The large rounded brown tuber gives rise to 2′ long and 1′ wide cordate (heart-shaped) to sagittate (arrow-shaped) leaves carried on 2½–3′ long petioles. In general, the leaves are peltate, that is, the petiole is attached inside the margin, usually near the center of the leaf. There are no stems; all petioles arise from the base of the plant.

Plants are grown for the shape and look of the leaves, but white to yellow flowers may occur at the base. The spathe is white to yellow, and the narrow spadix, found within, is shorter than the spathe. Some clones never flower. They are outstanding plants for gardeners looking for something blatant (no subtlety here) and—in the case of some hybrids on the market—quite beautiful.

An interesting story ran in *Vogue* magazine in 1998. It seems a Northwest Airlines flight from China to Japan served some ham on a bed of a raw taro leaf. Quite beautiful, but extremely dangerous, as food critic Jeffrey Steingarten

Colocasia esculenta   ASHA KAYS

found out. Having consumed a tiny morsel of the garnish, he experienced "an odd burning sensation" on his tongue and lips that spread slowly back along the sides of his mouth, toward his throat opening. Uncooked taro leaves contain oxalic acid, which can crystallize once ingested, causing serious breathing problems, not to mention pain. The good news is that Steingarten is fine—and uncooked taro is no longer part of the menu. And you thought airlines that served peanuts were bad!

Grow in full sun in moist soils. Propagate by division.

CULTIVARS

var. *antiquorum* (syn. *Colocasia antiquorum*) differs in having smaller leaves than *C. esculenta*. They are dark green with bronzy purple to black markings between the veins. True water lovers.

'Chicago Harlequin' has leaves spotted lime-green and cream. A reasonably handsome selection, although it sounds atrocious.

'Euchlora' has dark green leaves edged in violet. The petioles are also violet.

'Fontanesii' bears dark green leaves with violet veins and margins. The violet often extends to the leaf blade as well. Petioles are dark red to violet.

'Illustris' (imperial taro) produces light green leaves that are marked blue-black between the veins. One of the finest selections.

'Jet Black Wonder' has large solid dusky purple leaves. Also sold as 'Black Magic' and 'Cranberry' (at least they all look the same to me).

Additional reading

Posey, Patricia J. 1998. Elephant ears. *Flower and Garden* 42(3):15–16.
Steingarten, Jeffrey. 1998. Danger on the menu. *Vogue* 188(2):148–150.

Consolida (kon sal' ih da)   larkspur   Ranunculaceae

Larkspur is grown by the acre in this country as a cut flower crop, harvested in winter to early spring and sold as fresh and dried flowers to florists. The demand for larkspur continues to be strong even while other flowers come and go. In cool weather, the genus is among the cheapest, most persistent sources of cut flowers available to the home gardener, and its many cultivars offer a wide range of colors. Germination is relatively high even when seed is direct sown in the garden.

Unfortunately, the nomenclature of *Consolida* has been and continues to be confused with *Delphinium*, and catalogs have been slow in removing larkspurs from the pages of delphiniums. The two genera are certainly closely related. The foliage of larkspur is much more divided, however, and its flowers, thinner. And, of course, larkspurs are annuals (their other common name is annual delphinium), while delphiniums are mostly biennial or perennial. Another difference is that the upper petals of *Delphinium* are separate, while those of *Consolida* are fused. This "consolidation" thing would be a cute explanation for the generic name, which actually comes from the Latin, *consolido* ("make firm"), an allusion to the plant's purported wound-healing properties.

Approximately forty species are known, but the two used in the ornamental trade are *Consolida ambigua* and *C. regalis*. The differences between them are slight. *Consolida regalis* is shorter and more branched than *C. ambigua*, and its flowers are often in shades of bright pink and purple. *Consolida ambigua* is upright, with flowers of light pink or blue, usually. Nearly all garden selections are hybrids between these two species and *C. orientalis*, an upright form.

Garden cultivars and hybrids can reach 4' but are generally 2–3' tall in the garden; they branch from the upper parts of the plant only. The leaves are finely dissected, the lower leaves with long petioles, the upper ones sessile. The raceme carries dozens of spurred flowers in various shades, first terminal, then in branches from the upper leaf axils. Flowers are often semi-double and double, occasionally single.

Plants perform well in early to late spring everywhere; they persist longer where summers are cool (they are not hot-weather plants). Where winter conditions allow, seed can be sown *in situ* in the fall; seedlings can be placed under protection if necessary. Cold temperatures enhance germination, and fall planting is recommended. If fall planting is not possible in your area, mix the seeds with moist vermiculite or sand and place them in the refrigerator, then sow in early spring. Some sources claim that plants do not transplant well, but if they are purchased early enough and transplanted with normal care, there shouldn't be a problem. Most of these points are moot, however, because where it is comfortable, larkspur will reseed everywhere, on its own, with no help needed, thank you. They make stunning plantings with opium poppies; my good friend Laura Ann Segrest sows both poppies and larkspur in the fall in her cutting area, which is surrounded by blue flax. Fantastic and classy, just like the gardener herself.

Unfortunately, larkspurs are susceptible to powdery mildew and fusarium diseases, particularly when stressed. The biggest stresses are wet soils (use raised beds if possible) and heat. Pull them out when summer approaches. Don't be a sweetheart—yank with vigor.

Plant in full sun, cut when about one-third of the flowers are open. Some shattering of flowers may occur.

CULTIVARS

'Blue Bell', an old favorite with mid blue flowers, dates back to the late 1930s.

'Blue Cloud' is quite different from other larkspurs, bearing tiny blue flowers on 3-4' tall, many-branched, mounding plants. Great for fillers in the vase.

'Carmine King' has carmine-rose flowers on 3-4' tall stems.

'Dazzler' has brilliant scarlet flowers.

'Dwarf Hyacinth' is a mixture of colors about 2' tall. Useful where winds are a problem. Giant Double Hyacinth Hybrids are non-branched and about 4' tall. Both probably involve *Consolida ambigua*.

'Earl Gray' is 3-4' tall and bears flowers in slate gray. Quite different—not colorful, but interesting.

'Earlibird' is earlier to flower and about 2' tall. It occurs in a mixture of colors.

'Frosted Skies' produces semi-double white flowers with blue edges on 3-4' tall stems. Also sold as 'Blue Picotee'.

Giant Imperial series is a mixture of double flowers in several colors, including light blue, dark blue ('Blue Spire'), and pure white ('White King') on gangly 3-4' tall plants.

'Lilac Spire' has soft lilac-lavender flowers on 3' tall plants.

'Miss California' bears handsome salmon-pink flowers on 3' tall stems.

'Pink Perfection' has pale pink flowers.

'Rosalie' bears bright pink flowers.

'Salmon Beauty' produces bright salmon flowers.

Sublime Mix bears double and semi-double flowers in azure blue, pink, rose, and white.

'White Cloud' is the white cousin of 'Blue Cloud'.

Additional reading

Lee, Rand B. 1998. Larkspurs, the genus *Consolida. American Cottage Gardener* 5(2):24–26.

Convolvulus (kon vol' vew lus)   bindweed   Convolvulaceae

Woe to the gardener who fights bindweed! The weedy bindweed, *Convolvulus arvensis*, is a trailing, climbing, invasive pest that appears like magic and romps happily over its more sedate neighbors. Its reputation alone may be why the ornamental species have not exactly been embraced by American gardeners. No self-respecting grower wants bindweed in the greenhouse for fear of strangulation, resulting in a dearth of offerings.

But let's not panic here. Just because your cousin belches at the dinner table does not mean the entire family is uncouth. A few handsome annual species of this mostly perennial group are worth a look.

Quick guide to *Convolvulus* species

	Trailing	Height	Woody stems
C. cneorum	no	2–2½'	yes
C. sabatius	yes	6–9"	yes
C. tricolor	no	1–2'	no

-sabatius (sa bat' ee us)   trailing morning glory   6–9"/2'
   summer   light blue   Italy, North Africa

This species is not cold hardy north of zone 8, so much of the country should treat it as an annual, although it is generally listed as a perennial in catalogs (often under its old name, *Convolvulus mauritanicus*). The alternate, rounded leaves are slightly pubescent, with entire margins and short petioles. The stems become woody at the base, but new growth is continuously formed, especially if the plant is pinched. Pinching also helps to increase stems and flowering. The 1–2" wide light blue to violet flowers, often with a lighter throat, are formed in the axils of the leaves.

This great long-legged plant is particularly wonderful crawling out of window boxes and containers in sunny, dry areas. Does poorly in wet soils. Way underused, considering its excellent habit and flowers. Propagate by tip cuttings.

CULTIVARS

'Baby Moon' provides light blue flowers.
'Full Moon' has larger darker blue flowers.

-tricolor (tri′ kul er)   annual morning glory   1–2′/2′
   summer   blue   southern Europe, North Africa

The annual morning glory is so called because the three-colored flowers are similar to those of the popular morning glory vine, *Ipomoea tricolor*. The plants grow only about 2′ tall, lack any woody tissue, and make mounds of flowers rather than climb. The leaves are obovate and sessile. The light blue to dark blue flowers are borne in the axils of the leaves, and many flowers occur concurrently. The flowers are 1½–2″ across and generally have blue petals with white at the base and yellow in the center (thus the specific name). They are perfect in containers and do well in rock garden sites where drainage is excellent.

Full sun to partial shade, propagate by seed.

CULTIVARS

'Blue Ensign' has flowers that are bright blue, giving way to white and yellow toward the center.

'Cambridge Blue' produces pale blue flowers with similar white and yellow markings.

'Red Ensign' sports dark red petals around a yellow center.

'Rose Ensign' has rosy red flowers.

'Royal Ensign' is the best known, with intense dark blue flowers.

Alternative species

Convolvulus cneorum (silverbush) is a silver-leaved bushy plant, perennial to zone 7, that grows about 2′ tall. This relative of *C. tricolor* is often used as an annual silver accent in the North, where winters are too severe for overwintering. The fine white flowers, often overlooked because of the striking foliage, are 1–1½″ wide and quite welcome when they bloom. It is the foliage, however, that merits the plant's inclusion in the garden.

Quick key to *Convolvulus* species

A. Foliage silvery . . . . *C. cneorum*
AA. Foliage green, not silver
    B. Plant upright, leaves linear-oblong . . . . *C. sabatius*
    BB. Plant prostrate, leaves round-ovate . . . . *C. tricolor*

Coreopsis (kor ee op′ sis)   tickseed   Asteraceae

Everybody knows the perennial members of the genus, such as common tickseed (*Coreopsis grandiflora*) and thinleaf coreopsis (*C. verticillata*), but the annual forms are also popular. The most common annual is *C. tinctoria* (formerly in the genus *Calliopsis*), native to most of the United States, especially the East and the South. Plants are 2–3′ tall with four-sided stems that branch about two-thirds of the way up. The alternate 4″ long leaves are attached with short petioles, each

Coreopsis tinctoria   ASHA KAYS

leaf consisting of one or two pairs of linear segments. The many flowers are about 2″ wide and consist of seven or eight yellow ray flowers, which are reddish brown at the base, surrounding a dark red disk.

Coreopsis is a common ingredient of canned wildflower or native flower mixes. They are good for naturalizing: an inexpensive outlay will yield a great deal of color. To get really turned on, visit Monet's garden at Giverny, outside Paris. In my art-challenged opinion, his garden is far better than his paintings. Coreopsis, cleome, dahlias, zinnias, nasturtiums—you name it, it thrives there, despite the million or so people who troop through each day. The true meaning of tough. If you can't get quite that far, I saw a terrific mixture at Park Seed's trials in Greenwood, South Carolina, in which cleome dominated and annual coreopsis and queen anne's lace were outstanding complements. Flower color is highly variable, and many hues can be seen in the same planting. Coreopsis tend to reseed and will persist for a few years if weeds are kept down. In the garden, they can get a little weedy after flowering and often need some support.

Plant in full sun; shade results in an awful mess. Fertilize sparingly. Propagate by seed *in situ*, or start inside and transplant after threat of frost has passed.

CULTIVARS

'Mardi Gras' has 2–2½″ wide bicolor daisies, golden yellow with random markings of dull red. Plants are about 1½–2½′ tall.

'Nana' is an excellent selection of *Coreopsis tinctoria*, with similar flower color. Only about 2′ tall.

Alternative species

Coreopsis leavenworthii is a quick-growing yellow-flowered annual from Florida. Plants are 12–18″ tall. A neat little plant, definitely worth a try in the garden.

Additional reading

Dean, Molly. 1993. The carefree flower of summer. *Flower and Garden* 37(3):32–33.

Cosmos (koz′ mos)   Asteraceae

I love cosmos! They are so easy and so colorful, and they work so well throughout the season. Breeding efforts have yielded both tall and short forms, in numerous colors. They can be put in the ground in the spring throughout the country; where summers are hot, however, they may be replanted again in the summer.

Quick guide to *Cosmos* species

	Height	Flower form	Flower color
C. atrosanguineus	2–3′	single	maroon
C. bipinnatus	3–4′	single	red, rose, pink, white
C. sulphureus	2–3′	semi-double	orange, gold, yellow, scarlet

-*atrosanguineus* (a tro san gwin′ ee us)   chocolate cosmos   2–3′/2′
     summer   maroon   Mexico

This plant is always a favorite, no matter who is in the garden. It is pretty enough, with single, occasionally double flowers of purple to red, but not nearly as vigorous or as floriferous as other species. Half the time the dark color of the flowers gets lost among other, more sturdy plants, but that same hidden color fascinates people who get close to it—and getting close is the key. The petals are velvet, the color is maroon, but the real kicker is the unmistakable aroma of chocolate that fills your head as you approach. A great plant for the child in all of us, and a good cut flower too, making all the other flowers in the vase seem that much brighter by comparison.

Plants grow 2–3′ tall with 4–5″ leaves, mostly one- or two-pinnate. Flowers are about 2″ wide and borne reasonably profusely in full sun in the garden. The species, which grows from swollen tuberous roots, is a short-lived perennial in some gardens, but for most of us, it should be treated as an annual. It prefers cool nights and may not perform as well as other common species, particularly in warmer climates. Plants are hard to ignore, especially when one leads with their nose.

-bipinnatus (bi pih nay′ tus)	tall cosmos	3–4′/2′
all season	many colors	Mexico

The tall cosmos is an erect annual with sessile or short-petioled fern-like leaves consisting of narrow linear pinnate segments. The foliage is wispy and quite handsome when well grown. The flowers are 2–3″ across and are almost always single. But are they beautiful. The species has eight-ray (usually) flowers in shades of rose-pink to lilac, and cultivars offer whites and bicolors as well. Most are more suited for the back of the garden bed, where other plants can be positioned around them to lend a little support. Deadheading spent blossoms helps keep the plants in flower.

Cosmos is commonly produced as a specialty cut flower in the United States, and it is certainly excellent as a cut flower from the garden. Flowers persist well if cut when fully open.

Plant in full sun, either as small transplants or from seed. If they get "tired" as the season progresses, reseed around the last two weeks of July.

CULTIVARS

'Candy Stripe' produces bicolor flowers consisting of white petals splashed with crimson or with margins of crimson. The centers are golden yellow. Quite eye-catching. Plants grow 3–3½″ tall.

'Daydream' has petals of white, each with a rosy pink base, resulting in a blush bicolor effect. Flowers are about 2½″ across and sit atop 4–5′ tall plants.

'Dazzler' is an old-fashioned (1943) form with deep carmine flowers, growing about 5′ tall.

'Early Wonder' is an early-flowering tall form with a mixture of large (4–4½″ wide) red, rose, pink, and white flowers on 4–5′ tall plants. Essentially replaced the Sensation series.

'Gazebo' is among the most floriferous tall forms, producing many flowers on 3–4′ tall plants. Seeds are available in pink, red, white, and a mixture.

'Imperial Pink' has large flowers of deep lilac-pink with a darker ring around the center disk. Strong stems up to 4½′ tall. Sometimes available in other colors, such as 'Imperial White'.

'Pied Piper Red' is a selection from the popular Sea Shells Mix. The tubular petals are deep crimson on the inside and lighter on the reverse.

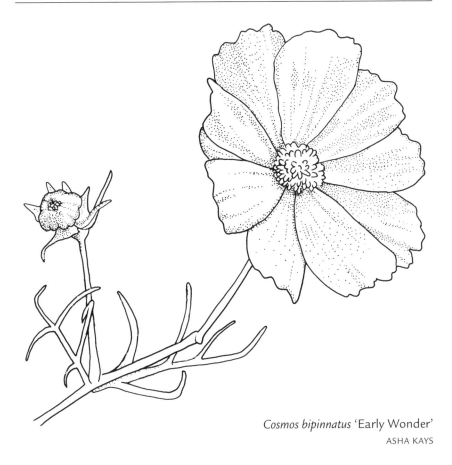

Cosmos bipinnatus 'Early Wonder'
ASHA KAYS

'Psyche' is an antique selection, bearing semi-double flowers on 3–4' tall plants in a mix of magenta and pink.

Sea Shells Mix has been around for years, but its unique rolled and quilled petal shape, along with a good color mix, has maintained its popularity. Petals on the same plant may or may not be inrolled—somewhat disconcerting. Single colors in carmine, pink, pink blush (light lavender-pink), and white are also available. Plants are 3–3½' tall.

Sensation remains an excellent flowering series. Similar to 'Early Wonder'. Colors available in rose, crimson, white, and a mix. A 1938 All-America Selection.

Sonata is the best series for gardeners with limited space. Plants branch with abandon, and handsome 2½–3" wide flowers smother them all season. The winning feature, however, is their short size: plants produce stout 2–2½' tall stems. The best selection is 'Sonata White', but carmine, pink, pink blush, and a mixture are also available.

Versailles Mix remains among the best selections for use as a cut flower. The large flowers of red, pink, rose, and white are held on strong 3–3½' tall stems. The cultivar of choice for commercial cut flower production.

| *-sulphureus* (sul fer ee' us) | sulphur cosmos | 1–3'/2' |
| summer | yellow, gold | Central America |

This species, having also gone through some serious hybridization, provides colorful plants for bedding or containers. The stems are four-sided, branched, and rather hairy. The 12″ long leaves are divided two or three times into linear segments. Its leaves are more dense than those of its taller cousin, *Cosmos bipinnatus*, and its flowers are even more abundant. Blooms are generally semi-double, occasionally double, and produced with such heartfelt passion that plants often flower themselves to death by mid summer. The saying "here today, gone tomorrow" was probably coined by a gardener with sulphur cosmos.

Plants generally grow about 2' tall, so they may be used in any part of the garden or in containers. Butterflies and bees love them as well. Plant in full sun, water abundantly, and try to deadhead if possible. Replace the planting by sowing new seeds around the base of the older plants in mid summer. When the seedlings are 6–9″ tall, pull out the old plants. The second planting will be terrific in late summer and fall.

CULTIVARS

'Bright Lights' is a mixture of bright yellow, gold, and red 2–2½″ blooms on rather tall (up to 4') plants.

Cosmic series offers outstanding uniformity and double flowers in yellow, orange, and gold. 'Cosmic Orange' was an All-America Selection for 2000.

'Diablo' is available in yellow and orange. An excellent floriferous series, a 1974 All-America Selection.

'Ladybird' is a fine dwarf (12–15″ tall) with excellent heat tolerance and staying power. Separate colors of yellow and gold are occasionally available as well as a mix with red.

'Lemon Twist' bears unique sulfur-yellow flowers on 2½' tall stems. Quite lovely—reminds me a little of *Coreopsis verticillata* 'Moonbeam'.

'Sunny Gold' is an excellent cultivar with 2″ wide golden flowers on 2' tall stems. 'Sunny Red', an All-America Selection in 1988, is almost as good, with scarlet-red flowers all season.

Quick key to *Cosmos* species

- A. Leaf divisions mostly linear or threadlike, flowers in many colors . . . . *C. bipinnatus*
- AA. Leaf divisions lance-like or broader, flowers mainly orange, yellow, or red
  - B. Color of flowers yellow or orange . . . . *C. sulphureus*
  - BB. Color of flowers rose or red . . . . *C. atrosanguineus*

Cosmos sulphureus 'Cosmic Yellow'   ASHA KAYS

Additional reading

Dean, Molly. 1996. Cosmos. *Flower and Garden* 40(4):42–43.

Craspedia (kras pee′ dee a)   billy buttons   Asteraceae

I was indeed fortunate to hike some of the mountains of New South Wales and Victoria, Australia, where I saw entire valleys cloaked with wildflowers, including the bright yellow buttons of *Craspedia*. No doubt in my mind: flowers look better at home than they do lined up like soldiers in a field. Until then, I had known *C. globosa* (glo bo′ sa; golden drumstick) only as a minor cut flower for bouquets.

Plants grow from basal rosettes consisting of white-woolly spatula-shaped 3″ long leaves. The flower stems are leafless and terminate in rounded yellow flowers, 1–1½" wide. Some species have small bracts at the base of the flowers, but this species does not. Handsome, even cute, button flowers are produced most of the summer. *Craspedia* is difficult to find except through retail seed companies, but it is fun to try every now and then.

Full sun, well-drained soils. Propagate by seed.

Alternative species

Craspedia uniflora (billy buttons) is similar to *C. globosa*, but its basal leaves don't have the white-woolly appearance and its flower stems often carry small leaves. Just as good for the garden and the vase.

Cuphea (kew′ fee a)   Lythraceae

Cuphea is a large genus, consisting of approximately 260 species, most native to tropical and subtropical areas of Central and South America. So many species translates to significant variability, with plants ranging in height from 6–8" to more than 4'. Petals too show remarkable variation: some species, such as *C. ignea* (cigar plant), have no petals; some, like *C. hyssopifolia* (Mexican heather), have the normal complement of six equally sized petals; and other species are characterized by all sorts of intermediates between the two. The generic name is thought to have come from the Greek, *kyphos* ("curved"), referring to the curved seed capsule. In general, the leaves are opposite, occasionally alternate or whorled, and the flowers are borne on one-sided racemes. Most species are grown from seed; others are propagated from cuttings.

This is a terrific genus of outstanding and often little-known plants for the American garden. As breeders discover its potential and tap its variability, hybrids and cultivars can only get better.

Quick guide to *Cuphea* species

	Height	Flower color
C. cyanea	1–2'	pink with yellow tips
C. hyssopifolia	1–3'	lilac, lavender
C. ignea	9–15"	scarlet with black edge
C. micropetala	3–4'	red, shaded green-yellow
C. pallida	8–12"	purple
C. ×purpurea	1–2'	bright red, pink

| **-cyanea** (si an′ ee a) | black-eyed cuphea | 1–2'/2' |
| summer | pink | Mexico |

This species varies dramatically in height. Plants can reach 4' in height in the southern garden; 1–2' is the norm in the North; and in pots and containers, where plants are usually grown, a height of 12–15" is not uncommon. The opposite leaves are ovate with a round base and attached by a short petiole. The flowers stems branch and form 1″ long tubular flowers that are mostly pink, turning yellow at the ends. Two maroon petals near the tip of the flower give it its unusual look of having ears or black eyes. Add the red stamens, which stick out as if to mock you, and you've got to wonder what the flower is thinking.

Best in containers in full sun. Propagate by seed or cuttings.

-hyssopifolia (hih sop ih fo′ lee a)   Mexican heather   1–3′/3′
    summer   lilac, lavender   Mexico, Guatemala

This heavy flowerer is probably the best-known species in the genus, forming small well-branched shrub-like plants useful for the front of the garden or for containers on the porch. The 1″ long leaves are handsome, usually dark green, glossy, and crowded together on the stems. They are linear to lanceolate in shape with slightly wavy or entire margins, a little like those of the herb hyssop. Even when not in flower, the species is a good-looking addition to the garden.

Flowers are formed in the axils of the leaves, which explains why the plant is often covered with bloom. They consist of six equal petals, usually pale lilac with lavender veins, and are borne on very short flower stems. Expect flowering from early summer until frost.

We have trialed many forms of *Cuphea*, but Mexican heather is always a favorite, with its hundreds of flowers and compact, full-bodied growth.

Full sun, propagate by seed or cuttings.

CULTIVARS

'Alba' bears a profusion of white flowers.

'Allyson' is marvelous, with many pink-lavender flowers on a bushy 12–15″ tall plant.

'Linda Downer' is a handsome compact form with many white flowers.

'Palest Pinkie' is one of several pink-flowered forms, all so pale pink that they fade into the foliage. 'Allyson' is better.

-ignea (ig′ nee a)   cigar plant   1–2′/2′
    summer   scarlet   Mexico, Jamaica

About the common name of this well-known species: it is fun and harmless, although plants with small cigars are not the norm in the plant kingdom, and mind you, I am not aware of any scarlet-colored smokes out there. Perhaps the other common name, firecracker plant, is more appropriate. *Cuphea ignea* (syn. *C. platycentra*) is woody at the base with oblong or lanceolate 2″ leaves. The flowers are produced in the leaf axils and, in the better forms at least, are not buried in the foliage. They are usually scarlet, with a black apex edged in white. All in all, a neat flower when you get on your hands and knees to admire it.

Doubtless other more colorful plants are out there, even within the genus, but the growing habit of this species complements taller plants and makes it an outstanding candidate for containers and window boxes. Full sun, propagate by seed.

'Black Ash' has small pearly flowers rimmed in maroon-black.

'Coan Flamingo' is a dwarf form with pink flowers.

'Coan White' bears white flowers.

'David Verity' is likely a hybrid involving *Cuphea ignea*. Plants grow 2' tall and carry bright orange-red tubes on dark green leaves.

'Dynamite' is similar to the species but about two-thirds the height. Filled with burning cigars—a fine low-growing selection.

'Pink Peculiar' produces light pink flowers.

'Variegata' has a sprawling habit and bears glossy green-and-gold foliage.

-llavea (lay′ vee a)	red cuphea	1–2′/2′
summer	red with black	Mexico

This compact shrubby species is characterized by opposite leaves and short spikes of showy flowers. Plants grow 2–2½' tall. Leaves are oval and pointed. Flowers have two deep red petals and a greenish calyx tinged purple. While working on *Cuphea* as a source of medium-chain fatty acids, Casimir Jaworski and Sharad Phatak at the University of Georgia bred a form of this species that accentuated the purple calyx; the overall appearance of the flower was somewhat like Mickey Mouse, with a smiling red face and two black ears. This 'Georgia Scarlet' was shorter than the species and really quite wonderful. It is spottily available in this country; in Australia, however, I saw masses of the plant under the name 'Tiny Mice'.

Full sun, well-drained soils. Propagate by cuttings.

-micropetala (mi kro pe′ ta la)	tall cigar plant	3–5′/3′
late summer, fall	red with green and yellow	Mexico

One of the Catch-22s of buying interesting new plants in the garden center is that the garden center succeeds or fails based on about six weekends in the spring. If a plant is not in full color at that time, it does not sell, therefore growers don't grow it. Many excellent garden plants don't flower until late summer and fall, and this is one of them. With its presence in retail centers thus limited, this species remains relatively unknown.

Plants are reasonably handsome, if not exciting, green shrubby things with 3–4″ long, opposite lanceolate, entire leaves. The midrib is cream-colored and quite visible. In mid to late summer, the 2″ long cigar-shaped flowers begin to form in the upper leaf axils, and by late summer and early fall, the plant is on fire. Without doubt, it is a highlight of the fall season in the trial gardens at the University of Georgia.

The flowers consist of six sepals and inconspicuous petals. They are reddish at the base, yellow in the middle, and green at the top. Sounds awful, but it is actually quite a wonderful combination and hummingbirds love them. Plants are hardy to about 20–25°F and may come back in mild winters.

Full sun, propagate by division or cuttings.

Cuphea micropetala   ASHA KAYS

Cuphea ×purpurea 'Firefly'   ASHA KAYS

Alternative species

Cuphea glutinosa is similar to *C. hyssopifolia* but has a hairy calyx tube, and two of its six petals are slightly larger than the other four. Petals are lightly veined. Casimir Jaworski and Sharad Phatak made three ornamental selections of this species in their *Cuphea* field studies at the University of Georgia. 'Lavender Lady', a prostrate form, is terrific in containers and falling out of raised beds; it has dark purple flowers on 6–9″ tall plants. 'Lavender Lei' bears light purple and white flowers with light stripes; plants grow 6–9″ tall. 'Purple Passion' is similar to 'Lavender Lei' but slightly more floriferous.

Cuphea pallida, a pendulous form seen flowing from the sides of hanging baskets and containers, is related to *C. ignea* but has much wider flowers. Its many branches bear small leaves and ½″ wide purple flowers. Reasonably heat-tolerant and a beauty in spring and early summer.

Cuphea ×*purpurea* is an outstanding red-flowered cross between *C. llavea* and *C. procumbens*. The most popular form of the hybrid is 'Firefly', with fire-engine red flowers with six conspicuous and unequal petals (the two top ones are much longer). Plants reseed like crazy but remain in flower all season. Stems may be about 15″ tall; in containers, they fall out and curve back up, like a goose's neck.

Cuphea rosea grows about 15″ tall and has many flowers in the summer. Quite similar to *C. hyssopifolia*. Cultivars include 'Lavender Lace', with purple flowers and shiny foliage, and 'Light Lavender', with light lavender blossoms.

Quick key to *Cuphea* species

A. Petals zero . . . . *C. ignea*
AA. Petals two to six
    B. Petals normally two, the other four abortive
        C. Petals red, half as long or longer than calyx . . . . *C. llavea*
        CC. Petals maroon, less than half the length of the calyx . . *C. cyanea*
    BB. Petals six
        C. Petals approximately the same size
            D. Petals obvious, flowers flared . . . . *C. hyssopifolia*
            DD. Petals minute, flower tubular . . . . *C. micropetala*
        CC. Petals not the same size . . . . *C.* ×*purpurea*

Additional reading

Armitage, Allan M. 2000. Is there a market for fall-flowering annuals? *Greenhouse Grower* 18(4):76–81.

Hardin, Ben. 1991. Cuphea, plants with a beautiful future. *Agricultural Research* 39(9):16–17.

Jaworski, C. A., and S. C. Phatak. 1991a. Flowering ornamental *Cuphea glutinosa* 'Lavender Lady'. *HortScience* 26:221–222.

———. 1991b. Flowering ornamental *Cuphea llavea* 'Georgia Scarlet'. *HortScience* 26:1243–1344.

———. 1992. Flowering ornamental *Cuphea glutinosa* 'Purple Passion' and 'Lavender Lei'. *HortScience* 27:940.

Curcuma (ker kew' ma)   hidden ginger   Zingiberaceae

I have included many tropicals in this book because I see them becoming popular, if not common, garden plants from Maine to Missouri. The gingers in particular are worth a closer look. One genus in the ginger family, *Curcuma*, offers great diversity of habit, foliage, and flower. Among the better known species in the genus is *C. longa* (turmeric), long cultivated for the bright yellow dye and spice prepared from the dried rhizome; other gingers grown as spices are *C. zedoaria* (zedoary) and *C. amado* (pickling spice). Some *Curcuma* species bear their flowers on short stalks amid the leaves, hence the common name for the genus; some won't flower in the North (sometimes not even in zone 8), but their foliage is reason enough to include them. All require bright light and do fine in the garden or in containers.

-alismatifolia (a lis ma tih fo' lee a)   Siam tulip   2–3'/1'
   summer   pink   Thailand

Around 1990, my friend Eddie Welsh, from New Zealand, sent me some of the weirdest rhizomes I had ever seen and told me to "go at it." Discounting their weirdness (they had swollen centers and other swollen parts hanging from long strings), I planted them in various areas, from greenhouse to garden, and waited, and waited, and waited for something to happen. This species came to be one of my favorite plants in the garden, but not until I learned a few things about it. First the bare or potted rhizomes require several weeks of heat (about 90°F) before they'll push out their latent buds. Once shoots are visible, the rest is easy. Without question, these fine flowering plants enjoy the heat of summer, and Maine may not be the place to enjoy them. Buying pre-started potted plants, not bare rhizomes, is essential—or you too will wait and wait and wait.

This species is one of the few hidden gingers that is not at all hidden. Plants grow to 2' in height and about 1' wide, much like a tulip. The foliage is also similar to tulips, but the pink flowers arise from the rhizomes to provide beautiful long-lasting spikes of flowers (bracts) on naked stems. They persist for weeks and weeks, either on the plant or in a vase. The only way to determine whether you have sufficient heat to flower the plants is to try them. In the North, place them in containers in full sun and let them to bake. In the South, they may be used in containers or in the garden.

CULTIVARS

'Rose' has rosy flowers. Not as vigorous as the species, nor as tall.
'White' bears white flowers with green tips.

| *-zedoaria* (ze dor' ee a) | zedoary | 4–7'/4' |
| spring | rose, pink | India |

This species can work in many warm-summer garden situations. The best part of the plant is the foliage, which consists of broad 2' long leaves on long petioles; the deep maroon midrib on each leaf lends the plant a noble and classy look. Flowers appear before the leaves, in handsome spikes of rose and pink. Of course, flowers are handsome only if plants overwinter, which will not occur north of zone 7 (and zone 7 is marginal). Plants have overwintered in the UGA Horticulture Gardens for two years, in mild winters; I grow ours in large containers, in case I need to take them inside when temperatures dip. Probably my favorite species in the genus.

Alternative species

Curcuma australasica (Aussie plume), a relative of *C. alismatifolia*, is native to Northern Australia and grows 4–5' tall. The 6–7" long leaves are lanceolate and held on 4" long petioles. The inflorescences consist of yellow flowers protruding from rose to red bracts.

Curcuma roscoeana (ros ko ee a' na; jewel of Burma) is similar to *C. zedoaria*. Plants grow 3–4' tall and about 2' wide. The beautiful waxy orange flowers arise at the base of the large light green leaves, which, if picked, last for weeks in the vase. They should be placed in partial shade in the South, full sun in the North.

Additional reading

Chapman, Timothy. 1995. *Ornamental Gingers*. 6920 Bayou Paul Rd., St. Gabriel, LA 70776.
San Felasco Nurseries: www.sanfelasco.com
Stokes Tropicals: www.stokestropicals.com
Wight Nurseries of North Carolina: www.wightnurseries.com

Cynara (sih na' ra)   Asteraceae

This genus is best known for the globe artichoke, *Cynara scolymus* (sko' lee mus)—a vegetable best known for the stares of disbelief on the faces of people expected to eat the thing. But sucking on artichoke bracts is something that mothers teach daughters every year, providing the greatest ratio of exercise-expended to useful-food-consumed for any known vegetable. Every now and then, however, gardeners value a plant for its architectural presence, and *C. cardunculus* (kar dunk' yew lus; cardoon) is such a plant. Why else would anyone put a seriously prickly 6' tall plant with mundane lavender-purple flowers in their garden? People love this species for its robust stature and the way its handsome deeply cut foliage, gray-green above and whitely hairy below, contrasts with surrounding green-leaved plants. Native to the Mediterranean, it is at its architectural best from spring to mid summer; thereafter, depending on the severity of the summer, it can look like a tired old field thistle. Use as a short-lived perennial in zones 7 to 10 and as an annual elsewhere.

Full sun, well-drained soils, and plenty of room. Propagate by seed.

Additional reading

Sussman, Elena. 1998. Artichokes anywhere. *Organic Gardening* 54(1):54–55.

Cynoglossum (sih no glos′ um)   hound's tongue   Boraginaceae

This genus—which belongs to the same hairy family as forget-me-nots and Virginia bluebells—definitely lost out in the common name department. When my Hannah dog licks me, her tongue is a little rough, but I figure she is a 60-pound lover who simply gets carried away. I surely don't think about hairy leaves. Such are the mysteries of nomenclature. The charm of hound's tongue is not in the leaves, but in the beautiful blue flowers, and the best annual (or biennial) species by far is Chinese hound's tongue, *Cynoglossum amabile*. Some creative catalog writers refer to it as Chinese forget-me-not. Works for me!

The species grows about 2′ tall, with alternate, soft hairy leaves. The basal leaves are 6–8″ long, and the stem leaves smaller and sessile as they ascend the stem. Wonderful sprays of sky-blue flowers, each measuring about ¼″ in diameter, stand well above the foliage. A beautiful color.

Plants are at their best in spring or during cooler weather; they tend to decline in areas of hot, humid summers. Full sun and well-drained soils are a must. Propagate by seed. In mild winters, plants may be transplanted to the garden in the fall. In cold winters, place out as early as possible.

CULTIVARS

'Blue Showers' has colorful turquoise flowers over gray-green foliage.

'Firmament', a dwarf form, is about 15″ tall and bears intense blue flowers. A 1939 All-America Selection.

'Mystery Rose' bears off-white flowers with a touch of pink or lilac.

Additional reading

De Jong, Tom J., Peter G. L. Klinkhamer, and L. A. Boorman. 1990. Biological flora of the British Isles: *Cynoglossum officinale* L. *Journal of Ecology* 78(4):1123–1144.

D

Datura (day tur′ a) thorn apple Solanaceae

Datura has a gruesome history: all parts of the plant are toxic, particularly the fruit and the flowers, causing trances, hallucinations, and eventual death. One species, *Datura stramonium*, was already well known as a plant to avoid when the British soldiers who were sent to quell Bacon's rebellion at Jamestown, Virginia, ate the cooked plants—thinking they were salad greens—and suffered mightily; that weed of pastures and fields became known as Jamestown weed, later shortened to jimson weed. Thomas Jefferson, who knew of its properties, wrote, "The risk overbalances the curiosity of trying it. . . . Every man of firmness carried it in his pocket [during the French Revolution] in anticipation of the guillotine. It brings on the sleep of death as quietly as fatigue does the ordinary sleep." *Datura* has even been implicated in deliberate poisonings, although toxicity varies with the age of the plant and where it is grown. Fortunately, its toxic compounds have been harnessed in part as an effective treatment for asthma. The genus presently consists of about eight species; many original species have since been moved to *Brugmansia* (which see).

In the garden and landscape, thorn apples are used as low-growing shrubby plants whose upward- or outward-facing white to lavender trumpet-shaped flowers are produced continuously from mid summer until frost. Flowers are single or double and wonderfully fragrant. Warm summers provide the best performance.

Quick guide to *Datura* species

	Flower color	Leaves
D. innoxia	cream, pink, lavender	hairy
D. metel	white, yellow, purple	smooth

-innoxia (in oks′ ee a) downy thorn apple 2–3′/3′
    summer cream, pink, lavender Central America

This species grows about 3′ tall with 6–8″ long broad leaves coming to a rather sharp point. The leaves are softly pubescent (downy), and the margins are usually entire but can be a little wavy (sinuate). A more sprawling plant than some other *Datura* species, it can easily cover a 6' wide swath in the garden. The 7–8" long tubular flowers are usually pink to lavender and open in early evening, or during the day when cloudy. The flowers have five lobes, which appear to be ten. The rounded fruit is somewhat pendent and covered in long thin thorns, hence the common name. Plants previously classified as *Datura meteloides* are now placed here, providing additional fragrance to this species.

Plant in full sun, feed heavily. Propagate by seed or cuttings.

CULTIVARS

'Leverne Haynes' has a spreading habit with soft green leaves and fragrant creamy white flowers.

-metel (me' tel)	horn of plenty	2–4'/3'
summer	white, yellow, purple	South China

This is the most common species in gardens and landscapes, and selection has yielded some colorful cultivars as well. The oval leaves are 6–8" long and wide and usually entire. Plants are smooth, not pubescent. Stems are reddish in purple-flowered forms and green in white- and yellow-flowered ones. The classic single flower tube is 8" long and 4" across at the mouth, but incredibly grotesque double- or even triple-flowered forms have been raised. Flowers may be purple, yellow, or white on the outside (white is the most common color, by far), but the inside of the flower is often pale violet. The globose fruit has cone-shaped thorns.

Plants can be brilliant in full sun and heat. Apply sufficient fertilizer to get them going in the spring. Propagate by seed or cuttings.

CULTIVARS

'Alba' bears double white flowers. Very fragrant.

'Aurea' has yellow semi-double flowers.

'Belle Blanche' bears fragrant cream-colored double flowers.

'Caerulea' produces lavender flowers.

'Cornucopia' bears double purple and white flowers.

'Evening Fragrance' produces 8" long white flowers over attractive gray-green foliage. Sweetly scented.

'Grand Marnier' has beautiful soft yellow single flowers.

'Ruffles' is about 3' tall with double ruffled flowers. 'Yellow Ruffles' has light yellow flowers and purple stems. 'Purple Ruffles' bears flowers that are lavender on the outside and creamy white on the inside. 'White Ruffles' is white.

'Triple Yellow Angel' has triple primrose-yellow flowers. Grotesque or spectacular, depending on your point of view.

Alternative species

Datura wrightii (syn. *D. innoxia* subsp. *quinquecuspida*), a spreading form, is native to western Texas and Colorado. The tomentose (hairy) leaves are gray-green,

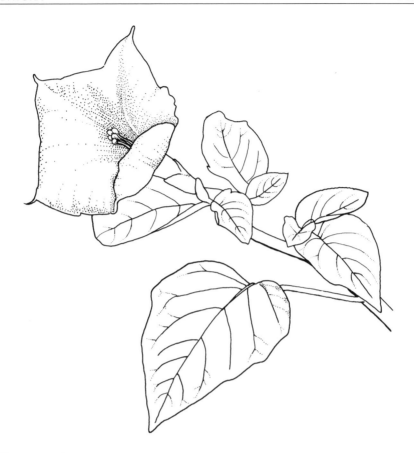

Datura metel   ASHA KAYS

and the 7–8″ wide five-lobed white flowers are usually tinged purple. Plants have wonderfully fragrant flowers that open in the evening. A commonly grown species.

Quick key to *Datura* species

A. Plant glabrous . . . . *D. metel*
AA. Plant hairy . . . . *D. innoxia*

Additional reading

Dunnett, Nigel. 1991. Annual additions. *Horticulture* 69(3):12–17.
Ellis, David. 1995. Devil in angel's petals. *American Horticulturist* 74(5):7.

Dianella (di a nel' a)   flax lily   Liliaceae

I first encountered *Dianella* in the Christchurch Botanical Garden (another great excuse to visit New Zealand). It was late fall: plants, although obviously vigorous, were no longer at their best; the broad sword-shaped leaves were rough around the edges. I saw the genus again at Mt. Stewart, a grand old nineteenth-century estate in Northern Ireland. This time, large panicles of small pale blue flowers had been produced with abandon on 4' tall plants. Each flower was about 1" across and reflexed; the leaves looked like large iris leaves armed with small sharp teeth. Finally, I saw the genus in its fruitful glory at Brian and Alice McGowan's outstanding Blue Meadow Farm in Montague Center, Massachusetts. In their greenhouse was a monster plant, 5' tall, whose flowers had been transformed to hundreds of beautiful bright blue berries, each 1" across.

In the first case, I was looking at *Dianella caerulea*, in the last two cases, *D. tasmanica*, native to southeastern Australia and Tasmania, respectively. The berries are the most spectacular thing about this genus: it is their color, size, and persistence (they hang on for months) that make these lilies so appealing. *Dianella caerulea* is a little shorter than *D. tasmanica*; it has blue to white flowers with yellow anthers and similar fruit. *Dianella intermedia* produces green leaves, white flowers, and small fruit; a variegated form occurs as well. Plants may be placed outside in containers when threat of frost has passed; flowering will occur in mid summer. Provide lots of moisture. Bring them in before the first frost. They are able to withstand temperatures in the low thirties, perhaps even a little lower, but no sense in taking a chance.

Full sun, propagate by seed or division.

Dianthus (di an' thus)   pink   Caryophyllaceae

Most pinks in gardens are perennials or biennials whose names—clove pink, maiden pink, sweet william, cheddar pink, cottage pink, and grass pink—are all part of the fabled family tree. But a world of wonderful annuals can provide outstanding color as well, in the spring and early summer in middle America and the South, and all summer in the North.

Quick guide to *Dianthus* species

	Bedding	Cut flower	Winter hardiness
D. barbatus	seldom	often	zone 3
D. chinensis	seldom	never	zone 8
D. chinensis × *barbatus*	often	never	zone 5

-*barbatus* (bar bay' tus)   sweet william   10–24"/12"
　　late spring   many colors   eastern Europe

The common name of this species honors the genial William, duke of Cumberland, who brutally crushed several uprisings in England, most notably the Jacobite Rebellion led by Bonnie Prince Charlie. Many adjectives were used by William's friends and foes, but "sweet" was very likely not among them. *Dianthus barbatus* is a true biennial, requiring a cold period for subsequent flowers; however, because of its reseeding tendencies, a garden may be with sweet william for ages, making the plant appear to be perennial. Certainly it is sufficiently winter hardy, overwintering as far north as Montreal (zone 3). The 2–3″ long lanceolate leaves are short-petioled and have a prominent midrib. Flowers are unscented, with toothed or fringed petals, often with a distinct eye. The easiest means of identifying the species is to look at the arrangement of buds and flowers: they are arranged in a flat-topped cluster (cyme), unlike nearly all other *Dianthus* species. This arrangement is most noticeable before the flowers open.

In the South, plants occasionally act as true perennials, particularly if spent flowers are removed before seeds mature and fall. Everywhere else, the apparent resurrection in the spring is actually new seedlings. Plants tolerate and even benefit from the addition of lime to the soil. Harvest when about half the inflorescence is open for an excellent long-lived cut flower for the vase.

Full sun, propagate by seed (sown at 70–75°F) or cuttings. Large plants may be divided.

CULTIVARS

'Blood Red' has exceptionally dark flowers.

Double Tall Mix is a descriptive name for a group of 15–18″ tall plants, suitable for cutting.

'Harlequin' provides semi-double to double pink and white flowers.

'Homeland' bears deep red flowers.

'Indian Carpet' is outstanding but is only 10–12″ tall. Available in many colors. A 6–8″ form is known as 'Dwarf Indian Carpet'.

'Messenger' is an excellent tall-growing selection in a mix of colors. The strong stems are up to 2′ tall and recommended for cutting.

'Midget' and 'Double Midget' are the antithesis of 'Messenger', growing about 4–6″ tall.

'Newport Beauty' is just that, with handsome pink flowers on 12″ stems.

'Nigrescens' has dark stems and deep red flowers.

'Pink Beauty' and 'Scarlet Beauty' bear flowers of salmon-pink and rich scarlet, respectively.

'Sooty', a maroon-purple selection, grows about 9″ tall.

-chinensis (chin en′ sis)	annual pink	12–15″/12″
summer	red, pink, bicolor	China

The small stature and numerous bright flowers of this species, among the more spectacular pinks, demand that one look, and look again. Leaves are alternate, slightly hairy, and lanceolate. The fragrant flowers are held in a ten- to fifteen-flowered inflorescence in early summer. The petals are deeply toothed or cut almost in half, normally pink to lilac with a purple eye.

If they are so beautiful, why aren't annual pinks in more gardens? The prob-

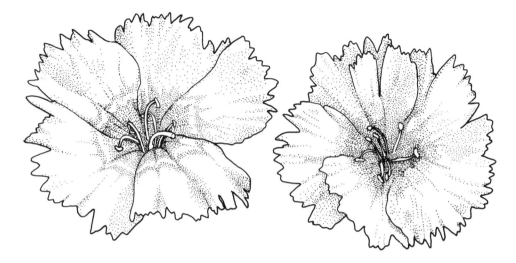

Dianthus chinensis   ASHA KAYS

lem is twofold. *Dianthus chinensis* has little heat tolerance, and except in the coastal areas, our summers are too hot for it, and often too humid. Plants melt out after a few hot spells and can look awful after a month or so in the garden. But they sure look good to unsuspecting gardeners in the retail area in the spring. The other problem for annual pinks is the explosion of hybrid pinks (*D. chinensis* × *barbatus*, which see), which offer far better garden performance. They simply left annual pinks in the dust by the side of the road.

Full sun in the North, partial shade in the South. Propagate by seed.

CULTIVARS

Carpet series consists of short plants with many ¾″ wide flowers. Selections include 'Fire' with salmon-red flowers, 'Crimson', 'Oriental' (crimson with darker tones), and 'Snow' (white).

Charms series produces 1½″ wide flowers on short, compact frames. Coral, crimson, pink, scarlet, white, and a mix ('Magic Charms') are available. 'Magic Charms' was an All-America Selection in 1974.

'Merry-Go-Round' acts as a ground cover with 6–7″ tall and 9–10″ wide plants. The flowers are white with a scarlet center.

Super Parfait series is early to flower and compact, and the plants are among the most eye-catching of all annual pinks. 'Raspberry Super Parfait' is crimson with dark eyes; 'Strawberry Super Parfait' bears scarlet flowers with dark eyes. Truly outstanding.

'Snow Fire' is a beautiful red and white form, with eye-catching color and uniformity in the garden. An All-America Selection in 1978.

-chinensis × *barbatus*

-chinensis × *barbatus*	hybrid pink	12–20″/12″
spring, summer	many colors	hybrid

Combining the long flowering time of the annual pink with the cold tolerance of sweet william yielded the revolutionary hybrid pinks (syn. *Dianthus* ×*heddewigii*). Seed breeding companies in America and Europe have jumped into this class with both feet, resulting in outstanding colors, garden performance, and availability for American gardens and landscapes. Any gardener who enjoys planting a pansy, in either the fall or early spring, will enjoy hybrid pinks as well. They produce 1–1½″ wide flowers in many colors on sturdy plants, from early spring on through the summer. They also have a wonderful fragrance, thanks to the annual pinks in the bloodline. The alternate leaves are 3–4″ long and usually broadly lanceolate.

Growers who produce hybrid pinks for fall planting often complain that gardeners don't buy them—but pansies rush out the door. Unforgivable. If growers have gone to the expense and trouble of producing good plants, gardeners must try them out—or next year there will be none to try. Hybrid pinks could and should be planted wherever pansies are commonly planted in the fall. They are nearly as cold-tolerant as pansies (*Dianthus barbatus* is cold hardy to zone 3) and will begin flowering at the merest hint of spring. They will not flower in the winter, as many pansies will, but they light up the place in early spring. Because so many other annuals vie to replace them for summer bloom, hybrid pinks are generally treated as a fall-planted biennial in southern gardens. They may also be planted in the spring anywhere except the Deep South, since they tolerate heat much better than do annual pinks. At the University of Georgia gardens, we plant them in May and in October. In warm areas of the country, hybrid pinks do fine in summer, but admittedly, they enjoy cool summers more than warm ones.

Full sun, propagate by seed.

CULTIVARS

'Bouquet Purple' stands about 24″ tall and provides slightly fragrant lavender flowers.

Diamond series, with flowers in blush pink, pink, purple, scarlet, and white, has done well in trials.

Floral Lace series has serrated (dare I say lacy?) petals in many colors on 8–10″ tall plants. Flowers are 1½″ wide. Colors include cherry, crimson, light pink, picotee (white with red center), purple, rose, violet, and violet picotee (large violet center, white margin).

Ideal series has for years been the finest performer in winter/spring trials at UGA. Plants grow about 15″ tall and are covered with flowers in every conceivable color except blue and yellow. Sixteen colors plus a mix have been developed. 'Ideal Violet' was an All-America Selection in 1989.

Melody series offers flowers in blush pink, pink, white, and other colors. 'Melody Pink' was an All-America Selection in 2000.

Princess series, available in seven colors and a mix, is similar to Melody series.

Telstar, one of the original series in this hybrid line, is still excellent. Many breeders took the Telstar genes and incorporated them into their own series. 'Telstar Picotee' was an All-America Selection in 1989. Bred in eight colors and a mix.

Tutti Frutti Mix is a palette of pastel and salmon hues.

Alternative species

Dianthus caryophyllus (ka ree a' fil us; carnation) is not a major garden species; a few cultivars have nevertheless been selected. 'Cinnamon Red Hots' has brilliant red flowers that bloom well even in the heat. 'Tiroler Gebirgshaengenelke', not a name designed to enhance sales, bears bright red flowers on lax stems; good for containers or window boxes. Deadheading is necessary.

Quick key to *Dianthus* species

A. Flowers in flat-topped cluster . . . . *D. barbatus*
AA. Flowers not held in flat-topped clusters
    B. Plant winter hardy to zone 5 . . . . *D. chinensis* × *barbatus*
    BB. Plant winter hardy to zone 8 only . . . . *D. chinensis*

Additional reading

University of Georgia Trial Reports: www.uga.edu/ugatrial

Diascia (di as' kee a)   twinspur   Scrophulariaceae

Diascia, an up-and-coming garden plant in America, is finding new life in Europe, where the history of twinspur in gardens is long. Plants are categorized as both annuals and perennials. The generic name comes from the Greek, *di* ("two") and *askos* ("pouch"), referring to the two sacs found on *Diascia bergiana*, the type species. The position of the pouches is marked with two translucent yellow patches, known as windows. Plants are usually no taller than 12″ and decumbent (low-growing), making them excellent for the front of the garden or in patio containers. Flowers are pink, rose, or salmon, and usually, but not always, have two small downward projecting spurs. They are held in terminal racemes.

Species of *Diascia* are handsome but not particularly eye-catching. They are also self-incompatible: even in the wild, a plant must receive pollen from a separate clone of the same species before pollination will take place. Pollination in the wild is generally accomplished by a specially evolved species of bee, whose forelegs are long enough to reach into the spurs to extract the plant's nectar. Hector Harrison of Appleby, South Humberside, England, overcame the natural incompatibility of the species and raised many of the hybrids that have rekindled interest in the genus, which had remained in relative obscurity until the late 1980s and early 1990s. Although some *Diascia* species spread by stolons and can be divided when necessary, most are commercially propagated by terminal or node cuttings.

Diascias have only recently been commonly available in the United States; therefore, although interest in the genus is high, information on its performance is limited. Cold tolerance of the many species native to the summer-dry Cape region of South Africa is questionable north of zone 7. Nor are diascias particularly happy in hot and humid summers. The few species that inhabit moister areas of the Drackensburg region tend to be more perennial.

This used to be another "good on the West Coast only" plant but not so any longer. In the northern part of the country, diascias will be increasingly available as annuals. In warmer areas of the country, diascia trials prove they can be fall-planted with pansies, violas, snapdragons, and pinks, making a terrific show in early spring. If cut back after flowering in April and May, some flower well into the summer as well.

Full sun in the North, full sun to partial shade in the South. All diascias prefer excellent drainage. Deadheading will keep plants in flower as long as possible. Cut back hard after flowering.

Quick guide to *Diascia* species

	Flower color	Sprawler	Height
D. barberae	rose	yes	10–12"
D. rigescens	rose-pink	no	12–24"
D. vigilis	pale pink	yes	9–12"

-*barberae* (bar′ ber ee)	Barber's diascia	10–12"/12"
spring, summer	rose	South Africa

Somewhat weedy-looking but handsome in flower, this species produces mats of small ovate-lanceolate leaves that cover the ground in late spring and early summer. The rose to salmon flowers have two patches of dark glands on either side and two ¼" long spurs. Native to marshy grounds in the Drackensburg area.

Plants are among the least cold hardy (zones 8 to 10) diascias and should be treated as annuals throughout most of the United States.

CULTIVARS

'Pink Queen' is 9–12" tall, with rose-pink flowers and a yellow throat.

-*rigescens* (rih je′ senz)	rigid diascia	1–2'/2'
spring, summer	rose-pink	South Africa

This is the most robust and impressive species, bearing 6–8" long racemes densely packed with two-spurred rosy pink flowers. *Diascia rigescens* has considerable natural range, roaming from southern KwaZulu-Natal to the mountains of the eastern Cape. It is distinct from other species in having sessile leaves that are sharply serrated. The foliage takes on a beige tint with age. Like all diascias, they require good drainage and are terrific in raised beds, especially if planted at eye-level—as they are at Savill Gardens in Great Windsor Park outside London, England, one of the finest eye-level displays I have seen. Unfortunately, I have not been so impressed in the United States.

Plants are as cold-tolerant as any species. They are propagated by node cuttings; take a piece of the stem with a solid node at the base (new stems are hollow). Cold hardy to zone 7.

CULTIVARS

'Forge Cottage' is 1–2' tall with copper-pink flowers in long racemes. The foliage is speckled yellow when young.

-vigilis (vih jil' is)		9–12"/2'
spring, summer	light pink	South Africa

This species is among the longest bloomers in the genus, with small pale pink flowers on long wiry stems. Vigorous and stoloniferous, it is easy to propagate from divisions. The light green foliage contrasts well with the flowers. The epithet is a reference to the huge volcanic rock, the Sentinel, that towers vigilantly over Royal Natal Park on the northern end of the amphitheater wall.

Alternative species

Diascia cordata is similar to *D. barberae*. Many authorities consider the names synonymous, and plants sold as *D. cordata* are more often than not *D. barberae*. The calyx segments of *D. barberae* are thin and slightly hairy whereas those of *D. cordata* are always glabrous (smooth). Talk about splitting hairs.

Diascia fetcaniensis is similar to *D. vigilis*, but its salmon-rose flowers are cup-shaped, unlike the open, slightly flat flowers of *D. vigilis*, and the entire plant is covered in glandular tipped hairs, making it feel moist when touched. Plants are extremely floriferous and are fairly decent garden subjects. *Diascia fetcaniensis* is among the most cold hardy species.

Diascia integerrima, a relative of *D. rigescens*, is native to rocky areas and is tolerant of dry conditions. It is distinct in having numerous wiry but rigid decumbent (low-growing, with tips ascending) stems from the crown. The foliage is blue-green and tufted in appearance. Plants are about 18" tall. The rose-pink flowers occur over most of the season.

Quick key to *Diascia* species

A. Plant stoloniferous, loose racemes <3" long
  B. Flowers rose-pink, leave bases slightly rounded . . . . *D. barberae*
  BB. Flowers light pink, leave bases more acute . . . . *D. vigilis*
AA. Plant stems mainly arise from central crown, dense racemes
  >3" long, leaves sessile . . . . *D. rigescens*

Diascia **hybrids**

Treat the exciting hybrids that have arisen from Hector Harrison's breeding program and other nurseries as hardy annuals. If they are perennial, consider it a bonus.

'Blackthorn Apricot' and 'Hopleys Apricot', both likely sports of 'Ruby Field', were named after the two nurseries who found them. 'Blackthorn Apricot' is particularly handsome, with its soft apricot blooms on spreading plants. Always a favorite color among passers-by.

'Coral Belle' is the standard by which other diascias should be judged for persistent flowering and plant longevity. I have been comparing diascias for many years, and this flowers in the spring as well as in the heat of the summer. The best of the low-growing twinspurs.

'Elliott's Variety' bears large pink flowers on 12–15″ tall plants. Widely available. Also sold as 'Jack Elliott'.

'Jacqueline's Joy' ('Lilac Belle' × 'Hopleys Apricot') is a low-spreading plant about 12″ tall, with large, bright purplish pink flowers.

'Joyce's Choice', named for Hector Harrison's wife, has salmon-apricot flowers on 12″ tall plants. A hybrid of 'Salmon Supreme' and 'Hopleys Apricot',

Diascia hybrid   ASHA KAYS

which cross also yielded 'Stella' (pink flowers) and 'Lady Valerie' (smaller flowers with a salmon tint).

'Langthorn's Lavender' has dozens of lilac-colored flowers on upright 12″ tall stems. A hybrid involving *Diascia lilacina*, a small-flowered but vigorous sprawling species with lilac-pink flowers.

'Lilac Belle' resulted from a cross between 'Ruby Field' and *Diascia lilacina*. The small lilac-pink flowers are held in long racemes. Most handsome.

'Lilac Mist' had 'Lilac Belle' and *Diascia rigescens* as its parents. Plants are 12–18″ tall and spread 3–4′ wide. The silver-lilac flowers age almost to white as they mature, providing a two-tone effect.

'Little Charmer' bears small strawberry-pink flowers.

'Pink Spot' is about 10″ tall with purple-pink flowers. A hybrid between two forms of *Diascia vigilis*.

'Red Ace' produces many dark rosy pink flowers. Plants grow vigorously even in the heat of summer, and flowering continues off and on throughout the season. Our most vigorous performer.

'Ruby Field', a hybrid between *Diascia barberae* and *D. cordata*, is more richly colored and floriferous than either species and probably the most popular diascia offered. In my garden, it flowered heavily in the spring and early summer but quickly succumbed to July's onslaught of heat and humidity. Plants, which resulted from a cross made by John Kelly of Abbotsbury, Dorset, England, were named for the wife of Paul Field of Lincolnshire.

'Rupert Lambert' has rosy red flowers on upright stems. Similar to 'Ruby Field' but larger in all respects.

'Salmon Supreme', a cross of 'Ruby Field' and *Diascia stachyoides* (a rose-pink species), bears beautiful salmon-pink flowers. Exceptional for flowing out of baskets or containers.

'Strawberry Sundae' is a vigorous hybrid from Australia, with pink-red flowers on long vigorous stems. Worked quite well in trials at Georgia. 'Raspberry Sundae', from the same Australian program, has rosy flowers but lacks the vigor of 'Strawberry Sundae'.

Sun Chimes, a new series from Hector Harrison, consists of low-growing plants in coral and red. The color of 'Sun Chimes Coral' shows up nicely; it should become a winner. 'Sun Chimes Red' did well in our trials, and much of the country can expect the same performance.

'Twinkle' ('Lilac Belle' × 'Ruby Field') has lilac-rose flowers.

'Wendy' ('Lilac Belle' × 'Hopleys Apricot') bears large rich dark pink flowers on 12″ spreading plants.

Additional reading

Benham, Steve. 1987. *Diascia*: a survey of the species in cultivation. *The Plantsman* 9(1):1–17.

Garbut, Simon. 1994. The up-and-coming *Diascia*. *The Garden* 119(1):18–21.

Kelly, John. 1987. *Diascia* 'Ruby Field' (letter to the editor). *The Plantsman* 9(2):128.

Rader, J. 1993. Elliott's variety diascia: *Diascia vigilis*. *GrowerTalks* 57(4):21.

Dicliptera (di clip′ ter a)   Acanthaceae

The family Acanthaceae is an interesting group of plants, many so similar that they trade names every now and then. Most gardeners don't notice the changes in *Dicliptera*, *Justicia*, *Belperone*, and *Pachystachys*, plants that are mostly encountered as houseplants or in gardens in the Deep South. Times are changing, however, and several of the affected species are being gardened in the North. The most common is *D. suberecta*, native to Uruguay. This species was in the genus *Justicia* (*J. suberecta*) until it was forced to change family homes—something about its conspicuous floral bracts, six-sided stems, and the way its stamens were attached to the floral tube's throat. I am not sure any gardener really cares.

The 2–3″ long velvety leaves of *Dicliptera suberecta* are covered with pale gray

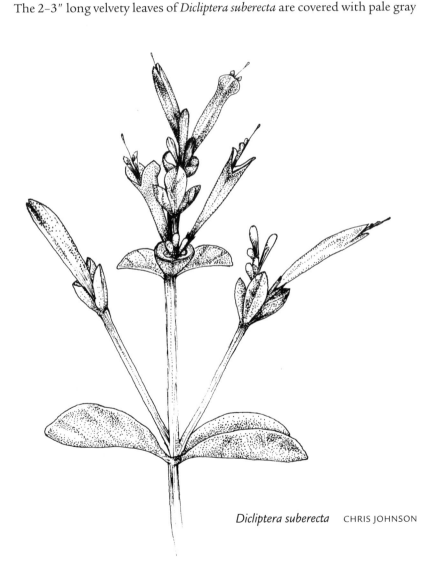

Dicliptera suberecta   CHRIS JOHNSON

down. Plants are erect to somewhat pendulous. Rusty orange-red tubular flowers, each 2″ long, are held in terminal and axillary clusters during the summer. These wonderful flowers are the plant's main claim to fame; they persist for weeks and will continue even longer in warm temperatures. Plants are useful as swaths of color in the garden and landscape but are equally good as a plant or two in containers. They attract lots of people and whiteflies too, unfortunately. Stems are very brittle, so keep plants away from traffic. The species is somewhat cold-tolerant: plants have returned three years for my colleague Meg Green, who lives outside Athens, Georgia (zone 7).

Full sun, propagate by cuttings.

Dioscorea (dee os ko′ ree a)   Dioscoreaceae

When I first saw a certain twining plant growing over a pergola, I looked at the unpronounceable label (*Dioscorea batatas*), noted the vigorous habit, and promised to learn a little more about it. The genus is best known for yams (*D. alata*)—goes to show how many yams I eat. In fact, there are more than 600 species and a few of them, including *D. batatas* (cinnamon vine), are hardy to about zone 6. This species is useful as a fast-growing vine for shade, which it brightens with its small white fragrant flowers. The angled stems twine around structures in a clockwise direction and produce green to green-purple foliage. The shiny 3″ leaves have heart-shaped bases and seven to nine veins, with short petioles. Interesting small tubers are formed in the leaf axils, which may be planted to produce another vine. The roots form large tubers that can be dug, with effort, in the fall of the second year. The flowers, which occur in the axillary racemes, are sweetly fragrant; cinnamon might come to mind, depending on your definition of that spice. Plants grow to 15′. Native to the Philippines and east Asia, they may become weedy in the South, so beware.

Some people enjoy the appearance of even larger tubers in the leaf axils. If you are such a person, *Dioscorea bulbifera* (air potato) might be fun to try. The 10 × 7″ leaves are usually alternate, sometimes opposite, and with 6″ long petioles. The flowers are in spikes in the leaf axils, and the female flowers give rise to variably sized "potatoes." Reasonably palatable, but more fun than functional. Few root tubers are formed. Plants are annuals for sure, not as hardy as *D. batatas*.

Full sun, propagate from roots, tubers, or cuttings.

Duranta (der an′ ta)   Verbenaceae

Members of the verbena family are often attractive, and *Duranta erecta* (pigeon berry, golden dewdrop), a native of South America, is beginning to charm a loyal cadre of supporters. The genus is named for noted Italian physician Castor Durantes, who practiced in Rome in the mid 1500s. Golden dewdrop, with its blue flowers and long ornamental value in the landscape, is one of my favorite specialty annuals.

Duranta erecta used to be called *D. repens*, which I could never figure out since it is neither sprawling nor prostrate. Plants are woody and, if they overwinter, can be quite large; in fact, in mild climates such as Australia and Greece, I have seen shrubs well over 15' tall. But as they seldom overwinter in most of this country, they are best grown as a 2–4' annual. Even when they die back in the fall and return in Athens (zone 7), plants seldom reach more than 5' in height, then die to the ground again in the winter. When plants do overwinter, they are slow to emerge in the spring and do not start flowering until mid summer, whereas newly planted material will begin to flower in late spring. The light green 2" long leaves are opposite and entire, and the stems may be either dangerously thorny or unarmed, depending on the plant source. Obviously, choose an unarmed specimen! The others can be hazardous to fingers. Flowers may be blue, lavender, or close to violet and are held in 6–8" long axillary racemes in summer and fall. The stems become woody over time and as fall approaches, plants resemble a shrub more than an annual.

The approach of fall makes this species even more wonderful, particularly in areas where cool nights and warm days persist for a month or so and summer does not rush into winter. The flowers give way to astonishing grape-like clusters of golden fruit, which persists until eaten by birds or dehydrated by cold. In the

Duranta erecta   ASHA KAYS

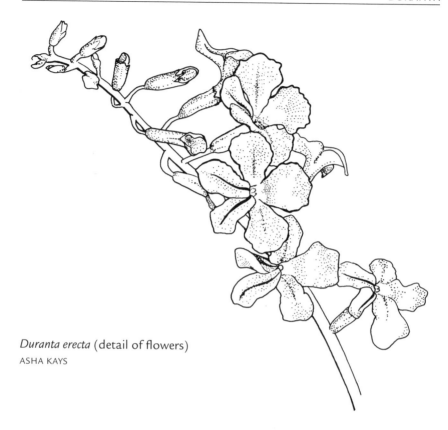

Duranta erecta (detail of flowers)
ASHA KAYS

Northeast and northern Midwest, fall may be too short for good fruit production, but the plant is worth a place in the garden for its flowers nevertheless.

Full sun, propagate by cuttings.

CULTIVARS

'Alba' has white flowers, but the stems in the selections I have seen carry more thorns than the species and flowering is much more sparse.

'Thornless' is almost, but not entirely, thornless. An introduction from the New Crop Program at the University of Georgia. Lavender-blue flowers, golden fruit.

'Variegata' is among the best variegated plants for the landscape, producing clean lines of white and green. Thorned and flowerless. Grow for foliage effect only.

Additional reading

Armitage, Allan M. 2000. Is there a market for annuals with ornamental fruit? *Greenhouse Grower* 18(5):140–146.

E

Eccremocarpus (e krem o kar′ pus)   Chilean glory vine   Bignoniaceae

A genus not often seen, this Chilean native requires more time and less winter than much of the United States can offer. I saw one vine in its glory at the Mercer Botanical Gardens, Humble, Texas, and was most impressed. Of course, Canadians like me are impressed whenever summer lasts more than six weeks and plants grow more than 3′ in a single year. But even my friends there were impressed—and admitted it, a rare occurrence for any Texan.

Eccremocarpus scaber, the most common species, is a terrific tendril climber, covering fences and pergolas and scrambling through shrubs. Plants can reach 20′ tall. The opposite divided leaves are about 3″ long, and the flowers are held terminally and in the axils. They are borne in 6–7″ long racemes, each 1½″ long flower consisting of a constricted tube that opens into a rounded mouth. This may sound a little gruesome, but the effect is quite handsome. Flowers are generally scarlet; other colors are also available. Flowering begins in mid to late summer, if plants are started early enough, and continues until frost.

Plants require some support and full sun. Propagate by seed indoors early, and place in the ground when threat of frost has passed.

CULTIVARS

Anglia Hybrids climb 6–10′ and occur in yellow, orange, pink, and scarlet.
'Aurea' has bright yellow flowers.
'Carmineus' bears deep red flowers.
'Roseus' produces flowers that are bright pink to red.
'Tresco Crimson' climbs to 6′ tall and bears scarlet to crimson flowers.
'Tresco Cream' produces creamy white flowers with a tinge of pink. From the wonderful garden on Tresco, England's "island of flowers."

Additional reading

Halpin, Anne. 1997. Annual vines. *Horticulture* 94(4):60–64.
Missouri Botanical Garden: www.mobot.org/research/bignoniaceae

Echium (e′ kee um)   bugloss   Boraginaceae

When you include *Echium* in the garden, you are sure to have dozens of bees buzzing about. About forty species of this amazing genus of annuals are members of the "conservatory gang" or the "somewhere-other-than-here gang," with travelogue names such as pride of Tenerife (*Echium simplex*) and pride of Madeira (*E. candicans*). They are truly beautiful in their native habitats; if you are lucky, you might see them in better conservatories, such as Longwood, or in gardens with Mediterranean climates. Seed may be purchased for some of these 5–8′ tall plants, but why would anyone in Vermont want to purchase seeds of something someone in Florida can't even grow? Go for it only if challenge is a necessity in your garden life. If not, several smaller species of bedding stature make a fine show, often reseeding to return in following years.

The best known is the biennial viper's bugloss, *Echium vulgare*, native to southern Europe. Plants are 1½–2½′ tall, with rough hairy, linear to lanceolate leaves. The basal leaves are about 6″ long; those on the stem are a little shorter. All are sessile. Dozens of blue to blue-violet, sometimes pink or white, flowers are produced in multiple scorpioid (like a scorpion's tail) inflorescences in spring to early summer. The five blue-purple stamen filaments are obviously exserted from the flower petals. I have grown this species for several years. In the spring to early summer, it makes an outstanding low-growing colorful plant; in the summer, it disappears, only to return the next spring from seed.

Full sun, propagate by seed.

CULTIVARS

'Blue Bedder' is the most popular selection, about 1′ tall, with blue-violet bell-shaped flowers.

Dwarf Hybrids are a mixture of 1′ tall plants in purple, lilac, pink, rose, and white.

Alternative species

Echium plantagineum (plan ta jin′ ee um; plantain bugloss) is similar to *E. vulgare* in habit and flower but has wider leaves (like those of plantain) and stamens that are only slightly exserted. Plants are generally a little shorter. Monarch Hybrids are 12″ tall and produce flowers in shades of blue, carmine, lavender, pink, and white.

Additional reading

Anonymous. 1989. Deep blue spires make it the Pride of Madeira. *Sunset* 182(3): 186.

Echium vulgare   ASHA KAYS

Emilia (e mee′ lee a)   Asteraceae

This little-known genus contains about twenty-four species, but seldom are they seen as garden plants. The most common is *Emilia coccinea* (syn. *E. javanica*; tassel flower)—not that it's popular by any means. This may be because its many fuzzy scarlet and orange flowers, borne on 12–15″ long stems, are only ½″ or so in diameter. The mostly basal leaves are about 6″ long, sessile, and oblong to lanceolate. Although the species may look like an orange weed, it is useful as a colorful filler for cut flowers; the many 6–8″ lateral flower stems produced on each main stem may also be used as short-stemmed fillers. Plants continue to flower even in heat and humidity, which means that such conditions do not inhibit flower initiation or development. They are annuals but self-sow prolifically.

Full sun, propagate by seed.

Alternative species

Emilia sonchifolia has 4" long wavy (lyrate) leaves and produces fewer flowers than *E. coccinea*. Young plants may be eaten in salads or soups or steamed as a vegetable. The species has purple-red flowers; 'Lutea' has yellow flowers.

Additional reading

Armitage, Allan M. 1993. *Specialty Cut Flowers*. Timber Press, Portland, Ore.

Erysimum (e rih' sih mum)   wallflower   Brassicaceae

All wallflowers were previously listed under the genera *Cheiranthus* and *Erysimum*; now many taxonomists have lumped everything into *Erysimum*. This is a good thing because I never could tell the difference between the two. In the old breakdown, differences between genera were found in insignificant parts of the flower and within the seed and fruit: *Erysimum* has no nectary glands at the base of the stamens, the fruit (silique) is not as flat as in *Cheiranthus*, and seeds within the fruit are in a single row (the compressed fruit of *Cheiranthus* has two rows). In general, plants of *Cheiranthus* bore orange-yellow flowers and *Erysimum* produced mauve to purple hues, but as more *Erysimum* species were introduced, it soon became obvious that flower color could not be used to discriminate between the two genera. A small victory for the lumpers in the taxonomic world! Many species are biennials, but the main species of interest is the sweet fragrant biennial, *E. cheiri*.

-cheiri (cheer' i)   wallflower   6–12"/12"
spring   many colors   southern Europe

Wallflowers act like biennials. Many flower the first year from seed; others may persist in the garden for three to four years, but, realistically, don't bet on much more than two years. They are common in gardens in the British Isles, southern Europe, and New Zealand. Their main problem in America is, well, America. Like so many European natives, they don't do well in climates with a wide range of temperatures. They are not particularly good in heat, and their limit for cold is around zone 7. That they are short-lived and need well-drained neutral to slightly alkaline soils also keeps them slightly out of reach.

All parts of the plant are highly variable. The alternate lanceolate leaves are 2–8" long and less than 1" wide; they are generally pointed, occasionally somewhat hairy, and usually with entire margins. All flowers have four sepals and four clawed petals and are arranged in a raceme; four of the six stamens are longer than the other two. The fruit is a silique (long, narrow, splitting open longitudinally). Flower color on the species and many cultivars is bright yellow-orange, often with red to purple stripes. Cultivars and hybrids abound, so finding the species itself is quite unlikely.

Good drainage is a must, and plants do better in alkaline soils than in acidic ones. In the South, fall plantings result in the best spring performance. Plant in full sun in the North, partial shade in the South. Plants will often perpetuate by self-sowing. Our plantings of 'Golden Bedder' in Athens are more than six years old, mainly by self-sowing. Propagate by seed.

CULTIVARS

Most of the following cultivars are seed-propagated and likely hybrids of various wallflowers, including *Erysimum cheiri*, *E. bicolor*, and *E. sempervirens*. Treat as biennials; some may also perform as annuals or occasionally as perennials.

'Aunt May' is only about 6″ tall, bearing rose-lavender flowers.

'Aurora' has apricot, bronze, orange, and mauve flowers.

'Bredon' is a well-known hybrid with reddish buds and golden yellow flowers. About 8″ tall.

'Butterscotch' has orange flowers.

'Cloth of Gold' bears large yellow-orange flowers.

'Constant Cheer' grows about 15″ tall and bears dull rose to amber flowers in late spring. Flowers start brownish orange before turning amber. Long-flowering.

'Covent Garden' bears fragrant, deep magenta flowers.

'Fire King' is an old-fashioned form with bright orange-scarlet flowers.

'Golden Bedder' produces dozens of golden flower heads on 9–12″ tall plants. An excellent performer in the UGA Horticulture Gardens. Also sold as part of Brilliant Bedder (Super Bedder) series.

'Golden Gem' produces deep yellow flowers on 9–12″ tall plants.

'Harper Crewe', a double-flowered form of *Erysimum cheiri*, was selected in the seventeenth century and is among the oldest wallflowers still in commerce. Very fragrant, often listed as *E. ×kewensis* (*E. cheiri* × *E. bicolor*).

'Ivory White' is just that, an unusual color for wallflowers.

'Jubilee Gold' has gold flowers over 6″ bushy plants. Similar to 'Bredon' but with toothed leaves. Among the shortest forms.

'My Fair Lady' is a mixture of apricot, cream, gold, lemon, mahogany, pink, purple, rose, and salmon.

Persian Carpet Mix offers bright colors in apricot, gold, orange, purple, and rose.

'Plant World Gold' and 'Plant World Lemon' are recent introductions from Ray Brown of Plant World Nursery in Devon, England. They are compact with two-tone flowers. 'Plant World Lemon' has more subtle flower color than 'Plant World Gold'.

'Ruby Gem' has velvety flowers in wine-red.

'Scarlet Bedder' has rich red flowers.

'Tom Thumb' is a mixture of 6–8″ tall plants in a wide color range.

'Turkish Bazaar' bears very fragrant yellow to gold flowers on 6″ stems in the spring.

'Variegatus' has leaves variegated with cream.

'Wenlock Beauty' produces yellow flowers with a bronze tint.

'White Dame' has creamy white flowers.

'Yellow Bird' is about 12" tall with yellow-gold flowers.

Eschscholzia (esh olts' ee a)   California poppy   Papaveraceae

How I enjoy California poppies! Their wonderful flowers provide an informal sheet of color in gardens and medians or even as escapees, hanging out on the side of the road. Not that I am the first to be enamored with them. The Spaniards who came to California called the land the Golden West and named the flowers *copa de ora* ("cup of gold").

That I love eschscholzias doesn't mean I can spell them. The number of *schs* can be attributed to the genus's being named for German physician and naturalist Johann Elsholz, who was aboard the Russian vessel *Rurik*, a ship organized to explore western North America in 1815. Elsholz's name was Russianized by the ship's captain, to "Eschscholz," and so you have it. Approximately eight to ten species of the genus have been recorded, but our native annual *Eschscholzia californica* (California poppy) is by far the most popular in American gardens.

Plants are native throughout the coastal areas of California (where it is the state flower) and Oregon and are naturalized in Europe; they also occur in India. They are short-lived perennials and often return through viable seed shed in the previous year. In most of the country, it is best to treat them as annuals.

The deeply dissected leaves are alternate, smooth, and often blue-green; the plant is eye-catching even when not in flower. The single flowers, borne on long flower stems, consist of two sepals, four petals, many stamens, and an interesting four- to six-lobed stigma. The silky flowers are 2–2½" across and typically bright yellow, but many color variants occur as well as gruesome double-flowered forms. They are persistent but tend to close like an umbrella in dull weather. Strongest colors occur in poor soils; overfertilization results in leafy plants with poor flower numbers and color.

California poppies are often used in wildflower mixes for highway planting or pastures. They transplant poorly; in the garden it is best to sow them in a prepared site in late summer or fall in mild climates or early spring in cooler areas. Harvest as a cut flower when fluted buds are about to open, or after initial opening and closing. Pick in early morning after dew has dried off. Many cultivars are available, but you can't go too far wrong with the species itself.

Full sun, propagate by seed.

CULTIVARS

'Alba' has white flowers.

'Apricot Flambeau' is an interesting name for an eye-catching plant. Semi-double to double flowers have light yellow fluted petals with coral edging.

'Aurantiaca' bears brilliant orange blooms.

Ballerina Mix produces fluted, double flowers.

'Buttermilk' provides semi-double creamy white fluted flowers above blue-green foliage.

Eschscholzia californica   CHRIS JOHNSON

'Carmine King' has masses of single rose-colored flowers, often with a creamy center. Introduced in 1931 and still a popular choice.

'Dalli' bears scarlet-red semi-double flowers with a golden base.

'Inferno' produces hot orange-scarlet single flowers. An appropriate name.

'Ivory Castle' has pure white single flowers.

'Mission Bells' is a mixture of semi-double flowers, mostly in oranges and pinks.

Monarch Mix provides an array of colors in single and semi-double flowers.

'Purple Gleam' has single flowers in shades of lilac and purple.

'Rose Chiffon' bears rosy pink semi-double and double flowers with a light yellow center.

Thai Silk Mix is an example of "look what they've done to my flower." Garish colors on awful double flowers. To each their own.

Alternative species

Eschscholzia caespitosa (ses pih to' sa; tufted California poppy) has many flower stems rising from a tuft of leaves. The finely divided grayish leaves may also occur up the 1' tall stems, which end in small (1½–2") bright yellow single flowers. They don't flower as persistently as *E. californica* but are certainly worth a spot in the sunny garden. 'Sundew' has dozens of pale yellow single flowers occurring in compact tufts. Nicely scented as well.

Additional reading

Springer, Lauren. 1997. Parade of poppies. *Horticulture* 94(6):41–45.
Swezey, Lauren Bonar. 1997. A poppy with panache. *Sunset* 199(4):59.

Euphorbia (yew for' bee a)   spurge   Euphorbiaceae

With more than 1600 species of *Euphorbia*, one would expect that a few would be
useful garden plants, but most of the approximately thirty-five species native to
the United States are unattractive weeds. We mainly encounter "euphorbs" at
Christmas, as the ubiquitous poinsettia (*E. pulcherrima*), or as perennials in the
garden (wood spurge, *E. amygdaloides*; Mediterranean spurge, *E. characias*; myrtle
spurge, *E. myrsinites*). All species are characterized by milky sap and unique clusters of flowers called cyathia, which are subtended by bracts of various size and
color.

Quick guide to *Euphorbia* species

	Leaf color	Flower color
E. cyathophora	red at base	green
E. lathyris	bluish green	yellow-green
E. marginata	variegated	white

-*cyathophora* (si ath o for' a)   fire-on-the-mountain   2–4'/2'
    summer   orange-red bracts   South Dakota, Oklahoma

I tried this native when it was called *Euphorbia heterophylla*: the common name of
fire-on-the-mountain set my greenhouse heart a-flutter. It didn't flutter long,
however, as the plant didn't deliver the fire or the mountain. The stems are erect,
branching but not freely; the ovate to linear leaves have variable margins and are
slightly hairy beneath. The cyathia are green, with a tinge of red. Flowering
occurs in mid to late summer. The trouble with this annual poinsettia is that
unlike the true poinsettia, the bracts don't turn uniformly red. Rather, they
become reddish only at the base of some and become more uniformly red as
they ascend the stem—not something that makes me want to invest more time
or money next year.

    Full sun, propagate by seed or cuttings.

-*lathyris* (la' thih ris)   gopher spurge, caper spurge   3–4'/3'
    summer   yellow-green flowers   Europe

Absolutely one of my favorite plants, this biennial pops up from seed each
spring, providing a classic-looking plant with reputed magical (at least for a
gardener) properties: it is said to repel gophers, moles, and voles, and while I
know of no scientific evidence that supports the lore, gardeners desperate to rid

their gardens of these obnoxious burrowers have often embraced the news as gospel. Even if such magic is nonexistent, this is a wonderful plant, producing erect stems with opposite 6 × 1″ leaves, the leaves above being in perpendicular planes to the set below (an arrangement described as decussate). The small flowers, which occur in the apices of the terminal leaves, quickly give way to the green caper-like fruit. Give the plant another glance in a few weeks and you will find two stems arising from either side of the fruit, ready to produce additional flowers and fruit.

In the Armitage garden, I have not verified their rodent-repellent properties, but I have verified their ability to reseed wherever they want. They never become a pest, and I look forward to the smooth unbranched appearance each spring.

Full sun to partial shade. Propagate by seed, or plant in the spring.

-*marginata* (mar jih na′ ta)   snow-on-the-mountain   2–3′/3′
   summer   foliage   western United States

I may be disappointed by the lack of fire on the mountain of *Euphorbia cyathophora*, but I put on my snowshoes in expectation of *E. marginata*, which never fails to impress. The snow is the plant's white-margined foliage; in some cases, leaves near the top of the plant are almost entirely white. Plants branch well; pinching in spring encourages an even fuller plant. The erect stems carry 3″ long pale green leaves that are softly hairy above and smooth below. In warmer climates, some staking may be necessary.

This species makes an outstanding contrast to the multicolored flowers and foliage of summer. It subtly softens yet is visible from the other side of the garden. It is tolerant of heat and humidity yet does well in cooler summers. You'd think this terrific plant would be more common. The problem is its milky sap,

Euphorbia marginata   CHRIS JOHNSON

which can be a contact irritant to some and is poisonous to all when ingested. The solution is to wear gloves and keep it out of your salads. Growers and retailers don't particularly like handling the plants either, so seed may be your best bet in acquiring them.

Full sun, well-drained soils. Propagate by seed *in situ*.

CULTIVARS

'Kilimanjaro' is probably a better choice than the species, being a little taller, more compact, and an earlier-flowerer. Good name, as well.

'Summer Icicle' is a dwarf form, growing 1½–2' tall. Quite striking.

'White Top' is 3–3½' tall, with almost white leaves at the top of the plants.

Quick key to *Euphorbia* species

```
  A. Upper leaves with white margins  . . . . . . . . . . . . . . . . . . . . . . E. marginata
 AA. Upper leaves without white margins
       B. Upper leaves and bracts blue-green or yellow . . . . . . . . . . . E. lathyris
      BB. Upper leaves and bracts red, at least at base . . . . . . . . E. cyathophora
```

Additional reading

Swezey, Lauren Bonar. 1992. Deer proof and deer friendly. *Sunset* 189(3):48–50.

Eustoma (yew sto' ma)   lisianthus   Gentianaceae

What a beautiful species this genus boasts, whose chalice-like flowers in a dazzling array of colors have kept prairies in Nebraska, Colorado, and Texas ablaze in spring color. The blooms have been captured by the commercial cut flower breeders, meaning that 3–4' tall stems are arriving in shops from greenhouses as close as California and as far away as Israel. The same species of lisianthus has also been bred to 6–9", so it can be grown in small containers on the dining room table, to be enjoyed with a glass of wine and the evening meal. A fine legacy for this great American native. It is not an easy plant to grow, however, and in many areas of the country, it works everywhere but in the garden. That is not to say it is not tried.

The cause of all this headache and joy? *Eustoma grandiflorum* (prairie gentian), once known as *E. russellianum*. The leaves of this 2–3' tall plant are thick and blue-green. The cupped to chalice-like flowers are produced singly; they are commonly violet to lavender but have been bred in white, pink, and purple, usually with a darker eye in the center. Flowers are 2–3" long and about 3" wide. They do well in the garden where gentians do well (they are in the same family): if you are a frustrated gentian gardener, lisianthus will lessen the frustration somewhat. To be fair, they tolerate a good deal more heat than most gentians, but they are most enjoyable in mixed containers, where protection from heavy summer rains may be provided, or as cut flowers in a vase. We have trialed lisi-

Eustoma grandiflorum
'Echo White'
ASHA KAYS

anthus for years at the University of Georgia, and the new cultivars are increasingly tolerant of normal garden abuse. If I had sufficient sun in my garden, I would try them again.

Well-drained soils, propagate by seed. Morning sun and afternoon shade are recommended but not necessary. Plants are best bought as seedlings as it takes a good deal of time before a mature plant is produced.

CULTIVARS

Single flowers
These are all greenhouse-grown and make good cut flowers.

Flamenco series is 2–3' tall in eight colors.

Heidi series branches more near the top of the stems, producing a spray of flowers in twelve colors.

Laguna series offers three colors. Taller than most series.

Malibu, an early-flowering series, is about 3' tall. Six colors available.

'Red Glass' is a deep violet (close to red) flowering form. Plants grow about 18" tall.

'Sentenial Porcelain' is 2–3' tall, bearing silvery white flowers with a touch of lavender.

Tyrol series bears large flowers in five separate colors.

Ventura series is an early-flowering form in seven colors.

'Winter Pink' produces sprays of rose-pink flowers atop 2–3' tall stems.

Double flowers

Again, all greenhouse-grown and useful for cut flowers.

'Blue Picotee' has blue margins on the many petals of the double flowers.

'Double Up Pink' bears fully double pink flowers on 3' tall stems.

Echo series is available in nine separate colors and a mix and bears fully double flowers.

Mariachi series bears large flowers in five colors.

'The Blue Rose' has large double flowers of deep blue on 20–24" tall plants.

Short forms

Useful for containers or interplanted in garden.

Florida series consists of 8–10" tall plants in blue, pink, and sky blue.

'Forever Blue' provides good basal branching and deep blue flowers on 8–10" tall plants. An All-America Selection in 2001.

Lisa series, about 12" tall, has reasonable heat and humidity tolerance. 'Lisa Blue' and 'Lisa White' are offered.

Lizzie series consists of blue, pink, and white flowers on 12" tall stems.

Mermaid series branches well and bears blue, pink, or white flowers on 9–12" tall plants. Probably the best choice for garden plants.

'Sapphire Blue' is a dwarf form (4–6" tall), with blue flowers. Better in a pot than in the ground.

Evolvulus (ee volv' yew lus)   Convolvulaceae

The generic name comes from the Latin, *evolvure* ("to untwist"), a hint that this member of the morning glory family is not a climber—rather unusual for that group of plants. Nor does it grow erect: its popularity stems from its use as a subject for hanging baskets. While there are about a hundred species, only *Evolvulus pilosus* (syn. *E. nuttallianus*) is seen in gardens. The stems have dense, silky hairs and many alternate 1" long spatula-like gray-green leaves, with little or no petiole. The round blue flowers, which occur singly, are only about 1" wide but are produced in ample numbers throughout the season. Blue flowers on gray foliage provides a stunning basket.

A good plant for baskets or containers; not good for normal border use. Full sun to partial shade, propagate by cuttings.

CULTIVARS

'Blue Daze' is more compact, with more ovate hairy leaves and blue flowers, often with a white center. A better choice than the species.

'Hawaiian Blue Eyes' has light blue blooms. New flowers are produced daily.

F

Felicia (fe lee′ see a) blue marguerite Asteraceae

A group of aster-like plants, usually with blue to lavender flowers. They may be shrubs, perennials, or annuals, with flowers occurring singly or in groups. The blooms are generally blue, but some variation occurs. None of the approximately eighty species identified are yet common in American gardens.

Quick guide to *Felicia* species

	Height	Pubescent
F. amelloides	1–2′	slightly
F. bergeriana	6–9″	densely

-amelloides (a mel oy′ deez) blue marguerite 1–2′/2′
  summer blue South Africa

Long a favorite blue-flowered plant in conservatories and greenhouse, blue marguerite is being used more and more as an outdoor annual, providing months of flowering. I have used them in our gardens at the University of Georgia, and they flower well until temperatures stay stubbornly in the nineties. Then they die. In Montreal, plants are shorter and flowers, a little bluer, but the biggest difference is continued persistence in the garden.

Plants are actually subshrubs, becoming woody at the base, then dying to the ground in the fall. The 1–2″ long opposite leaves are ovate in shape, entire or nearly so, and have no petioles. They resemble the leaves found on an aster native to southern Europe, *Aster amellus*, hence the specific name. The flowers are about 1½″ wide, borne singly on 6″ long flower stems, and consist of light blue ray flowers surrounding a yellow disk. On dull days, flowers may not open.

Plants must be situated in well-drained areas, preferably in full morning light and some afternoon shade. They are susceptible to root rots in wet, cool weather, and wet, hot weather is not a great deal better. Propagate by seed or cuttings.

'Astrid Thomas' has darker blue flowers than the species and grows about 1' tall.

'Monstrosa' (var. *monstrosa*) reportedly bears much larger flowers, up to 3" across, but I have not been able to locate it.

'Read's Blue' provides lavender-blue flowers around a yellow center. About 12" tall.

'Santa Anita' has somewhat larger flowers than the species but otherwise is similar.

'Santa Anita Variegata' produces stippled green-and-white foliage with 1½–2" wide flowers.

'Spring Merchen' grows 12–15" tall, with mostly blue flowers but some white and purple as well.

'Variegata' is the common variegated form, with heavy uneven white margins on the green leaves. An excellent choice for the garden or container.

-bergeriana (ber ger ee a' na)	kingfisher daisy	6–8"/2'
summer	blue	South Africa

This species is less well known than blue marguerite because it is less showy and not as readily available. Plants are ground huggers, producing densely hairy mats of leaves, which may grow to 12" tall (6–8" is more common). The 1–2" long opposite gray-green leaves are oval to lanceolate, hairy, and usually toothed. The bright blue flowers are about ¾" wide, on short flower stems. The flowers roll under in dull weather and open again in full sun.

Full sun to partial shade, well-drained soils. Propagate by seed or cuttings.

CULTIVARS

'Cub Scout' forms carpets of bright foliage and brilliant blue flowers with a tinge of turquoise.

Alternative species

Felicia echinata (ek in a' ta) is related to *F. bergeriana*. This subshrub grows 18–30" tall, with coarsely hairy to spiny leaves, each less than 1" long. The lilac to white flowers usually occur singly but also in groups of up to six flowers, on a sandpapery flower stem. Useful for containers or in well-drained soils.

Felicia heterophylla (he ter a' fil a) grows about 2' tall, producing alternate 2" long entire to dentate leaves. The solitary blue flowers are most common, but rosy pink flowers often occur in a mix of seedlings. 'The Blues' (sky blue) and 'The Rose' (pale pink) are 6–10" tall. Although not as easy to find as *F. amelloides*, it is a reasonable alternative.

Quick key to *Felicia* species

A. Plant slightly hairy or glabrous
  B. Leaves opposite, entire or nearly so . . . . *F. amelloides*
  BB. Leaves alternate, entire or dentate . . . . *F. heterophylla*
AA. Plant densely hairy
  B. Plant 6–9" tall, mat-forming, villous . . . . *F. bergeriana*
  BB. Plant 2–3' tall, upright, coarse to spiny hairs . . . . *F. echinata*

Fuchsia (few′ sha)   Onagraceae

I recently visited the botanical garden at Hohenheim University, one of the great gardens of southern Germany. The new gardens were wonderful, but the old botanical garden was of most interest to me, as the home of botanist, botanical illustrator, and herbalist Leonhart Fuchs. It is impossible to walk through any garden in Germany and not trip over shrubs, containers, and standards of his namesakes. Everybody in North America wants to trip over fuchsias in their garden as well, but alas, North America is not northern Europe, and fuchsias have been slow to embrace the warmer summers here. In fact, they simply don't flourish in significant portions of our country. I would guess that more fuchsia baskets have been killed by well-meaning American gardeners than any other basket item. The crammed 12" basket is the container of choice for many retailers, and it is difficult not to buy at least one when fuchsias are in flower. Better to purchase a standard (plants trained on a single woody stem, 4–5' tall and flowering at the top), if you can find one at an affordable price; standards have good root volume and are better looking anyway. Remember: the larger the basket or container, the greater your chance of success—and the keys to success, regardless of location, are water and reasonably cool summer temperatures.

It is quite difficult to find true species or even selections of one. Sometimes a plant of *Fuchsia magellanica*, an important parent in many hybrids, is offered at a retail center. *Fuchsia boliviana*, a three-leaved species used in the hybridization of the Triphylla Hybrids, is sold by mail order; the scarlet flowers are crowded into terminal pendulous racemes. *Fuchsia corymbiflora* is among the most beautiful species I have seen, with exceedingly long pale pink calyx tubes and red petals, in inflorescences of a dozen flowers or more. *Fuchsia magellanica* is a large shrub, a classic beauty seen throughout the British Isles and on the coastal Northwest and quite terrific if you can grow it; usually covered with hundreds of long narrow scarlet flowers, it may also have flowers of pink or white, or leaves that are golden ('Aurea') or variegated ('Versicolor', 'Sharpitor'). *Fuchsia triphylla*, with dull green leaves arranged in groups of threes, is also quite popular; its long flowers have short sepals and are usually orange to coral in color, with orange-red stamens.

Most plants in the trade are hybrids with at least three different species somewhere in their parentage. And, good Lord, I never realized how many were out there until I wore out my Nikon trying to shoot all I came across in Oregon,

Washington, and northern Europe. Apparently more than 8000 cultivars have been listed, which I suppose gives us license to keep killing them until we find one that lives through the summer. In the Northwest and parts of the Northeast, fuchsias can be grown in the sun, but partial shade, at least in the afternoon, is best for most everywhere else. *Fuchsia triphylla*, *F. boliviana*, and *F. splendens* have provided the popular group of fuchsias known as the Triphylla Hybrids, which are more tolerant of heat and humidity than many other forms. They should be actively sought out if you have grown dead fuchsias in the past.

With so many cultivars, it is not surprising that many flower forms have been developed. The showy part of the flower is usually the tubular calyx (sepals), whose five lobes may be flared or reflexed backward. The calyx surrounds the inner corolla (petals), which may be single, semi-double, or double. And adding to the chaotic brilliance of the flower, the stamens and style may be highly colored and exserted (they stick out) as well. To try to simplify habit and flowers a little, several garden forms have been identified, including those with single flowers ('Celia Smedley'), double flowers ('Pink Marshmallow'), upward or outward facing flowers ('Estelle Marie'), reflexed sepals ('Evensong'), reflexed petals ('Swanley Gem'), long-tubed ('Swanley Yellow'), very large flowers ('Texas Longhorn'), very small flowers ('Eleanor Lytham'), and variegated leaves ('Golden Marinka').

When treated as annuals, plants may be dug, repotted, and placed in a frost-free environment in winter months. That is difficult for most gardeners, but my grandmother did it with geraniums for years—and a $30 fuchsia standard, as opposed to a $10 basket, may just inspire you to change your overwintering philosophy.

Several cultivars are available as seed, but most gardeners don't have the time or facilities to tend to a fourteen- to eighteen-week crop. Cuttings are far easier. Retail outlets have a reasonable supply of newer cultivars and purchasing a few plants a year is the best bet.

CULTIVARS

I offer only a sampling of those I have seen; few are heat-tolerant.

Single flowers

Angel Earrings series consists of 'Cascading Angel Earrings' and 'Dainty Angel Earrings'. The latter is an average fuchsia, with red sepals and blue corolla. 'Cascading Angel Earrings', on the other hand, is among the most outstanding fuchsias I have trialed for heat tolerance. Large robust pink-rose flowers with a purple corolla drip down horizontal stems. And they actually flower in the heat! A Georgia Garden Gold Winner.

'Ballerina Blue' has cherry-red sepals and a blue corolla.

Belle series is a seed-propagated form consisting of 'Evening Belle', with red and white blooms, and 'Morning Belle', with red and purple flowers.

'Bluette' bears rose-pink sepals and lavender petals.

'Checkerboard' produces a red calyx tube and white calyx lobes. The petals are red, providing a checkerboard appearance. Outstanding.

'David' is a bushy form with red sepals and purple petals.

'Fete Floral' is a seed-propagated form with long tubular flowers of deep red.

'Gartenmeister Bonstedt' is a popular Triphylla Hybrid, with dull bronze-green leaves and long tubular red-brown flowers. Reasonably tolerant of heat and humidity.

'Hawkshead' has white sepals tinged green and pure white petals.

'Hidcote Pink' provides coral and white flowers. Often seen as a standard. Also sold as 'Hidcote Beauty'.

'Honeysuckle' is a terrific plant, with single coral flowers and maroon foliage. The sepals flare out, not as reflexed as in most others.

'Jingle Bells' is a dwarf plant, with rose and white flowers.

'Koralle' is a Triphylla Hybrid from Germany, quite similar to 'Gartenmeister Bonstedt' but with lighter green foliage and coral flowers.

'Lord Beaconsfield' bears single magenta and rose flowers.

'Lottie Hobbie' has small dark cerise flowers and very small leaves. Useful for bonsai work.

'Loveliness' has long tubes of pure white and a red corolla.

'Love's Reward' provides pink flowers.

'Madame Cornelissen' is a *Fuchsia magellanica* hybrid with long flowers of red sepals and white petals.

'Mrs. J. D. Fredericks' produces pink-on-pink flowers. Good heat tolerance and therefore a popular plant in the States.

'Mrs. Popple' is a common large-flowered form with spreading scarlet sepals and violet petals. The crimson stamens and style are long and exserted.

'Snowcap' is a dwarf form sometimes used as a bedding plant. The flowers consist of a red calyx and a white corolla with red veins.

'String of Pearls' ('Leinepearl') bears pink sepals and pink-veined white corollas.

'Swanley Yellow' bears yellow flowers with 3″ long tubes.

'Tom Thumb' is a miniature form with purple to red flowers on short upright stems.

'Voodoo' has plum-colored petals and crimson sepals.

'Yuletide' produces white double flowers.

Double and semi-double flowers

'Annabelle' has short, fat flowers in pale pink.

'Bagdad' has large flowers, with bright pink sepals and deep purple petals.

'Big Mama' has fat flowers of red sepals and purple petals.

'Blue Gown' is a dwarf form with scarlet calyces and deep purple corollas.

'Buttons and Bows' bears pink sepals surrounding folds of deep violet petals. Pink stamens protrude from the flowers.

California Dreamers is a collection of double trailing fuchsias from Euro-American. I have not trialed them and therefore cannot comment on their weather tolerance; however, they will be offered throughout most of the country. The collection consists of 'Bella Rosella' (rose flowers), 'Circus Spangles' (pink), 'Deep Purple', 'Eureka Red' (fire-engine red), 'Flamenco Dancer' (white and red), 'Peachy', 'Rocket Fire' (pink-purple), 'Royal Mosaic' (violet and rose), and 'Snowburner' (red and white).

'Dark Eyes' bears double red and violet flowers.

'Florabelle' is a seed-propagated F_1 hybrid that has enjoyed good success in baskets. Flowers are purple and red.

'Isis' provides plants with many very small-flowered rose-pink flowers.

'Sonata' has fat blooms consisting of white calyx and corolla flushed with pink.

'Swingtime' produces flowers with a rosy calyx and white petals. A seed-propagated form.

'Winston Churchill' has double red and lavender blossoms.

Variegated foliage

'Autumnale' provides leaves in gold, dull green, and russet tones, with purple to rose flowers. Foliage always seems to be changing color, particularly in the spring.

'Golden Marinka' has single red bell-shaped flowers and foliage variegated gold, red, and cream.

'Island Sunset' has leaves with white edges and red blooms.

'Sharpitor', a cultivar of *Fuchsia magellanica* var. *molinae*, has gray leaves edged in white. Flowers are pale pink.

'Sunray' has green-and-white variegated foliage, red sepals, and blue corollas.

'Versicolor' has gray-green leaves with a silver tint, edged white, and bright red variegation. The young leaves are red-purple in color. A selection of *Fuchsia magellanica*. Flowers are scarlet. Also sold as 'Tricolor'.

G

Gaillardia (gay lar' dee a)   blanket flower   Asteraceae

The genus was named for Gaillard de Charentoneau, an eighteenth-century French magistrate and patron of the botanical sciences. I often wonder why many native genera such as *Gaillardia* (all the approximately thirty species are native to North America, most to the southwestern United States) commemorate people from abroad. It turns out that *Gaillardia* was studied and named by French botanist Auguste Denis Fourgeroux (1732–1789), who then immortalized Monsieur de Charentoneau. Might have been worse—it could have been Charentonea or Fourgeroia.

Gaillardia is much better known as a group of fine perennials, particularly the popular *G.* ×*grandiflora*, one of the parents of which is the annual *G. pulchella*.

-pulchella (pul chel' a)   indian blanket, firewheels   1–2'/2'
    summer   red, yellow   United States, Mexico

This plant, also known as blanket flower, is a hairy annual, with 3–4" long leaves and many 2" balls of flowers on long flower stems. Flowering begins in late spring and continues to frost. The species is seldom seen in gardens, but several fine cultivars have enjoyed success. They are prone to leaf and root rot if summer rains and humidity are excessive or if drainage is poor. Like their perennial cousins, plants may be short-lived, flowering themselves to death, particularly in warm weather. Full sun, well-drained soils. Propagate by seed. Prepare to plant in spring and late summer.

CULTIVARS

'Lorenziana' is unusual with enlarged, quilled ray flowers and funnel-shaped disk flowers. The flower colors are red, yellow, or bicolored.

'Red Plume' is the best of the selections, bearing dozens of double brick-red flowers all summer. An All-America Selection in 1991.

'Yellow Plume' is a yellow version of 'Red Plume', not as well known but quite colorful.

'Yellow Sun' is likely the same as 'Yellow Plume'.

Alternative species

Gaillardia aestivalis var. *winkleri* (white firewheel) is an endangered species native to dry areas in Hardin County in southeastern Texas. They are characterized by flowers with deeply lobed white to magenta petals surrounding a yellow to purple eye. Plants grow 1–2' tall. I saw a beautiful population in the Endangered Species Garden at the Mercer Botanical Gardens, Humble, Texas. Unfortunately, plants are not available to gardeners, but seed may some day become available.

Additional reading

Lee, Rand B. 1998. Blanket flowers (*Gaillardia*). *American Cottage Gardener* 5(3):22.
Turner, B. L. 1979. *Gaillardia aestivalis* var. *winkleri* (Asteraceae): a white-flowered tetraploid taxon endemic to southeastern Texas. *Southwestern Naturalist* 24(4): 621–624.

Gazania (ga zay' nee a)   treasure flower   Asteraceae

The approximately sixteen species of this South African genus are best known as drought-tolerant bedding plants. Plants, usually only 6–12" tall, produce brilliantly colored daisy flowers throughout the season. Most material available from growers and retailers is of hybrid origin, with *Gazania rigens* as the dominant parent but with contributions from *G. linearis* and others. For differences among other South African daisies, see *Arctotis*.

-rigens (ree' jenz)   treasure flower   9–18"/18"
summer   many colors   South Africa

Nearly all the cultivars that involve this species consist of blooms with brown to black spots on the base of the ray flowers, making a dark ring around the disk. The flowers are held singly and borne on 4–6" long smooth peduncles. The leaves are also exceedingly handsome; the uppersides are green, and the undersides are often white and woolly. Some cultivars are white woolly on both sides, providing additional interest.

Without a doubt, some of the most brilliant daisies are to be found here, and I love them in the spring and early summer. They are not always carefree in the garden, however. They are drought-tolerant but not lovers of summer rains or humidity. The woolly leaves collect moisture, and if they don't dry out or if the excess water does not drain away, crown and root rots may occur. And the marvelous colors do not always persist throughout the growing season, a problem more common in the South than in the North.

Full sun, in raised beds, containers, or well-drained soils. Most cultivars, including hybrids, are raised from seed.

Gazania rigens Talent Mix   ASHA KAYS

CULTIVARS

'Aureo-Variegata' has lanceolate green leaves with yellow margins. The flowers are bright orange.

Chansonette series consists of a mix of compact 10–12″ tall plants with 2–2½″ wide flowers.

'Christopher Lloyd' has interesting rose-pink flowers with a green ring at the base.

'Cookie' has 2–3″ wide scarlet flowers with black centers over silvery foliage.

Daybreak series is among the most brilliant of this brilliant group of plants. 'Daybreak Bright Orange', 'Daybreak Garden Sun' (bright yellow), and 'Daybreak Red Stripe' (red stripes running down the deep yellow petals) have all received Fleuroselect awards. An outstanding series available in eight colors and a mixture.

'Dorothy' bears yellow flowers with narrow petals and black centers.

'Filigree' is different. Its orange to yellow blooms have narrow ray petals and are borne on long flower stems, and its attractive silver foliage is highly divided.

'Freddy' has rose flowers with a green ring. The plants form 12–15″ mounds of compact foliage and flowers.

Harlequin series is a tall form (up to 18″) with large flowers in flashy tones of yellow, orange, pink, and red.

Klondyke series is a mixture of colors on 12–14″ plants.

'Lolita' produces narrow silvery foliage and bright yellow flowers. The leaves also have narrow white margins.

Mini-Star series offers short, compact plants with bright 2″ flowers. 'Mini-Star Tangerine' was both an All-America Selection (1985) and a Fleuroselect award winner. 'Mini-Star Yellow' was also the recipient of a Fleuroselect award. White flowers ('Mini-Star White') are also available.

'Moonlight' is green on the uppersides of the leaves and produces excellent yellow flowers with a black ring at the base of the ray flowers.

'Northbourne' has leaves similar to 'Lolita' but with orange flowers with black rings.

'Orange Beauty' appears to have a good deal of *Gazania linearis* in the parentage, bearing pure orange flowers over green leaves.

'Silverlight' has narrow silver foliage and bright yellow single flowers.

Sundance series is an eye-catching mix of blooms with stripes on the ray flowers. About 12″ tall.

'Sundrop' is a compact selection with silver foliage and bright yellow flowers.

Sunshine series is a mix of 3″ wide flowers. Plants are about 12″ tall and feature cream, yellow, orange, pink, and red flowers.

Talent Mix is a beautiful group of plants. The foliage is as handsome as the flowers, obviously silver-green on both sides. Several flower colors are present in the mix, and 'Talent Yellow' is available as a single color.

'Torquay Silver' bears single orange flowers and silver foliage.

var. *uniflora* has silver to white lanceolate leaves and pure yellow flowers. Flowers are smaller than the species but equally handsome.

'Variegata' has leaves variegated gold and cream, with orange flowers. 'Waterlily' is a favorite of mine, with dozens of large creamy white flowers on green foliage.

Alternative species

Gazania linearis (lin ee ar' is; syn. *G. longiscapa*) has shorter more pointed leaves crowded at the apices of the stems. The leaves are slightly hairy above, white-woolly beneath, and often with inrolled margins. Plants have a mounded habit, and they can make excellent ground covers. The flowers are golden yellow, usually without the dark disk at the base of the ray flowers. 'Peggy's Pet' forms wonderful mounds of green-silver foliage and yellow flowers poking out on all sides. A double-flowered form, 'Flore-plena', is occasionally grown.

Geranium (jer ay' nee um)   Geraniaceae

Most plants grown as geraniums are the bedding plant species and scented forms of *Pelargonium*. Those we call geraniums are generally grown as perennials, and many a person has gone through a geranium stage of life in their evolution as a gardener. But being a collector of useful annual geraniums is quite simple, there are so few worth cultivating. The native species *Geranium robertianum* (ro ber tee ay' num; herb robert) is a reasonably good plant, but I cannot get past its weedy leaves and wild-looking flowers. Some people love them, and it is easy enough for those to gather seeds from the wild (a good dump is a fine place to explore) and plant them among other wildings.

I really do love spotted geranium, *Geranium maculatum* (mak yew lay' tum), probably our best native perennial form. Normally its flowers are lavender, but white and rose varieties can also be found. I seldom see spotted geraniums in garden centers. Look for them in native mail-order catalogs or in the gardens of geranium enthusiasts. They are tolerant of shady locations, reseed themselves readily, and should be tried more often, regardless of whether you consider them annual or perennial.

| *-incanum* (in ka' num) | geranium | 1–2'/2' |
| summer | pink | South Africa |

This fine bushy species has wonderful ferny foliage that is green above, whitish beneath, and slightly fragrant. The leaves are cut into five linear divisions with linear lobes and teeth; all divisions and segments are very thin, less than $1/8''$ wide. The pink to light lavender flowers, each with a white eye, measure $1\frac{1}{2}''$ across and occur in late summer, continuing for many weeks. Flowers are held in few-flowered inflorescences or singly. Quite lovely when weather is cool, but they can look tired in hot summers. Well worth a try, however: the take-home message is that even when not in flower, this plant will not disappoint with its delicate foliage.

Full sun in the North, a little afternoon shade in the South. Propagate by
seed or cuttings.

CULTIVARS

'Sugar Plum' has an obvious white eye in the blue to purple flowers.

Alternative species

Geranium robustum, another native of South Africa, bears three to seven finely
divided leaves, silvery above and below. The pale purple flowers have a white
base and are held in a many-flowered inflorescence. 'Frances Grate' is a 16–20"
tall hybrid between the two species with violet-blue flowers and handsome silvery foliage.

Gerbera (ger' ber a)   Transvaal daisy   Asteraceae

Gerberas are among the most popular cut flowers produced by European and
American greenhouses; they have been bred for long stems, and their semi-double brilliantly colored flowers are bought in florist shops all over the country. Of
the forty species, the gerbera daisies most often seen are cultivars of *Gerbera
jamesonii* or hybrids between it and *G. viridifolia*. These plants are stemless; all
produce foliage in a basal rosette, giving rise to a naked flower stem. The 2' long
leaves are usually entire, but may be dentate or lobed. The flowers are usually
semi-double and in shades of yellow, orange, dark red, white, or pink. The disk
flowers are dark brown to black.

As garden plants, they are outstanding in some years and awful in others.
They are susceptible to leaf spots and root rots in beds that remain wet during
rainy periods. They do produce dozens of flowers, however, and if cultivars are
selected for garden use, not cut flowers, some beautiful flowers will result. The
F_1 hybrids, all raised from seed, deliver the best garden performance. They are
generally compact and shorter than those selected for cut flowers; their flower
stems remain upright, rather than flopping around like a fish on a hook every
time it rains.

CULTIVARS

Festival series is 10–12" tall and produces 4" wide daisy flowers. Breeders
have produced thirteen separate colors, but they are often available as a mix.

Gigi Mix is a mixture of 3' long cut flowers with 3" wide flowers in five or so
bright colors.

Happipot Mix was among the first F_1 hybrids for pot use and landscape performance. Flowers are about 3" wide and grow 12–14" tall.

Mardi Gras series bears 4–5" wide semi-double flowers in four colors. Good
for garden use.

Masquerade series consists of 4" wide daisy flowers with dark centers in five
colors. The best for outdoor performance.

Gerbera jamesonii
CHRIS JOHNSON

Gilia (gil′ ee a)

Polemoniaceae

I am not sure why so few gilias are offered to the gardener. Perhaps it is because most hail from dry, desert habitats in the southwestern United States and southern South America. At one time or another, most genera in the family Polemoniaceae were lumped under *Gilia*, and even with those species now in *Collomia* and *Ipomopsis* removed, *Gilia* is still a bewildering genus—depending on the reference you pick up, the number of species is anywhere from twenty-five to a hundred.

When gilias are grown, it is for their finely divided foliage and tight clusters of flowers, usually blue, but also in lavender and white. The only species I know, and not particularly well, is *Gilia lepantha* (le pan′ tha), an 8–14″ tall blue-flowered form that flowers in the spring. The finely pinnately divided leaves are handsome prior to flowering, and the clusters of flowers cover most of the foliage for many weeks.

Afternoon rains and poorly drained soils are to be avoided; only one you can do something about. If humidity and rain are a problem, plants may decline in mid summer.

Full sun, propagate by seed *in situ*.

Glaucium (glo' kee um)   horned poppy   Papaveraceae

Approximately twenty-five species occur in this genus, many of them annual or biennial, and a few, such as *Glaucium flavum*, true perennials. The generic name comes from the Greek, *glaukos* ("gray-green"), a reference to the foliage color, and indeed, for most gardeners, the color of the foliage is the most handsome part of many of the species. The sap is yellow and the roots are poisonous. The striking horn-like seed pods have given rise to the common name.

I enjoy all the flowers of this genus, but they are troublesome in warm, humid summers. Full sun or afternoon shade is recommended and good drainage is a must. Beautiful foliage, handsome flowers; marginal performance unless cool and dry.

-*corniculatum* (kor nik yew lay' tum)   red horned poppy   2–2½'/2'
   summer   red   Europe, SW Asia

This species is considered biennial, but if plants are put in early in the spring, they will flower without a cold treatment. Flowers are 2½" wide, with two sepals and four petals, spotted red or orange at the base; they are often red but may be orange or yellow as well. The hairy gray-green leaves are pinnately divided, each division narrowly oblong. Plants are hardy to about zone 7, and easily propagated from seed at 65–70°F in humid conditions.

Glechoma (glay ko' ma)   Lamiaceae

To some gardeners, this genus represents nothing more than obnoxious weeds; others see indispensable plants for containers and baskets. There may be twelve species, but only the European *Glechoma hederacea* (ground ivy) is ever cultivated. This species is a creeper and rhizomatous, speedily moving along the ground, forming mats of green. The opposite leaves are 1–1½" long held on 2" long petioles attached to the squarish stems. Plants form small violet, pink, or occasionally white flowers in four- to six-flowered whorls in the leaf axils.

Gardeners seldom purchase the green species, although if a green ground cover is desired, this works just fine. With common names like alehoof, field balm, gill-over-the-ground, and runaway robin, it is pretty obvious that these are movers and shakers. If plants overwinter (zones 7 to 10), it will be either a terrific plant or a fast-spreading weed. Plant in full sun, although plants tolerate shade well, and water well.

CULTIVARS

'Variegata', by far the most popular form, has gained exceptional acceptance as the use of containers has become more common. The green leaves have broken edges and zones of white and silver throughout. Used as a trailer for containers and baskets.

Globba (glo′ ba)

This genus offers plants for the person who likes to garden on the edge—they are fascinating, romantic, and weird, at least to gardeners outside the Deep South. Like other members of the ginger family, *Globba* provides a tropical look, interesting foliage, and a promise of colorful flowers that, for most of us, remains unfulfilled. Plants grow from slender rhizomes and produce alternate 8″ long leaves on a reed-like stem. Flowers consist of showy bracts around small flowers in a pendulous raceme. Approximately seventy species are known; two or three are available as garden plants, propagated through tissue culture. Most are hardy to zone 9, with protection to zone 8. I have the same opinion of globbas and orchids: they are better for greenhouse culture and look good only when in flower.

-*marantina* (ma ran tee′ na)	yellow dancing lady	2–3′/2′
late summer	yellow	SE Asia

This species (syn. *Globba bulbifera*, *G. schomburgkii*) bears 10–15″ long elliptical leaves that are softly hairy beneath. The 3″ long inflorescence starts erect, then becomes pendulous as the flowers open. Flowers consist of ¾″ pale green bracts surrounding fleshy yellow flowers. The lips of the flowers are spotted orange or red at the base. Numerous small bulbils are formed in lowermost bracts of the flowers, which may be removed for propagation purposes.

Gardeners in moderate climates should use this species in containers, which can be easily removed in the fall for overwintering in a frost-free place. The containers may be freestanding or planted in the garden. Plants are not at all ornamental when not in flower; place them where they can be admired if flowers do occur, but treat them as a green filler otherwise.

Plants need copious moisture, high humidity, and indirect light. Plant in shady conditions, with a few hours of direct sun, for the best-looking plants. Propagate from bulbils in the flowers.

-*winitii* (win it′ ee i)	dancing ladies	1–3′/2′
late summer	mauve	Thailand

This is the most common globba on the market, which is not saying much; nevertheless, several cultivars are available to the gardener. The lanceolate leaves are about 8″ long with a heart-shaped base, attached to the stem by 3–4″ long petioles. The inflorescence is pendent, consisting of 1½″ long-lasting pink to mauve bracts around small yellow flowers.

It is fun to watch the ladies dance, and if you can find a globba or two, give them a try. Gardeners in Florida, the Gulf states, and southern California will find they can be both fun and extraordinarily beautiful. Temperate gardeners should consult my cultural comments for *Globba marantina*.

'Blushing Maid' is about 2' tall, with pendulous flowers consisting of white bracts around yellow flowers. The leaves are bronze on the undersides.

'Pristine Pink' has pink bracts surrounding the yellow flowers.

'Ruby Queen' produces flowers consisting of red bracts and yellow flowers.

'White Dragon' has white bracts and yellow flowers.

Additional reading

Chapman, Timothy. 1995. *Ornamental Gingers*. 6920 Bayou Paul Rd., St. Gabriel, LA 70776.

San Felasco Nurseries: www.sanfelasco.com

Stokes Tropicals: www.stokestropicals.com

Wight Nurseries of North Carolina: www.wightnurseries.com

Gloriosa (glor ee o' sa)   glory lily   Liliaceae

The glory lilies are glorious, no doubt about it, but they are for the most part denizens of conservatories and botanical gardens. Perhaps their popularity in gardens is limited because they are difficult to locate, expensive to buy, resentful of transplantation, and toxic to boot. The genus consists of but one species, *Gloriosa superba*, which arises from a hefty tuber. Plants are deciduous climbers, clinging and climbing by tendrils. The ovate glossy green leaves may be alternate, opposite, or whorled and are pointed at the tips. The 3–4″ long flowers, which are formed in the leaf axils on long pedicels, are nothing if not showy. The six wavy spreading tepals (sepals and petals together) are upright, their tips gently reflexed (bending) inwards. They may be bicolored or a single hue. The rest of the floral parts complement the distinctive tepals. The six stamens and single pistil at the base of the tepals resemble flared legs supporting a colorful table. Flowering occurs as plants mature, which is generally not until late summer or fall if young plants are placed in the garden.

As the roots of the tuber are quite brittle, care must be taken when transplanting to the garden. Alternatively, pot the tubers in containers and plunge the container in the garden. That way, it may be removed easily in the fall, if overwintering is in the plan. Withhold water in the fall as temperatures fall, and place the dried tuber in a dry, frost-free room.

Full sun, well-drained soils. Provide a shrub or other support. Water plentifully and feed with a dilute fertilizer solution in the spring. Seed propagation is not difficult.

CULTIVARS

'Abyssinica' has 2–3″ long smooth red tepals with gold bands down the center and golden base. Not as vigorous as most other cultivars.

'Carsonii' has purple-red tepals, yellow toward the centers. The tepals are wavy and strongly reflexed.

'Citrina' bears beautiful lemon-yellow tepals.

'Grandiflora' bears deep orange to scarlet tepals with yellow margins.

'Rothschildiana', once known as *Gloriosa rothschildiana*, is the largest, best, and best-known cultivar, with vigorous fast-growing stems. The 3–4″ long tepals are scarlet, yellow at the base and with a central stripe, strongly recurved.

'Superba' bears narrow tepals, deeply waved and reflexed, in deep orange and red.

'Verschuurii' has crimson undulated tepals that are yellow at the margins.

Gomphrena (gom free′ na)   Amaranthaceae

Plants of this genus, in the same family as *Celosia* and *Amaranthus*, are characterized by their dozens of tiny flowers held in colorful inflorescences throughout the growing season. These are excellent plants for heat, seemingly springing from the hottest places on earth. Or as Frank Arnosky of Texas Specialty Cut Flowers explains it, perhaps there is a "hell on earth."

> *Gomphrena* likes it hot because it originally grew in Hades's garden at the gates of hell. Hades kidnapped Persephone, the daughter of Demeter, while she was out picking flowers (of course). Zeus worked out a compromise to get Persephone back for at least half of the year (summer). Hades was none too happy about it. He decided to curse Demeter, the goddess of agriculture and fertility, by sending gomphrena seeds up with Persephone. Of course they grew like hell, and since then, all of us who farm flowers for a living share in Hades's curse. *Gomphrena* grows best here in Texas because our climate most closely matches that of [its] native environment.

Gomphrena is one of the best-known ornamental genera of the family, tough and colorful, and *G. globosa* is by far the best known of its approximately ninety species.

-globosa (glo bo′ sa)   globe amaranth   1–3′/1′
    summer   many colors   Central America

When someone asks me to recommend a tough plant that will tolerate heat and abuse, and still be colorful, I ask them if they have heard of globe amaranth. This species has been on the garden scene for a long time, having come over to this country with some of the first settlers. It has undergone many transformations in form and function: the taller forms are valuable for fresh and dried cut flowers; the dwarf ones fit well into landscapes and gardens.

Plants consist of opposite 3–4″ long, 1–1½″ wide leaves, entire, lanceolate, slightly hairy, and almost sessile. Dissecting a flower spike is an interesting exercise for plant nerds on a rainy day. At the base of the spike are a couple of small ovate leaves, which are easily seen and removed. Dozens of small flowers make up the spherical inflorescence, each one consisting of five tepals and subtended by two broad leafy bracts. The entire conglomeration is held together in a colorful inflorescence, produced at the end of the stems as well as in the leaf axils. Interesting exercise, but perhaps it's not worth wasting even a rainy day making a mess in the kitchen when you can be outside making a mess in the garden.

Plants are tough and available in enough colors and heights to fit most garden needs. Plant in full sun, provide sufficient water when young, and deadhead occasionally. Easily propagated by seed in the spring. If plants look a little tired, reseed in mid summer for fall flowering.

CULTIVARS

'Bicolor Rose' is among the best cultivars I have trialed, producing dozens of rose-pink heads on 2' tall plants. An excellent selection.

Buddy series grows only 9–15" tall. Plants are available in four or so colors. Susceptible to leaf spot diseases, at least in my experience.

Gnome series is a better, more consistent group than the older Buddy series. Equally dwarf and colorful, good for containers and gardens.

'Strawberry Fields' is among the finest globe amaranths on the market. The vigor of its strong upright stems and its striking strawberry-red color make it very popular with fresh and dried cut flower growers. About 12–18" tall.

Woodcreek series (Qis series) arose from Woodcreek Farms in Ohio and consists of lavender, orange, pink, purple, red, rose, and white blooms on 2' tall upright plants.

Alternative species

Gomphrena haageana (hay gee an' a) is 2–2½' tall and produces lanceolate leaves about ½" across that are often six times as long as wide. The plants used to be called *G. aurantiaca* and *G. coccinea*, referring to the common yellow and red flowers of the species. Not as much choice as *G. globosa* but as easy to grow. Propagate by seed.

Graptophyllum (grap to fil' um)   Acanthaceae

This genus consists of about ten species, all with beautifully marked foliage. The name comes from the Greek, *grapho* ("to write") and *phyllon* ("leaf"), alluding to the handsome leaves. Plants, which had been confined to conservatories in the past, are fast gaining converts among gardeners everywhere for their ease of growth, colorful foliage, and tolerance of heat and humidity. The species most commonly grown is *Graptophyllum pictum* and its fine cultivars.

-pictum (pik' tum)	caricature plant	2–4'/2'
summer	foliage	SE Pacific

I really like these plants for several reasons. They grow reasonably quickly but don't pour out of their growing spaces. They are unaffected by heat and humid-

Graptophyllum pictum 'Chocolate' ASHA KAYS

ity yet grow nicely, albeit more slowly, in cool summers. They provide excellent foliage color the entire season without any maintenance to speak of, and bugs and spores seem to stay clear. The scarlet to purple-red tubular flowers are attractive but generally seen only in the conservatory in the winter months. Plants are used as annuals in cold zones and pruned into hedges in the tropics.

So where is this plant? Why is it not more common? For a start, it is a slow grower and not a coleus. It requires more heat, so few growers want to try it. And so few gardeners know it, they don't buy it even when it *is* grown—the classic Catch-22 of new crops. Difficulties in propagation have also kept it an uncommon offering. All these challenges, although not insurmountable, will likely keep the plants in the hard-to-find category. That they are slightly off-the-wall is what makes some of these little-known plants so treasured.

The leathery oval to elliptical foliage is opposite and entire. The species has glossy green leaves irregularly blotched or marbled cream in the center of the leaves. The small scarlet to purple-red flowers are held in terminal racemes, but

I have never seen them while plants have been growing outdoors in the summer. Just as well, as they are not needed for color.

They tolerate considerable shade, as demonstrated by their sales as houseplants, but should be planted in full sun for best color. Propagate by terminal cuttings. Rooting can be slow, requiring three to four weeks, particularly the selection 'Tricolor'.

CULTIVARS

'Black Beauty' produces foliage that is almost completely deep purple to black.

'Chocolate' ('Lurido-sanguineum') has purple leaves with creamy to pink central veins running down the leaves. My favorite.

'Tricolor' bears green leaves mottled yellow and pink. Both this and 'Chocolate' are Athens Select plants.

Gypsophila (jip sa' fil a)   Caryophyllaceae

The perennial *Gypsophila paniculata* (baby's breath) may be found in every florist and bouquet, tempering raucous reds and stomach-wrenching oranges, and the alpine *G. repens* works wonders in rock gardens everywhere. But let us not forget the classy plants offered by two annual species, *G. elegans* and *G. muralis*.

Quick guide to *Gypsophila* species

	Height	Branching	Flower color
G. elegans	18–30"	moderately	white, rose
G. muralis	6–12"	strongly	pink

-elegans (el' e ganz)	annual baby's breath	12–16"/12"
summer	white, rose	Caucasus

The species has dark green lanceolate leaves on erect stems. The plants tend to branch in the upper parts only, producing clouds of flowers above the foliage. They are occasionally used as cut flowers by professional growers and can be cut out of the garden as well. The single flowers are usually white, with subtle pink or purple veins but rose, pink, and carmine flowers have also been bred by hybridizers. The many flowers are held in compound inflorescences (panicles) on long slender flower stalks.

Plants make a terrific show all summer, if temperatures do not climb above 85°F for a prolonged period. They tend to melt out in high humidity and heat. Plants are lime lovers and will persist longer if lime is added to the area of the garden in which they are to be planted. Those in raised beds or in rock gardens are more tolerant of abusive conditions.

Full sun to partial shade, propagate by seed.

'Carminea' ('Kermesina') has carmine-rose flowers on 1½–2½' tall plants.

'Covent Garden' is the best-known cultivar and bears large single white flowers on 2–2½' tall plants.

'Red Cloud' produces rose to carmine flowers.

'Rosea' has pale pink flowers.

-*muralis* (mer al′ is)	annual baby's breath	6–12″/12″
summer	pink	Europe

Gypsophila muralis differs from *G. elegans* in several ways: its stature is smaller, its habit is mounded rather than erect, and it has many more flowers. The linear dark green leaves are carried on strongly branched stems, resulting in a handsome mound. Flowers sit in showy clouds above the foliage.

The lack of recognition this small-flowered species suffered changed when flower breeders introduced a couple of vigorous growers with relatively large flowers. I trialed these two in the Georgia heat and humidity, assuming they would keel over at the first hint of bad weather. I was pleasantly surprised by both forms, which flowered for three to four months. Eventually, the triple barrels of heat, humidity, and afternoon thunderstorms caught up with them, but I have no trouble recommending them to southern gardeners as well as those in the rest of the country. They don't appear to be as lime-loving as most other species of *Gypsophila*. Excellent for containers and mixed baskets.

Full sun to partial shade. Keep out of afternoon sun in the South. Propagate by seed.

CULTIVARS

'Garden Bride' is about 10″ tall and bears handsome single light pink flowers, ⅛″ wide and often blotched with white. Very nice.

'Gypsy' is a double-flowered form of 'Garden Bride', with larger flowers (¼″ wide) and a more compact growth habit. Even better. An All-America Selection in 1997.

Quick key to *Gypsophila* species

A. Plant >15″ tall, erect habit, leaves lanceolate . . . . *G. elegans*

AA. Plant <15″ tall, mounded habit, leaves narrowly linear . . . . *G. muralis*

H

Hamelia (ha may' lee a) Rubiaceae

Named for French botanist and author Henri Louis du Hamel de Monceau (1700–1782), the genus consists of about forty species of tropical shrubs and small trees. The only one seen in cultivation as an annual in this country is the showy *Hamelia patens* (Texas firebush), which lights up the landscape in late summer and fall.

-patens (pa' tenz)	Texas firebush	3–4'/3'
summer	scarlet	tropics

I first saw *Hamelia patens* planted in containers on a sidewalk near the entrance of a building. It was still like an oven in San Antonio that October, and the sidewalk and surrounding building were even hotter, yet the abundant scarlet blossoms were flowering their heads off. The plants were actually enjoying themselves. They had obviously been flowering for a long time: the containers were full, and black to purple berries were numerous. I was a relative rookie to the heat, having come from Montreal, and I figured I had to try these things in Athens, a veritable oasis of cool compared to San Antonio. And I did.

In their native habitat, plants are small trees, growing up to 20' tall, but otherwise shrubby in habit, producing woody stems and four-sided branches as they mature. Perennial in Louisiana, south Florida, and south Texas, the species returns each year and is a popular landscape plant. The pointed leaves are 4–6" long, 2–3" wide, and handsome with their pinkish veins and red petioles; they are three- to five-whorled, sometimes opposite, and hairy beneath. The plant really comes into its own when the tubular scarlet flowers begin to appear in terminal flat-topped 3–5" wide inflorescences (cymes). The individual flowers are about 1" long, consisting of five sepals and a tubular corolla with five short lobes and five stamens; when present, they can be seen across a football field, and every hummingbird knows exactly when to visit. After flowering come scarlet berries, which turn black as they mature. These too are loved by all sorts of birds.

These plants love heat, which may be why they have not made it into garden jargon outside the most southern climes. Most annuals, from impatiens to zinnias, benefit from heat; after all most are native to warm areas of the world. But Texas firebush would not flower, even in Athens, until late summer, when temperatures had heated up to the point where even the dogs wouldn't go outside. This is good for the landscape but bad for the grower, who has to spend so much for heat just to get the plants to grow, and without growers to produce them, it is difficult to find the plants. Our best success occurred in containers placed outside the greenhouse door, where the sun beat down and heat reflected up from the sidewalk below. These are spectacular plants but won't flower well or for a long time in the North.

Plant in full sun. Pinch in early summer as soon as vigorous growth occurs; planting specimens in containers is a good way to keep their height under control. Propagate by terminal cuttings.

Alternative species

Hamelia ventricosa (ven trih ko′ sa) is a shrub or small tree with pointed smooth whorled leaves and yellow flowers. The tubular flowers are about 1½″ long and held in few-flowered inflorescences. Not as floriferous nor as spectacular as *H. patens*, but its handsome foliage is a nice change.

Additional reading

Armitage, Allan M. 1995. Photoperiod, irradiance and temperature influence flowering of *Hamelia patens* (Texas firebush). *HortScience* 30(2):255–256.

Helianthus (he lee an′ hus)   sunflower   Asteraceae

Although there are many more perennial species of *Helianthus* than there are annual, it was the annual sunflower that came into its own in the 1990s, appearing at florists everywhere and adorning coffee mugs and T-shirts as if no other flower existed. If you are fortunate enough to drive by a sunflower field in the Midwest or Europe, it is almost impossible not to stop and stare and set up an easel yourself. Was this all van Gogh's fault, or were we simply a little slow to catch on? The centenary of his death in 1990, combined with the introduction of "pollenless" F_1 hybrids from Japan around that time, jump-started interest in and mass sales of sunflowers as cut flowers. The lack of pollen shedding made the flower much more attractive to department stores, mail-order sources, and high-end designers, who no longer had to worry about messy pollen shed.

-annuus (an′ yew us)   annual sunflower   3–10′/3′
summer   yellow   western United States

By far the most common sunflower, *Helianthus annuus* is grown by the acre for birdseed, oil, and the flowers themselves, as well as enjoyed by gardeners throughout the world. It requires nothing but sun and water and provides

Helianthus annuus   ASHA KAYS

months of pleasure for little input. (If only people were more like sunflowers.) Without doubt, sunflowers can look awful once flowering is completed, particularly the big-faced ones; simply toss them out and reseed a few more.

Plants can grow to 10′ in height, but most cultivars are 3–7′, with a sandpapery stem and alternate leaves. The three-nerved leaves are rough-hairy, broadly oval to heart-shaped and coarsely toothed. The flowers consist of wide disks of purple or red, surrounded by yellow ray flowers. Flowers on some of the taller forms are so large and so heavy that it is too much to ask that the stems support themselves—a definite drawback to "bigger is better." Stalking is difficult and a pain in the derrière, and tall forms should be avoided by gardeners unless cut flowers are the reason for including them. Of course, you may plant the tall ones to challenge the world record, held since 1986 by a certain M. Heijmf, a fellow from Oirschot, the Netherlands, whose plant towered 25', 5½". All things being equal, I prefer the intermediate and short forms—heck, even the dwarf forms provide excellent cut flowers and also fit in the vases I keep in the cupboard. The height of plants, the color of the ray flowers, and the size of the flowers help to distinguish the dozens of cultivars out there.

Full sun, propagate by seed. Do not sow seeds too early indoors: plants will get leggy and never recover. In-ground sowing is best. Fertilize about a week after planting, or after plants are about 2' tall. Fertilize every ten days thereafter.

CULTIVARS

Tall forms (>5')
Excellent for cut flowers or the back of the garden, these often require staking.

'Chianti' bears 4" wide pollenless flowers on branched plants. The blooms are maroon and red, flecked with gold.

'Crimson Thriller' has a great name and is a huge thing. Orange-red ray flowers around a big black disk.

'Evening Sun' sports 8–10" wide flowers with red rays and dark maroon rings surrounding a dark center.

'Full Sun' bears golden yellow 6–7" wide flowers with black disks.

'Indian Blanket' has bicolor flowers of wine and lemon-yellow. Plants are 5–6' tall.

'Lemon Queen' provides creamy pale yellow ray flowers around a large brown disk. Plants branch well, forming many additional flowers. A lovely color.

'Mammoth Russian' is definitely mammoth, a blue-ribbon contender at the local fair. The yellow flowers are up to 10" across on 7' tall plants.

'Moonbright' has lemon-yellow flowers and a brown disk. Flowers are 6–7" across; they don't produce pollen, making them exceptional cut flowers.

'Moonshine' bears lemon-yellow flowers with a large black eye.

'Red Sun' produces large red flowers on 5' tall stems.

'Sunbeam' bears 5–6" wide golden yellow flowers around chartreuse-green disks. Pollenless and terrific.

'Sunbright' has bright yellow flowers around dark brown centers, otherwise similar to 'Sunbeam'. Pollenless.

'Sun Goddess' produces very large (8–10" wide) flowers consisting of golden yellow rays around a chocolate-brown center.

'Sungold' is a terrific golden yellow double-flowered form. I am not partial to double flowers, but I found this to be an excellent cultivar with strong stems and exquisite flowers. If you like double-flowered sunflowers, this one is worth seeking out. Also sold as 'Giant Sungold'.

'Sunrich Lemon' and 'Sunrich Orange' are 5–6' tall single-stem forms, extremely useful for cut flowers. The blooms are about 7" across and pollenless.

'Taiyo' is another large and large-flowered form, with 8' tall plants boasting 10" wide flowers. The flowers have short orange-yellow rays surrounding a wide brown disk.

'Titanic' is a double-flowered sunflower with a small dark disk. Plants grow 5–6' tall. May be the same as 'Sungold'.

'Velvet Queen' has deep velvety red flowers with dark centers on 5' tall plants. One of the better reds.

Intermediate forms (3–5')
Excellent for cut flowers or mid to back of garden.

'Del Sol' grows about 4' tall and produces many 5–6" wide yellow flowers with a black center.

'Floristan' has 5–6" wide flowers with unique bicolored ray flowers, burgundy at the base and light yellow at the tips. The center is burgundy with gold stamens. Branched, about 5' tall. Quite an eyeful.

'Helios' bears double lemon-yellow flowers with a small interior eye.

'Holiday' is another of the branching forms, with 6–8" wide golden yellow flowers.

'Ikarus' is about 4' tall, similar to 'Valentine' but with slightly brighter yellow flowers.

'Monet' is a bit wild-looking, as befitting the great garden of the man. Single yellow flowers.

'Moonwalker' produces branching plants with many flowers per stem. Blooms consist of lemon-yellow rays around a dark chocolate center.

'Orange Sun' is similar to 'Helios'.

Prado is a highly uniform series, with 4–5" flowers of either red or golden yellow. Pollenless.

'Sonya' bears tangerine-orange 4" wide flowers with dark centers on 3–4' tall plants.

'Soraya' is a multibranching form with bright orange flowers.

'Sun King' is another double-flowered orange form, about 4' tall.

'Tangina' produces 4" wide gold-orange ray flowers around a dark disk. Plants are 3–4' tall.

'Valentine' is well branched, seldom needing staking. The 6" wide lemon-yellow rays surround a dark center. My favorite intermediate.

Short forms (<3')
Excellent for containers or interplanted in the garden.

'Big Smile' is about 2½' tall with 5–6" wide single golden yellow flowers. Disks are burgundy.

'Elf' is 16–20" tall with 4" wide yellow flowers.

'Moonshadow' is only about 1' tall with 4" wide pale yellow ray flowers around a brown center. Pollenless.

'Music Box' is a mixture of yellow to mahogany colors on 2–3' tall plants. Multibranched with many flowers.

'Pacino' has 4–5" wide yellow flowers with pale centers.

'Sundance Kid' produces 4–6" wide yellow to bronze flowers.

'Sunspot' is a dwarf form of the van Gogh sunflower, growing 2–3' tall. Flowers are yellow and up to 6" wide.

'Teddy Bear' bears 3–5" wide yellow flowers. This plant with the cute name provides a nice balance of double-flowered form and dwarf habit.

Alternative species

Helianthus argophyllus (ar ga' fil us; silver-leaf sunflower) is usually sold as 'Silver Leaf'. It is native to Texas and Florida but was introduced from Japan and has become a favorite for those who are looking for something a little different. The multibranched plant really does have wonderful silver-gray leaves. The 4–5″ wide yellow flowers with brown disks are formed at the end of each branch. This terrific plant should be grown more often.

Helianthus debilis (dih bil' is; cucumber-leaved sunflower) differs from *H. annuus* by having more branches at the base and more slender stems. Plants are hairy throughout, and the branches are often mottled with purple or white. Flowers are generally 2–4″ across. Native to Texas and westward. 'Italian White' is the best-known form and bears ivory-white to light primrose 4″ wide flowers. The rays contrast well with the dark centers. Plants grow 5–7′ tall.

Additional reading

Poncavage, Joanna. 1997. Grow the sunniest flowers of all. *Organic Gardening* 44(5):26–31.

Rice, Graham. 1996. Rays of sunshine. *The Garden* 121(8):495.

Shepherd, Renee. 1998. Annual sunflowers. *Horticulture* 95(2):53–54.

Helichrysum (he lee kris' um)   strawflower   Asteraceae

This large genus of more than 500 species from South Africa and Australia is among the most diverse, containing some of the best-known plants for the arranger, the collector of potpourri, the herbalist, and the gardener. But taxonomic rumblings have been rolling over *Helichrysum*: some authorities have placed the Australian members, including the popular paper daisy (*H. bracteatum*), in a separate genus, *Bracteantha*, while the popular rosemary strawflower (*H. rosmarinifolium*) has been transferred to *Ozothamnus*.

Quick guide to *Helichrysum* species

	Everlasting	Silvery foliage	Use
H. ambiguum	no	yes	container, garden
H. argyrophyllum	no	yes	container, garden
H. bracteatum	yes	yes	cut flower, potpourri, garden
H. italicum	no	yes	garden, herb
H. petiolare	no	yes	basket, container
H. splendidum	no	yes	container, garden

-*bracteatum* (brak tee a´ tum)   paper daisy   1–3´/2´
    summer   many colors   Australia

Want to see a face come alive? Simply introduce someone to a real live strawflower (syn. *Bracteantha bracteata*). The first touch always inspires wide eyes and profound responses like "neat" and "geez." The flower head consists mostly of glossy papery bracts; that is the dried straw one feels. The actual soft flowers are much smaller than the bracts and are seldom even noticed. The flower heads are solitary and 2–3˝ across. The 4–5˝ long alternate leaves are oblong to lanceolate and usually pointed at the end.

Many cultivars have been developed, mostly from seed, but more and more are being produced vegetatively. All require full sun and well-drained soils. Too much shade results in lanky plants, and wet soils result in a higher incidence of root rots.

CULTIVARS

'Blushing Beauty' has pink-tipped cream-colored flowers with orange centers. Plants grow 12–15˝ tall. Vegetatively propagated.

Bright Bikini series bears 2½˝ wide double flowers in many colors on 12–18˝ tall plants. The flower centers are generally yellow. Seed-propagated.

Chico series grows 12–15˝ tall and produces 2˝ wide double flowers in orange, pink, red, white, and yellow. Seed-propagated.

Helichrysum bracteatum
CHRIS JOHNSON

Florabella series consists of 2–3′ tall strawflowers in pink, gold, lemon, and white. Good form, good colors, good plants.

'Gold on Bronze' is vegetatively propagated and grows about 2′ tall. It is loaded with gold and bronze flowers. Outstanding.

'Golden Beauty' is big and robust, with large bright golden yellow flowers.

'Lemon Blush' bears single lemon-yellow flowers with orange centers on 16–20″ tall plants. Vegetatively propagated.

'Matilda Yellow', among the best of the vegetative forms, grows about 12″ tall with bright yellow double flowers.

Monstrosum series has large 2½″ wide flowers in orange, purple, white, red, and rose. Plants grow 3–3½′ tall. Seed-propagated.

'Silver Bush' is a 16–20″ tall vegetative form with single white flowers on orange centers.

Sundaze series comes from Australia and grows about 14″ tall, with flowers of bronze-gold, golden yellow, lemon-yellow, pink, and white. Quite compact.

'Sunray' has large semi-double golden yellow flowers on 2–3′ tall plants. As it is too big for most greenhouse operators, this vegetative cultivar will be difficult to find.

Tom Thumb Mix consists of 12″ tall plants in a mixture of bronze, crimson, pink, white, and yellow.

'Yellow Beauty' is similar to 'Golden Beauty' but with slightly more yellow in the flowers.

-italicum (ih ta′ lih kum)	curry plant	15–24″/2′
late summer	yellow	southern Europe

Want to see a nose come alive? Simply introduce someone to a real live curry plant. (Isn't this genus the easiest one to explain?) The plant that smells just like the curry that fills the air at your favorite Indian restaurant is actually *Helichrysum italicum* subsp. *serotinum*, a subspecies far more common than the less-fragrant species itself. It is the only form of the species grown in this country.

Although the species is called the curry plant, the common name refers to the fragrance only. Unlike parsley, sage, rosemary, and thyme—which are produced from plants with those names—no single species is responsible for the curry powder found on the kitchen shelf. The curry we cook with is a blend of various spices, mainly ginger, coriander, and cardamom; sometimes turmeric and peppercorns are part of the mix as well.

The narrow silvery leaves are about 1½″ long, alternate, and with many glands beneath, which contain the fragrant oil; they are lightly hairy to smooth, with margins rolled slightly under. The foliage is the best part of the plant: the flowers are a nondescript washed-out yellow, occurring in late summer and fall. This is more of a fun plant, not one that offers extraordinary ornamental value.

-petiolare (pe tee o la' ree)   licorice plant   6–9"/3'
   winter   foliage   South Africa

This species is a common plant in baskets and containers, where it is included for its ability to complement and tone down its brighter neighbors. Its prostrate habit is a favorite among container designers as it flows out and away, extending the size and scope of the design. The 1–1½" wide alternate leaves, held on slender stems, are gray-green and slightly hairy. If you look closely at the petiole, you will see it is flat and often winged (such conspicuous structures resulted in the specific name). If you don't feel like looking at petioles, no problem: it is the foliage and overall habit that people enjoy seeing. Flowers occur in the winter in its native habitat, but since it is dead in the winter here, we seldom see the small opaque white flowers. Some cultivars are so much more handsome, the species is seldom used anymore, pleasant though it is.

Place in containers or baskets in full sun to partial shade. Plants are susceptible to root rots, and soil must drain water away readily; add extra drainage hole in baskets if possible. Propagate by cuttings.

CULTIVARS

Licorice series consists of three selections: 'Licorice Splash' has variegated creamy leaves (probably a rename for 'Variegatum'); 'Petite Licorice' has smaller, tighter leaves and is more compact; and 'White Licorice' bears leaves with a little more silvering.

'Limelight', the most popular cultivar, has lime-green leaves. Quite beautiful and complementary. Also sold as 'Aurea'.

'Variegatum' has leaves variegated in gray and cream.

-splendidum (splen' dih dum)   silver everlasting   2–3'/3'
   late summer   yellow   South Africa

This species grows into a woody shrub with woolly silver leaves and late summer and fall flowers. Plants branch freely, and each stem bears alternate 2–2½" long linear leaves, very hairy beneath but almost smooth on top. The bright yellow flowers are only about ½" wide, but they are held in many-flowered inflorescences. The plant is grown for the leaves; the flowers are secondary.

Full sun, well-drained soils. Propagate by terminal cuttings.

Alternative species

Helichrysum ambiguum (am big' yew um) has narrow 3–3½" long silver leaves, without the curry scent of *H. italicum*. The many small yellow flowers are held in a 2–3" wide inflorescence in summer. Plants grow about 2' tall and twice as wide. Native to Spain.

Helichrysum argyrophyllum (ar je ra' fil um) is similar to *H. splendidum*. It is a prostrate mat-former (rarely more than 6" high) with handsome satiny silver leaves. Faded lemon-yellow flowers occur in late summer. 'Moe's Gold' has golden yellow flowers. Excellent ground cover for a sunny, well-drained location.

Helichrysum thianschanicum (than shan' ih kum) is related to *H. petiolare*. This species has narrow intensely silver leaves that can look stunning in containers; its yellow to orange flowers simply detract from the foliage and should be removed. Also sold as 'Icicles' and 'Silver Spike'.

Quick key to *Helichrysum* species

A. Plant prostrate or mat-forming
    B. Leaves obviously silver . . . . *H. argyrophyllum*
    BB. Leaves gray (or lime-green in cultivars) . . . . *H. petiolare*
AA. Plant not prostrate or mat-forming, upright
    B. Leaves obviously silver
        C. Foliage with obvious curry fragrance . . . .
        . . . . *H. italicum* subsp. *serotinum*
        CC. Foliage without obvious curry fragrance
           D. Leaves >2" long . . . . *H. ambiguum*
           DD. Leaves <2" long . . . . *H. splendidum*
    BB. Leaves not obviously silver . . . . *H. bracteatum*

Heliotropium (hee lee o tro' pee um)   heliotrope   Boraginaceae

Heliotrope has been grown for centuries, partly for the blue color but mainly for the sweet fragrance of certain species. The flowers were considered somewhat magical, as they constantly turned toward the sun; the generic name is in fact derived from the Greek, *helios* ("sun") and *trope* ("turning"), for that very characteristic. Most of the 250 species are native to South America; several are also native to the United States. The most ornamental native is the large white-flowered *Heliotropium convolvulaceum* (morning glory heliotrope), whose 1″ wide flowers have a yellow throat and great perfume; someone needs to get this fragrant plant into the hands of gardeners. Other reasonably ornamental natives are the yellow-flowered *H. leavenworthii* and the white *H. parviflorum*, native to the southeastern United States. None of these three may even remotely be described as available to the gardener. Only two species are out there, and one, *H. arborescens*, dominates.

Quick guide to *Heliotropium* species

	Habit	Height	Fragrance
H. amplexicaule	prostrate	6–12"	no
H. arborescens	erect	12–24"	yes

-*amplexicaule* (am pleks ih kawl' ee)   prostrate heliotrope   12–24"/24"
    summer   light blue   Peru

This species is naturalized along roadsides in the Southeast. It is likely perennial to zone 7 or 8, but let's lump it with other annuals until more information

Heliotropium amplexicaule   ASHA KAYS

becomes available. I have tried this plant in the UGA Horticulture Gardens, where it makes a terrific ground cover, rapidly filling in large areas. Plants are highly useful for the garden as well as in containers and baskets. I really like the obvious heat and humidity tolerance of this species, its rapid growth rate, and its continuous flowering.

The decumbent stems carry alternate oblong leaves about 3″ long and 1″ wide on short petioles. The flowers are pale blue, although darker blue and white are occasionally found. They are held in many-flowered inflorescences and bloom from mid spring to frost. It does have one drawback: with a name like heliotrope, people can't help sticking their nose in the flowers. Mistake. In my opinion, which is shared by many but not all, they are not particularly inviting, and anyone would admit they are not sweet-smelling—especially growers, who have a tough time with the fragrance in the enclosed greenhouse and are therefore not particularly enthralled with producing them. That is really too bad, as the flowers are only obnoxious if you roll around in the plants like cats in catnip.

Plant in full sun, propagate by terminal cuttings.

CULTIVARS

'Azure Skies' is a new selection with vigorous growth and blue flowers.
'Irongate' is smaller and has light lavender flowers.

-arborescens (ar bor e′ senz)	heliotrope	1–2′/1′
summer	violet	Peru

The words "heliotrope" and "fragrance" are wedded, and so sweet is the smell to some that the other common name for the species is cherry pie. I love cherry pie, but I don't get it—doesn't smell like any kind of pie to me. Heliotrope was a popular cut flower for its fragrance in the 1950s, grown in greenhouses and forced for winter or early spring sales, but the old-fashioned fragrant heliotrope went through some major changes in the late 1990s, not all good. In the race for bigger, brighter flowers, much of the fragrance has been lost. Doubtless fragrance is highly variable, differing in strength from cultivar to cultivar, nose to nose, and among the plants themselves, and in all fairness to the breeders, it is difficult to complain about the garden performance and beauty of some hybrids. They offer significant improvements in weather tolerance over the old-fashioned forms and are still fragrant—just not nearly as sweetly or obviously so. Heliotrope is one of the easiest plants to combine with others because the violet, purple, or blue flowers complement others so well. I have seen some beautiful companion plantings here and there, such as the terrific combination of pink geraniums and heliotrope in Butchart Gardens in British Columbia and a most striking blend of heliotrope and burning bush (*Kochia*) in the gardens at the Isle of Mainau in southern Germany: the heliotrope was a sea of blue, and the upright fine-foliaged lime-green plants of kochia were like sentinels throughout. Tough not to appreciate gardening when you see such gardens.

The species ranges from dwarf 12″ forms to taller 3′ plants that are easily trained to standards. The alternate ovate leaves are 3″ long by 1½″ wide and usually dark green. The many blooms on each flowering stalk unfurl slowly, until a large inflorescence of violet is formed. Plants, which are useful for garden use and increasingly popular in mixed containers, are excellent for cool climates, doing well the entire season. In the South, they do well until about August 1, when the heat and humidity finally get the better of them. But they are glorious until then.

Full sun to partial shade, well-drained soils. Propagate by seed or cuttings.

CULTIVARS

'Alba' bears white flowers with a nice vanilla fragrance.
'Atlantis' has deep blue flowers on 1½′ tall plants.
'Blue Wonder' is about 12″ tall with a sweet fragrance. Deep blue flowers.
'Haskell's Form', an upright plant that grows 3–4′ tall, is offered by a few nurseries. Named for excellent Massachusetts plantsman Alan Haskell.
'Iowa' has large deep amethyst-purple flowers with a nice subtle fragrance. The leaves are light green. A favorite of mine for fragrance.

Heliotropium arborescens 'Atlantis'   ASHA KAYS

'Light Eyes' grows 18–24″ tall and bears light lavender flowers with an even lighter center. Nicely fragrant.

'Marine' is among the most popular cultivars. The leaves are dark green, and the slightly fragrant flowers are deep purple. Plants grow up to 2′ tall.

'Mini Marine' is similar to 'Marine' but about 1′ tall. The size of the flowers are large relative to the size of the plant. Also sold as 'Dwarf Marine'.

'Nagano' has darker flowers than 'Atlantis' and grows about 14″ tall.

Additional reading

Lee, Rand B. 1996. Heliotrope (*Heliotropium arborescens*). *American Cottage Gardener* 3(4):5–7.

Martin, Tovah. 1994. Fragrant indoor plants. *Flower and Garden* 38(1):48–50.

Helipterum (hel ip' te rum)   everlasting   Asteraceae

About fifty species with alternate leaves and entire margins are known in the genus, another of the many everlastings that are easily confused among gardeners and growers. In fact, according to some, but not all, taxonomists, several species of *Helipterum* have been reclassified under *Acroclinium* and *Rhodanthe*. Many people don't accept all these higgledy-piggledy changes, including those who argue one way or another. And I have a terrible time explaining the differences among everlastings like *Ammobium*, *Helipterum*, *Helichrysum*, and *Xeranthemum*—there simply is not much to distinguish one from another. Most people don't give a flip about the differences, but a few gardeners are curious. For the curious among us, here are a few similarities and differences among the everlastings.

The characteristic winged branches of *Ammobium* are easy to see with the naked eye, but other differences can be detected only with a 10× hand lens or by someone with a microscope and a lot of patience. All species lack ray flowers; the colors are provided by the papery bracts. A structure distinctive to the aster family is the pappus, a modified part of the calyx borne on the ovary but seen at the base of the flower and on the fruit. It may be plumose, bristle-like, scaly, or lacking, which variety of form is a useful identification point for the everlastings.

Quick key to everlasting genera

A. Pappus of bristles or bristle-like hairs
    B. Bristles of pappus plumose throughout . . . . *Helipterum*
    BB. Bristles of pappus plumose only at tip . . . . *Helichrysum*
AA. Pappus not bristly or lacking
    B. Branches conspicuously winged, bracts white . . . . *Ammobium*
    BB. Branches not winged, bracts purple . . . . *Xeranthemum*

In *Helipterum*, two of the better known species are now missing. *Helipterum roseum* is now *Acroclinium roseum* or *Rhodanthe chlorocephala* var. *rosea* (taxonomists are more confused than we are), and *H. manglesii* has been classified as *Rhodanthe manglesii* by some authors. Those plants left in *Helipterum* are usually yellow- or white-flowered, while those in the two species just named are white-, rose-, or pink-flowered. All taxa are native to South Africa and Australia.

-splendidum (splen' dih dum)   showy sunray   1–2'/2'
    spring   white   Western Australia

The only true *Helipterum* remaining for sale, *H. splendidum* is about 2' tall with gray-green, linear, 1" long leaves that are crowded at the base. Beneath the flowers are found 2" wide creamy white bracts, often with a purple band.

Push seeds into the ground after weather has warmed up, or plant transplants about 9" apart in early spring. Plants look best in spring to early summer but decline as temperatures and particularly humidity rise. Full sun.

Alternative species

Helipterum floribundum (flor ih bun' dum; common white sunray) is multi-branched and about 1' tall. The small 1" wide flowers are solitary but numerous, due to the branched nature of the plant. Flowers are creamy white. Native to Australia. Full sun.

Hemigraphis (hem e graf' is)   Acanthaceae

This genus consists of about ninety species native to tropical Asia. Those available to gardeners are prostrate and seldom more than 9" tall. The common species have maroon to purple leaves and are closely related to *Strobilanthes* although differing significantly in height and habit. The filaments of the outer stamens of *Hemigraphis* are quite hairy; the generic name comes from the Greek, *hemi* ("half") and *graphis* ("brush"), referring to the hairiness on half the stamens. The plants are quite beautiful but are too small except for the front of gardens or in containers, where their colorful leaves can be admired up close.

-repanda (re pan' da)   4–9"/12"
summer   foliage   Malaysia

This is a terrific showy prostrate species with red to maroon foliage. The glossy leaves are almost smooth, with a few hairs beneath; they are about 2" long, linear to lanceolate and with wavy margins. The whitish flowers are small but easily visible against the dark leaves. They are held in short terminal spikes, and, although you have to get on your hands and knees to appreciate them, are quite handsome. Plants flower in late spring and continue much of the summer. They are perennial to about zone 7, but I treat them as annuals in case the winter is tough.
Full sun to partial shade, well-drained soils.

Alternative species

Hemigraphis alternata (al ter nay' ta; red ivy, red flame ivy) is similar to *H. repanda* but with heart-shaped, larger leaves (up to 3" long) that are silver-gray above and flushed purple beneath. The uppersides of the leaves are considerably puckered or blistered. 'Red Waffle' is about 10" tall with glossy puckered purple foliage. Both *H. alternata* and *H. repanda* should be in more gardens.

Heterocentron (he ter o sen' tron)   Melastomataceae

The first time I planted representatives of this genus in the garden, I thought they were a low-growing form of princess flower, *Tibouchina*. In fact, I labeled them creeping tibouchina, because the flowers and leaves were so similar to the upright forms of that genus. Turns out they belong to the same family, so I don't feel too badly. This genus differs from *Tibouchina* by being prostrate. Its flower structure too is different: pull apart the flowers of *Heterocentron* and note the eight stamens, four of which are longer and more bristly than the others. The generic name comes from the Greek, *hetero* ("different") and *kentron* ("spur" or "sharp point"). If you pull apart *Tibouchina* flowers, you will find ten stamens. Most people don't really care about any of this flower hocus-pocus, and if you are one of them, simply enjoy *Heterocentron* for its beauty.

-elegans (el′ e ganz)	Spanish shawl	6–9″/12″
summer	mauve	Central America

The best planting of Spanish shawl I have seen was at the Mercer Botanical Gardens in Humble, Texas. Plants spread rapidly and quickly fill in areas with as few as one plant per square yard. The dull green ovate to oblong-ovate leaves are entire or slightly wavy with obvious veins. In general, three veins are common, but some leaves may have more. The leaves are opposite and seldom damaged by insects or diseases. The 1″ wide mauve to magenta flowers are formed only periodically and seldom bloom profusely, which is a problem for this annual: it forms a fine ground cover, but the flowering is too sparse for acceptance by gardeners. But if you are looking for a tough carpet, you might want to give this a try.

Full sun, propagate by terminal cuttings.

Hibiscus (hi bis′ kus) mallow Malvaceae

This genus contains about 220 herbaceous and woody species, all native to subtropical and tropical areas of the world. That all plants hail from warm climates ensures they are annuals in most areas of the United States. The perennial *Hibiscus coccineus* is perennial in zone 7, but annual in zone 4; similarly, Chinese hibiscus (*H. rosa-sinensis*), so prevalent in Florida, is a houseplant nearly everywhere else in this country. But that is true with almost all the genera in this book. I have selected just three species of mallow as annuals.

All hibiscus are characterized by their large bright flowers with stamens that appear to be attached to the pistil, in a column. The symmetrical flowers are usually solitary; they always have five veined petals, often with a basal purple spot, and five sepals, below which is the epicalyx, a bract-like structure, which consists of four to ten segments. People love hibiscus, and if they are planted sufficiently early, they will provide flowers all summer and then frost away.

Quick guide to *Hibiscus* species

	Height	Feature	Flower color
H. acetosella	3–4′	reddish foliage	purple-red
H. rosa-sinensis	1–3′	large flowers	varied
H. trionum	9–15″	flowers	creamy white with purple

-acetosella (a set o sel′ a)   red hibiscus   3–4′/3′
   summer   purple   east and central Africa

It is not often that a genus so well known for large colorful flowers provides a
species best grown for its foliage. Red hibiscus bears alternate, three- to five-
lobed dark green leaves with a red tint on long petioles. Plants grow up to 8′,
although 4′ is more common. The small (1½″ wide) purplish flowers often have
a deep purple base and are borne in the leaf axils. Beneath the sepals is an epicalyx of nine to ten segments. In the red-leaved cultivar, the flowers blend so
well with the foliage they are seldom noticed. I really enjoy this form. It always
look good and provides a nice color change from the common green foliage in
the garden and landscape.
   Full sun.

CULTIVARS

'Red Shield', the only form available, consists of brilliant maroon leaves and
can grow much larger than the species. In the UGA trials, it loomed at least 8′
tall, extraordinarily eye-catching.

-rosa-sinensis (ro za sih nen′ sis)   Chinese hibiscus   1–3′/3′
   summer   many colors   China

Formerly seen strictly as gift- or houseplants, this species is now offered by nurseries and garden centers as an annual for gardeners. They are all greenhouse-
grown and sold based on the large colorful flowers. In tropical areas of the country, plants are often used as hedging and screening; for the rest of us, they are
probably best in large containers, where they can show off their flowers when
temperatures warm up and be moved indoors when temperatures decline.
   The leaves are up to 6″ long and 3″ wide, always glossy green and serrated.
Their luster is a handsome addition to the plant as a whole. The flowers are up
to 5″ across and occur in an incredible range of colors and shapes. Flowers are
held in the upper leaf axils on short pedicels.
   While the flowers are certainly beautiful, heat is needed for continued flower
initiation and for good plant performance. Once temperatures drop below
60°F, plants decline; the foliage turns yellow, and flowers are sparse and small.
Like most members of this family, plants are also susceptible to insects, such as
Japanese beetles, so surround them with other plants in the container and enjoy
the terrific flowers.
   Full sun, fertilize well in the spring.

CULTIVARS

The hundreds of cultivars were mainly developed for the gift plant market.
Many are hybrids between *Hibiscus rosa-sinensis* and *H. schizopetalus*.
   'Cooperi', a popular selection, is grown mainly for the ornamental foliage.
The olive-green leaves are marbled with red, pink, and white. Flowers are rosy
red.

Hibiscus rosa-sinensis CHRIS JOHNSON

'Donna Lynn' produces flowers with a red throat fading to a pink hue and then to a light yellow edge.

'Fifth Dimension' has a yellow border around a whitish interior and a dark red throat.

'Flamingo' has single salmon-colored flowers.

'Gold Dust' is orange with yellow flecks throughout.

'Johore' produces hot pink flowers with pointed petals.

'Kona' is a pink double.

'Lady Elizabeth' bears magenta-pink 8″ wide flowers.

'Miami Lady' has pink flowers with a ruby-red throat.

'Morning Glory' produces flowers whose red and white centers give way to white edges.

'Peggy Henry' bears double yellow flowers.

'Ruth Wilcox' has creamy white double flowers.

'The Path' produces flowers with a yellow edge around an orange interior and a pink throat.

-trionum (tri o′ num)	flower-of-an-hour	9–15″/2′
summer	creamy white	western United States

With all the competition for flower size and beautiful foliage among species of *Hibiscus*, this species will not win any awards. Gardeners have been growing this little gem for many years, however, and for all its lack of pizzazz, it is still a favorite. Plants are bristly hairy, with deeply three-lobed (occasionally five-lobed) upper leaves; the lower leaves are often entire. The solitary 1½" wide flowers, borne in leaf axils on short pedicels, range from creamy white to pale yellow with a purple throat and yellow stamens, providing the three colors of the specific name. Beneath the base of the sepals is the seven- to ten-segmented epicalyx.

The plants grow upright early in the season, branching over time and producing flowers continuously, though not dozens at a time, from spring until temperatures fall below 45°F. They provide months of pleasure and look at home in any garden or in mixed containers. They often reseed in warm climates.

Full sun. Sow in the garden or in a protected area and transplant when threat of frost has passed. Fertilize early, then leave them alone.

Alternative species

Hibiscus schizopetalus (skit zo pe' ta lus; Japanese hibiscus) is related to *H. rosa-sinensis*. Native to East Africa, common name notwithstanding, plants grow to 10' in height and bear 5–6" long ovate, serrated leaves, on long petioles. The pendent flowers, held on long slender pedicels, are 3–4" wide, with cut petals in pink or red. The split petals provide a delicate look to the flowers.

Quick key to *Hibiscus* species

  A. Foliage tinged or heavily colored maroon, flowers about
      2" wide, red . . . . *H. acetosella*
  AA. Foliage not tinged red
      B. Flowers in many colors, 3–5" wide, leaves smooth or
         nearly so . . . . *H. rosa-sinensis*
      BB. Flowers creamy white or pale yellow, 1–1½" wide,
         leaves hispid . . . . *H. trionum*

Additional reading

Lee, Rand B. 1998. A feast of mallows. *American Cottage Gardener* 5(3):5–7.
Wesley, Trish. 1996. Hibiscus. *Horticulture* 74(2):52–53.

Hunnemannia (hun ee man' ee a) Mexican tulip poppy Papaveraceae

I first tried Mexican tulip poppy many years ago, when its handsome flowers and foliage suggested it be included in research I was doing on new crops for the greenhouse industry. I grew the plants from seed, but the plants proved unworkable from the start, with wide variability of seed vigor, plant vigor, height, and flowering. In the greenhouse, uniformity of a population is a critical characteristic, and although the plants were beautiful, they were going nowhere in greenhouse production.

None of this, however, precludes their use in the garden. The only species in the genus is *Hunnemannia fumariifolia* (few ma ree ih fo' lee a), which can indeed make a beautiful garden plant. Plants are native to the western highlands of Mexico and enjoy the same growing conditions as California poppy: cool nights and warm days. They are grown for their clear glossy 2-3" wide yellow flowers, held above gray-green finely dissected foliage. The leaves are cut in groups of threes (ternate) and are about 4" long. The flowers, which are produced at the terminals, consist of four shiny petals and two sepals. In the North, plants will be slow to get going but should do well in the summer and fall; in the South, just the opposite: they will do well early but decline as heat and humidity set in.

Place them about 9" apart in full sun for a good show. They are easily grown from seed, either direct sown in early spring or in the fall in frost-free areas. They may also be transplanted in the spring, but take care to disturb the roots as little as possible. Members of the poppy family don't appreciate too much abuse.

CULTIVARS

'Sunlite' is similar to the species but with larger (up to 3" wide) flowers. A 1934 All-America Selection.

Hypoestes (hih po es' teez)   Acanthaceae

The approximately forty species of this genus have opposite leaves, with margins varying from entire to serrated. I have grown these plants off and on in the UGA Horticulture Gardens for many years—for the foliage, not the flowers.

-phyllostachya (fi lo sta' kee a)	polka dot plant	2-3'/2'
summer	foliage	South Africa

This species is included in the garden so that its many 2" long, opposite, dark‐green leaves may be enjoyed. The foliage is spotted, splashed, and otherwise awash with all sorts of rose, pink, lavender, or white paint. The patterned leaves are so interesting that they have given rise to common names like measles plant, flamingo plant, and, my favorite, freckle face. So if you don't know this plant, names like those should give you a pretty good idea that it is not staid. Nor is it gaudy: the dark leaves and the dark freckles blend well with each other, and, except for the white painted form, people may not notice the different shades until they are on top of the plant.

They grow rapidly in sunny areas but will tolerate partial shade as well. In general, the bedding forms are seldom more than 2' tall, but shade and heat can cause additional stretch. They are fine in heat and humidity but better behaved in cooler climates. The lilac flowers are nothing to write home about, and I think they should be picked off, like a coleus, when they appear.

Plants are grown in the greenhouse from seed, but gardeners are best served by buying transplants in the spring.

CULTIVARS

Confetti series grows 1½–2′ tall and consists of splashes of burgundy, red, rose, and white. The white is the most noticeable splashing, burgundy the least.

Splash series has the same basic splattering of colors but is more dwarf, growing only 12″ tall. The best is 'Splash Pink'.

Hypoestes phyllostachya   CHRIS JOHNSON

Abelmoschus moschatus 'Pacific Light Pink' and 'Pacific Orange Scarlet'

Abelmoschus esculentus

Abutilon ×hybridum 'Bella Yellow'

Abutilon megapotamicum 'Variegatum'

Abutilon pictum 'Aureo-maculatum'

Alcea rosea 'Chaters Purple'

Alcea rosea 'Nigra'

Alocasia micholitziana 'Maxkowskii'

Alonsoa warscewiczii

Alpinia zerumbet 'Variegata'

Alternanthera dentata 'Wave Hill'

Amaranthus cruentus 'Hot Biscuits'

Amaranthus tricolor 'Aurora'

Ammi visnaga

Anagallis monellii 'Skylover'

Anoda cristata 'Opal Cup' and 'Snow Cup'

Arctotis ×hybrida 'Flame'

Arctotis ×hybrida 'China Rose'

Arctotheca calendula

Asperula orientalis 'Blue Surprise'

Ballota pseudodictamnus

Barleria cristata

Bidens ferulifolia with argyranthemum

Bidens cernua

Brassica oleracea

Browallia speciosa 'Marine Bells'

Brugmansia ×*candida* 'Ecuador Pink'

Brugmansia 'Charles Grimaldi'

Caladium bicolor 'White Queen'

Calibrachoa ×*hybrida* 'Million Bells Cherry Pink'

Callistephus chinensis Pompom series

Capsicum annuum 'Medusa'

Caryopteris incana

Centaurea americana

Cerinthe major 'Purpurascens'

Chrysanthemum segetum 'Prado'

Chrysocephalum apiculatum 'Nullarbor Golden Buttons'

Clarkia amoena Grace series

Cleome hassleriana 'White Queen' (from the Queen series)

Cobaea scandens

Coleus blumei 'Gay's Delight'

Coleus blumei 'Red Ruffles'

Colocasia esculenta 'Jet Black Wonder'

Consolida ambigua

Convolvulus cneorum

Convolvulus sabatius

Convolvulus tricolor 'Blue Ensign'

Coreopsis tinctoria in wildflower mix

Cosmos atrosanguineus 'Ace of Spades'

Cosmos bipinnatus 'Versailles Pink'

Cuphea llavea with *Rudbeckia hirta* 'Becky'

Cuphea micropetala

Curcuma alismatifolia

Curcuma roscoeana

Curcuma zedoaria

Cynara cardunculus

Datura metel with 'William Languth' geraniums

Diascia 'Coral Belle'

Duranta erecta (fruit)

Ensete ventricosum 'Maurelii'

Euphorbia lathyris

Eustoma grandiflorum

Felicia amelloides 'Read's Blue' with salvia

Fuchsia 'Koralle'

Gaillardia pulchella 'Yellow Plume'

Gloriosa superba 'Rothschildiana'

Graptophyllum pictum 'Black Beauty'

Helianthus annuus

Helianthus annuus 'Big Smile'

Helianthus annuus 'Chianti'

Helichrysum italicum

Heliotropium arborescens 'Marine' with geraniums

Hibiscus trionum

Iberis amara 'White Pinnacle'

Impatiens balfourii

Ipomoea alba

Ipomoea quamoclit

Kaempferia pulchra 'Bronze Peacock'

Lablab purpurea

Lantana camara 'Athens Rose'

Lantana trifolia (fruit)

Lavatera trimestris 'Loveliness'

Layia platyglossa

Leonotis leonurus

Limnanthes douglasii

Loasa triphylla

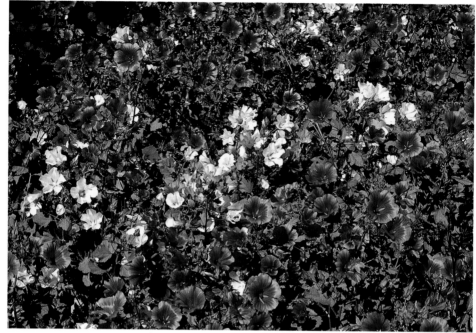

Malope trifida 'Vulcan' and 'White Queen'

Musa acuminata

Nicotiana sylvestris

Nigella damascena

Nierembergia scoparia

Odontonema strictum

Orthosiphon stamineus

Osteospermum Passion Mix

Osteospermum 'Silvia' (from the Sunny series)

Passiflora 'Amethyst'

Petunia 'Purple Wave' with 'Margarita' sweet potato and 'Amazon' coleus

Phlox drummondii Paloma Mix

Plectranthus amboinicus 'Athens Gem'

Plectranthus argentatus

Plumbago auriculata

Portulaca grandiflora 'Sundial Peach'

Ptilotus exaltatus

Quisqualis indica

Reseda odorata

Rhodochiton atrosanguineum

Ruellia brittoniana

Ruellia brittoniana 'Chi Chi'

Scaevola aemula 'Purple Fan' (from the Outback series)

Schizanthus pinnatus 'Floraboard'

Senecio confusus

Solanum wendlandii

Strobilanthes dyerianus with nicotiana and petunias

Thunbergia battiscombei

Thunbergia grandiflora

Thysanotus multiflorus

Tibouchina semidecandra var. *grandiflora* 'Athens Blue'

Tithonia rotundifolia with dahlias

Torenia flava 'Suzie Wong'

Torenia fournieri 'Summer Wave Blue'

Trachelium caeruleum

Trachymene coerulea

Turnera ulmifolia

Tweedia caerulea

Zinnia angustifolia 'Persian Carpet'

Iberis (i′ ber is)   candytuft   Brassicaceae

The Iberians, among the oldest European peoples, likely came from Africa in prehistoric times and settled in the peninsula now occupied by Spain and Portugal, which is still referred to as the Iberian peninsula. Iberia is no longer used as the name for Spain, and the Iberians have disappeared (the Basques of northern Spain are thought to be their closest descendants), but the name has been maintained in this fine genus.

Nearly all gardeners know the perennial species, *Iberis semperflorens*, the candytuft found in shimmering white in almost every state each spring. This perennial candytuft is so dominant that most gardeners don't realize that annual species are available. They tend to be seen in conservatories rather than in gardens, likely because insufficient information is available to review the performance of plants across the country. But these annuals are certainly worth a try in containers or as spring-flowering plants.

Quick guide to *Iberis* species

	Height	Color effect
I. amara	6–18"	white
I. umbellata	9–12"	varied

-*amara* (a mar′ a)   rocket candytuft   1–3′/2′
   spring   white   Europe

This species is stiff and erect in habit, with lanceolate leaves, toothed toward the apex. Plants branch readily, and dense inflorescences of white flowers occur at the end of the stems. The flowers are four-petaled and occur in corymbs, that is, the inflorescence starts off rounded or flat but elongates as the flower heads mature, providing the "rocket" look. The petals are white, perhaps with a tinge of purple, and wonderfully fragrant. Several forms with larger flowers have been introduced; these are more ornamental than the species, which is looked upon as a weed in Europe.

Place in full sun, provide good drainage. Cooler climates are desirable; heat and humidity cause plants to decline in early summer. Plants do well in limey soils.

CULTIVARS

'White Pinnacle' has some of the largest flowers I have seen, standing like newly laundered soldiers in formation. Rockets of flowers are formed by elongating inflorescences, and in cool climates, the persistence of the flowers results in beautiful popsicle-like flower heads. The white flowers are useful for cut flowers, and the seed pods are also dried. 'Giant Hyacinth Flowered', 'Giant Snowflakes', and 'Giant White' all appear similar.

-umbellata (um bel a' ta)   common candytuft   9–12"/12"
 spring   many colors   southern Europe

The first time I saw a clump of the annual common candytuft, in rose and purple shades, I exclaimed how wonderful it was that perennial candytuft occurred in so many colors—this species is that similar in habit and look to the perennial. The upper leaves are entire; those near the base are serrated. The main difference between this species and *Iberis amara* is that the flowers are held in umbels rather than corymbs. This is mostly garden trivia, except that since umbels do not elongate, no "rockets" will occur. Flowers of *I. umbellata* are commonly purple, but other colors have been selected and are sold as mixes.

Full sun to partial shade, well-drained soils. Plants are best in cooler climates; in the South, they provide outstanding spring color but melt out in early summer. They are also useful in limey soils.

CULTIVARS

Brilliant Mix has mounded, 10" tall plants in shades of red, lilac, purple, rose, and white.

Dwarf Fairyland Mix has lilac, maroon, carmine, and white flowers, about 9"' tall.

Flash Mix is 9–12" tall with many rose, lilac-pink, and white flowers.

Alternative species

Iberis crenata, a relative of *I. amara*, is an erect annual, growing about 1' in height. The leaves are spatula-shaped to linear, and plants bear clean white flowers with purple centers. The petals are about four times longer than the sepals, and the lobes on the pods are erect. Plants flower well in late spring and summer.

Iberis odorata (fragrant candytuft) is similar to both *I. amara* and *I. crenata* but differs in the shape of the fruit (lobes spreading) and size of the petals relative to the sepals (one and a half times larger). Very fragrant. 'White Pinnacle' is often offered as a cultivar of this species.

Quick key to *Iberis* species

A. Inflorescence an umbel, usually in a mixture of colors . . . . . . *I. umbellata*
AA. Inflorescence a corymb or raceme, flowers usually white
    B. Leaves lanceolate, flowers elongate as they mature . . . . *I. amara*
    BB. Leaves linear to spatulate, flowers elongate only slightly
        C. Petals four times longer than sepals . . . . *I. crenata*
        CC. Petals one and a half times longer than sepals . . . . . . *I. odorata*

Impatiens (im pay′ shenz)   balsam   Balsaminaceae

I suspect if you asked a hundred people to name five herbaceous plants, impatiens would be included on ninety-five lists, albeit in different guises, as people know it: the old-fashioned rose balsam; the wild but impressive jewelweed; the New Guinea impatiens; or busy lizzie, the number-one-selling bedding plant in the world. What accounts for this success? First of all, the genus is diverse, with about 850 species (and that they are all ornamental certainly doesn't hurt). Secondly, the genus has super-attracted the attention of breeders, who have placed many fine plants—particularly the New Guinea and busy lizzie hybrids—before the gardener. And finally, the genus is highly successful in shade. The last characteristic means every retailer, landscaper, and gardener places some plants of *Impatiens* in shady areas; after all, few other choices provide such long-lasting colorful flowers in the shade.

Plants in the genus produce succulent stems ranging from 6″ to 4′ in height. Leaves are mostly alternate, occasionally opposite or whorled. The flowers reward close study. They usually have three (sometimes five) sepals, one of which is much larger and almost like a bract, extending backward into a spur. The upper of the five petals is free; the lower four are united into two fused pairs. Some flowers resemble saucers, others, helmeted blooms, depending on how the petals are fused. There are also five stamens and a five-lobed pistil. Impatiens flowers are so common and numerous, no one stops to look at them, but they are a trip!

Add to the interesting and beautiful flowers the seed-bearing fruit capsule, the organ that is responsible for its generic name, and it is an almost irresistible plant. One year I began my fall class by collecting ripe capsules of bedding impatiens from the UGA Horticulture Gardens and placing one on each desk. As the students arrived, I simply asked them not to touch what was there. I starting introducing the class and myself, and waited. About thirty seconds later the first gasp (not a scream, but a yelp) occurred. The girl (it is always a girl) couldn't help herself. She had prodded the fruit, which then exploded. Others soon followed suit, more by curiosity than by science, and soon seeds were exploding like fireworks on the Fourth of July. Once I gave the word to have fun, the classroom became a virtual den of impatience, with popping fruit and popping eyeballs. Next time you walk through a garden with someone, gently pick a ripe capsule and place it in their hand, and watch them jump. No one who does this—no one—will forget where the impatiens gets its name. Gardening is supposed to be fun, after all. We can't be reading books all the time.

The genus has a wide distribution around the world, with flowers varying significantly in shape and size as well as color. Little-known species like *Impatiens racemosa*, with an abundance of small yellow flowers, and *I. stenantha*, with red-tipped upward-turned spurs, are slowly finding their way to gardeners willing to buy seed but are light-years from retailer shelves. Curiosity-seekers can track down *I. repens*, a creeping form with small leaves and small yellow flowers, or *I. niamniamensis*, the famous Congo cockatoo, with bright red and yellow flowers on 3′ tall plants. Hallucinogenic! These crazy plants may be found in special crazy catalogs and businesses, like Glasshouse Works in Stewart, Ohio, who offer all sorts of weird impatiens to plantspeople eager to try the unusual. These off-the-wall impatiens are definitely worth a little space, but it is the bedding impatiens (*I. walleriana*) that dominates, with New Guinea impatiens (*I. hawkeri*) a distant second.

Quick guide to *Impatiens* species

	Height	Flower color	Ornamental foliage
I. auricoma	10–20″	yellow	yes
I. balfourii	1–1½′	white, flushed pink	no
I. balsamina	1–2′	varied	no
I. capensis	3–5′	orange-yellow	no
I. glandulifera	3–5′	rose-purple	no
I. hawkeri	1–2′	varied	yes
I. walleriana	1–2′	varied	no

-*auricoma* (or ih kom′ a)	yellow impatiens	10–20″/12″
summer	yellow	Comoro Islands

I knew very little about this species, so I grew out a few recently. They are short annuals, perhaps better suited to containers than to the garden proper. The 3–6″ long leaves are alternate with wavy margins. The midrib is bright red on the top but somewhat pale beneath. The orange to yellow hooded flowers are 1–1½″ long and held on long flower stems; they have short spurs and are streaked with red, obvious in some, not so in others. I was quite pleased with my plants, which were different, handsome, and durable. Not as humidity-tolerant as I had hoped, perhaps, but I will try them again.

I knew little enough about the species but even less about Comoros, an African country made up of several islands in the Indian Ocean off the coast of Mozambique, between the mainland and Madagascar. Comoros was a French possession until 1975, when three of the four largest islands declared independence. The language is French, and the capital is Moroni on Grande Comore Island. Get yourself a few plants of *Impatiens auricoma* and invite some Comoran flora to your home.

Plant in containers in groups of at least three, in partial shade. Seed may be available somewhere, but cuttings may be taken to overwinter plants.

CULTIVARS

'African Queen', about 15″ tall, has less red foliar streaking than the species.

-balfourii (bal for′ ee i)	Balfour's impatiens	12–18″/12″
summer	white, flushed pink	western Himalayas

I don't know why this species is not more popular. Plants are not excessively tall or short, and they flower over a long period of time. I discovered them several years ago, and I loved them in my shady garden. But they did not reseed, and I couldn't find a source of seed or plants again. The species commemorates Sir Issac Bayley Balfour (1853–1922), a botanist and director of the Royal Botanic Garden, Edinburgh, Scotland.

The alternate leaves are ovate to elliptical, 1–5″ long and about 2″ wide. The tips are pointed, and the margins are slightly recurved. The hooded flowers are white, flushed with pink, with a pale yellow lower lobe; they are held in loose three- to nine-flowered racemes. They begin to flower in late spring and continue throughout most of the season. Their western Himalayan home precludes great performance under prolonged hot, humid conditions, but they look great in the Northeast until they tire out. I would love to see this plant being grown in commercial greenhouses, destined for the shelves of retailers.

Partial shade, well-drained soils. Propagate by seed or cuttings. Plant 9–12″ apart.

-balsamina (bal sa mee′ na)	rose balsam	1–2′/2′
spring	many colors	SE Asia

Rose balsam, an old-fashioned plant better known by your grandparents than your friends, was in every garden in the 1950s but is now relatively obscure. The fall from grace may be because plants have not changed significantly since that time; all breeding efforts have been focused on the enormously popular bedding impatiens.

The erect stems bear alternate leaves, about 3″ long and 2″ wide, on glandular, short petioles. Leaves have deeply toothed margins and are generally light green, although some variegated forms are available. The ¾–1½″ wide double flowers, which resemble tiny camellias, are held on short flower stems (pedicels) in the upper leaf axils, sometimes solitary, sometime in twos or threes. Flower colors include white, creamy yellow, pink, lilac, bright red, rose, and bicolors.

Partial shade, well-drained soils. Propagate by seed or cuttings.

CULTIVARS

'Blackberry Ice' has the habit of bedding impatiens but is thought to more closely resemble rose balsam in flower. The double flowers, purple splashed with white, are handsome enough, but it is the variegated foliage that sets them apart.

We grew the Ice series in the UGA Horticulture Gardens, and I thought they were excellent. They pooped out before the bedding impatiens, but they provided a terrific show for many months. Outstanding!

'Camellia Flowered' is a mix of double flowers on 2½' tall plants. Old-fashioned but effective.

'Carambole' bears fully double flowers in a mix of bright colors. Plants are 12–15" tall.

'Peach Ice' has variegated foliage, like 'Blackberry Ice', and salmon-peach double flowers.

'Strawberry Ice' is similar to 'Blackberry Ice' but with double red flowers splashed white. All the "Ices" are often sold as double bedding impatiens.

'Tom Thumb' is about 12" tall, with large double flowers in a mixture of colors.

Top Knot Mix consists of 9–12" tall plants in a mixture of double flowers.

-*capensis* (ka pen' sis)	jewelweed	2–5'/2'
summer	orange-yellow	northern United States

Take a walk by a stream bank that doesn't have houses and parking lots debasing it, and you are likely to see large stands of this species. In Canada and the northern United States, jewelweed is a fixture in damp, shady places. Beads of rain tend to form on the waxy leaves, glistening in the sun like jewels. Plants are certainly impressive, with their tall stout stems and smooth ovate leaves and coarsely toothed margins. The flowers are mostly orange-yellow with reddish brown spots and a spur hooked back to point forward; they may be found drooping from long pedicels from the upper leaf axils, sometimes solitary, sometimes in twos. Their look and habit accounts for another of the plant's common names, lady's earrings.

Some wonderful uses are associated with jewelweed, not least of which is that the sprouts are edible and delicious. Gently boil the 4–6" sprouts in water; pour the water off (good idea not to drink the water, it is poisonous); and enjoy the cooked sprouts with butter or cream sauce. Some people prefer them to asparagus tips, although I find that hard to believe. The most useful attribute of the species is its use as an astringent; it contains a natural fungicide effective in the treatment of athlete's foot, nettle stings, sunburn, bee and insect bites, abrasions, blisters, rashes, and itches—a veritable drug store on a stem. If you come into contact with poison ivy and spy some jewelweed nearby (the plants have similar soil and moisture requirements and are often seen side by side), crush jewelweed's stems and leaves in your hand and rub into the exposed skin area. If the salve is applied immediately, the rashes and bumps associated with poison ivy may not appear at all; if applied after their appearance, the salve will relieve some of the itching. Your skin will be a little orange in color but should feel better. Concoctions to soothe a reaction to poison ivy can also be made by boiling jewelweed's stems until half the water has evaporated; use the remaining solution to bathe affected areas.

In the garden, this species is not something people tend to plant, as lovely as its description sounds. It does not produce nearly as many flowers as other species of impatiens and can be a most noxious weed, too tall and too weedy in appearance for most tastes and turning some well-behaved gardeners into ranting maniacs, as plants come from nowhere and take over acres of garden real estate. Moist areas, which we like to think of as water gardens, are targets for the far-reaching seed; more prized water plants are then choked out. But if jewelweed reseeds occasionally in a damp area and appears at home, enjoy its visit: there are far worse "weeds" out there, and most are not nearly as useful.

Place in damp, shady areas. Propagate by seed.

-glandulifera (gland yew lih′ fe ra)   policeman's helmet   3–5′/2′
    summer   rose-purple   western Himalayas

Plants of *Impatiens glandulifera* (syn. *I. roylei*) have some of the thickest (up to 3″ in diameter) stems in the genus. Stems are also red-tinged, smooth, and sparsely branched. The serrated leaves are up to 8″ long and 3″ wide and are arranged in whorls of three to four. The 1½–2″ long rose to purple flowers are hooded (thus the common name) and abundantly produced in long many-flowered racemes in the upper leaf axils. The interior of the flowers is often yellow-spotted.

These are magnificent plants, but their tall stature and coarse habit seldom gain them a spot in polite garden schemes. Although native to faraway places, they have naturalized in the northern United States and Canada. The ability to self-sow provides populations from year to year. If you can find some seeds or plants, try them in the back of the garden, in a drift of a dozen plants or more. Impressive but also potentially aggressive. Be careful with all these upright impatiens.

Propagate by seed. Place in partial shade, in a reasonably damp, not wet, location.

CULTIVARS
'Candida' grows 4–6′ tall with pure white flowers.

-hawkeri (hawk′ er i)   New Guinea impatiens   1–3′/2′
    summer   many colors   New Guinea

New Guineas are a floricultural success story. Their introduction resulted from a joint USDA and Longwood Gardens expedition to Southeast Asia in 1970, from which a few plants arose, some with variegated leaves and large pink flowers. Over the years additional vegetatively propagated cultivars were put out by the greenhouse grower, mainly as gift plants, but they languished, never promoted as garden plants and not really catching on with the gardening public. Several fine cultivars, including several from seed, were available, but the tip of the iceberg had barely been seen. In the early 1990s, new cultivars from Kientzler in Germany were introduced to American growers by the Paul Ecke Ranch in California, and the market exploded. Cultivars with large (up to 3″ across) flowers and green, variegated, or bronze leaves are now seen in American landscapes —everywhere. I bet I have looked at hundreds of different forms in gardens and in trials; the fact is, there are no "dogs," and for the most part, distinguishing one from another is getting more and more difficult. In our trials, we look for persistence of flowering, particularly in the summer heat.

The foliage is in whorls of three to seven leaflets, usually dark green or bronze; the variegated forms are variegated or pink along the midribs. The leaves, held on short petioles, are ovate to elliptical with sharply toothed margins. Of course, as handsome as the leaves are, it is the flowers that have caused all the excitement. And exciting they are. Their size is probably the first thing that people notice: flowers are one and a half to two times larger than those of the bedding forms. Colors range from the gaudiest scarlets to pastel blushes and bicolors. The long spur on the back just adds a little more excitement to an already exciting plant. Most cultivars produce little seed, therefore few popping capsules occur.

Full sun in the North is possible, but partial shade is recommended even there. It is a must in the South (although they can tolerate more sun than bedding impatiens). They are heavy drinkers but do not do well in wet soils. Nearly all cultivars are vegetatively propagated by cuttings.

CULTIVARS

Baby Bonita series is a dwarf form, growing less than 1' tall. 'Kijal' (lavender), 'Kimpque' (scarlet), 'Kimptol' (rose), 'Kinar' (salmon), 'Kinic' (mid-pink), and 'Kisar' (purple) make up this series. I get upset with consumers who are too lazy to ask for plants by cultivar name, but the companies who named this and other New Guinea series share the blame. Give us a break!

'Ballet' has white flowers on dark shiny leaves.

'Calypso' has purple flowers with a white center.

Celebration series has been trialed extensively around the country and provides 15–30" plants in many colors. Apricot, bright coral, cherry red, deep red, light lavender, orange, purple, raspberry, rose, and salmon are among the available choices.

Celebrete series is an excellent group of dwarf plants, around 12–15" tall. Appleblossom, cherry, grape crush, hot rose, lavender, orange, peach, and scarlet are among the colors we trialed and were pleased with.

'Danova' has orange bicolored flowers.

'Foxtrot' produces violet-purple flowers.

Gem series is a double-flowered series, in blush pink, lavender, orange, orange pinwheel (red striping on light pink), pink, purple, red, and white.

Harmony series is a compact and well-developed series in twenty-five colors.

Java series is grown from seed, providing compact well-branched plants in lilac, orange, frosty white, and pink.

Lasting Impressions series often has markings on the foliage, either highly distinctive or just a tone here and there. 'Ambience' (reddish orange and pink bicolors), 'Blazon' (scarlet flowers with tinge of cream on foliage), 'Cameo' (salmon-pink), 'Heathermist' (lavender flowers, red midribs on leaves), 'Illusion' (light pink flowers, red midribs), 'Impulse' (bright pink), 'Purity' (white), 'Rhapsody' (deep purple), 'Serenade' (light lavender), 'Serenity' (cherry red), 'Shadow' (purple and carmine), and 'Tempest' (reddish orange and white bicolor).

Impatiens hawkeri 'Celebration Apricot'   ASHA KAYS

'Macarena' has 3″ wide bright orange flowers with glossy green foliage.

'Minuet' bears large bright pink flowers.

Ovation series comprises well-branched compact plants in several colors, including bright white, bright pink, blush pink, deep orange, hot pink, lavender, purple, red, salmon, 'Orange Swirls' ("swirls" generally means white streaks radiating from the center, in a picotee pattern), 'Orchid Star', 'Red Peppermint' (dark lavender with red stripes), 'Rose Swirls', and 'Salmon Pink Swirls'.

Paradise series offers compact, persistent flowering plants in many colors. Most have dark green to bronze leaves. Cultivars are sold either as a color or as the nonsensical cultivar name: 'Anguilla' (cherry rose), 'Antigua' (scarlet), 'Bonaire' (deep pink), 'Bora Bora' (violet), 'Grenada' (salmon), 'Guadeloupe' (fuchsia on lavender), 'Lanal' (red), 'Lopinga' (deep coral), 'Martinique' (cherry red), 'Moala' (true red), 'Moorea' (white), 'Nocturna' (wine), 'Pago Pago' (red on pink), 'Pascua' (orchid), 'Samoa' (pearl white), 'Tarawa' (bright red), 'Timor' (electric orange), 'Togo' (lavender-blue), 'Tonga' (orchid on blue), 'Woya' (light pink), and 'Xanthia' (orange).

Petticoat series consists of about eight colors and grows 12–15″ tall. Among the best is 'Petticoat Fire', whose dazzling scarlet flowers earned it a Georgia Garden Gold Winner in 1999.

Pizzazz series is 12–15″ tall in many colors.

'Polka' bears violet flowers with dark foliage.

Pretty Girl series includes 'Alexis' (deep pink), 'Flora' (coral pink), 'Kim' (cherry red), 'Sarah' (pink), 'Tina' (pink blush), and 'Vicky' (deeper pink blush).

Pure Beauty series is an excellent group of plants. Compact and free-flowering, they have looked good across the country: 'Aglia' (rose), 'Anaea' (red), 'Apollon' (fuchsia), 'Aruba' (purple), 'Dark Delias' (pink), 'Jolana' (magenta), 'Kallima' (light pink), 'Lycia' (orange on white), 'Marpesia' (scarlet), 'Melissa' (light coral), 'Neptis' (red on pink), 'Octavia' (lavender on purple), and 'Prepona' (bright red).

Riviera series has performed well in UGA trials. The 12–15″ tall plants can be found in several colors.

Spectra series from seed superseded 'Tango' and bears 2–3″ wide flowers in five colors.

'Sugar' bears large white flowers.

'Swing' produces bright purple bicolored flowers.

'Tango', among the first seed-propagated forms introduced, was an All-America Selection in 1989. The large orange flowers were outstanding, but plants were too tall. A shorter form may now be found as 'Tango Improved'.

'Tarantella' has purple-pink flowers.

-walleriana (wal er ee a′ na)   bedding impatiens, busy lizzie   1–3′/2′
    summer   many colors   East Africa

John Kirk, a British consul in Zanzibar (now part of Tanzania) in the mid 1860s, sent some seeds of this species to Europe in 1865. The seeds were grown in Kew Garden and were named, by Sir Joseph Hooker, *Impatiens sultanii*, after "that distinguished potentate, the Sultan of Zanzibar, to whose enlightened philanthropic rule eastern Africa owes so much." The name was later changed to *I. walleriana*, in honor of Horace Waller, a missionary in central Africa.

The bedding impatiens is the number-one-selling bedding plant. After turf grass, more bedding impatiens are likely planted than any ornamental plant in North America, and after begonias, they are probably the least demanding: put them in the shade and get out of the way. Mounds of flowers begin when plants are placed in the ground and continue until frost knocks them down. The leaves are mostly alternate, although they may be opposite near the top, wavy to toothed, and held on long petioles; they may be green-red, sometimes red-tinged beneath, but in general, bedding impatiens have less color in their foliage than New Guineas. Their flowers are smaller than New Guineas too, although present cultivars are larger than their predecessors. They are ¾–2″ wide and in almost all colors under the sun.

All breeding companies associated with bedding plants have established aggressive programs to introduce new series of impatiens (the market has been so strong that even a 5% share is significant). Such intensity has resulted in outstanding cultivars, and, as with the New Guinea impatiens, it is difficult to complain about any of them.

Although some claim that bedding impatiens perform well in full sun, do so at your own risk. North or South, I have never seen plants grow and flower as well in full sun as they do in partial shade. They are tolerant of deep shade and are obvious choices for deeply shaded areas: if hostas are the perennial kings for shade, then impatiens are the annual kings. Too much shade will result in lanky plants, so select shorter cultivars for heavily shaded areas.

CULTIVARS

Most series differ from each other only in seed germination, time to flower in the greenhouse, and height in the growing container; the differences in the garden performance of these modern hybrids are negligible. Unfortunately, as with most bedding plants, even if you ask for a cultivar by name, plants are too often labeled generically in the retail center.

Dwarf (9–15″), single flowers

Accent series is one of the most popular forms, growing about 12″ tall in twenty-four colors.

Butterfly series comes in cherry and peach shades with contrasting centers of darker colors.

Cajun series has bright colors on 12–15″ tall plants.

Carnival series is about 15″ tall in many colors. Among the better performers in our 1999 trials.

Dazzler series is well-branched and free-flowering in twenty colors.

Deco series is a little taller than other dwarfs, with dark green foliage. Flowers are available in eight colors.

Firefly Mix is a blend of colors on 8–10″ plants.

Impact series is an excellent and full series with 2″ flowers available in fourteen colors.

Infinity series has large flowers and is available in orange-scarlet, light pink, pink, salmon, and white.

'Mega Orange Star' has orange and white 2" wide flowers.

Mosaic series is unusual in that the flowers are streaked and textured with silvery lines. Lilac, rose, and violet are available. Terrific for "up-close and personal" work.

Stardust Mix provides white star-shaped patterns on pink, scarlet, and rose flowers.

Super Elfin series is a leading impatiens, with abundant flowering and compact habit. Available in only twenty-two colors. 'Super Elfin Blue Pearl' is a favorite of mine.

Swirl series is among the most beautiful impatiens and highly desirable for baskets or containers where people can appreciate the individual blooms. Flowers are swirled with darker color around the margin. Available in coral, peach, and pink.

'Wild Thing' bears deep magenta flowers with a slightly orange center.

Intermediate (15–20"), single flowers

Blitz series, among the first major introductions, made impatiens a staple. Flowers were large (2" wide); plants were vigorous and floriferous. The series was an All-America Selection in 1981. They were too tall for many landscapers and were improved in the Blitz 2000 series, which provides more compact habit.

Pride series has larger flowers (up to 2½" wide) in seven colors.

Shady Lady series has been around for many years and is still a fine series for the gardener. Available in fourteen colors.

Showstopper series has large flowers in sixteen colors. Excellent in baskets.

Starbright Mix is a mixture of colors with 2" wide flowers.

Tempo series is a fine group of plants, available in twenty-seven colors. (Impatiens breeders do not lack creativity. I bet none of us could name twenty-seven colors of anything.)

Double flowers

Cameo is a wonderful series of double-flowered impatiens. Colors are light pink, pink, scarlet, and white. Outstanding.

Carousel series has rosebud-like flowers, good branching, and vigorous growth. Available as 'Red Carousel' and a mix of colors.

Confection series has been bred in four colors and a mix.

Fiesta series is a popular double form, with good reason. Compact plants in six colors, vigorous and free-flowering on 16–22" tall plants. They performed very well in our trials at the University of Georgia.

Golden series takes a little getting used to, but some people like their look. They bear double flowers over variegated leaves. Dramatic for sure. 'Golden Anniversary' has lilac flowers, 'Golden Girl' bears pink blossoms, and 'Golden Sunrise' produces rosy pink blooms.

Rose Parade series has miniature rose flowers in four colors and a mix.

Tioga series is popular, providing several wonderful colors on 16–20" tall plants.

Impatiens walleriana 'Fiesta White'   ASHA KAYS

'Victorian Rose' offers bright rose semi-double flowers and good compact habit. An All-America Selection in 1998.

Alternative species

Impatiens noli-tangere (no lee tan′ je ree; touch-me-not) translates as "do not touch," a reference to the seed capsules. It is highly variable, ranging from 4′ to less than 1′ in height. The alternate leaves are up to 5″ long, ovate and pointed. The European equivalent of *I. capensis*, it has yellow flowers with red-spotted interiors, which, as in *I. capensis*, are held in three- or four-flowered racemes in the upper leaf axils.

Impatiens tinctoria is related to *I. glandulifera*. Native to cool areas of East Africa, this species grows up to 6′ tall with stout bamboo-like stems. The 8″ long leaves are spirally arranged and have an obvious red midrib. The hooded white flowers are held in many-flowered racemes. It is a tuberous impatiens; the tuber is reported to be perennial in temperatures as low as 1°F.

Quick key to *Impatiens* species

A. Leaves mostly alternate
    B. Flowers borne close to main stem, mainly double . . . . . . *I. balsamina*
    BB. Flowers held on long flower stems
        C. Plants >3' tall, flowers yellow-orange . . . . *I. capensis*
        CC. Plants <3' tall
            D. Flowers fused, helmet-like
                E. Flowers mainly yellow, leaf midrib red . . . . *I. auricoma*
                EE. Flowers white flushed pink, midrib not red . . . .
                 . . . . *I. balfourii*
            DD. Flowers not fused into helmet-like shape . . . . . *I. walleriana*
AA. Leaves mostly opposite or whorled
    B. Leaves obviously whorled, plants upright . . . . *I. glandulifera*
    BB. Leaves mostly arising from base, whorled or opposite . . . . *I. hawkeri*

Additional reading

Grant-Downton, Robert. 1992. In praise of *Impatiens tinctoria*. *The Garden* 117 (12):584–585.
Grey-Wilson, Christopher. 1997. Impestuous balsams. *The Garden* 122(8):583–587.
Shear, William A. 1997. Impatiens for summer. *Flower and Garden* 41(2):38–43.
Soucie, Gary. 1993. A poison ivy potion. *Field and Stream* 97(12):73.
University of Georgia Trial Reports: www.uga.edu/ugatrial

Ipomoea (ih po mee′ a)   morning glory   Convolvulaceae

Next time you see a vine that kind of looks like a morning glory, but kind of doesn't, know this: it is probably a cousin from this genus of about 450 species —exuberant trailers, runners, and vines all, and a terrific group of plants from which to choose a thug for your garden. Plants go under wonderful names like moonflower, red star vine, cypress vine, cardinal climber, sweet potato, and morning glory; nearly all contain ornamental flowers on enthusiastic stems.

Sometimes when I am looking at plants with morning glory–like flowers, I wonder if plants belong to *Ipomoea* or *Convolvulus*. In general, plants of *Convolvulus* are not as vigorous as those of *Ipomoea*, and they have smaller flowers and leaves than most species of *Ipomoea* one is likely to encounter. Sprawlers and climbers that cover significant ground are mostly ipomoeas, although *Convolvulus sabatius* and *C. tricolor* do trail somewhat. For a more scientific treatment, look at the top of the flower's pistil. Pistils of *Ipomoea* have one or two stigmas, globose or rounded; those of *Convolvulus* always have two stigmas, and they are oblong or linear in shape.

Quick guide to *Ipomoea* species

	Habit	Flower color
I. alba	climber	white
I. batatas	trailer	no flowers in ornamental forms
I. coccinea	climber	red
I. lobata	climber	scarlet to yellow
I. quamoclit	climber	scarlet
I. tricolor	climber	blue, violet, white

-*alba* (al′ ba)   moonflower   vine
    late   summer white   tropics

How can anyone not love the blooms of moonflower, with large white fragrant flowers on long narrow tubes? The flower buds, which appear during the day and consist of spiraled petals, are as handsome as the flowers. The anticipation of opening flowers is deliciously wonderful; head to the vine as early as 5:00 p.m. or "when the moon comes out," and you can watch the 6″ wide flowers slowly spiral open. Then stick your nose within to appreciate the fragrance. The flowers consist of exserted stamens (longer than the petals) and a two-lobed stigma. The deep green, heart-shaped leaves are 6″ across and equally long. The base of the stems are woody, and if parts of the plant are pulled off, a milky latex may be seen.

    The vines climb rapidly and will attain the height of whatever structure they climb on. We grow ours on a 10′ tall trellis, and it still topples over the top. Ours does not flower until late summer or fall and continues throughout the au-

Ipomoea alba   CHRIS JOHNSON

tumn. The large leaves, dense growth, and rapid rate of growth allow vines to be used as shelter on the balcony or deck. If the spiraled buds are cut prior to opening, they will open that evening in the house.

Full sun to partial shade. The hard seeds are difficult to germinate and should be soaked overnight or nicked with a chisel (scarified) to boost germination percentage.

-batatas (ba ta' tas)	sweet potato	vine
all season	foliage	South America

Who would've thunk it? The sweet potato, a star in the ornamental arena! Next thing you know, ornamental okra, ornamental corn, and ornamental cabbage will be poking through "normal" plants. If I have seen one 'Margarita' sweet potato, I have seen ten thousand, combined with almost anything, including other chartreuse-colored plants like 'Amazon' coleus, a truly nauseating sight. Don't get me wrong—I introduced 'Margarita' to the unsuspecting population (see "Cultivars" for story), but never did I think it would become so popular. Sweet potatoes have been, and are, an extraordinarily important food crop in the tropics, their tubers providing carbohydrates to millions of people. Stan Kays and Wayne Maclaurin, only a few doors down from me in the University of Georgia's department of horticulture, have been working with scientists the world over in the search for a perfect sweet potato. We get along famously, even though I have patiently explained to them that "perfect sweet potato" is an oxymoron. When Stan and Wayne try to get us together to taste-test their breeding efforts, you should see the place empty.

Plants consist of alternate heart-shaped to lobed leaves, in some cultivars 6" wide and equally long. Although the vegetable forms may have lavender to purple flowers, 2" wide, ornamental forms seldom produce flowers. Their claim to fame is their extraordinary growth rate, some 2' per week, particularly in areas with warm temperatures; I have seen some cultivars foaming out of containers in cool Portland and Seattle as well as hot Miami. The soft-fleshed tubers expand over time and may reach the size of basketballs—wrinkled, convoluted basketballs to be sure, but they are quite the hit when dug out of the garden in the fall. We just leave them on the ground, and people exclaim at the size and shape. The tubers of the ornamental forms too may be prepared and eaten, but they are not as tasty as those bred for flavor.

Full sun, propagate by terminal cuttings. Plants expand rapidly and grow rapidly, therefore copious moisture is needed. Sweet potato weevils and flea beetles, which riddle the leaves with tiny holes, can be quite destructive.

CULTIVARS

'Black Heart', a fine vigorous grower, is similar to 'Blackie' but has entire heart-shaped leaves. Foliage is as purple as 'Blackie'. Also sold as 'Ace of Spades'.

'Blackie', the first of the accepted ornamental forms of sweet potatoes, was apparently discarded from a USDA breeding program. The purple leaves are deeply five-lobed, 6" long and 4" wide.

'Ivory Jewel', less known than others, bears heart-shaped leaves with splashes of cream and bright green.

'Margarita' has lobed chartreuse leaves with a hint of thin purple margins. In the fall of 1993, I was speaking in Raleigh about potential new crops. When I mentioned 'Blackie' as a plant with terrific landscape potential, I was greeted with polite snickers; most in the audience were not ready to accept a vegetable as an ornamental. After the talk, one of North Carolina's finest horticulturists, Hunter Stubbs, said he had an unusual sweet potato with yellow-green leaves and asked if I would like to trial it at Georgia. We discussed potential names, and he suggested 'Margarita'. I placed it in the garden the following spring; growers were incredibly impressed, cuttings disappeared like no tomorrow, and the rest—as they say—is history. 'Margarita' differs from 'Sulphur', an older form, which we put beside it in the garden; 'Sulphur' was more upright and not as vigorous. Also sold as 'Marguerita' and 'Marguerite'.

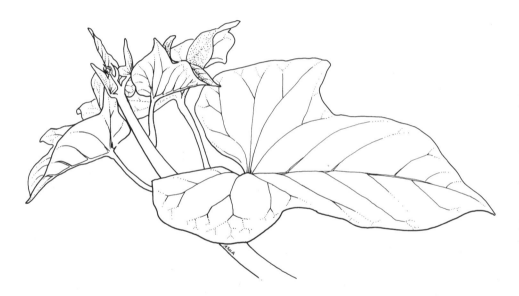

Ipomoea batatas 'Margarita'   ASHA KAYS

'Pink Frost' has 3″ wide leaves, each three-lobed leaf looking like a finger painting of pink, green, and white. It is beautiful and not nearly as vigorous as other cultivars out there, which may not be a bad thing; but if you are looking for the exuberant growth associated with 'Blackie' and 'Margarita', you will be disappointed. Also sold as 'Tricolor'.

'Terrace Lime', introduced in 1999, is so similar to 'Margarita' that when planted side by side in the UGA Horticulture Gardens, no one asked could tell the difference.

-*coccinea* (kok sin' ee a)   red morning glory   vine
summer   scarlet   eastern United States

This species is often seen as a roadside weed or scrambling through thickets in the central and eastern United States. The ovate leaves, 4–5″ long, are entire or with slightly toothed margins. The scarlet flowers consist of a 1″ long tube and flattened 1″ wide five-lobed disk. If fed and provided with a little care, the plants may put on a reasonable show.

Full sun to partial shade. Plants appear through seed distribution and may be propagated from seed reasonably easily. Plant in wilder areas among shrubs or plants that can support the twining stems.

-*lobata* (lo ba' ta)   Spanish flag   vine
summer   red and yellow   Mexico

Long known as *Mina lobata*, this species was recently folded into the genus *Ipomoea*. I loved the name Mina, but I'll get over it. Plants are different from most others in the genus, not as vigorous and with many-flowered forked racemes of curved flowers. I learned about Spanish flag from my friends Linda Copeland and Marilynn Kohla, who grew it in their gardens and during a greenhouse production course. It was great fun to see it twining up from their containers in the middle of a space otherwise filled with staid chrysanthemums and bedding plants.

The 2–3″ wide leaves are deeply three-lobed; a fourth "mini lobe" can be found to one side. The margins are coarsely toothed, and the base is heart-shaped. The 1″ long flowers are borne in the upper axils, and as the plant grows up, the flowers follow. Each one is narrowly tubular and slightly curved, with protruding stamens. They start scarlet and gradually mature to yellow; as many as thirty flowers can occur on a single raceme. Spanish flag does well climbing up a trellis or post or in combination in a large container. Much easier to use than other species of *Ipomoea* because it is a little less exuberant. On the other hand, it is not as easy to grow nor is it as eye-catching from a distance. A unique experience, nevertheless.

Full sun to partial shade, propagate by seed. Provide some structure for climbing.

-*tricolor* (tri' kul er)   morning glory   vine
summer   many colors   Mexico, South America

Fine garden writer Reginald Arkell offered this advice regarding morning glories, "If you don't look at them before breakfast, you probably don't see them at all." Morning is certainly the best time to see these flowers; looking for them when you get home from work just doesn't do it. A morning glory can be very beautiful or very weedy, depending on how long it has been reseeding all over the place. I love a well-grown morning glory, but boy, I get tired of the seedlings. Just like bindweed, and just as bad. Having said that, I am sure I am in the minority since most people I talk to are in love with this species. They probably don't worry about those seeds!

The smooth 2–3″ wide leaves are ovate to heart-shaped and borne on long petioles. The stems twine around any fence or support they can find and will grow up to 20′, although 10–15′ is more common. The funnel-shaped flowers are borne singly to severally and are 2–3″ wide. The common form is lavender with a yellow throat, but several other colors have been selected. Heat and moisture are needed for vigorous growth and enthusiastic flowering.

Propagate by seed, nicking or soaking the seed as suggested for *Ipomoea alba*. Place in full sun, provide shrubs or structures for support.

CULTIVARS

'Blue Star' produces fragrant pale blue flowers marked with a deeper blue star. An All-America Selection in 1949.

'Crimson Rambler' bears large crimson flowers with a white throat.

'Grandpa Ott's', an old form, has magenta flowers with a red star.

'Heavenly Blue' is probably the best-known cultivar, with large sky-blue flowers. 'Improved Heavenly Blue' has similar flowers but with a paler center.

'Pearly Gates' is one of my favorites, with large white flowers and a little blue color as well. An All-America Selection in 1942.

'Summer Skies' produces light blue flowers.

'Tie Dye' has 6″ wide blooms with deep purple swirls and splotches on a lavender background. To each his own. Leaves have a silvery sheen to them.

'Wedding Bells' bears rose-lavender flowers.

Alternative species

Ipomoea hederacea (he de ray′ see a), a relative of *I. tricolor*, has three-lobed ivy-like leaves with small blue or lavender funnel-shaped flowers. Its neatest form is 'Roman Candy', with green-and-white variegated leaves and rose to white flowers.

Ipomoea nil is also similar to *I. tricolor*, climbing with abandon and bearing large flowers. Plants are more hairy than *I. tricolor*. 'Chocolate' has unique chocolate-brown flowers; Early Call Mix, an All-America Selection in 1970, is a fast-flowering mixture of colors; 'Flying Saucers' bears 4–5″ flowers marbled white and blue; 'Scarlett O'Hara', an All-America Selection in 1939, consists of fiery (just like Scarlett) red flowers; 'Scarlet Star' produces scarlet flowers with a star-shaped white throat.

Ipomoea quamoclit (cypress vine) has 1″ wide scarlet flowers with distinct pointed lobes, like *I. coccinea*. The feathery leaves are pinnately divided into hair-like segments. Plants are seen from Florida to Texas and northward to Virginia and Kansas. Quite beautiful, although most people still look upon it as a weed.

Ipomoea ×sloteri (*I. ×multifida*; cardinal climber), a cross between *I. coccinea* and *I. quamoclit*, has 1–2″ wide scarlet flowers similar to cypress vine. Its foliage is much more ornamental: the 3″ wide leaves are palm-shaped and deeply cut into three to seven lobes. The three stamens of the flowers are exserted. Terrific plant.

Quick key to *Ipomoea* species

A. Flowers predominantly red or scarlet, 1–1½" wide
   B. Flowers long tubular with five equal lobes
      C. Leaves finely divided into narrow hairlike segments . . . .
      . . . . *I. quamoclit*
      CC. Leaves cordate . . . . *I. coccinea*
   BB. Flowers curved, turning yellow with age . . . . *I. lobata*
AA. Flowers usually lavender or purple, >2" wide, or no flowers produced
   B. Plant with smooth stems
      C. Stems long trailing, not climbing, no flowers . . . . *I. batatas*
      CC. Stems twining, climbing, flowers >2" wide
         D. Leaves cordate, 4–6" wide, flowers white, open
         in evening . . . . *I. alba*
         DD. Leaves cordate, 2–4" wide, flowers many colors,
         open in day . . . . *I. tricolor*
   BB. Plant with hairy stems
      C. Leaves obviously three-lobed, 2–3" long, flowers
      <2" wide . . . . *I. hederacea*
      CC. Leaves shallowly three-lobed, 3–4" long, flowers
      >2" wide . . . . *I. nil*

Additional reading

Armitage, Allan M. 1999. Sweet potato. *Greenhouse Grower* 17(3):103–104.
Baggett, Pam. 1997. The humble morning glory and its exotic kin. *American Cottage Gardener* 4(3):6–7.
Jesiolowski-Cebenko, Jill. 1998. Twining for morning glories. *Organic Gardening* 45(3):52–53.
Sanchez, Janet. 1996. Raising morning glories from seed. *Horticulture* 74(4):34–35.

Ipomopsis (ih po mop′ sis)   Polemoniaceae

I have grown this supposedly impressive group of plants (*ipo* is Greek, "to impress") in Georgia for a couple of years, and I've seen it elsewhere. Seldom have I been impressed. The genus consists of twenty-four species, but the only one grown is *Ipomopsis rubra* (standing cypress). Now, I love all cypress tree species, and to call this any kind of cypress is really pushing it. To be honest, I have seen some beautiful plantings, but mostly in the Northwest or the British Isles. In the Southeast and Midwest, plants lack vigor, heat tolerance, and weatherability; they never look as good as they do in catalog photos, which is a bit puzzling, as the species is native from South Carolina to Florida and west to Texas.

Ipomopsis rubra is 2–3′ tall, erect and unbranched, with leaves both in a basal rosette and alternate on stems. Leaves are about 1″ long, pinnately compound or divided, and light green. The flowers are held in a narrow terminal compound inflorescence, made up of trumpet-shaped flowers consisting of narrow sepals and 1″ long scarlet petals, yellow- or red-spotted inside. When its bright and vivid flowers are at their best, standing cypress can be impressive, just don't hold your breath.

Full sun to partial shade, propagate by seed. Plant no more than 9″ apart.

CULTIVARS

'Scarlet Surprise' bears deep scarlet flowers.

Iresine (er e see′ nay)   bloodleaf   Amaranthaceae

The genus consists of about eighty species, the cultivated ones of which are grown for their colorful leaves, as with *Alternanthera* and other leafy genera used for formal plant displays. The genus differs from *Amaranthus* by having opposite leaves (leaves are alternate in *Amaranthus*), and from *Alternanthera* by having larger flowers in spiky panicles (heads are axillary in *Alternanthera*).

-herbstii (hairbst′ ee i)   beef plant   9–18″/12″
summer   red   Brazil

In the tropics, this species easily attains 6′ in height, but in most areas of this country, it is of bedding plant height. The species has either purplish red leaves with lighter midrib and arched side veins or, occasionally, green leaves with yellowish veins, but cultivars with more scarlet in the foliage have been selected to provide the red in floral clocks or floral flags. The leaves are 1–2″ long, heart-shaped to nearly circular, and often notched at the apex. The creamy white flowers are small and bundled together in 2–4″ long panicles. This species is chiefly used for plant painting. Plants also make fine specimens for containers and edging, although they seldom see their way into the gardener's domain.

CULTIVARS

'Aureoreticulata' bears reddish green leaves with yellow veins.

'Beefsteak', which grows about 12″ tall in containers, has brilliant red heart-shaped leaves.

'Brilliantissima', the most coveted form, has rich crimson leaves.

'Wallisii' is a dwarf selection (<9″ tall) with dark purple, almost black foliage.

Alternative species

Iresine lindenii (lin den′ ee i) differs from *I. herbstii* by having pointed lanceolate (rather than circular) leaves. It is often even redder in leaf color, with stems just as red. 'Formosa' has yellow leaves with crimson veins.

J

Jasminum (jas min' um) jasmine Oleaceae

Jasmines are seldom considered annuals in American gardens. Most are sold as slow-growing shrubs or climbers, such as winter jasmine (*Jasminum nudiflorum*), showy jasmine (*J. floridum*), primrose jasmine (*J. mesnyi*), and common white jasmine (*J. officinale*). Greeted heartily as perennial shrubs by gardeners in zone 6 (*J. nudiflorum*) and zone 8 (the other three species), they are otherwise ignored—except when snowbirds wander south in the winter. I too see little use for jasmine as an annual, but one plant might be worth a try in gardens, at least in the South.

-sambac (sam' bak) Arabian jasmine 1–3'/2'
summer white India

I have tried and rather like Arabian jasmine as a fragrant addition to the sunny garden. We tried *Jasminum sambac* for a couple of years in Athens, and I saw excellent plantings at Cheekwood Botanical Garden in Nashville. In both locations, plants die quickly with frost. Plants, which bear shiny green opposite or whorled leaves, are the bushy rather than the climbing sort of jasmine. The single clean white flowers open in three- to seven-flowered clusters and appear constantly over the summer (although plants are never covered with flowers). As with other jasmines, it is the wonderful fragrance that brings people back to the plant time and again. They are slow growers, and patience is a must. Disappointing in cool summers; dry climates are best for most vigorous growth and flower power.

Full sun, propagate by cuttings.

CULTIVARS

'Arabian Knights' is an upright plant that bears single white flowers.

'Grand Duke of Tuscany' has 1½" fully double flowers, similar at first sight to small carnations. Fragrant.

'Maid of Orleans' is similar to 'Arabian Knights'.

K

Kaempferia (kemp fer′ ee a)   peacock ginger   Zingiberaceae

Here is a genus just waiting to be discovered. (That it has been used for years in Texas and Florida simply reflects the good taste of people from those states.) The generic name recognizes the contributions of German botanist Engelbert Kaempfer (1651–1716), who studied plants in Sweden, Indonesia, Japan, and the Middle East. He described such new genera as *Hydrangea* and *Ginkgo*, as well as new varieties of magnolias and azaleas.

Plants, which are sometimes referred to as the southern hosta, are characterized by a large rosette of handsome leaves, which start out like large curled-up tongues and unfold over a few days. The leaves may be green or bronze, splotched with white or edged in white, and are 6–12″ long and almost as wide. The phlox-like white and blue flowers are borne singly or in pairs in the center of the plant. Species are seldom more than 1′ in height and up to 2′ wide. All species are native to the tropics of Asia, which is why they are not enjoyed throughout the country. They require lots of heat, and many greenhouse operators cannot afford to produce them in cold winters. Plants grow fine outdoors when temperatures are above 75°F, but they are slow to move below that.

I have tried only a few of the fifty known species, but people who see them can't get enough. Among the most attractive is *Kaempferia atrovirens* (silver peacock), which has striking silver-patterned leaves and white flowers with purple on the lip; 'Brownie' has chocolate-brown leaves with a small amount of silver. *Kaempferia gilbertii* has white margins around the green leaves, which are more narrow than many of the species; plants are 6–9″ tall and flowers, very pale blue to white. Its selection '3-D' has more intense variegation, with leaves white, dark green, and light green. I really enjoy some of the cultivars of *K. pulchra*, which species has highly patterned foliage and light purple flowers, often with white centers: 'Bronze Peacock' has wonderful bronze leaves with a feather pattern; 'Roscoe' has larger leaves with a similar pattern; and 'Silverspot' produces a mound of green foliage with white to silver spots. *Kaempferia rotunda* is known as the resurrection ginger because the white and purple flowers appear before the leaves break the soil. Its leaves are silvered, often with a bronze hue underneath; plants grow to 2′ tall, but 'Snow Queen' can top out at 4′.

Kaempferia pulchra   CHRIS JOHNSON

Kaempferias require deep shade. Full sun in the South will cause leaves to bleach within a few days, and in the North, the damage is done a few days after that. Provide sufficient moisture and fertilize in the spring once temperatures rise above 70°F.

Related genera

The genus *Kaempferia* was larger until some species were split off and assigned to other genera. *Cornukaempferia aurantiaca* has dark maroon markings on the uppersides and is slightly purplish on the undersides of the green leaves; 'Jungle Gold' bears bright golden flowers at the base of the foliage—a fabulous plant! The approximately seven species that were placed in *Siphonochilus* (si fon o chil' us) have ornamental leaves and also want deep shade; they differ from

Kaempferia in subtle flower characteristics and by being more upright. *Siphono-chilus decorus* (yellow trumpet) and *S. kirkii* (pink trumpet) have canary-yellow and lavender flowers, respectively.

Additional reading

Chapman, Timothy. 1995. *Ornamental Gingers*. 6920 Bayou Paul Rd., St. Gabriel, LA 70776.

San Felasco Nurseries: www.sanfelasco.com

Stokes Tropicals: www.stokestropicals.com

Wight Nurseries of North Carolina: www.wightnurseries.com

Kochia (ko′ kee a)   burning bush   Chenopodiaceae

Where have all the kochias gone? I remember a time, not so long ago, when *Kochia* (syn. *Bassia*) was common in landscapes. Not like marigolds or petunias, certainly, but not as difficult to find as it is now. They were grown in abundance for their light green feathery foliage and columnar habit, which harmonizes so well with low-growing plants. I have seen fabulous combinations of *Kochia* with heliotrope, geraniums, and bidens, or as a simple contrast in containers with prostrate petunias. And it looks wonderful in the summer even before it does its biblical thing, that is, become a burning bush. In the fall, cool temperatures cause the leaves to turn purple-red, like the leaves of maple trees. The color is far more obvious in the Northeast (and other places where temperatures fall quickly in the autumn) than in the Southeast. If leaf color is good in the fall, then so will the bush burn lively. During hot summers, plants languish and look poor before turning crimson. In the South, they may be planted in mid summer and will enjoy a modest color change in the late fall.

Kochia scoparia (sko pa′ ree a; summer cypress), native to southern Europe and Asia, is the only species grown; its most common form is the erect f. *tricho-phylla*, which has many alternate, smooth, three-veined leaves. The narrow leaves are soft, accounting for the plant's common name. The small inconspicuous flowers are of little interest.

Full sun, well-drained soils. Propagate by seed *in situ*, when threat of frost has passed.

CULTIVARS

'Acapulco Silver' produces two-tone leaves that are silvery white at the ends. The bush resembles an ice cream cone during the summer, its season of interest, but plants are not quite as vigorous as *Kochia scoparia*. An All-America Selection in 1983.

'Autumn Red' is an improved form of *Kochia scoparia*, meaning that plants are more uniform and fall color is more consistently red.

'Evergreen' is 2–3′ tall and stays green, which kind of defeats the purpose. A handsome plant, nevertheless.

Alternative species

Kochia trichophylla (trih ka' fil a; burning bush) may in fact be the common form cultivated in gardens. The leaves are more narrow than those of *K. scoparia*, and plants always turn reddish in the fall. It is difficult to know just what one is purchasing; happily, if the plant performs well, it really doesn't matter.

L

Lablab (lab′ lab)   hyacinth bean   Fabaceae

"Plant them beans here, son, and get outta the way." Everyone needs a mentor, and what this fine gentleman lacked in grammar he more than made up for with plant know-how. I did what he said, and sure enough, like Jack's beanstalk, seedlings ripped through the ground and started reaching for the sky. "Them beans" were the seeds of the hyacinth bean, *Lablab purpureus*, the only species in the genus, and they produced 10–20′ tall vines of purple flowers and purple beans. The young pods are edible fresh (after soaking) or dried and are not uncommon as a foodstuff in the tropics, particularly in India. Smaller-fruited forms are valued for food production. Plants were previously classified as *Dolichos lablab*; luckily the word "lablab," whatever its position, assures this plant is recognizable in garden conversation.

The alternate leaves are trifoliate, each triangular leaflet about 6″ long and wide, held on long slender petioles from the twining stems. The stems require something strong to grow on; bamboo poles will be pulled down by the weight of the plant. I use strong metal fencing held between two stout posts and allow the stems to clamber to the top. I also let hyacinth bean grow through woodies, like hollies. When the vine reaches the top of its support, whatever it is, it simply falls back upon itself. The ornamental value of this thug-like plant is the dark green leaves, followed by fragrant purple flowers in the leaf axils. The bean-like flowers occur throughout the summer and give way to flat purple beans, 6″ long. The vine makes a terrific shade cover for the west or south side of a porch or patio.

Propagate by seed. Fruit (with seed within) may be collected from the vines and stored in a cool, dry area. Sow seed *in situ*, in full sun, and get out of the way.

CULTIVARS

'Albus' has white flowers and fruit. Not nearly as handsome as the species. Also sold as 'Giganteus'.

'Ruby Moon' has bicolored pink flowers and purple pods. Quite fascinating.

Lantana (lan tan′ a)   shrub verbena   Verbenaceae

The differences between annuals and perennials becomes blurred, depending on where one lives and the plant in question. To Floridians, Californians, and Texans, *Lantana* can be a serious weed, cropping up everywhere and never going away, while for the rest of the country, it is a sought-after colorful annual, dying at the first major frost. What *Lantana* brings to the table is season-long flowering in a diversity of heights and colors. In general, its members are happy in moderate climates and ecstatic in hot summers, but some species are not as tolerant of hot, humid climates as others are.

I must admit, even to my students, that I sometimes have trouble telling *Lantana* from the annual species of *Verbena*. The genera have similar flower heads and flowers, and some species are similar in habit as well. To be sure, the leaves of *Lantana* are smoother, less hairy, and more fragrant than those of *Verbena*; and most lantanas are bigger and more upright, but those qualities are so variable it is hard to count on them as defining characteristics. For most people and for most plants, the two genera are easy to tell apart, but some of the differences require a 10× hand lens:

	Leaves	Stamens	Ovary
Lantana	opposite or whorled, dentate, often wrinkled	two pairs, unequal lengths	two-celled
Verbena	always opposite, toothed, incised	two pairs, equal lengths	four-celled

Quick guide to *Lantana* species

	Flower color	Fruit	Height	Cultivars
L. camara	orange, yellow, often bicolored	black, inconspicuous	1–6′	many
L. montevidensis	rosy lilac	black, inconspicuous	2–3′	none
L. trifolia	lavender	lavender, conspicuous	2–3′	none

-camara (ka′ ma ra)   lantana   1–6′/2′
  summer   many colors   tropics

The most common and colorful lantanas belong to this species or are hybrids involving it. Where summer heat wreaks havoc with other annuals or perennials, they are outstanding plants, producing dense heads of flowers throughout the season. The leaves are opposite and roughly hairy above but not as rough beneath. Some of the "wilder" forms have thorns, particularly near the base, and several cultivars have a decidedly prickly feel. In general, the dentate leaves are held on 1″ long petioles. Leaves often have a heavy fragrance (some say it smells like lemon) when crushed; the scent is more conspicuous on some cultivars than on others, and more pleasant to some noses than others. The flowers are usually bicolored, changing colors from bud to open flower. The dense flower heads are formed in leaf axils, the inflorescences expanding as the flowers mature. The fruit starts green and turns black on maturity.

Plants show extraordinary variation in vigor and height: some forms grow less than 1' tall, others grow 4' in a single year. This species is grown throughout the country, often as a trained standard in public gardens.

Full sun, propagate by cuttings.

CULTIVARS

Many, many cultivars are offered. Subtle differences set some apart, some are identical but bear different names. Some are more upright, many others are low-growing. They all flower with flair. I have trialed many available cultivars of *Lantana* over the years, trying to sort out those that were remarkably similar and those that were distinctive, with these results.

Lookalike cultivars
That the following pairs are similar in no way means they are not fine cultivars; similarities in such a large genus seems unavoidable. The news for the gardener is this: if a favorite taxon is not available, then perhaps its twin will suffice.

'Bronze' and 'Lady Olivia' have identical leaves, size, and upright habit, and both have pale coral buds that open to a soft pink to yellow flower.

'Confetti' and 'Patriot Rainbow' have virtually identical flowers of yellow, orange, and pink. And although their upright habit is *supposed* to be different ('Confetti' much more open and tall vs. the super-compactness of 'Patriot Rainbow'), in our trials, both were very compact.

'Gold Mound' and 'Patriot Moonshine' have the same golden flower, but 'Patriot Moonshine' is more upright than spreading. Both are incredibly floriferous and vigorous.

'Irene' and 'Spreading Sunset' share the same multicolor flowers (bright yellow, red, and pink). 'Irene' is more upright; 'Spreading Sunset' is, as the name implies, more spreading!

'Lemon Drop' and 'Yellow' are another set of identical twins: butter-yellow flowers, small leaves, and sprawling, trailing habit.

'Patriot Bouquet' and 'Patriot Desert Sunset' offer a similar effect at several paces: orange-gold, pink, and coral blooms (although from a bug's-eye view, the order in which these colors appear on each flower head may differ). Both are upright, extremely vigorous, and very colorful.

'Patriot Firewagon' and 'Radiation' have similar gold to deep orange-red flowers. 'Radiation' is the low-grower of the two; 'Patriot Firewagon' is more upright.

'Silver Mound' and 'Snowfall' offer identical flowers (creamy white with a gold eye). Again, exuberant both in number of flowers and in spreading habit.

Distinctive cultivars
'Athens Rose', from Perth, Western Australia, grows 3–4' tall in a single season. The flower buds start red, then open rose and yellow. A vigorous upright grower, woody at the base. Appears to be cold hardy in zone 7.

Lantana camara 'Athens Rose'   ASHA KAYS

'Clear White' has a low, spreading upright habit and all-white flowers with no eye.

'Greg Grant', named for the fine Texas plantsman, bears handsome gold and cream variegations on the foliage. The flowers are light pink fading to yellow. Upright grower.

'Miss Huff' was found in a garden in north Georgia and propagated and grown by Goodness Grows Nursery in Lexington, Georgia. She is the tallest upright and the most vigorous lantana known, accruing 5–6' of new growth in height and width in a single season. The flowers are orange and yellow and appear all season. Definitely cold hardy in zone 7.

'New Gold', a spreader, is among the finest cultivars of recent years. Plants are 9–15" tall and absolutely covered with bright golden flowers throughout the growing season.

'New Red' is actually a crimson-orange with an upright yet compact habit.

'Orchid' is a lovely soft lavender with a vigorous sprawling and cascading habit.

'Patriot Honeylove' lends a faded effect, with flowers in shades of pale pink, butter yellow, and ivory. Very low and spreading.

'Patriot Rainbow' is beyond compact, with flowers of bright gold and pink. Many fine cultivars may be found under the Patriot name, all bred by Jack and Jo Roberson.

'Pink Lace' is a vigorous upright and a prolific bloomer, offering a strong pastel effect of lavender and pink flowers with gold eyes.

'Samantha' is a very compact spreader with excellent lemon-and-lime variegated foliage and bright yellow flowers. Eyepopping! And about 1' tall.

'Tangerine' produces small, loose flower heads in citrusy shades of orange to gold. Low habit.

'Yellow/White', whose flowers resemble those of both 'Silver Mound' and 'Snowfall', has bigger leaves and a drastically more compact, and upright, habit than either.

-trifolia (tri fo' lee a)	lavender popcorn	3'/3'
summer	lavender	West Indies, Mexico

I can hardly contain my glee when I see this shrubby species in the garden. I get excited, and people want to know why I enjoy this—to all appearances—dull, lanky, lavender-flowered plant so much. Like a kid eager to tell the ending of a movie, I have a hard time not letting the secret out of the bag.

The 3–4″ long leaves are oblong to lanceolate, whorled (usually in threes but sometimes in fours), and very roughly hairy; the 1½–2″ wide flat-topped inflorescence consists of small lavender flowers, sometimes with more pink or occa-

Lantana trifolia   ASHA KAYS

sionally white. But the best part of the plant is the fruit that follows the flowers. The inflorescences lengthen, and the lavender fruit expands to form what appears to be a delicious-looking ear of corn. People invariably smile when they stop to look. The fruit (which in shape and color recalls the fruit of beautyberry, *Callicarpa*) remains on the cob unless it is handled, in which case it falls off readily.

Plants are shrubby, but a hard pinch or two early in the growing season will help tame the lanky tendencies somewhat. Fertilize as needed; too much nitrogen results in too leafy a plant.

Propagate by seed (remove the lavender skin) or cuttings.

Alternative species

Lantana montevidensis (mon tee vih den' sis; weeping lantana) is related to *L. camara* but is more prostrate. This species, native to Montevideo, boasts trailing stems without any hint of thorns. The ½" wide flowers are held on many-flowered 1–1½" wide heads and are always lavender to rosy lilac in color. Excellent in containers and falling out of raised beds.

Quick key to *Lantana* species

A. Flowers lavender or rosy lilac
    B. Flowers lavender, fruit elongated, lavender, highly
       conspicuous .... *L. trifolia*
    BB. Flowers lavender to rosy lilac, fruit rounded, not
       elongated .... *L. montevidensis*
AA. Flower many colors, often bicolored .... *L. camara*

Additional reading

Allen, Oliver E. 1987. Step-by-step: training a standard lantana. *Horticulture* 65(8):30–31.

Armitage, Allan M. 2000. Is there a market for annuals with ornamental fruit? *Greenhouse Grower* 18(5):140–146.

———. 2000. Lavender popcorn, *Lantana trifolia*. *Horticulture* 97(3):76.

Armitage, Allan M., and H. Scoggins. 1996. Lantana. *Greenhouse Grower* 14(10): 90–93.

Bender, Steve. Flowers through thick and thin. *Southern Living* 24(5):106–108.

Riley, Ellen. 1999. Perfect planters in sun or shade. *Southern Living* 34(4):55–56.

University of Georgia Trial Reports: www.uga.edu/ugatrial

Lathyrus (la' thih rus)   wild pea   Fabaceae

The genus consists of more than a hundred species, from those used for silage in dairy farms to fragrant garden ornamentals. While half a dozen species can be found occasionally in seed catalogs, it is the sweet pea, *Lathyrus odoratus*, that people think of when this genus is discussed. The rise in popularity of ornamental horticulture reflected the rise in popularity of the sweet pea. Sweet peas were introduced in England around 1699 and were first offered for sale in catalogs in 1730. The Invincible series appeared in 1866 and was introduced to America in 1870; they were originally intended to be grown as sweet pea hedges and screens and included for their fragrance in bouquets. The first miniature sweet pea, 'Cupid', was introduced by the Burpee Company in 1893, and by the late 1800s, more than 130 cultivars had been bred. The love of sweet peas, as representatives of the taste and spirit of post-Victorian years, was at its height in 1914. In the garden, sweet peas remain popular for their subtle flower colors and wonderful fragrance.

Interestingly, unlike most of its edible fellow peas, the sweet pea is poisonous, bringing on convulsions, leg paralysis, and unconsciousness when consumed. Fortunately, a lot of seeds must be eaten before lathyrism, as the condition is called, occurs, and few cases have been reported. Unfortunately, European seed catalogs still offer a wider choice of cultivars than American seed catalogs, in which perhaps a dozen choices may be available. Other species may be had, in particular *Lathyrus latifolius* (perennial sweet pea; zones 4 to 8), but the annual sweet pea remains the most popular.

-odoratus (o dor a´ tus)		sweet pea	vine
spring	many colors		southern Europe

Sweet peas are vines, growing to 10′ when given a support to which the tendrils can clasp. The winged stems bear alternate one-paired leaflets, 1–2″ long and ½″ wide. The keeled flowers, which are held on short flower stems, occur in groups of two to four and in a wide range of colors. Fragrance is a prime incentive for growing sweet peas—walk by a fence full of flowers or a vase with even one or two to gain some understanding of the sweet pea mania of Victorian times. Tall forms with long stems are now grown as a commercial crop for cut flowers under elaborate systems in greenhouses, mainly on the West Coast, and dwarf pot types have also become popular. They all require cool temperatures to do well and are therefore far more popular on the West Coast than on the East.

I am terribly jealous of gardeners who can grow sweet peas as easily as autumn clematis. Essentially, plants require a cool root run, good air circulation, and plenty of light. Soak seeds overnight and sow indoors in winter; place out in early spring, once the threat of frost has passed, but while cool days and nights are common. They may be sown outdoors in fall if a cloche or mini-greenhouse is used over the seeds. They may also be sown *in situ* in very early spring, where the ground does not freeze or only slight freezes occur; however, germination will not occur until soils reach 60°F. Plants grow well until temperatures reach 75–80°F; as temperatures rise, the quality of the plants declines. Removing flowers and fruit helps maintain continued flowering.

Seed catalogs are the only source of sweet pea cultivars, so look through some of your favorites and find something that looks enticing. Do not overlook the non-climbing bush forms of var. *nanellus*, which is about 2' tall and fragrant; the Explorer series is one such offering.

Additional reading

Ganter, Mary N. 1995. Charming sweet peas. *Flower and Garden* 39(1):28–32.
Inge, Dominique. 1999. Sweet peas. *Horticulture* 96(5):34–36.

Laurentia (lor en' see a)   isotoma   Campanulaceae

This genus is a bit confused, as experts pull plants from *Isotoma* into *Laurentia*. I am not sure if one is more correct than the other, but three species of this mostly Australian genus are sold in this country under *Laurentia*. (In Australia, *Laurentia* appears to be a synonym of *Isotoma*, in this country, the other way around.) A related genus, *Pratia*, is equally confused. According to Rodger Elliot, "*Pratia*, *Isotoma*, and *Lobelia* have many similarities, and it is often only the differences in fruit which separate them from each other. *Pratia pedunculata* is very difficult to separate from *Isotoma fluviatilis*. The pratia has bisexual, male, and female flowers, whereas *I. fluviatilis* nearly always has bisexual flowers, with possibly a few females, and its tubular flowers are split nearly to the base, while the pratia has more fan-shaped flowers. All double dutch!"

How about double Greek? Have no fear! Try out any plant you can find with any of the above names. If you like it, try to figure out what it really is; if it dies, who cares? One caution first: the milky sap of some *Laurentia* species, including *L. axillaris*, can cause severe irritation and swelling on contact with skin and eyes. People with sensitive skin are more susceptible. If that describes you, be sure to wear appropriate clothing when gardening in the vicinity of laurentias. (Rodger Elliot further mentions that the genus has been implicated in the deaths of cattle and sheep, but this has not been substantiated by analytical research.)

Quick guide to *Laurentia* species

	Habit	Leaf margin
L. axillaris	upright	pinnately divided
L. fluviatilis	spreading	slightly toothed

-*axillaris* (aks il ar' is)   upright isotoma, star flower   6–15"/1'
summer   blue-violet   Australia

Laurentia axillaris (syn. *Isotoma axillaris*) is a terrific plant, with multibranched stems bearing deeply divided alternate leaves. Leaves are about 1" wide along the midribs and 2–3" long, with linear lobes. When not in flower, the green plants look a little like a thistle. They grow about 1' tall, but I have seen plants at least double that. The axillary flowers are somewhat similar to those of *Lobelia*; the corolla has five equal, uncut linear lobes, presenting a star-like appearance. The stamens are attached near the top of the corolla of the blue-purple flowers, although hues vary significantly. Some people claim cold hardiness to zone 6, but I have had no success in Athens (zone 7). They are at their best flowing out of mixed containers.

Full sun, propagate by seed.

CULTIVARS

'Blue Stars', the most common cultivar, is probably just the species with a spiced-up name.

'Pink' is just that.

'Shooting Stars', the modern name for var. *alba*, has white flowers.

'Stargazer' is a mixture of blue-, white-, and pink-flowered forms.

-fluviatilis (floo vee a' tih lis)	blue star creeper	2–4"/1'
summer	blue	Australia

I grow this creeping species (syn. *Isotoma fluviatilis*) in my garden, among the rocks surrounding a small pond. For me, it is much hardier than *L. axillaris* and comes back regularly. The specific name refers to its preferred habit of "belonging to a river." The stems bear dozens of small leaves, oblong-ovate and less than 1" long. The small light blue star-shaped flowers are held in the leaf axils and almost cover the plant in late spring and early summer. Flowers appear off and on later, but it is essentially a spring flowerer. Outstanding plant for a moist area.

Partial shade, moist conditions. Propagate by seed or cuttings.

Alternative species

Laurentia anethifolia (syn. *Isotoma anethifolia*) is related to *L. axillaris* but with leaves even more deeply divided. Flowers are about 1" across and usually white, sometimes pale pink. Flowering is sporadic, usually from mid summer through early fall.

Quick key to *Laurentia* species

A. Leaves deeply divided, plants upright . . . . *L. axillaris*
AA. Leaves not divided, plants prostrate . . . . *L. fluviatilis*

Lavatera (la va ter' a)   tree mallow   Malvaceae

The genus is named for physician and naturalist J. R. Lavater, who lived and worked in sixteenth-century Zurich. Some of the most beautiful plants in the large mallow family reside in this genus of perennials, biennials, and annuals.

Lavatera can be distinguished from other members of Malvaceae, such as hibiscus and flowering maple, by the three pointed and joined bracts under the flower and by the slightly lobed leaves. Plants are highly sought after for the profusion of bloom they provide in spring and summer. Of the twenty-five species in the genus, only *Lavatera trimestris* is widely grown as an annual.

-*trimestris* (tri mes′ tris)   3–5′/3′
summer   pink   Mediterranean

This species is among the most beautiful flowering annuals. In British Columbia, people stop in their tracks when they happen upon the pink mallow blossoms covering the shrub-like plants at Butchart Gardens; in California, where it is grown as a cut flower, it is shockingly beautiful while it is showing off its wares, row after row. But for me, living in the challenged Armitage garden, desire for this species is like wanting to ask out the prettiest girl in school but knowing there is no chance she would consider a twit like me. So it is with many gardeners in the Midwest and East, who end up with a less-than-satisfactory blind date with *Lavatera trimestris*. They shouldn't be surprised: this is a Mediterranean species, and not too much of North America is particularly Mediterranean-like. Cool nights, warm days, and dry climates are to its liking, and we all have some of those. Thus, in the South for example, plant them, enjoy them, and then—when plants start taking exception to the less-than-Mediterranean summers—move on. This is true for many fine plants: perhaps the term "short-lived perennial" should be extended to include "short-lived annual." That all annuals

Lavatera trimestris
CHRIS JOHNSON

must look like the catalog five months of the year is simply a mind-set that needs changing.

The 3″ wide lower leaves are rounded to heart-shaped and sparsely covered with stiff hairs; the upper leaves are slightly three-, five-, or seven-lobed. The solitary 2½–3″ wide white or pink flowers are held in the upper axils and are saucer-shaped. Beneath the petals, you can see the small green sepals, and beneath those, the three ovate and mostly united bracts (epicalyx) characteristic of the genus. Flowers persist for many days, depending on temperature, and flower buds continue to form. Plants may have some problems, but abundance of flowers is surely not one of them. They flower and flower, totally covering the plant when they are happy. The stems may be cut and flowers brought in; harvest in the morning and place with other flowers in a floral preservative.

Flowers in particular, but also the foliage, are prey to Japanese beetles in the summer and can be badly disfigured, especially if plants are under stress. Most members of the family are so disposed, but this species seems unfairly chosen. Perhaps the damage inflicted upon it by those rotten little beetles just seems worse because its flowers are so perfect.

Full sun in the North, partial shade in the South. Propagate by seed or cuttings.

CULTIVARS

'Dwarf White Cherub' is covered with white flowers and grows only 12–15″ tall.

'Grandiflora' has large rose-red flowers with darker venation.

'Loveliness' grows 3–3½′ tall and produces trumpet-shaped deep rose flowers.

'Mont Blanc' is only about 2′ tall with pure white blossoms. A Fleuroselect award winner.

'Mont Rose' is the darker equivalent to 'Mont Blanc'.

Parade Mix is a mixture of flower colors including pink, cherry red, and white.

'Pink Beauty' bears delicate pink flowers with violet veins and a dark eye. Plants are bushy, growing 2–2½′ tall.

'Ruby Regis' bears large (3–4″ wide) cerise-pink flowers on 2½–3′ tall plants.

'Salmon Beauty' has salmon-rose flowers with dark rose veins. Height is 2½–3′.

'Silver Cup' produces large flowers (4″ wide) of iridescent pink. The many-branched plants are 2–2½′ tall. A Fleuroselect award winner.

'Splendens' produces large white or rose flowers on 3′ tall plants.

Alternative species

Lavatera arborea (tree mallow), a biennial whose seed is occasionally sold, flowers first year from seed and is often treated as an annual. It is a large plant, growing 6–8′ in a single year and producing clusters of small lilac to purple flowers in the leaf axils. Most areas are too cold for this species, but it may be worth a try.

Additional reading

Byers, Peggy. 1988. Seed packet annuals. *Flower and Garden* 32(2):56–57.

Layia (lay' ee a)   Asteraceae

Between 1825 and 1828, the ship *Blossom*, captained by Richard Beechey, visited the Pacific Northwest and the Bering Straits. It landed in 1827 on the coast of California, where the ship's botanist found many marvelous coastal plants, one of which was *Layia*, named for naturalist George Tradescant Lay. Of the fifteen species in the genus, only *L. platyglossa* is used to any extent.

-platyglossa (plat ee glos' a)	tidy tips	10–15″/12″
spring	yellow with white	California

This species is characterized by its ten- to twelve-ray yellow flowers, each tipped with white and about 1″ wide. Black anthers within the flower add a little more color. The flowers are formed on small plants with entire to pinnately divided linear leaves. Plants are easy to grow from seed and may be direct sown in early spring or transplanted while cool. They abhor heat of any kind and will likely tire out by early summer in most areas of the country, West Coast excepted. I saw these plants growing beautifully in a trial site managed by Roger Ditmer, a fine horticulturist on Sea Island, off the coast of Georgia. They were fabulous in the spring and certainly turned my head, but their beauty was fleeting. But for gardeners, fleeting is normal, and beauty, sometimes, all too rare.

Full sun to partial shade, propagate by seed.

CULTIVARS

'Alba' is a pure white form.

Lechenaultia (lech en al' tee a)   Goodeniaceae

I was fortunate to spend a sabbatical in Australia several years ago, and although most people who go to that great country end up in the east, we spent our time in Western Australia. Like a kid in a candy store, I would wander out of Perth every chance I got and stick my fingers into the bins of colorful wildflowers painting the countryside. That I didn't know it all was not a surprise, but the extent of my ignorance shocked me completely. I expected not to recognize many genera, but that I had never even heard of most of the plant families was a lesson in humility. In the end, I could hardly restrain my glee at recognizing *Chorizema, Dampiera, Pimelia, Scaevola,* and *Thysanotus*. Spring in Australia is magical—in Western Australia, it is kaleidoscopic.

| ***-biloba*** (bi lo′ ba) | blue lechenaultia | 9–15″/12″ |
| spring | blue | Western Australia |

Blue lechenaultia is the very definition of the term "wildflower" in Western Australia. Many plantspeople consider that the flowers of this species are the most beautiful of all the world's blue flowers. Quite a claim, and I cannot disagree with it. Coming upon a native stand of it by the roadside invariably means a workout for the car brakes and camera shutter.

A dozen flowers per inflorescence may be formed during the bloom season, which occurs in winter and spring in Australia. Flowers consist of five-lobed petals in gentian blue and persist for many weeks. Plants are heath-like, consisting of thin stems covered with short linear leaves; as plants mature, stems become woody.

As beautiful as the plants are, few are grown on this continent. They require significant greenhouse time to reach flowering and do not look particularly outstanding in a retail outlet, but the main problem is that very few climates and soils are similar to those of Western Australia, and plants have difficulty adapting. They may be planted in containers, but unless you can grow finicky plants like meconopsis, your attempt to plant them in the ground will likely be futile. Would I spend a great deal of money for them? Absolutely not. Would I plant them if I could find them for sale? Absolutely yes. They will probably die in a heartbeat, but so what? How many plants have you killed lately? None, I bet, that could lay claim to having the world's most beautiful blue flowers.

Some excellent hybridization work has been conducted at King's Park, a must-see botanical garden in Perth, and at the University of Western Australia, Julie Plummer and her colleagues have been studying environmental limitations to the hybrids. The more we know about the plant, the greater our chance for success. But no matter how many plants eventually thrive in North America, *Lechenaultia* will remain a great excuse for visiting Western Australia.

Full sun, sandy, well-drained soils. Propagate by tip cuttings.

Alternative species

Lechenaultia formosa (red lechenaultia) bears scarlet flowers but occasionally occurs in pinks and oranges as well. Prostrate in habit, best used in containers.

Leea (lee′ a)   Leeaceae

A little-known genus closely related to the grape family, Vitaceae, *Leea* consists of about thirty-five species of tropical shrubs and trees. Most species display few flowers; the handful grown in this country are found in conservatories, trained to posts to show off their handsome foliage. *Leea amabilis* is occasionally offered for its special foliage and habit.

-amabilis (a ma' bih lis)   leea   3–6'/3'
    all season   foliage   Borneo

This erect plant is sparsely branched with glossy deep bronze leaves, noteworthy for their broad white central strip above and claret color beneath. They are similar to those of *Nandina*, with five to seven pinnately arranged lanceolate leaflets. The leaflets are pointed at the tips and have serrated margins. No flowers occur in gardens.

    Warm, humid temperatures are needed for significant growth to appear and plants will simply sit in areas of cool summer nights. Full sun in the North, partial shade in the South. Propagate by cuttings.

CULTIVARS

'Splendens' is more handsome than the species: the entire plant is flushed dark claret to bronze. Quite attractive.

Alternative species

Leea coccinea (kok sin' ee a; West Indian holly) is the only species that may flower in a temperate garden. Plants produce a 3" wide flat-topped inflorescence of scarlet buds, which open to pink flowers with yellow stamens. Each flower is about ½" across. The foliage is not as handsome as *L. amabilis*, which makes it doubly disappointing if the plant does not flower.

Leonotis (lee o no' tis)   lion's ear   Lamiaceae

Lion's tail, lion's mane, maybe—but lion's ear? Apparently the common name of this genus refers to the hair-fringed lip of the flower, which looks something like an ear. Since I have never been, nor plan to be, close enough to a lion to examine its ears, who am I to disagree? Of the thirty species that occur in the genus, nearly all from southern Africa, only one is commonly available.

-leonurus (lee o noo' rus)   lion's ear   3–5'/3'
    late summer   orange   South Africa

The first thing you notice when you come across a well-grown planting of this species (syn. *Phlomis leonurus*) is the remarkable color of the flowers and then the classy upright stature of the plants themselves. The opposite leaves are lanceolate and about 2" long, coarsely serrated and hairy. Whorls of orange flowers are carried on the stem like the tiers of a chandelier, each whorl consisting of dozens of lipped flowers. The petals are about three times longer than the sepals, the upper lip large, hairy, and concave, and the lower lip small and three-lobed. Flowers, which also include a two-lobed style and four stamens, are about 1½" long. After flowering is complete, large balls of seed clusters remain on the stem. This species reminds me of the whorled shrub *Phlomis fruticosa* (Jerusalem sage) but is not as cold hardy.

In flower, this species makes gardeners salivate, but in truth, it is not the easiest plant to grow. It is actually a woody shrub, and northern growers generally treat it as a tender biennial. This means that plants need to be brought in for overwintering or started very early in the spring to obtain some cold, not excessive frost. In the South, plants may flower early if direct-sown early, or started in the greenhouse and transplanted in March. If they flower the first year from seed, flowering generally occurs in late fall; if they are started sufficiently early or overwintered, flowering occurs in late spring and summer.

Full sun, propagate by seed.

CULTIVARS

'Alba' is a white form, but I have not seen it.

'Staircase' is 3–5′ tall and produces many large tubular flowers of reddish orange.

Alternative species

Leonotis sibiricus is an interesting stately plant, 6–7′ tall, and although seldom seen (I have come across it only a couple of times), it is worth a try in the garden if seeds become available. The dark green opposite leaves are pinnately lobed and become smaller as they ascend the stem. The pink-mauve flowers, whorled at each node, are borne on the upper 3–4′ of each stem; they are much smaller than those of *L. leonurus* and not nearly as showy.

Related genera

Leonurus, an occasional presence in the herb garden, was used to ease the aftereffects of childbirth, hence its common name, motherwort. The main taxon is *L. cardiaca*. The 4–6′ tall plants have light green opposite lobed leaves, nearly palmate in shape, and small whorled pale pink flowers, often with purple spots. European in origin, probably a perennial but usually acts like an annual.

Limnanthes (lim nanth′ eez)   meadow foam   Limnanthaceae

The name comes from the Greek, *limne* ("marsh") and *anthos* ("flower"), referring to the habit of the genus, which consists of seven species of annuals. Flowers are beautiful—and plants are absolutely unknown outside the West Coast and the British Isles. The one hope for the genus is the species known as poached egg plant, a name that stirs curiosity, if not sales.

-*douglasii* (dug las′ ee i)   poached egg plant   9–12″/12″
summer   yellow   California

It is hard to believe that Scottish explorer David Douglas, after whom the stately fir is named, took the time to send back seeds of a relatively diminutive plant like the poached egg plant. An explorer of unbelievable grit and horticultural insight, he discovered so many plants that he apologized for seeming to "manufacture" them "at [his] pleasure."

This species, native to marshlands in the western United States, has rather fleshy light green pinnately divided leaves, each leaflet dentate. The 1″ wide flowers consist of five sepals, five petals, a five-headed stigma, and ten stamens. They are fragrant and usually bright yellow and white toward the tips of the notched petals. The combination of yellow and white looks a bit like a poached egg, especially if someone tells you that it does. Where plants are comfortable, seedlings appear in large numbers. Their California and Oregon roots say a lot about where they are comfortable: most of the country has too much fluctuation of temperature to qualify. Plants can look good almost anywhere, however, if planted early and removed before temperatures rise. Just don't expect longevity.

Full sun, propagate by seed in spring. Consistent moisture is necessary.

CULTIVARS

var. *sulphurea* has sulfur-yellow flowers without the white edges.

Limonium (lih mo′ nee um)   statice   Plumbaginaceae

So much statice is grown for the cut flower trade that hardly anyone thinks of it as a garden plant. German statice, Caspian statice, and Siberian statice are nearly always greenhouse-grown and enjoyed only in the vase, although acres of German statice (*Limonium latifolium, Goniolimon tataricum*) can be seen in that country. But *L. sinuatum* can be enjoyed both as a cut flower and a fine garden plant.

-sinuatum (sin yew a′ tum)   statice   1–3′/2′
summer   many colors   Mediterranean

Admittedly, more plants of *Limonium sinuatum* are cultivated for commercial use than for the garden, but they are so easily grown—why not enjoy their flowers in the vase without having to pay someone else? The densely hairy leaves are 3–4″ long, 1″ wide, and pinnately divided. The obvious characteristic is the winged flowering stem, the terminal of which ends in the dense, compact inflorescence. The flowers consist of outer bracts, sepals, and petals, all of which provide color to the flower heads. Pick flowers at the first sign of color if you intend using them fresh; wait until most of the inflorescence is colored if you wish to dry them.

Full sun, propagate by seed.

CULTIVARS

Many of these cultivars are more accessible to commercial growers than to gardeners.

'Blue River' has intense blue flowers with somewhat shorter stems than Fortress series.

Excellent series is produced more rapidly than others, and its uniformity of colors, including deep yellow, light blue, purple, rose, pink, salmon, and sky blue, is excellent.

Fortress is among the most popular series for cut flower production. Individual colors are apricot, dark blue, heavenly blue, purple, rose, white, yellow, and a mix.

'Kampf's Blue Improved' has rich dark blue flowers.

'Lavandin' bears clear lavender flowers and appears to resist sunburn better than other cultivars.

'Market Grower Blue' produces tall, uniform blue stems.

'Midnight Blue' has uniform flowers of a rich dark blue.

'Oriental Blue', a longtime standard for cut flower production, offers a rich deep blue that is consistent and uniform.

Pacific Strain is available as a mix or in individual colors, including 'American Beauty' (deep rose), 'Apricot Beauty', 'Gold Coast' (deep yellow), 'Heavenly Blue', 'Iceberg' (white), 'Midnight Blue', 'Roselight' (rose-pink), and 'Twilight' (lavender-pink). Some growers, particularly in the Northwest, claim that yield of the Pacific Strain is significantly higher than Fortress.

Pastel Shades series is a mixture of lavender and purple shades on 2–3' tall stems. One, 'Sophia', consists of rose and pale pink flowers.

Qis series (formerly Sunburst series) is excellent for greenhouse and field production. This fast-flowering series grows 2½' tall and has uniform colors of dark blue, pale blue, rose, white, and yellow, among others.

'Rose Strike' has rose-pink shades and a loose flower habit.

Soiree series offers flowers of apricot, rose, purple, light blue, white, deep blue, and a mix.

Sunset series bears flowers in fall colors. Shades of yellow, orange, salmon, rose, and apricot are available.

Turbo series is known for its pastel shades, early flowering, and long stems. Plants grow 2½' tall. Colors are blue, carmine, peach, purple, white, and yellow.

Alternative species

Limonium suworowii (syn. *Psylliostachys suworowii*; rat tail, Russian statice) has a terminal spike, up to 1' long, of lavender flowers that are excellent for drying. The flower stems are 2–2½' long. Cut while in full flower (no less than four-fifths open) and hang upside down with leaves remaining. This species is not tolerant of warm summer conditions and should be avoided in the Midwest and South. Plants are best grown in a cool greenhouse in the Southeast but may be produced in the garden in winter in Florida and California.

Linaria (lih na′ ree a)   toadflax   Scrophulariaceae

Common toadflax (*Linaria vulgaris*), better known as butter-and-eggs to those who observe it, is a European escapee that usually populates waste places or roadsides, where it does little harm; it is quite a lovely plant, if perhaps not lovely enough to be planted beside the snapdragons. The genus, in fact, is closely related to *Antirrhinum*, having similar leaves and flowers, except that flowers of *Linaria* have a spur at the base of the petals (snapdragons are swollen on one side, not spurred). Most species of toadflax are not considered garden members in much of North America, but a couple of annuals are fun to try. All love cool temperatures and have environmental needs similar to those of calendulas and nasturtiums.

Quick guide to *Linaria* species

	Height	Flower color	Cultivars
L. maroccana	9–15"	violet-purple	many colors
L. reticulata	6–9"	bicolor	bicolors

-maroccana (mar o ka′ na)   bunny rabbits   9–15"/9"
   spring   violet-purple   Morocco

Of the 150 or so species of *Linaria*, this is the most common. Plants are native to North Africa but have become naturalized in northeastern United States and eastern Canada. The slender stems are branched, and the linear, 2″ long leaves are generally whorled below and remotely alternate above. Leaves are usually smooth beneath and somewhat hairy on the top. The flowers are always held in a terminal raceme, which becomes lax as it matures. The individual flowers of the species, less than 1″ wide, are brilliant purple-violet with orange to yellow markings within. The spur is easy to see, hanging vertically and longer than the rest of the flower.

Plants do not like warm temperatures and are at their best in early spring. If cool summer temperatures persist, they can be grown all summer beside the pansies, and if flowers are cut back as they fade, flowering may be prolonged. In much of the country, they will be planted early, enjoyed briefly, and removed for summer annuals. They make terrific cut flowers, although short stems limit their usefulness in many vases.

Full sun, well-drained soils. Sow seed *in situ* in the fall or early spring, or plant transplants as soon as the ground is workable.

CULTIVARS

'Carminea' bears rosy carmine flowers on 9–12″ tall plants.
'Diadem' is 6″ tall with violet and white flowers.
'Fairy Bouquet' has large flowers in a range of colors on 9–12″ tall plants.
'Fairy Bride' bears white flowers.
'Fairy Bridesmaid' produces lemon-yellow flowers on 1′ tall plants.
'Fairy Lights' is a mixture of pastel flower colors, with contrasting white throats.

Fantasy is a modern series in a mixture of flower colors, including blue, magenta-rose, speckled pink, white, and yellow. They are about 1′ tall and loaded with flowers. Exceptional and arguably the best of available cultivars.

'Lemon Twist' has lemon-yellow flowers.
'Northern Lights' is similar to 'Fairy Lights' but has brighter flowers.
'Ruby King' has blood-red flowers.
'Yellow Prince' produces pure yellow flowers on 12" tall plants.

-reticulata (rih tik yew la´ ta)	purple-net toadflax	6–9"/9"
spring	purple bicolor	North Africa

Linaria reticulata is difficult to obtain and therefore not as commonly cultivated as the abundantly available *L. maroccana*. Its linear leaves are channeled, whorled below and alternate above, and bear no hairs. The short racemes are made up of deep purple flowers with obvious netted veins throughout, and orange or yellow within. The spur is only about half the length of the petals.

Full sun, well-drained soils. Propagate by seed. Same cultural recommendations as for *Linaria maroccana*. Plants dislike warm climes and shine in cool springs and summers.

CULTIVARS

'Aureo-purpurea' has deep purple flowers with orange or yellow throat.
'Crown Jewels' is a mixture of bicolors of maroon, red, gold, and orange.

Alternative species

Linaria aeruginea (ar oo jih´ nee a), a relative of *L. reticulata*, grows about 12" tall with ascending stems. Flowers are small and vary from yellow to purple-brown with a bright orange marking on the lower lip. Var. *nevadensis* is smaller in all respects, with flowers usually yellow. The selection 'Gemstones' is semi-trailing and bears many red and scarlet flowers with a yellow spur.

Linaria triornithophora (tri or nih tha´ for a; three birds flying) is similar to *L. maroccana* and worth growing if only for its common name. Plants are 2–3' tall with long spurred 1" wide purple and yellow flowers and broad gray-green foliage. They are considered perennial in mild winters but should be grown as annuals everywhere else. Wherever, however, it's great fun to see the birds on the wing.

Quick key to *Linaria* species

A. Plant >18" tall .... *L. triornithophora*
AA. Plant <18" tall
    B. Spurs shorter than corolla
        C. Flowers violet or purple with obvious netted
           venation .... *L. reticulata*
        CC. Flowers red or scarlet, no obvious venation .... *L. aeruginea*
    BB. Spurs longer than corolla .... *L. maroccana*

Linum (li' num)   flax   .   Linaceae

About 200 species of *Linum* have been named, many of which are perennials, annuals, biennials, and shrubs native to the United States. Most have smooth, simple, alternate leaves and close clusters of flowers consisting of five petals and five sepals. Although flowers fall apart rapidly, they are continuously formed so plants always seem to be in flower. The most famous and well-known species is *L. usitatissimum* (yew sih ta tih' sih mum), grown by the acre in Europe for its fiber content (linen) and the oil content of the seeds (linseed oil). Give me an English field of flax before cathedrals and castles any day. Beats the heck out of soybean fields. The best-known garden species are the perennial forms, *L. perenne* and *L. narbonense*, valued for their many flowers and graceful habits. Of the numerous annual species in the genus, only flowering flax, *L. grandiflorum*, is used to any extent.

-grandiflorum (gran dih flor' um)   flowering flax   15–24"/24"
   summer   rose-red   North Africa

This erect graceful species has 1–1½" long sessile broadly lanceolate leaves, always smooth and always alternate. One expects flax flowers to be blue, but this species offers blooms in various shades of red. They are held in loose inflorescences, each flower consisting of five broad petals and small lanceolate sepals beneath. The 1½–2" wide flowers usually have a darker eye and decline within a day of opening. Happily, other flowers rapidly take their place, and plants bloom for a long period of time. They are terrific as annual fillers in the garden and need not be planted as "drifts as color." They are most successful when weather is cool; although they are tolerant of heat, flowering is then limited. In warm summers, they may need to be lifted in mid summer and replaced with more heat-tolerant species, but months of pleasure may be had before then.

Propagate by seed *in situ*, or start inside in winter a few weeks before last frost is expected. Place in full sun and raised beds for best results. If too much shade is present, plants stretch and may require staking.

CULTIVARS

'Album' is a white form. I've never seen it, but I understand it's of easy culture and a reasonably clean white.

'Bright Eyes' has ivory flowers with a deep brown center—really something for a species thought to consist solely of red flowers.

'Caeruleum' bears purple-blue flowers.

'Coccineum' has flowers of deep scarlet.

'Roseum' is a rather washed-out flower of rose-pink.

'Rubrum' is the most common form, consisting of bright red flowers with a satiny sheen. The center is darker red. Probably the best of the reds.

Alternative species

Linum flavum (yellow flax) is actually a perennial but flowers first year from seed and acts like an annual in many areas of the country. The flowers are golden yellow, similar in size and shape to *L. grandiflorum*. Plants grow about 2′ tall and can become woody at the base. 'Compactum' is shorter, growing only about 8″ tall.

Loasa (lo a′ sa)   Chilean nettle   Loasaceae

Such a beautiful flower, such a nasty disposition. I first met this genus in southern Germany and approached it as I do most others, with excitement at seeing something different and anticipation of learning something new. Of course, the common name was not listed, and so, ignorance being my middle name, I picked and poked about, only to be painfully reminded that not all plants appreciate such tenderness. Turns out the entire plant, flowers included, is covered with stinging hairs, many of which dislodged to greet my skin intimately. I then read accounts of this genus of a hundred or so species, native from Mexico to South America; some authors actually had the gall to call it "quaint and rather charming." Others were a little more forthcoming and let me know that "these plants are too much like nettles to deserve general culture" and that "the pain from their pricks may last several days." I wish I had read up before donating my hands to science.

Although the plant sets you up for pain, even I must admit that the flowers are almost "quaint and rather charming." But we are being set up again: the white to yellow flowers are nodding, and in order to be properly admired, they must be flipped up. Bending down and looking up makes more sense in this case, however.

-triphylla (tri fil′ a)	whorled Chilean nettle	12–18″/18″
summer	white	South America

This is probably the most common species of *Loasa*. Plants grow 12–18″ tall with 2–3″ long trifoliate leaves, with toothed or serrated margins. The leaves may be alternate at the base, becoming three-whorled near the top. The peculiar nodding flowers consist of spreading white petals, each with a colorful yellow nectar scale, whose bars of red and white form wonderful concentric rings in the inner core of the flower. You might want to take my word on this one (or find some gloves before attempting to verify). A little pain and discomfort never stopped gardeners: these plants make effective fillers in the garden, but you might want to post a warning for the curious. In Athens, plants transplanted to the garden in May grew and flowered well until they succumbed in early August. We will try again next year.

Full sun. Propagate by seed *in situ*, or start inside in winter six weeks before last frost is expected.

Alternative species

Loasa acanthifolia (a kan thih fo' lee a) is similar but with beautiful 1″ wide yellow flowers. Leaves are opposite and divided, each division sharply pointed (acuminate). They are even more bristly and cantankerous than *L. triphylla*.

Related genera

Several native genera belong to this family, all excrutiatingly beautiful. The genus *Mentzelia* (stickleaf), native to the western United States, has lovely yellow flowers and barbed leaves. *Mentzelia laevicaulis* and *M. decapetala* are handsome species. Not as lethal as *Loasa*: most barbs are on the leaves, not the flowers.

Lobelia (lo beel' ee a)   Campanulaceae

This is a genus of immense diversity, offering everything from 10′ tall African trees to handsome upright perennials to popular low-growing annual species. Little did Mathias de L'Obel, a Belgian physician and royal botanist to James I of England, realize that his legacy rested not in the moods of a king but in the pleasure of gardeners. No doubt the perennial lobelias are most appreciated. It is hard to argue with the well-known flame of cardinal flower (*L. cardinalis*) and the many brilliant colors of the hybrids (*L. ×speciosa*), but the purples and blues of the bedding lobelia need make no apologies.

-erinus (e ri' nus)	bedding lobelia	6-9″/12″
spring	blue, purple	South Africa

Success can be boring, and bedding lobelia can be both, lining every path and garden walk from Antigonish to Nanaimo. But does it work. Growing up in Montreal, it was among the few plants I could name, even from a distance; it spilled out of every container and was even part of our floral clock in the town of Mount Royal. The stuff was in flower from June to frost and wouldn't go away. Alas, I took the plant for granted and wish I could view it in my garden in Athens as easily as I did in Montreal. Plants do not tolerate heat well. Now I enjoy them for a couple of months in spring and early summer, then replace them. At least they no longer bore me.

The toothed lower leaves of the species are ovate and attached by a short petiole; the stem leaves are linear and almost sessile. The blue to violet flowers, held in lax spikes, usually have a white or yellow throat, and the stamens are exserted (they stick out).

Breeding has resulted in even more diversity: bred for compactness and tightness, bedding lobelia is most useful for edging; as a sprawling, prostrate plant, it is best for baskets and containers. All forms are propagated by seed, and unless a greenhouse is available, they are best purchased in the spring and transplanted to the garden. Provide full sun, plant early, and remove when foliage becomes stretched and flowering declines. In the South, plants persist and flower longer in containers.

Trailing forms

Excellent for baskets and containers.

'Big Blue' performed exceptionally well in mixed containers in our trials, flowering well throughout the season.

Cascade series offers flowers of blue, crimson, lilac, red, sapphire, and white.

Fountain series comes in blue, crimson, rose, and lilac.

Regatta series consists of light blue ('Marine Blue'), lilac, midnight blue, rose, sapphire, and white flowers with blue throats ('Blue Splash').

'Sapphire' is an older cultivar with sapphire-blue flowers and cascading bronze foliage.

Upright forms

Used for edging or plant painting.

'Blue Sky' bears clear, bright blue flowers.

'Cambridge Blue' has light blue flowers.

'Emperor William' is about 4″ tall with deep blue flowers and bronze foliage.

'Laguna Blue' bears light blue flowers.

Moon series consists of green-leaved plants in blue ('Blue Moon') and pure white ('Paper Moon'). Very compact.

'Mrs. Clibran' bears deep blue flowers with white eye.

Palace series offers rounded habit and flower colors including blue, dark blue with bronze leaves ('Royal Palace'), and white. 'Crystal Palace', an older variety, is still quite popular; flowers are dark blue and foliage is slightly bronzed.

Rapid series was developed for faster flowering in the greenhouse. Flowers are blue, violet-blue, or white.

Riviera series is only 3–4″ tall in blue with white eye ('Blue Flash'), lilac, marine blue, midnight blue, sky blue, rose, and white.

'Rosamund', a short form, has carmine flowers with a white eye over bronze foliage.

'Royal Jewels' has dark blue flowers with a white center. 'Compact Royal Jewels' is more compact and grown from cuttings.

'Snowball' has white flowers.

'String of Pearls' is a seed mix available in a variety of colors.

'Tioga Blue' has good sky-blue flowers on 12″ tall plants.

'White Lady' bears clean white flowers.

Alternative species

Lobelia tenuior (ten yew′ ee or), native to Western Australia, grows 1–2′ tall and is covered with 1″ wide blue flowers in the summer. Provide full sun, shelter from wind. 'Blue Wings' has gentian-blue flowers.

Lobularia (lob yew la' ree a)   alyssum   Brassicaceae

Once included in the genus *Alyssum*, this bedding plant has forever been tagged with its old generic name as its common name. Differences between the two genera are mostly technical (two nectary glands in *Lobularia*, only one in *Alyssum*), but the obvious difference is that most *Alyssum* species have yellow flowers, while flowers of *Lobularia* are generally white or pink.

-*maritima* (mar ih tee' ma)   sweet alyssum   6–9"/12"
   spring   white, pink   southern Europe

Edges and borders of gardens have always been the domain of sweet alyssum, as they have been for annual lobelia. Plants grow in a mound and are covered with flowers from spring until mid summer, at which time higher temperatures reduce the amount of flowers. This species is highly branched. Leaves are linear, somewhat silvery, and tiny (<¼"). The four-petaled blooms are held in compact racemes, which elongate after flowering. The wonderfully sweet smell of the flowers enchants on a warm spring evening and fills the kitchen when they are brought in.

Plants are easy to grow from seed and may be started indoors or *in situ* in the spring. The species, which is native to maritime climes, tolerates winds and even salt spray. What it will not tolerate is 90°F days and 80°F nights. When such conditions persist, flowering declines and plants lose their ornamental value. It is said that sweet alyssum is a poor choice for the South—not so! They bloom profusely all spring and through mid summer, and some cultivars appear sufficiently heat-tolerant to do well the entire season. I am sure they would prefer to be in Halifax, but so would many of us in the middle of the summer.

Full sun to partial shade, well-drained soils. Propagate by seed.

CULTIVARS

Aphrodite Mix is a blend of apricot, pink, rose, purple, salmon, and white flowers on 3–6" tall plants.

'Apricot' is an unusual color for sweet alyssum. Reasonable heat tolerance.

'Creamery' produces a mixture of pale cream colors.

'Crispy White' is a compact sweet alyssum from the Netherlands, with clean white flowers.

Easter Bonnet is an excellent series with flowers in deep pink, deep rose, lavender, and violet.

'Golf' provides a pastel mixture of flower colors.

'New Carpet of Snow' has snow-white blooms. Highly popular.

'Rosie O'Day' bears rose-pink flowers on 6" tall plants.

'Snow Crystal' produces larger flowers than other white-flowering forms on 6–9" mounds.

'Snowdrift' is a fine white, producing clean flowers on a mounded habit.

'Violet Queen' has deep violet flowers.

Wonderland is a very common series, consisting of deep rose, pastel pink, purple, and white. Excellent heat tolerance.

Lotus (lo' tus)   Fabaceae

The word "lotus" means different things to different people. Farmers use lotus as a pasture crop but know it as bird's foot trefoil (*Lotus corniculatus*); in fact, this prostrate European weed is occasionally used for rock gardens, especially the double yellow-flowered form. Students of anthropology know that the fruit of the Cyrenean lotus was eaten by North African tribes, who became known as lotus eaters; these plants probably belonged to the genus *Ziziphus*. Water gardeners think of lotus as a beautiful water lily of the genus *Nelumbo*, with outstanding foliage, flowers, and fruit. But gardeners seeking plants with silver leaves and handsome pea-like flowers, usually pouring out of a hanging basket, look for the genus *Lotus*.

| *-bertholetii* (ber to let' ee i) | parrot's beak, coral gem | 12–18″/18″ |
| spring | scarlet | Canary Islands |

An exceptionally pretty mounded plant for hanging baskets, this much-branched slender bush is as much admired for its leaves as for its odd-looking flowers. Three to five leaflets are whorled or costapalmate (appear to be palmate) in arrangement. The soft linear silver-gray leaflets, ½″ long, are the best part of the plant; the blossoms are no slouches either, but they come and go rapidly, while the wonderful foliage remains. The 1½″ long orange-red to scarlet flowers have a prominent beak with a long curved keel (some see it as a lobster's claw, others as a parrot's beak). Flowers are formed in bunches of fifteen to twenty near the end of the branches. They flower in the spring and early summer then produce pea-like fruit.

Cool weather is needed for good flowering, but even when the bush is not in flower, its foliage makes a welcome contrast with other plants. At least as good as *Helichrysum* 'Limelight' and dusty miller. Full sun in the North, partial shade in the South. Well-drained soils are a must—the best reason for planting them in baskets or containers, where soil and water can be controlled.

CULTIVARS

'Amazon Sunset' has wonderful blue-green leaves that fill containers and baskets. Flowering is sparse in the summer, at least in my experience, but the foliage needs no help.

'Atrococcineus' has glossy dark scarlet flowers with black spots.

'Kew Form' has silver leaves, and its red flowers continue to bloom longer than others.

Alternative species

Lotus sessilifolius (ses ih lih fo' lee us) has gray-green palmate leaflets and handsome yellow flowers. Almost as good as *L. bertholetii*. 'New Gold Flash' has orange-scarlet flowers. Beautiful in flower, cool temperatures necessary.

Lunaria (loo nar' ee a)   honesty, money plant   Brassicaceae

Honesty has been a popular garden plant since Victorian times, when it was grown for the round paper-thin fruit (silicles). The most common species, and the only one listed in the majority of garden catalogs, is the biennial *Lunaria annua* (dollar plant); *L. rediviva* (perennial honesty) too is occasionally offered and in many gardens may be grown as an annual.

Lunaria is not difficult to grow and does well in almost any garden soil if some afternoon shade is provided. The leaves are opposite, toothed, and heart-shaped. The purple or white flowers are held above the foliage, and fruit forms while the uppermost flowers are still opening.

-annua (an' yew a)	dollar plant	2–3'/2'
spring	purple	Europe

While technically a biennial species, *Lunaria annua* (syn. *L. biennis*) self-sows so readily that it is always somewhere, although probably not where originally planted: it's always a delight to visit my friend Laura Ann Segrest in April, when dollar plant is in flower and fruit all over her garden. A great deal of variation occurs in the species, and the heart-shaped leaves may be opposite or alternate. They are coarsely toothed, and the upper leaves are sessile. The flowers of the species are purple, but the white-flowered var. *alba* is just as common; chances are good that both colors will be present in purchased seed or plants. In my garden, I try to keep the purple-flowering plants where the yellow daffodils flower; the late daffodils and early lunarias make a wonderful combination. I leave the white-flowered ones in the spring shade garden; light reflects off the flowers and brightens up the surrounding greenery.

The fruit, the best known part of the plant, is 2″ wide, round, and papery thin. If you intend to bring the stems inside, cut them just as the green color disappears from the fruit and hang them upside down in a cool, well-ventilated place for three to five weeks. They dry exceptionally well and make wonderful additions to winter bouquets. The down side of this species is that they seed everywhere; you had better not get tired of them, because they will be your partners in the garden for a long time. Susan is brutally honest in her evaluation of these weeds in the summer, wondering why I have left so many around.

Full sun in the North, away from afternoon sun in the South. The species and varieties can be raised from seed (although var. *variegata* yields both variegated and green-leaved forms). Seed germinates irregularly over time; place seed at 35–40°F for four weeks to enhance uniformity. Flowering occurs in April in north Georgia (zone 7), in mid May in Iowa (zone 5). Plants are winter hardy to zone 4.

CULTIVARS

var. *alba* has white flowers.
var. *atrococcinea* has deep red flowers.
'Munstead Purple' has flowers of rich purple.
var. *variegata* bears leaves with irregular white margins, resulting in a plant that has interesting foliage, good-looking flowers, and desirable fruit. This cannot be said of many other plants.

Alternative species

Lunaria rediviva is larger overall than *L. annua*. It has finely toothed, petioled leaves; smaller, lighter purple, more fragrant flowers; and 2–3″ long, 1″ wide elliptical fruit (the fruit of *L. annua* is round). May be dried as with *L. annua*. Hardy to zone 4.

Additional reading

Askey, Linda. 1995. Money plant: an old-fashioned treasure. *Southern Living* 30(4):74.
Brandies, Monica. 1986. Lunaria. *Horticulture* 64(8):26–27.

Lupinus (loo pi′ nus)   lupine   Fabaceae

For many, this genus conjures up magical scenes of colorful rockets igniting gardens in the British Isles; but I assure you, coming across a stand of our native bluebonnet in Texas, Colorado, or California is even more magical, almost a religious experience. There is no such thing as an unattractive lupine—all species would be welcome in my garden. Most lupines sold in garden outlets are the perennial hybrids, mainly the Russell Hybrids, which in most areas of this country should be treated as biennials. The annuals species include those with yellow, blue, and bicolor flowers. All lupines are susceptible to root-rot organisms where drainage is poor; and leaf-spotting organisms proliferate on plants stressed by high heat and humidity.

Quick guide to *Lupinus* species

	Height	Flower color
L. *hartwegii*	1½–2′	blue and rose or yellow
L. *luteus*	2–2½′	yellow
L. *nanus*	½–1′	blue and white

-hartwegii (hart weg′ ee i)	Hartweg lupine	2–3′/2′
late spring	bicolor	Mexico

This beautiful species is particularly popular for the sweet smell of the flowers, to say nothing of its softly hairy foliage. The compound leaves consist of seven to nine oblong leaflets, each about 2″ long and less than 1″ wide. The many ½″ long flowers are held in crowded 8″ long racemes, each flower bicolored in blue and white or yellow. The fragrant flower stems may be brought in for long-lasting cut flowers.

Full sun, well-drained soils. Propagate by seed *in situ* in the fall in the South, or in early spring in the North. Plants are native to Mexico and tolerate more heat than the perennial forms do. Still, they do best in cooler weather. In cool summers, plants will flower for six to eight weeks.

CULTIVARS

'Sunrise' is the only form of *Lupinus hartwegii* easily found in seed catalogs. The flowers are blue, white, and yellow on the same inflorescence. Wonderfully fragrant.

-luteus (loo′ tee us)	yellow lupine	2–3′/2′
spring	yellow	southern Europe

The stem of the yellow lupine is densely hairy and supports compound leaves consisting of seven to eleven lanceolate to oblong leaflets. The bright yellow flowers, whorled around the 10″ long racemes, are nicely fragrant. A beautiful plant but somewhat finicky.

Full sun, excellent drainage. Propagate by seed *in situ* in early spring, as plants don't transplant particularly well. Nor do they perform well in high humidity or late afternoon rains. This is true of most lupines, but this species, native to the Mediterranean, seems worse than others, at least in the East.

-nanus (nay′ nus)	sky lupine, dwarf lupine	1–2′/1′
spring	blue and white	California

Plants bear slightly hairy upright stems, which are often branched at the base. The five to seven linear leaflets are only 1–1½″ long, hairy on both sides, and carried on 3″ long petioles. The blue and white flowers are whorled on loose racemes up to 10″ long.

Full sun, well-drained soils. Propagate by seed *in situ* in early spring.

CULTIVARS

'Pixie Delight' is about 12″ tall and has flowers in pastel shades of white, pink, and light blue.

Alternative species

Lupinus texensis (bluebonnet) is one of our loveliest wildflowers. Plants, which are 12–18″ tall, produce five to seven acute leaflets and vivid blue and white flowers. They are no easier to grow in the garden than *L. luteus*, but who cares? Buy some seeds and sow them anyway.

Quick key to *Lupinus* species

A. Flowers yellow . . . . *L. luteus*
AA. Flowers bicolor
    B. Plant 2–3′ tall . . . . *L. hartwegii*
    BB. Plant 1–2′ tall . . . . *L. nanus*

Lychnis (lik′ nis)   campion   Caryophyllaceae

The generic name comes from the Greek, *lychnos* ("lamp"), an apt description of the flame-colored flowers of certain species. Older literature occasionally refers to these plants as "champions" because some species were used to make garlands for victors in public contests, hence the common name. About twenty species are presently included in the genus, although the number changes constantly. Most are considered perennials, including the well-known *Lychnis coronaria* (rose campion) and *L. chalcedonica* (Maltese cross); a couple of species flower the first year from seed and should be considered annuals in most areas of the country.

Flowers have five petals, and plants have opposite leaves and swollen nodes, as do other members of the family. Several genera in this family are so alike, in fact, that it can be hard to tell which plant is which. *Lychnis* may be distinguished from *Silene* by its five styles, the female part of the flowers (*Silene* has only three). Many species originally placed in *Lychnis* have been transferred to *Silene* and *Agrostemma*—the fluidity of plant classification in action.

Quick guide to *Lychnis* species

	Height	Flower color
L. ×*arkwrightii*	18–24″	orange-scarlet
L. coeli-rosa	18–24″	pink-purple with eye

-×*arkwrightii* (ark ri′ tee i)   Arkwright's campion   18–24″/12″
early summer   orange-scarlet   hybrid

This hybrid between *Lychnis chalcedonica* and *L.* ×*haageana* (Haage's campion), with its brilliant orange-scarlet flowers, is increasingly popular. The 1½″ wide flowers, carried in a three- to ten-flowered cyme, contrast well with the dark bronze foliage. They have notched petals and are often borne singly the first year. Garden longevity is a little better than *L. ×haageana* but not as permanent as *L. chalcedonica*. Although they may live as long as three years, plants benefit from replacement each year. Plants should be pinched early in the season to force additional shoots and reduce legginess. In their first year in the UGA Horticulture Gardens, plants flowered in early spring. After flowering, the swollen seed pods turned from green to brown, providing additional interest in the season. Shade should be provided in zones 7 and 8; full sun is acceptable further north.

Propagate cultivars from seed or cuttings. Little variation occurs with seed-grown plants, which flower the first year.

CULTIVARS

'Vesuvius' is similar but has vermilion flowers, a color one either loves or hates. Very popular, best treated as an annual.

-*coeli-rosa* (ko lee ro′ za)	rose of heaven	15–18″/2′
summer	purple-pink with eye	Mediterranean

This species, although it has gone through all sorts of name changes, has been known by gardeners since the early 1700s. Most people (and I am one of them) like to include this plant under *Lychnis* because it has five styles; however, it has been under *Agrostemma*, *Viscaria*, and more recently, *Silene*, where some authorities believe it should be. Enjoy its beauty, whatever its name.

Plants, which are often seen along the roadsides and in the meadows of southern Europe, are not particularly fond of heat, and even less so of humidity. They are quite beautiful in the spring, however, if seeds are sown sufficiently early in the house or greenhouse. The hairy leaves are linear-lanceolate and sharp pointed. The 1″ wide flowers are on short flower stems and are generally purple-pink or rose-pink with a white eye.

Full sun, afternoon shade in the South. Propagate by seed *in situ*.

CULTIVARS

Angel Mix is a seed combination of peach, rose, and blue. 'Blue Angel' produces clear blue flowers with a darker eye.

'Candida' is all white, all the time.

'Cherry Blossom' is about 2′ tall with white centers and soft pink edges.

'Kermisena' has deep red flowers.

'Oculata' bears light pink flowers with a purple eye.

'Peach Blossom' has peach to light pink flowers.

'Rose Angel' produces bright rose flowers with a dark eye.

Quick key to *Lychnis* species

A. Flowers orange to orange-scarlet . . . . *L. ×arkwrightii*
AA. Flowers usually purple-pink to rose-pink . . . . *L. coeli-rosa*

Additional reading

Armitage, Allan M. 1997. *Herbaceous Perennial Plants*, 2nd ed. Stipes Publishing, Champaign, Ill.

Lawrence, G. H. M. 1953. The cultivated species of *Lychnis*. *Baileya* l:105-114.

Lysimachia (lih sih mok' ee a)   loosestrife   Primulaceae

This genus is extraordinarily diverse, ranging from 3-4' tall white-flowered runners like *Lysimachia clethroides* to diminutive yellow-flowered *L. japonica* 'Minuitissima'. Nearly all the 150 or so species are perennials, and most are aggressive. It is interesting then, with such diversity, that so few are annuals. I am intimately acquainted with the many perennials I have killed and yanked, but I know of only one annual.

-congestiflora (kon je stih flor' a)   golden globes   12–16"/12"
    summer   yellow   Japan

I was immediately taken by *Lysimachia congestiflora* (syn. *L. procumbens*) when first introduced to it in the early 1990s. The rounded 2" long dark green leaves are basal and a handsome part of the plant. The bright yellow flowers, about 1" wide and generally with a small purple eye, are held in many-flowered clusters, like golden globes. That the clusters are held so tightly may account for the specific epithet. I have seen the plants used effectively in baskets, as masses of bright flowering plants, and even as upright standards.

Full sun in the North, partial shade in the South. Propagate by division. Well-drained soils are recommended.

CULTIVARS

'Eco Satin', from the famous Eco Nursery in Decatur, Georgia, has a larger purple eye than the species.

'Outback Sunset' has the same yellow flowers combined with variegated chartreuse and green foliage.

M

Malope (mal o′ pee)　　　　　　　　　　　　　　Malvaceae

Of the dozens of genera in the mallow family, this is among the least known. Flowering maple, hibiscus, hollyhock, lavatera, even ornamental okra and cotton, are better known than the lowly malope. Its flowers are smaller than those of lavatera and hollyhock but otherwise quite similar—with one subtle difference: note the three distinct heart-shaped bracts behind the colorful flowers (lavatera and hollyhock usually have six to nine bracts). Definitely a group of plants worth trying in the flower garden. *Malope* consists of about four species, but only one is used.

-trifida (tri fih′ da)	three-lobed malope	2–4′/2′
spring	purple-red	Mediterranean

The 3–4″ long leaves are three-nerved, three-lobed, and borne on unbranched 2–4′ tall stems. The leaves have long petioles, and the lobes are somewhat triangular in shape. Solitary 2–3″ wide flowers may be found in the leaf nodes, particularly near the top of the plant; they have five petals and are usually rose to purple, with darker veins and darker centers.

This species is well known in Europe as an old-fashioned cottage garden plant. It is not nearly as coarse as hollyhock and, with its informal habit, is much easier to incorporate in a mixed garden. Plants are native to sandy soils around the Mediterranean and do badly in poorly drained soils, high temperatures, and high humidity. They perform best in cool weather and should be deadheaded as flowers finish.

Full sun, propagate by seed.

CULTIVARS

‘Grandiflora’ has dark rose flowers; a mix of colors is also available as Grandiflora Mix.

‘Pink Queen’ has light pink outer petals, red inner petals, and darker purple veins.

'Vulcan' is tetraploid and therefore quite vigorous, bearing larger flowers than other forms. It has rosy purple blooms with darker venation.

'White Queen' bears large silky white flowers with green centers.

Mandevilla (man da vih' la)   Apocynaceae

Formerly seen strictly as a conservatory vine or a greenhouse plant, mandevilla enjoys more garden fans every year. Despite the abundance of choice tropicals, more people seeking a tropical look for their temperate gardens are choosing mandevilla to decorate their mailboxes or outdoor light fixtures. (That mailbox mentality also plagues clematis, the postal carrier's nightmare.) But only a handful of the more than a hundred species of *Mandevilla* are offered to gardeners; all are woody vines, with opposite leathery leaves, each leaf with pinnate venation. They climb by twining around a structure or, in nature, another vine, shrub, or tree. Their showy funnel-shaped flowers, which are often sweetly fragrant, are produced over long periods in summer and fall.

Most of us neophytes to tropical plants can't tell a mandevilla from an allamanda from a dipladenia. What else is new? For those who need to know, the stamens of *Mandevilla* are united around the stigma, as they are in hibiscus flowers (stamens of *Allamanda* are not united). And the good news is that most taxonomists have agreed to fold *Dipladenia* into *Mandevilla* (their differences were so minimal as to make them synonymous), so we don't really have to know it at all.

-sanderi (san' der i)   Brazilian jasmine   vine
  summer   rose-pink   Brazil

Brazilian jasmine, like most other species of *Mandevilla*, twines and has outstanding foliage and large funnel-shaped flowers. The shiny leaves are 2–3″ long, broadly elliptical and with a sharp apex. The pointed flower buds expand into 1–

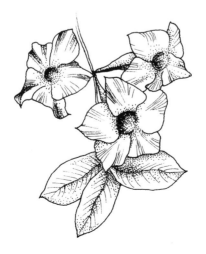

Mandevilla sanderi
CHRIS JOHNSON

2″ long rosy pink flowers held in three- to five-flowered one-sided racemes. The flowers essentially face the strongest rays of the sun (south or west, depending on the garden). It is a great vine, best suited for warm summers and sunny skies. Flowering is slow and does not occur until plants reach maturity, but once begun, it continues until temperatures reach 40°F. Plants are vigorous in their native habitat, reaching 12–15′, but in garden situations, 5–8′ is more common; in baskets or containers, 3′ tall plants are normal. The further north one gardens, the more established the roots should be when planted, if tall plants are desired.

Place in full sun when the risk of frost has passed. Provide support and water well. Reduce watering as light and temperatures are reduced in the fall. Plants overwinter to zone 8 but can be propagated by 3–4″ softwood nodal cuttings.

CULTIVARS

'Red Riding Hood' has bright red 2″ wide blossoms with a light yellow throat. Flowering occurs all season.

'Rosea' is similar but less bright.

Alternative species

Mandevilla ×*amabilis* (a ma′ bih lis) grows 10–12′ tall. Leaves are 6–8″ long; flowers are 4″ wide, rose-pink with a crimson center and a yellow throat. The lobes of flowers are pointed. 'Alice Dupont' has rich pink-rose flowers and, in fact, may be synonymous with the hybrid species.

Mandevilla boliviensis (bo lih vee en′ sis; white dipladenia) grows 10–12′ and has handsome creamy white flowers with pointed petals and orange-yellow throats.

Mandevilla laxa (syn. *M. suaveolens*, *M. tweediana*; Chilean jasmine) has creamy white flowers that are probably the most fragrant of the available species. Leaves are glossy green above and often purple or gray-green below. 'Tropical Dreams' has 3″ wide yellow flowers with a golden margin and may be a hybrid with this species.

Manettia (man e tee′ a)   Rubiaceae

Signore X. Manetti, for whom this genus is named, was a keeper of the royal gardens in eighteenth-century Florence. Plants are favorites among plant connoisseurs, not so much for their growth habit as for their explosive flowers. Of the approximately eighty species that are known, a couple are reasonably popular.

-*luteorubra* (loo tee o roo′ bra)   Brazilian firecracker vine   vine
        summer, fall   red with yellow   Paraguay, Uruguay

Manettia bicolor, *M. inflata*, and *M. discolor* have all been folded into the current specific epithet, which describes the color of the flowers. The opposite, ovate to lanceolate, pale to dark green leaves are 2–4″ long and held on four-sided many-branched twining stems. The stems will trail unless provided with a trellis, bamboo poles, or some other support to climb. The axillary flowers are held singly on short flower stems and consist of a leafy four-lobed calyx (sepals) and a four- to five-lobed cylindrical corolla (petals). The vibrant orange to scarlet corolla is about 2″ long and is painted yellow at the end of the four lobes. Flowering occurs in late summer on spring-planted material: the earlier plants are placed in the soil, the more rapidly they will flower. Flowers are more abundant if plants are trained to climb.

This is a fun plant to try in the garden or in containers. The flowers intrigue all who see them, and although not a vigorous climber, the plant, given warm temperatures and sunny conditions, will provide interest and color. Plants are highly susceptible to spider mites and whiteflies, much more an indoor problem than in the garden.

Full sun to partial shade, propagate by softwood cuttings.

Alternative species

Manettia cordifolia (kor dih fo′ lee a; firecracker vine) is similar in growth habit to *M. luteorubra*. It differs in that the base of the leaves is heart-shaped, and the flower lobes are slightly or not at all yellow. I used this species in containers and allowed them to grow without support; plants flowered in late summer on 2–3′ long trailing stems.

Matthiola (ma tee o′ la)   stock   Brassicaceae

Herbalist John Gerard wrote, "Stocke Gillo-floures [have little use] except amongst certaine Empericks and Quacksalvers, about love and lust matters, which for modestie I omit." The term "gillyflower" described clove-scented flowers and was associated with carnations and pinks; a "stock gillyflower" was one with a woody stock or stem, hence the common name of this genus. Stocks, long appreciated for their sweet fragrance, have graced English gardens since the early sixteenth century and have been bred at least that long. A highly fragrant and vigorous form arose in the Brompton Park Nursery, near London, in the early 1700s; it was so popular that plants are often still referred to as Brompton stocks.

Gardeners do not commonly grow stock for their own vases, but the flower has been a mainstay of the cut flower industry for many years. Populations occur as single or double flowers; the double form is much more esteemed than the single. Many colors and habits, from dwarfs to those over 2′ in height, have been bred.

| *-incana* (in ka' na) | Brompton stock | 1–2½'/1' |
| spring | many colors | southern Europe |

The taxonomic breakdown of the garden forms has been much discussed. Most current stocks are hybrids with *Matthiola incana, M. sinuata,* and *M. odorata* and to find an original species is nearly impossible. Plants consist of gray-green entire lanceolate leaves, often quite hairy. Plants branch out as they mature and are usually 1–2' tall. The flowers are held in terminal racemes and may be single or double. The fragrance can be quite strong, particularly in the evening—so sweet that some find it overwhelming.

Plants are all raised from seed, which means that the percentage of double-flowered forms may be less than desired. In the greenhouse industry, growers use temperature to determine which seedlings to grow on (doubles) and which to throw out (singles). Once the seedlings have emerged, temperatures are lowered to about 45°F, and in some strains, differences in cotyledon and early leaf color is obvious: the leaves of the double-flowered forms become yellow or pale-colored, the singles remain green. Growers discard the good-looking ones, keep the bad stuff, and raise the temperatures. Modern strains were bred so that the differences between leaf color is more obvious; it is not always an easy call with older strains, however, which can be quite frustrating. Commercial cut flower and pot plant growers are adamant about double flowers, but gardeners need not be quite so straitlaced. The single forms are still fragrant, and some people even prefer them for their simplicity.

Stock is a cool-loving plant; many hybrids in fact benefit from some cold weather and are best grown as biennials. Some cultivars may overwinter as far north as Pennsylvania, but overwintering is not consistent in much of the country. In the North, they are best planted as early as possible after the threat of a hard frost has passed. Flowering will occur as temperatures warm up but will not occur well when day temperatures rise above 75°F. In the South, they may be planted in the fall, but problems are not uncommon. We fall-plant stock at the UGA Horticulture Gardens. They flower well in early spring and until temperatures rise. The drawback is that if a few deep freezes occur, the winds and lack of snow cover results in ripped-up foliage or dead plants. It is difficult therefore to recommend them for fall planting anywhere except the West Coast.

Full sun, well-drained soils. Propagate by seed *in situ* in a well-prepared site.

CULTIVARS

Bedding forms
Plants are about 12" tall and generally single-stemmed. Somewhat more heat-tolerant than taller forms.

'Appleblossom' is about 12" tall, with double flowers in blush pink to white.
Cinderella series, available in five colors, is 10–12" tall and basally branched.
Echo series is about 10" tall and bred in five colors.
Harmony series is only 9" tall, in cherry red, red, and purple.
Legacy Mix grows to 15" tall and consists of about seven colors.
Midget series is just that, 8–10" tall.

Vintage series is mostly double with copper, lavender, pink, and white flowers. 'Vintage White' is the best.

Upright forms

Hard to find and generally available only to the commercial cut flower industry. Cool temperatures are necessary for best development.

Beauty of Nice Mix has well-branched plants in various shades of rose, pink, violet, and yellow. Plants are 1½–2' tall.

Cheerful series is about 80% double in white and yellow.

Column series is the best for garden stocks, up to 3' tall. Non-branching, about 55% double.

Giant Imperial Mix is self-branching, with a stem more central than that of Beauty of Nice Mix but less central than that of the Column series. Height is 2–2½'.

Alternative species

Matthiola longipetala (syn. *M. bicornis*; night-scented stock) is grown for its wonderful sweet scent rather than its ornamental value: the flowers are smaller than Brompton stock, plants are rather straggly, and the flowers close during the day. Leaves are pinnate at the base and entire near the top. Place in an out-of-the-way spot and enjoy the mysterious wafting fragrance.

Additional reading

Lee, Rand B. 1995. Stocks. *American Cottage Gardener* 2(2):15–16.

Mecardonia (me kar do' nee a)   Scrophulariaceae

Not much has been written about the garden potential of this genus, which contains moisture-loving plants native to Florida and Texas as well as tropical Central America. Our native species *Mecardonia acuminata* has small white flowers and is usually seen in marshy conditions or even in water, but both *M. dianthera* and *M. procumbens*, which carry their yellow flowers above the foliage, have the potential to be as successful in hanging baskets as their relatives in *Sutera*. This may all come to nothing, but then again, nobody heard of *Sutera* or *Angelonia* five years ago either.

Full sun, propagate by seed, lots of moisture.

Melampodium (mel am po' dee um)   Asteraceae

This genus from western North America and Mexico is poorly known but tough as nails. Of the thirty-five species identified, only *Melampodium paludosum* is available.

-paludosum (pa loo do' sum)   medallion flower   15–24"/12"
   summer   yellow   Mexico

My work with this plant began in the mid 1980s, when seed first became available to the greenhouse industry. Bright yellow flowers and ease of culture suggested it might be a good pot plant for gift occasions, but as a lark, I also put a few plants in the trial gardens. Since then, I have abandoned the potted idea. These are excellent landscape plants: they grow in the worst heat and humidity and have no trouble with poor soils, flowering from spring to fall.

The alternate pale green, entire leaves are not particularly memorable, but they are carried on purple-black stems. The foliage remains in good shape until the short days of fall. The 1" wide blooms—bright yellow ray flowers with a pale center—are extraordinarily numerous, never going out of flower. This is simply a gutsy plant, providing color without complaint. The only criticism I have is that plants, even the cultivars, are a little tall; they can flop over in mid summer and may need to be removed.

Full sun. Propagate by seed indoors or *in situ* when the ground warms up.

CULTIVARS

'Derby' is similar to 'Showstar' but is somewhat shorter and a bit more compact.

'Medallion', the first cultivar selected, provides persistent yellow color on 2–3' tall plants.

'Million Gold' is about 12" tall, flowering all season.

'Showstar' is excellent, 15–18" tall, compact, and as floriferous as 'Million Gold'.

Melampodium paludosum 'Showstar'   ASHA KAYS

Additional reading

Bender, Steve, 1989. Flowers through thick and thin. *Southern Living* 24(5):106–108.

Mimulus (mim' yew lus)   monkey flower   Scrophulariaceae

Next time you look at the grinning face of a mimulus flower, you may be reminded of George, the curious monkey who lived with the man with the yellow hat. More than 150 species have been cataloged, and many are grown as perennials, particularly in temperate areas of Europe and the West Coast of the United States. They are all handsome of flower and very colorful. Most prefer at least moist soils; many, such as *Mimulus guttatus*, require standing water to do well. Some are more tolerant of "normal" garden conditions, and a few, such as the desert species *M. fremontii*, require excellent drainage. All—particularly the moisture lovers—can be invasive. Many, many hybrid annuals have been bred, a few of which should enjoy popularity in American gardens in the future. Most are grouped under *M. ×hybridus*.

-×*hybridus* (hi' brih dus)   monkey flower   1–2'/2'
summer   many colors   garden

The hybrids are mainly the result of crossing *Mimulus guttatus* (large monkey flower) and *M. luteus* (yellow monkey flower), although other species have recently entered the mix as well. The light green opposite leaves are toothed. The irregular 1–2" wide flowers are two-lipped, with two upper and three lower lobes and four stamens, two long and two short, inside; they look a little like gaping snapdragons but without the closed throat or spur on the calyx. Plants enjoy moist conditions (but watering as needed will suffice), and even with all the hybridizing, they still prefer warm days and cool nights. As fine as these hybrids are, they remain a local item that has yet to catch on in much of the country. Some newer cultivars are cold hardy to zone 7 and more heat-tolerant than their predecessors; they may simply need a champion to tell gardeners of their attributes. Time will tell.

Full sun in the North, partial shade in the South. Propagate by seed *in situ* or start inside and transplant.

CULTIVARS

'Andean Nymph' has ivory-white flowers with pink spots.

Calypso series consists of 1–1½' tall flowers in many shades, all with spotted petals.

'Highland Red' is a dwarf mat-forming plant with deep red flowers.

Jelly Bean series has large flowers in apricot, white, and yellow. Plants are potential winners, performing well in containers in our trials. They should probably be purchased for the outrageous name alone, even if you don't like jelly beans.

Magic series has large flowers with essentially clear faces; the throats have spots, mainly of the same color as the petals.

Malibu series is taller, about 18″, and has petals that are lighter on the margins and darker in the throats.

Mystic series is about 12″ tall with spotted flowers.

'Viva' has yellow flowers with large red blotches.

Alternative species

Mimulus guttatus (goo ta′ tus; large monkey flower) is an outstanding species for those fortunate enough to have a boggy area in the garden. Chrome yellow flowers with reddish brown spots. Plants are probably the most cold hardy species, often returning from the roots as far north as zone 6. Plants will likely reseed.

Mirabilis (mih ra′ bih lis)   marvel of Peru   Nyctaginaceae

Of the fifty or so species in this genus, the most common by far is Peruvian native *Mirabilis jalapa*, an old-fashioned favorite as an individual specimen and even, years ago, as a hedge.

-jalapa (ha lap′ a)	marvel of Peru, four o'clock	2–3′/3′
summer	many colors	Peru

A stout plant results from the regularly two- or three-branched stems of this species, each bearing dozens of smooth entire opposite leaves. One common name, four o'clock, refers to the fact that the flowers don't open until late afternoon and not at all on cloudy days, although newer cultivars are less responsive to dull times. Flowers will stay open all night or until they are pollinated by a night visitor. Each 1½″ wide five-lobed funnel-shaped flower is borne in a leafy sepal-like involucre and occurs in various colors including purple, crimson, yellow, and white, often striped or mottled; it is not unusual to find flowers of different colors on the same plant. The stamens are prominent, adding to the allure of the fragrant flowers. Bend down to get a whiff, but keep your mouth away: all parts of the plant are poisonous. The roots are tuberous, and tubers may be lifted, like those of dahlias, and overwintered. The combination of free seeding and deep tubers can make for obnoxious weeds.

Full sun, well-drained soils. Propagate from the large black seeds, in a seed flat or *in situ*.

CULTIVARS

'Broken Colors' is a mixture of yellow, rose, and pink flowers on 2–3′ tall plants.

Tea Time series, the best of current offerings, has outstanding flowers in red, rose, and yellow on plants 2–3′ tall. 'Tea Time Rose' stands out from the others.

Alternative species

Mirabilis longiflora (lon gih flor′ a) has a similar, if smaller, habit than *M. jalapa* and bears long narrow white flowers. I tried this plant and was most disappointed, as it is billed as being among "the most exotic of garden plants." It is also supposed to be more cold hardy than *M. jalapa*. Just my luck: it was not exotic, and it did come back.

Additional reading

Lee, Rand B. 1996. Four o'clocks. *American Cottage Gardener* 3(3):4–5.

Moluccella (mo loo chel′ a)   Lamiaceae

This is a genus you're likely to encounter in the florist shop, not the garden; in a vase, not the ground; as a cut flower, not a real plant. But *Moluccella laevis* (bells of Ireland) is a real plant from western Asia, and how many gardeners can boast of a plant with green flowers? Actually, the inflated bell-shaped calyces provide the Irish green, and it is their shape that accounts for two other wonderfully imaginative common names: shell flower (each calyx resembles a small clam) and lady-in-a-bathtub (a reference to the flower within the calyx) are as creative as bells of Ireland. The small white to pink petals are bilabiate, with four extending stamens, and are held within the calyx, as they are in most other plants in the mint family. The flowers are in sixes, whorled around the leafy flower stems. The 3–4′ tall plants have multiple four-sided stems and 2″ long opposite rounded light green leaves.

Flowers may be enjoyed in the garden in late summer, where they blend in well with brighter yellows and oranges, or they may be picked for fresh arrangements when about three-quarters of the whorls are open. If you intend drying them, harvest when all flowers are open and hang upside down in a dark airy location. Flowers have been dyed absolutely gruesome colors by obviously colorblind people who ought to be locked up for flower abuse, and the cut stems, if allowed to wilt slightly, may be bent into various shapes, which they will retain when rehydrated—more abuse by well-meaning people. Every now and then the plant extracts a little revenge: simply ask those who have felt the pain of the five small thorns at the ends of the sepals.

Full sun. Propagate by seed *in situ*.

Monopsis (mon op′ sis)   Campanulaceae

Few gardeners know this relative of *Lobelia*, and it is unlikely that this genus of South African natives will become common in the near future. They are nevertheless undemanding annuals for cool, moist summers, with numerous small axillary blue to violet flowers. About eighteen species are known; I have seen but a few. *Monopsis campanulata* (kam pan yew la′ ta), a prostrate plant, is especially

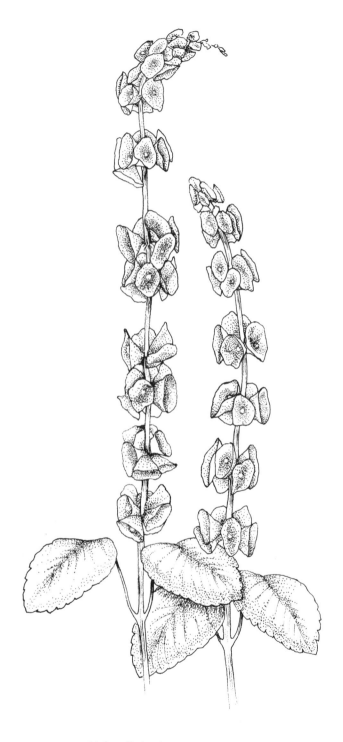

Moluccella laevis   CHRIS JOHNSON

appropriate for mixed containers and baskets; the small variable leaves are only ½″ long, obovate to lanceolate, entire to slightly dentate. *Monopsis unidentata* (yew nih den ta′ ta) is also prostrate with slightly bigger leaves, often whorled, and with two-lipped violet to blue flowers. I suspect these plants would do fine in most areas, other than those that experience hot, humid summers.

Full sun, propagate by seed or terminal cuttings.

Musa (moo′ sa)   banana   Musaceae

Good grief, the ornamental garden is more edible by the day. From ornamental kale to bronze-fruited okra, from chartreuse sweet potato to black-leaved taro, Aunt Zelda's homestead garden is a study in biodiversity. For years bananas have been used for their tropical effect in large landscapes and botanical gardens, where space (and money) is not a big issue, but unless one lives in the banana belt of the Deep South, growing bananas outdoors for the fruit is a bit of a stretch. (Fruit can sometimes be gathered from greenhouse-grown trees, but even if you have a large greenhouse and lots of time, the joy will be in the growing, not the eating.) The allure of these plants, without question, is their tropical foliage, and ornamental, more dwarf forms of bananas are now available and ready for your garden. The question is, what species or cultivar does one begin with? Like tomatoes, there are a lot of bananas out there.

Chances are, the ornamental bananas you've seen in the botanic garden or the landscape downtown are not the true banana, but rather its more ornamental cousin, *Ensete* (en se′ tee). *Ensete* resembles *Musa*; it bears huge paddle-shaped leaves, some measuring up to 18′ long by 3′ wide, but does not produce particularly edible fruit. Of the seven species in the genus, *E. ventricosum* (Abyssinian banana) is most commonly drafted for ornamental uses. The olive-green leaves have a green or reddish midrib and are usually clustered at the top of the stem. This is a big plant in its native habitat, growing up to 40′ tall; in containers or in a northern landscape, however, plants reach only 8–10′, providing handsome unfolding foliage and perhaps a cluster or two of flowers; its selection 'Maurelii' (syn. *E. maurelii*; red Abyssinian banana) is the best of the ensetes, with outstanding red leaves, red leaf surfaces, and a red midrib. Plants grow up to 10′ and are excellent in containers. *Ensete gilletii* (jil et′ ee i), smaller at 4–5′ tall and with sunken midribs of bright red, may sometimes be found.

The banana sliced over your cereal is probably a cultivar of *Musa acuminata* or *M.* ×*paradisiaca* (*M. acuminata* × *M. bulbisiana*). The more than 300 cultivars of edible banana differ in many ways, including bunch size, firmness of fruit, and degree of resistance to disease. In this mélange of a gene pool, many offer quite ornamental foliage, and all have handsome fruit as well (to banana aficionados, there are no bad-looking bananas). 'Bloodleaf' (Sumatran banana) is a beautiful form whose large leaves are striped and stained with burgundy; plants (also sold as 'Rojo' and 'Zebrina') grow 6–8′ tall, but in containers, 4′ is not uncommon. For outstanding foliage, 'Ae Ae' (variegated Hawaiian banana) provides leaves in dark green, medium green, and creamy white. Difficult to locate, expensive to buy, but quite eye-catching. Plants grow up to 12′ tall. Gardeners in tropical areas or with conservatories might want to try 'Red Iholene'; the leaves have a burgundy underside, the flower bracts are dark red, and the beautiful fruit starts out pale yellow.

Musa basjoo (bas′ jo; Japanese banana) also offers some exciting possibilities. Plants grow about 15′ tall under favorable conditions, half that size in most of our gardens. In the species, the leaves are thin and light green, but the inflorescence is among the most beautiful. The species is probably the most cold hardy of ornamental selections, plants being recorded as root hardy in the ground at −3°F, with mulching, down to −20°F! Perhaps root hardy to zone 5. The selection 'Variegata' has foliage banded or flecked lime-green, cream, and white but is less available and not as cold hardy.

In all cases, when growing plants outdoors, find a place where there is plenty of room, plenty of sun, plenty of moisture, and little wind. The first three are self-evident; the last is important because the thin leaves are easily torn by strong wind—and that this is normal does not make the ragged appearance any more appealing. In most states, plants should be brought in when temperatures move into the thirties. Buy started plants from a mail-order nursery or a firm specializing in tropical plants.

Additional reading

Stokes Tropicals: www.stokestropicals.com
Waddick, James W., and Glenn M. Stokes. 2000. *Bananas You Can Grow*. Stokes
     Publishing, New Iberia, La.

Mussaenda (mew sayn′ da)   Rubiaceae

Grace Price, a colleague of mine and a wonderful plant breeder, has forgotten more about this genus of tropical shrubs—some of them useful annuals—than I will ever know, and she sent me some of her work to help sort it out. Heat is a requirement for rapid growth, but normal American summers in most locales provide sufficient warmth. Some of the hundred or so species are climbers; most are upright plants with opposite or three-whorled leaves. These plants are difficult to find; look in catalogs that provide tropical material. Unfortunately, choices will be few until plants become better known.

| *-incana* (in ka′ na) | white mussaenda | 1–3′/3′ |
| summer | yellow, white | Asia |

I have no idea when these plants first appeared in the greenhouses at UGA, but there they were, asking for a little attention. I decided to try them in mixed containers in the Horticulture Gardens and darned, if people didn't think they were interesting—not necessarily impressive, but at least curious. Of course, I took full credit for scouring the earth to find them.

Mussaenda incana   ASHA KAYS

The unique floral structure, which I just love showing to my students, is what makes this species so curious. The flowers are small (ca. ½"), consisting of a funnel-shaped yellow or orange corolla and a five-lobed calyx. One of the lobes, however, is greatly expanded (2–2½" long) and is clean white, occasionally cream or yellow. The flowers are persistent, remaining on the plants for many weeks. The plants themselves are not particularly outstanding, but the ovate 6" long leaves certainly do not detract from the overall look of the plant. These are simply fun plants that add good color and heat tolerance from Washington, D.C., to Miami.

Full sun, propagate by terminal cuttings (allow three to four weeks to root).

Alternative species

Mussaenda erythrophylla is a large plant with bright red sepals and yellow petals.

Mussaenda frondosa has orange petals and white sepal lobes but is much larger than *M. incana*.

Additional reading

Price, Grace R. 1974. Cultivated mussaendas in the Philippines. *Philipp. J. Biol.* 3: 37–55.

N

Nelumbo (ne lum′ bo)   lotus   Nelumbonaceae

Water plants, like water gardeners, are always a little bit out there on the edges of the garden mainstream. We all love water features, we all want waterfalls, brooks, and gaudy fish, but the flora and fauna required to fill and surround them are so unique that entire stores have been created to help us figure out what we want. From *Thypa* and *Elodea* to *Vallisneria* and *Eichhornia*, the plants are in a league of their own, doing ornamental and cleaning duties and loved only by those who love to garden with water up to their knees. Ponds are an integral part of all good gardens. One dictum I share with people who mistakenly ask me about design: a garden is incomplete without some water feature. Be it a bird bath or a waterfall, the sound and sight of water makes a yard a garden. Heavy, isn't it?

Water features have been part of garden design as long as records have been kept, and from the tombs of the pharaohs along the Nile, to Chinese and Japanese cultures, surviving illustrations and writings show gardeners tending ponds that included water lilies and lotus. The sacred lotus, *Nelumbo nucifera* is still part of garden design. I can't think of a prettier scene than the one devised by our good friends Vince and Barbara Dooley, whose handsome pond and marvelous lotuses are sited to gently dominate one area of their outstanding garden. That the offspring of plants valued 5000 years ago brightens their garden today makes it more than a pretty face.

-nucifera (noo sih′ fer a)   sacred lotus   3–5′/3′
    summer   yellow, pink, white   Asia

These are extraordinarily beautiful plants for the still-water pond, beloved for their waxy gray leaves, their fragrant handsome flowers, and their decorative seed heads. The peltate leaves, which can rise 3–5′ above the surface, may be up to 30″ wide with undulating margins. So beautiful is the foliage that I believe every botanical artist has either sculpted or painted lotus leaves. The flowers are held well above the leaves and may be 12″ wide, single or double. Both petioles and peduncles are hairy and rather rough. The highly fragrant flowers are usu-

Nelumbo nucifera   CHRIS JOHNSON

ally yellow, pink, or white, with four to five sepals, many spirally arranged petals, and 200 to 400 stamens. Upon fertilization, the flowers give way to large flat-topped spongy seed heads, within which are the persistent hard seeds. The seed head, with its distinctive holes in the top, is often cut and dried for indoor use.

Set root stalks horizontally in tubs or baskets in compost-enriched soils; place them in shallow water (2–3″ deep) initially, then move to deeper water (as deep as 2′) as plants begin to grow. Rate of growth is dependent on water temperature; the deep planting common in the tropics is generally impractical in temperate areas. Remove faded foliage during the growth season. Plants are considered annual north of zone 9; some cultivars can be overwintered as far north as zone 7. Plants may also be planted in tubs on the deck, where they are more easily moved to a warm area in the winter. Maintain moisture over winter regardless of where they reside.

Plants may be propagated by division, but carefully, as rhizomes resent disturbance. They may be placed in small containers in warm shallow water, then moved to deeper water as they grow. To propagate by seed, chip the hard seed coats and place seeds in shallow containers. Plants flower about three years after germination.

CULTIVARS

'Alba' has single white flowers
'Alba Plena' produces double white flowers, with a green tinge initially.
'Empress' bears white flowers with crimson margins.
'Lotus Blossom' has lovely white flowers heavily tinged in pink.
'Mrs. Perry D. Slocum' produces large deep pink flowers that turn creamy yellow over time.
'Pekinensis' bears carmine flowers; 'Pekinensis Rubra Flora' has double flowers.
'Red Lotus' has deep red flowers.
'Shiroman' produces double creamy white flowers with a greenish center.

Alternative species

Nelumbo lutea (loo' tee a; American lotus, yanquipin) has smaller leaves (1–2' across) and pale yellow flowers. Not quite as classic as *N. nucifera*, but sacred lotus, however beautiful, cannot boast yellow blossoms. Plants are native to eastern Kentucky, Tennessee, and northern Oklahoma, and as far north as the Plain states. Americans should be proud of this ornamental and impressive native son: when well established and in flower, it is a sight worth traveling out of one's way to see. 'Flavescens' has green leaves splashed with red.

Nemesia (ne me' see a)   Scrophulariaceae

About sixty-five species of South African nemesias are known. The genus is characterized by opposite leaves and colorful blossoms, often with a pouch or sac at the front of the flower. The flowers are two-lipped (bilabiate), and the calyx is five-lobed. Plants are not terribly successful in mainstream American gardens, but hybrids of *Nemesia strumosa* have been developed for use as pot plants or colorful bedding plants in the spring and summer.

-strumosa (stroo mo' sa)	nemesia	1–2'/2'
spring, summer	many colors	South Africa

Plants have four-sided stems and 3″ long sessile, spatula-like dentate to entire leaves; the upper leaves become lanceolate and are reduced to less than 1″ long. The flowers, each about ½–1″ wide, are held in terminal racemes, 2–4″ long. The blooms are white or in shades of yellow and purple, often veined purple outside and yellow within the throat. The throat is also bearded.

Numerous cultivars have been offered with larger and more colorful flowers, but all require cool temperatures to do well. They thrive in spring, as long as temperatures remain below 70°F, and are best pulled before they become lanky

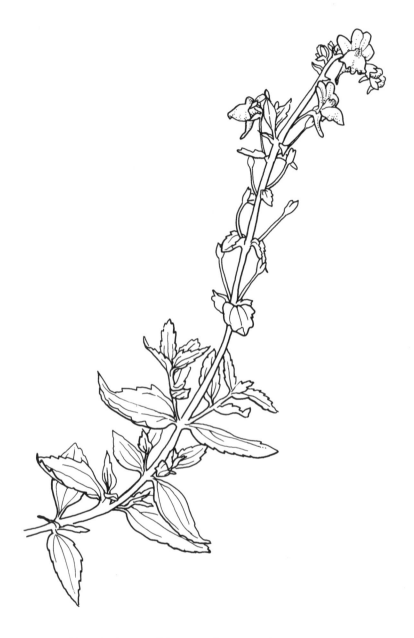

Nemesia strumosa 'Compact Innocence'   ASHA KAYS

and cease flowering. Plants may also be planted in late summer for a few months, as temperatures fall again. They are beautiful—little doubt of that—and colorful to the point of being gaudy, but they can be temperamental. Plants are quite cold-tolerant; if fall temperatures harden them off, they can tolerate 22°F and still flower when temperatures warm up again. All the same, they should be considered annuals.

Full sun in the North, partial shade in the South. Propagate by seed, at temperatures of 60–70°F.

CULTIVARS

'Blue Bird' is an outstanding selection with bright blue flowers and a small white and yellow throat.

'Compact Innocence' has been a pleasant surprise in gardens across the country. White flowers with a small yellow center bloom most of the summer on 9–12″ plants. They are best used in mixed containers, where they can fall out and be partially shaded by other plants.

'Innocence' bears white flowers and is bigger than its sister, 'Compact Innocence'.

'Joan Wilder' has mauve flowers with yellow centers. Not quite as vigorous as 'Compact Innocence'.

'KLM' bears blue and white flowers, the colors of the Royal Dutch Airline.

Mello series has red, rose, and white flowers.

'National Ensign' produces deep red and white bicolor blooms on 9–12″ tall plants.

'Orange Prince' provides vivid orange flowers on 9″ tall plants.

Sachet series offers relatively large flowers of 'Blueberry' (purple), 'Lavender', 'Peach' (pink), and 'Vanilla Sachet' (white).

'Tapestry' is a mixture of colors on 10″ tall plants.

'Woodstock' has dark blue flowers with a yellow eye. Plants are 15–18″ tall.

Alternative species

Nemesia versicolor (ver′ sih kul er), a seldom-seen parent of the hybrids, usually has upper and lower lobes of different colors, providing flowers in variable colors including blue ('Blue Gem'), mauve, yellow, and white. Same cultural recommendations as for *N. strumosa*.

Nemophila (ne ma′ fil a)   Hydrophyllaceae

This genus of unique flowering plants, native to western North America, was first discovered by David Douglas (see *Limnanthes*). Most genera belonging to Hydrophyllaceae prefer at least moist soils, and *Nemophila* is no exception. About eleven species occur; two are reasonably well known.

Quick guide to *Nemophila* species

	Flower color	Height
N. maculata	white with violet blotch	9–12"
N. menziesii	blue with white center	4–6"

-*maculata* (mak yew la′ ta)   five spot   9–12"/9"
    spring   white with violet spot   central California

The leaves are opposite. The basal foliage is lyrate (pinnately lobed but with a large rounded terminal lobe and smaller lateral lobes, diminishing in size toward the base); the five to seven smaller lobes are blunt and entire. The upper leaves are wedge-shaped, only three-lobed, and borne on erect or semi-prostrate stems. The 2" wide, five-lobed flowers are easy to distinguish: they are solitary, on long flower stems, and axillary. The specific epithet is Latin for "spotted"; plants are so named because each of the five white lobes has a violet blotch at the tip (the five spots of the common name). Often the blotches are obviously defined, sometimes they are less so. Flowers appear in early spring to early summer and stop flowering if temperatures become too warm. In much of the country, plants become leggy and fall over in summer; they should be thought of as spring flowerers only.

Full sun, moist but not wet soils. In mild winter climates, seeds may be planted in fall or late winter. Plants may be started indoors in winter and placed outdoors as soon as frost is not a threat.

CULTIVARS

var. *albida* has white flowers without the blotches.
var. *variegata* has variegated leaves. Both varieties are difficult to find.

-*menziesii* (men zee′ see i)   baby-blue-eyes   4–6"/8"
    spring, summer   light blue with eye   California

British naval captain George Vancouver is best known for his four-year exploration of the Pacific Islands and coast of North America, from 1790 to 1795. The surgeon and botanist who accompanied him was Archibald Menzies, a Scotsman who was remembered by Hawaiian natives as "the red-faced man who cut off the limbs of men and gathered grass." He is also commemorated by the genus *Menziesia*.

The succulent stems are procumbent and up to 12" long, with pinnatifid (deeply pinnately lobed) leaves. The nine to eleven lobes are ovate, nearly entire, and slightly hairy. The flowers are solitary, long stalked, and axillary. They are about 2" wide and highly variable in color. Blossoms are sky-blue, sometimes creamy white, often with a white or yellow center, or dotted or stained dark blue to purple.

Same cultural recommendations as for *Nemophila maculata*. Plants flower best in cool weather and do poorly in hot, humid climates.

CULTIVARS

'Alba' has white flowers with a black center.

var. *atomaria* is almost white but is spotted in black-purple. Also sold as 'Snowstorm'.

'Coelestis' produces white flowers edged in sky blue.

'Crambeoides' produces pale blue unspotted flowers with purple veins.

'Insignis' bears pure blue flowers.

'Oculata' has pale blue flowers with purple-black centers.

'Pennie Black' has deep purple flowers edged in white.

Quick key to *Nemophila* species

A. Flowers white, with deep purple spots at tip of each petal
   lobe .... *N. maculata*
AA. Flowers blue or white, dotted or veined, without spots at
   lobe tips .... *N. menziesii*

Nicandra (nih kan' dra)   shoo-fly, apple of Peru   Solanaceae

Only one species, *Nicandra physaloides* (fi sa loy' deez), named for the similarity of its fruit to that of Chinese lantern (*Physalis alkekengi*), is known. The erect branching stems are 3–4' in height and bear 3–3½" long slightly lobed, lanceolate leaves. The alternate leaves have a somewhat pointed apex and slightly triangular base. The 1–1½" wide bell-shaped corolla is lilac-purple to white, and the purple calyx beneath is strongly five-parted. Flowers are produced through late summer and fall and tend to stay open only for a few hours around midday. After flowering, the attractive rounded fruit is enclosed by the inflated green and purple calyces and may be picked and dried for winter decorations. The common names refer to the plant's supposed value as a fly repellent and the shape of its fruit, respectively. I really enjoy this large plant, which provides architectural form, handsome flowers, and interesting fruit.

Full sun, well-drained soils. Propagate by seed *in situ* early in the spring. Plants reseed vigorously and can become a bit of a nuisance.

CULTIVARS

'Black Rod', which bears 1" wide light blue flowers, gets its name from the purple to black stems.

'Splash of Cream' has blue flowers with a white center and leaves splashed and mottled in creamy yellow.

'Violacea' has larger violet flowers, white beneath. Its leaves, which are smaller than those of the species, are often spotted with purple on the upper surfaces.

Nicotiana (nih ko shee a' na)   tobacco   Solanaceae

Nicotiana is very like another genus that man has managed to exploit: the genus *Papaver*. They both contain members whose beauty provide a great deal of joy, but both contain substances that have caused incredible amounts of pain. Addiction to their beauty besots gardeners; addiction to their drugs enslaves far too many others. The species that keeps farmers, doctors, and lawyers busy is *N. tabacum*, but the genus is bursting with other beautiful members.

All sixty-seven species are characterized by large wavy alternate leaves and terminal panicles of tubular or campanulate flowers, often quite fragrant. The flowers of many species open only at night, but the flowers of the garden forms were bred to open during the day, except on very hot days. These garden plants range from bedding forms, about 12" tall, to mammoth specimens up to 20' in height. Hummingbirds and aphids are attracted to the flowers in equal numbers.

Quick guide to *Nicotiana* species

	Height	Flower color
N. alata	3–5'	white with pale violet
N. glauca	12–20'	yellow-green
N. langsdorffii	2–3'	green
N. ×sanderae	1–2'	varied
N. sylvestris	3–5'	white

-alata (a la' ta)   winged tobacco   3–5'/2'
summer   white with pale violet   South America

The common bedding forms of flowering tobacco, of which I am quite fond, are usually listed in catalogs as cultivars of *Nicotiana alata*, but they are not (they are hybrids, *N. ×sanderae*). The true winged tobacco is taller, more slender, and far more fragrant. I have grown the bedding forms of this species for years; in areas where plants reseed, some of the parents arise 3' in the air, covered with creamy white flowers, each with pale violet inside and wonderfully nocturnally fragrant. The subtle fragrance accounts for the plant's other common name, jasmine tobacco. I saw terrific populations of free-flowering plants when I visited June Collins, whose exuberant Portland, Oregon, garden is a plantsman's dream.

The stems, scarcely branched and somewhat sticky, bear 12" long spatulate leaves. The basal leaves are attached to the stem by a winged petiole (*alata* means "winged"), but the upper leaves tend to be sessile, with the base of the leaves encircling the stem. These tall plants are wonderful, but not low maintenance; they often fall over in wind and rain and can attract aphids and whiteflies. The five-lobed trumpet flowers open at dawn and dusk but can wilt like wet rags when the sun beats down. This is a bit disconcerting if one never ventures out after dinner, but a joy to the evening gardener. It is a plant with charm and romance, but I kind of like to see my flowers open during the day every now and then. It is better in areas with a good deal of cloud cover than in ones with lots of sun. Seed can be obtained through seed catalogs and seed-saver organizations. The species is difficult to find, obtainable only from packet seeds, but the hybrid forms (see *Nicotiana* ×*sanderae*) are as common as petunias.

Plants require full sun in the North, tolerate partial shade in the South. Propagate by seed started indoors.

-*langsdorffii* (langs dor' fee i)   lime tobacco   2-3'/2'
    summer   lime-green   Brazil

Probably the most interesting of all tobacco species, these plants are normal as far as leaves are concerned but unique as to flowers. The stems are branched, somewhat sticky and hairy. The leaves are ovate to lanceolate and sessile. The many flowers are arranged in drooping panicles, each blossom consisting of a ½" long tube. The tube swells into a little hoop, at the end of which are the spread, fused petal lobes. The entire flower is chartreuse-green, the intensity of which deepens down the tube. The color is magical, consorting well with almost all other colors in the garden, including the deep green of evergreen shrubs and hedges. It is a subtle plant, for the gardener who doesn't need to be hit over the head with the newest and the gaudiest. Plants can grow 3–4' tall, winding themselves through taller plants, but 2–3' is more common in most gardens.

Plants prefer moderate temperatures and have trouble in areas of high summer heat and humidity. They are always beautiful in the spring, however, and self-sown seedlings may appear. Enjoy this plant, there is nothing else quite like it.

CULTIVARS

'Variegata' has similar flowers but with leaves splashed in cream. I have not seen this plant, and I am not sure I want to.

-×*sanderae* (san' der ay)   hybrid flowering tobacco   1-2'/1'
    summer   many colors   garden

I have great admiration for the plant breeders who created these outstanding plants in an unmatchable range of excellent colors, particularly those in tones of lime-green and salmon. I must admit, I love them when they look good. Plants are crosses between *Nicotiana alata* and *N. forgetiana* (Brazilian tobacco), a scentless, scarlet-flowered species. Unfortunately, as is far too often the case, the scent genes got lost in the cross, and little fragrance can be attributed to the hybrids.

Leaves, stems, and flowers are all smaller on these hybrids, which are otherwise morphologically similar to their parents, down to the winged petioles. These much shorter plants perform particularly well in moderate temperatures and low humidity but still look good in most of the country—perhaps not for the entire season, but long enough to enjoy in the garden. Susceptibility to aphids and other sucking insects is a problem, but if any kind of tobacco is grown, insects are cultivated along with it. When day temperatures rise above 85°F, flowers tend to close, especially if combined with high humidity. From the previous statements, you may have discerned that plants can look bad much of the time; if they poop out in mid summer, a late summer planting will provide additional color until frost.

Plants are grown from seed, but transplants of the hybrids are best used in the spring.

CULTIVARS

All are F_1 hybrids. Differences in habit, color selection, or performance are subtle; most differences are based on greenhouse production criteria.

'Avalon Bright Pink' is about 15″ tall with handsome pink flowers. An All-America Selection in 2001. Other colors are also offered.

Domino series consists of 1–2″ wide flowers on 12–14″ tall plants. Flower colors include lime-green, picotee (white with rose margins), pink with white eye, purple, purple with white eye, red, salmon-pink, and white.

Havana is a good compact series in about seven colors. 'Havana Appleblossom', which provides pastel white flowers blushed with rose, is a favorite of mine.

Heaven Scent series provides more fragrance than many of the hybrids, at least in the evening, and may be found with red, dark rose, light rose, bright purple, and icy white flowers on 3–3½′ tall plants.

Nicotiana ×*sanderae* Domino series   ASHA KAYS

Hummingbird series, among the most dwarf offerings, is 9–12″ tall in seven separate colors and a mix. Also sold as Starship series.

'Merlin Peach' has bright salmon-peach flowers on 1′ tall plants.

Nikki, one of the earlier series, is still popular. Self-branching 14–16″ tall plants occur in red and white. 'Nikki Red' was an All-America Selection in 1979.

Prelude series is similar to others, with numerous flower colors on 12–15″ tall plants.

Saratoga series is 10–12″ tall in five colors and a mix.

-sylvestris (sil ves′ tris)	white shooting stars	3–5′/3′
summer	white	Argentina

My travels take me here and there in this country and to a few others as well, and as a horticultural tourist, I keep my head down, my camera shooting, and my pencil scrawling. I am a cheap tourist: I refuse to pay entrance fees to museums and galleries, preferring to save my money for seeds and film. A perennially great place to visit is Montreal, my hometown, where I not only enjoy the city landscaping gratis but even pay to visit their outstanding botanical garden. I first saw a 5′ white shooting star in a median planting on St. Denis Street, holding center court surrounded by red amaranthus. Big, bodacious, and gaudy—a great French Canadian painting.

Plants are robust and branched and eventually produce woody stems. The wavy, somewhat puckered leaves are sessile, broad, and oblong to spatulate, slightly clasping the stem at the base. They are also big, 12–15″ long, slightly glandular and hairy throughout. Aphids have a ball! The fragrant tubular flowers are produced in drooping panicles, resembling exploding shooting stars as they open. The spindle-like corolla tube is about 4″ long, seven times longer than the five-angled calyx, and ends in five equal white lobes. The diameter of the flowers is about 1½″. Hummingbirds, butterflies, and moths are all attracted to the open flowers.

Seedlings often reappear in the garden and may be left in place or moved around. When these plants are in their prime (late summer and fall, generally), they are full of shooting flowers and wonderfully fragrant. If I had to choose just one ornamental tobacco species, I would make space for this one.

Full sun, propagate by seed. Transplant seedlings in the spring. As with all species, aphids and whiteflies can be a problem. The honeydew formed by these insects is an excellent medium for sooty fungus, which is black and messy.

Alternative species

Nicotiana glauca (tree tobacco, mustard tree) is a relative of *N. langsdorffii*. It can grow to 10′ even in a New England summer. Plants are impressive, not only for their size but for their large smooth blue-green foliage and pendulous clusters of creamy yellow to yellow-green trumpet flowers. Late fall flowers seldom open in northern states, but the plants are worth growing for their stately habit and unusual foliage.

Nicotiana knightiana (ni tee a′ na) is similar to *N. sylvestris*. It is a robust species, 3–4′ tall, with large soft leaves and panicles of white-and-green tubular flowers. A good specimen plant.

Quick key to *Nicotiana* species

A. Plant usually >2′ tall
   B. Plant usually >10′ tall, leaves blue-green, flowers yellow . . . *N. glauca*
   BB. Plant usually <10′ tall, leaves green, flowers white or chartreuse
      C. Flowers mostly white or cream-colored, corolla tube 3–4″ long
         D. Flowers closed during day, corolla four to five
            times longer than calyx . . . . *N. alata*
        DD. Flowers drooping, open during day, corolla
            seven times longer than calyx . . . . *N. sylvestris*
     CC. Flowers chartreuse, corolla tube ½–1″ long . . . . . *N. langsdorffii*
AA. Plant usually <2′ tall, many-colored flowers, mostly bedding . . . .
. . . . *N. ×sanderae*

Additional reading

Lee, Rand B. 1997. Jasmine tobacco (*Nicotiana alata*). *American Cottage Gardener* 4(3):4–5.
Winterrowd, Wayne. 1998. Nicotianas. *Horticulture* 95(8):45–48.

Nierembergia (neer em ber′ gee a)   cupflower   Solanaceae

The genus is named for Spanish Jesuit Juan Eusebio Nieremberg, who wrote a book on the marvels of nature, published in 1635. Plants are native to South America, not to the city of Nuremberg, Germany, as some creative writers have attested. The twenty-three species have slender stems, alternate leaves, and cup-shaped flowers. The flowers are five-lobed with four normal stamens and one staminode (distorted stamen).

Quick guide to *Nierembergia* species

	Height	Flower color
N. frutescens	1–3′	blue, purple, white
N. hippomanica	9–12″	violet-blue
N. repens	4–8″	white, tinged yellow or pink
N. scoparia	2–3′	light blue

-frutescens (froo te′ senz)   cupflower   1–3′/1′
    summer   pale blue   Chile

The species itself is a shrublet, that is, a small shrubby plant up to 3′ tall. All selections available to gardeners are considerably shorter (<12″) but still become woody at the base with age. The stems are densely branched, and the foliage is nearly glabrous (no hairs). The linear to lanceolate leaves are alternate, sessile, and about 1″ long and half as wide. The flowers consist of a ten-lobed calyx, from which extends the petal tube and the five-lobed petals. In the species, the throat is yellow, and the petal lobes are pale blue fading to white at the margins.

The upturned flowers are colorful and classy, like small bellflowers. They are produced profusely in the spring and continue through the summer, although humidity and heat can result in foliar diseases that slow flowering. Plants benefit from a trim in early summer to enhance flowering branches and to curb rapid expansion of some of the stems. Provide a sheltered position, if possible, because flowers can be damaged by wind and rain; this is one reason plants have been more popular as pot plants or conservatory items than as garden subjects.

Partial shade to full sun, propagate by seed.

CULTIVARS

'Purple Robe' is a dense plant growing about 6″ tall with deep violet-blue cup-shaped flowers. An All-America Selection in 1942.

'White Robe' is similar to 'Blue Robe' but with white flowers.

-hippomanica (hih po man′ ih ka)	cupflower	9–12″/12″
spring, summer	violet-blue	Argentina

This species stands about 1′ tall. Plants are highly branched and dense, bearing pubescent linear leaves less than ½″ long and even more narrow. The five-lobed flowers, 1–1½″ wide, are blue-tinged violet. This is a true herbaceous species; it does not become woody at the base. Its habit and needs in the garden, however, are similar to those of *Nierembergia frutescens*.

Partial shade to full sun, propagate by seed.

CULTIVARS

'Mt. Blanc' is 4–6″ tall with clean white flowers, 1″ wide. The very best, an All-America Selection in 1993.

var. *violacea* (syn. *Nierembergia caerulea*) is probably what most blue species of *Nierembergia* are. Flowers are violet-blue, and leaves are a little longer than the species.

-repens (re′ penz)	white cupflower	4–6″/12″
spring, summer	creamy white	South America

This species is grown for its trailing habit and handsome flowers. Plants are slender creepers freely rooting at the nodes, forming a dense mat. The oblong to spatulate leaves, about 1″ long and ¾–1″ wide, are attached to the stem by long slender petioles. The 1″ wide, five-lobed flowers, held close to the stems, are creamy white, tinged yellow or rose-pink at the base. Plants are hardier than other *Nierembergia* species, overwintering to zone 7. Plants make excellent mats of flowers in sandy soils and where warm afternoon rains are not common. I love this plant in the spring, but it tends to disintegrate later in the summer.

Partial shade to full sun. Propagate by division, cuttings, or seed.

CULTIVARS

'Violet Queen' has dark violet-blue flowers.

-scoparia (sko par' ee a)	tall cupflower	1–2'/2'
summer	light blue	Argentina

Without doubt, this species is the least behaved of the cupflowers, with long slender stems going this way and that. The leaves are less than 1″ long and even more narrow. When not in flower, plants look kind of frazzled, but with a little patience, they soon become winners. The 1–1½″ wide pale blue to violet flowers can smother the plant, bringing on gasps of unadulterated joy. But like most members of this fickle genus, smothering flowers cannot be promised every year: when summers become very hot, flowers stall or simply do not open, and when flowers aren't present—well, think of Don King's hair. Still, it is my favorite. I'll take the exuberance any day, and when smother time rolls around, I'll be there.

Full sun to partial shade, propagate by seed or cuttings.

Nierembergia scoparia   ASHA KAYS

Quick key to *Nierembergia* species

A. Plant prostrate, root at nodes . . . . *N. repens*
AA. Plant upright, doesn't root at nodes
     B. Stems usually <12" long
         C. Plant woody at base, leaves about 1" long . . . . *N. frutescens*
         CC. Plant herbaceous, leaves <1" long . . . . *N. hippomanica*
     BB. Stems usually >12" long . . . . *N. scoparia*

Nigella (ni jel′ a)   love-in-a-mist   Ranunculaceae

A most interesting genus in a most interesting family. Ranunculaceae contains such ornamental plants as *Anemone*, *Clematis*, and *Paeonia*, so the fact that *Nigella* competes in this class makes it pretty special. The genus is not nearly as colorful or showy as the genera just mentioned, but the feathery foliage, hazy weird flowers, and outstanding fruit sustain its popularity. In some species, an obvious leafy involucre beneath the sepals adds to the ornamental aspect of the bloom. The plants are not only ornamental but of economic and culinary importance as well. The fruit of *N. damascena* and *N. hispanica* is harvested for dried arrangements, while the seed of *N. sativa* (black cumin) is a culinary spice. The generic name comes from the Latin, the diminutive of *niger* ("black"), a reference to the seed.

Quick guide to *Nigella* species

	Flower color	Height	Involucre
N. damascena	blue, white	1–2'	present
N. hispanica	blue	1–2'	absent
N. orientalis	yellow	1–3'	absent

-*damascena* (da ma see′ na)   love-in-a-mist, wild fennel   1–2'/18"
    summer   blue, white   southern Europe, North Africa

Easily raised from seed, this species is commonly grown in gardens throughout the country. The dark green alternate leaves are pinnately divided numerous times into many thin segments, providing a feathery look to the plants, somewhat like that of fennel. The flowers are interesting—take one apart if you're curious. At the base is the leafy structure called an involucre, then the five large rounded sepals, above which are the smaller upright petals. The light blue sepals are the colorful part, and the involucre gives the flower its misty appearance. After flowers are fertilized, large five-sided inflated bronze capsules occur, with erect horn-like styles on the top. They are wonderfully handsome on their own and are commercially harvested for the cut flower trade. You may do the same, so they can be dried and gather dust in the foyer.

    Plants were thought to have come from Damascus, thus the specific epithet. The one common name, however, is a little harder to explain, especially to my students. Evidently, the hair-like involucre was quite suggestive to Western authors: in more primitive times, close living quarters made refinement difficult, and many flower names had overt sexual connotations. Love-in-a-mist was one of them; the French, less coyly, call the plant *chevaux de Venus*. Living conditions had improved by Victorian times, when it became popular to give girls, admiringly compared to flowers, such names as Rose, Violet, and Daisy.

Full sun to partial shade, propagate by seed. Plant in drifts if possible, and allow the flowers to produce the seed capsules. I think they do better sown *in situ* than when transplanted. Thin to 10–12″ centers.

CULTIVARS

'Albion' bears double white flowers, which then produce deep purple pods.
'Dwarf Moody Blue' is only 6–9″ tall with blue flowers.
'Miss Jekyll' has semi-double flowers in sky blue. Also found in white ('Miss Jekyll White').
'Mulberry Rose' produces double pale pink flowers.
'Oxford Blue' bears large double, dark blue flowers.
Persian Jewels is a mixture of mauve, purple, and white flowers.
'Red Jewel' produces deep rose flowers.

-hispanica (his pan′ ih ka)   fennel flower   1–2′/2′
     summer   blue   Spain, France

The leaves of this species are divided but less so than in *Nigella damascena*. The 1–2″ wide blue flowers are similar to those of *N. damascena*, except they don't have the involucres at the base. The lack of these spidery structures makes for a "cleaner" look, but many gardeners miss them—after all, they are one reason love-in-a-mist is so misty. The color comes from the broad sepals and the red stamens. The capsules are inflated, longer than wide, and topped by the five spreading styles. The shape of the fruit and the spreading habit of the styles help to differentiate this species from the more common *N. damascena*.

Full sun, propagate by seed.

CULTIVARS

'Exotic' has lavender sepals, purple petals, and deep red stamens, which combination makes the sepals appear to be spotted in red. An apt name.

Alternative species

Nigella orientalis (or ee en ta′ lis; Asian nigella) differs considerably from *N. damascena* and *N. hispanica*, mainly by producing smaller yellow flowers with red spots. The involucre is also absent. The inflated fruit is united in the middle and divergent above. 'Transformer' bears yellow flowers and curious seed pods, which are excellent for cutting.

Quick key to *Nigella* species

A. Flowers with a basal involucre .... *N. damascena*
AA. Flowers without involucre
    B. Flowers yellow or yellow with red spotting .... *N. orientalis*
    BB. Flowers blue, sometimes white, not yellow .... *N. hispanica*

Additional reading

Sargent, Joan. 1988. Winter annuals for cutting. *Horticulture* 66 (12):60–64.

Nolana (no la′ na)   Nolanaceae

The genus, the only member of the family, is characterized by solitary flowers, five fertile stamens, two-celled ovaries, and a regular corolla. Seldom seen in American gardens, *Nolana* is used primarily to cover poor or rocky soils. But they are attractive small plants for edging gardens or paths, and their showy flowers are produced in great profusion. *Nolana paradoxa* is the main species found, but a couple of others are sometimes offered.

Quick guide to *Nolana* species

	Height	Flower color
N. humifusa	4–6"	light blue
N. paradoxa	7–10"	blue

-paradoxa (pa ra doks′ a)   nolana   7–10"/3′
   summer   blue, purple   Chile, Peru

Plants produce 7–10″ tall smooth or sparsely hairy decumbent stems and opposite leaves. (A decumbent stem lies horizontally along the ground but with the tip ascending and almost erect.) The basal leaves are ovate and are attached by long petioles; the stem leaves are mostly sessile or with a short winged petiole. The large 1–2″ wide flowers resemble those of *Convolvulus*, with five lobes, usually blue, with a white ring in the center and a yellow throat. They are produced singly at the upper nodes of the stems.

Flowers tend to open only in bright sunshine. These handsome plants grow rapidly, and while they are not considered a ground cover like periwinkle, they do cover a considerable area. Their habit allows them to be produced and grown as hanging baskets.

Full sun, propagate by seed *in situ*.

CULTIVARS

'Alba' has white flowers.

'Blue Bird', the most common form, has large dark blue trumpet-shaped flowers with a white throat, fading to yellow.

'Cliff Hanger' has a trailing habit, blue flowers, and a pale yellow throat.

Alternative species

Nolana humifusa (hew mih few' sa) is more or less decumbent and bears small (¾") light blue flowers, striped in dark purple. 'Shooting Star' is nicely floriferous, with lilac flowers and purple veins. Excellent for hanging baskets.

Nolana ×*tenella* (te nel' a), a hybrid between *N. paradoxa* and *N. humifusa*, is highly variable. Flowers are usually pale purple-blue, with a white throat and purple veins.

Quick key to *Nolana* species

A. Flowers 1–2" wide, not striped . . . . *N. paradoxa*
AA. Flowers <1" wide, striped with dark purple . . . . *N. humifusa*

O

Ocimum (o see′ mum)   basil   Lamiaceae

This is a large genus of aromatic plants, mainly cultivated for the culinary properties associated with common basil, *Ocimum basilicum*. Not only are basil leaves
used in soups, casseroles, sauces, and certain liqueurs; some species, such as *O.
tenuiflorum* (holy basil), have long been cultivated for medicinal and religious
reasons. As much as I enjoy some basil on my plate, I enjoy it more in my garden.

-basilicum (ba sil′ ih kum)   common basil   1–3′/2′
   summer   foliage   tropical Asia

Margins, apices, and leaf shapes are highly variable in the cultivated forms of
this species. The sessile ovate leaves are ½–2″ long, ¹⁄₁₆–½″ wide. The leaf surfaces are usually glandular, accounting for the unique fragrances. The short
inflorescences are typical for the family, that is having two-lipped white to
creamy yellow whorled flowers, with slightly exserted stamens. Small floral
leaves or bracts are found at the base of each whorl, with approximately three
flowers per node. Purple forms are quite common and can be confused with
purple *Perilla* (for differences between the two genera, see *Perilla*). Basil grows up
to 3′ tall but is generally in the 18–24″ range and may be globe-shaped. If spaced
close together, plants act almost like a ground cover.

   Full sun, propagate by seed.

CULTIVARS

   'Ararat', an old form of basil, has green mottled foliage, no more ornamental
than many but highly aromatic.

   'Aussie Sweetie', about 2′ tall, is useful for trimming into shapes. Plants are
compact growers with dense green foliage.

   'Citriodorum' (lemon basil) has lemon-scented leaves.

   'Crispum' (curly basil) produces curly-edged foliage.

   'Dark Opal' has reddish purple leaves with a bit of a clove scent. An All-America Selection in 1962. Also sold as 'Purpureum'.

   'Minimum' (Greek basil) bears small leaves, less than ⅓″ long.

'Purple Delight' has ovate purple leaves without the curliness of 'Purple Ruffles'. Very similar, if not identical, to 'Dark Opal'.

'Purple Ruffles' is a handsome form with curled dark purple leaves. An All-America Selection in 1987.

'Siam Queen' grows 2–3' tall and 2' wide, with larger leaves and purple flowers.

'Spicy Globe' is a mounding form, quite different from others. Good foliage and white flowers.

'Sweet Dani' has a strong lemon scent. About 2' tall. A 1998 All-America Selection.

Odontonema (o don to ne' ma)   Acanthaceae

That such beautiful plants are essentially unknown outside the South can perhaps be explained by the fact that the genus flowers only in late summer and fall. What a waste! About twenty-five species have been identified, evergreen in their native habitats, with opposite leaves and usually with late-season crimson-red flowers in a panicle. The only commonly available species is *Odontonema strictum* (firespike).

-*strictum* (strik' tum)   firespike   4–5'/3'
fall   crimson-red   Central America

This species offers outstanding dark green glossy foliage on stout plants for the spring and summer landscape. The opposite glabrous leaves are about 6" long and half as wide, oblong, pointed, and somewhat wavy around the margins. I have yet to see insect or disease problems on the leaves. An erect compact inflorescence, about 1' long and composed of many small (1") waxy crimson flowers, is formed in late summer. Flowers open over a three- to four-week period and remain in bloom for weeks or until frost takes them out. After a long hot summer, when thoughts of giving up this gardening obsession are ever-present, the fresh foliage and emerging flowers of this species are wonderfully welcome. Gardeners in the far northern states and Canada may not have a fall lengthy enough to allow flowers to form before frost. To everyone else, I highly recommend this species for adding zip and zow to the fall garden.

Full sun, propagate by cuttings.

CULTIVARS

'Variegata' has pale green-and-white leaves, equally glossy and quite handsome. Plants don't flower as well as the species, however.

Additional reading

Armitage, Allan M. 2000. Is there a market for fall-flowering annuals? *Greenhouse Grower* 18(4):76–81.

Orthosiphon (or tho si' fon)   Lamiaceae

The generic name sounds like a representative of a chemical company doing
something illegal at the gas pump. Of the hundred or so species, all easily confused, the only plant commonly offered is *Orthosiphon stamineus*, which binomial trips off the tongue as easily as, say, *Adlumia fungosa*, the most singsong of
singsong names in gardening lore.

| *-stamineus* (sta min ee' us) | cat's whiskers | 2–3'/3' |
| late summer, fall | white, lavender | India |

The common name of this species refers to the long stamens, which stick out of
the flowers at right angles, like Sylvester's whiskers. Cat lovers are always taken
by the plant; those who think cat lovers are crazy, much less so. When people
look at the plant, they may be moderately impressed. Tell them the common
name, and two warring factions immediately result. The same thing would
probably happen if the common name were dog's whiskers. Rhetoric aside, cat's
whiskers can be a beautiful, dramatic flowering plant in the late summer and fall
garden.

Plants, which are native to warm areas of India, have little trouble with heat
and humidity in American gardens. They have square stems, opposite leaves,
and long whorled flowers. The pointed ovate leaves are coarsely toothed and
attached to the stem by a long petiole. One of the criticisms of this species is that
the foliage seldom is dark green: the leaves usually have a pallor; they look as if
they need fertilizer but do not. This might be a pH problem, although nothing
we have done in the UGA Horticulture Gardens has remedied the problem.

Plants produce many stems, which form terminal racemes in late summer.
Individual flowers consist of a long two-lipped corolla, about three times longer
than the five-toothed calyx, and the four stamens, three times longer again. The
1" long flowers are white or lavender, generally with three to six flowers per
whorl. Many stems do not flower, and certainly they do not all bloom at the
same time, resulting in full plants with few flowers. They blossom over a long
period of time, however, and while flowers occur from mid summer to frost,
most open in the fall. Many people really like these plants, problems and all,
and it is a shame they are so difficult to locate in retail outlets. Well worth a
spot in the garden.

Full sun, propagate by cuttings.

Alternative species

Orthosiphon hyoseroides (hi o ser oy' deez), from South Africa, blooms with yellow to orange ray flowers with yellow centers. Plants stand about 2' tall and produce fine flowers in spring and fall. Usually available only from seed. 'Gaiety
Orange' produces rich orange flowers with a darker center than the species.

Osteospermum (os tee o sper' mum)

Cape daisy, South African daisy   Asteraceae

This South African genus has been in European gardens for many years, its plants flowering freely in areas where summer temperatures—or at least evening temperatures—are relatively cool. In the 1980s and early 1990s, I enjoyed them in gardens in the British Isles and wondered if they could be successful in the States. While in Australia in the mid 1990s, I saw outstanding taxa, including variegated foliage forms, in full flower in spring, but they stopped flowering in summer. In Sydney, Perth, Dublin, Edinburgh, or London, plants had their moments, but most of them were during cooler times of year. American gardeners—so spoiled by the season-long flowering of begonias and petunias—expect all plants that flower in spring to continue to bloom all season; still, I was convinced that American breeders should be working on the genus. The two main species, *Osteospermum ecklonis* and *O. jucundum*, initiate flowers around 50°F, but when temperatures routinely rise above the sixties, flower initiation decreases. As summer progresses, plants form handsome, albeit flowerless, shrubby plants. Happily, breeders in Denmark, Australia, South Africa, and America are developing cultivars that address the problem and flower in warm temperatures.

Of course, telling so many daisies apart literally requires a hand lens or microscope. The closest relative to the osteos is probably *Dimorphotheca*, another South African genus cultivated in southern California for the greenhouse trade. *Osteospermum* has fertile ray flowers and is usually more robust, growing to 2' tall; *Dimorphotheca* has sterile ray flowers and usually grows only about 16" tall. Some cultivars on the market may be called *Dimorphotheca* (the Dandenong series, for example), but I have included them under *Osteospermum* because recent taxonomic changes have lumped several common *Dimorphotheca* species in *Osteospermum*.

Osteos are subshrubs, meaning they become woody at the base of the plants, with alternate linear to oblong leaves. They are well branched and form handsome 1–2' tall plants with beautiful daisy flowers. In *Osteospermum ecklonis*, the ray flowers are generally white above and indigo beneath, with a bright blue disk. In *O. jucundum*, the ray flowers are generally red on both surfaces, with dark purple, almost black disks. Both species have a few selections associated with them, but nearly all plants now offered are hybrids, within and among species. I have trialed many of the hybrids and continue to believe that great plants will result; however, most present-day plants should be expected to dazzle in spring, flower sporadically in the heat of the summer, and possibly recover in the fall. In semi-tropical areas of the country (zone 8 and south), they are best planted in the fall to be enjoyed in early spring, then replaced with more appropriate taxa.

CULTIVARS

Cape Daisy series offers 2–4" wide flowers in various colors. Good plants, but something has to be done about these awful names. 'Bamba' has deep rose-

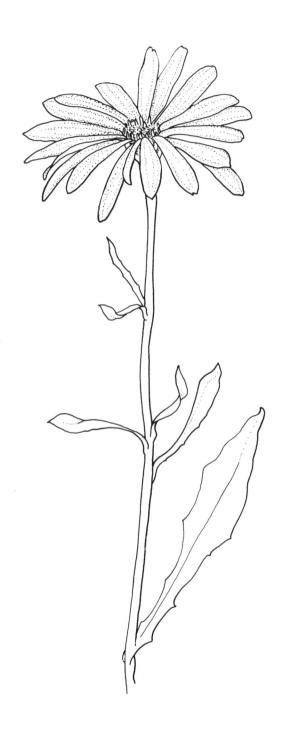

Osteospermum 'Sirius'   ASHA KAYS

red blooms; 'Beira' is bluish white; 'Dondo' is cherry red; 'Durban' has creamy white petals and deep blue eye; 'Kalanga' is a handsome pink blushed form; 'Lusaka' produces purple flowers; 'Nasinga' is a group of spoon-tipped flowers in cream, purple, and white—quite an eye-catching flower shape; 'Oringa Peach' has beautiful peach-colored flowers; 'Volta' produces pinkish petals with redder tips; 'Zimba' is medium-sized with white on top and creamy yellow on the underside of the ray flowers; and 'Zulu' has bright yellow flowers that contrast well with the cinnamon disk. "Awful" is perhaps an understatement.

Dandenong, bred in Australia, is a lower-growing, more spread-out series of plants. They may be cultivars or hybrids of *Dimorphotheca* and performance has been a little better than *Osteospermum*, at least in the South. Available in creamy white ('Vanilla Cream'), mauve, pink ('Daisy Pink'), purple blush, rose, variegated, and white. 'Dandenong Variegated' was an excellent performer in the University of Georgia trials; the green-and-white splashed leaves were colorful all season, and the blue-centered flowers bloomed most of the summer.

Passion Mix is grown from seed and available in shades of purple, lavender, and white with blue centers. The daisy flowers appear on 12–18″ plants. An All-America Selection in 1999.

Side series, bred by the Sakata Seed Company of Japan, is more compact than others and its flowers stay open longer into the evening. 'Brightside' bears white flowers with a blue center; 'Highside' is rose and white with blue disk; 'Riverside' has handsome yellow flowers and a dark disk; 'Seaside' is a pink and white bicolor form; and 'Wildside' bears deep purple flowers with bluish centers.

Spring Star series, another fine example of German breeding, is available in four colors. 'Arctur' performed well in our trials and has good white ray flowers around a blue center. Others are 'Aurora' (magenta), 'Mira' (deep magenta, also an excellent performer at UGA), and 'Sirius' (rosy red).

Sunny series consists of 'Ingrid' (dark purple flowers), 'Sonja' (spoon-tipped ray flowers with blue centers), and 'Silvia' (white and pink bicolored flowers).

Symphony series, from Japan, is about 12″ tall. 'Lemon Symphony', 'Orange Symphony', and 'Cream Symphony' have bright yellow, orange, and creamy white large single daisy flowers, respectively. Outstanding color. If outdoor performance can be maintained, they should do well in the marketplace.

'Variegata' has wonderful green-and-white foliage with white flowers and a purplish reverse. Even when not in flower, which is often, it is a good-looking plant.

Additional reading

University of Georgia Trial Reports: www.uga.edu/ugatrial

Otacanthus (o ta kan' thus)   Scrophulariaceae

I was introduced to this genus in 1992, on a visit to a Southwest nursery. Always on the hunt for upright, blue-flowered plants, I brought a few of these bloomers back to Georgia for trialing that summer. *Otacanthus caeruleus* (Brazilian snap-

Otacanthus caeruleus ASHA KAYS

dragon), the species that ended up in our display beds in Athens, is now in green-houses and retail outlets throughout the country.

-caeruleus (sa roo' lee us)	Brazilian snapdragon	2–4'/3'
late summer	lavender-blue	Brazil

The alternate leaves of this species are 2–3" long, serrated, and deep green. The flowers are held in few-flowered racemes; each 1" wide flower is two-lipped, but each lip is almost semicircular, making a rounded individual flower. The base of the petals is fused into a long tube that sticks out from the foliage. Flowers are lavender-blue to purple, and the white center is small but obvious. The blooms are quite beautiful, and although flowering will occur throughout the season, most prolific flowering is mid to late summer and fall.

The plants I brought back with me passed their first tests in the gardens in Athens: they rooted easily enough and their habit was good. They grew well with little care and fuss and were admired, if not lusted after, by visitors that first summer. (This lack of lust stemmed from their late flowering and the fact that flowers never fully covered the plants.) These are not "knock your socks off" plants. They are more classy, inspiring people to come back for a second look. Their flower color goes well with the yellows of summer and bronzes of fall, and few insects and disease problems have been encountered in the many years we have grown them. In our greenhouse trials, we could not induce massive flow-ering through photoperiodic control. Warm temperatures and bright light were the switches that induced flowering.

Full sun, propagate by terminal cuttings.

CULTIVARS

'Caribbean Blue', introduced in 1999 by Bodger Botanicals, is perhaps more compact but otherwise similar to the species. I am pleased someone took the opportunity to introduce this fine plant to American gardeners.

Additional reading

University of Georgia Trial Reports: www.uga.edu/ugatrial

P

Papaver (pa pa′ ver)   poppy   Papaveraceae

From Flanders Field to the Wizard of Oz, from fresh rolls and pastries to blighted city streets, poppies are woven into our poetry, literature, and social structure. That they have been memorialized and cursed with equal vigor underscores the longevity and the beauty of some of the species. About forty species of poppies are known, and they are all beautiful: some coarse, others frail, some persistent, others lasting no longer than a one dollar bill. They are usually represented in American gardens by the perennial Oriental poppy, *Papaver orientale*. I would be hard pressed to find an ugly poppy among the perennial forms, except when they are in my garden, suggesting that cooler temperatures are a necessity.

Many species can be treated as annuals in many gardens in North America, either because they are true annuals, or because they behave like biennials, enjoying the cold of winter, exploding in spring, and disappearing in summer. I have met a few people who I wish were as considerate. Only about three species are commonly grown as annuals or biennials, but many others are out there for the poppy collector. As with *Phlox* or *Salvia*, collecting all the species of *Papaver* is a full-time job. My poppy stage of life was brief: I managed to try half a dozen or so of the fanciful species, but they kept dying on me, so my stage quickly changed.

Poppies are characterized by nodding flower buds, solitary flowers on long flower stalks, milky juice, and leaves that are lobed or dissected. The seed capsule is hard, oval, and decorative. Many self-sow prolifically, and new plants can often be counted on year after year.

Quick guide to *Papaver* species

	Height	Flower width	Gray-green foliage
P. nudicaule	12–24"	3–4"	yes
P. rhoeas	9–18"	1–3"	no
P. somniferum	24–36"	3–4"	yes

-nudicaule (noo dih ka′ lee)   Iceland poppy   1–2′/1′
  spring   many colors   subarctic regions

This northern species is increasingly popular throughout the country in both public and private gardens, where fall plantings produce spectacular drifts of vibrant flowers in the spring. Although unable to survive the hot summer in most of the United States, Iceland poppies are perennial in the North, living two to three years and flowering from early spring to early summer.

Plants are rosetted and stemless and produce 4–6″ long, gray-green pinnately lobed leaves. The silky flowers, up to 4″ wide, are borne on 12″ high leafless flower stems. Most are seed-propagated, and mixes are common. The selections from the species also make wonderful potted plants for indoor use, and more plants will be seen in florists displays and mass market outlets. It is also the only species suitable for cut flowers.

Seed-propagated plants flower the first year. Seeds collected from F_1 hybrids, however, result in plants dissimilar to the parent plant. Plant in the fall in full sun; pull out of the ground when plants start to decline, generally late April to early May in the South, late May to early June in the North.

CULTIVARS

Iceland poppy cultivars offer specific colors and heights, with each new entry providing larger and more vibrant flowers than its predecessors. As the majority are propagated from seed, some variation is inevitable.

'Champagne Bubbles' is an F_1 hybrid with 3″ wide flowers in white, orange, pink, and yellow shades.

'Coonara Pink' has 2″ wide flowers in pastel pink shades.

'Flamenco' offers pastel pink flowers with white fluted edges. They are a mixture of colors from light to dark pink and probably should be thought of as pink shades.

Garden Gnome series is about 1′ tall in shades of scarlet, salmon, orange, yellow, and white.

Kelmscott Strain is 12–18″ tall and consists of mostly pastel colors.

Meadow Pastels series is a mixture of pastel and bicolored flowers on 2–2½′ tall plants.

Monarch Mix bears flowers up to 2″ wide in many bright colors.

Oregon Rainbows series grows 20″ high, with large 6″ wide blooms in about five colors.

'Party Fun' produces sturdy upright stems with 4″ wide flowers in a wide range of colors. Plants stand about 12–14″ tall.

'Popsicle' has 3–4″ wide flowers in an assortment of colors.

'Red Sails' bears 5″ wide orange-scarlet flowers on 30″ tall plants.

'Solar Fire Orange' is useful as a cut flower, growing nearly 2′ tall. One of the few choices in a single color: its bright orange flowers are eye-catching.

'Summer Promise' contains both solid and bicolor 2–3″ wide flowers on 2′ tall stems.

Wonderland Mix is more compact than the type and bears 2–3″ wide flowers. Bright orange 3″ wide flowers are available as 'Wonderland Orange'. The best

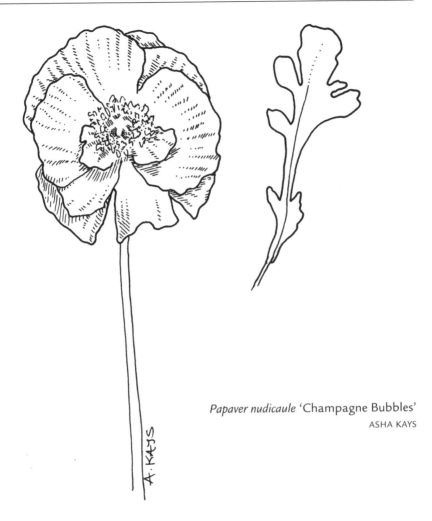

Papaver nudicaule 'Champagne Bubbles'
ASHA KAYS

selection for windy areas, it has proven resilient even in the windswept beds of Auckland Botanical Gardens.

-rhoeas (ro ee′ as)	corn poppy, Flanders poppy	9–18″/12″
spring	red	Europe, Asia

This most famous poppy species was immortalized by Canadian poet John Mc-Crae in the hauntingly beautiful "In Flanders Field." I bore my students to death with the story of the red poppy, partly because it is an interesting part of horti-cultural sociology and also because I feel very close to two main figures in the Flanders story. McCrae lived in the small college town of Guelph, Ontario, and his small house on Water Street is marked with a brief inscription, which I read every now and then on my way to school. He wrote the poem, but the person

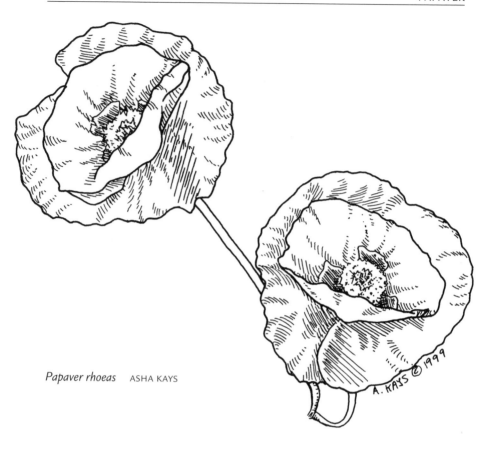

Papaver rhoeas   ASHA KAYS

who made the red poppy famous was Moina Michael, an unassuming country teacher who lived outside Athens, Georgia. The "poppy lady" was so inspired by McCrae's poem that with nothing but determination and spirit, she single-handedly made the poppy the Veterans Day flower, sold to raise money in the United States, England, and Canada on every Veterans Day since 1925.

The green foliage is hairy and coarsely toothed, more or less pinnatifid (not quite pinnate, but close). Plants can grow up to 3', but those used for wildflower plantings along the median are usually half as tall. Flower color is diverse, from the usual cinnabar-red to deep purple and even white, often with dark spots. The fruit is a typical poppy capsule, somewhat rounded and with many black seeds. The seeds fly everywhere, and plants reappear for many years.

CULTIVARS

'Angels Choir' is a gruesome variation of the classic poppy, producing awful double flowers in half a dozen colors. Plants are about 2' tall.

'Mother of Pearl' is a robust group of 2–2½' tall plants in shades of lilac, pink, white, lavender, and peach. Single flowers.

Shirley poppies were selected and reselected by the Reverend W. Wilks of Shirley, England. Wilks began to select this strain in 1880, and I find it interesting that they are still the leading form of this plant in gardens in America. The history of the Shirley poppy is a story of one man's perseverance. Following are excerpts from a 1932 article Wilks wrote for volume 57 of *The Garden*:

In 1880 I noticed in a waste corner of my garden abutting on the fields a patch of the common wild field poppy [*Papaver rhoeas*], one solitary flower of which had a very narrow edge of white. This one flower I marked and saved the seed of it alone.... [I continued selecting plants over the years,] all the while getting a larger infusion of white to tone down the red until they arrived at quite pale pink and one plant absolutely pure white. I then set myself to change the black central portions of the flower from black to yellow or white, and having at last fixed a strain with petals varying in color from the brightest scarlet to pure white, with all shades of pink between and all varieties of flakes and edged flowers also, but all having yellow or white stamens, anthers and pollen, and a white base.

Wilks distributed plants freely to all and continued to select plants to keep the strain as pure as possible. According to Wilks, "The true Shirley poppies (1) are single, (2) always have a white base, (3) yellow or white stamens, anthers and pollen, (4) never have the smallest particle of black about them." And he too found it "rather interesting that the gardens of the whole world—rich man's and poor man's alike—are today furnished with poppies which are the direct descendants of one single capsule of seed raised in the garden of the Shirley Vicarage."

-somniferum (som nih fe' rum)	opium poppy	2–3'/2'
late spring	many colors	Greece, western Asia

This species, the oldest poppy in cultivation, has enjoyed a diverse history. Opium, which is made from the sap of the green seed capsules, was known by the Greeks and Egyptians several centuries before the birth of Christ. The narcotic properties of the species have long been recognized (poppy juice was even mixed with baby food to make babies sleep), but plants are also used for the edible seeds, which, besides turning up on your poppy-seed bagel or bun, are also sold as birdseed under the name of mawseed. Cut flower growers have been producing opium poppy for the decorative pods for years—there is as much chance of getting high on these things as seeing the man on the moon. But laws concerning this species are changing in the United States, and many states aggressively prohibit the growing of it, period. Crazy! If you are a serious athlete, you know one thing very well: if you ingest the seeds of this plant, you will test positive in drug tests. But since most of us have trouble running down the driveway for the paper, we need not worry about random drug tests. Let's enjoy these plants for their beauty and be done with all this legislative mumbo-jumbo!

The lack of branching on these 2–3' tall plants further accentuates their height. The gray-green leaves are unequally toothed at the base and clasp the

Papaver somniferum   ASHA KAYS

stem. The plants themselves are not particularly attractive, but the flowers, which can be 4–5″ across, more than compensate. The scarlet flowers of the species are beautiful, and the many available cultivars range in color from white through pink, red through purple (no yellow or blue flowers yet exist). In most flowers, showy black blotches at the base of the petals provide additional beauty. Flowers drop their petals quickly and make poor cut flowers, but when the seed capsules are standing tall, they can be enjoyed as an outdoor ornament or brought in to dry in the vase.

Papaver somniferum is a short-lived plant, but it flowers profusely and the seed is viable, particularly after being chilled in the winter. Every spring, southern gardens come alive with seedlings of opium poppies, many not exactly where they were last seen. Each spring, I take my students across town to the beautiful garden of Laura Ann Segrest. We stand in awe of the symphony of color provided by this magnificent plant, now better known for its ability to cause pain than for its potential for beauty.

Full sun. Plants and seeds overwinter to zones 6 and 7.

CULTIVARS

Two flower forms are common in gardens: carnation-flowered and peony-flowered. The former has fringed petals, the latter does not. Blooms of the peony-flowered strain, sometimes listed as *Papaver paeoniaeflorum*, resemble those of double peonies. Colors vary in both forms.

'Oase', a carnation-flowered form, is bright red with some white.

var. *setigerum* is a hairy form of the opium poppy. Flowers are violet-purple and leaves are deeply incised.

'White Cloud', a peony-flowered form, has double white flowers.

Alternative species

Papaver commutatum (kom yew tay' tum) is similar to *P. rhoeas*, except that its petals are blotched. The 1″ wide flowers are red with black splotches in the middle. 'Lady Bird' has deep crimson flowers with a similar black blotch.

Papaver glaucum (glaw' kum; tulip poppy) is related to *P. somniferum*. Its common name was suggested by its scarlet color, the texture of its petals, and especially its cup-shaped flowers. Plants grow 12–18″ tall and bear smooth, blue-green leaves and stems.

Papaver triniifolium (trin ee ih fo' lee um) is a biennial and another relative of *P. rhoeas*, with a basal rosette of blue-green filigreed leaves that is as handsome as any part of the plant. As temperatures warm up, the 12–18″ tall scapes bear dozens of 1″ wide salmon to apricot papier-mâché flowers. If cool spring temperatures persist, plants will flower for a month or more, but they stop flowering at the first sign of summer heat. Lots of seed is produced, which may be saved for next year.

Quick key to *Papaver* species

A. Leaves usually green, seldom gray- or blue-green . . . . *P. rhoeas*
AA. Leaves usually gray- or blue-green
    B. Flowers on leafless scapes, leaves all basal . . . . *P. nudicaule*
    BB. Flowers on more or less leafy scapes, stem leaves
       clasping . . . . *P. somniferum*

Additional reading

Bender, Steve. 1992. Poppies Parr excellence. *Southern Living* 27(11):66.

Christopher, Thomas. 1981. Poppies. *Horticulture* 59:24–29.

Cullen, James. 1968. The genus *Papaver* in cultivation. Part 1: the wild species. *Baileya* 16(3):73–90.

Dean, Molly. 1996. The pleasures of poppies. *Flower and Garden* 40(2):40–43.

Pollan, Michael. 1997. Opium, made easy: one gardener's encounter with the war on drugs. *Harper's* 294(1763):35–58.

Springer, Lauren. 1997. A parade of poppies. *Horticulture* 94(6):41–45.

Passiflora (pa sih flor′ a)   passion flower   Passifloraceae

The interest in these fascinating vines increases as more people see them. The flowers of the genus are certainly among the more exotic blossoms in the garden, evoking the perfection of divine creation, biblical tragedy, or an appreciation of the diversity of living things, depending on your imagination. Passion flowers are so called in reference to the Crucifixion: the corona represents the crown of thorns; the five anthers, the wounds; the three styles, the nails; the five sepals and petals, the apostles (less Peter and Judas); and the hand-like leaves and tendrils, the hands and scourges of Christ's persecutors. Who says plants don't evoke passion! While I understand how such stories could evolve, I simply see a beautiful flower in vivid colors growing from handsome vines. That I see so few of them has nothing to do with my religious leanings; it is simply that they are plants for zones 8 to 10, in the main, and most people think of them as indoor plants or conservatory specimens rather than as garden annuals. But with the renewed interest in tropicals in mainstream gardening, why not let a few exotic passion flowers loose through shrubs or on a trellis?

As the stories suggest, this is a terrific flower to pull apart in order to understand some of the lesser known flower structures. Starting at the base, the five sepals below the petals are often the same shape and color as the petals, as with the tepals on many bulbs. Notice the slender filament-like structure coming from the center of the flower; this is the corona. Coronas are seldom seen in flowers (the tube of a daffodil flower is the best-known example). In the passion flower, the ornamental corona, which comprises much of the color of the bloom, consists of one to several rows of filaments, whose main function appears to be to make the bloom attractive to insects.

More than 500 species of *Passiflora* have been cataloged, some of which are themselves making a rapid comeback. Flowers are available in a color palette that includes brilliant reds (*P. coccinea*), handsome whites (*P. subpeltata*), and shocking yellows (*P. citrina*). And the numerous cultivars and hybrids that are available to the collector offer bicolored and tri-colored flowers to enliven the place as well. Passion fruit, known as granadilla in the subtropics and tropical highlands, is harvested from many species, including *P. edulis*, *P. ligularis*, *P. mollissima*, and *P. quadrangularis*. Some species and their offspring are hardy to zone 7 (some to zone 6) and can be grown like hardy perennials, resprouting from the base in the spring. Most should be considered annuals, however, even in zones 8 and 9. Hardy species include *P. caerulea*; *P. incarnata* (maypop), a field weed that some believe should be eradicated; and *P. lutea*, as well as some of the hybrid forms that use them as parents. Semi-hardy forms such as *P. antioquiensis*, *P. edulis*, and *P. manicata* generally defoliate below 40°F and are best maintained at 45–50°F (zone 9). The remaining tropical forms and hybrids require a minimum temperature range of 55–60°F (zone 10). Most are kept in a greenhouse over winter and placed outside as established, perhaps even budded, plants.

Full sun, fertilize sparingly. Too much nitrogen results in an overabundance of leaves and few flowers. All plants may be propagated by cuttings in mid summer; some species are available from seed. Plantlets placed in the ground or in containers in the spring may not grow sufficiently or flower well, particularly north of zone 7.

Quick guide to *Passiflora* species

	Sepal/petal color	Corona	Leaf shape
P. caerulea	blush pink	sky blue	five-lobed
P. citrina	yellow	yellow	two-lobed
P. coccinea	red	black	simple, not lobed
P. coriacea	yellow-green	ivory	two- to three-lobed
P. vitifolia	scarlet	red	three-lobed

-caerulea (se roo′ lee a)	blue passion flower	vine
summer	blue	Brazil

This species has better cold hardiness than others and is therefore the most common passion flower for gardeners. The robust stems are somewhat angular and furrowed and bear alternate lobed leaves. The 4″ long leaves are usually palmately five-lobed but can have from three to nine segments. The tendrils and two stipules (small leaf-like structures) as well as the flowers occur at the nodes. The slightly fragrant flowers are about 4″ wide, with blush-pink sepals and petals. The filaments that make up the corona are blue at the top, white in the middle, and purple at the base, resulting in circles of color. The ovoid fruit is orange or yellow.

A terrific plant for beginners, this species is also parent to some popular cultivars and hybrids. Plant in containers, or in the ground, in full sun.

CULTIVARS

'Constance Eliott' has creamy white sepals and petals and is often sold as the species. Very common.

'Grandiflora' has similar but larger flowers, up to 6″ in diameter.

-citrina (sih treen′ a)	lemon passion flower	vine
summer	yellow	Honduras

Discovered in Central America in 1991, this vine has not yet enjoyed the popularity of older hybrids and species. Its leaves and flowers, however, offer a classical rather than a multicolored look. The flowers are relatively small, only about 1½″ wide; they consist of a long tube that explodes into a star of sepals and petals at the base. The leaves are two-lobed and feel like felt. The vigor of the plant and the many leaves tend to hide the flowers, although the fact they are completely yellow makes them difficult to miss.

This is an excellent plant for containers, with everblooming flowers. They cannot be considered miniatures but will likely reach no more than 4′ tall. Full sun, do not fertilize.

-coccinea (kok sin′ ee a)   red passion flower   vine
   summer   scarlet   South America

The 4–5″ wide deep red flowers and the 5–6″ simple leaves make this an easy passion flower to recognize. The leaves are oblong, and the margins are wavy to serrated. The scarlet sepals and petals are linear in shape and almost vertically oriented from the center. The corona is pale pink to white at the base, deep purple toward the top. All in all, a brilliant palette of color. Its fruit, known as red granadilla, is also harvested.

   Full sun. Plants will grow 5–6′ in containers.

-coriacea (kor ee ay′ see a)   bat-leaf passion flower   vine
   summer   yellow-green   Mexico

The common name is reason enough to include this plant in the conservatory or garden. The leathery (*coriacea* means "leathery") peltate leaves consist of two broadly divergent lobes that resemble the wings of a bat. The small flowers, 1–1½″ wide, consist of yellow-green sepals and no petals. Flowers are reasonably handsome, with an ivory-colored corona, but are no match for other species and hybrids. I wonder if the Joker would like them?

   Full sun, plant in containers or ground. Since leaves are the important feature in this species, plants may be fertilized relatively heavily.

-vitifolia (vih tih fo′ lee a)   grape-leaf passion flower   vine
   summer   red   Central America

The leaves are three-lobed, much like a grape leaf, and about 6″ long and 7″ across. The lobes are pointed, and the leaves are usually three- to five-veined. The flowers, which are about 4″ across, consist of strap-like deep red sepals and petals and red to bright yellow filaments. The slightly hairy 3″ oval fruit is edible, although not the fruit of choice for passion fruit lovers.

   Full sun, do not overfertilize. Plants will grow 3–4′ in containers.

CULTIVARS

   'Scarlet Flame' has deep scarlet flowers and fruit that supposedly tastes like strawberries.

Alternative species

   Passiflora ×*alato-caerulea* is a common hybrid between *P. alata* (winged passion flower), a large red- to blush-flowered species, and *P. caerulea*. It has purple and blush petals and sepals and a deep amethyst corolla. The 4″ wide flowers are fragrant. Plants bear larger and more fragrant flowers than *P. caerulea* but are not as cold hardy as that species (perhaps to zone 9).

   Passiflora ×*decaisneana* is a cross between *P. alata* and *P. quadrangularis*. The brilliant carmine flowers are topped with long wavy purple and white filaments. Large fruit and fragrant flowers.

Passiflora quadrangularis (kwod rang yew la' ris; giant granadilla), a relative of *P. caerulea*, is widely cultivated for its large smooth fruit. The 5″ wide flowers consist of mauve petals and sepals and many series of purple filaments, which make a dense corona. Leaves are simple and ovate-lanceolate. 'Variegata' has leaves splotched yellow.

Passiflora sanguinolenta (san gwih no len' ta) is botanically related to *P. citrina*. It has small flowers and is more dwarf in habit. The flowers also have a long tube with starry pink sepals and star-shaped petals. The leaves are slightly two-lobed.

Quick key to *Passiflora* species

A. Leaves usually two-lobed or simple (not lobed)
    B. Leaves usually two-lobed
        C. Leaves peltate, leathery, two lobes divergent,
           flowers blue . . . . *P. coriacea*
        CC. Leaves not peltate, flowers yellow . . . . *P. citrina*
    BB. Leaves simple, not lobed
        C. Margins serrated to wavy, flowers red . . . . *P. coccinea*
        CC. Margins entire, flowers mauve to purple . . . . . *P. quadrangularis*
AA. Leaves three- to many-lobed
    B. Leaves three-lobed, flowers red . . . . *P. vitifolia*
    BB. Leaves five-lobed or more, flowers blue . . . . *P. caerulea*

Passiflora hybrids

'Amethyst' has three-lobed leaves with intense blue petals and dark purple filaments. Sometimes confused with *Passiflora amethystina*, which has larger flowers with mauve petals and many rows of purple filaments.

'Blue Boutique' has light blue sepals, petals that point downward, and beautiful filaments, blue at the top, white near the base. Quite lovely.

'Coral Glow' has linear petals, sepals of rich coral to scarlet, and essentially no corona. Best for indoor use, as flowering is heaviest in the winter.

'Debbie' produces large flowers with creamy white sepals and petals and many long thin mauve-purple filaments. Leaves are three-lobed.

'Elizabeth' bears large (5″ wide) fragrant flowers with lilac sepals and petals and dozens of crinkled lavender and white filaments. The center of the flower is rosy purple.

'Incense' provides large royal purple flowers, highlighted with wavy blue-purple filaments, which overlay the entire bloom. Fragrant.

'Jeanette' produces many flowers on a vigorous plant. The petals and sepals are purple and wine-colored, with deep purple centers and purple filaments that are white at the base.

'Little Orchid' has three- to five-lobed dark green leaves with light lavender to orchid flowers. The light lavender filaments contrast with the light-colored sepals and petals.

'Pura-Vida', among the most handsome passion flowers, bears blue-lavender sepals and petals and a dark blue corona.

'Saint Rule' has small (2″ wide) clean white fragrant flowers on small three-lobed leaves. The white filaments have a small lavender band in the middle.

'Sapphire' is a favorite of mine, providing relative ease of culture and many flowers. The sepals and petals are light lavender to cream, and the filaments are purple at the base and white at the top.

'Star of Bristol' bears large flowers with strap-like lavender-white petals and green-white sepals, which together form a star-shaped flower. The filaments are lavender.

'Star of Clevedon' bears flowers of creamy white downward-pointed sepals and petals, and purple filaments that have central band of white.

'Star of Kingston' is similar to 'Star of Clevedon', but the sepals are tipped with mauve and the petals are light mauve.

'Sunburst' has large two-lobed pointed leaves with three main veins. The small orange flowers are about 2″ across with lemon-yellow filaments. Not as showy as some, but beautiful contrasting colors between flowers and foliage.

Additional reading

Vanderplank, John. 1996. *Passion Flowers*, 2nd ed. MIT Press, Cambridge, Mass.

Patersonia (pa ter so′ nee a)   leafy purpleflag, wild iris   Iridaceae

It is highly unlikely that gardeners will be able to find plantlets of this genus of iris in their garden center or even their favorite mail-order catalog, but since I noticed seeds for sale, I thought it would be fun to include it. This iris should probably be called the Australian wild iris as it is endemic to that country, mainly in the states of Queensland and New South Wales but now escaped to Victoria and Western Australia as well. The genus was named for William Paterson, an early botanical collector for Australian gardens and the Lieutenant-Governor of New South Wales from 1800 to 1810.

The only species I can find offered is *Patersonia occidentalis* (ok sih den ta′ lis), although about twenty species are included in the genus. The 6–18″ long linear leaves are less than ½″ wide and clustered at the base of the plant, forming a fan, like most plants in the iris family. The margins of the leaves are entire. The flowers are held in few- to many-flowered 6″ tall spikes, enclosed in thin, translucent bracts. The purple iris-like flowers consist of three broad, spreading outer tepals, and three small, erect inner tepals. Flowers open in summer but are short-lived, persisting only a day. They do not open fully in cloudy and cold weather.

Plants may have no future in American gardens, as their ability to tolerate the great diversity of our climate has not been established. Certainly they are capable of surviving heat, even some humidity, but they will likely not be cold-tolerant below 28°F. Their slow growth may eliminate them from serious use as annuals as well, but who cares? Trying things out never hurt anyone, and buying a few seeds is a lot cheaper than going to Australia to see them.

Full sun, excellent drainage. Propagate by seed.

Alternative species

Patersonia umbrosa (um bro′ sa) is native to Western Australia. Plants are about 20″ tall, with narrow rigid linear leaves, about the same length as the flower spikes. The flowers are blue, obovate in shape. Var. *xanthia* has striking yellow flowers.

Pelargonium (pe lar go′ nee um)   geranium, cranesbill   Geraniaceae

The geranium is among the most popular plants of all times and all places. As a young landscaper, I was asked to plant more geraniums in gardens than all other annuals combined, and even now, with the explosion of perennials, new genera of annuals, and hundreds of new cultivars and varieties, the simple red geranium still rules many a small garden. That apparent simplicity, however, is anything but. The common bedding geranium is a trampoline of a complex hybrid that has launched hundreds of cultivars. Species of the genus were first introduced to European gardens in the seventeenth century; hybridization was well under way by the nineteenth century. On the forefront of the geranium wave are several excellent breeding companies—such as Oglevee and Pan American in the United States and Fischer Geraniums in Germany—as well as many seed companies, which have made sure the gardener has plenty to choose from. But if the bedding geranium were to disappear today, would the *Pelargonium* cupboard be bare? Absolutely not! At least 249 other species are known, all native to South Africa, and at least a dozen are as ornamental as the common geranium. Those who travel to South Africa and view the incredible variety of the genus keep scratching their heads, wondering why breeders don't take advantage of such diversity.

Gardeners are sometimes confused by the differences between the members of the family Geraniaceae, which consists of only three genera, *Pelargonium*, *Geranium*, and *Erodium*. Lesson one is that *Geranium* and *Erodium* are mostly perennial, *Pelargonium* is annual. To further separate plants, look at the leaves. Nearly all species of *Erodium* have pinnately compound leaves; most species of the other two genera have palmate-lobed leaves. *Pelargonium* differs from *Geranium* in two ways: the individual flowers of *Pelargonium* have a small spur, and some of the stamens (usually three of the ten) don't have anthers (the pollen bearing portion). If such detail is of no interest, you will not enjoy geraniums any less than the person with a 10× hand lens around his neck. Have fun. All geraniums have alternate leaves and flowers arranged in umbels.

The main groups of geraniums for gardeners are the common bedding geranium (*Pelargonium* ×*hortorum*), the ivy geranium (*P. peltatum*), the regal geranium (*P.* ×*domesticum*), and the scented geranium, which consists of about half a dozen different species. The former two species are most common outdoors; regal and scented geraniums are more often sold as pot or gift plants and seldom find their way into mainstream gardens.

Quick guide to *Pelargonium* species

	<u>Use</u>	<u>Leaves obviously scented</u>
P. ×*domesticum*	indoor, container	no
P. ×*hortorum*	outdoor	no
P. *peltatum*	outdoor, basket	no
scented geraniums	indoor, container	yes

-×*domesticum* (do mes' tih kum)

	regal geranium, Martha Washington geranium	1–2'/2'
spring	many colors	hybrid

Plants are likely the result of crosses between *Pelargonium grandiflorum, P. cucullatum*, and others; no "regal geranium" actually exists in nature. These hybrids have non-succulent stems and 2–4″ wide cordate to kidney-shaped leaves, with many sharp, unequal teeth on the margins. The showy flowers are up to 2″ across and are held in an umbel (a few flowers per umbel) well above the leaves.

Regals have a number of fine attributes, such as really beautiful flowers and . . . well, that's about it, actually. On the other hand, they produce light green anemic leaves, are marked with a bull's-eye for every whitefly in a thirty-mile radius, and aren't worth a tinker's damn in 99% of the gardens in America. Did I mention the lovely flowers?

But, having been forced into flower in greenhouses under favorable environmental conditions, they are useful as pot or gift plants, to be enjoyed on the balcony or on the coffee table. In such a spot, they are a joy to behold. After beholding them, however, put them in the compost heap, not in the garden; they will provide far more service in this secondary way. Regal geraniums require six weeks of around 40°F for flowers to form; without that cool temperature, few flowers will see the light of day. Six weeks of 40°F nights, even 50°F nights are hard to come by in the summer, so one doesn't see a whole lot of regal geraniums in American gardens. On the West Coast, in parts of Canada, and in some European countries, they are sometimes successfully grown as a flowering outdoor plant, but even in such places, one finds far more petunias than regals.

But all this is no reason not to enjoy them. Purchase some in the winter from a florist and bring some of Martha Washington's favorite plants home. Partial shade, propagate by cuttings.

CULTIVARS

'Candy Girl' produces beautiful pink flowers with a darker marking.
'Carisbrooke' has ruffled pink petals that are marked with maroon.
'Carnival' bears rosy red flowers with purple markings.
Elegance series consists of large plants with large flowers. The series includes 'Brilliance' (white), 'Dandy' (melon red), 'Dapper Burgundy' (deep red-purple

flowers with red markings), 'Debutante' (pink with dark red markings), 'Enchantment' (orchid petals marked with purple), 'Erin' (salmon-pink with scarlet blotches), 'Fantasy' (burgundy on white), 'Fascination' (pink and red petals with carmine-red blotches), 'Lois' (magenta and light lavender bicolor), 'Rapture' (pink-salmon with red markings), 'Sandra' (light pink and scarlet bicolor), 'Symphony' (pink with burgundy markings), and 'Tiara (white petals highlighted with magenta).

'Empress of Russia' provides burgundy flowers.

'Flower Basket' has bicolored flowers, light pink with a darker center.

'Georgia Peach' bears large salmon flowers.

'Grand Slam', a well-known hybrid selection, has rosy red petals with dark markings.

'Lord Bute' has maroon flowers with a darker marking in the center.

Maiden series from Oglevee consists of smaller plants in six colors. They are 'Maiden Lilac', 'Maiden Orange', 'Maiden Petticoat' (white flowers with dark purple markings), 'Maiden Rose-Pink', 'Maiden Red' and 'Maiden Sunrise' (salmon flowers with dark red markings and white eyes). Quite compact, quite lovely.

'Pompeii' has dark purple to nearly black flowers.

Royalty series offers vigorous plants with large flowers. Look for "royal" names like 'Baroness' (raspberry red), 'Emperor' (lavender flowers with red purple markings), 'Empress' (dark purple and white bicolors), 'Enchantment' (orchid with purple markings), 'Excalibur' (cherry-red and light pink bicolors), 'Imperial' (dark purple with white margins), and 'Monarch' (light lavender with purple splotches).

'White Chiffon' bears white flowers.

-×*hortorum* (hor tor′ um)	zonal geranium	1–3′/3′
summer	many colors	hybrid

In sales surveys taken by the greenhouse industry each year, bedding plants are always the top-selling annuals. Different bedding plants rise to the front, some lose popularity, others are popular only in certain regions, but a constant in all surveys, year after year, is the market for geraniums. In these surveys, zonal geraniums usually rank number three; they have never fallen out of the top five. Red geraniums signal the onset of summer just like red poinsettias ring in the winter holiday season. Everybody loves geraniums, with the possible exception of those who must maintain them, and their popularity has spawned hundreds of cultivars in dozens of colors.

Flowers are held in umbels, each flower consisting of five petals, but often the stamens have been transformed to petals, resulting in semi-double or double flowers. Flowers are formed in the upper nodes, and as plants continue to grow, flowers continue to initiate and open throughout the summer. The leaves are orbicular to kidney-shaped, often with a horseshoe-shaped darker zone on the leaf blade, referred to as a zonation, thus the common name.

The zonal is a complex hybrid, the two dominant parents being *Pelargonium inquinans*, a bright scarlet-flowered South African species, and *P. zonale*, which

Pelargonium ✕*hortorum*   ASHA KAYS

accounts for the zonation. The zonation is quite variable, depending on parentage of the hybrid and night temperatures. The cooler the temperature, the more anthocyanin is produced, and it is this reddish pigment that accounts for the dark zonation. While the zone provides a nice look to the foliage, the flowers are what make geraniums so popular. Plants have been bred from 6″ to 3′ tall, with flowers in all hues but blue and yellow, and are easy to grow from Yellowknife to Mobile. In southern California or other Mediterranean climates, geraniums act like perennials and grow like shrubs. But the rest of us can count on geraniums being frost sensitive at around 25°F, lower if the fall was cool. Maintain your favorites by bringing them into the house to overwinter, or take cuttings. Most often it makes sense simply to purchase new material. Breeding continues, and every year additional named varieties from seed or cuttings find their way to the grower, the retailer, and the consumer. And people keep buying them.

Having raised, maintained, and evaluated thousands of plants in my time, however, from Montreal to Athens, I sometimes wonder why; for as popular as they are, they are not without problems. They are one of the most high-maintenance plants in the garden, requiring constant deadheading (removal of spent flowers), or they can look awful. If plants are not deadheaded, their flowering will be greatly reduced, and they become highly susceptible to gray mold (a fungal disease caused by *Botrytis*)—this in addition to the several root and leaf diseases (such as those caused by *Pythium*, *Rhizoctonia*, and *Sclerotinia*) to which they are already susceptible, particularly in hot, humid, rainy weather. They are heavy feeders, requiring more fertilization than most other plants in the landscape; yet too much fertility also increases their risk of becoming diseased. To be honest, they are not terribly good in the South, although they look beautiful in the spring and, if late-summer planted, are outstanding in the fall (they prefer cool weather). In our trials at University of Georgia, we must evaluate fifty cultivars a year, often three-quarters of them new to the trial that year. We have awarded excellent marks to a handful (see "Cultivars"), but most are not at all happy with us. Gardeners everywhere can find a time when geraniums look good, however; for some, that time is simply shorter than it is for others.

In the early 1970s, all zonal geraniums were vegetatively propagated, but many cultivars introduced since are seed-propagated. Propagation of F_1 hybrids revolutionized the growing of geraniums by greatly reducing the threat of disease carried through vegetative stock plants. Add to this the benefit that bedding plant growers could now produce geraniums in flats, and the volume of geraniums exploded. Some excellent series were produced, whose main claim was their germination percentage, greenhouse performance, and cheaper price; flower color, zonation, and vigor were extremely variable. But the advent of seed material shook up the complacency of vegetative breeders, and vegetatively propagated cultivars were soon improved and cleaner. The advent of the F_1 hybrids meant not only more geraniums but better geraniums—regardless of how they were propagated.

One wouldn't think that the method of propagation would make a big difference in the performance or appearance of the end result, but in this case it does. Next time you are looking at geraniums, look at the individual flowers.

With rare exception, the flowers of seed-propagated hybrids are single; the flowers of vegetatively propagated hybrids are semi-double, that is, with more petals. Thus, in general, vegetatively propagated forms have larger flowers. The single flowers of the seed hybrids tend to fall off the plant more readily; this self-dead-heading is bad for the look of the plant, but good in the sense that the occurrence of gray mold is reduced. If plants are placed side by side, consumers tend to choose the bigger flowers of vegetative material over the singles of seed; landscapers who are planting large beds, on the other hand, often use the seed material because of cost and performance. It is impossible to say that one form of propagation is better in gardens than the other. Over the years I have found that few differences in a plant's performance could be attributed to how it was propagated; performance is cultivar specific.

Full sun, propagate by cuttings. Provide good drainage; afternoon rains in hot climates can be devastating. Fertilize in spring and twice in summer. The main breeders of geraniums have subjected their propagation material to a process that gets rid of viruses. Culture virus indexing was an important step toward getting clean vegetative material to the consumer.

CULTIVARS

Vegetative

All are propagated from cuttings, nearly all are culture virus indexed. All have semi-double to double flowers unless otherwise noted.

'Alba' has white flowers.

Americana, a popular series with growers and retailers (and by default, gardeners), is bred in over a dozen separate colors. Plants are vigorous, with large flowers and mid-green leaves, and reasonably heat-tolerant.

'Atlantis '96' produces raspberry-red flowers.

'Aurora' has dark lavender-pink flowers with a white eye.

'Blues' bears pink blooms.

'Bravo' provides dark pink flowers. 'Bravo Light Pink' is also available.

'Brazil '99' has strong zonation and single magenta blossoms.

'Calypso' bears dark lavender flowers.

Candy series features seven selections with dark green leaves, which contrast well with the flowers. All flowers are semi-double unless otherwise noted and have "candy-like" names: 'Bubblegum' (bicolor dark pink and magenta single flowers), 'Cotton Candy' (salmon-pink), 'Fireball' (scarlet), 'Lollipop' (coral red), 'Raspberry Ice' (blush pink with magenta centers, good bicolor), 'Sweet Temptation' (lavender-pink), and 'White Truffle' (white).

Charleston 2000 series offers compact plants in coral and salmon.

'Charmant' has flowers of light salmon and strong zonation.

Designer series has many flower colors with good zonation.

'Diablo '98' produces leaves with strong venation and bright red blooms.

'Dolce Vita' bears light salmon blooms.

Eclipse, the sister series to Americana, has smaller plants and bronzier leaves. Five flower colors have been raised.

'Evening Glow' has dark salmon semi-double flowers with medium zonation.

Fantasia series is 12–18″ tall in numerous colors. Good zonation.

'Fox' provides deep magenta flowers.

'Gloria '98' bears bright orange flowers.

'Grand Prix' has scarlet flowers with strongly zoned leaves.

'Jazz '99' produces salmon-blush blooms.

'Joy' has pink to deep purple flowers.

'Kardino' bears purple-red blossoms.

'Kim', among the most popular scarlet-flowered geraniums, is an excellent plant with good heat tolerance.

'Laura' provides lavender-pink flowers with white eyes. I knew this would be beautiful—it bears the same name as my beautiful daughter.

'Lavender Lady' consists of lavender blooms with magenta markings.

'Lotus' has excellent white blooms.

'Magic '99' produces dark purple blooms over leaves with strong zonation.

Melody series offers compact semi-double forms consisting of 'Melody' (pink flowers with red and white markings), 'Melody Blue' (lavender blooms), and 'Melody Red'.

'Merker 2000' bears scarlet flowers.

'Montevideo' produces salmon blossoms.

'Noblesse '99' has dark salmon flowers.

'North Star' bears large semi-double white flowers.

'Omega 2000' has large rose-violet blooms.

Patriot series features medium-green leaves and semi-double flowers. The Patriot name is found in bright pink, cherry rose, pink, salmon blush, and violet.

'Peaches' have fully double blooms of salmon with peach accents throughout.

Pillar series is more a way of growing geraniums than breeding. 'Pillar Salmon', with single coral flowers, is the best by far. Five plants in at least a 12″ pot and a tomato cage or other supporting material help make the pillar.

'Pink Expectations' is a best-selling pink cultivar with double flowers and good zonation.

'Pink X2' provides salmon-pink blossoms.

Pinnacle series provides many colors, about 16″ tall.

'Rio' bears pink flowers.

'Ritz' has bright scarlet-red blooms.

Rocky Mountain series consists of bright red, deep salmon, red, salmon, scarlet, and white flowers. 'Rocky Mountain White' produces excellent white flowers.

Romance series consists of two cultivars with "romantic" names. They have semi-double bicolor flowers. 'First Kiss' bears large pink flowers with magenta eyes, 'Valentine' has pink flowers with magenta eyes.

Rosebud series provides double flowers in a tightly bunched umbel, almost like a rosebud. 'Appleblossom Rosebud' has double pink and white flowers, 'Red Rosebud' bears double red flowers, 'Pink Rosebud' provides double pink blossoms.

'Rumba Fire' has bright scarlet flowers and strong zonation.

'Samba' provides dark red blooms with strong zonation.

'Sarah' consists of large rosy pink flowers.

'Sassy Dark Red' has magenta blooms.

'Schoene Helena' is among the best lavender-flowered cultivars.

'Shalimar' has star-shaped pink flowers with distinctly zoned foliage.

Showcase series is available in seven colors.

'Sincerely Yours' appears to be gaining popularity as a scarlet-flowered selection.

'Skies of Italy' is a tricolored geranium, with leaves of yellow, bronze, and red. The small single flowers are orange-red.

'Sparkler Red' provides streaks of magenta against a background of pale pink. Semi-double.

Starburst series bears plants with pink or red starry flowers.

Stardom series offers the class of geraniums known as floribundas, which consist of hundreds of double flowers with light zonation and reasonable heat tolerance. Good for containers and window boxes: 'Elizabeth' (red), 'Gypsy' (lavender), 'Jessica' (pink-magenta), 'Julia' (coral), 'Lucille' (coral), 'Maureen' (orange and white bicolor), and 'Sophia' (bright pink).

Summit series provides zoned foliage in many flower colors.

Tango series is available in dark red, light salmon, orange, red, and violet. Strong zonation occurs with 'Tango Light Salmon' and 'Tango Orange'.

'Tiffany '96' has lavender-pink blooms.

'Veronica' bears vivid magenta blooms.

'William Languth', the best green-and-white variegated form, has beautiful variegated foliage and scarlet flowers. Outstanding and an excellent performer.

'Yours Truly' is a very popular vigorous scarlet-flowered form that has stood the test of time.

Seed-propagated

Single-flowered unless otherwise noted.

'Cameo' has round heads of coral-salmon.

'Dolly Varden' has variegated foliage and red flowers.

Elite series, originally bred for earliness to flower, is a good performer available in six colors.

'Freckles' is unique: a white spotted with pink. An All-America Selection in 1991.

Glamour series is lightly zoned, available in six colors.

'Lone Ranger' has carmine-red flowers.

Maverick series is available in coral, pink, red, salmon, scarlet, violet, and white, and a rose and white bicolor ('Maverick Star').

Multibloom series, a breakthrough in the geranium field, produces many flower stems at once. Not as vigorous in the garden but excellent in the spring. Available in ten colors.

'Neon Rose' is a compact form with large heads of neon rose.

'Orange Appeal' is probably the best orange geranium and a good garden performer as well.

Orbit series has been in garden centers for years, with good reason. Available in seventeen colors.

Pinto series too has stood the test of time. Eleven colors, many with strongly zoned leaves.

'Raspberry Ripple' bears salmon flowers flecked with red.

Ringo 2000 series has flowers in ten colors, with excellent zonation.

Video series, a more dwarf form, is available in a mix only.

-peltatum (pel tay′ tum)	ivy geranium	1–3′/3′
summer	many colors	South Africa

Although zonals are sometimes used for the same purpose, this species is the geranium most often seen in hanging baskets. Its habit and look—of long trailing supple stems and alternate ivy-shaped leathery leaves—lends itself to this use. The peltate leaves often have a circular zone and five triangular lobes. The single flowers are held on three- to nine-flowered umbels and have been bred in an incredible array of colors.

They prefer some shade even in the North, but afternoon shade is a requirement in the South. Plants do not have as many problems as the zonals, but they are not entirely without them. The main headache for growers is less noticed by gardeners: oedema, a physiological leaf problem characterized by brownish blisters, particularly on the underside of the leaves. In some cultivars, it can be devastating, interfering with the plant's normal growth. Neither a fungal nor a pest problem, it is best avoided by a simple inspection of the undersides of the foliage before purchase. Growers, realizing the implications, do everything possible to reduce its incidence.

CULTIVARS

Many are complex hybrids that definitely have *Pelargonium peltatum* as the dominant parent.

'Amethyst '99' has amethyst-purple flowers.

Balcon series, which came from extensive trialing in northern Europe for balconies, offers single star-shaped flowers: 'Balcon Pink Star', 'King of Balcon' (light coral pink), 'Princess of Balcon' (orchid), and 'Balcon Royale' (red); see also 'Desrumeaux'.

'Barock '99' produces deep red flowers.

'Beach '99' bears good orange-red flowers on vigorous plants.

'Beauty of Edinburgh' has magenta-red flowers.

'Belladonna '99' produces double pink flowers.

'Blanche Roche' has double lavender and white flowers.

Blizzard series consists of trailing forms in lavender-blue ('Blue Blizzard'), dark red, pink, red, and white.

'Bolero' provides deep purple flowers with white borders. Solid burgundy flowers are more common under bright light conditions.

'Butterfly' produces light purple flowers.

Cascade series has single flowers that cover the basket, in various colors. They are available as Blizzard Cascades in blue, pink, red, and white (see Blizzard series); Cascades such as 'Bright' (red) and 'Sophie' (lavender-pink); Compact

Pelargonium peltatum   ASHA KAYS

Cascades with 'Acapulco' (rosy red) and 'Lila' (lavender); and Mini Cascades like 'Evka' (variegated foliage and scarlet flowers), 'Lavender', 'Pink', 'Red', and 'Lila' (lavender). They are essentially identical apart from flower color: they all cascade and work well with baskets.

Chirocco series has lavender-pink flowers with well-zoned foliage.

Colorcade series provides burgundy, lavender, lilac, and pink flowers.

'Comedy' bears rosy red blooms.

'Crocodile', an old-fashioned ivy form, has bright single pink flowers but is grown for the net of yellow over the soft green leaves.

'Desrumeaux' is another of the many Balcon, or balcony, geraniums, which are outstanding for trailing baskets. Bright pink flowers with darker pink venation.

'Duke of Edinburgh' has variegated white-and-green foliage with pink single flowers.

Freestyle series is available in burgundy, cherry rose, dark red, and white.

Global series bears double or semi-double flowers in bright purple, coral rose, lavender, light lavender, burgundy ('Merlot'), light pink ('Misty Pink'), coral pink ('Neon'), pink ('Pink Pearl'), purple ('Sangria'), red, rose, and deep red.

'Lambada '98' bears rosy red flowers.

'L'Elegante' is a beautiful old form, with leaves of off-white and green shaded with pink. The single white flowers have purple veins.

'Luna '98' provides white flowers.

'Mandarin' has dramatic bright scarlet flowers.

'Marimba' produces bright rose flowers.

Matador series is a terrific group for heat tolerance. 'Matador Burgundy' was a major hit at UGA trials, and 'Matador Light Pink' was almost as good.

'Mexicana' produces white flowers with pink edges.

'Molina' bears cherry-red flowers.

'Nicole' has bright pink blooms.

'Nutmeg Lavender' has nutmeg-scented leaves with a dark central zone and double lavender flowers.

'Peppermint Candy' produces variegated leaves with crimson and white flowers.

'Picasso' has marvelous flowers with a white center and rose-purple edges. When placed in overbright light, flowers tend to lose their white center.

'Ragtime 2000' produces open plants with double cherry-red flowers.

'Reggae Red' provides bright red flowers.

'Rose Sybil' is similar to 'Sybil Holmes' but with flowers that are more salmon.

Summer Showers, the first accepted series propagated from seed, consists of pink, rose-lilac, and rose-red colors. Quite beautiful.

'Sunset Ivy' produces star-shaped green leaves with pink edges. The single white flowers have maroon streaks. Unique.

'Sybil Holmes' is a popular cultivar with double pink and white flowers.

'Taj Mahal' bears deep purple flowers.

Tornado is a seed-propagated series of hybrids in lilac and white.

'White Nicole' produces clean white flowers.
'Wico' has single flowers of light cherry pink.

Scented *Pelargonium* species
summer

scented geraniums   1–3'/3'
foliage   South Africa

Fragrance is a complex thing. Books, manuscripts, and scientific papers debate the meaning of fragrance, perfume chemists make their reputations with their noses, and childhood memories can be stirred with a familiar scent. What we smell is seldom a single molecule or chemical; more often it is a whole group of substances, usually in the form of chemicals called esters or terpenes. The leaves of scented geraniums are covered with oil-bearing glands, particularly on the undersides of the leaves, and when the leaves are rubbed slightly, those complex molecules are volatilized to reach your nose. An amazing number of scents are reputed by sensitive noses to be found in the leaves of these geraniums: caraway, clove, apple, lemon, rose, eucalyptus, peppermint, nutmeg—anything, it seems, that has a pleasant smell. With so many scents, it is not surprising that numerous *Pelargonium* species and many hybrids are collectively known as scented geraniums. The leaves are seldom as ornamental as those of the more popular garden species, and if the leaves don't turn you on, the flowers won't either. Flower they do, however, and the beauty is in the details. They are not good garden plants, tolerating neither rain, wind, nor heat. But they are effective as fillers in containers and sure are fun to have by a chaise longe, where they can be caressed every now and then.

Quick guide to scented *Pelargonium* species

	Foliar scent	Leaf shape	Flower color
P. capitatum	rose	three- to five-lobed	mauve-pink
P. crispum	lemon	three-lobed to kidney-shaped	pink
P. denticulatum	pine	deeply cut	purple-pink
P. fragrans	apple, nutmeg	three-lobed	white
P. graveolens	rose	triangular, pinnately cut	white to pale pink
P. odoratissimum	apple, nutmeg	entire	white
P. tomentosum	peppermint	three- to five-lobed	white

-*capitatum* (kap ih tay' tum)
summer

rose-scented geranium   1–3'/2'
mauve-pink   South Africa

A rose is a rose, unless it is a geranium. All sorts of geraniums have some rose scent, some stronger than others, but this species is among the more common sources of rose scent, if not the most obvious. Plants are weak-stemmed and may be decumbent (lie horizontally along the ground, with stem tips ascending and almost erect), although stems become woody with age. The 1–3" wide velvety leaves are three- to five-lobed, roughly heart-shaped, and with crinkled margins. The inflorescence is compact, consisting of ten to twenty small flowers; the two upper petals are rose with purple venation, the shorter, lower three petals are rose-colored.

Partial shade, propagate by cuttings. Plant in well-drained containers; the habit of the species lends itself well to containers.

CULTIVARS

'Attar of Roses', the most common form, is more upright and rougher. Excellent rose fragrance.

-*crispum* (kris' pum)	lemon geranium	1–3'/2'
summer	ink	South Africa

The margins of the leaves are said to be crispate, that is, they are curled and twisted irregularly, one of the characteristics of this lemon-scented species. The small leaves are less than 1″ wide and are slightly three-lobed to kidney-shaped (reniform). The 2' tall plants are upright, branched, and woody when mature. Only one or two flowers, about 1″ wide, are produced per inflorescence, each pink and marked with deep pink veins. This species is thought to be the parent of several hybrids as well.

Partial shade, well-drained soils. Plants are best used in containers to provide fragrance rather than stand-alone beauty.

CULTIVARS

'Cinnamon' has a compact habit and crispy-margined leaves with an obvious scent of lemon and a hint of cinnamon.

'Major' has larger leaves than the species.

'Peach Cream' bears peach-scented green leaves with white splashes.

'Prince Rupert' has ruffled leaves, upright habit, and ruffled lemon-scented leaves. The pink flowers have darker pink throats.

'Prince Rupert Variegated' provides cream-and-white leaves with a lemon scent. Light pink single flowers occur.

'Variegatum' has leaves edged in cream. Also sold as 'Prince Rupert Variegated'.

-*fragrans* (fray' grans)	spicy geranium	1–2'/2'
summer	white	South Africa

Taxonomists have been arguing over this plant for years: some consider it a true species; others suggest it should be called *Pelargonium* Fragrans Group, since so much variability as to fragrance exists from plant to plant. In general, plants have a strong, spicy scent, variously described as apple or nutmeg. The leaves are gray-green, velvety, and usually three-lobed with blunt teeth. The flowers are clustered in four- to eight-flowered umbels and are white, often marked with red lines.

Partial shade, well-drained soils, as recommended for most scented forms.

CULTIVARS

'Logeei' has gray-green crinkle-edged leaves that smell like aftershave, or so I am told. From Logee's Greenhouses, Ltd., Danielson, Connecticut. Also sold as 'Old Spice'.

'Snowy Nutmeg' produces small leaves, with large white margins, whose center is gray. The fragrance is decidedly nutmeg-like.

'Variegata' bears leaves edged in creamy yellow, becoming nearly green as they mature.

Alternative species

Pelargonium denticulatum (pine-scented geranium), a relative of *P. fragrans*, is an erect branched plant that can grow 3–4' tall. The rough, sticky leaves are about 3" wide and strongly balsam- or pine-scented. The leaves are deeply cut into small narrow-toothed segments. The purple-pink flowers are less than 1" and grouped about six to an inflorescence.

Pelargonium graveolens (gra vee o' lenz; rose geranium) is similar to *P. capitatum* and is probably the most common rose-scented form sold. The 1–2" wide leaves are gray-green, more or less triangular, and so deeply cut they appear to be compound. The four to five flowers are white to pale pink. This is the species from which geranium oil, used in the flavoring of jellies, is collected. The nomenclature of the "rose" geranium is mixed up, and hybrids and cultivars may include this or *P. capitatum* or *P. radens*, another rose form. Gardeners don't care about parents, and in this case, they may choose from among several excellent forms. 'Lady Plymouth' has yellow variegated leaves with rose and mint fragrance, 'Radula' has less finely divided leaves and a less pungent smell, and 'Rober's Lemon Rose' has soft gray-green leaves with lemon to rose fragrance.

Pelargonium odoratissimum (apple geranium), another species related to *P. fragrans*, is the most apple-scented of the geraniums. The light green leaves are rounded, about 2" wide, and wavy-margined. The small white flowers are marked with red lines.

Pelargonium tomentosum (peppermint geranium) too is related to *P. fragrans*. This species is a low-growing spreader with peppermint-stick fragrance. The palmate leaves consist of three to five rounded lobes and are very soft and velvety to the touch. Flowers are white marked with purple. A variegated form ('Variegatum') with creamy margins also exists.

Quick key to *Pelargonium* species

  A. Leaves with obvious fragrance (scented geraniums)
     B. Leaves deeply cut
       C. Obvious scent of rose, flowers white to pale pink . . *P. graveolens*
       CC. Obvious pine scent, flowers purple-pink . . . . *P. denticulatum*
     BB. Leaves lobed or entire

      C. Leaves three- to five-lobed
         D. Obvious rose or mint fragrance
            E. Obvious rose fragrance, flowers pink . . . . *P. capitatum*
           EE. Obvious mint fragrance, flowers white . . . .
                              . . . . *P. tomentosum*
        DD. Obvious lemon or apple fragrance
            E. Obvious lemon fragrance, flowers pink . . . . *P. crispum*
           EE. Obvious apple fragrance, flowers white . . . *P. fragrans*
      CC. Leaves entire or almost so, apple fragrance . . . *P. odoratissimum*
AA. Leaves not obviously scented
    B. Stems thin supple, plants with trailing habit . . . . *P. peltatum*
    BB. Stems not thin and supple, plants not trailing
      C. Stems succulent when young, leaves slightly
        lobed, usually with a broad color zone within
        the margin . . . . *P. ×hortorum*
      CC. Stems not succulent, leaves angled, sharply
        toothed, no color zone within the margin . . . . . *P. ×domesticum*

Pelargonium hybrids

Scented geraniums
'Atomic Snowflake' has light green leaves with white crinkled margins. To some, leaves smell like roses; others detect lemon and lilac.

'Candy Dancer' provides deeply cut dark green lemon-fragrant leaves.

'Chocolate Mist', perhaps a selection of *Pelargonium tomentosum*, has deeply lobed velvet leaves with a chocolate spot. Not as obviously peppermint-scented, but noticeable. May be the same as 'Chocolate Peppermint'.

'Chocolate Peppermint' produces peppermint-flavored leaves with a chocolate-brown spot.

'Citronella' has deeply cut leaves with an intense lemon fragrance. The efficacy of this "mosquito plant" as a mosquito repellent is hotly debated, particularly by those who have just paid $9.95 for a scrawny plant.

'Clorinda' has rose-scented lobed leaves (others insist it is redolent of cedar and eucalyptus) and large rose-pink flowers.

'Concolor Lace' provides fern-like foliage with a nutty fragrance.

'Dean's Delight' is a pine-scented form with deeply cut oak-shaped leaves. The blush-pink flowers have darker eyes.

'Joy Lucille' is gray-green, deeply cut, and scented of peppermint.

'Lady Mary' smells strongly of lemon and was once called *Pelargonium ×limoneum*.

'Little Gem' is another of the rose-scented group. The small lacy leaves are topped with lilac blossoms.

'Mabel Gray' is strongly lemon-scented, with small pale purple flowers.

'Mary's Mabel' has crinkled slightly lobed leaves and smells strongly of lemon. Pansy-faced flowers have wine-colored streaks.

'Mrs. Kingsley' has rosy red flowers and rose-scented curled leaves.

'Peacock' produces rose-scented variegated leaves.

'Prince of Orange' has orange-scented light green leaves and mauve flowers.

'Red Flowered Rose' has various shades of pink and red flowers and rose-scented leaves. May be the same as *Pelargonium capitatum*.

'Roger's Delight' has some of the largest flowers in the scented group of geraniums. The large deep pink flowers fade to a light pink. The leaves are lemon-scented.

'Sweet Miriam' bears bright pink flowers with a light rose scent.

Unscented fancy-leaf geraniums

There is so much more to geraniums than simply the red bedding plant or the hanging basket form, which in fact are relatively recent introductions to the horticulture trade. In the 1800s and early 1900s, geraniums were far more common as houseplants (parlor plants) and in containers, admired for their foliage as much as their flowers. Fancy-leaf geraniums are a mixture of species, but most are placed in the *Pelargonium* ×*hortorum* group. In their heyday, they were highly sought after and cherished. The zillions of bedding geraniums now available have obscured the variability of this genus; however, some wonderful companies (Atlantic Nurseries of Dix Hills, New York; Blue Meadow Farm of Montague Center, Massachusetts; Logee's Greenhouses, Ltd., of Danielson, Connecticut; and Glasshouse Works of Stewart, Ohio) have kept these plants and many other fine annuals alive and available to us. So if you want beautiful—rather than plentiful—geraniums, give some of these a try. Don't expect great garden performance, but in containers, they shine.

'A Happy Thought' has bright green ruffled leaves with lemon-yellow centers and a maroon zonation, fading to cream. Flowers are scarlet.

'Bird Dancer' produces many small but bright salmon flowers over small leaves of chartreuse and maroon. Quite bushy. Also sold as 'Stellar Bird Dancer'.

'Black Tartan' bears some of the darkest green (close to black) leaves of any geranium. The double scarlet flowers are also distinctive.

'Butterfly Lorelei' produces white flowers over light green leaves with interior creamy splashes.

'Chelsea Gem' has creamy leaf margins and pink double flowers with a white eye.

'Crystal Palace Gem' was named for the great glasshouse built for the Exposition of 1851 in England. The yellow leaves have splashes of dark green, combined with magenta flowers. Still one of my favorites.

'Frank Hedley' has highly serrated green leaves with white edges. The flowers are pink.

'French Lace' has both green and gold leaves as well as a lemon fragrance. The edges of the leaves are pink.

'Greengold' has rounded leaves with yellow-green edges and thin red zonation in the middle.

'Grossersorten' bears dark green leaves with a handsome black zonation. Single salmon-pink flowers.

'Marshall McMahon' has bright scarlet flowers over olive-green foliage with maroon zonation.

'Mrs. Pollack' has at least three colors on the curly leaves, including green, orange and creamy white. Topped with red flowers.

'Mrs. Quilter' produces ruffled leaves of chartreuse, sometimes almost yellow, with dark zones. Single salmon flowers.

'Persian Queen' bears golden yellow leaves that contrast beautifully with the purple flowers.

'Platinum' has white margins on dark green leaves and single rosy pink flowers.

'Sorcery', an exquisite form, has dark bronze foliage with lighter green margins. Leaves are also zoned red. Flowers are orange-red.

Stellar is an old-fashioned series with deeply incised leaves and deeply lobed petals with serrated edges. Both the leaves and the blossoms are said to resemble a star, thus the name. 'Stellar Golden Staph' has golden leaves with a faint zonation and orange-pink flowers.

'Vancouver Centennial' has salmon flowers and fan-shaped leaves with maroon centers and chartreuse margins and veining. Terrific plant—highly popular and with good reason. Also sold as 'Vancouver'.

Additional reading

Armitage, Allan M., and Mark Kaczperski. 1992. *Seed-Propagated Geraniums and Regal Geraniums*. Timber Press, Portland, Ore.
Fischer Geraniums: www.fischerusa.com
Oglevee Geraniums: www.oglevee.com

Pennisetum (pen ih see' tum)   Poaceae

Most of the eighty species of this genus are considered perennials, including such well-known grasses as *Pennisetum alopecuroides* (zone 5), *P. orientale* (zones 6 and 7), and occasionally *P. villosum*. Most are native to the savannahs and woodlands of the tropics and have many economic uses in those areas, from fodder (*P. clandestinum*) to forage and pulp (*P. purpureum*) and grain (*P. glaucum*). The ornamental forms are valued for their feathery panicles of flowers, which consist of long spikes with slender bristles. Some of the more popular choices are doubly prized for their purple foliage.

Quick guide to *Pennisetum* species

	Height	Bristles	Purple color available
P. glaucum	4–7'	no	yes
P. setaceum	3–4'	yes	yes
P. villosum	3–4'	yes	no

-setaceum (se tay' see um)   fountain grass   3–4'/3'
   summer   white tinged pink to purple   Africa

Fountain grass became a fairly popular landscape plant with the recent grass movement (plants, that is), especially the cultivars of the perennial *Pennisetum alopecuroides*. 'Hameln' and 'Moudry' are well-known selections of that fine perennial, and *P*. 'Burgundy Giant', the wide-leaved favorite, is a hybrid of this popular species.

Fountain grass has many fans for many reasons. Plants can easily attain heights of 4' and equal widths. The thin green elongated leaves are about ½" wide and 1–2' long, bristly and quite rough to the touch. The plumed inflorescence, 1' long, is usually slightly inclined, much of its girth made up of 1" long unequal bristles. The overall look is a big green thing with creamy white plumes of flowers in the summer. The species is available, but it is the cultivars that have become widespread.

Full sun, propagate by division. As with most grasses, division is not easy. Don't hurt your back.

CULTIVARS

'Purpureum' is a popular form with wider leaves (up to 1"). Inflorescences are more darkly tinged but still contrast well with the darker foliage. Also sold as 'Atropurpureum'.

'Rubrum' is similar to 'Purpureum' but is bigger, and the leaves and inflorescences are creamy to deep burgundy. The two are constantly confused: unless they were grown side by side, they are probably mislabeled. In any case, both make beautiful bull's-eyes, providing a place for the eye to rest as they tower over other, low-growing colorful plants. Also sold as 'Cupreum'.

-villosum (vih lo' sum)   feathertop   2–3'/3'
   summer   white   tropical Africa

The species is considered perennial on the coasts and generally can be expected to return in zones 7 and warmer, but I think of it as an annual in my garden. Of course, many plants behave like annuals in my garden, regardless of what I tell them they are supposed to be. The leaves of feathertop are flat or slightly folded, about ½" wide, and 12–18" long, descending toward the ground. The common name, however, gives a hint that these leaves are not its raison d'être, but rather the soft feathery inflorescences of fine long bristles, with thin secondary bristles, that appear in summer. They are white with tinges of tawny brown. Quite lovely to see and fine to touch.

Full sun to partial shade, propagate by division or seed.

Alternative species

Pennisetum glaucum (glaw' kum; millet), a relative of *P. setaceum*, is well known to farmers and birds as an agronomic crop. There is nothing particularly ornamental about the species, with its long compact inflorescences. The lack of bris-

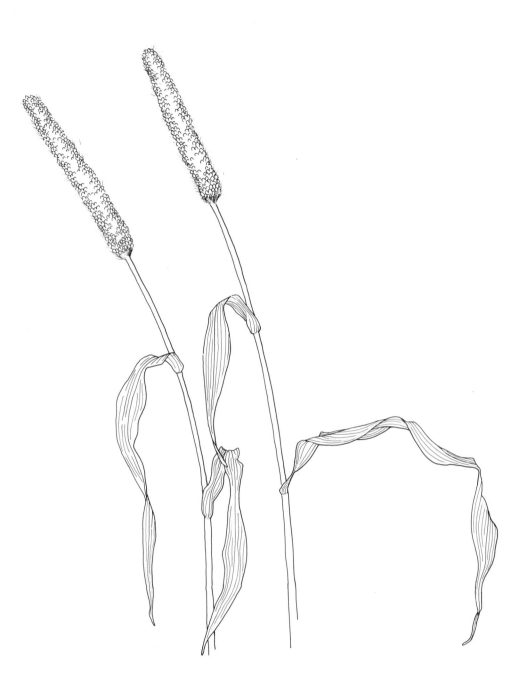

Pennisetum glaucum   ASHA KAYS

tles on the upright inflorescences make them look more like cat-tails than fountain grass; and I would exclude millet if not for an exceptionally fine purple-leaved form we have trialed for several years. Its deep purple foliage is 2″ wide, and the erect flowers range from purple to light crimson; the cultivar is unnamed presently, but it will be widespread within a year or so.

Quick key to *Pennisetum* species

A. Long obvious bristles to the inflorescences, inflorescences not erect
    B. Bristles naked, not feathery, unequal . . . . *P. setaceum*
    BB. Bristles branched, feathery . . . . *P. villosum*
AA. Bristles short, if any, not obvious, inflorescences erect . . . . *P. glaucum*

Pentas (pen′ tas)   Rubiaceae

Pentas is a popular member of the Rubiaceae, the madder family, which is best known for such economically important crops as coffee and *Cinchona* (which yields quinine). Of the ornamentals discussed in this book, only *Asperula, Hamelia, Manettia,* and *Mussaenda* are similarly related, and none are exactly household words in American gardening jargon. The family is characterized by opposite, entire leaves and four or five united petals. *Pentas* is so called because it has floral parts in five (*pente* is Greek for "five"), including sepals, petals, and stamens. *Pentas* has always had followers; the genus is fringe plant for gardeners in the North and Midwest but of more importance further south. Fans cite the relative ease of cultivation, range of flower colors, and tolerance to summer heat. Dissenters cite susceptibility to disease, lack of vigor, and insufficient flower power. Approximately thirty-five species reside in the genus, but only *P. lanceolata* is grown to any extent.

-lanceolata (lan see o la′ ta)   Egyptian star cluster   1–3′/2′
    summer   many colors   East Africa, Arabia

The species can reach 6′ in height in its native habitat, but most garden forms are 1–2′, seldom taller than 3′. The less heat plants receive, the shorter they will be. Stems are erect and pubescent, becoming woody at the base as plants mature. The opposite lanceolate leaves are 4–6″ long and 1–2″ wide; they have pointed ends and softly hairy margins and are held on 2″ long petioles. Flowers are star-shaped and held in clusters (thus its common name) in a tightly packed many-flowered corymb. (The easiest way to conjure up the look of a corymb in your mind is to think of yarrow, whose flowers are also held in corymbs.) Individual flowers are ¼–1½″ wide, but the entire inflorescence may consist of a hundred flowers. Flower color is usually in the pink to scarlet range, but lilac and white also occur.

    Plant hybridizers have rediscovered this fine plant, and newer, more vigorous cultivars are appearing. The newer hybrids have many of the attributes we

Pentas lanceolata 'Nova'   ASHA KAYS

want in garden plants: upright habit, a range of bright colors and sizes, persistent flowering, and heat tolerance. These plants are poised to be mainstream annuals.

Full sun, propagate by division. Many of the new cultivars are seed-propagated in greenhouses, but the seed is tiny and likely won't produce the same plant as the parent if collected and grown at home.

CULTIVARS

Butterfly series is an excellent entry in the *Pentas* game, and one which we have trialed extensively. Vigor is excellent, numerous flower colors are available, and plants flower the entire summer. I think this will become a mainstay.

'Cranberry Punch' is 2–4' tall with magenta flowers.

'Ivory Stars' has clusters of white flowers.

'Jessica' bears soft pink flowers on compact 2–3' tall plants.

'Lavender Delight' is 10–12" tall with dark green foliage and light lavender flowers.

New Look is a much-needed series of vigorous seed-propagated plants. They are reasonably vigorous, but at 12–15" tall, plants can be overrun by neighboring plants. Colors are good, however, and they are excellent in containers. Cherry, pink, red, rose, violet, and white are available. Mainstream plants.

'Nova' is one of the most vigorous forms I have trialed, growing to about 3' and bearing large flowers of red or pink. My favorite, useful as a cut flower as well as a garden plant.

'Orchid Illusion' provides clusters of orchid flowers.

'Pink Profusion' has many pink flowers on compact plants, about 15" tall.

'Polar White' bears dark green foliage and clean white flowers.

'Ruby Glow' provides large clusters of rosy red flowers and bright green leaves.

'Scarlet Turbans' has the best name of all the cultivars and some terrific scarlet flowers as well.

Star series consists of 'Star Lavender' and 'Star White'.

'Starburst' bears bicolor flowers of pink and white.

Perilla (pe ril′ a)   Lamiaceae

The interest in foliage has made this purple weed more popular than I ever thought it would be—once again, my inability to prognosticate has been bared. Some six species of *Perilla* are known, but *P. frutescens* appears to be the only one out there. I admit to confusing both the green-leaved species and especially the ornamental purple-leaved forms of *Perilla* with *Ocimum* (basil). *Perilla* can even be purchased from some Asian-vegetable specialty markets as Chinese basil, for its aromatic leaves are used in some Asian cuisines. I don't believe raw perilla is poisonous, so I tell the two apart by tasting a small piece of leaf. For those with a lower risk threshold, I outline here a few minor differences between the two genera.

	Leaf shape	Leaf size	Flower habit
Ocimum	ovate	usually <2" long	floral leaf subtends three flowers
Perilla	broad-ovate	usually >2" long	floral leaf subtends one flower

-frutescens (froo te′ senz)		shrubby perilla	1–2′/2′
summer	foliage		Himalayas, east Asia

These fast-growing annuals have become favorites in gardens where reseeding plants are welcome and formality is a no-no. Plants can attain heights of 3′ or more, but in most gardens, 1–2′ is more common. The opposite broadly ovate leaves are 2–4″ long and 1–2″ wide, pointed at the tip and serrated on the margins. The aromatic green leaves, often speckled with purple, are held on 1–1½″ petioles. The small two-lipped white flowers are held in 4″ long inflorescences with prominent floral leaves, which subtend one or two flowers. Inside the flowers are four stamens, in two pairs.

Plants are invaluable for their disdain of heat, drought, and disease. They reseed with abandon and pop up everywhere; in some gardens, they are a nuisance, in others, a constant source of delight. Full sun, well-drained soils. But plants tolerate partial shade, particularly in the South, and though they prefer good drainage, moisture is not a problem. Propagate by seed or terminal cuttings.

CULTIVARS

'Atropurpurea' is a common form, with deep red-purple leaves.

var. *nankinensis* (syn. *Perilla crispa*) bears deep bronze or purple leaves, each coarsely toothed with fringed and crisped margins. Arguably the most handsome and vigorous form.

Petunia (pe too′ nee a)   Solanaceae

A seedsman with a major flower breeding company recently mused, "If I could sell one half of one percent of the petunias sold today, I would be a rich man." The highs and lows of many a company have mirrored the highs and lows of petunia popularity for decades now, so important have petunias become in America's short landscape history. The petunia was the number-one-selling bedding plant from the 1950s through the 1980s. The love affair with petunias has soured a little since, worldwide (now they are in second place in bedding plant sales, after impatiens); but new high-performance hybrids have been developed continually since the late '80s, and despite the all-time high interest in diverse and unusual annuals and perennials, petunias still sell in record numbers and still enjoy tremendous success and visibility. Readers of this book, newly besotted with the odd and unique, may never buy another petunia, but look around the landscapes of public and commercial properties and reality will quickly dawn. Petunias don't maintain their popularity because of promotion and hype: they remain popular because they perform well in many areas of the country, they flower throughout the season, and they have a lovely fragrance to boot. That they are readily available each spring simply makes the choice to purchase petunias that much easier.

Although 99% of what you see in 99% of the outlets are hybrids, this mostly South American genus has many species. I've had the good fortune of knowing Grace Price, a longtime flower breeder. Every time I see her, she is working with another species, and even though she has introduced dozens of hybrids (the Wave series is among her finest), her eyes sparkle as she talks about her seedlings and the potential of the crosses yet to come. It is the Grace Prices of the floricultural world whose passion makes this wonderful gardening habit so exciting.

The hybrids mostly arose from two species, each one occasionally found in garden centers or mail-order catalogs. *Petunia integrifolia* (violet-flowered petunia) was sent to the Glasgow Botanical Garden in 1831 by intrepid South American explorer James Tweedie (see *Tweedia* for more on him). *Petunia integrifolia* has elliptical to lanceolate leaves and small lavender to purple flowers. The stems are spreading with upright tips, and the overall habit is more wild. More and more plants of this and 'Alba', its white-flowered form, are being sold. They exhibit better weather tolerance than many of the grandiflora forms and provide a glimpse of a simpler time in the petunia world. *Petunia axillaris* (large white petunia, night-scented petunia) was sent to Paris in 1823 by a French commission sent to South America to evaluate resources for the French throne. The buff-white flowers, with a longer, thinner tube and more flattened opening, are wonderfully fragrant in the evening. Try to find these wonderful plants. Who could have foreseen that two rather plain South American weeds could have so influenced plant commerce in the twenty-first century?

All petunias have soft alternate entire leaves, often sticky, and flowers that consist of a five-parted calyx and five-lobed funnelform corolla. The flower tube is long and sits loosely on the calyx. I can't think of a color that is not available, other than brown (except when dead) or black (except when diseased). As popular as petunias are, they are not without problems. *Sclerotinia* (stem rot and wilt), *Phytophthora* (late leaf blight), *Botrytis* (gray mold), and *Rhizoctonia* (root rot) are some of the disease organisms that plague petunias in the landscape. Viruses and insects too afflict them. The warmer the summer, the more likely problems will develop, and the further south one gardens, the more important cultivar selection becomes. Fungicides are effective; so are raised beds. But look closely at the cultivar name (if provided) on the beautiful flat of petunias in the garden center, particularly south of zone 6.

Full sun, well-drained soils. Plant in raised beds if summers are wet.

Petunia hybrids

In an attempt to help growers decide what to grow, breeders grouped petunia hybrids into different classes, originally based on flower size. What is provided here is a hybrid of industry classes and Armitage classes, which may help cut through the fog of new forms. Having to choose among the cacophony of colors, habits, and sizes is, for most sane people, like trying to penetrate a rose thicket. For years, all petunias were developed from seed, but many new vegetative forms have now hit the market. In general, the vegetative material is used for baskets and containers.

Cascading forms bear long pendulous stems that drip out of baskets and containers, for which look they were bred. Often vegetatively propagated (Surfinia series, for example) but also from seed. Flowers occur in many colors and size varies from small (1″ wide) to medium (2–2½″ wide).

Grandifloras have the biggest flowers and are always the most showy in the retail center. If petunias struggle in your area, stay away from the grandifloras. They simply don't have the weather tolerance of the other classes. For areas that offer the combined stress of summer rain, heat, and humidity, I wouldn't recommend a grandiflora to save my life. Flowers may be singles or doubles.

Miniatures form tight mounds covered with small flowers. The main series of this class, Fantasy series, has shown excellent weather tolerance and fine flower power. 'Fantasy Pink Morn' was an All-America Selection in 1998. Vegetative miniature forms tend to be much more cascading in habit.

Mounding forms are just that, large mounds for the landscape. Best shown by the Tidal Wave series.

Multifloras have smaller flowers than the grandifloras but usually carry more of them. In general, weather tolerance is better; plants rebound more quickly from rains and winds. Forms are single or double, upright or cascading (as in the Wave series). Breeding in the 1990s blurred the distinction between multifloras and grandifloras, and we now have large-flowered multifloras called floribundas.

As with impatiens, salvias, and the other main classes of bedding plants, many petunia cultivars were bred specifically for greenhouse performance (fewer days to production, short, compact habit, uniformity), but they are often similar both in appearance and in garden performance. Choosing a petunia will be easier if you deal with a retailer that provides reasonable labeling and then look for the cultivar name.

Cascading

Cascadia series is vegetatively propagated, excellent for baskets and containers. Available in white ('Choice'), soft pink ('Charme'), pink, veined ('Pink Spark', 'Blue Spark'), dark purple ('Cherie'), red, violet-blue, deep rose ('Champagne'), blue ('Charlie'), white with yellow eye, salmon-pink ('Chipper'), and yellow.

Ruffle series bears trailing semi-double and double flowers, in about four colors.

Supertunias have had a significant impact, with many colors in cascading, energetic plants. Lavender-pink, rose ('Mariposa Rose'), bright pink, lilac, pastel pink, purple, strawberry-veined pink, lavender ('Priscilla'), 'Purple Sunspot' (among the very best in the series), 'Royal Velvet' (purple), and white.

Surfinia series is vegetatively propagated and was an instant success in the garden and landscape trade. Trailing habit and medium-sized flowers, combined with vigorous growth helped these plants find a niche in the crowded petunia field. Available in eight colors including solids ('Surfinia White') and veined ('Surfinia Purple Veined'). Excellent heat tolerance.

Floribunda

Double Madness is among the best series with double flowers, with 3″ fully double flowers in burgundy, red and white, rose, rose and white, salmon, sheer (pink with darker veins), and silver shades.

Madness series is an excellent group of single-flowered plants. Approximately 2½″ wide and in nineteen colors, named for the flower color as well as for the four seasons ('Spring Madness', and so on), plus two mixes.

Grandiflora

Aladdin series is available in twelve colors and three mixes.

'Blue Skies' has 3–3½″ wide light blue flowers.

'California Girl' has soft yellow flowers but lacks vigor and has shown poor garden performance in most areas of the country.

Cloud series provides good performance and a slightly cascading habit. Ruffled, veined, and solid colors offered in seven separate colors and a mix.

Countdown series, well-branched and compact, is available in five colors and a mix.

Daddy series has veined flowers of high ornamental value in six colors and a mix.

Dreams series offers free-flowering plants in nine colors. 'Appleblossom Dreams' is a lovely soft pink, 'Midnight Dreams' bears dark violet-blue flowers.

Falcon series provides early-flowering plants, fifteen colors plus a mix.

Flash is a compact series of plants, with 3″ flowers in ten colors plus a mix.

Frost is an interesting series, bearing bicolor flowers with white edges. The center of the flowers are blue, cherry, red, white ('Fire Frost'), and wine and red ('Velvet Frost').

'Happiness' has rose-pink single flowers on well-branched compact plants.

Hulahoop series is similar to the Frost series, with bicolor flowers and white edges. Four colors plus a mix.

Picotee is another bicolored white-edged series in four colors plus a mix.

'Prism Sunshine' is among the better yellow-flowering forms in terms of performance. An All-America Selection in 1998.

Storm series bears 3–4″ wide flowers in four colors and a mix. 'Lavender Storm' is particularly excellent.

Supercascade series has exceptionally large flowers in nine colors and a mix.

Trumpet series has a mounding habit in the garden and bears large flowers in red, pastel pink, chiffon, pink, purple, and neon rose.

Ultra is a popular series with large flowers with star patterns ('Ultra Blue Star') and veining ('Ultra Light Pink Vein'); eighteen solid colors ('Ultra Blue') and three formula mixes are also available.

'Yellow Magic' bears ruffled 3–4″ flowers in deep yellow.

Double grandiflora

Double Cascade series bears 2″ wide double flowers veined in burgundy, pink, and plum.

Petunia 'Ultra White'   ASHA KAYS

'Duet' has salmon and white double flowers.

Pirouette series produces ruffled flowers with white edges. Available in purple and rose.

'Sonata' produces white flowers with fringed edges.

Miniature

Dream series is a vegetatively propagated mounding petunia with small flowers, recently bred in Israel. Not to be confused with the Dreams series of seed-propagated grandiflora types. Offered in white ('Bright Dream'), pink with darker veins ('Pink Dream'), and purple ('Purple Dream'). They are often referred to as petitunias and are best for containers. Terrific plants.

Fantasy is the best seed-propagated miniature series I have trialed. Many 1–1½" flowers cover the small, compact plants all season. Best for small areas and containers. Available in nine colors and a mix.

Multiflora

Carpet series produces low-growing plants with 1½–2″ wide flowers. Sixteen colors plus a mix.

Celebrity series offers twenty-two colors, including include solid flowers ('Celebrity Blue'), veined ('Celebrity Peach Ice'), star flowers ('Celebrity Rose Star'), and white-throated forms ('Red Morn'). Six mixes, each a blend of different colors, are also available. 'Celebrity Chiffon Morn' was an All-America Selection in 1995.

Hurrah series provides small but colorful flowers in numerous colors.

Kahuna series has been an excellent performer in the UGA trials—outstanding even in truculent weather. Half a dozen colors are available.

Pearls, an earlier series, is nevertheless heat- and disease-tolerant and always full of flowers. 'Azure Blue Pearls' is among the best.

Primetime is as full as Celebrity series. No moss growing under these breeders' feet. Twenty-four named colors plus seven mixes.

'Summer Sun' has dull yellow flowers.

Supermagic series, a longtime entry, has large plants in numerous colors.

Surprise series was indeed a most pleasant surprise in the UGA trials. These low-growing mounded plants are filled with flowers most of the season.

Symphony series cascades more than others and therefore looks good falling out of containers and raised beds. Numerous colors from which to choose.

Wave series revolutionized the petunia market in the 1990s. They are low-growing but spread wildly, filling large areas in no time—the antithesis of the Fantasy series. Outstanding garden performance from northern states to the Deep South. 'Purple Wave', an All-America Selection in 1995, was the first entry to the marketplace. Then 'Misty Lilac Wave', 'Pink Wave' and 'Rose Wave' were introduced; all are somewhat more upright than the prostrate 'Purple Wave'. In 1999 I trialed the most vigorous of all petunias, watching mounding plants covered with hundreds of flowers all season; these became known as the Tidal Wave series. Cherry and hot pink have been exceptional but are not for small areas—they have been known to swallow small dogs.

Double multiflora

Doubloon series consists of double flowers in pink, rosy lavender ('Pink Star'), soft lavender ('Blue Star'), and lilac-blue. Vegetatively propagated.

'Heavenly Lavender' has deep lavender-blue double flowers. An All-America Selection in 1996. Seed-propagated.

Marco Polo, a series with an upright, somewhat mounding habit, consists of 'Adventurer' (magenta), 'Odyssey' (a terrific pink), 'Silk Road' (white), and 'Traveller' (lavender-blue).

Additional reading

Armitage, Allan M. 1998. Petunias are strutting their stuff. *Greenhouse Grower* 16(10):127–128.

Shaw, Jolie. 1998. Growing today's cutting petunias. *GrowerTalks* 62(9):49–50.

University of Georgia Trial Reports: www.uga.edu/ugatrial

Phacelia (fa see' lee a)   scorpion weed   Hydrophyllaceae

Few gardeners know these plants, but that doesn't mean that most gardeners would not love to have them in their landscape. The genus consists of about 150 species, most native to the western North America (mainly California and Mexico); only one or two are native to the East. Flowers are usually blue or lavender and consist of five lobes, with a flower tube beneath the lobes. Most species used in gardens are annuals or biennials and often will persist by reseeding. All love cool weather and require excellent drainage, particularly those from the West.

Quick guide to *Phacelia* species

	Nativity	Flower color	Leaves
P. bipinnatifida	East	violet-blue	pinnate
P. campanularia	West	gentian blue	simple

-*bipinnatifida* (bi pih na tih' fih da)   scorpion weed   8–12"/12"
   spring   lavender-blue   SE United States

This biennial is a common species of *Phacelia*, mainly for its reseeding ability and its tolerance of eastern climate extremes. Where plants do well, the shaded spring garden is a carpet of violet-blue. Plants are somewhat downy throughout, with pinnately compound leaves on long petioles. The leaves consist of three to five ovate leaflets, pointed and deeply toothed. The five-lobed, wide-mouthed, bell-shaped flowers occur in the spring; they are about ½" in diameter and an outstanding soft lavender-blue color. They are formed on single-sided racemes, usually coiled up like a scorpion's tail before they open. The length of time they remain in flower depends on the spring weather and how soon warm weather arrives.

Plants do best in shaded areas, such as the shade of pine or high deciduous canopies. Heavy soils are not a problem, and consistent moisture is recommended. Plants are grown from seed, either started in late winter then transplanted in early spring, or sown directly in a well-prepared soil. Plants flower the first year from seed and may be treated as annuals.

-*campanularia* (kam pan yew la' ree a)   California bluebell   6–9"/12"
   spring   blue   California

Among the most beautiful blues to be found in garden plants, this southern California native inspires all who see it—and frustrates almost as many others. It is a true annual, flowering first year from seed. Plants generally have reddish stems, bearing oval, pointed, toothed leaves. Some say stems have a pleasant fragrance when crushed; I have smelled something upon crushing, but I believe I thought it pleasant only because I was told to expect it to be so. Maybe it is just me. Flowers are a beautiful gentian blue, measuring about 1" across, with five purple stamens and white anthers. The anthers make the flowers appear to be spotted white.

Plants need excellent drainage; they often grow best in rock gardens, or between rocks in a patio or walkway. Sandy soils are far better than heavy ones. Cool temperatures, especially cool nights, are needed to keep plants alive (much less flowering) in eastern gardens. That they often perish in warm summers does not diminish their beauty—just don't bet the farm on their success. If you garden on the West Coast, enjoy.

Full sun to partial shade, in open soils. Moisture must be provided. Propagate by seed, as with *Phacelia bipinnatifida*.

CULTIVARS

'Alba', a white-flowered form, doesn't hold a candle to the blue flowers of the species.

Alternative species

Phacelia parryi (par′ ee i) is another of the many southern California natives, like *P. campanularia*, producing sticky stems and ovate lobed leaves, 4″ wide. The 1″ wide dark blue flowers are spotted white or yellow in the center. 'Royal Admiral' has unmarked soft purple flowers.

Phacelia purshii (per′ shee i; Miami mist), a most handsome member related to *P. bipinnatifida*, is native north to Minnesota and south to Alabama. Flowers are light blue to white and beautifully fringed around the margins. The basal leaves are pinnately divided, the upper leaves, lobed. 'Lavender Lass' bears 1″ wide flowers, each with a lavender margin and large creamy white center.

Quick key to *Phacelia* species

A. Leaves pinnate, leaflets three to five
    B. Flowers fringed . . . . *P. purshii*
    BB. Flowers not fringed . . . . *P. bipinnatifida*
AA. Leaves simple, no leaflets
    B. Lobes of corolla exceeding flower tube . . . . *P. parryi*
    BB. Lobes of corolla half or less as long as flower tube . . *P. campanularia*

Phlox (floks)   Polemoniaceae

When one talks *Phlox*, the conversation nearly always concerns the perennial forms and usually mildew as well. So many perennial species (*P. paniculata, P. divaricata, P. subulata*, to name but a few) have provided so much pleasure for so long, we seldom remember the annual species. Long before garden phlox became popular, however, the annual *P. drummondii* was a mainstay of English gardens, providing season-long color in Victorian England. Annual phlox is still being bred, but its relative lack of weather tolerance and competition from other tougher annuals have reduced its place in American gardens, particularly those in the eastern half of the country.

-drummondii (drum un' dee i)   Drummond phlox, annual phlox 6–15"/12"
    spring   many colors   Texas

The history of garden plants goes hand in hand with those crazy people who collected plants all over the world, but equally important and less well known are the people or nurseries who sponsored their trips. Among these sponsors was Veitch's Nursery in Chelsea, England, which establishment not only introduced several good plants that bear its name (*veitchii, veitchianus*, and so forth) but also supported the efforts of several plant explorers. E. H. Wilson is one famous Veitch alumnus; another is Thomas Drummond (1790–1835), who collected in North America, mainly in Canada and Texas. Drummond endured incredible hardships in the name of plant exploration: he barely survived a shipboard epidemic of cholera; he almost starved to death on Galveston Island; he suffered from snow blindness and such severe boils that he was unable to lie down for weeks; and on several occasions, he was nearly killed by grizzly bears. Among the last items he sent home were seeds of a small annual he'd collected in Texas. Drummond was very taken by his find: "A bed of this plant has hardly yet been seen, for it is far too precious and uncommon to be possessed by anyone except in small quantities." He died soon after of unknown causes in Cuba. Sir Joseph Hooker of Kew Garden named the plant in Drummond's honor "to serve as a frequent memento to its unfortunate discoverer."

Plants are usually only about 9" tall; they are branched, with quite variable leaves, ranging from narrow to oval leaves, sessile at their base. The variability of structure extends to the leaf arrangement: opposite at the base, and alternate above. The fragrant flowers are generally arranged in dense flat-topped heads, each flower about 1" wide, and consisting of five petals, fused for one-third of their length; they are often paler inside the petal tube with markings around the throat. Color of the flowers varies, from pale lavender to brilliant scarlet. Breeding has resulted in flowers with broad circular outlines, typical of most phlox flowers; those with narrow, often fringed petals, are referred to as star phloxes.

Plants are sold in bedding plant mixes in the spring. It is ironic that one of our native plants, so successful in Europe, has never been truly accepted in its own country. No one disputes the brilliance of the flowers, but many American gardeners find that plants are not sufficiently weather-tolerant to survive the extremes of their native climate. I was pleased when I saw some good-looking examples in the Brooklyn Botanic Garden and ecstatic to see them look as good in August as they had in May in the Butchart Gardens in Victoria—but disappointed nearly everywhere else. Deadheading helps prolong the season of flowering. They are good to excellent in northern gardens, useless after June in the Southeast.

Full sun in the morning, partial shade in the afternoon. Propagate by seed. Good drainage is needed; in difficult locales, rock garden situations offer the best chance for success.

CULTIVARS

Beauty Mix is a combination of pastel colors on 1' tall plants. Also sold as 'Border Beauty'.

'Cecily' is a combination of colors, about 8" tall, in many bright colors, most with an eye of a different color.

'Chanal' is a double-flowered form, with appleblossom-pink flowers on 12" plants. Terrible thing to do to our phlox.

'Coral Reef' has many rounded flowers in shades of apricot, coral, cream, pink, and white.

Crystal Mix has many colors on 12" tall plants.

Dolly Mix comes in single colors or a mix consisting of burgundy, deep rose, purple, and salmon. Plants are about 8" tall.

Dwarf Beauty Mix is made up of rounded flowers in clear colors of blue, crimson, lilac, pink, salmon, scarlet, white, and yellow. Plants are about 10" tall.

Globe Mix is an old standard mix of colors, mostly in pastels. About 8" tall.

Paloma is an excellent mix consisting of free-flowering 8–10" plants with pastel colors.

Petticoat Mix is made up of many-colored flowers with pointed star-shaped petals.

'Phlox of Sheep' (has to be one of the best names I've heard) consists of pastel colors, including apricot, bicolor, pink, rose, white, and yellow.

'Promise Pink' is a double form with large heads. More rose-pink than pink.

'Tapestry' is similar to 'Phlox of Sheep'. May be the same thing with a different name.

20th Century Mix consists of blue, crimson, magenta, salmon, scarlet, and white flowers, also sold separately.

Twinkle Mix is an excellent mix of star-shaped flowers in carmine, pink, rose, and white, usually with a different-colored eye.

Unique Mix has some heat tolerance and consists of pastel colors on a mounded habit.

Additional reading

Lovejoy, Ann. 1996. Pick of the phlox. *Horticulture* 74(7):40–43.

Plectranthus (plek tran' thus)   Lamiaceae

Nothing reveals how mixed-up a genus is like having one or two species suddenly become popular in mainstream landscaping. As soon as one taxon becomes useful, all sorts of others are introduced, often by gardeners or growers who got them from their grandmothers. That's the fate of *Plectranthus*: a couple of new interlopers stirred interest in a genus nobody (it turns out) knew much about (and that includes me). But this shouldn't be too surprising in a genus with more than 300 classified species, many of which show great foliar diversity and not a great deal of floral interest for gardeners. Few species grown in temperate gardens flower, and since we all know that leaf color, shape, and even arrangement are greatly influenced by environment, it is no wonder so many of us are scratching our heads.

And as far as these plants becoming an everyday choice for gardeners—well, first we have to at least find a common name that doesn't sound like a sore throat. Of course, some of the members do have less painful names, but they seem to be lifted from other plants. *Plectranthus verticillatus*—a common hanging houseplant and seen in malls ad nauseam—is known as Swedish ivy. But this most famous plectranthus is neither an ivy nor from Sweden; even the Swedes are tired of it, in fact. Others are known as French thyme (neither French nor a thyme), Spanish thyme (ditto), and even country borage (not even the same family). So if you are a little confused, you're in good company.

Most species in the genus *Plectranthus* have the same family characteristics as other members of the mint family, that is, square stems, opposite leaves and whorled flowers; the genus is further characterized by fleshy scalloped leaves, two-lipped corolla, and four stamens. Many species are either slightly or obviously decumbent, meaning that the stems grow horizontally along the ground but with the tips ascending to appear almost erect. The flowers are remarkably similar to coleus but differ morphologically by having the stamens free rather than being united at the base. All taxa are used for their foliage; flowers will seldom be seen outdoors, except in areas that do not experience freezing temperatures until December.

Quick guide to *Plectranthus* species

	Fragrant foliage	Foliar color	Height
P. amboinicus	oregano-like	usually variegated	1–2'
P. argentatus	slight	gray-silver	2–4'
P. ecloni	slight	green	3–4'
P. forsteri	minty	green or variegated	1–2'

-amboinicus (am boy' nih kus)   oregano plectranthus   1–2'/3'
   all   season foliage   South Africa

It's easy to recognize this species if you forget about your eyes and rely on your nose. All plectranthus have a fragrance, some more pleasant than others and usually rather medicinal or minty. To help my students identify this plant, I ask them to rub a leaf and smell their fingers. I then ask, "What restaurant are you eating in?" Nine times out of ten, recognizing the heavy oregano smell, they say Italian (I have brilliant students). Plants are slightly decumbent and appear erect and upright. The thick leaves, 2–4" long, have scalloped margins, and the species itself is a deep green. The flowers, when they occur indoors, are lilac-mauve to white and are held in dense whorls. The species is seldom seen in commerce, but a couple of cultivars are being used quite regularly.

Full sun to partial shade, propagate by terminal cuttings.

CULTIVARS

'Athens Gem' was a stem sport of 'Variegatus' and bears yellow-and-green variegated foliage. Plants stand 1–1½' tall and are tough as nails, spitting out heat and humidity while maintaining a sense of decorum.

'Variegatus' is taller (up to 2') than 'Athens Gem' and more common, with handsome white margins around the green leaves. Both taxa are Athens Select plants.

| *-argentatus* (ar jen ta' tus) | silver plectranthus | 2–3'/3' |
| all season | foliage | Australia |

Gray- or silver-foliaged plants will always have a place in the garden; the simple addition of their benign hues are welcome for their own sake and actively calm the screaming tones of their neighbors. Although this species is too large to be an everyday substitute for dusty miller, it offers a similar effect. Plants are branching erect subshrubs that become woody at the base with age; they can grow quite rapidly, particularly in areas of hot summers. The opposite ovate leaves are about 4" long and 2" wide, the apex is bluntly pointed, and the margins are evenly scalloped. They are densely covered with silvery hairs and short, gray-white pubescence, both of which contribute to the look landscapers and gardeners seek. Flowers, when they appear, are pale blue to white and held in 1' long whorled racemes.

Plants can grow rapidly and get out of control in a small landscape. Cutting them back when they are young helps reduce height and increase branching. The leaf color, however, does not significantly fade over time. An excellent foliage plant in the summer garden.

Full sun, propagate by terminal cuttings.

| *-ecloni* (ek lon' ee) | purple plectranthus | 4–6'/4' |
| late | fall purple | Asia |

It is hard to love plectranthus: nobody knows what you are talking about, no flowers are formed, and leaves are smelly. So when I saw this big, bold plant with highly ornamental purple flowers at San Felasco Nurseries in Gainesville, Florida, I had to have some. Alan Shapiro, the patient owner, once again put up with my plant ravings and kindly sent me a few cuttings. Plants rooted easily, and they were plunked into the trial gardens in Athens as soon as possible in the spring.

They grew nicely, producing only slightly aromatic dark green leaves, 4–6" long and 4" wide. Plants are useful for the garden, but it is the flowers that make this plant worth spending money on: the dark purple flowers grow about 15" long and are held in whorled racemes. Unfortunately, like most species in the genus, short days are needed for flower initiation. Although this species requires less short days than most, flowers still do not appear until late fall, late October at the earliest in Athens. That is not a problem if October is benevolent, and several plants, like *Cuphea*, *Odontonema*, and *Tibouchina*, are much welcomed in late fall. Folks in Montpelier or Pierre, however, do not stand a chance of seeing flowers before frost.

Full sun to partial shade, propagate by terminal cuttings.

-forsteri (for' ster i)	plectranthus	1–2'/3'
all season	foliage	SW India

Plectranthus forsteri (syn. *P. coleoides*) is probably more confused than most other species of *Plectranthus* because there is nothing unique about it. Plants are decumbent in habit, and the straggling stems bear mid-green aromatic leaves, somewhat minty to my nose, with scalloped to serrated margins. Measuring less than 1″ long and about 1½″ wide, they are ovate in shape and hairy on both surfaces. The pale blue to mauve flowers are clustered in six- to ten-flowered whorls and held in racemes.

Full sun to partial shade, propagate by terminal cuttings. It is most useful as a basket or container plant, filling in nicely in mixed containers.

CULTIVARS

'Green and Gold' is a colorful low-growing form that brightens up containers or the garden's edge. Leaves are bright gold with irregular green centers.

'Marginatus' is popular and quite different from the species. Plants are more bushy, and leaves are scalloped, thick, and succulent. They are variegated with creamy margins. Also sold as 'Variegatus'.

Alternative species

Plectranthus hilliardiae (hil ee ard' ee ay) has large flowers, similar to those of *P. ecloni*, that appear in late fall and winter. Usually sold as a conservatory and indoor plant; little information is known about its performance outdoors. The lavender flowers are tubular, ending in slightly flared lobes with purple spots.

Plectranthus oertendahlii (er ten dal' ee i; candle plant), a relative of *P. forsteri*, is a common denizen of greenhouses and conservatories but is also sold to gardeners as a basket for the summer or a filler for containers. Decumbent stems bear leaves that are 1½″ long and a little wider. They are ovate to almost circular, greenish above but purple beneath. The margins are scalloped and slightly hairy. Flowers mauve to pale blue, occasionally white. Partial shade.

Quick key to *Plectranthus* species

  A. Plant appears erect, decumbent but only slightly so
      B. Leaves silver to gray, covered with silver pubescence . . . *P. argentatus*
     BB. Leaves not silver or gray
        C. Plant 1–2' tall, leaves highly aromatic, like
           oregano, small lilac flowers in winter . . . . *P. amboinicus*
       CC. Plant 4–6' tall, leaves not highly aromatic, large
          purple flowers in late fall . . . . *P. ecloni*

AA. Plant obviously decumbent
    B. Leaves green on both sides . . . . *P. forsteri*
    BB. Leaves green above, purple below . . . . *P. oertendahlii*

Additional reading

Armitage, Allan M. 1998. Mexican mint. *Greenhouse Grower* 16(8):55–56.
Kleine, Adele. 1998. Welcome the prodigal plectranthus. *Flower and Garden*
    42(5):32–34.

Plumbago (plum bay′ go)   leadwort   Plumbaginaceae

The generic name—which comes from the Latin, *plumbum* ("lead"), because the
plant was thought to be a cure for lead poisoning—rolls off the tongue about as
readily as the common name, which, unfortunately, is also the common name
for the perennial *Ceratostigma*, a close relative in the same family. About fifteen
species occur in the genus; only *Plumbago auriculata* (Cape leadwort) is grown in
American gardens.

-*auriculata* (or ih kew la′ ta)   Cape leadwort   1–3′/3′
    summer   light blue   South Africa

Traveling in south Texas was quite a change for this Canadian boy. The town of
McAllen was certainly interesting; no doubt McAllenites would never live anywhere else, but I found little there that would inspire one to put down roots.
One of the things I did see, however, almost everywhere, was great drifts of light
blue plumbago. I renamed the town Plumbagoville, and immediately it was a
more pleasant place.

    Cape leadwort is a perennial evergreen shrub in zones 8 to 10, but everywhere
else, it should be treated as an annual. Plants grow up to 3′ tall in a single year
and bear alternate, simple entire leaves whose bases are ear-shaped (auriculate)
and may clasp the arching stems. The flowers are in a spike-like raceme. They
consist of five united sepals, from which a long tube extends, forming the five
fused petal lobes. Five stamens and five filaments are found within. Color ranges
from white to light to dark blue. After each flower is spent, a fruit capsule is
formed, bearing small hooks that cling tenaciously to clothing of passers-by or
to my dog, Hannah. Plants flower all season; if they get a little lanky, simply cut
them back. Great for large containers.

    Full sun. Propagate by seed or terminal cuttings.

CULTIVARS

    'Alba' is a white-flowered form.
    Escapade series consists of 'Escapade Blue' and 'Escapade White'. Both are 2–
2½′ tall and performed well in the UGA trials.
    'Imperial Blue' has darker flowers than the type and is a popular form.

Polygonum (pa lee go' num)   knotweed   Polygonaceae

As with many ornamentals, *Polygonum* is far better known for its taxa treated as perennials than for its annual members. Only one species (other than the several obnoxious weeds that seed everywhere in the garden) is cultivated, and it is an effort to find even that.

-*capitatum* (kap ih tay' tum)   magic carpet   4–8"/12"
   spring   pink   Himalayas

Seldom have I seen this species live through zone 7 winters, unless the weather was unseasonably mild. More often than not, however, plants reseed themselves, and the colony persists as if it were perennial. And a colony it is, forming a dense creeping ground cover in a matter of weeks. Plants are only about 4" tall when not in flower, 6–8" tall in bloom. The ovate to elliptical leaves are about 1" long and as wide, green with a V-shaped band in the middle; they are held to the prostrate stems by a short petiole. Dozens of small pink flowers are held together in many spherical heads (*capitatum* means "dense head"), each measuring about ½ to ¾" in diameter. Plants can roam freely even in a single year, so plant them where they'll have plenty of room.

   Plants do well in moist areas and without suitable irrigation seldom grow as rapidly as advertised. I have seen handsome colonies beneath the high shade of deciduous or coniferous trees, and some shade, at least in the South, results in larger leaves and a better-looking ground cover. Placing plants in baskets and containers shows off the well-marked foliage to advantage and reduces the invasive tendencies. Hot baking sun is not recommended. Propagate by seed or terminal cuttings.

CULTIVARS

   'Magic Carpet' was probably a selected cultivar, and everything sold is likely that selection. So common, the species itself has taken it on as a common name.

Alternative species

   Polygonum orientale (or ee en ta' lee) possesses the magical name of kiss-me-over-the-garden-gate, a name only the British could think up. Sometimes a plant is worth trying if for no other reason than that. Plants are hardy to about zone 7 and are sometimes considered perennial. Large heart-shaped leaves and long drooping flower spikes of rosy purple blooms are arranged over 3–5' tall plants. The flowers gave rise to another common name, prince's feather, but give me that garden gate any day. Invasive.

Portulaca (por choo la' ka)   purslane   Portulacaceae

In some places, this genus is thought to offer nothing more than fast-moving weeds that are vigorously eliminated to the compost heap. In America, we have chosen instead to use the genus with the wide, colorful flowers as a tough garden plant. All species of *Portulaca* have fleshy leaves and a prostrate habit, which allows them to be used as a ground cover and in mixed container plantings. Two closely related species, of the forty or so, are used in American gardens.

Quick guide to *Portulaca* species

	Flower form	Leaves
P. grandiflora	single, often semi-double and double	usually <1" long
P. oleracea	always single	usually >1½" long

-*grandiflora* (gran dih flor′ a)

	moss rose	4–8"/12"
summer	many colors	South America

Moss rose has been a favorite for many years, enjoyed throughout the season for its small cylindrical leaves and colorful flowers. The stems are prostrate with the ends somewhat ascending; they can grow to 1' tall, but present hybrids are generally less than 6" tall. The ½–1" long leaves have long thin hairs but are not prominently woolly; they are thick, succulent, and usually alternate, although they may be opposite or even whorled occasionally. Leaves are also terete (cylindrical in cross section). The size of the leaves and the close-to-the-ground branched habit are reminiscent of moss; combine these characteristics with the flowers, and you have a common name that is most apropos. Flowers consist of four to six petals (usually five), two sepals, and eight or more stamens; they measure 2" in diameter and are usually semi-double to double, in a wide assortment of colors. As with all portulacas, the flowers tend to remain closed until the sun shines and may remain closed on cloudy days; the breeding of double flowers has reduced this problem only slightly.

Moss rose has the reputation of being exceedingly tough, and indeed, they are by no means wimps. Good drainage is essential, however, for the season-long health of plantings used to provide color in the landscape. In areas of high heat, humidity, and afternoon rains, plants often succumb to root diseases by mid to late summer; in dry summers, plants remain healthy to frost.

Propagate by seed. Place in full sun in raised beds or containers.

CULTIVARS

Calypso series is an F_2 hybrid mix of bright 1–2" wide double flowers. No single colors are available.

Double Mix, often sold in seed packages, provides a random mix of double flowers.

Margarita series consists of compact, well-branched plants with semi-double flowers in six colors. 'Margarita Rosita', with vibrant hot pink flowers, is particularly colorful—an All-America Selection in 2001.

Sundial, an F_1 hybrid and the best series by far, provides many semi-double colors on vigorous plants. Available in cream, fuchsia, golden yellow, apricot-orange, orange, peppermint, pink, scarlet, tangerine, white, yellow, and a mix. 'Sundial Peach' was an All-America Selection in 1999.

Sunnyside series is an open-pollinated form in a random assortment of colors. Open-pollinated simply means that bees or other insects pollinated uncontrolled parents: that is, no hand pollination occurred, and therefore control of certain traits (for example, keeping flowers open even on cloudy days) is impossible. This does not mean poor garden plants; it does mean plants are generally less uniform and single colors are seldom possible.

-oleracea (o le ray' see a)	purslane	4–8"/12"
summer	many colors	India

In many parts of the world, this species is cultivated as a culinary herb for its iron-rich succulent leaves, which are eaten raw when young or cooked with other mature leafy vegetables, such as spinach; it is common in Indian, French, Italian, Greek, Central American, and Middle Eastern cuisine. The leaves are rather broad and flat, not terete. The spatulate to ovate leaves are not hairy and usually more than 1½" long. The entire plant is prostrate and trailing and therefore used to best effect hanging from the sides of mixed containers or raised beds. The single flowers are spectacular in the modern hybrids, easily measuring 2" across and in bright magnificent hues. In general, eight stamens, which move when even gently touched, may be found in the flowers. Flowers close under stress or in cloudy weather.

Full sun, well-drained soils. Propagate from cuttings,.

CULTIVARS

Duet is a bicolor group, with large flowers. 'Candy Stripe' (white with red margins), rose (yellow on rose), and yellow (red on yellow) make up the series.

Hot Shot series comes in a mix of colors and has performed well.

Samba series consists of flowers even larger than those of Yubi Summer Joy, some in rose and white. Quite striking.

Summer Baby series came from the single Yubi series introduced in the late 1990s. I'm not convinced double purslanes will be a big hit, but they looked much better in our trials than I thought they would. The series consists of orange, lemon-yellow, pink, red, rose, white, and bicolors ('Sunset Red' is a yellow and red bicolor). Large wild foliage.

Yubi Summer Joy is the series by which others are judged, combining excellent colors, large flowers, and terrific garden performance. Available in nine colors, including yellow, rose picotee, and white. These are no-brainers for summer color.

Quick key to *Portulaca* species

A. Leaves terete, usually <1" long, more or less hairy, flowers
   usually semi-double or double . . . . *P. grandiflora*
AA. Leaves broad and flat, usually >1½" long, plant smooth,
   flowers single . . . . *P. oleracea*

Portulaca oleracea 'Yubi Summer Joy White'   ASHA KAYS

Additional reading

Armitage, Allan M. 1998. Purslane. *Greenhouse Grower* 16(1):131–132.

Pseuderanthemum (soo der an' tha mum)   snow bush   Acanthaceae

Approximately sixty species are known in this little-used genus. A few tropical members are used for their wonderfully variegated foliage; handsome pink to purple tubular flowers can occur on them as well. All are native to the tropics but perform well in most areas of the country, providing temperatures remain above 75°F for a length of time.

Quick guide to *Pseuderanthemum* species

	Height	Leaf color	Flower color
P. alatum	2–2½'	bronze	purple
P. atropurpureum	2–3'	purple	white with rose spots
P. laxiflorum	2–3'	bronze-green	lavender

-alatum (a lay′ tum)   chocolate soldiers   2–2½′/2′
   summer   purple   Central America

Chocolate soldiers is a fair description of this species, which has heart-shaped bronze to chocolate-brown leaves. They have a slightly curved apex and are held by long-winged petioles; the leaf blades can measure 6″ to over 1′ in length. The veins are deeply depressed, and the leaf blade is quilted and puckered between them. Leaf color varies from milk chocolate–brown to greenish brown to reddish brown; the midrib and parts of the main lateral veins are always painted in silver or gray, and small dots of the same color occur toward the margins. The more sun, the redder the leaf. Plants grow up to 3′ in the tropical areas; in temperate zones, 1–2′ is more common.

The small purple summer blooms are held in upright racemes; they are pretty enough to enhance the look of the leaves, but the foliage makes the plant, for me.

Full sun in the North, partial shade in the South. They may be placed in full sun but will wilt badly if not watered often and well. Propagate by seed or cuttings. Plants will reseed if flowers remain.

-atropurpureum (at ro per per′ ee um)   red pseuderanthemum   2–3′/3′
   summer   white   Polynesia

This species is an erect shrub, growing 5–6′ in Florida and other frost-free areas but attaining about 3′ in more temperate areas. The 4–6″ long ovate to elliptical leaves are borne on long, rather weak branches. Plants are coveted for their purple to deep metallic green foliage. The foliage color is darkest when plants are young, then tends to fade somewhat; full sun also tends to fade the color, which is brightest in partial shade. Flowers are handsome but would not be missed if removed. The 1″ wide flowers, which are held in terminal racemes, range from white to lilac color, each with fuchsia to rose spots.

Full sun in the North, partial shade in the South. Propagate by seed or cuttings.

CULTIVARS

'Variegatum', the most common form, bears bronze-purple foliage, marked pink, with distinctive cream-yellow variegations. Quite eye-catching.

-laxiflorum (lak sih flor′ um)   shooting stars   2–3′/3′
   summer   lavender   Fiji Islands

I must admit—my excitement about this genus is somewhat lukewarm, but this little-known species is worth a closer look. Plants are smooth all over. The ovate to lanceolate leaves may have a bronze-green appearance, although they are not nearly as deeply colored as those of other species. The axillary flowers, however, which are larger than those of other species, are well worth retaining; they are a striking lavender-purple, with five distinct pointed petal lobes at the end of the tube, resembling a star. Flowers continue to form as long as temperatures remain 75°F.

Full sun in the North, partial shade in the South. Propagate by seed or cuttings.

CULTIVARS

'Amethyst Stars' has star-like raspberry-rose flowers on 1–2' tall plants.

'Variegatum' has green, pink, and white leaves and flowers similar to those of the species.

Alternative species

Pseuderanthemum reticulatum (re tik yew lay' tum) has flowers similar to those of *P. atropurpureum*. It is grown for its foliage, dark green leaves with obvious yellow-netted veins.

Quick key to *Pseuderanthemum* species

A. Flowers lavender-purple to pink
    B. Leaves chocolate-brown with silver-gray venation, flowers
       lavender-purple .... *P. alatum*
    BB. Leaves dark green, no obvious colored venation, flowers
       lavender to pink .... *P. laxiflorum*
AA. Flowers white or light lavender-white, usually with rose to red spots
    B. Leaves dark green with obvious yellow venation ...... *P. reticulatum*
    BB. Leaves red to wine-purple, no yellow venation ..... *P. atropurpureum*

Ptilotus (ti lo' tus)   mulla mulla   Amaranthaceae

Walk into any garden center and ask for some mulla mulla. You'll get stares of disbelief, then probably the old heave-ho—unless you are in eastern Australia, where mulla mulla is native and occasionally used as a cut flower. The family Amaranthaceae is better known for amaranthus and celosia; conjuring up those feathery spike-like flowers helps take a bit of the mystery out of *Ptilotus*. I believe the genus has some potential as a cut flower in this country (seeds will soon be available to those growers who want to try it), and a couple of the hundred or so species may have garden value as annuals.

Ptilotus exaltatus (ek sal ta' tus; tall mulla mulla) has 3–4" long blue-green lanceolate leaves with a blunt point at the tip. The plant grows to 3' in height and is topped with cylindrical 6" long woolly spikes of pinkish tan flowers. Each tomentose stem terminates in an inflorescence, and although the plant itself is not particularly well behaved, the flowers could make excellent cut flowers. All plants are grown from seed, and germination and growth is erratic. Some are well branched, others weak and ugly. Much has to be done with the species before it is acceptable as a garden plant even for the Australians, and it will be awhile before we see it offered here. Full sun, well-drained soils. Plants hate wet feet.

Two other species with potential as small border plants are *Ptilotus spathulatus* (spath yew lay' tus; pussytails) and *P. grandiflorus*. They both stand only 1–1½' high and produce many hairy spikes of golden to pink flowers and large rose-pink flowers, respectively. The former is native to eastern Australia, the latter to Western Australia. If seed can be obtained, you might want to try a few. Same cultural recommendations as for *P. exaltatus*.

All species are propagated easily from seed.

Q

_____

Quisqualis (kwis kwal′ is)   Combretaceae

A good friend introduced me to the Mercer Arboretum and Botanical Gardens in Humble, Texas. On that first visit, we came upon a display of tropical vines; they were climbing everywhere, devouring anything that dared linger in their path, blinding the eyes with color and the nose with fragrance. Well, okay, maybe not quite that extreme—but it was an education in color, form, fragrance, and habit for this northern lad. And apparently I was not the only fellow scratching his head: the generic name (Latin for "who? what?") was bestowed by an awestruck botanist astonished by the plant's behavior. Pen in hand, my friend lost out there somewhere, I took notes, not knowing when I would see these vines again.

One species in particular I have seen occasionally in Florida and Texas gardens and in many conservatories. Its botanical name, *Quisqualis indica*, is one of the few unpronounceable names I usually remember; its common name, Rangoon creeper, sort of sticks to the palate, too. Plants are climbers, producing long stems that clothe arches, pillars, and pergolas and even climb up trees. The 7–8″ long, 3″ wide opposite leaves, usually entire and pointed at the tip, are held by a 2″ long petiole. Of course, it isn't the leaves that people notice but rather the 4″ drooping inflorescences, consisting of up to a dozen long tubular flowers. The tubes are long and narrow, with five petal lobes at the end. Each fragrant flower usually opens white then changes to pink or pale red over time. The flowers are formed in the axils as well as terminally, so flowering continues for a long time. The resulting dry leathery fruit is also quite interesting, being acutely five-angled and containing a single seed.

It is doubtful that temperatures in temperate gardens will allow for sufficient growth and flowering the first year, so plants will have to be brought in and overwintered. They survive to about zone 8 with protection. Freezes occur in the Houston area, and plants come back fine the next year, growing to about 15′. This plant is not for everyone, but if a warm garden or heated conservatory has an empty spot, the Rangoon creeper may be just the ticket.

Propagate by softwood cuttings or seed. Seed-propagated plants may take on a bushy habit before climbing.

R

Reseda (res e′ da)   mignonette   Resedaceae

Reseda comes from the Latin, *resedo* ("to calm"), an allusion to the sedative properties of the genus. The genus is little known, consisting of about fifty species,
only one of which has found favor. *Reseda odorata* (sweet mignonette) was very
popular in Victorian times and well into the first half of the twentieth century,
when hundreds of acres of mignonette were grown under glass for the fragrant
cut flowers.

-odorata (o dor a′ ta)   sweet mignonette   2–2½′/2′
summer   white   Mediterranean

I'll admit it. Although I'm sure I could find a photogenic clump here and there
in gardens in the West Coast or eastern Canada, I've seen few good garden plantings of sweet mignonette in North America. The species is mostly grown as a cut
flower or as a pot plant in greenhouses. It grows well in cool weather, planted on
stony or sandy soils, and as garden material it can provide a rich source of nectar to bees.

The branched plants bear obovate alternate entire leaves, 4″ long and ¾″
wide; upper leaves may have one or two lateral lobes. The white flowers, sometimes tinged green or yellow, are held together in upright racemes; at first glance,
they look a little like those of *Iberis amara*, rocket candytuft (another of the common names for this plant is bastard rocket). The individual flowers are small and
made up of four to seven unequal petals and seven to forty small stamens attached on one side of the flower. They are wonderfully fragrant and are held
tightly to the flower stem, but as the flowers age, the racemes become loose and
open. When being used as a cut flower, they should be picked when about a fifth
of the flowers are open. They persist for at least five days in water alone, longer
with a floral preservative.

Full sun to partial shade, propagate by seed. Excellent drainage is a must.
Plant early in the spring; replace with other annuals when plants begin to decline in the heat of the summer. Plants are exceptionally good for cold frames
and cool conservatories.

'Fragrant Beauty' has fragrant reddish lime-green flowers.

'True Machet' has red-tinged highly fragrant flowers. Quite similar to 'Fragrant Beauty'.

Alternative species

Reseda alba (white mignonette) is more erect than *R. odorata* and has larger, more ornamental clean white flower stems. This is an easier plant to grow, rising 2–3′ in height. Its only drawback: the sweet fragrance is not there (some find it malodorous, in fact). I don't think they smell bad, but they can't compare to *R. odorata* for essence.

Rhodanthe (ro dan' thee)   everlasting   Asteraceae

As discussed at *Helipterum*, taxonomy of the everlastings is sorely debated; species move among *Acroclinium*, *Helipterum*, and *Rhodanthe*, with *Ammobium* and *Helichrysum* getting their fair share of attention also. Unless equipped with microscopes and lens—and unless you are ready to look at the bristles on the pappus, the shape of the phyllaries, the size of the capitulum, and the other structures that make up the flower—you will simply have to believe the label, and that can be a scary thought. As a plant geek, I enjoy looking at those flower parts, but most of my colleagues and I could not tell you definitively if you are looking at *Rhodanthe* or *Helipterum*. The truth is, even the taxonomists can't agree, as they are still discussing what characteristics belong to what genus. Up-to-date reference books and papers list a favorite Australian plant of mine, *Rhodanthe chlorocephala*, under either *Helipterum* or *Acroclinium*, so whom am I to believe? In this case I go with my Australian experts, Rodger and Gwen Elliot, who after all, have been surrounded by this plant for years. They also speak English, as opposed to taxonom-ish.

-chlorocephala (klor o sef' a la)   pink everlasting, rosy sunray   10–20″/12″
   spring   white, pink   Western Australia

In Western Australia, wildflowers are still as common as dandelions, and spring is truly alive with all sorts of colorful flora. This species is among the most numerous. A springtime drive through the bush there is always a thrill: you will learn more, see more, and photograph more wildflowers than you dreamed possible. Bring with you a camera and—this is critical—a driver who has no interest in plants, because you will drive off the road, and maybe hit a kangaroo, if you attempt to pilot and observe at the same time. A visit to King's Park Botanical Garden in Perth during the wildflower festival in October is a must, if for no other reason than to find out the names of all those marvelous flowers you saw.

Rhodanthe chlorocephala (syn. *Acroclinium roseum*, *Helipterum roseum*) used to consist of two main varieties, var. *rosea* and var. *splendidum*. The latter, however, was caught in the taxonomic crossfire and is listed, for this month anyway, as *Helipterum splendidum* (which see).

Variety *rosea*, the most common variety, is exceptionally diverse. Plants have numerous branched erect stems and are quite variable in height, ranging from 6" to 24" tall (10-20" is most common). The alternate leaves are 1-2" long, linear, sessile, and quite smooth. The margins are entire, and the tips are pointed. The terminal flower heads are about 2" wide and the colored parts consist of papery-dry bracts called phyllaries. The bracts are commonly rose-pink (sometimes white) with yellow disks, single or double. The color fades over time, but the bracts remain on the plant long after the color has faded. They are striking even after seed has formed and they are no longer particularly colorful. Everlasting is a most appropriate name. Flowers may be cut before fully open for fresh arrangements, or cut and hung upside down in cool, dry conditions away from direct light. If dried in this manner, they will retain their color for at least a year.

Full sun, well-drained soils. Propagate by seed *in situ*, or start inside in winter about eight weeks before last frost is expected. Seedlings are particularly susceptible to slugs and snails.

Alternative species

Rhodanthe manglesii (man gles' ee i; Swan River everlasting) is also native to Western Australia and grows about 2½' tall. The leaves are much longer (to 3") than *R. chlorocephala* and ovate rather than linear. Flowers are similar but usually light pink, although 'Maculatum' has red spots on the petal-like phyllaries. Same cultural recommendations as for *R. chlorocephala*.

Additional reading

Elliot, Gwen. 1998. *Australian Plants for the Garden*. Highland House, South Melbourne, Australia.

Rhodochiton (ro do ki' ton)   Scrophulariaceae

So many fine vines in the world of annuals—and so few people who take advantage of them. No doubt that they must attain a certain size before they flower, and that they persist only a year deters people from attempting them, but what a waste not to try one every now and then. The generic name of this vine comes from the Greek, *rhodo* ("red") and *chiton* ("cloak"), a reference to the calyx (sepals), which envelops the flower like a cloak. The genus consists of only three species; the one most grown is *Rhodochiton atrosanguineum*.

-atrosanguineum (at ro san gwin' ee um)   purple bell vine   vine
    summer   purple   Mexico

I love seeing this vine growing over fences or pergolas, where the dark red flowers are shown to advantage. I have also seen it grown in window boxes and large hanging baskets, where the pendent stems and flowers can be easily admired. The leaves are alternate, cordate or slightly five-lobed, and darker on the upper surface than beneath, often with a little purple tinge. They climb by twining their 3″ long petioles around anything they can find, as twining snapdragon (*Asarina*) does. The pendent flowers are unique. The papery magenta calyx forms an acutely five-lobed umbrella, under which hangs a 2–2½″ long-tubed magenta corolla; the total effect is that of a lantern. The tip of the corolla is expanded into five blunt petal lobes. They appear over a long period of time and are followed by balloon-like fruit, from which the seeds can be raised to form new plants.

This is a great vine, one which if propagated early inside will flower abundantly the first year. Seeds may be saved for next year's crop (sow seed when fresh) or semi-hardwood cuttings may be taken. In frost-free area, plants will be evergreen.

Rhodohypoxis (ro do hi poks′ is)   Hypoxidaceae

Rhodohypoxis can be included in both annual and perennial discussions. Species of this genus occur naturally in the Drackensburg Mountains of South Africa at elevations of 7000–8000′, providing winter hardiness to 25–28°F. But for most of us, plants are best treated as annuals. They are so beautiful, with six tepals colored in various shades of pure white to pale pink to deep red, that they are well worth a try, if only for a season.

-baurii (bor′ ee i)   red star   1–3″/3″
  spring   many colors   South Africa

The small flowering plants of this species are perfectly suited to the nooks and crannies of a rock garden. They enjoy plenty of moisture in the spring and early summer but abhor wetness in the winter, a problem in all but the most well-drained, water-retentive soils (there is an oxymoron, for sure). Plants produce keeled narrow leaves and flowers in ones or twos on 5–6″ tall scapes. In the wild, three distinct forms of *Rhodohypoxis baurii* are found: var. *baurii*, with deep pink to red flowers; var. *platypetala*, with white flowers; and var. *confecta*, with bicolored flowers. Named cultivars have arisen through hybridization and selection, but most catalogs simply offer a mixture of white-, pink-, and red-flowered forms. The species is sometimes found in florist shops, produced as a pot plant for sale on Valentine's or Mother's Day. One way to enjoy them more than a year is to grow the bulbs in pots and plunge them in the garden in the early spring. Bring them in before winter sets in and store them at cool but not freezing temperatures.

Gardeners on the Pacific Coast and those with protected locations might be pleasantly surprised by leaving them in the garden over the winter. Nothing ventured, nothing gained!

CULTIVARS

'Albrighton' has deep red flowers.
'Dawn' opens pale pink and fades to white.
'Eva Kate' is a vigorous selection with deep pink flowers.
'Fred Broome' consists of light pink and rosy pink flowers.
'Harlequin' has flowers which change from pink to white.
'Helen' bears white flowers with smudges of pink on the edges of the tepals.
'Pictus' is a vigorous white, with pink blushing on the tepals.
'Ruth' provides clean white flowers.
'Tetra Red' has intense red blossoms.

Alternative species

Rhodohypoxis milloides (mil oy′ deez) is more vigorous and has flowers in which the tepals are in two layers of three, separated by a noticeable gap. No such gap occurs in *R. baurii*. This species is also more tolerant of wet feet, so drainage is less of a problem. Of the several existing colors, 'Claret', with deep red flowers, is especially beautiful.

Additional reading

Robinson, Allan. 1996. Rhodohypoxis. *The Garden* 121(6):345–347.

Ricinus (ri sin′ us)   castor oil plant   Euphorbiaceae

Any reader who grew up in the 1950s or earlier will associate the tall handsome plants of this monotypic genus with the vile taste of castor oil, floating in a spoon about to be thrust down one's throat. Castor oil was obtained from great acreages of the plants in India, Italy, and California. The oil (where abundant and cheap, such as Calcutta at the beginning of the twentieth century) extracted from the seeds was also used as a fuel for lanterns.

Let me share with you a portion of an account of castor oil manufacture in California, written in the early 1900s:

> The seeds are submitted to dry heat in a furnace for about an hour to soften them, then pressed in a large powerful screw press, and the oily matter which flows out is caught and diluted with an equal volume of water, and boiled to purify it from mucilaginous and albuminous matter. After boiling for about an hour, it is allowed to cool, the water is drawn off, and the oil is transferred to zinc tanks or clarifiers capable of holding from 60 to 100 gallons. In these it stands for about eight hours bleaching in the sun, after which it is ready for storage. By this method, approximately 100 pounds of good seeds yield 5 gallons of pure oil.

All that, for a putrid concoction that was supposed to be good for you. It was given by well-meaning mothers as a purgative for constipation. It worked. (I have not had that problem since my mother forced the stuff on me when I was five—just the thought of it clears up any difficulties.) Ricin, the plant's active ingredient isolated in the early 1900s, is now known to be highly poisonous and can be fatal even in small doses; but, no fears, ricin is not found in castor oil. Castor oil is still used in the manufacture of paints, varnishes, and lacquers, which makes sense: taking castor oil was like drinking varnish, with approximately the same results.

The extraordinary genus in question consists of a single species, *Ricinus communis*, the variants and cultivars of which made quite a comeback as ornamentals at the dawn of the twenty-first century. Castor oil plant perfectly fits the concept of a tropical plant for temperate gardens: it grows rapidly, takes up significant space, and provides colorful and interesting foliage and flowers. Plants are many-branched, growing to 12' tall and equally wide in cultivation, although 6–8' is more common. The alternate, palmately lobed leaves are the most attractive part of the plant; they are peltate (the long petiole attaches to the middle of the leaf) and resemble a hand (in the Middle Ages, plants were called *palma Christi*, "hand of Christ," a name still seen in publications). Leaves may be dark green to blood red to variegated. The flowers are held in terminal panicles, with male flowers borne at the base and female flowers toward the top. The flowers are apetalous (they lack petals); the male flowers consist of numerous stamens and branched filaments, while the female flowers form feathery pistils. Flowers, usually a vivid red, are later encapsulated in spiny ovoid fruit. The ripe seeds are released explosively and may be shot for a considerable distance; seedlings may arise a long way from the mother plants.

Gardeners in most areas of the country will do well with castor plant, but plants will be smaller where summer temperatures are moderate. Leaf color, however, will be equally good. I have seen beautiful 10' specimens in Cleveland, so those in Duluth should be successful also. Some people are allergic to the leaves and seed pods, so be a little cautious when handling the plants. Propagate by seed (soak seeds overnight), plant in the back of the bed in a sunny location, and get out of the way.

CULTIVARS

'Carmencita' bears large bronze leaves and bright red flowers and fruit. Plants grow 5–6' tall. One of the best.

'Carmencita Pink' is similar to 'Carmencita' but with pink flowers and fruit.

'Gibsonii' (var. *gibsonii*) is a dwarf form that usually grows only 3–4' tall. The stems are deep purple, and the leaves are purple-red with a metallic luster.

'Impala' is 5–6' tall with maroon to carmine young growth. The flowers are sulfur-yellow, quite unlike other cultivars, followed by maroon fruit.

'Laciniatus' (var. *laciniatus*) has deeply divided green leaves.

'Sanguineus' (var. *sanguineus*) provides dark red to burgundy leaves.

'Scarlet Queen' (var. *carmineus*) has burgundy leaves and bright orange-red flowers.

'Zanzibarensis' (var. *zanzibarensis*) bears some of the largest leaves of the entire species. The green leaves should be suffused with white veins, but a great deal of variability occurs, and white venation is not always apparent. The plants with entirely green leaves have been termed 'Zanzibarensis Viridis'. Plants grow 8–10' tall.

Additional reading

Thigpen, Charlie. 2000. Castor bean, an age-old beauty. *Southern Living* 35(8): 221.

Rosmarinus (ro sma ree' nus)   rosemary   Lamiaceae

Rosmarinus officinalis is the ultimate ornamental herb, providing beauty, fragrance, and persistence. Everyone is familiar with its aromatic leaves, which are used for potpourri, perfumes, and seasoning. These gray-green Mediterranean plants are woody shrubs and can easily grow 4–6' tall over time. The flowers, usually light blue to white, occur in late winter to early spring and attract bees from miles away. Plants are grown by herb specialists as culinary companions to thyme, oregano, and lavender, or as ornamental standards (small potted trees). For much of the country, rosemary is an annual or container plant brought in during the winter, but some of the numerous cultivars, offering different habits and leaf and flower colors, are hardy to zone 7. The roots are more cold-tolerant than the tops; winters may cause top death, but new growth will occur in the spring. The biggest threat to winter persistence in zones 7 to 10 is poorly drained soils.

Full sun. If a sheltered dry area is available, rosemary can even be pruned and groomed as a hedge. Both acid and basic soils are appropriate.

CULTIVARS

'Albus' has white flowers.

'Arp' has light blue flowers and is quite cold hardy.

'Athens Blue Spires' is an upright vigorous hardy form whose light blue flowers absolutely cover the erect branches in late winter or early spring. Probably one zone more cold hardy than others. From the New Crop Program at the University of Georgia.

'Aureus' bears leaves speckled with yellow.

'Blue Boy' is a dwarf form with small leaves.

'Golden Rain' has yellow variegated foliage.

'Lockwood de Forest', a procumbent form, is otherwise very similar to 'Tuscan Blue'.

'Majorca Pink' bears pink flowers.

'Prostratus' is a common low-growing prostrate form.

'Silver Spires' may be the silvery plant grown in seventeenth-century Europe and then lost to cultivation. This upright sport was re-found in 1996, in Mayfields Nursery, Surrey, United Kingdom, by Christine Wolters. The plant has pale green leaves with white margins and in full sun can almost appear white.

'Tuscan Blue' has dark blue flowers and narrow leaves.

Additional reading

Hildebrand, I. 1993. Herbs as bonzi. *Prairie Gardener* 54:31–33.
Moore, S. 1994. Growing: pray, love, remember, from Aphrodite to Ophelia. *Garden Design* 13(5):35–36.
Ocone, L. 1993. Robust and rugged rosemary. *Sunset* 54:60–62.
Wolters, Christine. 1996. *Rosmarinus officinalis* 'Silver Spires'. *The Garden* 121 (8): 503.

Rudbeckia (rud bek' ee a)   coneflower   Asteraceae

This marvelous genus of the American countryside honors father and son, Olaus Olai Rudbeck and Olaf the Younger. The elder, a well-known Swedish naturalist and founder of the Uppsala Botanic Garden, spent his life creating more than 11,000 woodblocks of plants; however, nearly all the work was destroyed in the Uppsala fire of 1702, and he died soon after. His son, also a professor at Uppsala, befriended Carl Linnaeus when he was a poverty-stricken student. Being a good fellow, Linnaeus named the genus for both of them. (Um... I think I got an apple once.)

Rudbeckia hirta (black-eyed susan) is often sold as a perennial, although it is best treated as an annual. It is favored by gardeners for its ease of cultivation, its long flowering time, and its range of colors. With all the hype, well deserved though it may be, surrounding the perennial coneflowers such as *R. maxima*, *R. laciniata*, and especially the inescapable 'Goldsturm' rudbeckia, *R. hirta* has kind of gotten lost in the shuffle.

-hirta (her' ta)	black-eyed susan	2–3'/2'
summer	gold, yellow, orange	central United States

Native throughout the Plains and east to the Carolinas, plants had been as numerous as the buffalo before their natural habitat too declined. The alternate leaves are 2–4" long, narrowly lanceolate, usually three-ribbed and entire. The plant is characterized by bristly hairs, which occur all over the stems and on the undersides of the leaves and flower head. The presence of stem and foliar bristles is one of the easiest ways to distinguish this species from perennials such as *Rudbeckia fulgida* var. *sullivantii* 'Goldsturm'. The 2–4" wide solitary daisy flowers can be single or double, and the ray flowers are generally in shades of yellow, gold, and orange. The ray flowers are usually darker near the center; the disks are brown to black.

Flowers occur in mid summer and continue throughout the season, particularly in dry summers. In humid or rainy climates, however, the hairs tend to hold water, and fungal diseases often set in by mid summer. Flowering persists longer in dry summers than in wet ones. Removing flowers as they decline promotes further blooms and reduces the incidence of disease. In the UGA Horticulture Gardens, plants decline around late June; we replace them with seed-

Rudbeckia hirta   ASHA KAYS

lings to keep susans in the garden until frost. Buying seeds or plants of the species itself is just fine—they will provide lovely color—but many beautiful and increasingly diverse cultivars have been offered to the American gardener. My wife, Susan, thinks this is a good thing.

Full sun, well-drained soils. Propagate by seed. Plants often reseed in the garden and return for many years. Refrain from overhead watering, if possible. Deadhead often.

CULTIVARS

'Becky' is a compact mix in yellow, orange, and gold flowers, 3-4" wide. Plants grow only about 1' tall.

'Gloriosa', an old-fashioned form, has large semi-double to double flowers (up to 6" across) in orange and rust shades. Plants too are large, 3-5' tall. An All-America Selection in 1981. Also sold as 'Gloriosa Double Flowered' and 'Double Orange'.

'Goldilocks' is a semi-double to double daisy, about 18-24" tall. The 3-4" wide flowers are golden yellow. The doubleness is quite attractive, if you like double daisies, but flowers are then even more susceptible to disease when exposed to summer rain and humidity.

'Green Eyes' bears narrow yellow ray flowers surrounding a greenish disk.

'Indian Summer' is among the finest black-eyed susans I have seen. Developed in the late 1990s, plants are about 30" tall and absolutely smothered in single clean yellow flowers, 6" wide. Plants are compact, not gangly, and seldom need support. An All-America Selection in 1995. If I had but one choice, this would be it.

'Irish Eyes' is a handsome form, with yellow-orange ray flowers around a green eye.

'Kelvedon Star' grows 3-3½' tall and has interesting bicolor flowers. The 4" wide yellow flowers have mahogany-purple centers.

'Marmalade' is an old standard, providing large golden yellow flowers with a contrasting dark disk. Plants grow 2½-3' tall.

'Monarch' is a mix of 4" wide flowers in shades of bicolors, oranges, and yellows on 3' tall plants.

'Rustic Colors' are just that, a mix of bronze, gold, mahogany, and yellow with a contrasting black center. Plants are 2' (sometimes called 'Rustic Dwarf') to 3½' tall.

'Sonora' is the best of the bicolors, bearing 5" wide flowers with a mahogany-red center zone on the ray petals, then golden yellow beyond. Plants are only 15-20" tall.

'Toto' is my choice for a dwarf selection, with clean single gold-yellow rays surrounding a dark center. At 8-10" tall, it is useful anywhere good, persistent color is required and is the least maintenance-needy of any cultivar.

Ruellia (roo el' ee a)   Acanthaceae

The genus commemorates naturalist Jean de la Ruelle (1474–1537), who so impressed François I of France that he named Ruelle his personal botanist and physician. Ruelle was respected by his peers and wrote a well-known botanical text just before his death. The genus consists of more than 150 species, most native to the tropics of South America, mainly Brazil; the best-known species reside mainly in Mexico and Texas, and others are native to Pennsylvania, New Jersey, Florida, South Carolina, Kansas, and Arkansas, among other states in this country.

The genus has been grown in the Southwest for so long, gardeners are getting tired of it, but it has been unjustly ignored by the rest of the country. Plants are thought to be too big, or too wild; they self-sow too much, or they don't have enough flowers. But the wonderful diversity of the genus furnishes a rebuttal to each claim. I have grown a small percentage of the 150 species, and with taxa ranging from 6″ to 6′ tall, and flower colors from scarlet to white, I have a ways to go before I want them gone from my garden. I don't understand why seeds of at least some of the species or cultivars are so hard to find in national catalogs— the rest of the country should have a chance to get tired of them too.

Quick guide to *Ruellia* species

	Height	Flower color
R. brittoniana	3–5′	lilac-blue
R. devosiana	12–18″	white with lavender markings
R. elegans	8–12″	red
R. humilis	1–2′	lilac-blue

-*brittoniana* (brih to nee ay' na)   Mexican petunia, Texas petunia   3–5′/3′
summer   lilac-blue   Mexico

I was shown these large, lanky plants years ago in Texas, where they are generally dismissed as weeds and thugs, but I thought they weren't half bad. Perhaps they might respond to a little food and water—spruce them up a bit. I took a few urchins back to Georgia—not exactly the hot bed of *Ruellia* gardening—and began teaching my students about an entirely new genus. After about five years' observation of this species and several selections, I can positively say it is not for everyone. Plants are tall, produce only a few stems, do not flower until mid summer, produce flowers which when temperatures get hot tend to stay closed, and reseed everywhere. Having said that, I also can say that they are terrific plants if you are looking for a tall background specimens, don't need flowers until mid summer, can enjoy the flowers in the morning or evening on particularly stinking hot days, and appreciate free plants in the spring. One man's ceiling is another man's floor!

The three to four upright stems are dark green to purple, and the leaves are deep green. The 4–8″ long, opposite, linear to oblong leaves are essentially smooth, and entire and about ½" wide. The petunia-like flowers are formed in the upper axils of the stems and arise from a creamy spiraled bud. The spiraled buds are characteristic of *Ruellia* and are quite handsome in their own right. From the flower stem (pedicel), the petal first makes a long cylindrical tube then expands to form five broad rounded lobes, which floral structure is very similar to a petunia's, at least at first glance. Once flowering begins, plants bloom until frost.

In the heat of awful summers, plants remain upright and turgid, but flowers flag, either not opening at all or staying open only for an hour before temperatures get too warm. They may open again in the evening. Since flowers remain on the plant only for a day at the best of times, a constant stream of new flower buds is essential, and, if plants are provided with water, this generally occurs. In mid summer or late spring, seedlings may become a problem; from our single plant, we have spawned a compost heap. But that does not diminish its potential as a plant to try, anywhere in the country. In cooler summers in the Midwest and Northeast, plants will not grow as rapidly and flowering may not occur until later in the summer. Plants have been winter hardy to zone 7.

Full sun, propagate by seed. Irrigate well.

CULTIVARS

'Alba' provides white flowers, but flowering is sporadic.

'Chi Chi' has stunning pink flowers, bigger than those of the species, on plants about two-thirds the height; its drawback is that flowers are not nearly as numerous, and the heat-closure problem is worse. Its smaller size and handsome flowers have nevertheless gained it many fans. Plants reseed, and plants are true from seed.

'Katie' is the best and worst selection of the species. The dwarf habit (only 6–9" tall) and its rosetting habit make it a no-brainer for the front of the garden. The lilac-blue flowers are large relative to the size of the plant and crowded on the top. When in full flower, it is out of this world. When not in flower, which occurs more often than one would like, it is simply a pile of dark green leaves taking up space. I love this plant and dislike it as well. Start new plants each spring; if they overwinter, they tend not to flower as well (at least in zone 7). Plants reseed, and the seed comes true. Named after nurserywoman Katharine Fulcher Ferguson of Conroe, Texas.

-elegans (el' e ganz)	red ruellia	9–12"/12"
summer	red	Brazil

This is among the few of the many red-flowered ruellias in the genus that flowers during the gardening season and can be enjoyed outdoors. Many of the other red species are beautiful but tend to flower in winter, and their use is therefore limited to conservatory or indoor enjoyment. The mid-green opposite ovate leaves of this species are about 2" long and 1" wide and entire. Plants spread rapidly; in a single season, they will have doubled their area. The scarlet to red flowers rise above the foliage and continue to open most of the summer. They are relatively small (up to 1″ wide) compared with many other species, with five flared petals arising from the same spiraled buds common to the other species of *Ruellia*. The two top petals are seemingly attached, although close inspection dispels that notion. The throats of the flowers are whitish to yellow, reflecting the color of the stamens, and the pistil pokes out from the center as well.

This is a fine plant, little known but becoming more common as people recognize the genus. They require warm temperatures (>60°F) before they start growing rapidly. Place in full sun, in containers or in the garden.

-humilis (yew mih′ lis)	short ruellia	2–3′/3′
summer	violet-blue	United States

This highly variable species is native to New Jersey, Florida, Texas, and southern Pennsylvania to Nebraska. The plants are somewhat pubescent with branching stems. Leaves are 2–2½″ long, ovate to oblong, and essentially sessile (no petiole). The violet-blue tubular flowers are clustered from the upper axils with short flower stalks, each flower about 2″ across.

Full sun. Plants are often hardy to about zone 7 or 8 and will reseed with abandon.

Alternative species

Ruellia caroliniensis (kar o lin ee en′ sis) is a taller version of *R. humilis*. Flowers are similar in color and size; *R. caroliniensis* differs by having petioles and longer flower stalks.

Ruellia devosiana (da vos ee a′ na), a relative of *R. brittoniana*, is a low-growing species with white veins on the uppersides of the leaves and purple beneath. The white flowers, spotted or striped with lavender, are about 1½″ wide. Plants are grown more for the foliage than for the flowers.

Ruellia macrantha (ma kran′ tha; Christmas pride) is a bushy shrub 2–3′ tall, related to *R. elegans*. The rosy pink flowers are often 3″ across with a paler throat. Beautiful as this plant is, do not expect it to flower in the garden. Flowering occurs in winter, so it must be enjoyed indoors.

Ruellia makoyana (ma koy a′ na; monkey plant), another relative of *R. elegans*, has some of the prettiest foliage in the genus, bearing large ovate olive-green leaves with contrasting silver veins on top and purple beneath. The long tubular rosy red flowers are 1–1½″ wide but occur in the winter only. This spreading plant grows only 12–15″ tall.

Ruellia malacosperma (ma la ko sper′ ma) is similar in height and flower color to *R. brittoniana*, and the two are often sold interchangeably. Leaves of this species are somewhat hairy, especially when young, more oblong, shorter, and mostly toothed.

Quick key to *Ruellia* species

A. Flowers red, rose, or scarlet
    B. Foliage not particularly ornamental, no obvious venation color
        C. Flowers up to 3" wide .... *R. macrantha*
        CC. Flowers <2" wide .... *R. elegans*
    BB. Foliage ornamental, often with colored veins .... *R. makoyana*
AA. Flowers lilac, violet, or white
    B. Flowers white with lilac markings, foliage purple
       beneath .... *R. devosiana*
    BB. Flowers lilac or violet, foliage not purple beneath
        C. Plants 3–5' tall .... *R. brittoniana*
        CC. Plants <3' tall .... *R. humilis*

Ruellia hybrids

'Ground Hugger' is a wonderful low-growing form, useful for baskets and mixed containers or as a ground cover. Lavender flowers occur all season on 4–8" tall plants. An Athens Select plant.

Additional reading

Armitage, Allan M. 1998. Texas petunia. *Greenhouse Grower* 16(4):107–108.

Ruellia 'Ground Hugger'   ASHA KAYS

Russelia (roo sel' ee a)   Scrophulariaceae

Few of us know of the city of Aleppo, the second-largest city in Syria, with nearly a million inhabitants. Aleppo, an important trading center since 1500 B.C., has a history of prosperity too often interrupted by feuds, raids, skirmishes, and wars. The British influence at Aleppo was first felt in 1581, and by 1662 the "English factory," as it was called, numbered about fifty merchants. John Russell was the factory's physician from around 1740 to 1768; a noted naturalist, he also wrote the *Natural History of Aleppo* in 1756. The genus commemorates his work.

I admit to knowing very little about this shrubby genus except to sense that it has some garden potential for much of the country. The genus consists of about fifty evergreen species, but I am sufficiently schooled in only a couple of them. And even that could be debated.

Quick guide to *Russelia* species

	Height	Flowering time	Flower color
R. equisetiformis	2–4'	summer	red
R. sarmentosa	2–3'	summer	red

-equisetiformis (ek wih see tih for' mis) coral plant, fountain plant 2–4'/3'
summer   red   Mexico

When I first saw this plant many years ago, I could only think that if this was the best the genus had to offer, then obscurity would likely be its middle name. Of course, those who grew it thought it was the cat's meow and told me of its charms: tough, colorful, reliable.

The stems reminded me of horsetail (*Equisetum*), with their scale-like whorled leaves, but with a much more shrubby appearance. Those familiar with the genus *Ephreda* will admit its marked similarity to that genus as well. The stems, which are ridged or angled, start erect but become pendulous as the plants mature. The red flowers open in early summer and fall and are quite eye-catching, but to me the overall effect is that of a plant evolved to survive its surroundings rather than to enhance them. Plants are perennial in the Southwest and Deep South, withstanding temperatures around freezing or a little below.

Full sun. Propagate by division. Stems will also root where they touch the ground.

-sarmentosa (sar men to' sa)   running russelia   2–3'/3'
summer   red   Mexico, California

I believe this species has more garden potential than *Russelia equisetiformis*, mainly by virtue of its habit and foliage. It is still shrubby but not as hard-looking as coral plant. The basal stems are prostrate and run along the ground, rooting at the nodes of the angled stem if given the opportunity. The central stems rise up and arch over—an excellent habit for containers and baskets. The opposite leaves are nothing like horsetails; rather they are ovate and dentate, around 2½" long and about 1" wide. The bright red flowers are held in a lax many-flowered inflorescence at the end of the stems; they form in mid summer and continue until frost. This species will struggle to find acceptance as a mainstream garden plant, but in containers or in a "wildish" garden, it is worth a try.

Full sun. Propagate by division or from nodal cuttings (like an ivy).

Quick key to *Russelia* species

A. Leaves very short and narrow, scale or needle-like, stems
upright . . . . *R. equisetiformis*

AA. Leaves ovate, stems prostrate . . . . *R. sarmentosa*

S

Salpiglossis (sal pih glos' is) painted tongue Solanaceae

Only two species of this unusual genus have been described, and all representatives grown in gardens are probably hybrids between the two. The dominant species in the hybrids is *Salpiglossis sinuata* (sin yew a' ta), an erect, sticky 2–2½' tall plant with beautiful, large petunia-like flowers.

The 4″ long alternate leaves are narrow and hairy and have wavy margins. The flowers, however, are the reason for buying some painted tongues. The generic name comes from the Greek, *salpinx* ("trumpet") and *glossus* ("tongue"), a reference to the style (the female tube), which is elongated and trumpet-shaped. The beauty of the plant comes from the 2½″ wide pale yellow flowers striped with lavender and purple. The flowers are formed in axils in the upper part of the plant and, if deadheaded, will continue to form.

If this plant is so beautiful, why don't we see it more often? Simply put, it is a wimp. It looks robust in the greenhouse and conservatory but is a coward when placed outdoors. Cool springs, bright sunshine, and balmy breezes are tolerated, but ask not for painted tongues when the weather turns hot, the sun beats down, and breezes are no longer balmy. In short, they look great at Lake Louise, Alberta, and Victoria, British Columbia. In our trials in Georgia, they elicited delight in the spring and despair in the summer. As an early spring plant in much of the country, they are wonderful—but not for too much longer.

Partial shade, propagate by seed. Excellent drainage is necessary.

CULTIVARS

Casino Hybrids are about 15″ tall and have flowers veined in shades of red, yellow, orange, rose, and purple.

Royale Hybrids offer exceptionally beautiful flowers in dark purple, lavender, yellow, and rose, with deeper, darker veins. Best of the hybrids.

Salvia (sal' vee a)   sage   Lamiaceae

If all the world's a stage, then all the salvias must be players. And the stage is crowded: more than 900 species share it, each one vying for the attention of those who have been bitten by the salvia bug. All gardeners pass through the salvia stage of life—it is a rite of passage. The challenge is to emerge unscathed. Been there, done that—but the pull, for me, to try yet one more is still strong. Although many species are woody shrubs in their homeland, and although they do produce tough woody stems here, most are annuals in much of the country; only a handful survive north of zone 7. Biennials are not uncommon in the genus, and these species may enjoy cold hardiness to zone 4 or 5.

Salvias are found throughout the world. Species originate from Mexico, South America, North Africa, Asia, and southern Europe, and a few are native Americans. Many species are fall-flowerers, some so late as to be almost useless in the North, especially in years of early frosts. But the fall-flowerers can be outstanding, bringing color back to landscapes that have become boring or tired. Fragrance too is part of the salvia charm; the leaves entice us with the perfumes of pineapple (*Salvia rutilans*), currants (*S. microphylla*), and, of course, sage (*S. officinalis*).

The genus is characterized by opposite leaves, squarish stems, and whorled two-lipped flowers.

Quick guide to *Salvia* species

	Height	Flower color
S. argentea	2–4'	whitish yellow
S. coccinea	1–3'	scarlet
S. farinacea	1–2'	purple, lavender
S. greggii	2–3'	red
S. involucrata	3–5'	rose-pink
S. leucantha	3–5'	violet-blue and white
S. madrensis	3–5'	yellow
S. patens	2–4'	violet
S. regla	2–3'	salmon
S. rutilans	2–3'	scarlet
S. splendens	1–2'	varied
S. viridis	2–3'	varied

-*argentea* (ar jen' tee a)   silver sage   2–4'/3'
      summer   foliage   southern Europe

Plants are true biennials (flowering the second year from seed), although new plants may arise from root stalks or seeds and therefore appear to be perennial north to zone 5. Plants are often found in perennial catalogs, but if you grow them for a few years, you'll find they've moved all over the garden. This species is among the few salvias whose large white-woolly leaves are the main attraction of the plant, the flowers being secondary. The wedge-shaped, wrinkled, and irregularly toothed leaves are sessile, 6–8″ long and 6″ across; they provide a wonderful contrast to green-leaved garden plants.

Flowers appear the second year on seed-propagated plants but are not particularly exceptional. They appear in a slightly branched large panicle, each whorl consisting of six to ten whitish yellow flowers. The inside part of the flower, the corolla, is about three times longer than the calyx. Having given the details of this flower's structure, I now recommend their removal as soon as possible. This insures the plant produces leaves rather than marginally attractive flowers. The foliage should remain the dominant feature of the plant.

In late summer, plants often look the worse for wear, particularly if the summer has been hot and rainy. Hairy-leaved plants such as this and *Stachys* tend to retain moisture, allowing leaf diseases to become established. Although short-lived, plants rebound from seed the next year in most areas of the country. This is a terrific plant for containers and requires well-drained gritty soils to do well. In the North, plants do well down to zone 5, in the South, they perform well north to zone 7a, struggle in 7b, and quickly melt out further south.

Propagate by seed or by self-rooting lateral offshoots, which may be detached in the spring and replanted.

-coccinea (kok sin′ ee a)		bloody sage 1–3′/2′
summer	scarlet	tropical South America

This species is a favorite summer-flowering sage of mine because it has not been bred to death in the name of short and compact. It is short, relative to many other species, but can grow to 3′ in height (1–2′ is more common). The 1–2″ long leaves are ovate, with a heart-shaped base and wavy margins. The foliage is thin and more or less translucent (pluck off a leaf and hold it to the sun, to see for yourself); this is one of the best ways to differentiate *Salvia coccinea* from other red-flowering species, especially common bedding sage, *S. splendens*. The whorled flowers are held quite distant from each other on many-flowered racemes, again a departure from the crowded flowers of common bedding sage. All in all, the species is more refined and elegant than other red salvias.

Full sun in the North, partial shade in the South. Afternoon shade in general promotes better performance. Propagate by seed.

CULTIVARS

'Cherry Blossom' has lovely salmon and white bicolored flowers on 15–24″ tall plants.

'Lactea' has white flowers. The precursor of 'Snow Nymph'.

'Lady in Red', an earlier introduction, bears scarlet flowers on 2–2½′ tall plants. Excellent for containers and still very popular.

Nymph, an outstanding and eye-catching series, produces flowers in white ('Snow Nymph'), white and red bicolor ('Coral Nymph'), salmon, and pink.

-farinacea (fa rih nay´ see a)   mealy-cup sage   1–2´/2´
   summer   purple, lavender   Texas, Mexico

A most popular bedding sage, this species provides drifts of purple and lavender flowers for towns and gardeners' gardens. Plants are 1–2´ tall, with 3″ long, ovate to lanceolate leaves, minutely pubescent on the veins beneath. The flowers are held densely in ten to fifteen whorls on the 8″ tall racemes. The cup-like calyx (sepals) is violet but is densely covered with long white woolly hairs, thus the common name (the specific epithet is Latin for "flour"). The corolla (petals) is purple and does not obviously protrude from the calyx, as it does in many other salvias.

Full sun in the North, partial shade in the South. Propagate by seed.

CULTIVARS

'Argent' is an older white-flowered form. The silver plants do not stand out as well as the blue and violet forms.

'Cirrus' is about 15″ tall with white flowers on silver-white flower stems. More compact and slightly whiter flowers than 'Argent'.

'Reference' has bicolor flowers, similar but not as well known as 'Strata'.

'Rhea' is a short, compact form (12″) with dark blue to violet flowers.

'Strata' makes a most interesting addition to the garden, bearing bicolored blue and white flowers. I find it a washed-out color, uncertain whether it wants to be blue or white and not fully either. But I am in the minority for sure: this cultivar was a Fleuroselect award winner in Europe and a 1996 All-America Selection in the United States.

'Victoria' is by far the most common cultivar, with large intense violet-blue flowers. Bigger and more vivid than 'Rhea'.

-greggii (greg´ ee i)   Texas sage   2–3´/3´
   summer   red   Texas, Mexico

This fine Texas native has found its way into mainstream gardens and provides more winter hardiness than most other red salvias. The typical form has scarlet flowers and was found near Saltillo, Mexico, by Mexican trader Josiah Gregg in 1870. The 1–2″ long ovate leaves have entire margins and emit a heavy sage fragrance when rubbed. The two-lipped flowers, which may be red, pink, violet, or white, are held in whorls of two or three and have a wide lower lip and smaller upper lip. Flowering begins in mid to late summer and continues well into the fall. Plants are a bit unruly and get rather messy as the season progresses. Cutting them back after a month in the garden helps keep them more compact.

Many handsome hybrids, some of which share their popular parent's welcome tolerance for heat, humidity, and drought, have resulted from crossing Texas sage with other species, in particular with *Salvia microphylla* (small-leaved sage) and *S. blepharophylla* (eyelash sage). A few of these hybrids are listed in "Cultivars." Many have shown cold hardiness to zone 7.

Full sun, propagate by seed or cuttings.

CULTIVARS

'Alba' has white flowers with a green calyx. Also sold as 'White'.

'Big Pink' produces flowers of deep pink and lavender with an obviously larger lower lip.

'Cherry Queen' (*Salvia greggii* × *S. blepharophylla*) is among the many hybrids produced by Richard Dufresne of North Carolina. We have had this sage in the UGA Horticulture Gardens since 1995, and every year it starts flowering in May and continues until frost. An absolutely outstanding plant for southern gardens.

'Chiffon' produces light yellow flowers on 2–3' tall plants.

'Dark Dancer' bears fuchsia flowers.

'Desert Blaze' has variegated leaves with narrow white edges. Plants are only about 18″ tall and bear red flowers in spring and fall.

'Furman's Red' (named for plantsman William Furman of Kerriville, Texas) grows much more upright than the former cultivars, stretching up to 3' in height. The bright red flowers occur throughout the season but are heavier in late spring and fall. Hardy to zone 6b.

'Keter's Red' has an orange-red flower.

'Pale Yellow', likely a hybrid, bears pale yellow flowers on 18″ tall plants.

'Peach La Encantada' produces handsome peach-colored flowers on 15–18″ tall plants. Also sold as 'La Encantada'.

'Purple Haze' has deep violet-blue flowers. Introduced by Pat McNeal of Austin, Texas.

| *-involucrata* (in vol yew kray′ ta) | roseleaf sage | 3–5'/2' |
| late summer | rose-pink | Mexico |

These large subshrubs bear long unbranched stems and smooth 2–3″ long ovate leaves with pointed tips and triangular base. The flowers are held in 12″ long whorled racemes, each whorl consisting of four to six rosy pink flowers. Small bracts surround the flowers, from which comes the specific epithet, Latin for "ring of bracts." The bracts fall off rapidly and are best seen in newly emerging blooms. The corolla is about 1½″ long and obviously exserted (sticks out from the calyx). The racemes form in mid to late summer. The most obvious and curious part of the inflorescence is the globose tip, which looks like an Irish shillelagh.

This is a beautiful but lanky and difficult-to-tame species. It grows rapidly and even when pinched just waits until your back is turned to grow another 3' overnight. After wrestling the thing to the ground a few times, perhaps encasing it in a small supportive jail, it is time to sit back and enjoy the late summer and fall flowers. With their rounded tips and lovely color, they are worth waiting for. If the plant is still too big and lanky, cut the flowers and bring them indoors to enjoy. This one requires tough love!

Full sun, propagate by cuttings.

'Bethellii' (named for the man who raised it) was touted as more compact but that is not the case, at least not in my garden. The leaf bases are heart-shaped, and the flowers are rosy red to rosy crimson. In my opinion, little enough difference indeed.

'El Cielo' has darker flowers than the species.

'Mulberry Jam' has darker magenta flowers and a better, more compact habit. From the garden of Betsy Clebsch.

| *-leucantha* (loo kan' tha) | velvet sage, bush sage | 3–5'/4' |
| fall | violet-blue and white | Mexico |

This arguably perennial plant is often cold hardy to zone 7, perhaps a little colder; however, reliability is suspect, and I prefer to consider it an annual in most gardens. In any case, this is a truly outstanding species in a genus filled with them. It is often the dominant plant in the fall garden, towering above others and, like a magnet, drawing all visitors to it.

Plants grow 3–5' tall in southern gardens, less tall in the North. The softly pubescent leaves are ovate to lanceolate (4×1"), whitish below, and velvet to the touch, thus one of its common names. Not highly aromatic, but we often go out of our way to rub a leaf just for the feel of it, the lamb's ears of sages. Plants branch well, forming a vase-shaped bush with woody stems. The calyx of the flowers is lavender to violet, and the lipped corolla is white, producing a bicolor effect. They are initiated by shortening day lengths in late summer and are in their glory in late summer and fall. Unfortunately, in some northeastern states, such as Vermont, frost may arrive before days become sufficiently short. There is no doubt that this is a better plant for the South than for the North.

Full sun, propagate by cuttings. Mulch in zones 6 and 7 to induce overwintering.

'Midnight' has both purple calyces and corollas. More eye-catching and more elegant and therefore a better plant than the species. Also sold as 'Purple on Purple' and 'Blue on Blue'.

'Santa Barbara' is a dwarf form, growing only about 3' tall before flowering. A welcome addition to the garden.

| *-madrensis* (ma dren' sis) | forsythia sage | 3–5'/3' |
| late fall | yellow | Belize |

Among the brightest and yellowest of the salvias, this species is a slow-developing late-bloomer from the Sierra Madre Oriental (the specific epithet describes its origin). These are large plants, with large felty ovate leaves and obviously square stems, so robust they could be used as plant stakes. The coarse heart-shaped leaves are larger at the base, becoming smaller as they ascend the plant. The whorled 1–1½" long flowers, held on a 12" long inflorescence, are a wonderful shade of yellow. Unfortunately, forsythia sage is among the latest plants to flower. Again, flowering results from shortening days; the nights must be at least thirteen hours long. Unless plants are brought inside, or if you garden in zone 8 or further south, it is likely that cold weather and frost will destroy the stems before flowers open.

A big plant in every way, and a great plant for gardeners in coastal areas and the Deep South. It will disappoint many gardeners in temperate zones. Full sun, propagate by cuttings.

| *-patens* (pa′ tenz) | gentian sage | 2–3′/2′ |
| summer | violet | Mexico |

People who come upon *Salvia patens* in full flower are compelled to exclaim over its color and the size of the flowers. At Butchart Gardens, a crowd actually gathered to admire a planting, wonderfully sited to catch people as they rounded a corner. Of course, crowds gather at every corner of this great garden, arrested by the beauty on all sides.

The 6–8″ long leaves are deltoid (an equilateral triangle) and have 2–3″ long petioles; occasionally they are sessile. The 1½–2″ long gentian-blue flowers are borne sparsely in two- or three-flowered whorls. The lower lip is much larger than the upper one and resembles the hanging tongue of an exhausted dog, or at least the hanging tongue of my Hannah. Although the flowers are among the largest in the genus, the lack of floriferousness necessitates a large planting to really make a show. Whether for one or ten plants, however, people will stop. The 30″ tall plants may overwinter in zone 8. Some consider them half-hardy perennials, but they should be treated as annuals in most of the country.

Full sun, propagate by seed.

CULTIVARS

'Alba' is a white-flowered form I have not yet seen. I just can't imagine what I would do with a white gentian sage.

'Cambridge Blue' bears flowers of a lighter, less violent blue than the species. Quite beautiful.

'Chilcombe' has mauve-blue flowers.

| *-splendens* (splen′ denz) | scarlet sage | 12–15″/12″ |
| summer | many colors | Brazil |

The species itself is unrecognizable, but its offspring are everywhere: the frenzy in salvia breeding peaked in the 1970s and 1980s, but new cultivars of scarlet sage are still rolling off breeders' benches. It is easy to criticize overbred bedding plants, and I hear holier-than-thou comments about "ghastly" colors, "plastic" plants, and "gaudy" appearances all the time. Get a life! If people don't like them, they shouldn't buy them. And the next time someone offhandedly skewers salvias (or marigolds, or petunias . . .), they should realize they are truly in the minority. Many gardeners and landscapers love these plants: they provide color all season, require little maintenance, and simply look good. I too feel

Salvia splendens   ASHA KAYS

it is time for salvia breeders to incorporate other species into scarlet sage, but I don't make the rules or pay their salaries.

In general, scarlet sage has deep green opposite $2\frac{1}{2} \times 2''$ ovate leaves with somewhat pointed tips and serrated margins. The flowers are held in densely flowered racemes, each whorl consisting of two to six flowers. The calyx and corolla are scarlet, and the corolla is obviously exserted. But the painful details of plant description quickly evaporate when the long corolla tube is plucked, then sucked, on a warm summer day. The nectar is exquisite, and you will be flooded by old forgotten feelings of your past life as a hummingbird. Be sure the plants haven't been sprayed with some pesticide, or your first taste may be your last. Plants flower all season, but they are absolutely magnificent in cooler weather, and fall can often be their most glorious show.

The selection and propagation of cultivars have been going on for at least a century, but it is only since the 1950s that scarlet sage became an established bedding plant item, that is, short and compact. The first selections—slight color variations of the 3' tall species—have all but disappeared from culture. The exception is the wonderful 'Van Houttei', an extremely popular form that was understandably but incorrectly elevated to the rank of species by some authorities. But this must-have plant (see "Cultivars") is increasingly difficult to find—which brings to mind the question posed by gardeners (and city historians and plant ecologists): "What other excellent selections (and period buildings and medicinal plants) once existed that no longer do?"

Dozens of modern bedding cultivars have been selected, nearly all F_1 hybrids, and except for flower color and height, it is difficult to tell one from another. As with most bedding plants, the labeling is atrocious, so the best you may find in the retail store is "red salvia." With any luck, your nursery or garden center is better than that, for one thing is doubtless: salvias are not all red anymore.

In the South, place in an area of afternoon shade, in the North, the same recommendation may be made, but not as forcibly. Plants need a good deal of fertility after planting, otherwise they take weeks to become established. Deadhead in the middle of summer, and plants will return in full dress.

CULTIVARS

Tall forms (20–24")

'Bonfire' and 'Early Bonfire' are 2–3' tall with scarlet flowers. 'Early Bonfire' flowers a little earlier.

'Faye Chapel', a vigorous bright scarlet, arose as a sport from 'Van Houttei' in the greenhouse of Phil Gibson, a Georgia grower with a great eye. Plants flower much earlier than the species and remain in flower until frost. We trialed them for two years at the University of Georgia, where they were excellent—and eye-catching—performers. Named by Gibson for one of Georgia's leading ladies of horticulture.

'Paradiso' has bright red flowers.

'Van Houttei' commemorates celebrated Belgian nurseryman Louis Benoit van Houtte (1810–1876), the editor of *Flore des Serres* (he is better known for the popular white-flowered spiraea that also bears his name). This rather lanky plant is up to 3′ tall, well-branched but rather open in appearance. The long flowers are a most interesting color. Some call them burgundy, a nicer description than the more apt mauve-puce. Plants generally form in late summer and fall. Partial shade is recommended.

Intermediate forms (14–18″)

Dress Parade Mix is a blend of pink, purple, scarlet, rose, and white flowers.

'Dwarf Early Bird' is a scarlet-flowered form with deep green foliage.

'Etna' has deep scarlet flowers.

'Flare' bears tall spikes of scarlet red.

'Garden Leader Firecracker Red' has large scarlet flowers. 'Garden Leader Rose' is equally large.

Marbella series provides pink, purple, rose, salmon, scarlet, and white blossoms.

'Red Pillar' bears dark green leaves with scarlet flowers.

'St. John's Fire', long a popular form, provides fire-engine red flowers over dark foliage.

Short forms (6–12″)

'Blaze of Fire' is just that, on a compact frame.

'Dwarf Little Tango' has scarlet flowers.

Empire series has dark green foliage and flowers in burgundy, lilac, orange bicolor, purple, red, rose, salmon, and white.

'Fuego' bears brilliant scarlet flowers.

Hotline series is a compact form with burgundy, red, salmon, and white flowers.

'Melba' bears scarlet and white bicolor blooms.

'Red Arrows' has dark green leaves and brilliant scarlet flowers.

'Red Hot Sally' was among the best names ever given a plant—and she is red and hot.

Salsa series provides a compact plant with burgundy, light purple, purple, rose, rose bicolor (rose and white), salmon, salmon bicolor, scarlet, scarlet bicolor, and white flowers.

'Scorpio' is a dwarf red-flowered selection.

Sizzler series has flowers in burgundy, lavender, orchid, pink, plum, purple, red, salmon, salmon bicolor, and white.

'Vista Red' bears dark green foliage and bright scarlet flowers. An alternative for the old Carabiniere series. 'Vista Salmon' is equally good.

-viridis (ver ih′ dis)	green sage, clary	1–2′/2′
summer	many colors	southern Europe

This plant was at one time a most important salvia, the namesake of all salvias in the Greek language. Until about 1980, it was known as *Salvia horminum* (which specific epithet is Greek for "sage"). The species is now seldom grown, at least in American gardens. Plants consist of 1–1½′ tall erect stems with 2″ long, 1″ wide simple leaves. Terminating the stems are long racemes of small (<1″

long), purple- or lilac-whorled flowers. The flowers are handsome enough, but the color and beauty of the plants result from the wide bracts at the base of the whorls. The broad bracts are somewhat pointed at the tips, about ½″ long and persistent. Many salvia species have bracts, but none are as large, relative to the flowers, nor as persistent as these.

Plants are reasonably handsome, particularly in groups of a dozen or so. The bracts are often striped as opposed to deeply colored and blend rather than stand out in the garden. No doubt this is a most interesting species and quite different from the other large-flowered salvia forms. It is simple to raise and grow and worth a spot in the garden, for the interest alone. Plants are native to the Mediterranean and do not tolerate extremes of temperature or humidity. Better in the North than the South.

Full sun to partial shade. Propagate by seed *in situ* in early spring.

CULTIVARS

'Alba' has white bracts.

'Bluebeard' produces pale violet bracts with darker veins.

'Claryssa' is a dwarf form in a mix of purple, pink, and white bracts.

'Oxford Blue' bears blue-purple bracts.

'Pink Sundae' has rosy carmine bracts with darker veins. Similar to 'Purpurea'.

'Purpurea' is quite common and has rosy red to purple bracts.

'Rose Bouquet' has pink bracts.

'Violacea' bears violet bracts with darker veins.

'White Swan' has clean white bracts but is essentially the same as 'Alba'.

Alternative species

Salvia aethiopis (African sage), a relative of *S. argentea*, is a biennial with basal rosettes of large toothed leaves. The leaves are dull green but have long white hairs (tomenta) in the center in the winter and early spring. The flowers are dull white.

Salvia blepharophylla (ble fa ra′ fil a; eyelash sage), a relative of *S. coccinea*, has three to six whorls of scarlet flowers, each with a longer lower lip. The margins of the leaves are notched and ciliate (edged with tiny hairs), thus the common name. 'Diablo' produces new foliage in purple and flowers that are fire-engine red. 'Sweet Numbers' has longer hairs on the margins of the leaves, but flowers are similar to those of the species.

Salvia ×jamensis (jay men′ sis) is the name given by James Compton to the naturally occurring yellow-flowered hybrid between *S. greggii* and *S. microphylla* found in 1991 near the town of Jame, in a Mexican mountain pass at elevations of 2000–3000′. Other colors also occur, and names have been published. All these recent introductions are alive with hummingbirds and butterflies and are well worth a try, if salvia space allows; some are hardy to zone 7, all are hardy in zones 8 to 10: 'Cienaga de Oro' has pale yellow flowers and grows 15–18″ tall; 'El Duranzo' bears peach-colored flowers; 'La Luna' has creamy yellow flowers; 'Maraschino' is an excellent maraschino-cherry sage; 'Pat Vlasto' produces pale peach flowers; 'Raspberry Royale' bears magenta flowers in late summer and fall, and the similar 'Red Velvet' is about 3' tall and has velvet red flowers; 'San Isidro Moon' is blessed with gray calyces and peach and cream corollas; 'Sierra San Antonio' has peach-rose flowers with a yellow lower lip.

Salvia regla (Hildago sage) is related to *S. greggii*. Among the most beautiful shrubby sages in the genus, plants of this species grow 2–3' in a season; then, in late fall, they come alive with orange-scarlet flowers, an almost-salmon that inevitably stops people in their tracks. Native to Mexico and south Texas, plants are hardy to about zone 8 (maybe zone 7 with excellent drainage). Unfortunately, flowers occur too late for many northern gardeners, but southerners should take note. Several named selections are available, among them 'Mount Emory', from Texas A&M, with 2" red flowers, and 'Warnock's Choice', a 4–6' tall form from Yucca Do Nursery.

Salvia rutilans (syn. *S. elegans*; pineapple sage) is related to *S. coccinea*. This species has scarlet-red flowers and ovate leaves and grows up to 3' tall. The leaves truly do smell like pineapple, especially if you are suggestible. Hardy to zone 7. The names *S. rutilans* and *S. elegans* are used interchangeably, with taxonomists divided as to splitting or lumping them. 'Honey Melon', a dwarf pineapple sage, is only about 1½' tall.

Quick key to *Salvia* species

A. Leaves <1" long
  B. Flowers obviously larger than bracts . . . . *S. greggii*
  BB. Bracts persistent, most obvious part of "flower" . . . . *S. viridis*
AA. Leaves larger
  B. Leaves highly pubescent, green-silver . . . . *S. argentea*
  BB. Leaves not highly pubescent
    C. Flowers blue, violet, puce
      D. Flowers >1½" long . . . . *S. splendens* 'Van Houttei'
      DD. Flowers <1½" long
        E. Flower stems hairy (mealy) . . . . *S. farinacea*
        EE. Flower stems not mealy
          F. White corolla, <1" long . . . . *S. leucantha*
          FF. Violet corolla, >2" long . . . . *S. patens*
    CC. Flowers red, rose, yellow, not blue, violet
      D. Flowers yellow . . . . *S. madrensis*
      DD. Flowers rose-salmon or pink, red, scarlet
        E. Flowers red, scarlet
          F. Flowers >1½" long, leaves unscented . . . .
            . . . . *S. coccinea*
          FF. Flowers <1½" long, leaves fruit-
            scented . . . . *S. rutilans*
        EE. Flowers rose-pink or rose-salmon
          F. Flowers >1½" long, rose-pink . . . . . *S. involucrata*
          FF. Flowers <1½" long, rose-salmon . . . . *S. regla*

Additional reading

Armitage, Allan M. 1997. *Herbaceous Perennial Plants*, 2nd ed. Stipes Publishing, Champaign, Ill.

Bloom, Alan. 1980. Salvias. *The Garden* 105(7):290–291.

Caye, D. 1994. Clary sage: simple, beautiful. *Flower and Garden* 38(3):64.

Clebsch, Betsy. 1997. *A Book of Salvias*. Timber Press, Portland, Ore.

Compton, James. 1985. Some worthwhile Mexican salvias. *The Garden* 110(3): 122–124.

——. 1993a. Mexican salvias in cultivation. *The Plantsman* 15(4):193–215.

——. 1993b. Salvias from the high Sierras. *The Garden* 118(2):499–501.

Lacy, Allen. 1990. Late-season salvias. *Horticulture* 68(10):36–39.

Martin, Tovah. 1984. Salvia savvy. *Horticulture* 62(7):12–20.

Ogden, Scott. 1993. Tender and hardy salvias. *Fine Gardening* 33:62–67.

Sanvitalia (san vih tal' ee a)   Asteraceae

The genus is named for Federico Sanvitali (1704–1761), who was a professor in Brescia, Italy. About seven species of low-growing annuals occur, but only *Sanvitalia procumbens* has received any garden attention.

-procumbens (pro kum' benz)   creeping zinnia   4–8"/12"
summer   yellow, orange   Central America

This little daisy creeper is easy to raise from seed and is undemanding as to soil and location. The many-branched stems are procumbent, and the opposite, lanceolate to ovate leaves have entire margins. The flowers, which are less than 1" wide, have a purple center and bright yellow to orange ray flowers. Flowering begins in summer and continues most of the season. Plants are pretty enough, but I have seldom seen them covered in flowers, nothing close to what an impatiens can look like. But we have enough impatiens, and some good selections of creeping zinnia would be greatly appreciated.

Flowering is quite good in the North; flowers form well and foliage remains healthy if drainage is adequate. In hot summers, the foliage declines by mid summer, and flowers are sparse at that time. They rebound well as temperatures fall in the autumn but are at their best in spring and early summer. They are better used in patio containers, mixed with upright flowers, than in the ground. Avoid baskets.

Partial shade in the South, full sun can be tolerated in the North. Afternoon shade is recommended most everywhere. Good drainage is essential. Propagate by seed or cuttings.

CULTIVARS

'Gold Braid' has golden double flowers with a brown center.

'Golden Carpet' and 'Yellow Carpet' are very low-growing dwarf forms with small orangish and lemon-yellow flowers, respectively.

'Irish Eyes' is a favorite of mine, with bright orange petals surrounding a green center.

'Mandarin Orange', among the best-known forms, has bright orange single flowers with a black center.

Scabiosa (ska bee o' sa)   scabious   Dipsacaceae

Many of the sixty species of this genus are perennial, and, of these, only two or three are used to any extent in gardens. Similarly, only one annual, *Scabiosa atropurpurea*, is seen, although a couple of others may occasionally be found in florist shops. All make exceptionally good cut flowers.

Quick guide to *Scabiosa* species

	Height	Fragrance	Grown for
S. atropurpurea	2–3'	yes	fresh flowers
S. prolifera	1–2'	no	dried flowers and fruit
S. stellata	1–2'	no	dried flowers and fruit

-*atropurpurea* (at ro per per' ee a) pincushion plant, sweet scabious 2–3'/2'
    summer   purple, crimson   South Africa

This annual species earned one of its common names for its dark purple flower head, whose tufted appearance was thought to resemble a velvet pincushion. The dark flower color also brought death to mind, accounting for another of its common names, mournful widow. The erect branched stems stand upright, without need of support. The basal leaves are lanceolate-ovate and coarsely toothed but become pinnately compound as they ascend the stems. The fully double flowers are sweetly fragrant, forming in late spring and continuing through the summer. Borne singly on long flower stems, they are purple to crimson, but other fine colors have been bred. At the base of the flowers are the whitish overlapping bracts—one way to distinguish the genus from others in the family. Flowers should be deadheaded for persistent bloom.

This species is similar to the popular perennial *Scabiosa caucasica*, but it is available in many more colors and flowers for a longer period of time. Full sun to partial shade, propagate by seed *in situ*.

CULTIVARS

'Ace of Spades' is a terrific plant, with dark purple to almost black honey-fragrant blooms. About 2½' tall. Everyone enjoys this one.

Double Mixed is 2½–3' tall in numerous colors.

Dwarf Double Mixed is only about 15" tall, in many colors.

-*stellata* (ste la' ta)   drumstick scabious   1–3'/1'
   summer   bronze   Mediterranean

Seldom seen in gardens, *Scabiosa stellata* is nevertheless interesting, if not particularly colorful, and a fine everlasting flower, grown by cut flower growers in
this country and abroad. Stems are branched, and the alternate leaves and stems
are covered with short hairs. The leaves are lyrate (similar to pinnately lobed,
only the terminal lobe is much bigger than the side lobes), with a long terminal
lobe. The flowers are pink or bluish white in rounded heads; they dry to a tan-
bronze. Once the seeds form, the entire fruit head becomes everlasting and can
be cut for long-term arrangements.

Full sun, well-drained soils. Propagate by seed.

CULTIVARS

'Drumstick' is 2½' tall, with light blue flowers turning into bronze, globe-
shaped heads.

'Ping Pong' has small white flowers that form rounded seed heads with a
touch of maroon.

Alternative species

Scabiosa prolifera (pro lih' fer a; carmel daisy), a relative of *S. stellata*, is 2' tall
with 2 " creamy yellow flowers arranged in a rounded head. When the petals fall
off, the remaining parts of the flowers form a dense globe that is useful for dried
arrangements.

Quick key to *Scabiosa* species

  A. Flowers borne singly, fragrant . . . . *S. atropurpurea*
AA. Flowers borne in a hemispherical head, not particularly fragrant
      B. Leaves lyrate . . . . *S. stellata*
     BB. Leaves oblong to oblong-lanceolate . . . . *S. prolifera*

Scaevola (skay vo' la)   Goodeniaceae

Australia is known for many things, different things to different people, and to
choose favorites from Down Under is indeed a challenge. Some choose the kangaroo in the bush, others the barrier reefs, or the opera house, or the beaches.
Me, I choose *Scaevola*. The genus has a wide distribution on that continent, ranging from Western Australia to New South Wales. Upon its introduction to the
United States in the mid 1990s, gardeners immediately embraced the color,
habit, and performance of this tough genus. Few plants native to Australia suc-
ceed in mainstream American gardens, where the climate is often too cold for
perennials and too wet and humid for annuals; *Scaevola*, *Helichrysum*, and *Brachycome* are the exceptions.

The generic name is Latin for "left-handed," a reference to the fact that all five petals are on one side (or that the dried flowers look, to some, like a withered hand). Roman lore too supposedly had something to do with the name. Around 506 B.C. (according to Livy), Mucius Cornelius, the king of Clusium, demonstrated his loyalty to Porsenna by placing his right hand in a fire; he was thenceforth known as Scaevola ("Lefty"). Although ninety-six species have been identified, only *Scaevola aemula* has been successful in American landscapes.

-aemula (ay mew′ la)		fan flower	4–9″/18″
summer	blue, purple	eastern Australia, South Australia	

The common name of this species makes more sense to me. Stems are procumbent. The small alternate fleshy leaves, 2″ long by 1″ wide, are lanceolate to oblong, with sharp serrations on the margins. The foliage is tough and somewhat thick and seldom wilts. The solitary flowers occur in the leaf axils, beginning early in the summer and continuing throughout the summer. Plants have no trouble with heat, chewing it up and spitting it out with disdain. I have grown various cultivars for many years, through the hottest, worst summers, and plants just keep on flowering.

Full sun, well-drained soils. The only situation that deters growth is wet soil; heavy soils are not a problem if drainage is adequate. Plants are slow to propagate from cuttings, which problem growers have overcome to produce plants for retailers.

CULTIVARS

'Blue Shamrock' provides dark blue flowers on vigorous plants. Excellent performance in the University of Georgia trials.

Outback series consists of several colors. The most popular and best performers are in the bluish purple range: 'Colonial Fan' is 6–8″ tall with flowers 1″ wide; 'Purple Fan' is about 1′ tall with purple flowers and spreads rapidly, without a doubt among the best cultivars I have tested; 'Royale Fan' is about 18″ tall with light lavender flowers. Other colored forms are less vigorous and have fewer flowers: 'Mini Pink Fan' is 8–12″ tall with bluish pink flowers; 'White Fan' is quite lovely, with many small white flowers. 'Sun Fan' bears small flowers in light blue.

'Sapphire Blue' is similar to 'Purple Fan' and has performed just as well in our trials. Also sold as 'Saphira'.

'White Charm' is a terrific white-flowered form with many small flowers. A nice change from all the blues.

Wonder is another popular series of plants that did well in the Georgia trials. 'Mini Wonder' has small lavender-blue flowers on vigorous but low-growing plants; 'Blue Wonder' bears blue 1″ flowers and spreads rapidly; 'New Wonder' is a fine vigorous selection with 1″ wide flowers, essentially superseding 'Blue Wonder'.

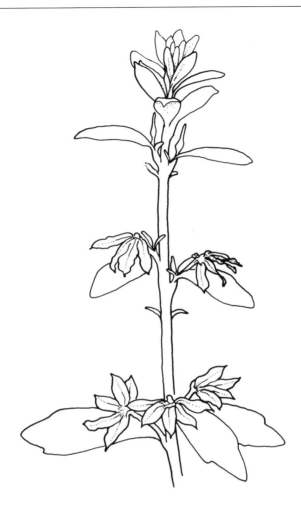

Scaevola aemula 'Blue Shamrock'   ASHA KAYS

Alternative species

Scaevola calliptera (kal ip' ter a; royal robe) is more upright than *S. aemula* and bears flowers that appear to be more open because of the wider distance between the petals. Used in breeding but seldom seen by itself.

Scaevola nitida (tree scaevola) is an upright shrub, growing 6–10' in the Australian bush. I had no luck in Americanizing the species (a long time is needed to obtain a mature plant), but it is well worth a look in frost-free climates.

Scaevola striata has thicker leaves than *S. aemula* and is much slower to colonize. Some of the pink forms have arisen from this species.

Additional reading

Armitage, Allan M. 1997. Scaevola, a well-traveled plant. *Greenhouse Grower* 15(4):61–62.

——. 1998. Fan flower. *Greenhouse Grower* 16(3):87–88.

Schizanthus (shih zan′ thus)
butterfly flower, poor man's orchid   Solanaceae

The deeply divided petals of this relative of the tomato explain one of its common names: the cut petals, particularly in a breeze, resemble a butterfly. When, as a destitute student at the University of Guelph, I first discovered the genus, I thought its beauty and my poverty were particularly well suited for the other common name, and so do many others, as it is known as poor man's orchid throughout North America and the British Isles. Of the twelve or so species, *Schizanthus pinnatus* and hybrids involving it are the most common.

-pinnatus (pih nay′ tus)	butterfly flower	1–2′/2′
summer	many colors	Chile

This is the species responsible for the hybrids most commonly encountered in conservatories, greenhouses, and occasionally gardens. The erect stems branch near the top of the plant, each bearing 3–4″ long leaves that are pinnately cut almost to the midrib, forming six to eight pairs of leaf segments. The segments themselves are about 1″ long and may be serrated or entire. The flowers are formed in a branched inflorescence. The calyx is deeply divided into five linear segments, but it is the corolla that provides the color. The corolla tube is short, not much longer than the calyx, and flares out to form two lips, which are divided into three segments. Two sterile stamens stick out from the flower. The flowers vary in depth of color; the lower lip is usually violet or lilac, the upper, paler, its middle lobe with a yellow blotch at the base, spotted with purple. Obviously, not an easy flower to portray—in fact, as I reread this description, it sounds awful. But in spite of me, the flowers are brilliant. Many variations of those colors appear in the hybrids.

Succeeding with this plant in the garden is not easy in most of the country. The cultural recommendations for *Salpiglossis* may essentially be repeated here: plants tolerate cold climates much better than they do warm climates, and except in northern provinces and states, mountain areas, or gardens on the West Coast, *Schizanthus* will seldom make you proud all season.

Propagate by seed *in situ* in early spring, or by cuttings. Afternoon shade is recommended.

CULTIVARS

Angel Wings Mix is a colorful selection of flowers on 18″ tall plants.
'Cherry Shades' bears 2″ wide flowers in shades of red with maroon stripes.

Disco Mix produces pink and crimson flowers on 6–9" tall plants.

Dr. Bodger's Mix is a time-tested mixture of plants in every conceivable color.

Dwarf Bouquet Mix is about 15" tall, with amber, crimson, pink, rose, and salmon flowers.

'Floraboard' has large brilliant purple flowers with a yellow eye.

Hit Parade Mix grows in a bushier habit, about 15" tall, and produces blooms in shades of pink and mauve.

Star Parade Mix is similar to Hit Parade mix, only shorter.

'Sweet Lips' has orchid-like flowers striped and veined in strong colors.

Alternative species

Schizanthus grahamii (gray ham' ee i) is similar to *S. pinnatus*, but the corolla tube is much longer than the calyx, and the stamens barely stick out from the flower.

Schizanthus ×*wisetonensis* (wise to nen' sis) is a hybrid between *S. pinnatus* and *S. grahamii*, with the habit and foliage of the former and the flower shape of the latter. Most cultivars just listed probably belong under this hybrid form.

Schizopetalon (skit zo pe' ta lon)   Brassicaceae

Another of the many terrific plants in the mustard family, which includes such mainstays as kale and candytuft. But while many gardeners would recognize the genera associated with the names just mentioned, few have heard of *Schizopetalon*. The name comes from the Greek, *schizo* ("to cut") and *petalon* ("petal"), referring to the cut petals. And cut they are. Although the handsome white flowers of the species *S. walkeri* (wal' ker i) have only four petals, each one is deeply cut and appears to consist of four to six claws. There are four green sepals and six stamens. The 5" long alternate leaves are also deeply cut. The other wonderful thing about the flowers is their ephemeral almond scent.

Plants grow 12–15" tall and are best used in rock gardens and areas with good drainage. They do not tolerate much abuse and have been slow to be adopted by American gardeners. Full sun, well-drained gritty soils. Propagate by seed *in situ* after the threat of frost has passed.

Schoenia (sho en' ee a)   Asteraceae

Another of the treasures enjoyed by Australians every spring but only recently discovered by North American gardeners, this genus was named for German ophthalmologist and one-time botanical artist Mattheus Albrecht Schoen. *Schoenia cassiniana* (ka sih nee a' na), a colorful spring-flowering garden plant, is even more well-known as an everlasting cut flower. The 2–4" leaves are linear to lanceolate and mostly basal, although some alternate stem leaves occur. The beautiful pink, papery flowers are held singly in loose inflorescences, and in dry, warm climates, they open in the spring. If deadheaded, they continue for many weeks; if not deadheaded, the flowers will dry on the plants and form interesting vistas of silvery preserved flower heads. In most areas, plants should be cut for arrangements or removed in late spring.

Although only *Schoenia cassiniana* is recognized, a yellow-flowered form is also found in gardens around Perth, Western Australia. It is called *S. filifolia* and is as pretty as any yellow-flowered everlasting I have seen. Unfortunately the name keeps floating around in Never Never Everlasting Land.

Full sun, well-drained soils. Propagate by seed *in situ* in early spring.

Senecio (sen ee' see o)   Asteraceae

This is a huge and diverse genus of about 1000 species, many hardly ornamental and, indeed, often noxious and invasive. Very few species are used in American gardens, with good reason, but such a diversity of germ plasm is bound to contain a hidden gem or two.

-cineraria (sin er ar' ee a)	dusty miller	1–2'/1'
all season	foliage	Mediterranean

Dusty millers have evolved from an interesting gray-leaved plant that was kind of cute to an essential part of the landscaper's palette. Everywhere one looks, one sees circles of red begonias surrounded by dusty millers, like grain farmers holding hands and circling the milkmaids in a May Day dance. No doubt they are terrific plants: they work and are popular because they show off other flowers to their fullest. But let's use a little creativity every now and then—can't we loosen up a little and at least mix them with heliotropes or marguerite daisies?

The leaves are all basal, sometimes entire but often cut into narrow lobes, the terminal lobe being the largest. The silvery gray color is mostly the result of dense white tomentosum or farina on the leaves, which, if you are so inclined, can be rubbed off. The small yellow daisy-like flowers are rather unattractive and seldom occur on the more popular forms. If they do appear, remove them, as they do nothing but detract from the picture.

Full sun to partial shade, propagate by seed.

CULTIVARS

'Cirrus' has a dwarf habit and rounded leaves with shallow lobes. Plants are 8–10" tall.

'New Look' is about 10" tall with almost white leaves in a rounded oakleaf-shape.

'Silver Dust' has deeply lobed (almost filigreed) silver leaves. Up to 15" tall.

Alternative species

Senecio confusus (orangeglow vine) was introduced to me by Lori Crane, a fine nurserywoman in Maryland. My first impression was of bright green narrow foliage and glowing orange daisy-like flowers, flowing down 3' or more from a basket. Flowers by no means cover the vine, but they are brilliant enough to hold your attention. 'Sao Paulo' is offered, but I cannot tell the difference between it and the species. Full sun in the North, afternoon shade in the South. Some taxonomists have reclassified this plant as *Pseudogynoxys* (soo do jin ok' seez) *chenopodioides* (chen o pod ee oy' deez), a charming name obviously designed to further endear this plant to gardeners. Native to Colombia.

Setcreasea (set kres' ee a)   purple heart   Commelinaceae

How many plants of purple heart were killed in dorm rooms, porches, and living rooms when it was sold by the bazillions as a hanging houseplant in the 1960s and 1970s? Then we knew it as wandering jew, and if we didn't kill it, we probably abused it until a few scraggly stems hung disconsolately down from the ugly green plastic pot. Times have changed, however, and the old houseplant has been transformed into a popular ground cover, providing purple color at the base of whatever upright plants it complements. An amazing transformation—which required nothing more than a new look at an old plant.

Plant nomenclature bounces back and forth between *Setcreasea purpurea* and *Tradescantia pallida*. I am not sure which name will finally be agreed upon, so for now, I leave it here. The stems are around 18" long and follow the ground until the end, where they bend toward the sky (decumbent). The succulent smooth leaves are trough-shaped and are sheathed to the stem. They are purple on both sides, but some of the color may change to a burnished green under stress. (The species itself is greener than the far more popular 'Purpurea'; see "Cultivars.") The flowers are handsome but secondary to the foliage. They are three-lobed, pink, and mainly produced in the winter, in the greenhouse; they are not often seen in summer.

This is a species whose terrific abuse tolerance, fine color, and capacity for growth have catapulted it to an important spot in landscape and garden. Beats the heck out of what I used to do to this poor plant back in my college days.

CULTIVARS

'Purpurea', the only cultivar available, offers soft purple leaves all season.

Additional reading

Armitage, Allan M. 1999. Purple heart. *Greenhouse Grower* 17(2):97–98.
Druitt, Liz. 1999. Plunge into purple. *Southern Living* 34(5):18GA.

Silene (si lee′ nee)   campion, catchfly   Caryophyllaceae

Most of the 300 or so species of this genus are cold hardy, and those we grow are generally found in perennial or wildflower gardens, such as Carolina pink (*Silene caroliniana*), fire pink (*S. virginica*), or wild pink (*S. regla*). The few that are grown as annuals seldom have the promotion or visibility of the perennial forms. They are much more widespread in European gardens and roadsides, as many are native to the Mediterranean and throughout Europe. One common name, campion, is also used for *Lychnis*, and the other common name, catchfly, is also used for *Viscaria*. That confusion occurs in identifying such similar plants is not surprising, so for the amateur taxonomists among you, try counting the number of styles (female part of the flower). In *Silene*, there are usually three; in *Lychnis*, there are usually five. The species that seems to jog back and forth between genera most is rose of heaven, which I've discussed as *L. coeli-rosa* in this book. All this taxonomic infighting is exhausting, and normal people need pay those weird style-counting gardeners no attention. They are not dangerous.

Quick guide to *Silene* species

	Height	Flower color	Pubescent
S. armeria	12–20″	pink	no
S. compacta	12–15″	pink	no
S. pendula	6–9″	pink	slightly

-*armeria* (ar me′ ree a)   sweet william, catchfly   12–20″/2′
summer   pink, rose   southern Europe

This showy species from southern Europe is much more widely used on that continent than in North America. The erect stems rise 12–18″ in height, to which clasp smooth gray-green oval leaves, 1–3″ long. The lower leaves are spatula-shaped and wither early in the plant's life. The upper part of the stems is somewhat sticky, giving rise to one of the plant's common names.

The flowers are held in dense terminal clusters of flowers measuring about ¾″ in diameter. The shallowly notched petals range from bright pink to rose. In general, plants do not fare well in warm, humid summers, which tend to sap their strength, but can look fine in the Northeast and upper Midwest. They are best treated as biennials in all climates.

Full sun to partial shade, propagate by seed.

-*pendula* (pend′ yew la)   Mediterranean campion   6–9″/10″
summer   pink   Mediterranean

Plants consist of many weak stems, ascending to about 6″ high. The soft hairy leaves are ovate to ovate-lanceolate and somewhat sharply pointed. The flowers are beautiful, held in loose, drooping sprays, each flower measuring about ½″ across. The five petals are shallowly two-parted. Flowering tends to start in spring and persists until hot, humid weather shuts it down. Beautiful in rock gardens or in containers, where soil and water can be better controlled. Not very good for the South.

Full sun in the North, afternoon shade in the South. Good drainage. Propagate by seed.

CULTIVARS

'Peach Blossom' has light pink to peach-colored flowers. Quite beautiful. 'Snowball' is a white version of 'Peach Blossom'.

Alternative species

Silene compacta (kom pak' ta; syn. *S. orientalis*) is similar to *S. armeria* but with shorter stems and broader leaves. The flowers are a little larger, and the petals are not notched. It too is a biennial.

Quick key to *Silene* species

A. Plant pubescent, to 10" tall, petals two-parted . . . . *S. pendula*
AA. Plant not pubescent, 1–2' tall
    B. Flowers subtended by ovate stem leaves, petals entire . . . *S. compacta*
    BB. Flowers subtended by lanceolate bracts, petals slightly
       notched at tips . . . . *S. armeria*

Additional reading

Armitage, Allan M. 1997. *Herbaceous Perennial Plants*, 2nd ed. Stipes Publishing, Champaign, Ill.
Swezey, Lauren Bonar. 1993. Low growing ground cover for rock gardens. *Sunset* 191(3):42.

Solanum (so la' num)   nightshade   Solanaceae

With about 1400 species, it is no surprise that such a wide range of niche, habit, and flower occurs in this genus. From such economically important crops as potatoes (*Solanum tuberosum*), pepino (*S. muricatum*), and eggplant (*S. melongena*) to vines and houseplants, the diversity is exceptional indeed. Poorly represented in temperate North America, the genus finds its greatest provenance in tropical America and seems to abound in species with poisonous properties. It is difficult to argue with the toxicity of some members, such as bittersweet (*S. dulcamara*); however, the bad reputation has been exaggerated. As an ornamental, only half a dozen species are grown, and while one or two of them enjoy some local acclaim, few are known throughout the country.

Quick guide to *Solanum* species

	Habit	Flower color	Grown for
S. crispum	vine	violet	flowers
S. jasminoides	vine	white	flowers
S. pseudocapsicum	shrubby	white	fruit
S. rantonnettii	shrubby	purple	flowers
S. wendlandii	vine	lilac-blue	flowers

-jasminoides (jaz min oy' deez)   potato vine   vine
summer   white with blue   Brazil

This much-branched vine is spineless and has smooth stems and leaves. The leaves are divided into three entire ovate leaflets, each leaflet 2–3″ long but greatly reduced in size, almost simple, toward the top of the plant. The 1″ wide star flowers are tomato-like and held in short racemes of eight to twelve flowers. The beauty of the flowers is attributable in part to the lemon-yellow stamens, which contrast so well with the white petals.

The vines, like all climbers in the genus, are stem twiners and often require some support to climb. They do well in warmer areas of the country and will tolerate frost to about 28°F. They are terrific in conservatories, where they can attain a fuller size not found in the open. If started in a glass patio in late winter and transplanted to a bright warm area, plants will grow well even in the North.

Full sun, propagate by cuttings.

CULTIVARS

'Alba', by far the most popular form of this vine, has clean white flowers, darker green foliage, and a vigorous habit.

-pseudocapsicum (soo do kap' sih kum)   Jerusalem cherry   1–3′/3′
summer   white   Madeira

I have never seen 3′ tall Jerusalem cherries in a garden; the only ones any of us would recognize are the 9–15″ tall pot plants produced in greenhouses for Christmas sales. And even then I hardly see it: growers and florists probably fear the litigation that would result if someone decided to use the fruit, which is highly toxic, as part of a salad—not a good idea. The leaves are elliptical with pointed tips and wavy margins, and the veins are prominent beneath the leaf, rather than above. The white, star-like flowers are small and usually carried singly (sometimes in twos or threes) in an inflorescence. They are somewhat pendulous in flower but erect when in fruit. It is the rounded fruit, about ½″ wide and bright orange, that has appealed to florists and consumers. When full of fruit, the plants really stand out, and it is not surprising that they are a popular impulse-purchase item. The fruit is succulent and poisonous: not a good plant to have if toddlers are anywhere about.

Partial shade, propagate by seed. Plants are useful in mixed containers and could be produced for garden sales as well as a Christmas crop if the market demanded.

CULTIVARS

'Cherry Jubilee' has multicolored fruit, in white, yellow, and orange.
'Giant Red Cherry' bears large 1″ wide orange-red fruit.
'Paterson' bears many orange-red fruits on a dwarf plant.

-rantonnettii (ran ton et′ ee i)	purple nightshade	3–5′/3′
summer	purple	Argentina

In the States, I occasionally see this species as a container plant in botanical gardens, and even then, plants are uncommon, if not rare. In European gardens, I see it far more often, albeit mostly in public gardens, and nearly always as a trained standard in containers or as an architectural feature rising up from a garden bed. I was pleased to see plants in the rock garden of the Royal Botanic Garden in Burlington, Ontario, where they were competing successfully with blazing amaranths and other colorful annuals. The large stems have dark ridge lines, an easy identification feature for the plant. The simple leaves are entire with slightly wavy margins; they are elliptical to oval and 2–4″ long.

The tomato-like flowers, dark purple to violet with yellow stamens, are slightly lighter colored in the center. They are produced singly or in a few-flowered cluster in the upper leaf axils. They are never produced copiously, but when in good shape, they always draw comment. I think they look far better trained as a standard, where the flowers can be enjoyed, rather than as a multibranched shrub. The 1″ wide red fruit that follows is heart-shaped, drooping, and quite ornamental.

I like this plant, but it will likely remain the pet of greenhouse and botanical garden personnel, who bring out trained material for the public. Most homeowners don't have the time or facilities for training. If a well-trained specimen can be found at the garden center, however, it is definitely worth a try.

Full sun in the North, afternoon shade in the South. Propagate from cuttings.

-wendlandii (wend lan′ dee i)	paradise flower	vine
summer	lilac-blue	Costa Rica

This has to be one of the most beautiful species of the genus, and I am fortunate to have seen it growing profusely both in its native home in Costa Rica and all over a trellis at Heronswood Nursery in Victoria, Australia. Plants bear large stems attached to which are 6–10″ long pinnately divided leaves, consisting of two or three pairs of rather small leaves and a larger (and usually three-divided) terminal segment. It is easy to recognize the plant from the large flowers and stout stems; the formidable hooked spines on the midrib, petiole, and young stems are also painful give-aways. The lilac-blue 2–2½″ wide flowers are held in large forked clusters at the terminals of the many stems. Stunning. The globose fruit is 1–2″ wide.

Plants are grown in Florida, southern California, and the southern Gulf States. In the North, if started plants can be found, put them on a sunny wall and get out of the way. Propagate by cuttings.

CULTIVARS

'Albescens', a form I have not seen, bears off-white flowers.

Alternative species

Solanum capsicastrum (kap sih kas′ trum; false Jerusalem cherry) bears fruit similar to those of *S. pseudocapsicum*, only slightly more oval and less rounded. Plants are hairy compared to the true Jerusalem cherry. Sometimes used by florists. A variegated leaf form, 'Variegatum', is quite handsome.

Solanum crispum (kris′ pum) is better known by well-traveled gardeners than *S. wendlandii* because it is all over such European gardens as England's Sissing-hurst and Ireland's Glasnevin. The lilac-blue flowers are clustered on the woody 6–12′ tall vines, but the cultivar 'Glasnevin' has larger clusters of darker blue flowers and golden yellow stamens. Leaves are simple, not compound. More cold hardiness has been attributed to 'Glasnevin' than to *S. jasminoides*, but I have not noticed it.

Solanum seaforthianum (see for thee a′ num; St. Vincent lilac), like *S. jasminoides*, is a beautiful "unarmed" vine with three leaflets, each 1½–2″ long. Plants grow 10–15′ if given the chance. The light purple to blue flowers are about 1″ in diameter and are held in long drooping racemes. Native to Brazil and more often cultivated in the tropics than in America.

Quick key to *Solanum* species

A. Plant vining
    B. Flowers blue to lilac
        C. Stems prickly . . . . *S. wendlandii*
        CC. Stems not prickly
            D. Leaves simple . . . . *S. crispum*
            DD. Leaves pinnately divided . . . . *S. seaforthianum*
    BB. Flowers white . . . . *S. jasminoides*
AA. Plant not vining
    B. Plant 3–6′ tall, flowers dark purple to violet . . . . *S. rantonnettii*
    BB. Plant 9–24″ tall (at retail), flowers white . . . . *S. pseudocapsicum*

Additional reading

Askey, Linda. 1993. Twine a new vine. *Southern Living* 28(12):4.

Spraguea (spray´ gee a)   Portulacaceae

The genus is named for Isaac Sprague, a nineteenth-century botanical and zoo-logical artist in Cambridge, Massachusetts, who worked for Asa Gray, the au-thor of *Gray's Manual of Botany*, which classic was first published in 1858. About nine species are known, but only the Northwest native, *Spraguea umbellata* (pussy-paws), is grown to any extent, mostly in European or western American gardens.

Plants grow only 4–8˝ tall. The somewhat fleshy 1˝ long leaves are spatula-like and mostly occur in basal rosettes. The flowering stems bear reduced alter-nate leaves and umbellate inflorescences of white or pink flowers. The small flowers consist of two persistent sepals, four petals, and three stamens, which are produced all season long in cool climates. They are native to high elevations and dry, sandy soils and therefore do not perform particularly well in hot or wet summers.

Full sun in the North, afternoon shade in the South. Propagate from seed. Best for containers or rock walls, where drainage can be controlled.

CULTIVARS

'Powder Puffs' has many pink to whitish umbels of flowers on 4˝ tall plants. Similar to the species.

Sprekelia (spre keel´ ee a)   Jacobean lily   Amaryllidaceae

In 1658, Linnaeus was sent a new plant by Johann Heinrich von Sprekelsen of Hamburg, Germany, a lawyer, gardener, and collector of botanical literature, for whom the genus is named. Its sole member is *Sprekelia formosissima* (for mo sis´ ih ma), native to Mexico and also known as St. James lily and Aztec lily.

Plants bear some similarities to the amaryllis but differ by having solitary flowers and irregular petals. The orchid-like flowers, which consist of six deep crimson tepals, are exotic in appearance. The uppermost tepal is wide, the two lateral tepals are strap-shaped, the lowermost is two-lipped, and the two other lower tepals curl toward the base and form a tube. Even the stamens are crim-son. It must be seen to be appreciated. The flowers are borne on sturdy 12–18˝ tall stems, seldom more than one per bulb. The three to six narrow strap-like leaves are 15–20˝ long and arise after the flower from the large brown bulb.

Bulbs are frost tender and are best treated as conservatory plants or placed in containers on the patio for spring or early summer bloom. Wherever conditions support an amaryllis, a sprekelia can be enjoyed too. Plant the bulb with the top barely exposed, and refrain from watering until the leaves start to appear. Increase irrigation until the foliage begins to decline, after the flower has come and gone. In most gardens, bulbs should be lifted in fall and overwintered at around 40–45°F.

Partial shade, well-drained soils. Propagate by seed. At least three years are needed for flowering-size bulbs.

Stachytarpheta (sta kee tar' fe ta)
false vervain, snakeweed   Verbenaceae

The sixty-five species of the genus are in the verbena family, meaning they are all characterized by four-sided stems; opposite or alternate leaves, mostly toothed and wrinkled; and a five-lobed flower. These annuals or small shrubs are already valued by the few who cultivate them for their erect spikes of blue, pink, or white flowers, and they are gathering more of a following as people learn about them. But don't hand one to a Florida gardener; they are weed-like in that state.

-jamaicensis (ja may sen' sis)   Jamaica vervain, blue snakeweed   2-4'/3'
   summer   blue   tropical America

The species is sometimes called by its old name, *Stachytarpheta indica*, and may be mixed up in the trade with *S. urticaefolia* (blue rat's tail) and *S. ×intercedens*. Plants have been naturalized in frost-free areas but originate throughout the tropics of Central and North America, including the island of Jamaica (hence the specific epithet). The branches are four-sided, and the leaves are 2-4″ long, opposite or alternate. They are variable, mostly ovate to oblong, coarsely serrated on the margins, and slightly pointed at the tips. The inflorescence can be up to 12″ long.

Oh, but what a tease this plant is! No doubt about it: until you, the unsuspecting gardener, realize how it flowers, you will not enjoy it. Don't expect a column of blue, all at once. The long thick spike (the generic name comes from the Greek, *stachys*, "spike," and *tarphys*, "thick") releases only two or three flowers at a time; every day, for weeks on end, a few more ½″ wide light to dark blue flowers open while yesterday's disappear. The flowers consist of a five-lobed calyx, small bracts at the base, a blue corolla, and two stamens. The spike is constantly in flower, but never in its glory. Obviously, a plant only plant lovers can love. We have had them in the Georgia gardens in beds and containers, and they have done well in both.

Full sun, propagate by cuttings.

Alternative species

Stachytarpheta ×intercedens (in ter see' denz), a hybrid between *S. urticaefolia* and *S. jamaicensis*, is intermediate but closer to the latter than the former. Leaves are darker green, plants more upright, and the flowers larger than those of Jamaica snakeweed. Flowers are usually dark blue.

Stachytarpheta mutabilis (mew ta' bih lis; pink snakeweed) is taller (up to 8') than *S. jamaicensis* and has thick leaves that are softly hairy on the undersides. The inflorescence can be up to 2' long with showy flowers that start crimson or red and fade to different shades of pink.

Stachytarpheta urticaefolia (er tis ay fo' lee a; blue rat's tail) can be distinguished from *S. jamaicensis* by the conspicuously blistered or puckered leaves, which are always opposite and decussate (adjacent pairs of leaves are at right angles to each other).

Stachytarpheta jamaicensis   ASHA KAYS

Steirodiscus (steer o dis' kus)   Asteraceae

About five species of this little-known genus occur, but only the South African species, *Steirodiscus tagetes*, is occasionally offered. Plants are only about 10″ tall and prove useful in small beds or mixed containers. The variability of the leaves is great: they may be alternate or spirally arranged; they may be shallowly or deeply cut into linear segments, providing a ferny appearance. The flowers look somewhat like small marigolds (thus the specific name), with yellow to orange ray flowers and deeper orange centers. They are less than 1″ wide and sit on 3″ long flower stems.

Full sun in the North, afternoon shade in the South. Propagate by seed.

CULTIVARS

'Gold Rush' is 6″ tall with ½″ wide flowers over fern-like foliage.

Streptocarpus (strep to kar' pus)   Cape primrose   Gesneriaceae

Perhaps you are familiar with the popular houseplant Cape primrose (also known as Bavarian belles), with its large tubular flowers and long crinkled lanceolate leaves. Many of the more than 130 species in this genus, like that houseplant and many others, are stemless; all the stemless forms are in the subgenus *Streptocarpus*, and the houseplant you recently bought is a hybrid of many species (generally classified as *S.* ×*hybridus*).

Species with stems are grouped into the subgenus *Streptocarpella*; species in this subgenus are excellent plants for hanging baskets and outdoor containers. Some members of subgenus *Streptocarpella*, such as *Streptocarpus kirkii, S. holstii*, and *S. stomandrus*, are winter-flowering and best seen in the conservatory or winter greenhouse.

Species that are useful for summer baskets and containers are similar in appearance, with small ovate leaves and 1–1½″ long lavender tubular flowers. They may be *Streptocarpus glandulosissimus, S. orientalis*, or *S. saxorum*, but it is difficult to know just what is being sold out there. Quite truthfully, this really doesn't matter: given low light and consistent moisture, plants are full of flowers throughout the summer into the fall.

Whatever is bought under the name *Streptocarpus* or *Streptocarpella* will enjoy filtered light and moist, but not wet, soils. Propagate by cuttings. Plant when temperatures are above 65°F.

CULTIVARS

'Concord Blue' bears many lavender-blue flowers.
'Dancing Flowers' are 8–12″ tall with violet-blue flowers on wiry stems.
'Sparkle' bears wine-colored flowers.

Strobilanthes (stro bih lan' theez)   Acanthaceae

A terrific genus for every garden—except the one that receives little sun. Plants are grown for the colorful foliage; flowers seldom occur during the growing season in temperate climates. Some 250 species are known to taxonomists, yet only recently have we been able to find even a single representative of this genus at the garden center.

-dyerianus (di er ee ay' nus)	Persian shield	3–5'/3'
winter	foliage	Burma

I remember seeing this species grown as a houseplant, in 4" containers, many years ago. Most of the time plants died in record time for lack of light on the coffee table, or too much or too little water. Someone must have planted a near-gone specimen outside—instead of flushing it down the toilet, like a pet crocodile—and eureka, it too grew. The simple fact is this: all you have to do is put it in the ground and watch it grow. Persian shield has become a popular garden plant for beds and containers, a purple foil in the summer garden.

The opposite, ovate to lanceolate leaves, measuring 6–9" long and 3–4" wide, are the most dynamic part of this robust shrub; they are sessile, toothed, and flushed purple with silver iridescence above, dark purple beneath. Plants look best when they are young; they sometimes become too woody and overgrown by

Strobilanthes dyerianus   ASHA KAYS

late summer. An early pinch helps branches to form and plants to remain attractive. Flowers seldom occur in the growing season but may be seen in the winter greenhouse; when plants flower in greenhouses, it is impossible to obtain sufficient cuttings for production, resulting in a shortage of plants the following spring—a secondary problem for consumers. The pale blue flowers are held in short cone-like inflorescences at the top of the stems. The tubular flowers are five-lobed with two to four stamens. In research at University of Georgia, it appears that a combination of cool temperatures and shorter days results in flower initiation. Cool weather causes leaves to blanch and the iridescent look to disappear, so some feel it is a southern plant only. Wrong. Some of the most exuberant specimens I have seen were in the New York Botanical Garden, and landscapers as far north as Cleveland have found plants to be excellent.

Full sun or afternoon shade, propagate by terminal cuttings.

Alternative species

Strobilanthes isophyllus (bedding conehead) is quite different, grown more for the flowers than the essentially green foliage. The willow-like leaves are equal, narrow-lanceolate, and 2–4″ long. Flowers are gathered in a blunt cone-like terminal inflorescence, each blush-pink, blue, or white bloom about 1″ long.

Additional reading

Armitage, Allan M. 1997. Persian shield. *Greenhouse Grower* 15(14):93–94.

Stylomecon (sti lo me′ kon)   flaming poppy   Papaveraceae

Hardly known outside California, this western genus consists of a single species, *Stylomecon heterophyllum* (he ter a′ fil um), native to California. Plants grow about 2′ tall, with alternate deeply cut 4″ long leaves. Each segment of the cut leaves is usually entire but may be dissected again. If the stem is broken or a leaf removed, yellow sap will bleed. The copper-orange flowers are borne on 6–8″ long flower stems, which occur in mid summer. Although you may have to sniff a couple of times to place it, the distinct fragrance of lily-of-the-valley is given off by the flowers.

Full sun in the North, afternoon shade in the South. Propagate by seed *in situ* in early spring.

Sutera (soo ter′ a)   bacopa   Scrophulariaceae

Originally known as members of *Bacopa*, plants have now been accepted under *Sutera*, which genus itself is undergoing further taxonomic study. In fact, some recently introduced plants, first included in *Bacopa*, belong to yet another closely related genus, *Jamesbrittenia*, not *Sutera*. We'll all get it right one of these days.

People who grow these plants should use bacopa as a common name, so we will improve our chances of knowing what plant we are talking about. All are trailing plants, probably *Sutera grandiflora*, and most consist of small (<½" long) opposite leaves with slightly wavy margins and small star-shaped five-petaled flowers. The flowers are generally less than 1" across, but well-grown plants may be covered with blooms and can be brilliant. I have seen baskets flowing 6' to the ground with the flowers of the common color, lavender-white, all along the stems, and new colors are being introduced constantly.

In the North and West, these are outstanding fillers, consorting well with many plants and swelling baskets and containers to a plumpness seldom seen. In hotter climates, they are not as vigorous, and, while they are fine fillers, they don't have the pizzazz found elsewhere.

Afternoon shade is recommended, as is copious water when plants mature. Best for hanging baskets and containers; it's a poor "in-ground" plant.

CULTIVARS

'African Sunset' was a breakthrough in color, with large (1") flowers of an interesting dusky red. The plants are quite lanky and must be combined with other plants, or they will look ragged.

'Candy Floss Blue' bears deep blue flowers. Perhaps a selection of *Sutera cordata*.

Sutera grandifolia 'African Sunset'
ASHA KAYS

'Giant Snowflake' has larger white flowers than other whites. Plants fared well in the University of Georgia trials.

'Lavender Storm' has lavender flowers on green foliage.

'Olympic Gold' is certainly different, with clean-looking yellow-and-green variegated foliage and small white flowers. The variegation tends to fade in the summer, but small flowers are produced for a long period of time. Its performance is not yet established throughout the country, but it should gain some popularity.

Penny Candy series, which properly belongs in *Jamesbrittenia*, provides flowers in pink, rose, and violet. The foliage is thinner and more divided than that of *Sutera*, and the flowers are bicolored and bigger. They are good-looking plants: the flowers of pink and rose are about ¼" wide, while those of violet are nearly 1" in diameter.

Showers series consists of 'Bridal Showers' (white), 'Blue Showers' (lavender-blue), and 'Lavender Showers' (excellent lavender flowers). All have flowers around ½" wide.

'Snowstorm', an earlier form, remains extraordinarily popular. Spreading habit, small white flowers.

Swainsona (swayn so' na)   Fabaceae

One plant I can't get enough of is *Swainsona formosa* (for mo' sa), the Sturt desert pea. I first saw this species grown as a greenhouse crop in Perth, Western Australia, and figured growers there simply knew what they were doing. But when I saw plants looking just as good in the botanical garden at King's Park, I knew that, even though Australian plants are notoriously difficult to grow in the States, I had to try some in Athens. I obtained some seed, and lo and behold, they germinated easily. We had no trouble growing a sufficient number to plant out in the spring. Troubles, however, were just around the corner.

The species is actually a small shrub in its native habitat and is short-lived even at home. The long prostrate stems are silky-pubescent, with alternate 5–6" long leaves consisting of nine to twenty-one leaflets, each ½–1" long. The gray-green leaves are sparsely pubescent above, densely downy beneath. Plants grow only about 1' tall but may spread to 3' in width. The flowers are spectacular, consisting of brilliant scarlet keeled flowers with a glossy black slightly protruding eye. The most obvious part of the flower, the keel, is 2–3" long. The flower must be seen to be appreciated—no amount of prose can do it justice.

Unfortunately the species is susceptible to numerous plant fungi, which attack the plant's roots and then its crown—and the plant, beautiful though it may have been, tends to lose its charm when it dies. Death does that to charm, particularly in plants. In Athens, all plants succumbed to heat and humidity by mid summer, and Athens was not unique. Even in King's Park, the Sturt desert pea was known as a somewhat wimpy plant, susceptible to many stresses. In Australia, the species is often grafted to rootstock of perennial relative *Swainsona puniceus*, or to *Colutea arborescens* (bladder senna), a small tree from southern

Swainsona formosa ASHA KAYS

Europe, which practice increases the resulting plant's vigor and decreases its susceptibility to root diseases.

Greg Kirby of Flinders University in Adelaide, South Australia, has been on the hunt for stronger plants and different-colored flowers for many years, and breeding work in Australia has already provided more robust plants as well as salmon, rose, and off-white flowers. And Jeff Adkins, another of our fine graduate students at Georgia, worked to select stronger plants from a large population. Nevertheless, plants will remain uncommon in American landscapes for the foreseeable future. We will continue to make selections, and people will continue to "ooh" and "aah" over plants in our trial gardens—until early July.

I was pulling my hair out trying to decide if I should put these plants under *Swainsona* or the other genus that taxonomists have been using, *Clianthus*. Since I was probably the only one who cared, I decided to consult my Australian experts, Rodger and Gwen Elliot. I wish I had not! Apparently both names are being dropped in favor of *Willdampia formosa*, named after British explorer William Dampier, who first collected plants in 1699. No wonder my students say I drive them crazy—I drive myself crazy! I will keep the plant under the genus *Swainsona* for now, pretending I never consulted the Elliots, but things will surely change.

Full sun to afternoon shade, propagate by seed. Excellent drainage is mandatory; plants are best placed in containers, where sharp drainage can be assured.

Additional reading

Elliot, Gwen. 2000. Sturt desert pea. *Australian Hort.* 98(2):14.

Williams, R. R. 1996. *Swainsona formosa*. In *Native Australian Plants*, Krystyna Johnson and Margaret Burchett, eds. University of New South Wales Press, Sydney, Australia.

T

Tagetes (ta jee′ teez)   marigold   Asteraceae

Tages is an obscure figure in Etruscan mythology, but he had pretty good parentage. The son or grandson of Jupiter, he supposedly sprang from newly plowed fields in Etruria (present-day Tuscany, Umbria, and Latium, in Italy) and taught the Etruscans the omens for lightning, winds, and eclipses—not an easy task. For all his trouble, Linnaeus named the marigold in his honor. This common name will mean different plants to different people. In Europe, it is often synonymous with the pot marigold, *Calendula*; in Africa, species of *Dimorphotheca* are the sun marigolds, and *Caltha palustris* is the marsh marigold. But in America, the genus *Tagetes* is the undisputed owner of the marigold moniker. The term "marigold" may be traced back to earliest English writings. Monks and nuns assumed that the Virgin Mary wore a yellow flower on her breast as a material symbol of the golden glow radiating from her head. By medieval times, the flower was called "Mary's gold," later "marygold"; finally the spelling we now use evolved. In the language of flowers, marigolds represent sorrow and despair; in Mexico, they are called *la flor de la muerte* ("the flower of death"). Here, they are simply referred to as bedding plants. The roots of several species, the best known being *T. minuata* (mister-john-henry), produce insecticidal or allelopathic herbicidal compounds. Various species deter such weeds as celandine, ground elder, and even bindweed, and bedding plant forms have been used effectively around potatoes and tomatoes as a barrier to non-beneficial nematodes. These chemical deterrents are not produced until plants are fully mature, so plants used for such purposes should be started in the greenhouse early and planted out as mature specimens.

The enormous success of marigolds has of course led to badmouthing; they are the constant brunt of disdain from plant snobs, who "would not have a marigold" in their garden to save their life. To have such an attitude is to dismiss an outstanding genus, which has and continues to provide season-long color in landscapes and gardens all over North America. I do nevertheless have a first-hand frontline warning about this genus: it has a particularly peppery odor and a debilitating effect on those of us who suffer from hay fever. I worked on marigolds as part of my Ph.D. thesis, and never have I gone through more tissue, handkerchiefs, and anything else available to blow my nose in. I would be in the lab measuring and sniffing, in the garden, planting and crying—and totally useless by the end of the day. In the trials at the University of Georgia, we still evaluate dozens of cultivars every year, but I refuse to do the sniff test any longer. I admire with eyes only. Thank goodness for others with less marigold-sensitive noses.

Approximately fifty species are known. Three are used extensively in gardens, but others have their moments in regional gardens.

Quick guide to *Tagetes* species

	Height	Flower width	Cultivars
T. erecta	1–4'	2–4"	few
T. patula	6–12"	1–2"	many
T. tenuifolia	8–18"	½–1"	many

-erecta (e rek′ ta)	African marigold, American marigold	1–4'/2'
summer	yellow, gold	Mexico

Other common names for this species are big marigold, which makes sense, and Aztec marigold, based on its origins; both official vernacular names, African marigold and American marigold, make no sense whatsoever. I suppose trying to understand plant names is futile—we should simply enjoy their beauty. In general, this species is distinguished by angular stems and the eleven to seventeen leaflets on the pinnate leaves, which often have large purple glands near the margins. The segments are sharply toothed and lanceolate in shape. Until about 1985, it was easy to tell African marigolds from others because they were always big and robust. In fact, I remember using Crackerjack marigolds as a 3–4' tall hedge, a common enough procedure that prompted yet another common name, hedge marigold. Most cultivars are around 2' tall, and some bred as dwarfs are barely taller than a common French marigold.

The solitary flowers are terminal, generally 2–4" across, and made up of numerous ray flowers forming double globes in orange, yellow, and gold. The weight of these large flowers can be a drawback: snapping of the flower stem is not uncommon, particularly after rains. And deadheading, a particularly odious and boring task, is essential for prolonged bloom; if plants are not deadheaded, flowers turn black with the fungus *Botrytis*. Spider mites and thrips are also problems. In fact, in the UGA Horticulture Gardens, where we trial dozens of cultivars, marigolds demand a significant portion of maintenance time; we often remove them in mid summer and reseed in late summer, enjoying the flowers a second time, in cooler fall climates, when disease and insect pressure is diminished. After all, seed is easier on the pocketbook than deadheading is on the back.

Dozens of cultivars have been bred. All should be planted in early spring, or sown *in situ* at that time. Full sun and deadheading are musts.

CULTIVARS

Antigua series bears 3″ wide double flowers on 2′ tall plants. Flowers occur in gold, orange, primrose, and yellow. Performed well in the University of Georgia trials.

Atlantis series bears well-rounded double 3-3½″ flowers on 12-15″ tall plants. Available in orange and yellow.

Crackerjack is an older series still available from seed. Plants are 3-4′ tall with large flowers that fall over with the first rain. Other, more compact series are far better, unless a marigold hedge is desired.

Crush series is 15-18″ tall with 3-3½″ wide double flowers in gold ('Papaya Crush'), bright yellow ('Pineapple Crush'), and orange ('Pumpkin Crush').

Discovery, an excellent series and a major breakthrough in African marigolds, combines the large double African flower with the height of the French marigold. Available in gold and orange.

Excel series is a winner. Plants are up to 2′ tall, bearing 3-3½″ wide double flowers in gold, orange, primrose, and yellow.

'French Vanilla' tries to answer the question, "Is there a white marigold out there?" The answer is no, but this is somewhat whiter than others. Seed is seldom available.

Galore series offers fully double forms in gold, orange, and yellow. Plants are 2-3′ tall. 'Yellow Galore' was an All-America Selection in 1977.

'Gold and Vanilla' is about 2½′ tall with a mix of orange, yellow, and gold, and a whitish flowered form as well.

Gold Coin series is 3-3½′ tall with 3-4″ wide double flowers of light orange ('Double Eagle') and yellow ('Doubloon').

Guys and Dolls series is only 15″ tall with large gold, orange, and yellow double flowers.

Inca series made African marigolds popular. They are compact with 4″ wide double blooms of gold, orange, and yellow. Superseded by other more compact forms, they are still excellent performers.

Jubilee series is 3-4′ tall with 3″ wide flowers of yellow ('Diamond Jubilee') and orange.

Lady series has 3½″ wide flowers on 3-4′ tall plants. Colors include gold, orange, primrose, and yellow ('First Lady').

Marvel series is 18-12″ tall with double flowers of gold, orange, and yellow.

Perfection series bear ball-shaped double flowers of gold, orange, and yellow. Plants are 2-3′ tall.

Sumo series has 3″ wide double flowers in a mixture of orange, primrose, and yellow.

Triploid forms

These plants, the result of interspecific crosses, are vigorous and set little seed. Seed is therefore expensive, but the resulting hybrids are long-flowering and can be quite impressive.

'Little Nell' provides single gold-yellow flowers with a red blotch. Plants are 12-15″ tall.

Tagetes erecta 'Inca Yellow'   ASHA KAYS

'Nell Gwynn' bears large semi-double golden yellow flowers on 12–15″ tall plants.

Nugget series has large double flowers in three or so colors.

Solar series is a double form, only 9–12″ tall. Flowers are gold, orange, red (red blotch), and sulfur.

'Suzie Wong' is shorter than others but with single gold-yellow flowers.

Zenith series is a semi-double (crested) to double-flowered form in golden yellow, lemon-yellow, orange, orange and red, red and gold, and yellow. Outstanding for initial color and form.

| *-patula* (pa′ chew la) | French marigold | 6–12″/12″ |
| summer | yellow, orange with red | Mexico |

French marigolds are so common that they hardly require description, and the cultivars continue to roll off the breeding line. In general, they are distinguished from the African forms by their shorter stature, more bushy habit, and smaller flowers. The flowers occur in many forms, including single, semi-double, and double, and often as not have a touch of red in the ray petals.

Plants have circular stems, usually stained purple, with pinnate leaves in nine to twelve lanceolate segments, each ½–1″ long. The solitary flowers are held on 1–2″ long flower stems and continue throughout the summer. The ray flowers occur in many colors, including red, red-brown, and multicolored. French marigolds are more popular than African marigolds: their smaller flowers cover the plants at times; their flowers do not become so heavy after a rain that they fall over, snapping the flower stems; and their smaller size allows them to be used in more situations than the bigger, taller Africans.

French marigolds do however present the gardener with the same maintenance challenges as African marigolds: deadheading is necessary, as is war against the numerous diseases and insects that gather for ravaging and fine dining. A second planting in mid to late summer in warmer climates ensures beauty into the fall.

Full sun. Propagate by seed *in situ* or start inside and transplant in spring.

CULTIVARS

Aurora series is about 12″ tall with 2–2½″ wide double flowers. They come in gold, light yellow, orange, red, and red with yellow.

Bonanza series is highly popular, showing good performance in most of the country. The double flowers are about 2″ wide, and plants are 10–12″ tall. Besides gold, orange, and yellow, selections include Bee (mahogany with yellow edges), Bolero (maroon petals with gold edges, an All-America Selection in 1999), Harmony (deep orange with maroon edges), and Spry (yellow with maroon edges).

Bonita series is generally 10–12″ tall in a mixture of colors. 'Baby Bonita' is smaller.

Bounty series is available in gold, orange, yellow, and bicolors (Flame and Spry).

Boy series is dwarf (6–10″ tall) with double flowers in gold, orange, yellow, Harmony (deep orange with maroon centers), Spry (yellow with maroon edges), and a mix ('Boy O' Boy').

Disco is a single-flowered series with 2″ wide flowers on 12″ plants. Selections include Flame (red and gold bicolor), golden, yellow, Marietta (golden yellow with mahogany center), orange, Queen (yellow and maroon), and yellow.

Gate is an impressive series with 2½–3″ wide flowers on 12–14″ tall plants. They appear to be intermediate between French and African forms. 'Golden Gate' (mahogany with gold) is outstanding, an All-America Selection in 1989; 'Orange Gate' and 'Yellow Gate' round out the series.

'Golden Guardian', with single golden orange flowers, is being sold as a nematicide. Reports concerning its effectiveness are glowing. I have not trialed it as an ornamental nor as an allelopathic companion plant, but it is certainly worth a try if nematodes are a problem in the vegetable patch.

Hero series is only 8–10″ tall with double flowers: Bee (mahogany with yellow edging), Flame (golden orange with red centers), gold, Harmony (deep orange with maroon centers), orange, Spry (yellow with maroon edges), and yellow.

'Honeycomb' has large mahogany-red flowers edged with gold.

Jaguar series is similar to the better-known Disco series, but the gold petals are splotched with maroon.

Janie series, an All-America Selection in 1980, is 6–10″ tall with 2″ wide double flowers in bright yellow, deep orange, Flame (golden orange), Harmony (primrose), and Spry (tangerine).

Little Devil series produces flat-topped double flowers about 1½″ wide. They include Bicolor (yellow centers with maroon edges), Fire (maroon petals with yellow edges), Flame (red and orange bicolor), and yellow.

Little Hero is similar to Hero series but is only 6–10″ tall and more compact, with smaller flowers. Can be recommended for hotter summers.

Marietta is an old but wonderful series—single flowers, various colors, and vigorous (too vigorous for many tastes). 'Golden Marietta' (gold flowers) and 'Naughty Marietta' (golden yellow flowers sporting a large maroon blotch) are still available.

'Mr. Majestic' sports single flowers with mahogany-red stripes on bright yellow petals. Quite impressive.

Safari series is well known and enjoys immense popularity. Double flowers are 2½″ wide on 12″ plants. Gold, orange, primrose, 'Queen' (russet red edged with gold), red, scarlet, tangerine, and yellow flowers make up the series.

'Spanish Brocade' bears 2″ wide gold and red bicolored semi-double flowers.

Sunspot series is about 12″ tall in gold, orange, and yellow.

'Tiger Eyes' has rounded flowers with yellow centers and red edges.

| *-tenuifolia* (ten yew ih fo′ lee a) | signet marigold | 8–18″/1′ |
| summer | yellow, orange | Mexico |

The signet marigold, arguably the prettiest species, is far less known than *Tagetes patula*. Its lack of popularity reflects a lack of breeding efforts, not a serious deficiency in the plant itself: there are simply fewer cultivars in front of the gardening public. That it is a marigold means it brings to the table many of the same deadheading, insect, and disease problems as other species, but to a lesser degree. Several excellent cultivars display great vigor and provide a totally different marigold look.

This different look is courtesy of the leaves, which are pinnately divided into thirteen to twenty-three very narrowly lanceolate segments; such fern-like foliage makes plants reasonable garden subjects even when not in flower. Plants can be big; although most cultivars have been bred to remain about 12″ tall, 18″ is not uncommon. The drawback to this beautiful mounding foliage is that in mid to late summer, particularly in warm, moist summers, foliar diseases can be a serious problem, as can be thrips and mites. Flowers are single, consisting of only a few ray flowers, generally yellow or bicolored. Deadheading is beneficial, as is an occasional foliar spray. If problems become serious, simply pull the suckers out and reseed *in situ* for additional plants in late summer and fall.

Full sun. Propagate by seed *in situ* or start inside and transplant in spring.

CULTIVARS

Gem series is 6-12″ tall with 1-1½″ wide single flowers of gold, lemon, and tangerine-orange.

'Lulu' is packed with single lemon-yellow flowers on mounded plants. Among the best I have seen.

'Ornament' has maroon-colored single flowers.

'Paprika' has red petals edged in gold.

Starfire Mix bears 1½″ wide single bicolored flowers of orange, red, and yellow. Outstanding.

Alternative species

Tagetes lucida (loo′ sih da; sweet marigold) is similar to *T. tenuifolia* but has simple, not pinnate, leaves and small two- to three-petaled flowers. The flowers have a far more agreeable odor, even to my nose. The foliage has been used as a substitute for tarragon, which it resembles in flavor. Terrific for southern gardeners.

Quick key to *Tagetes* species

A. Leaves simple, not pinnately divided . . . . *T. lucida*
AA. Leaves pinnately divided
    B. Rays few, usually about five, heads <1″ wide . . . . *T. tenuifolia*
    BB. Rays many, heads >1″ wide
        C. Flowers often marked with red, heads usually around
          1½″ wide . . . . *T. patula*
        CC. Flowers not marked with red, heads usually 2–4″ wide . . . .
        . . . . *T. erecta*

Additional reading

Askey, Linda. 1993. The Smith's answer to tarragon. *Southern Living* 28(6): 82.
Smittle, Delilah. 1997. Magnificent marigolds. *Organic Gardening* 44(1):54–59.
Winterrowd, Wayne. 1998. Marigolds. *Horticulture* 95(7):50–52.

Tecomaria (te ko ma′ ree a)   Cape honeysuckle   Bignoniaceae

Native to the Cape area of South Africa, the genus is represented by a single species, *Tecomaria capensis* (ka pen′ sis). Plants are closely related to our native trumpet creeper (*Campsis radicans*) and to the not-so-common trumpet bush (*Tecoma stans*), from Central America; the former is a vigorous climber, the latter, a tropical shrub seldom seen in this country except in the most tropical areas. Both bear large showy tubular flowers. Cape honeysuckle, by contrast, is a plant that can be used as an annual in much of United States to spectacular effect. In temperate areas, plants grow 3–4' tall, but where they perennialize (zones 8 to 10), they are small shrubs to small trees.

The leaflets are in three to five pairs, each about 1" long and half as wide, with serrated margins. The tubular flowers are formed in terminal inflorescences in mid to late summer; they are deeply two-lipped and show off the exserted stamens and pistil. Flowers range from scarlet to orange as well as yellow. We trialed this species in Athens, and although it seemed a long time before plants flowered, once they did, they were quite beautiful. Flowering occurred on 3–4' tall shrubs in early September. Overwintering may occur as far north as zone 7.

Full sun, propagate by terminal cuttings.

CULTIVARS

'Apricot' is a compact grower, about 3' tall, with orange flowers.
'Aurea' has 2" long glossy green leaves and bright gold flowers.
'Coccinea' bears wine-colored flowers.
'Lutea' is a low grower with strong yellow blooms.
'Salmonea' produces pale pink to orange flowers.

Thunbergia (thun ber′ gee a)   Acanthaceae

In the latter part of the eighteenth century, a young man from Sweden began studying medicine at the University of Uppsala, where he soon came under the influence of Linnaeus. After graduating in 1770, he was talked into joining the Dutch East India Company as a physician and was asked by the Dutch growers to send back plants from his travels, mainly in South Africa and Japan. He spent about ten years traveling, collecting, and studying. His name was Carl Peter Thunberg, and his reward was immortality every time a gardener plants a seed of black-eyed susan vine, clock vine, or any number of plants with the epithet *thunbergii*. After his travels, he became a professor at the University of Uppsala, teaching and preparing his botanical works.

This genus is represented by about a hundred species, most but not all self-twining vines. Some are well known, but a few should be used more often. Most are tender annuals or perennials to zone 8, occasionally zone 7.

Quick guide to *Thunbergia* species

	Habit	Flower color
T. alata	vine	yellow-orange with black eye
T. battiscombei	bush	violet-blue
T. grandiflora	vine	sky blue
T. gregorii	vine	orange

-alata (a la′ ta)   black-eyed susan vine   vine
   late summer   yellow-orange   tropical East Africa

I don't remember too many plants in our garden in Montreal, other than grass for cutting, a few scraggly hollyhocks, and this plant, which we treated as an annual. The memory from many years ago is clear: I can still see it, flowing down from a basket or climbing up some wooden posts, providing cheerful color. And although newer cultivars provide wonderful new colors, the old orange vine is still around and still brings a smile to my face.

The species produces opposite, somewhat triangular bright green leaves, 2–3″ long, along skinny twining squarish stems. The distinctive petiole appears to have two "wings," one on either side, and it is to this winged petiole that the epithet *alata* refers. The 2″ long, 1″ wide solitary flowers consist of small sepals surrounded by two large inflated bracts and five colorful petal lobes; they are borne in the upper leaf axils. Flowers always have a dark eye. The common color is yellow-orange, but that common color is not so common in the newer cultivars. Primrose and white are also grown.

Full sun or afternoon shade. Water well. Can be propagated from cuttings, but seed is just as easy. Soak the seeds overnight and sow *in situ* after frost, or start indoors. Plants grown from seed *in situ*, or transplanted to the garden in the spring, generally begin to flower in late summer; if plants are started indoors earlier, flowering begins a little earlier. Plants may either be left to spill over baskets or containers or placed near structures around which the stems can twine.

CULTIVARS

   'Alba' has creamy white petals with a dark eye.
   'Aurantiaca' is a brilliant orange.
   'Beauty Spots' is a collection of white, sulfur, and orange flowers.
   'Sulphurea' bears sulfur-yellow blooms.
   'Susie Orange' is outstanding—orange flowers without the dark eye.

-battiscombei (ba tis kom′ bay)   bush thunbergia   1–2′/4′
   late summer   violet-blue   tropical Africa

When I first grew this species, I was not impressed. I thought it should climb, but it wouldn't. Shows who the real boss is out there. It did its own scrambling thing, and I realized that if I left it alone, it wouldn't disappoint. I did, and it didn't.

Plants have thick stems with dark green triangular leaves, measuring 3–4″ long and half as wide. The foliage is glossy, clean, and handsome. Plants will slowly scramble over and through other perennials or even small shrubs. They really show off their beauty if allowed to grow near light green or golden foliage; even in flower, plants can get lost among dark green material, simply because the contrast is poor. At times, they can look weedy, especially when they are just scrambling around, apparently getting in the way of other plants you are trying to grow. But when the five-lobed, 2″ wide violet-blue flowers form in the upper axils of the stems, they will be noticed once, and then again and again. The classical appearance of the blooms is heightened by their nicely contrasting yellow throats. Plants have returned for us (zone 7) for two winters, but I still consider it an annual, even in Athens.

Full sun to afternoon shade, propagate by cuttings.

-*grandiflora* (gran dih flor′ a)   sky vine, clock vine   vine
   fall   light blue   northern India

A favorite in the genus *Thunbergia*, this large-flowered vine teases most of the summer with nice vigorous growth, but no flowers. The large 7–8″ long glossy green leaves are roughly pubescent, with toothed margins and palmate veins, and while this vegetative growth is certainly a welcome effect, where are the flowers? All things come to those who wait. The large 3″ wide light blue flowers appear in the upper axils in late summer or fall; they consist of five large petals, with a creamy white to yellowish throat that contrasts well with the blue. Flowers may be solitary or clustered together in three- or four-flowered racemes. Plants are considered annuals and conservatory subjects, but they have returned more than three years in our trials at Georgia (zone 7). Plants need something to twine about, such as a metal mesh or rough strings. If not allowed to climb, they can be grown as container plants. This is a fabulous vine!

Full sun. Propagate by seed or cuttings.

CULTIVARS

'Alba' is a white-flowered form with a yellow throat.

Alternative species

Thunbergia erecta (e rek′ ta; king's mantle) is a nonclimbing twining shrub, growing to 4′ in height in temperate gardens. The 2–3″ long leaves are shiny, and the solitary flowers are blue-violet with yellow throats. A white form, 'Albiflora', is also grown. Same cultural recommendations as for *T. battiscombei*.

Thunbergia gregorii (gre gor′ ee i; orange clock vine) is a twining climber with triangular palmately veined 3″ leaves. The petiole is slightly winged, as in *T. alata*. The flowers, however, are a brilliant deep burnt orange with no eye, and when in flower, plants cannot be passed without stopping. Those I have seen do not appear to be as vigorous as *T. alata* and are not as covered with flowers. A stunning color—hard to find, but worth the hunt.

Quick key to *Thunbergia* species

  A. Plant not a climber . . . . *T. battiscombei*
AA. Plant climber
      B. Flowers light blue . . . . *T. grandiflora*
     BB. Flowers orange to yellow
         C. Flowers with dark eye, yellow-orange, petioles
            obviously winged . . . . *T. alata*

CC. Flowers burnt orange, petioles not obviously winged . . . .
. . . . *T. gregorii*

Thymophylla (ti ma′ fil a)   Dahlberg daisy   Asteraceae

Plants were for many years considered members of the genus *Dyssodia* (di so′
dee a), but most taxonomists now agree they should be placed in *Thymophylla*,
which name comes from the Greek, *thymos* ("excrescence") and *phyllon* ("leaf"), a
reference to the scent from the glands on the leaves. Of the approximately ten
species identified, only one is occasionally gardened.

-tenuiloba (ten yew ih lo′ ba)   golden fleece   4–8″/8″
    summer   golden yellow   Texas, Mexico

The short frame, the scented leaves, and the many fragrant golden yellow single
daisy flowers help to distinguish this species from the million or so other daisies
out there. The 1″ long leaves are opposite and deeply divided in five to twelve
narrow segments, usually with bristly tips. The upper leaves are often alternate.
Many flowers are produced, each about ½″ wide, and if deadheaded, they continue for many months. Surrounding the ray flowers, the papery involucre
(bracts at base of ray flowers) bears many scent-producing glands. As with the
spore cases on ferns, the arrangement of these glands is used to identify various
species in the genus. (Being a taxonomist sure sounds like fun!) The disk is
raised slightly and is golden orange, like the ray flowers.

Seed companies offer this species under the name Golden Fleece, as a bedding plant or container plant. I have not seen many successful plantings of it—
perhaps gardeners would more easily accept its demise if they realized this short-
lived wildflower reseeds. Best in containers. Full sun, excellent drainage. Propagate by seed.

Thysanotus (thi sa no′ tus)   fringed lily   Liliaceae

In the first few weeks of my sabbatical in Western Australia, I pestered my guide
mercilessly as to the name of this plant and that plant. How is it grown? where
did it come from? and so on—which is likely why I found myself alone in King's
Park that day. Whoever said there was no such thing as a dumb question never
had to spend time with me. I was already shell-shocked by the number of beautiful and totally mysterious plants featured in that botanical garden. Then, the
most lovely fringe-flowered plant I had ever seen—in blue yet—appeared. A whole
colony of them. Fortunately, so many people had inquired as to this plant's
identity that a label had been provided, indicating that the fringed lily was native
to Western Australia.

There are about forty species of *Thysanotus*, the most common being *T. multiflorus* (mul tee flor′ us; many-flowered fringed lily). The basal, glabrous leaves, 8–
12″ long, are linear to lanceolate in shape. From the center of the foliage arise

many leafless scapes, each bearing an umbel of five to twenty flowers, although mature clumps can sport as many as sixty flowers in an umbel. Only one or two flowers in each inflorescence are open at a given time, each lasting but a single day; nevertheless, sufficient blooms are formed in the spring that flowering continues for a couple of weeks. The six tepals consist of three narrow blue-violet outer segments and three much wider inner segments with long lavender hairs on the margins, forming fringes around each of those segments.

Obviously, few of the fringed lilies are grown here, nor are they commonly cultivated even in Australia. They may be grown from seed or divided, but they require excellent drainage, warmth, and low humidity. A Mediterranean climate suits them well. I brought some fringed lilies back to Athens, but they were not happy. Who knows? Maybe someone will be more successful than I was and try a few in the garden. The world awaits your success.

Alternative species

Thysanotus dichotomus (di kot' a mus) is similarly handsome but with smaller flowers, which appear after the foliage has started to wither. The stems are dichotomously branched, thus its name. Same cultural recommendations as for *T. multiflorus*.

Additional reading

Corrick, Margaret, and Bruce A. Fuhrer. 1996. *Wildflowers of Southern Western Australia*. Five Mile Press, Noble Park, Victoria, Australia.

Tibouchina (tih boo chee' na)
glory bush, princess flower   Melastomataceae

This South American genus has been discovered by North American gardeners and landscapers—the only thing slowing its popularity is the difficulty in finding it in garden centers and catalogs. Of the 350 species known, none are consistently cold hardy above zone 8, although warmer winters have allowed our plants to overwinter in zone 7 for several years. I consider them annuals; if they come back, it's a bonus. The genus has large leathery entire leaves on long petioles, four-sided stems, and showy violet-blue flowers, usually in late summer and fall. In general, they are big plants, growing 4–8' in temperate areas, taller in tropical gardens. Plants have been classified in different genera, starting in *Pleroma*, then *Lasiandra*, and now *Tibouchina*.

Quick guide to *Tibouchina* species

	Height	Flowers	Flower color	Flowering time
T. grandifolia	5–7'	long panicle	violet-blue	fall
T. urvilleana	3–5'	solitary	violet-blue	summer

-grandifolia (gran dih fo′ lee a)   large-leaf princess flower   5–7′/4′
     fall   violet-blue   Brazil

This is a spectacular species for both summer and fall landscapes. In the summer, the large 10–12″ long, 4–5″ wide opposite leaves are formed on long petioles along the obviously square stem. All parts of the plant, from stem to petiole and leaves are softly hairy. You must touch the light green leaves to fully appreciate their velvety texture.

In most areas of the country, flowering does not begin until mid September. The 1″ wide blooms are held in 12–18″ long terminal branched panicles (a compound inflorescence), with dozens of flowers per panicle. They are an awesome sight, assuring this species will be the dominant plant in the fall landscape. Even when not in flower, plants are impressive. But since impatient gardeners expect flowers on annuals all summer, they must be told that none will occur until the fall. As the weather cools down, the foliage turns reddish before dropping. Take cuttings in the fall or, if room allows, dig up the plant to save for next spring. Temperatures above 50°F are needed to initiate growth, which then continues all season.

Full sun. Propagate by terminal cuttings.

-urvilleana (er vil ee a′ na)   bush princess flower   3–5′/4′
     summer   violet-blue   Brazil

Taxonomy on this genus is in flux; this species alone has been *Tibouchina grandiflora*, *T. semidecandra*, and *T. urvilleana*, in that order. I can only tell the reader that plants sold under one of these names have excellent attributes for the temperate garden, not least of which are the dark green leathery foliage and the beautiful large violet-blue flowers that appear sporadically throughout the warm growing season.

I first came across this plant as a 10′ tall hedge in Palmerston North, New Zealand. I couldn't believe my eyes when the 4–5″ wide flowers opened all over that hedge. Spectacular, to say the least. I inquired as to its identity and was told it was *Tibouchina semidecandra* var. *grandiflora*, the large-flowered form of princess flower. I did some research there to see if it would be useful as a pot plant for the greenhouse industry (it is not), and I brought a single cutting back with me to Athens. From this one cutting we propagated many plants, some of which wound up in the trial gardens at UGA. They reached 3–5′ tall, half the size I had seen in New Zealand, before they were cut down by the winter. The foliage was wonderfully handsome all season, however, and flower buds were present from June onward. The best flowering time was late summer and fall, but the flowers formed off and on most of the season. We called the plant 'Athens Blue', and growers propagated it and propagated it. Most of what is grown in temperate gardens since 1990 came from that single cutting, which journeyed back with me many years ago. They may not be labeled 'Athens Blue', but that is likely what they are.

Plants are shrubby, the ovate leaves are about 5″ long and pubescent. The five-petaled flowers also bear beautiful stamens, ten in number and markedly

Tibouchina semidecandra var. *grandiflora* 'Athens Blue'   ASHA KAYS

unequal in length. Flowers are borne singly, persist only a single day, and never cover the entire plant. The foliage appears resistant to chewing bugs and diseases and makes for a handsome green shrub even when the plant is not in flower. Plants do best in Mediterranean climes and just fine in most temperate gardens. They have overwintered reasonably consistently in zone 7.

Quick key to *Tibouchina* species

A. Leaves 8–12" long, highly pubescent, flowers in terminal
  panicles . . . . *T. grandifolia*
AA. Leaves 3–5" long, less pubescent, flowers borne singly
  (occasionally in threes) . . . . *T. urvilleana*

Additional reading

Armitage, Allan M. 2000. Is there a market for fall-flowering annuals? *Greenhouse Grower* 18(4):76–81.

Tithonia (tih tho' nee a)   Mexican sunflower   Asteraceae

The name *Tithonia* comes from the mythological Tithonus, the much-loved companion of Aurora, the goddess of the dawn. Although about ten species are known, only one is cultivated to any extent. Beloved and respected Southern writer Celestine Sibley once wrote a column for an Atlanta paper about *Tithonia*, lauding "this sunflower which fill[s] my yard with large brilliant orange flowers . . . on immense shrubs." Her columns were read by everyone, and thus she sparked enormous interest in "this sunflower." Unfortunately, she mentioned the common name, Mexican sunflower, only in passing and the genus but once. People were scrambling to find sunflowers that grew like shrubs and produced large orange flowers. After a few dead ends, persistent gardeners found what she was writing about and were not disappointed. Sibley, who died in 1999, is sorely missed.

-rotundifolia (ro tun dih fo' lee a)   Mexican sunflower   3–8'/4'
  late summer   orange   Central America

Plants of this species are usually big, 5–8' in height, although a dwarf form has been selected. Leaves are alternate, up to 12" long and 8" wide, entire to three- to five-lobed and carried on a long petiole. The flowers are 2–3" wide, with two series of bracts beneath, and range in color from orange to orange-scarlet; the disk is lighter than the ray flowers. Plants are easy to grow and attract butterflies in droves when they are in peak bloom, from mid to late summer; flowering is poor until then.

Its large size has been a problem for this plant, as have its susceptibility to sucking insects, such as aphids and thrips, and its late flowering. When grown

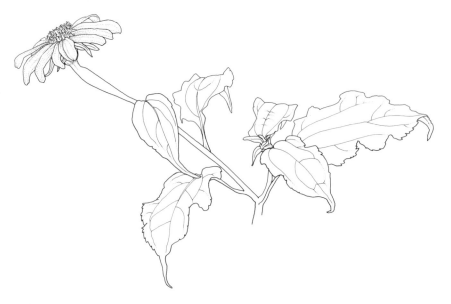

Tithonia rotundifolia 'Fiesta del Sol'   ASHA KAYS

well, it is really outstanding, but I have seen too many struggling specimens that do nothing more than take up room.

Full sun to afternoon shade, propagate by seed.

CULTIVARS

'Aztec Sun' has golden flowers on 4' tall plants. An excellent and unusual color for this species.

'Fiesta del Sol' was an All-America Selection in 2000, mainly because of its dwarf (2–3' tall) habit. I have seen some gorgeous specimens, but it has been inconsistent in growth and bloom, sometimes not flowering until late summer and occasionally staying too stunted.

'Goldfinger', the most common cultivar, bears large orange-scarlet flowers on 4–5' tall plants.

'Torch' is taller than 'Goldfinger', easily growing 6' tall. 'Fiesta del Sol' is a better choice if size is a concern.

Torenia (tor ee′ nee a)   wishbone flower   Scrophulariaceae

I have long known of the Dutch East India Company, populated by such interesting people as Carl Peter Thunberg (see *Thunbergia*). I later discovered that the Swedes had their own trading empire in India, known fittingly as the Swedish East India Company. The chaplain to this company resided in Surat, India, and later in China; his record of his travels was published by Linnaeus in 1759. His name was Olof Toren, and we commemorate him whenever we plant a wish-bone flower.

This genus of forty species has many fine attributes, but as for me, I mostly like the fun it provides when you open a typical flower. Take away the petals (your thumbnail will do) and notice the joined pair of stamens, looking just like the Thanksgiving wishbone. Show that to your kids, and they won't remember Olof, or the generic name, or whether sun or shade is required—but they will remember the wishbone.

Quick guide to *Torenia* species

	Height	Flower color
T. flava	6–12"	yellow
T. fournieri	6–12"	mixed, not yellow

-flava (flay' va)	yellow wishbone	6–12"/6"
summer	yellow with purple	Indochina

Hardly anyone knows or grows this little plant, but when they see it, they are enchanted. The ovate leaves are entire or wavy, and may be sessile or slightly petiolate. Plant habit is erect, but the species also can be a trailer, terrific for containers and baskets. The 1" flowers are unique. Beneath the corolla is a slightly keeled calyx, but it is the color of the petals that enamors people. The upper lip of the corolla is red-purple, and the lobes of the lower lip are yellow with a single purple spot. Plants are short-lived, but they are sufficiently different to warrant a try.

Full sun in the North, partial shade in the South. Propagate by seed.

CULTIVARS

'Suzie Wong' is the only selection of this species I know. She has brilliant orange-yellow flowers with a deep black throat. Outstanding.

-fournieri (for nee ayr' ee)	wishbone flower	6–12"/6"
summer	many colors	Vietnam

This is the only species commonly grown in North America. Historically all torenias were seed-propagated, but more vigorous vegetative forms have recently emerged. In general, plants have square stems and opposite, ovate to heart-shaped pale green leaves, 2–3" long. The flowers consist of ribbed sepals beneath the two-lipped corolla; the larger lower lip is deep violet-purple, the upper lip, paler blue. In the colored forms, splashes of color are found on the outside lobes of the upper lip. The throat is usually yellow. Flowers are formed all summer in small racemes or may be solitary. Numerous colors have been bred.

Plants generally grow only 6–9" tall and are used as bedding plants. They are better in cool summers than in warm humid ones.

Full sun in the North, afternoon shade in the South. Propagate by seed.

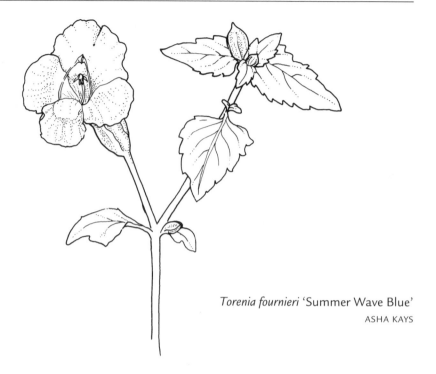

Torenia fournieri 'Summer Wave Blue'
ASHA KAYS

CULTIVARS

Clown is an excellent series of seed-propagated plants in many colors, including blue, blue and white, blush (white with pink spots), burgundy, light orchid, rose, and violet. The standard in dwarf torenias.

Duchess Mix is a mixture of colors in blue, deep blue, light blue, pink, and white. Excellent performers, about 8″ tall.

Panda Mix is similar to Duchess Mix but slightly shorter.

'Summer Wave Blue', a Georgia Gold Medal winner, is the standard vegetative form, with deep blue flowers much larger than the species. Outstanding in containers and baskets.

'Yellow Heart Moon' is another vegetative form whose yellow throat is the key color. Not as good as 'Summer Wave Blue'.

Quick key to *Torenia* species

A. Flowers yellow . . . . *T. flava*
AA. Flowers many colors, none yellow . . . . *T. fournieri*

Trachelium (tra keel′ ee um)   throatwort   Campanulaceae

The generic name comes from the Greek, *trachelos* ("the neck"); the plants were supposedly useful for afflictions of the throat (trachea). Only seven species have been identified, all native to Mediterranean countries; one is used ornamentally in this country.

-caeruleum (sa roo′ lee um)	blue throatwort	3-4′/2′
summer	blue, white	Mediterranean

This species is more common at local florists than local gardens, as it is a popular specialty cut flower in this country and abroad. It is grown by the acre under protection in the greenhouse and in the field in coastal California. Plants bear 3″ long, alternate lanceolate leaves with doubly serrated margins and pointed tips; they are widely branched toward the top, bearing terminal clusters, 2-4″ across. The clusters consist of dozens of small tubular flowers, each measuring less than ¼″ across. This species is not much seen in North American gardens; it ought to be tried more, particularly in cooler climates with low humidity. When harvesting for cut flowers, allow one-quarter to one-third of the flowers to open before cutting.

Full sun to partial shade, excellent drainage. Propagate by seed or cuttings.

CULTIVARS

'Blue Umbrella' has lavender-blue flowers and is perhaps a little less rangy than the species.

'Blue Veil' has violet-blue flowers.

Devotion series provides blue, purple, and white flowers.

'Passion in Violet' is a pretty name for a violet-blue form. May be the same as 'Blue Veil'.

'White Umbrella' bears creamy white flowers.

'White Veil' has whiter flowers than 'White Umbrella'.

Alternative species

Trachelium rumelianum (roo mel ee a′ num; Grecian throatwort) is native to Greece and Bulgaria. Plants are short (about 12″ tall) and tend to sprawl but can be covered with balls of sky-blue flowers in spring and early summer. Quite beautiful before heat and humidity take it down.

Additional reading

Armitage, Allan M. 1993. *Specialty Cut Flowers*. Timber Press, Portland, Ore.

———. 1988. Effects of photoperiod, supplemental light, and growth regulators on growth and flowering of *Trachelium caeruleum*. *J. Hort. Sci.* 63:187-194.

Trachymene (tra kih′ me nee)   Apiaceae

Approximately twelve species of the genus *Trachymene* (syn. *Didiscus*) are known, all native to Australia and the western Pacific. Only one of the two available species is common.

-coerulea (sa roo' lee a)   Rotnest daisy, blue lace flower   1–2'/2'
   summer   blue   Western Australia

This species—long enjoyed as a container plant and as an excellent, although short-stemmed, cut flower—seems to fade in and out of popularity. Plants are erect, somewhat hairy, with 3–4" long alternate divided leaves, each section quite variable, sometimes entire, sometimes divided again into three. The young leaves and stems are covered with soft, sticky hairs. The many lavender-blue flowers are slightly scented, pleasantly so, and are held in a long-stemmed umbel, 2–3" across. The entire plant, even the flower buds, has a lacy appearance, thus the most common of the common names. The native habitat for the species is Rotnest Island, a small island off the coast of Perth, Western Australia, thus its lesser known name. Flowering in North American gardens generally occurs from July to October in the North, a few weeks earlier in the South.

    Full sun in the North, partial shade in the South. Propagate by seed.

CULTIVARS

'Madonna' has off-white flowers with a hint of blue.

Alternative species

   Trachymene pilosa (pih lo' sa; hairy lace flower) is only 4–6" tall and bears deeply cut leaves. Eight to twelve white flowers with a purple tinge are held in short-stemmed umbels. Nice in rockery or as edging.

Tropaeolum (tro pay o' lum)   nasturtium   Tropaeolaceae

This genus, consisting of eighty-six species of annuals, perennials, and vines, offers great diversity of form and color. The well-established tendency of gardeners to allow nasturtiums to climb up tepees of poles and netting reminded Linnaeus of a Roman battlefield, where the victors would hang the shields (the rounded leaves) and helmets (flowers) of the vanquished on pillars as a trophy of conquest. He provided this seemingly harmless plant the name *Tropaeolum* after the Greek, *tropaion*, and Latin, *tropaeum*, for "trophy." I guess even Linnaeus had a few bad days. Do not confuse these plants, because of the common name, with the true *Nasturtium officinale* (watercress): these two genera are not even in the same family.

    Nearly all species of *Tropaeolum* are climbers or can be trained to climb by providing a support around which they can twist their leafstalks. Flowers are distinctive for the long slender spur that arises from one of the sepals. The young pods and seeds of *T. minus* and *T. majus* are pickled as a substitute for capers, while the peppery tasting leaves and colorful flowers are used as a garnish, like cress, accounting for the common name indian cress. Flower color is all over the spectrum: the bright yellow of *T. peregrinum*, the brilliant red of *T. speciosum*, and even blue, *T. azureum*. Common bedding forms are in yellows, oranges, and pinks. Many species arise from tuberous roots and show a remarkable amount of perenniality under mild winters.

Quick guide to *Tropaeolum* species

	Habit	Flower color
T. majus	prostrate, climber	many
T. peregrinum	climber	yellow

-majus (may′ jus)   nasturtium   vine
        spring   many colors   South America

This common nasturtium is grown as a compact bedding plant as well as a vigorous climber. The pale green, alternate leaves are smooth, orbicular (rounded) in shape, and held on long petioles. The 1–2″ wide flowers consist of five rounded, often clawed, petals and five sepals, one of which is extended into a long spur. Many of the variations of color and form are the result of hybridization of this species with *Tropaeolum peltophorum* and *T. minus*.

All nasturtiums abhor hot weather and should be considered early spring-flowering plants in the South, although they do well all summer in cool nights, well after the first frost. Remove plants when night temperatures consistently remain over 70°F.

Full sun. Propagate by seed *in situ* in late winter or early spring. Seed should be soaked or filed (scarified) before sowing.

CULTIVARS

'Alaska', the most common variegated form, is 12–15″ tall and comes true from seed. The small leaves are more splashed in white than they are variegated. Flowers occur in a mixture of colors. Plants are trailing and quite useful for baskets and containers.

Climbing Hybrids Improved grow to about 5′ and bear flowers in a wide range of colors.

'Dwarf Cherry Rose' is a compact double-flowered form.

'Empress of India' has dark green foliage and vermilion-red flowers. Plants are 12″ tall.

Gleam is a compact trailing series with double flowers in yellow ('Golden Gleam') and red ('Scarlet Gleam'). Can also be trained to climb. The two Gleams mentioned were All-America Selections in 1933 and 1935, respectively.

'Golden King', introduced over a century ago, bears dark green leaves and golden flowers on compact plants.

'Hermine Grashoff' has beautiful double orange-scarlet flowers over round pale green leaves.

'Jewel of Africa' is a climber, bearing a mixture of yellow, red, cream, and peach flowers over interesting marbled foliage.

'King Theodore' is a dwarf form with intensely dark crimson flowers over dark green leaves.

'Moonlight' is a 6–7′ climber with creamy yellow flowers.

'Peach Melba' bears salmon-peach blooms on 12″ tall plants. Can also be trained to climb.

'Red Wonder' is 10–12″ tall with bright red flowers.

'Salmon Baby' has fringed deep salmon-pink flowers over compact plants. A favorite for salad garnish.

'Strawberries and Cream' produces creamy white flowers with splashes of red.

'Strawberry Ice' consists of creamy yellow flowers with scarlet markings. About 9" tall.

Tip Top series is a mixture of mahogany, gold, apricot, and scarlet flowers over 5–8" tall plants.

'Tom Thumb' is only 6–9" tall with flowers in a wide range of colors.

'Vesuvius' has blue-green leaves and flowers in shades of salmon-pink with a dark spot on the upper petal.

Whirlybird is a compact series with upward-facing flowers in cherry red, cream, gold, mahogany red, and tangerine.

-peregrinum (per ih gree′ num)		canary creeper	vine
spring	yellow		Peru, Ecuador

This climbing species is characterized by deeply five-lobed leaves, about 2" across and orbicular in outline, carried on long petioles. The foliage is full, and if plants are given support, they can grow vigorously and rapidly, flowering in late spring. The small ¾–1" wide flowers are reminiscent of canaries—yellow, fringed, and flying all over the foliage. Well, maybe not, but still quite wonderful when in flower. The upper two petals are larger than the others, and the short curved spur is green.

A great plant, but in hot summers, it must be planted early to enjoy good flowering before heat arrives. It doesn't do particularly well in northern summers either. Full sun to afternoon shade, propagate by seed.

Alternative species

Tropaeolum minus is similar to *T. majus* but smaller in every way. Seldom seen, it acted as a parent in the dwarfing of nasturtiums.

Tropaeolum polyphyllum (pa lee fil′ um) is a prostrate plant that can, like *T. peregrinum*, be trained to climb. Many five- to seven-lobed large blue-green leaves provide color even when the plant is not in flower. Flowers are yellow, orange, or ochre. Fantastic but a poor performer in heat.

Tropaeolum speciosum (spee see o′ sum; flame nasturtium) is related to *T. peregrinum*. A fabulous climber with scarlet-red flowers, it arises from tuberous roots. It is perennial in mild winters but does poorly in hot summers.

Quick key to *Tropaeolum* species

A. Leaves orbicular, not lobed . . . . *T. majus*
AA. Leaves divided or deeply lobed
    B. Leaves lobed, flowers yellow and fringed . . . . *T. peregrinum*
    BB. Leaves divided to base
        C. Plants prostrate, flowers yellow to orange . . . . . . *T. polyphyllum*
        CC. Plants climbing, flowers scarlet . . . . *T. speciosum*

Turnera (ter′ ner a) Turneraceae

The Protestant views of clergyman, physician, and herbalist William Turner (1510–1568) were unpopular during his day, and he spent several years exiled from England. His ardent interest in botany led him to write *A New Herbal*, published in 1551, the first botanical work in English with any claim to originality. Turner, the "father of English botany," is far better known than the genus of about sixty species that honors him. One of its members, *Turnera ulmifolia*, has the potential for increased visibility in much of the country.

-ulmifolia (ul mih fo′ lee a)   sage rose, buttercup flower   2–4′/3′
summer   yellow   tropical America

Alan Shapiro of San Felasco Nurseries in Gainesville, Florida, gave me a rather weedy shrub and suggested that I might find some good things to say about it. I was thrilled: with its butter-yellow flowers and dark green leaves, *Turnera ulmifolia* looked like a winner to me. It has long been grown from Key West to Jacksonville, but I have never seen it in the Midwest or Northeast. I have grown it for several years in the UGA Horticulture Gardens, and while it may not be the next impatiens, I believe it has a place in American landscapes and gardens.

The lanceolate to oblong leaves, 2–3″ long, are alternate, dark green, and serrated, somewhat like alder leaves (hence its other common name, yellow alder). They are slightly hairy on the upper surface, more so beneath. A small pair of glands may be found just where the leaf blade meets the petiole. The 2″ wide flowers are intensely yellow, consisting of five petals, five stamens, and a single fringed stigma; they form in the upper axils and open all season without cessation. But the plant has one disadvantage: flowers open and close in a single day, often closing in late afternoon. A bit of a downer when you go to work before flowers unfurl and come home after they shut. They also close in cloudy and dull weather—but the same can be said for sundrops, purslane, portulaca, and daylilies. Plants will perennialize in frost-free areas and will certainly reseed in warm climates. They are well worth a second look.

Full sun to afternoon shade, propagate by seed or cuttings.

Tweedia (twee′ dee a) Asclepiadaceae

Absolutely one of the finest blues found in the plant kingdom. This is not to say it is the finest plant, but oh, the color of the flowers is to die for. Combine the wonderful color with the wonderful generic name, and who can resist? The former name for the genus, *Oxypetalum*, comes from the Greek, *oxys* ("sharp") and *petalum* ("petal"), referring to the pointed petals, but it is the present name that slides off the tongue and makes you want to know why a blue-flowered plant seems to be named after a yellow cartoon canary. As with most things horticultural, the history of the plant far predates the history of animation. The generic name comes from Scotsman James Tweedie, who lived in the mid 1800s and

Turnera ulmifolia ASHA KAYS

was the head gardener at the Royal Botanic Garden in Edinburgh. He left his comfortable surroundings and emigrated to South America, where he kept a small shop in Buenos Aires. He botanized throughout the continent, sending material back to Scotland for study. As records of this plant were further studied, taxonomists have placed this plant in the monotypic genus *Tweedia*, and *Oxypetalum* is now no more than a synonym.

-caerulea (sa roo' lee a)		tweedia	vine
all season		blue	Brazil, Uruguay

This species is more than just a pretty face, call it what you will. It's a climber, by twining stems, capable of growing 3' tall. Only a few long, lax stems are formed; if not provided with support, they will be shorter and less upright. The 2–3" long leaves are alternate, long, ovate, and, like the stems, minutely white-pubescent throughout. They feel like felt. The 1–2" long flowers are formed by ones or twos in the axils and consist of five narrow powder-blue petals. In the garden, plants grow about 2' tall. After flowering, long narrow milkweed-like pods form. Flowers and fruit continue throughout the season.

While I can gush on and on about the beauty of the flowers, this plant comes with a few drawbacks. The leaves do not have a pleasant smell, and while the stems make long-lasting cut subjects, they too have a rank odor; when cut, they bleed the white latex common to the family. The beauty of the flowers is easily marred by rain; if their perfection is to be maintained, they need protection from the elements. The fruit, although handsome, is so messy (like a milkweed) and so numerous that the beauty of the plant gives way to weediness. But, having said all this, I still enjoy sowing some seeds and marveling at the beauty of the beast.

I became the quasi-expert on this plant when I spent five months in New Zealand researching its response to photoperiod, light, and temperature for the cut flower industry. High light and moderate temperature (72°F) were the best criteria for production; photoperiod had little effect.

Full sun in the North, partial shade in the South. Propagate by seed or cuttings. Plants do fine in moderate summers; high heat is not needed, nor preferred. Good drainage is recommended.

Additional reading

Armitage, A. M., N. G. Seager, I. J. Warrington, D. H. Greer, and J. Reyngoud. 1990. Response of *Oxypetalum caeruleum* to irradiance, temperature and photoperiod. *J. Amer. Soc. Hort. Sci.* 115(6):910–914.

U

Ursinia (er sin' ee a)

Asteraceae

The genus, which consists of about forty known species of daisies, is named for Johann Ursinus, a mid seventeenth-century German botanical author. It is among the many little-known South African daisy genera that are occasionally offered as seed in this country (for more on South African daisies, see *Arctotis*).

-anthemoides (an the moy' deez)

summer   orange, yellow

15–18"/15"
South Africa

The alternate leaves are about 2" long, slightly pubescent on the underside and bipinnately dissected into linear segments; the overall look somewhat resembles the foliage of *Anthemis*. Leaves are strongly scented by glands on their underside. The 1½–2" wide flowers are solitary, held on an almost leafless 6–8" long scape. The flowers usually have twenty rays, often three-toothed, and are yellow or orange with dark purple spots at the base. The rays are the same color on both sides, or may be purplish coppery underneath. Both yellow and orange flowers may be found on the same plant—a beautiful effect. Flowers will not open in dull weather.

Plants share the soil and climatic preferences recommended for *Gazania* and *Arctotis*. Mediterranean climates suit them well: dry and warm, but not hot, with little summer rain and low humidity. Such conditions are not common in the bulk of North America, although in much of Canada, the northern states, and the West Coast, plants thrive into mid to late summer. Deadheading promotes longer flowering.

Full sun, propagate by seed. Plant after threat of frost has passed.

CULTIVARS

'Versicolor' has orange-yellow rays with brown-purple bases.

Alternative species

Ursinia calenduliflora (kal end yew lih flor' a) is about 10" tall, with yellow disk flowers (like a calendula's), dark purple toward the base.

V

Verbena (ver bee′ na)　　　　vervain　　　　Verbenaceae

Verbena consists of approximately 250 species, six or seven of which are in cultivation. The perennial species, such as *V. bonariensis* and *V. rigida*, are well known, even if they are only reliably hardy south of zone 6. Canadian verbena (*V. canadensis*) and cutleaf verbena (*V. tenuisecta*) are also thought of as perennials in zone 7 and south but can disappear quickly in wet and cold winters; I therefore include them here, along with the bedding plant verbena, *V. ×hybrida*. *Verbena ×hybrida* is always propagated from seed; *V. canadensis* and *V. tenuisecta* are propagated vegetatively, usually from terminal cuttings. Hybrids grown as annuals so dominated the market that the vegetative forms (*V. canadensis*, *V. tenuisecta*) hardly saw the light of day until the mid 1990s; significant breeding efforts have since been devoted to all three.

Plants generally have four-sided stems, terminal flowers, and opposite, dentate foliage. The annuals are all colorful and usually low-growing, performing best in well-drained soils in full sun. They are highly susceptible to root rots when drainage is poor. A good rule of thumb is to plant them on hillsides, or in containers where sunny, dry conditions can be maintained. Whiteflies and spider mites get out their steak knives when they hear verbena is in their neighborhood, and thrips can also be a problem. But hey, everyone has to eat. Powdery mildew can be an awful blot on the verbena landscape as well.

Several historical references are associated with the genus. *Verbena officinalis* was the classical name for certain sacred branches and is said to have been used to staunch Christ's wounds on Calvary. Plants were also used medicinally; the common name, vervain, is rooted in the Celtic, *fer* ("to remove") and *faen* ("stone"), referring to their use in treating bladder stones.

Quick guide to *Verbena* species

	Height	Flower color	Habit
V. canadensis	8–18"	red, pink	spreading
V. ×hybrida	8–15"	varied	upright
V. tenuisecta	8–12"	purple	spreading

-canadensis (ka na den' sis) clump verbena, rose vervain 8–18"/36"
summer red, pink North America

Native from Virginia to Florida and west to Colorado and Mexico, *Verbena cana-densis* is occasionally treated as a short-lived perennial in zones 7 to 10, and some hybrids will persist into zone 6 (the species is not native to present-day Canada; its specific epithet was bestowed when Canada extended further south than its present boundary). The many-branched pubescent stems lie on the ground with the ends ascending (decumbent), and rooting can take place where the lower stems touch the soil. The deeply lobed ovate leaves are 1–3" long and about 1" wide with a triangular to wedge-shaped base. The corolla tube is about twice as long as the calyx, but each flower is only about ½" wide. They are often rose-colored with a small white eye, hence one common name, rose vervain. Up to twenty flowers may be present on each of the stalked spikes.

This species has an excellent clumping habit and may be cut back severely if the stems lose leaves or become too long. A sunny place in the border with excellent drainage is a necessity. If drainage is poor, plant vigor declines rapidly, and no amount of corrective surgery will improve its demeanor. Like other members of the genus, susceptibility to mildew and spider mites is a problem.

Many hybrids in which *Verbena canadensis* is the dominant parent were bred in the late 1990s, thanks to private plant enthusiasts and large companies, who have realized that vegetative verbenas are in demand. Most differences among them have to do with color and vigor.

Full sun, excellent drainage. Propagate by terminal cuttings.

CULTIVARS

Lavender
'Abbeville' was found by Rick Berry of Goodness Grows Nursery, Lexington, Georgia, near the town of Abbeville, South Carolina. Flowers are a cool light lavender with a tiny hint of white. Vigorous.

Pink
'Appleblossom' has pale pink lightly fragrant flowers. More dwarf than most canadensis forms. Moderate vigor.

'Pink Parfait' bears handsome pink and white flowers. Not as vigorous as many other cultivars in our trials, it still attracts many followers.

'Sarah Groves', named for Sarah Groves of Oxford, Georgia, bears clusters of soft pale pink flowers, which change to a richer pink with age. Almost a bicolor.

'Silver Anne', from England, is one of the best warm pinks around. Vigorous and handsome, without being gaudy. I have seen plants called 'Homestead Pink', but they are identical to 'Silver Anne', and 'Silver Anne' they should be called. Let's not get carried away with this Homestead thing.

Red
'Big Red' (formerly 'Homestead Red'), from Robrick Nursery in Florida, has good red flowers, a little smaller than 'Evelyn Scott' and 'Taylortown Red'.

'Evelyn Scott' is a good true red from Goodness Grows Nursery. Floriferous with moderate vigor.

'Summer Blaze' (formerly 'Clear Red') supposedly has clear red flowers and good vigor. I have not yet trialed this and so do not know if it differs from the others mentioned here.

'Taylortown Red', from McCorkles Nursery in Georgia, is similar to 'Evelyn Scott'. Good red color, perhaps a little more vigorous and more floriferous than Evelyn.

Purple, magenta

'Homestead Purple' kicked the verbena market in the backside, rekindling interest in many other cultivars. The dark purple flowers are early, and plants are vigorous, eating up the surrounding competition. Merely a nod to the Georgia homestead where the plants were found, the Homestead name does not designate a series of colors, nor do other cultivars with the word "homestead" in their names have anything to do with 'Homestead Purple' in vigor, flower, or form.

'Ultramarine' is as vigorous as 'Homestead Purple', in a slightly different shade of purple.

White

'Snowflurry', from Garden Delights Nursery, Raleigh, North Carolina, is a semi-upright vigorous "virtual flowering machine." White flowers and true from seed. Formerly sold as *Verbena canadensis* 'White'.

Two- and three-tones

'Carrousel' is an older form with lavender and white flowers. Not especially vigorous.

'Fiesta', introduced by Greg Grant, has large bright pink flowers with flecks of purple that intensify with age.

'Lulu Norris' is a tricolor form selected by the outstanding proprietor of Lady Slipper Nursery in north Georgia herself: the top of the flowers is purple-violet, the bottom, light purple and set off with a clear white center.

Series

Aztec series includes bright lavender, bright purple, dark purple, lavender, pink, and rose-pink. In our trials, 'Aztec Lavender' outperformed other colors.

Babylon series includes light blue, lilac, neon rose, pink, silver, and white. 'Babylon Pink' was the best performer of the series; 'Babylon Silver' was the most popular color.

Freefall series includes colors in burgundy, light lavender, and purple.

Tortuga series produce some of the biggest flowers of all the verbenas, in double purple, hot pink, light pink, peach, red, and white. Without a doubt, 'Tortuga Peach' has a great future: good heat and humidity performance, plus a flower color that combines with almost anything.

Tukana series has denim blue (shades of blue), salmon, and scarlet flowers.

Twilight series consists of blue (with a white eye), mauve, pink, and a pink and white bicolor. 'Twilight Mauve Shades' was the best performer in the series, growing more vigorously and flowering later than the others.

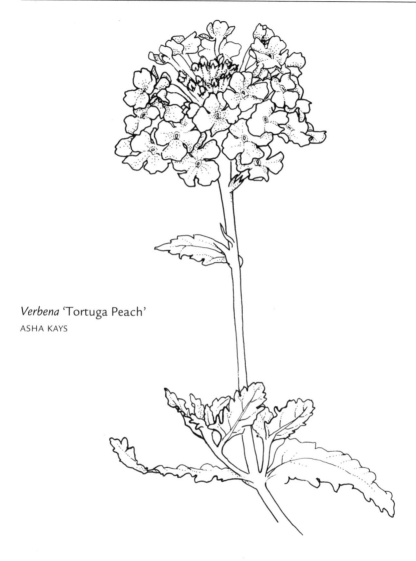

Verbena 'Tortuga Peach'
ASHA KAYS

Wildfire series includes blush and purple, both of which were the hit of the verbenas. Trial manager Meg Green simply blushed with delight when she showed off 'Wildfire Blush' in our containers.

-×***hybrida*** (hi′ brih da)	bedding verbena	8–15″/12″
spring	many colors	hybrid

Verbena ×*hybrida* results from the crossing of *V. peruviana*, *V. incisa*, *V. phlogiflora*, and *V. teucroides*. Demand is high, and additional species are being incorporated into the stew every year. This is probably still the most common verbena in retail stores—particularly the large box stores, which carry mostly bedding plants in the spring. The flowers, which come in a variety of colors, tend to be more up-right than *V. canadensis* and are beautiful, especially in the spring. Unfortunately, this hybrid is not as weather-tolerant as the vegetative forms in much of the country and is highly susceptible to disease when weather becomes inclement.

Full sun, excellent drainage. All cultivars are seed-propagated.

CULTIVARS

Amor series is only about 10″ tall but has a lovely mixture of colors. 'Amor Light Pink' is especially handsome.

'Blaze' is an old-fashioned but highly effective scarlet form.

'Blue Lagoon', a late 1990s introduction, is the bluest of the purple verbenas. Nice color.

Novalis series has a rounded habit and is even more upright than most of the others on this list. Plants are available in bright rose, bright scarlet, deep blue with eye, rose-pink with eye, scarlet with eye, and white.

'Peaches and Cream' is among the prettiest verbenas ever produced. The flowers are peachy pink and creamy white, and when they look good, they are show-stoppers.

Quartz series is a fine mixture of colors, both solid and with a white eye. In separate colors, scarlet- and burgundy-flowered plants are the best. 'Quartz Burgundy', a 1999 All-America Selection, is a vigorous grower with burgundy flowers on 8–10″ tall plants.

Romance was a breakthrough series in verbena production for its reasonably high seed germination. Plants are available in carmine with white eye, deep rose, pink, scarlet, scarlet with eye, silver, violet with eye, and white.

Sandy series grows 8–10″ tall and is available in magenta, scarlet, and white. All colors proved quite durable in tests under rugged southeastern conditions.

Showtime series is a mixture of bright colors.

-tenuisecta (ten yew ih sek′ ta)   moss verbena   8–12″/spreader
　　spring   lavender   southern South America

Here is a plant that is as common in the South as bedstraw is in the North. Naturalized from southern Georgia to Louisiana and south to Florida, *Verbena tenuisecta* (syn. *V. erinoides*) flourishes by roadsides and in fields. Many decumbent stems bear triangular leaves, 1–1½″ long, which are divided into linear segments. The spikes are terminal, solitary, and composed of five to fifteen small (½″ wide) lavender flowers. The flowers are about 1″ long and compactly arranged when they first open but elongate to 1½″ or more as the flowers mature.

Plants root in less than two weeks; eight terminal cuttings I had taken from a south Georgia roadside carpeted twenty to thirty square feet in the first six weeks. The species overwinters in zone 7 two years out of five (I take cuttings in the fall and overwinter them); given sufficient protection, it may be considered hardy in zone 8. If plants become leggy, they may be sheared with a lawnmower to 2″ tall and will return as fresh as ever; if sheared too close to the ground, they take a long time to fill in. Although not as colorful as some of the other forms

of verbena, new hybrids more than hold their own by requiring far less maintenance and providing excellent garden performance.

Many new hybrids have been bred, mostly from crosses between *Verbena tenuisecta* and *V. tenera*. They are usually lower to the ground, have deeply cut, almost
lacy leaves, and flower throughout the summer.

Full sun, excellent drainage. Propagate from 2–3″ terminal cuttings.

CULTIVARS

'Alba' is sometimes available from seed. Not quite as floriferous or vigorous
as the species itself, it does provide a low-growing white.

'Cotton Candy' bears medium pink flowers with a white center. Slow-growing but handsome. Raised by Greg Grant. Also sold as 'Texas Cotton Candy'.

'Edith', named for Edith Eddelman of the North Carolina Botanic Garden
in Raleigh, has lavender-pink flowers over deeply cut foliage. Compact and
floriferous.

'Flamingo Border Pink', from Edith Eddelman, is a lacy foliaged plant with
red-violet flowers.

'Imagination', from Benary Seed, is the most well-known purple and among
the few available from seed. Very similar to the wild *Verbena tenuisecta* of the
Southeast.

'Maonettii' has purple flowers with white edges. A low grower and not as
rapid a grower as many others. Also sold as 'Aphrodite'.

'Michelle', from Garden Delights in Raleigh, North Carolina, produces vivid
purple flowers on mats of foliage.

'Royalty', from Greg Grant, bears dense cutleaf foliage over which dark purple flowers abound. Very low-growing, quite vigorous.

'Sissinghurst' is an excellent cultivar (more likely of *Verbena tenera*) with coral-
pink flowers and lacy foliage. Also sold as 'St. Paul', 'Rosea', and 'Tex Tuf Pink'.

'Sterling Star' is a new cutleaf form with lighter lavender-blue flowers than
'Imagination'. Also seed-propagated.

Tapien is among the finest, toughest series of verbenas we have trialed. It
consists of 'Tapien Blue', a vigorous lavender-blue form, and 'Tapien Pink', a
vigorous grower that appears to be less susceptible to mildew. Among the most
cold hardy of the verbenas, 'Tapien Pink' is often in flower in early March in
Athens.

Temari series has received a lot of positive strokes, with good reason: these
plants are tough, colorful, and excellent garden performers. Available in bright
pink, burgundy, cherry blossom, patio hot pink, and patio rose.

'Tex Tuf Purple' has small violet-purple flowers over cutleaf foliage. Also sold
as 'Texas Peruviana'.

Alternative species

Verbena peruviana (Peruvian verbena) hugs the ground (3–6″ tall) and bears
bright scarlet flowers. The leaves are not as incised nor as deeply cut as those of
V. canadensis, nor are plants as tall or as winter hardy (zones 7 to 10).

Quick key to *Verbena* species

A. Plant upright . . . . *V. ×hybrida*
AA. Plant spreading
    B. Foliage cut into linear divisions . . . . *V. tenuisecta*
    BB. Foliage not cut into linear divisions . . . . *V. canadensis*

Additional reading

Armitage, Allan M. 1997. *Herbaceous Perennial Plants*, 2nd ed. Stipes Publishing,
    Champaign, Ill.
University of Georgia Trial Reports: www.uga.edu/ugatrial
Vanderlan, Darcy. 1997. Verbenas. *Flower and Garden* 41(5):46–47.

Viola (vi o′ la)   pansy, violet   Violaceae

So many stories, mostly romantic, concern the growing of pansies. In the language of flowers (used effectively in works by Homer, Virgil, and Shakespeare),
they signify remembrance. Napoleon's supporters sprinkled their sentences
with the word *violette* as a secret sign of recognition, and they wore violet-colored
items to identify themselves to each other. Aubrey deVere penned "To a Wild
Pansy," and Shelley waxed poetic "On a Faded Violet." What can I say? It is obvious that these writers were not surrounded by damn pansies every day, and if I
read any more of this romantic nonsense, I fear I will become bilious.

More than 500 species of violets are distributed in the north and south temperate zones. For garden purposes, violets may be divided into two large groups.
The first group is the true violets, such as *Viola cornuta* (tufted violet) and *V. odorata* (sweet violet), which are treated as perennials and flower in late fall and early
spring. The true pansies and violas constitute the second group.

It's not that I don't like pansies—I am simply overwhelmed. Perhaps it is that
I live in the Southeast, where pansy is the regional winter color (northerners
have their snow and slush, we have our pansies). And no doubt I've been trau-
matized by trying to evaluate hundreds of different varieties over the last five
years or so. Ever try to tell the difference between 'Regal Yellow with Blotch' and
'Crown Yellow with Blotch'? Talk about nightmares. So I am probably not the
one to tell you to go buy this particular variety or that one, as I have suffered near
mortal pansy blows to the brain. Pansies and violas didn't get to be so popular
because they are poor plants, however; that they perform so well has caused the
biliousness. My problem, not the pansies'.

Quick guide to *Viola* species

	Flower width	Stems	Reseeds true
V. tricolor	1"	obvious	yes
V. ×wittrockiana (viola)	1–2"	moderate	no
V. ×wittrockiana (pansy)	2–4"	short	no

-*tricolor* (tri′ kul er)   heart's-ease, johnny jump up   6–9″/9″
  spring   many colors   Europe, Asia

Tricolor doesn't tell the half of it. It is hard not to love these little plants, even though they can be a pest. Some people don't like plants that reseed in the garden; others, like me, welcome the families of good-looking plants, as did our mothers and grandmothers before us, and in the Armitage garden, these particular plants can jump up wherever they please. The leaves of this species are ovate to cordate, with a wavy margin, and held on obvious stems. Stems can get somewhat lanky and lax, and plants tend to slouch in the garden. The many-colored small flowers are made up of two violet to mauve upper petals, two white lateral petals with a black stripe, and a white lower petal with a yellow base.

No actual cultivars of johnnies are offered, although seedlings can vary significantly from each other. There is, however, a good deal of *Viola tricolor* in some of the old-fashioned cultivars still occasionally found in retail stores and mail-order outlets (see "Cultivars," "Old-fashioned pansies," under *V.* ×*wittrockiana*).

Full sun to partial shade, propagate by seed.

-×*wittrockiana* (wit rok ee a′ na)   pansy, viola   4–15″/12″
  spring   many colors   hybrid

Breeding of *Viola tricolor* (heart's-ease), *V. lutea*, *V. altaica*, and other true pansies has given rise to the modern hybrid pansies and violas. Nothing botanic distinguishes a pansy from a viola; they are horticulturally distinct, however, in that violas have smaller flowers than pansies and carry them in greater numbers. (A similar distinction separates multiflora and grandiflora petunias.) Some purists claim that the root system of true violas is multi-stemmed or stoloniferous, whereas the root system of pansies is single-stemmed. I can't say I've really noticed that when I am gleefully removing the pansy and viola trials in late spring.

Plants have ovate to nearly cordate leaves, with scalloped margins on lower leaves. The spurred flowers may be a single color, or possess a blotch of a different color. I think they all smell pleasant, and on a warm spring day, the trials are alive with their fragrance. Only good thing about it.

Pansies and violas love cool weather, and in a cool summer area, such as in the mountains of Colorado and Utah, they can be terrific summer flowers. In much of the country, they are removed when summer temperatures hover consistently above 75°F or simply to make way for summer material. In the South and Southeast, pansies are the number-one-selling bedding plant—witness the large numbers that are planted around office buildings, parks, and gardens each fall. Flowering so long as temperatures remain above freezing, they sure beat the dreariness of that snow and slush in colder climates, and I'd love them too if I didn't have to evaluate them or read poems about them.

Most pansies are F_1 hybrids, raised by the large seed companies and sold in pots or trays in the spring and fall; the old days of bare-rooted pansies, twenty-five to a bundle, are essentially gone. Pansies are available in clear-faced or

Viola ×*wittrockiana*   ASHA KAYS

blotched, and recently the clear faces have become quite popular, particularly where flowers are seen from a distance. Cultivars also offer small- to large-flowered forms, and in the real world of freezes, wind, and rain, those with smaller flowers are, in general, more tolerant of inclement weather than larger forms. Unfortunately, tags in the plants are usually smaller than the small plants themselves, and cultivars are seldom asked for by name. On the up side, there is surely no shortage of them.

Full sun.

CULTIVARS

So many, it is impossible to keep up with them, but at least we know we are being well served. Blended mixes are available too, which combine certain colors of various series. None are bad.

Small-flowered (2–2½" wide) pansy series
Many flowers, excellent weather tolerance.

Baby Bingo series provides clear and blotched blooms in five colors.

Crystal Bowl series is known for its approximately twelve clear colors. Crystal Bowl Supreme series has superseded the popular original.

Joker is among the more interesting series, with unique color combinations. 'Jolly Joker' has striking orange and purple flowers. A 1990 All-America Selection.

Maxim series (Maxim Supreme series) provides blotched forms only, in about fourteen colors.

Melody series has clear and blotched blossoms in six colors.

Rally series has clear and blotched forms in nine colors.

Sky series provides both clear (Clear Sky series) and blotched forms.

Ultima series has some of the prettiest colors in various pastel shades. Mainly blotched faces, in about fifteen colors.

Universal Plus series consists of clear and blotched forms in twenty-one colors.

Velour series, called a mini-pansy, is similar to violas in flower size. Six colors.

Wink series bears small mainly blotched flowers of red and yellow, and purple and white.

Medium-flowered (2½–3½" wide) pansy series
Many flowers, good weather tolerance.

Accord series provides many colors and specialty mixes. Both blotch- and clear-faced forms.

Crown series (Crown Supreme series) is a group of clear-flowered forms in eleven colors.

Dancer series consists of about sixteen colors in clear and blotched forms.

Delta series provides both clear and blotched forms in twenty colors.

Fama series consists of blotch- and clear-faced forms in about twenty colors.

Imperial series has clear and blotched forms in fourteen colors. The unique 'Imperial Antique Shades' is particularly beautiful.

Panache series has wonderful bright colors, both clear and blotched.

Regal series (Regal Supreme series) provides blotched forms only, in eleven colors.

Roc series consists of both clear and blotched forms in many colors.

Skyline series has clear and blotched members.

Vernale series provides clear and blotched forms in about twenty-two colors.

Large-flowered (3½–4" wide) pansy series

Fewer flowers, fair weather tolerance.

Atlas series is a group of clear-faced forms in six colors.

Banner series has sixteen colors in clear and blotched faces.

Bingo series has both clear and blotched forms in eleven colors.

Happy Face is a blotched series with six colors.

Majestic Giant is one of the oldest and most recognized series. The name itself seems to be magical, as sales continue even though better cultivars are available. Super Majestic Giant is a similar series with even larger flowers. Terrible plants in bad weather.

Scala series provides clear and blotched forms in about nineteen colors.

Turbo series has twenty colors of clear- and blotch-faced flowers.

Pansy independents

Some good flower colors and forms, although not part of a series, are still worth looking for.

'Blue Jeans' is a mix of blue colors.

'Brunig' has dark mahogany flowers with an edging of gold.

'Padparadja' has solid orange blooms, very striking.

'Purple Rain' has somewhat cascading flowers and spreading mounding plants. Good for baskets and containers. Also sold as 'Purple Trails'.

'Rippling Waters' has dark purple-blue flowers with white margins.

'Silver Wings' combines silver and dark purple on small flowers.

'Springtime Black' is one of several nearly black pansies. A neat flower.

Old-fashioned pansies

Before the mega-series and large breeders, many fine colors and forms were bred. *Viola cornuta* or *V. tricolor* (or both) contributed greatly to these beautiful old-fashioned—and still available—cultivars.

'E. A. Bowles' has deep purple, almost black flowers. Also sold as 'Bowles' Black'.

'Fiona' bears beautiful flowers tinged light blue.

'Helen Mount', an old-fashioned johnny jump-up, is among the best. She has purple upper petals and orange-yellow lower ones.

'Irish Molly' has flowers the size of garden violas, bronze-orange with a darker center.

'Maggie Mott' has mauve flowers with a lovely silver tinge. The centers are cream-colored.

'Molly Sanderson' bears small dark purple to black flowers with a yellow center.

'Thalia' is compact, with lower petals cream and upper ones purple.

Viola series

Alpine series consists of several colors. 'Alpine Summer' (purple and yellow) is outstanding.

Babyface series is somewhat similar to Sorbet series and is available in many colors.

Contessa series bears solid and blotched forms in about five colors.

Jewel series, among the first hybrid violas offered, is still excellent and available in five colors.

Penny series has great uniformity in eleven colors.

Princess series has seven colors.

Skippy series, an excellent performer in our trials, bears about eight colors. Who makes up these names anyway?

Sorbet, the premier series, provided breakthrough colors when first introduced by Waller Seed Co. Twelve colors. 'Yesterday, Today and Tomorrow' is fabulous, with white flowers that turn blue at maturity.

Splendid series consists of three colors.

Quick key to *Viola* species

A. Flowers usually <1" wide, always with at least three obvious
   colors, stems obvious . . . . *V. tricolor*
AA. Flowers usually >2" wide, often with single colors or
   bicolored, stems not as obvious . . . . *V. ×wittrockiana*

Additional reading

Armitage, Allan M. 1997. *Herbaceous Perennial Plants*, 2nd ed. Stipes Publishing, Champaign, Ill.

University of Georgia Trial Reports: www.uga.edu/ugatrial

X

Xeranthemum (ze ran' tha mum)

immortelle   Asteraceae

Immortelle is another everlasting flower (see *Helipterum* for a discussion of others). This genus of erect annuals is characterized by densely hairy leaves, alternate and entire, and heads that lack ray flowers. The large bract-like scales (involucre) are persistent and colored. Of the approximately five known species, *Xeranthemum annuum* is the most commonly cultivated.

-annuum (an' yew um)

	immortelle	1–2'/1'
spring	pink, white	SE Europe

The stems are branched at the base of the plant, but few branches occur from each stem. The linear to oblong leaves are 1–2" long and ½" wide; they are white, slightly hairy above and densely hairy beneath. The flower heads are 1–1½" wide, and the inner "bracts" are spread out and star-like. The flowers are usually pink, but sometimes white.

This is an excellent everlasting species that, whether the flowers are cut or allowed to remain on the plant, provides color and handsome foliage for many weeks. For cut flowers, harvest just before the blooms are fully open, then hang upside down. Plants prefer dry, well-drained conditions; they are tolerant of heat but do poorly when temperatures remain above 70°F at night. Best grown in spring and resown in the fall.

Full sun. Propagate by seed, *in situ* or in containers. Plants flower about twelve weeks after sowing.

CULTIVARS

Mixed Hybrids have velvety white leaves and 1–2" wide flowers in white, pink, rose, red, and purple.

'Purple Violet' is about 2' tall with semi-double deep purple flowers.

'Snowlady' has single white flowers.

Alternative species

Xeranthemum cylindraceum (sih lin dra see′ um) is 1½–2′ tall with the "bracts" almost upright. 'Lilac Stars' is a handsome plant with lilac-purple bracts.

Z

Zaluzianskya (za looz ee an' skee a)
Scrophulariaceae

This African genus is named for Adam Zaluziansky von Zaluzian, a seventeenth-century Polish physician. About thirty-five species of annuals, perennials, and shrubs are known; perhaps a couple are grown every now and then in American gardens.

| *-capensis* (ka pen' sis) | night phlox | 20–30"/12" |
| summer | white | South Africa |

Best known for the delicate fragrance that the flowers provide just after dark (thus the common name), this species is increasingly popular in rock gardens. The linear leaves are entire or slightly toothed, and the stems are hairy. The ½" wide phlox-like flowers are deeply notched and held in short spikes. Part of the allure is the red buds, which open to fragrant orange-eyed white flowers, the backs of which are glowing red. The fragrance, which occurs only in the evening, is subtle and memorable on a still night; planting a group together enhances the fragrance. Plants fare better in Mediterranean climates but are certainly worth a try in the Northeast and Midwest; they can tolerate cold to about 25°F. For best results, place them in a gritty, well-drained soil, where rain can drain away quickly.

Full sun. Sow seed *in situ* in late winter or in the fall in mild climates.

Alternative species

Zaluzianskya villosa (vih lo' sa) bears many small lilac to purple flowers on 10–12" tall plants. Good in containers or rock garden. Not as fragrant as *Z. capensis*. Quite striking.

Quick key to *Zaluzianskya* species

A. Flowers white, leaves linear . . . . *Z. capensis*
AA. Flowers lilac, leaves obovate . . . . *Z. villosa*

Zingiber (zin' jih ber)   ginger   Zingiberaceae

This is a genus of tropical plants, suitable wherever summer temperatures are warm and summers persist for more than two months. More than a hundred species of herbs with branching, thick, aromatic rhizomes and leafy reed-like stems are known, but for mainstream American gardeners, one or two may be useful for the highly ornamental flowers. The flowers of ginger are similar to those of *Hedychium* and *Globba*; they occur in the axils of colorful inflorescences in the upper leaf nodes of the plants. The inflorescence is long-lived, although the individual flowers last only a short time. The foliage is also pleasantly fragrant. The true culinary ginger is *Zingiber officinale*, native to the tropics of Asia and widely cultivated around the world.

Quick guide to *Zingiber* species

	Height	Cone color
Z. spectabile	5–7'	yellow, turning scarlet
Z. zerumbet	4–6'	green, turning red

-*spectabile* (spek tab' ih lee)   beehive ginger   5–7'/3'
   late summer   scarlet   Malaysia

The leaves are 10–20" long, deep green above, paler, downy beneath. The flowers are held in an 8–12" long loose cylindrical inflorescence, the bracts of which begin yellow and then turn scarlet. The small creamy white flowers within the bracts are about 1" wide. The two-lobed lip is dark purple with yellow spots. Flowers occur in late summer and continue through fall in areas of warm summers.

   Full sun, propagate by division.

-*zerumbet* (ze rum' bet)   pine cone ginger   4–6'/3'
   late summer   red   India

This probably should be the most popular ornamental form of *Zingiber* in this country. Plants grow upright with little or no branching. Large green cone-like inflorescences are produced in late summer and fall and persist for weeks. Small creamy yellow flowers appear under some of the bracts that make up the cone. The flowers have three petals; the middle petal (lip) is larger than the two lateral ones. As the inflorescence matures, it turns bright red. The inflorescences may be cut for long-lasting cut flower arrangements.

   Full sun, propagate by division.

CULTIVARS

   'Darceyi' is similar to the species but produces leaves with cream-colored margins. Flowering will not occur except in long warm summers, so, for gardeners in the North, the ornamental foliage of this species makes sense.

Alternative species

Zingiber mioga (mee o' ga; Japanese ginger) is related to *Z. zerumbet*. Plants of this species are only 2–3' tall and produce basal inflorescences, on which are borne light yellow flowers.

Quick key to *Zingiber* species

A. Inflorescence mostly basal . . . . *Z. mioga*
AA. Inflorescence mostly axillary
    B. Inflorescence >10" long, yellow-white corolla, lip with
       purple . . . . *Z. spectabile*
    BB. Inflorescence <6" long, white corolla, pale yellow lip . . . *Z. zerumbet*

Zingiber hybrids

'Chiang Mai Princess', from Thailand, produces cones that are initially green and then mature to a brilliant red. The bracts are sharply pointed. Inflorescences are produced at the stem base.

'Milky Way' has white cones, mostly produced at the base of the stem, suffused with pink.

Additional reading

Chapman, Timothy. 1995. *Ornamental Gingers*. 6920 Bayou Paul Rd., St. Gabriel, LA 70776.
San Felasco Nurseries: www.sanfelasco.com
Stokes Tropicals: www.stokestropicals.com
Wight Nurseries of North Carolina: www.wightnurseries.com

Zinnia (zin' ee a)   Asteraceae

Linnaeus did not shy away from honoring his fellow botanists; he named this genus for Johann Gottfried Zinn (1727–1759), a professor of botany at Göttingen, Germany, who lived a short but productive life. Zinnias have been garden favorites for many years, as traditional bedding plants and as cut flowers. Like other bedding plants, breeding has produced a bewildering array of cultivars, from dwarf forms to 4' giants, with single and double flowers, in almost all colors under the sun. Approximately twenty species are known, and although the majority of garden zinnias are selections of the common zinnia, *Zinnia elegans*, some of the better breeding in recent years has involved selections of *Z. angustifolia* and, to a lesser extent, *Z. haageana*.

A great deal of confusion surrounds the lesser known species, whose names have been used interchangeably. According to various sources, *Zinnia angustifolia* is synonymous with both *Z. linearis* and *Z. haageana*. Others disagree, and since nobody agrees with anyone else, I have filtered the literature for you: I believe that *Z. angustifolia* is synonymous with *Z. linearis*, and *Z. haageana* is still on its own.

Quick guide to *Zinnia* species

	Height	Flower color	Form
Z. angustifolia	10–18"	mainly yellow and gold	single
Z. elegans	1–4'	all colors but blue	single, semi-double, double
Z. haageana	1–2'	usually bicolored	single

-*angustifolia* (an gust ih fo' lee a)   narrow-leaf zinnia   12–15"/12"
   summer   orange, gold, yellow   SE United States, Mexico

When people ask, "Is there a zinnia that doesn't get leaf spots all the time?", I simply say, "Try some narrow-leaf." This is great stuff. *Zinnia angustifolia* (syn. *Z. linearis*) flowers continuously throughout the season, with little need of deadheading or maintenance of any kind. The hairy stems are branched and bear alternate, linear or linear-lanceolate leaves. They are less than ½" wide and sessile, not clasping on the stem, a characteristic that helps distinguish this species

Zinnia angustifolia   ASHA KAYS

from the bedding zinnia. The seven- to nine-ray flowers are only about 1″ wide (some newer cultivars are a little wider); the common flower color is orangish, and the disk is purplish orange.

This is a choice plant, with terrific performance and disease resistance in all climates. While other zinnias are declining in abusive weather, narrow-leaf zinnia keeps on like the Energizer bunny.

Full sun, propagate by seed.

CULTIVARS

'Classic Golden Orange', the granddad of the group, bears 1½″ flowers on 6–9″ tall plants.

'Crystal White' did exceptionally well in the University of Georgia trials, producing many clean white flowers with yellow centers all season.

Star series produces 1½–2″ wide flowers in gold, orange, and white.

'Tropical Snow' bears 2″ wide white flowers. Similar to 'Crystal White'.

| *-elegans* (el′ e ganz) | bedding zinnia, youth and old age | 1–4′/1′ |
| summer | many colors | Mexico |

This species is the most common of all zinnias and one that will likely remain popular, even though plants are plagued by several diseases. The green stems are prickly-hairy (strigose), with lanceolate to ovate leaves. The leaves, which more or less clasp the stem, are 1½–4″ long and 1–2″ wide. The flower heads are 2–4″ wide with broad, showy ray flowers and a black or green disk. In double forms, the disk is absent. If deadheaded, flowers will keep forming (and the appropriateness of one common name will be apparent). If not deadheaded, flowers become moldy, particularly the double forms.

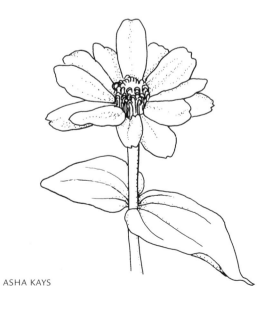

Zinnia elegans   ASHA KAYS

Plants are susceptible to gray mold (*Botrytis*), leaf blight (*Alternaria*), and root rots (*Rhizoctonia, Phytophthora*). In the South, zinnias are planted in early spring, then pulled out in mid summer and replaced with fresh plants. This way, two good summer seasons of flowering can be enjoyed, and the headaches—related to the diseases that gang up on the plants under stressful conditions—avoided altogether. I recommend this practice wherever zinnias decline in summer heat and humidity.

Full sun, propagate by seed. Many of the tall forms are best purchased from the seed rack at the garden center and sown *in situ*.

CULTIVARS

Tall forms (>2')

'Big Red' has 4–5" wide blood-red flowers on 4' tall plants.

Cactus Flowered Mix bears 5" wide flowers with long thin petals. Popular and different—and named for their resemblance to cactus-flowered dahlias, not to cacti.

'California Giants' is another cactus-flowered type, with 4½" wide flowers on 3' tall plants. It is usually offered in a mix, but separate colors are sometimes available: 'Canary Bird' (yellow), 'Purity' (white), and 'Scarlet Queen' (red).

'Candy Stripe' bears 4" wide fully double white flowers that are variously striped and splashed with red, rose, and pink. A veritable candy cane.

Dahlia Flowered Mix offers flowers that resemble big dahlias. Old-fashioned, popular, and in many colors. About 4' tall.

'Desert Sun' consists of 3' tall plants with primrose, ivory, and gold flowers.

'Envy Double' provides unusual chartreuse-green double flowers. About 2' tall.

'Liliput' has 2" wide double flowers on 2' tall plants.

Oklahoma is an excellent series of 3–4' tall plants in five colors. Good weather tolerance. Selected as the cut flower of the year in 1999 by the Association of Specialty Cut Flower Growers.

Peppermint Stick Mix recreates the joy and confusion of 'Candy Stripe', except with more combinations of even more colors.

Ruffles Mix has good weather tolerance and bears a mixture of cherry and yellow flowers on 30" stems.

'Splendor Pink' is about 2' tall with 4–5" wide pink flowers on 2–3' tall stems.

State Fair Mix, an old-fashioned dahlia-flowered form, is still a popular mix, with 4" wide flowers on 4' tall plants. Used mainly as cut flowers.

Sun series is excellent. Look for 3" wide Sun flowers in cherry, gold, red, and creamy white ('Silver Sun'). Plants are 3' tall.

'Whirligig' is a coat of many colors, with patterned flowers in red, yellow, and gold. About 2' tall, eye-catching indeed.

Short forms (10–20")

Blue Point Mix is an outstanding mixture of good flower colors and excellent form. Relatively disease-resistant.

Dasher Mix has 3" wide flowers on plants that are 4–6" tall. Fair weather tolerance.

Dreamland series is beautiful but not particularly weather-tolerant. Seven separate colors and a mix are available. If pinched early, plants form compact bushes laden with blooms.

Peter Pan series is 10–12″ tall in nine colors. Poor weather tolerance.

Profusion series is by far the best zinnia on the market today. Plants are weather- and disease-resistant; leaf-spotting seldom appears until very late in the season. 'Profusion Cherry' was a 1999 All-America Selection; 'Profusion Orange' and 'Profusion White' (the 2001 All-America Selection gold medalist) are just as good. Plants are 15–18″ tall.

Pulchino is a mix of colors on 15″ tall plants. Moderate weather tolerance.

Short Stuff is another beautiful series for the greenhouse but declines rapidly in the garden. Seven colors available.

'Small World Cherry' is an excellent selection with deep cherry blooms.

Thumbelina Mix, an old selection, offers small flowers in many colors on 10″ tall plants. Moderate weather tolerance.

| *-haageana* (hay gee a′ na) | Haage's zinnia | 1–2′/1′ |
| summer | bicolors | Mexico |

J. N. Haage was a mid nineteenth-century seed grower in Effurt, Germany. The species named after him is the least-known garden zinnia but not for lack of trying. It has been around for a hundred years but simply cannot compete with the bedding zinnia. Nor have a lot of exciting cultivars been selected recently, so it has not received much positive press. The branched stems bear sessile lanceolate leaves, 1–2″ long and about ½″ wide. As with other species, the stems and leaves are covered with short stiff hairs. Flowers may be gold or yellow, but those in commerce are usually bicolored gold and maroon. The flower heads are about 1″ wide, consisting of eight or nine ray flowers around an orange disk.

Plants are effective in containers or as a bedding plant combined with other low growers. Like *Zinnia angustifolia*, the species displays excellent disease resistance but benefits from deadheading. If you get tired of large-flowered zinnias, give this one a try.

Full sun, propagate by seed.

CULTIVARS

'Old Mexico' forms mounds of flowers, each about 1½″ wide. The flowers are bright yellow, gold, and mahogany.

'Persian Carpet' is a beautiful selection, with 2″ wide double flowers in colors as varied as a Persian carpet. Resistant to almost all abuse, highly recommended.

Alternative species

Zinnia peruviana, a relative of *Z. angustifolia*, is 2–3′ tall with 3 × 1″ leaves and spatula-shaped ray flowers of yellow or yellow-red surrounding a black disk. Good for cut flowers. 'Bonita Yellow', which is sometimes offered, provides creamy yellow and orange flowers.

Quick key to *Zinnia* species

  A. Leaves clasping or almost so, flowers 2–4" wide . . . . *Z. elegans*
AA. Leaves sessile, flowers <2" wide
      B. Leaves linear to linear lanceolate, flowers single color . . . .
      . . . . *Z. angustifolia*
     BB. Leaves lanceolate to ovate, flowers usually bicolored . . . *Z. haageana*

Additional reading

Lee, Rand B. 1998. Zinnias. *American Cottage Gardener* 5(2):4–6.
Winterrowd, Wayne. 1999. Zinnias. *Horticulture* 96(6):29–30.

SELECTED BIBLIOGRAPHY

Many resources were used in putting together this book, including scientific and trade literature, dozens of catalogs, and Internet sites; they are listed in "Additional reading" at the appropriate genus. The following reference books, some now out of print, were consulted constantly.

Armitage, Allan M. 1993. *Specialty Cut Flowers*. Timber Press, Portland, Ore.
———. 1997. *Herbaceous Perennial Plants*, 2nd ed. Stipes Publishing, Champaign, Ill.
Bailey, L. H. 1930. *The Standard Cyclopedia of Horticulture*. 3 vols. Macmillan, New York.
———. 1951. *Manual of Cultivated Plants*. Macmillan, New York.
Bales, Suzanne Frutig. 1991. *Annuals*. Prentice Hall, New York.
Beckett, Kenneth A. 1983. *Climbing Plants*. Timber Press, Portland, Ore.
Booth, C. O. 1957. *An Encyclopedia of Annual and Biennial Garden Plants*. Faber and Faber, London, U.K.
Corrick, Margaret, and Bruce A. Fuhrer. 1996. *Wildflowers of Southern Western Australia*. Five Mile Press, Noble Park, Victoria, Australia.
Huxley, Anthony. 1992. *The New Royal Horticultural Society Dictionary of Gardening*. 4 vols. Stockton Press, New York.
Johnson, Krystyna, and Margaret Burchett, eds. 1996. *Native Australian Plants*. University of New South Wales Press, Sydney, Australia.
Marston, Ted. 1993. *Annuals*. Smallwood and Stewart Inc., New York.
Rickett, Harold William. 1966–73. *Wild Flowers of America*. 6 vols. McGraw-Hill, New York.
Riffle, Robert Lee. 1998. *The Tropical Look*. Timber Press, Portland, Ore.
Stern, William T. 1996. *Stearn's Dictionary of Plant Names for Gardeners*. Cassell Publishing, London.
Ward, Bobby J. 1999. *A Contemplation Upon Flowers*. Timber Press, Portland, Ore.
Winterrowd, Wayne. 1992. *Annuals for Connoisseurs*. Prentice Hall, New York.

APPENDIX: USEFUL LISTS

Biennials

The following plants take two years to flower or significantly benefit from a cold treatment.

Adlumia fungosa
Alcea rosea
Ammobium alatum
Anchusa capensis
Angelica archangelica
Angelica gigas
Campanula medium
Campanula pyramidalis
Dianthus barbatus
Echium vulgare
Erysimum cheiri

Euphorbia lathyris
Glaucium corniculatum
Lavatera arborea
Lunaria annua
Papaver triniifolium
Phacelia bipinnatifida
Salvia aethiopis
Salvia argentea
Silene armeria
Silene compacta

Half-hardy perennials

The following taxa may sometimes be grown as half-hardy perennials. These plants will consistently overwinter in areas of frost-free winters. In areas of mild winters, however, these plants are best treated as annuals; if they overwinter and come back in the spring, treat their return as a bonus.

Abutilon ×hybridum
Alpinia zerumbet
Angelica archangelica
Angelica gigas
Brachycome iberidifolia
Calibrachoa hybrida
Canna ×generalis
Centratherum punctatum
Colocasia esculenta
Consolida ambigua
Consolida regalis

Cuphea hyssopifolia
Cuphea micropetala
Duranta erecta
Euphorbia lathyris
Gaillardia pulchella
Heliotropium amplexicaule
Hemigraphis repanda
Laurentia fluviatilis
Odontonema strictum
Otacanthus caeruleus
Plumbago auriculata

Rosmarinus officinalis
Ruellia brittoniana
Ruellia humilis
Ruellia macrantha
Salvia argentea
Salvia greggii
Salvia leucantha
Salvia rutilans

Solanum jasminoides
Tecomaria capensis
Thunbergia battiscombei
Thunbergia grandiflora
Tibouchina urvilleana
Verbena canadensis
Verbena tenuisecta

Winter annuals

The following plants are produced commercially and made available for late fall planting in areas of mild winters.

Antirrhinum majus
Bellis perennis
Beta vulgaris
Brassica oleracea

Cichorium intybus
Dianthus hybrids
Matthiola incana
Viola ×*wittrockiana*

Shade-tolerant plants

Performance of the following plants is enhanced when they are placed in a shady location. All tolerate morning sun; those marked with an asterisk will tolerate full sun.

Acalypha hispida
Adlumia fungosa
Alocasia macrorrhiza
Ballota acetabulosa
Ballota nigra
Ballota pseudodictamnus
Begonia ×*argenteoguttata*
Begonia bolivensis
Begonia clarkei
Begonia cucullata
Begonia davisii
Begonia dregei
Begonia fuchsioides
Begonia gracilis
Begonia masoniana
Begonia minor
Begonia pearcei
Begonia rex-cultorum
Begonia schmidtiana
*Begonia semperflorens-cultorum
Begonia sutherlandii
Begonia tuberhybrida-cultorum

Begonia veitchii
Browallia americana
Browallia speciosa
Browallia viscosa
Caladium ×*hortulanum*
Cardiospermum grandiflorum
Cardiospermum halicacabum
*Coleus blumei
Cornukaempferia aurantiaca
Fuchsia hybrids
*Globba winitii
Impatiens auricoma
Impatiens balfourii
Impatiens balsamina
Impatiens capensis
Impatiens glandulifera
Impatiens hawkeri
Impatiens niamniamensis
Impatiens noli-tangere
Impatiens racemosa
Impatiens stenantha
Impatiens tinctoria

Impatiens walleriana
Kaempferia atrovirens
Kaempferia gilbertii
Kaempferia pulchra
Kaempferia rotunda
Lunaria annua
Mimulus guttatus
Mimulus ×hybridus
Nemophila maculata
Nemophila menziesii

Phacelia bipinnatifida
Phacelia campanularia
Salpiglossis sinuata
Schizanthus grahamii
Schizanthus pinnatus
Schizanthus ×wisetonensis
Streptocarpus ×hybridus
Stylomecon heterophyllum
Torenia flava
Torenia fournieri

Fragrant plants

The following plants have scented flowers or foliage—and sometimes both.
Remember: not all noses have similar sensitivities, and not all fragrances are
necessarily pleasant!

Abelmoschus moschatus
Agastache foeniculum
Agastache mexicana
Alpinia zerumbet
Artemisia annua
Brachycome iberidifolia
Brugmansia ×candida
Brugmansia hybrids
Cardiospermum grandiflorum
Centaurea cyanus
Centaurea moschata
Cosmos atrosanguineus
Datura innoxia
Datura metel
Dianthus hybrids
Dioscorea batatas
Erysimum cheiri
Galium odoratum
Helichrysum italicum
Heliotropium amplexicaule
Heliotropium arborescens
Iberis amara
Iberis odorata
Ipomoea alba
Ipomoea tricolor
Jasminum sambac
Lantana camara
Lathyrus odoratus
Limnanthes douglasii
Lobularia maritima

Lupinus hartwegii
Lupinus luteus
Lupinus texensis
Mandevilla sanderi
Matthiola incana
Matthiola longipetala
Mirabilis jalapa
Nelumbo nucifera
Nicotiana alata
Nicotiana glauca
Nicotiana knightiana
Nicotiana langsdorffii
Nicotiana ×sanderae
Nicotiana sylvestris
Ocimum basilicum
Passiflora ×alato-caerulea
Passiflora caerulea
Passiflora ×decaisneana
Passiflora hybrids
Pelargonium capitatum
Pelargonium crispum
Pelargonium denticulatum
Pelargonium fragrans
Pelargonium graveolens
Pelargonium odoratissimum
Pelargonium tomentosum
Petunia integrifolia
Petunia hybrids
Phacelia campanularia
Phlox drummondii

Plectranthus amboinicus
Plectranthus forsteri
Quisqualis indica
Reseda odorata
Rosmarinus officinalis
Salvia greggii
Salvia leucantha
Salvia rutilans
Scabiosa atropurpurea

Stylomecon heterophyllum
Tagetes lucida
Thymophylla tenuiloba
Tweedia caerulea
Viola odorata
Viola ×wittrockiana
Zaluzianskya capensis
Zingiber spectabile
Zingiber zerumbet

Climbing plants

The following taxa are climbing plants, or plants that can be trained to climb.

Adlumia fungosa
Allamanda cathartica
Allamanda violacea
Asarina antirrhinifolia
Asarina barclaiana
Asarina erubescens
Asarina procumbens
Asarina purpusii
Asarina scandens
Basella alba
Cardiospermum grandiflorum
Cardiospermum halicacabum
Clerodendrum splendens
Clitoria ternatea
Cobaea scandens
Dioscorea batatas
Eccremocarpus scaber
Gloriosa superba
Ipomoea alba
Ipomoea coccinea
Ipomoea hederacea
Ipomoea lobata
Ipomoea nil
Ipomoea quamoclit
Ipomoea ×sloteri
Ipomoea tricolor
Lablab purpureus
Lathyrus odoratus
Mandevilla sanderi
Manettia cordifolia
Manettia luteorubra
Passiflora alata

Passiflora ×alato-caerulea
Passiflora antioquiensis
Passiflora caerulea
Passiflora citrina
Passiflora coccinea
Passiflora coriacea
Passiflora ×decaisneana
Passiflora edulis
Passiflora incarnata
Passiflora ligularis
Passiflora lutea
Passiflora manicata
Passiflora mollissima
Passiflora quadrangularis
Passiflora sanguinolenta
Passiflora subpeltata
Passiflora vitifolia
Quisqualis indica
Rhodochiton atrosanguineum
Senecio confusus
Solanum crispum
Solanum jasminoides
Solanum wendlandii
Thunbergia alata
Thunbergia grandiflora
Thunbergia gregorii
Tropaeolum majus
Tropaeolum minus
Tropaeolum peregrinum
Tropaeolum polyphyllum
Tropaeolum speciosum
Tweedia caerulea

Everlastings

Ammobium alatum
Gomphrena globosa
Helichrysum bracteatum
Helichrysum splendidum
Helipterum splendidum
Rhodanthe chlorocephala

Rhodanthe manglesii
Scabiosa stellata
Schoenia cassiniana
Schoenia filifolia
Xeranthemum annuum

U.S.D.A. HARDINESS ZONE MAP

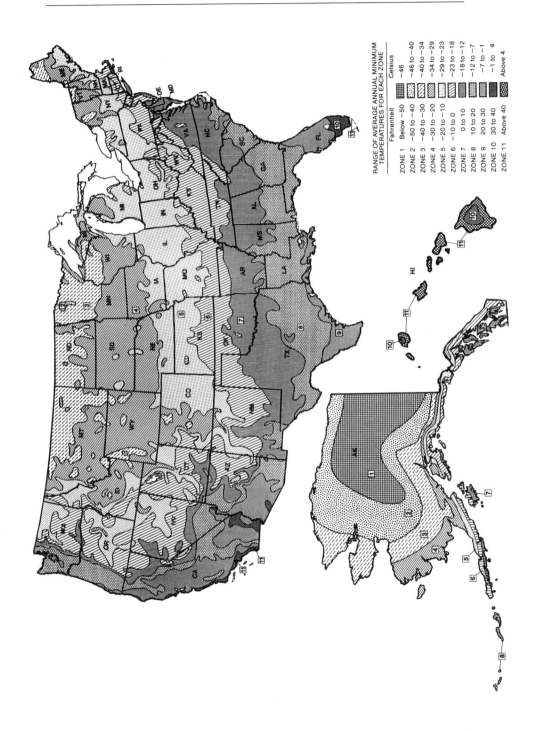

RANGE OF AVERAGE ANNUAL MINIMUM TEMPERATURES FOR EACH ZONE

	Fahrenheit	Celsius
ZONE 1	Below −50	−46
ZONE 2	−50 to −40	−46 to −40
ZONE 3	−40 to −30	−40 to −34
ZONE 4	−30 to −20	−34 to −29
ZONE 5	−20 to −10	−29 to −23
ZONE 6	−10 to 0	−23 to −18
ZONE 7	0 to 10	−18 to −12
ZONE 8	10 to 20	−12 to −7
ZONE 9	20 to 30	−7 to −1
ZONE 10	30 to 40	−1 to 4
ZONE 11	Above 40	Above 4

INDEX OF BOTANICAL NAMES

INDEX OF COMMON NAMES